Readings in Anthropology

942-3413

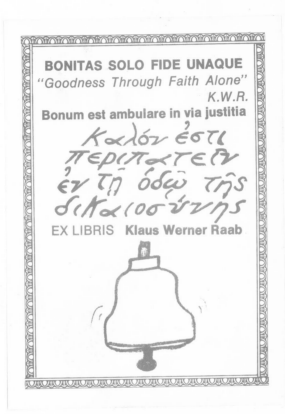

third edition

Readings in Anthropology

Jesse D. Jennings
University of Utah

E. Adamson Hoebel
University of Minnesota

McGraw-Hill Book Company
New York   San Francisco   St. Louis   Düsseldorf   Johannesburg
Kuala Lumpur   London   Mexico   Montreal   New Delhi
Panama   Rio de Janeiro   Singapore   Sydney   Toronto

This book was set in Helvetica by Black Dot, Inc. and printed on permanent paper and bound by The George Banta Company, Inc. The designer was Janet Bollow; the drawings were provided by the contributors. The editors were Ronald D. Kissack and Eva Marie Strock. Charles A. Goehring supervised production.

Cover: photograph of two Inca musicans courtesy of Hamburgisches Museum Fur Völkerkunde

Readings in Anthropology

Printed in the United States of America.

Library of Congress catalog card number: 71-174617

1234567890 BABA 798765432

To Our Colleagues in Anthropology

Contents

part 3   physical anthropology

part 4   primates

part 5   primitive technology

part 6   primitive society

part 7   language

part 8   society and culture

part 9   ecology

part 10   economic anthropology

part 11   applied anthropology

Preface to Third Edition

In this third edition of *Readings in Anthropology* some of the trends in anthropological theory and method that have grown stronger in recent years are exemplified. One trend is toward an increasing application of ecological principles to the interpretation of cultural data; articles attempting ecological explanations of aspects of both extinct and contemporary cultures are included in a separate Ecology section. Some selected sections also discuss the present-day efforts of certain archaeologists to apply more rigorous "scientific" methods to their data. Twenty-one of the sixty-eight selections in the second edition have been deleted, and nineteen new articles have been added (but rarely as one-for-one replacements). Such deleted articles as "The Importance of Radio-carbon Dating" and "The Outlines of New World Prehistory" contained information that is now widely known; these sections have been replaced by selections that cover the newer trends.

I was guided by the several considerations specified in the previous edition, the most important being the omission of any explanatory comments by the editor and the inclusion of a few contradictory selections. Treatment of references, bibliographies, and footnotes is the same as it was in the second edition.

Again I acknowledge the extremely valuable advice of seven anonymous reviewers. They not only offered penetrating critiques of the second edition and recommended what articles should be omitted, but they also suggested dozens of new articles for possible inclusion in this edition (I have used several of these articles).

Once more it is my privilege to mention with greatest thanks the generosity of my colleagues—a few of whom I have never even met—in allowing the use of their work in this volume; no one denied my requests. And I certainly appreciate the perceptive skill of Edith Lamb, who handled the correspondence necessary in soliciting authors' permissions, copyright releases, and other inescapable details. Finally, again I credit my wife Jane for the final review of the manuscript before its submission. The finished work attests to the advantage of having at least one perfectionist in the house.

Jesse D. Jennings
1971

Preface to Second Edition

When Professor E. Adamson Hoebel, the late Professor Elmer R. Smith, and I were compiling the first version of the *Readings,* we were aware of two things. First, we undertook the task because we felt the need of a selection of readings to be used in conjunction with introductory anthropology texts since, from experience, we knew that any text requires supplementary material. Therefore we tried to pull together a reader composed of wellwritten classic articles that were interesting and readable and that contained solid documentation of certain ideas. Second, we realized that any piece of good anthropological writing could be used to exemplify or clarify more than one idea or concept and would often be used by various teachers to make theoretical points quite different from those which led to its inclusion. Therefore, we decided against the preparation of explanatory materials either for the major sections of the book, or for the individual excerpts.

In preparing this revision, the same considerations are held as valid, but through the years, I have come to see another value in *Readings.* Whereas the textbook by its very nature tends to represent orthodoxy or, one should possibly say, widely held and agreed upon ideas, the reader can "run ahead" of generally agreed upon concepts. This helps the student to move beyond the orthodoxy of the text. I have also learned that students are stimulated and excited when they discover strong differences of opinion and real controversies raging beneath the placid prose of the day-to-day text. Therefore, I have included a few articles which are contradictory. Many of the added excerpts offer the student a view of subareas within anthropology which I expect to become stronger and to contribute importantly to the understanding of human behavior although they may receive scant, if any, attention in standard texts. Articles included in the present edition have been selected not only for relevance but for the interest they may have in broader terms for the undergraduate.

Editorial changes have involved deletion of some passages and the elimination of explicit bibliographic citations. The author being quoted, of course, is indicated as he is in the original, but source citations have been removed. Other deletions involve references to figures that are not reproduced. Footnotes are also removed.

Because Professor Smith had passed away and Professor Hoebel was committed to other work, I undertook this revision alone. The selections include some of the many I have found interesting, readable, and helpful over the years.

Although each author's permission to use his material is appropriately acknowledged, I should like to mention here with extreme gratitude the generosity that my friends and colleagues have shown in allowing me to draw freely on their professional writings. My especial thanks go to the several anonymous reviewers whose candid advice guided me in the final selection of the articles included. This assistance has made possible a reader which can support and supplement any of the standard introductory texts in anthropology.

And with appreciation, I mention the assistance of Caralee Price who efficiently took care of voluminous correspondence needed in securing permissions, checked copyrights, and did other chores. To my wife, Jane C. Jennings, who assembled the manuscript, reviewed my editing and assisted with all other phases of the job, I offer my special thanks.

Jesse D. Jennings
1965

part 1

The Study of Anthropology

Anthropology and an Education for the Future

Margaret Mead

From *The Teaching of Anthropology*. American Anthropological Association Memoir 94, 1963, pp. 595–607.© 1963, David G. Mandelbaum. By permission of the author, the publisher, and the copyright holder.

. . . Anthropology is a uniquely situated discipline, related in diverse ways to many other disciplines, each of which, in specializing, has also inadvertently helped to fragment the mind of modern man. Anthropology is a *humanity* [italics added], represented in the American Council of Learned Societies, concerned with the arts of language and with the versions that human cultures have given of the definition of man and of man's relationship to the universe; anthropology is a science, concerned with discovering and ordering the behavior of man-in-culture; anthropology is a *biological science* [italics added], concerned with the physical nature of man, with man's place in evolution, with the way genetic and racial differences, ecological adaptations, growth and maturation, and constitutional differences are implicated in man's culture and achievements; anthropology is a *historical discipline* [italics added], concerned with reading the record of man's far past and establishing the links which unite the potsherd and the first inscription on stone, in tying together the threads between the preliterate and the literate world wherever the sequence occurs, in Egypt, in China, in Crete, or in a modern African state. Anthropology is a *social science* [italics added], although never only a social science, because in anthropology man, as part of the natural world, as a biological creature, is not separated from man as a consumer or producer, member of a group, or possessor of certain psychological faculties. Anthropology is an art. The research skills which go into good field work are as complex as the skills of a musician or a surgeon; a disciplined awareness of self is as essential.

Partly because anthropology is a late comer on the scene, including a curiously assembled set of subject matters—such as the preliterate past, the body of man, the behavior of preliterate surviving people, the formal study of spoken language—and partly because of the diversity of anthropological interests, it is an uncommitted discipline. Because it includes all of them, it does not fall, with relentless traditionalism, into any category of science or of humanities or of social science. It has sheltered under the wings of philosophy and anatomy, botany and history, aesthetics and geology. Wherever it has been placed it has been restive, not for the simple imperialistic reasons that all part-departments seek to be whole departments but because there was always, when anthropology was placed within any category, such a large part that did not fit. How did a course in primitive art fit into a sociology curriculum, a course in the diffusion of material culture into a psychology department, a course in child training into philosophy?

It is in this very anomalousness that I believe anthropology can make a unique contribution to a liberal education. As a part of liberal education, it is peculiarly fitted to fill a tremendous need.

I should like to review briefly some of the gaps in the knowledge and understanding of modern man, so fragmented, so myopically limited and specialized, even at this very moment when we are journeying into space. Then I will consider how anthropology can be taught not by professional anthropologists alone, but by those who have studied under anthropologists and, like all great teachers of the adolescent mind, are willing to immerse themselves in their material sufficiently to convey it to their students "with the dew still on it."

The gaps in men's minds and imagination which we need to bridge are appallingly conspicuous today: the gap between the understanding of the past, the grasp of the present, and an ability to deal with the future; the gap between the lively pursuit of natural science wherever it leads and the statesmanship which will be able to control the results of such pursuits; the gap between the mathematical and formal analyses of systems and the ability to analyze and predict the behavior of human beings; the gap between the scientist who "understands" a single approach to the natural world and the poet and painter who can find no foothold in modern man's response to changes which he does not understand; the gap between man's knowledge of things and his knowledge of people; between his awareness of the external world,

which has never been so great, and his awareness of himself, which has seldom been so impoverished; the gap between our small ethnocentric, narrowly racial, class and time bound senses of identity and the grandeur of our membership in one human species, now bound together as denizens of one planet. On the verge of leaving that planet, we still fail to conceive our full place upon it, in time and in space.

The fully educated man, whether he was the young adult male member of a primitive tribe who had learned all that the elders had to tell him, the man of Greece or Rome, thinking about and understanding the known world, Renaissance man stirred to an aware excitement of the ancient world from which he had been cut off, and moved by the new discoveries—the great and the small seen for the first time through telescopes and microscopes—all of these had, in different measure, what we now seek to re-establish for our own time. In contrast, many members of great societies—the peasant, taught for centuries that his is a limited place in the world, the urban proletarian, starved and cynical in his slums near the palace, the bitter contentious member of one of the cults and sects that seek to narrow truth to the limits of their own impoverished emotions and intellects—these have never, no matter how great the civilization within which they resided, been men of a liberal education. The essence of a liberal education is to share the full identity made possible by the state of civilization within which one lives: today that identity stretches back to the beginning of life on this planet, and soon perhaps in other parts of the universe; it comprises all members of the human species, all their work and marvels of hand and brain, heart and eye, the intricacy of their languages, the significance of their myriad experiments in human relationships, the cunningness with which their bodies are made, their relationships to all living creatures—to birds who are bipeds and build nests, and dolphins who, handless and lipless, devise ballets of their own in the sea; it reaches back into the past, out into the present, deeper beneath the sea and farther into the atmosphere than man has ever gone, and onward into a future for which each one of us, and each nation, holds today a terrible responsibility. Modern man is offered today an identity far greater than he has ever known. It is a task of a liberal education to help him develop it.

In order to appreciate fully how anthropology can contribute to this stupendous but rewarding task, something must be said of the way in which an anthropologist is educated, and what he does, when, as a research worker, he goes into the field. Every smallest research report, and every more generalized publication for the layman, bears the stamp of this education, of the presuppositions on which his work is based, and of the methods that, whatever his temperamental bent, he must pursue in the field. It is this experience of the field anthropologist, particularly of the field cultural anthropologist, which provides the possibility of integration. It is not that the anthropologist is widely read in the literature of the world, that he has an encyclopedic grasp of the history of science, that he has traveled and understood the ancient ruins of Angkor Wat or Crete, or undergone the rigorous disciplines of medicine, or one of the arts. His inclusiveness and universality are of quite another order. It is in his education and his research, based as they are in the whole of human history, embedded in the simplest and the most solemn moments of human life, that his integration lies.

In the United States anthropology has remained an inclusive and integrating discipline by successfully resisting the fragmentation which has occurred in most disciplines, which, as they became more specialized, with more workers, in more countries of the world, have progressively shattered into mutually non-communicating parts. Anthropology has kept its own media of intradisciplinary communication. Just as the fragmented and over specialized biological sciences can still communicate through observation of scientific canons of presentation, argument, and experimental style, and the humanist in many tongues can still invoke the names of Plato and Aristotle, or physicians refer to a well-described case and lawyers to a carefully stated legal precedent, so too anthropologists have remained in communication with each other through the concrete materials with which they deal. They work not only with generalizations about culture, but also with the descriptions of particular cultures; not only with generalizations about language, but also with the auditory records of the speech of particular Indians or particular South Sea Island tribes; not only with tables of prehistoric time, but also with the actual artifacts and skeletal bits from which these tables are constructed. In their field work they go to various parts of the world, among living peoples who are different and speak different languages, or at a second remove, to the detailed accounts of those who did travel, and to the concrete specimens that they brought back.

Although it looked during the 1940's as if American anthropology, which had stood for such a unified approach to man in all his aspects, might fragment, it did not fragment. Graduate students in our universities today still learn about man's past, his place in evolution, the remains of his past civilization, the complexity of his languages, the nature of his culture and how to study it, and, increasingly, how to apply this knowledge, professionally, [to] various contemporary social problems as practitioners. In such an education the student is not lectured about the various parts of the subject but is forced to experience some small part of each, to read monographs about the Chukchee and the Koryak, to learn the shape of a bone, to undergo the discipline of analyzing an unknown language straight from an informant's lips, to arrange an assemblage of potsherds and/or the contents of a single archaeological dig. Where this ideal is not fully realized, contact with those who have spent many years doing just these concrete things serves, to some extent, as a surrogate for the experience itself. . . .

The World into which Darwin Led Us

George Gaylord Simpson

From *Science,* Vol. 131, No. 3405, 1960, pp. 966–974. Copyright 1960, American Association for the Advancement of Science. By permission of the author, the publisher and copyright holder.

. . . It has often been said that Darwin changed the world. It has less often been made clear just what the change has been. Darwin did not—to his credit he did not—make any of the discoveries that have led to our present overwhelming physical peril. Most, although not quite all, of our technology would be the same if Darwin's work had not been done, by him or anyone else. . . . The influence of Darwin, or more broadly of the concept of evolution, has had effects more truly profound. It has literally led us into a different world.

How can that be? If evolution is true, it was as true before Darwin as it is today. The physical universe has not changed. But our human universes, the ones in which we really have our beings, depend at least as much on our inner perceptions as on the external, physical facts. That can be made evident by an elementary example. Suppose a stone is seen by a small boy, an artist, and a petrologist. The small boy may perceive it as something to throw, the artist as something to carve into sculpture, the petrologist as a mixture of minerals formed under conditions. The stone is three quite different things to the three people, and yet they are seeing exactly the same thing. The stone has identical properties whatever anyone thinks about it.

In that trivial example all three conceptions of the stone, although profoundly different, are equally true. The stone can indeed be thrown, be sculptured, or be analyzed petrologically by procedures suitable to each of the three perceptions. But there are differing perceptions of objects and of our whole world that are not equally true in the same sense, which is the scientific sense of material testability. Perceptions that are not materially testable or that have been contradicted by adequate tests are not rationally valid. As they petrify into tradition and dogma they become superstitions. Perception of the truth of evolution was an enormous stride from superstition to a rational universe.

The Changing Universe

Years ago I lived for a time with a group of uncivilized Indians in South America. Their world is very different from ours: in space, a saucer a few miles across; in time, from a few years to a few generations back into a misty past; in essence, lawless, unpredictable, and haunted. Anything might happen. The Kamarakoto Indians quite believe that animals become men and men become stones; for them there is neither limitation nor reason in the flux of nature. There is also a brooding evil in their world, a sense of wrongness and fatality that they call *kanaima* and see manifested in every unusual event and object.

That level of invalid perceptions might be called the lower superstition. It is nevertheless superior in some respects to the higher superstitions celebrated weekly in every hamlet of the United States. The legendary metamorphoses of my Indian friends are grossly naive, but they do postulate a kinship through all of nature. Above all, they are not guilty of teleology. It would never occur to them that the universe, so largely hostile, might have been created for their benefit.

It is a quite wrong to think that uncivilized Indians are, by that token, primitive. Nevertheless, I suppose that the conceptual world of the Kamarakotos is more or less similar to that of ancient, truly primitive men. Indeed, even at the dawn of written history in the cradles of civilization, the accepted world pictures do not seem very different from that of those Indians.

The world in which modern, civilized men live has changed profoundly with increasingly rational, which is to say eventually scientific, consideration of the universe. The essential changes came first of all from the physical sciences and their forerunners. In space, the small saucer of the savage became a large disc, a globe, a planet in a solar system, which became one of many in our galaxy, which in turn became only one nebula in a cosmos containing uncounted billions of them. The astronomers have finally located us on an insignificant mote in an incom-prehensible vastness—surely a world awesomely different from that in which our ancestors lived not many generations ago.

As astronomy made the universe immense, physics itself and related physical sciences made it lawful. Physical effects have physical causes, and the relationship is such that when causes are adequately known effects can be reliably predicted. We no longer live in a capricious world. We may expect the universe to deal consistently, even if not fairly, with us. If the unusual happens, we need no longer blame *kanaima* (or a whimsical god or devil) but may look confidently for an unusual or hitherto unknown physical cause. That is, perhaps, an act of faith, but it is not superstition. Unlike recourse to the supernatural, it is validated by thousands of successful searches for verifiable causes. This view depersonalizes the universe and makes it more austere, but it also makes it dependable. . . .

To those discoveries and principles, which so greatly modified concepts of the cosmos, geology added two more of fundamental, world-changing importance: vast extension of the universe in time, and the idea of constantly lawful progression in time. Estimates of geological time have varied greatly, but even in the 18th century it became clear to a few that the age of the earth must be in millions of years rather than the thousands then popularly accepted from Biblical exegesis. Now some geological dates are firmly established, within narrowing limits, and no competent geologist considers the earth less than 3 billion years old. (Upper estimates for the solar system range from 5 to 10 billion.) That is still only a moment in eternity, but it characterizes a world very different from one conceived as less than 6000 years old.

With dawning realization that the earth is really extremely old, in human terms of age, came the knowledge that it has changed progressively and radically but usually gradually and always in an orderly, a natural, way. The fact of change had not earlier been denied in Western science or theology—after all, the Noachian Deluge was considered a radical change. But the Deluge was believed to have supernatural causes or concomitants that were not operative throughout earth's history. The doctrine of geological uniformitarianism, finally established early in the 19th century, widened the recognized reign of natural law. The earth has changed throughout its history under the action of material forces, only, and of the *same* forces as those now visible to us and still acting on it.

The Higher Superstition and the Discovery of Evolution

The steps that I have so briefly traced reduced the sway of superstition in the conceptual world of human lives. The change was slow, it was unsteady, and it was not accepted by everyone. Even now there are nominally civilized people whose world was created in 4004 B.C. Nevertheless, by early Victorian times the physical world of a literate consensus was geologically ancient and materially lawful in its history and its current operations. Not so, however, the world of life; here the higher (or at least later) superstition was still almost unshaken. Pendulums might swing with mathematical regularity and mountains might rise and fall through millennia, but living things belonged outside the realm of material principles and secular history. If life obeyed any laws, they were supernal and not bound to the physics of inert substance. Beyond its original, divine creation, life's history was trivial. Its kinds were each as created in the beginning, changeless except for minor and obvious variations.

Perhaps the most crucial element in man's world is his conception of himself. It is here that the higher superstition offers little real advance over the lower. According to the higher superstition, man is something quite distinct from nature. He stands apart from all other creatures; his kinship is supernatural, not natural. It may, at first sight, seem anomalous that those scientists who held this view did classify man as an animal. Linnaeus, an orthodox upholder of the higher superstition, even classifed *Homo* with the apes and monkeys. No blood relationship was implied. The system of nature was the pattern of creation,

and it included all created things, without any mutual affinities beyond the separate placing of each in one divine plan.

Another subtler and even more deeply warping concept of the higher superstition was that the world was created for man. Other organisms had no separate purpose in the scheme of creation. Whether noxious or useful, they were to be seriously considered only in their relationship to the supreme creation, the image of God. It required considerable ingenuity to determine why a louse, for example, was created to be a companion for man, but the ingenuity was not lacking. A world made for man is no longer the inherently hostile and evil world of *kanaima,* but that again is offset in some versions of the higher superstition by the belief that man himself is inherently evil or, at least, sinful.

Those elements of the higher superstition dominated European thought before publication of *The Origin of Species,* but various studies of the centennial year have exhaustively demonstrated that evolutionary ideas existed and were slowly spreading among a minority of *cognoscenti* long before Darwin. Some believed that a species, although divinely and separately created, might change, and in particular might degenerate from its form in the original plan of creation. That is not a truly evolutionary view, since it does not really involve the origin of one species from another, but it does deserve to be called pro-evolutionary in that it recognized the fact that each separate species may change. In the 18th century Buffon went that far, but hardly further, in spite of some apologists who now hail him as an evolutionist.

Some 18th-century worthies—among them Linnaeus in his later years—did go one step further. They conceived that each of the separately created "kinds" of Genesis might later have become considerably diversified, so that the unit of separate creation might be what we now call a genus or even a family or higher group, and the species or subgroups might have arisen, or indeed evolved, since the creation. Just as the many breeds of domesticated dogs are all dogs and of common origin, so the wolves, coyotes, foxes, jackals, and other wild species might all descend from a single creation of the dog-kind. That would still admit no relationship between the dog-kind and the now likewise diversified but singly and separately created cat-kind, for example. . . .

By the end of the 18th century there were a few true and thorough-going evolutionists—Charles Darwin's grandfather Erasmus was one, as has so often been pointed out. Their number increased during the first half of the 19th century. Some of them even had glimmerings of Darwin's great discovery, natural selection, although (contrary to some recent historians whose aim seems to be to denigrate Darwin) none of them elucidated that principle clearly and fully.

Darwin

Practically all of the ideas in *The Origin of Species* had been dimly glimpsed, at least, by someone or other before 1859. . . .

The reason why *The Origin of Species* carried conviction was that it did supply sufficient evidence of evolution and also provided an explanation of the phenomena of evolution. That twofold nature of Darwin's accomplishment has certainly been pointed out often enough, but the statement has also been criticized, and perhaps some small notice should here be given to some of the criticisms. It has, for one thing, been maintained that previous evidence *was* sufficient. It had persuaded Erasmus Darwin, Lamarck, Chambers . . . and others, so (some critics say) it should have persuaded anyone without Charles Darwin's needing to recompile it. That conclusion is simply ridiculous. What anyone thinks *should* have happened has nothing to do with the question of historical fact. Previous evidence *did not* convince a majority of interested scientists; therefore it was insufficient for that purpose. Darwin's evidence *did* in fact convince them; therefore it was sufficient. (It may of course be recognized, as Darwin himself implied, that the way had been prepared by a changing climate of opinion and that even his evidence might

have been insufficient if adduced at an earlier date.)

It has further been suggested that evolution could have been, perhaps should have been, established as a fact without requiring an explanation, and also that Darwin's explanation was not really adequate. The first proposition is debatable, certainly, and examples can be produced to support both sides. The inheritance of acquired characters was accepted by practically everyone, down to and including Darwin, even though no one had adequately explained it. Darwin himself did not like to deal with unexplained facts, and he did belatedly attempt to explain the inheritance of acquired characters. Since in this case the "facts" were not true, that particular Darwinian theory is now charitably forgotten. (Fortunately it was not really essential to his broader theory explanatory of evolution as whole.) In any case, belief in the inheritance of acquired characters did not depend on any explanation of the supposed phenomena. (Is there perhaps a warning in the fact that the unexplained phenomena did not in truth occur?) On the other side of the argument is the modern example of extrasensory perception. A great mass of facts is claimed to demonstrate the reality of that unexplained phenomenon, and yet it is not generally accepted. It seems quite clear that it will not carry conviction unless some credible explanation is produced.

It does seem to me highly improbable that the fact of evolution would have been accepted so widely and quickly if it had been unaccompanied by an explanatory theory. Again, to question whether it *should* have been would be childish arguing with history. . . .

The Fact of Evolution

The fact—not theory—that evolution has occurred and the Darwinian theory as to how it has occurred have become so confused in popular opinion that the distinction must be stressed. The distinction is also particularly important for the present subject, because the effects on the world in which we live have been distinct. The greatest impact no doubt has come from the fact of evolution. It must color the whole of our attitude toward life and toward ourselves, and hence our whole perceptual world. That is, however, a single step, essentially taken a hundred years ago and now a matter of simple rational acceptance or superstitious rejection. How evolution occurs is much more intricate, still incompletely known, debated in detail, and the subject of most active investigation at present. Decision here has decidedly practical aspects and also affects our worlds even more intimately, and in even more ways, than the fact of evolution. The two will be separately considered.

The import of the fact of evolution depends on how far evolution extends, and here there are two crucial points: does it extend from the inorganic into the organic, and does it extend from the lower animals to man? In *The Origin of Species* Darwin implies that life did not arise naturally from nonliving matter, for in the very last sentence he wrote, ". . . life . . . having been originally breathed by the Creator into a few forms or into one. . . ." (The words *by the Creator* were inserted in the second edition and are one of many gradual concessions made to critics of that book.) Later, however, Darwin conjectured (he did not consider this scientific) that life will be found to be a "consequence of some general law"—that is, to be a result of natural processes rather than divine intervention. . . .

Until comparatively recently, many and probably most biologists agreed with Darwin that the problem of the origin of life was not yet amenable to scientific study. Now, however, almost all biologists agree that the problem can be attacked scientifically. The consensus is that life did arise naturally from the nonliving and that even the first living things were not specially created. The conclusion has, indeed, really become inescapable, for the first steps in that process have already been repeated in several laboratories. . . .

At the other end of the story, it was evident to evolutionists from the start that man cannot be an exception. In *The Origin of Species* Darwin deliberately avoided the issue, saying

only in closing, "Light will be thrown on the origin of man and his history." Yet his adherents made no secret of the matter and at once embroiled Darwin, with themselves, in arguments about man's origin from monkeys. Twelve years later (in 1871) Darwin published *The Descent of Man,* which makes it clear that he was indeed of that opinion. No evolutionist has since seriously questioned that man did originate by evolution. Some, notably the Wallace who shared with Darwin the discovery of natural selection, have maintained that special principles, not elsewhere operative, were involved in human origins, but that is decidedly a minority opinion about the causes or explanations, not the fact, of evolution.

It is of course also true that the precise ancestry of man is not identified in full detail and so is subject to some disagreement. That is a minor matter of no real importance for man's image of himself. No one doubts that man is a member of the order Primates along with lemurs, tarsiers, monkeys, and apes. Few doubt that his closest living relatives are the apes. On this subject, by the way, there has been too much pussyfooting. Apologists emphasize that man cannot be a descendant of any living ape—a statement that is obvious to the verge of imbecility—and go on to state or imply that man is not really descended from an ape or monkey at all, but from an earlier common ancestor. In fact, that common ancestor would certainly be called an ape or monkey in popular speech by anyone who saw it. Since the terms *ape* and *monkey* are defined by popular usage, man's ancestors *were* apes or monkeys (or successively both). It is pusillanimous if not dishonest for an informed investigator to say otherwise.

Evolution is, then, a completely general principle of life. (I refer here, and throughout, to organic evolution. Inorganic evolution, as of the stars or the elements, is quite different in process and principle, a part of the same grand history of the universe but not an extension of evolution as here understood.) Evolution is a fully natural process, inherent in the physical properties of the universe, by which life arose in the first place and by which all living things, past or present, have since developed, divergently and progressively.

This world into which Darwin led us is certainly very different from the world of the higher superstition. In the world of Darwin man has no special status other than his definition as a distinct species of animal. He is in the fullest sense a part of nature and not apart from it. He is akin, not figuratively but literally, to every living thing, be it an ameba, a tapeworm, a flea, a seaweed, an oak tree, or a monkey—even though the degrees of relationship are different and we may feel less empathy for forty-second cousins like the tapeworms than for, comparatively speaking, brothers like the monkeys. This is togetherness and brotherhood with a vengeance, beyond the wildest dreams of copy writers or of theologians.

Moreover, since man is one of many millions of species all produced by the same grand process, it is in the highest degree improbable that anything in the world exists specifically for his benefit or ill. It is no more true that fruits, for instance, evolved for the delectation of men than that men evolved for the delectation of tigers. Every species, including our own, evolved for its own sake, so to speak. Different species are intricately interdependent, and also some are more successful than others, but there is no divine favoritism. The rational world is not teleological in the old sense. It certainly has purpose, but the purposes are not imposed from without or anticipatory of the future. They are internal to each species separately, relevant only to its functions and usually only to its present condition. Every species is unique, and it is true that man is unique in new and very special ways. Among these peculiarities, parts of the definition of *Homo sapiens,* is the fact that man does have his own purposes that relate to the future. . . .

Synthesis

Adaptation and the apparent purposefulness of evolution are basic problems that a successful theory *must* solve. The rising science of genetics early in this century not only failed to solve the problem but also made it appear insuperably difficult. That explains why almost no students of other disciples were inclined to accept mutationism, and why Neo-Lamarckism, an elegant but as we now know incorrect solution, hung on for so long. It also was one of several reasons for continued popularity of non-naturalistic theories, to which I allude below.

The way out of the dilemma seems simple now that it has been found. Mutationism is not an alternative to Neo-Darwinism but a supplement to it. If mutation is the source of new variation and yet is substantially nonadaptive, and if the actual course of evolution is to a large extent adaptive, then some additional factor or process must frequently intervene between the occurrence of mutations and the incorporation of some of them into evolving populations. The intervening process must be literally selective, because it must tend (not necessarily with full efficiency) to weed out disadvantageous mutations and genetic combinations and to multiply those that are advantageous in existing circumstances. Natural selection is just such a process, and the principal modern theory of evolution, although it contains much besides, is in large part a synthesis of selection theory and mutation theory.

Evolution is an extremely complex process, and we are here interested mainly in the effects of the concept on our world rather than in the process for its own sake. For that purpose I must, however, briefly note the main elements of the process now known. Genetic systems, governing heredity in each individual case, are composed of genes and chromosomes, discrete but complexly interacting units at different levels of size and complexity. The genes themselves, their organized associations in chromosomes, and whole sets of chromosomes have a large degree of stability as units, but all the kinds of units are shuffled and combined in various ways by the sexual processes of reproduction in most organisms. Thus, a considerable amount of variation is maintained, and, so to speak, genetic experimentation occurs in all natural populations. Mutations, in the broadest sense, affecting individual genes, chromosomes, or sets of chromosomes, introduce wholly new variation, which is fed into the processes of recombination.

Populations of similar animals, usually interbreeding among themselves and definable as species, have genetic pools, characterized by the total of genetic units in the included individuals and the distribution of combinations of those units through the population. Evolutionary change involves changes in the genetic pool, in kinds of included units, in frequencies of them, and in kinds and frequencies of combinations of them. Recombination alone does not tend to change the genetic pool. Only three processes are known to do so: mutation, fluctuation in genetic frequencies (what are known statistically as "sampling errors"), and differential reproduction. The first two of those processes are not oriented toward adaptation. They are in that sense essentially random, and are usually inadaptive, although they may rarely and coincidentally be adaptive. By "differential reproduction" is meant the consistent production of more offspring, on an average, by individuals with certain genetic characteristics than by those without those particular characteristics. That is the modern understanding of natural selection, including but broader than the Darwinian or Neo-Darwinian concept, which emphasized mortality and survival more than reproduction. Natural selection in the Darwinian sense and still more in this expanded sense is nonrandom, and its trend is adaptive. It also tends, not always with complete success, to counteract the random effects of mutation and sampling error.

Evolutionary processes are tremendously more complicated in detail than this bald outline suggests. The point of the outline is that here is a mechanism, involving only materials and processes known beyond a doubt to occur in nature, capable (as one of its proponents has said) of generating just the degree of improbability evident in the phenomena of evolution.

Further information pertinent to our theme is provided by paleontology, the actual record of events in the history of life. Observation and experimentation with living organisms can extend over a few years, at most. There is always a possibility that processes there evident worked out differently over spans of millions of years, or that the actual history involved principles undetectable in shorter periods of time. There is admittedly some difference of opinion, but I think it fair to say that there is now a consensus for the view that the fossil record is fully consistent with the modern synthetic theory of evolution and that it neither requires nor suggests any alternative explanation.

There is one thing demonstrated by the fossil record that is decidedly pertinent here and that probably would never have been inferred from study of living organisms. Throughout the whole history of life most species have become extinct, without issue. The statistically usual outcome of evolution is not, then, the progressive appearance of higher forms but simply obliteration. There has, indeed, been progression and even (still more rarely) progress, but this has been in the comparatively few, exceptional lines of descent. The adaptive mechanism of natural selection has guaranteed that some lineages would win, that the world would indeed be filled and kept filled with adapted organisms, but just as inexorably it has insured that most lineages would lose. It has, moreover, had the result that even the winners, the lineages that have survived so far, have not necessarily been progressive, from a human point of view at least. The primitive ameba has remained adapted, hence has survived, while the lordly dinosaurs lost adaptation and therefore life. The degenerate tapeworm is to all appearances as well adapted as the—we like to think—progressive man. . . .

The World of Man

Let me summarize and conclude as to this world into which Darwin led us. In it man and all other living things have evolved, ultimately from the nonliving, in accordance with entirely natural, material processes. In part that evolution has been random in the sense of lacking adaptive orientation. As a rule, however, it has been oriented or directed toward achieving and maintaining adaptive relationships between populations of organisms and their whole environments. Nevertheless, this blind, amoral process has not guaranteed indefinite maintenance of adaptation for any given lineage of populations. On the contrary, it usually leads to eventual extinction and a repeopling of the world by the newly divergent offspring of a minority of earlier successful lineages. The mechanism of orientation, the nonrandom element in this extraordinarily complex history, has been natural selection, which is now understood as differential reproduction.

Man is one of the millions of results of this material process. He is another species of animal, but not just another animal. He is unique in peculiar and extraordinarily significant ways. He is probably the most self-conscious of organisms, and quite surely the only one that is aware of his own origins, of his own biological nature. He has developed symbolization to a unique degree and is the only organism with true language. This makes him also the only animal who can store knowledge beyond individual capacity and pass it on beyond individual memory. He is by far the most adaptable of all organisms because he has developed culture as a biological adaptation. Now his culture evolves not distinct from and not in replacement of but in addition to biological evolution, which also continues.

Concomitant with these developments is the fact that man has unique moral qualities. The evolutionary process is not moral—the word is simply irrelevant in that connection—but it has finally produced a moral animal. Conspicuous among his moral attributes is a sense of responsibility, which is probably felt in some way and to some degree by every normal human being. There has been disagreement and indeed confusion through the ages regarding to whom and for what man is responsible. The lower and the higher superstitions have produced their several answers. In the post-Darwinian world another answer seems fairly clear: man is responsible to himself and for himself. "Himself" here means the whole human species, not only the individual and certainly not just those of a certain color of hair or cast of features.

The fact that man knows that he evolves entails the possibility that he can do something to influence his own biological destiny. The fact that uncontrolled evolution often leads to degeneration and usually to extinction makes it highly advisable that man take a hand in determining his own future evolution. If man proceeds on the wrong evolutionary assumptions—for instance, on those of Neo-Lamarckism or Michurinism—whatever he does is sure to be wrong. If he proceeds on the right assumptions, what he does may still be wrong, but at least it has a chance of being right.

A world in which man must rely on himself, in which he is not the darling of the gods but only another, albeit extraordinary, aspect of nature, is by no means congenial to the immature or the wishful thinkers. That is plainly a major reason why even now, a hundred years after *The Origin of Species,* most people have not really entered the world into which Darwin led—alas!—only a minority of us. Life may conceivably be happier for some people in the older worlds of superstition. It is possible that some children are made happy by a belief in Santa Claus, but adults should prefer to live in a world of reality and reason.

Perhaps I should end on that note of mere preference, but it is impossible to do so. It is a characteristic of this world to which Darwin opened the door that unless *most* of us do enter it and live maturely and rationally in it, the future of mankind is dim, indeed—if there is any future.

Perspectives Gained from Field Work

Laura Nader

From *Horizons in Anthropology,* Sol Tax (ed.), Aldine Publishing Company, 1964, pp. 148–158. Copyright © 1964, Aldine Publishing Company. By permission of the author, and the publisher and copyright holder.

As part of their training, professionals in every discipline develop a particular way of looking at the world—especially that part of the world which is the subject of their study. This paper will be about how anthropologists look at the world of man.

It is no exaggeration to say that nearly everybody, at one time or another, exhibits an interest in the language, physical type, and customs of other groups, whether they be foreign nationalities or minority groups at home. This was true of the Egyptians and, even more, of the Greeks, who touched on most modern anthropological interests in their philosophical explorations. However, it has been only during the past century that Western scholars have really grappled with the problem of understanding *all* the cultures of the world, from those of the Germans and Chinese to those of the Eskimos and Australian aborigines. This development in scholarship came after Europeans had been traveling to distant corners of the globe for something like four hundred years; ever since the age of Columbus, explorers had been voyaging to all parts of the globe, sometimes entranced and sometimes repelled, but always reacting to the diverse customs of the peoples with whom they visited, traded, and lived.

These early explorers were soon followed by missionaries, traders, and government officials who wrote reports of what they had seen, reports which pointed out to other Europeans that human life was much more varied than anyone had before supposed. The field reporters of that day were first and foremost nineteenth-century Europeans, so it was only natural that the things which impressed them most about non-European cultures were exactly the customs that were unknown to European civilization: things like cannibalism and plurality of wives. It was only natural, too, that societies with such strange and barbarous habits should be thought of as somehow lesser developments in the total history of mankind. When some of the earlier explorers came to the New World they found Indian tribes in which no one seemed able to tell the difference between uncles and cousins; but this was because the Indians used one term for what the Europeans thought of as two distinct categories. In the same way the early explorers believed that primitive people who always spoke in proverbs did not know how to think properly. The problem here was that Europeans saw everything in terms of the values, attitudes, and ideas that they had learned from European civilization. Their thinking was circumscribed by a lack of self-awareness. Regardless of their biases however, it is interesting that these early observers did think it was worth writing down their observations. The information that they made available stimulated the minds of many, and by the nineteenth century anthropologists were reading these detailed collections of facts and trying to find some sort of order in the great potpourri of data.

Following this initial period of anthropology—the study of man primarily based on the accounts of travelers, missionaries, and government men—a new practice developed, that of firsthand, systematic exploration of the variety of human cultures by the anthropologist himself. This foray into the field was the exciting step which was to force a twentieth-century revolution in thinking about the many questions asked by the nineteenth-century anthropologists. The very fact that the anthropologist abandoned his comfortable armchair for the rigors of life in the field was destined to expand the field of factual knowledge upon which theories of human behavior are built. It functioned also to affect radically the anthropologist's image of himself as scientist and humanist.

In the early days of field work, which began in wide-scale form at the turn of the century, a man went to live with a group of aborigines, either accompanied by several other scientists or alone. When he proceeded alone it meant that he was isolated from his family, from his friends, from the whole of his cultural setting. He found himself among a people whose culture was often quite alien to his own, but which need not be truly alien if he learned something about it.

The early fieldworkers—men like Rivers, Boas, Malinowski, and Radcliffe-Brown—began, in a sense, to find new identities by learning about the people they found themselves living among. What they learned they painstakingly recorded. Their notebooks were filled with details of what they saw and heard, and their resultant monographs attempted to render their experiences intelligible in terms, not of Western European culture, but of the native culture itself. A prime problem the field anthropologist has to face was expressed by the famous jurist Cardozo, "No matter how objective we may try to be, we must never forget the fact that we see with our own eyes."

The early fieldworker, somewhat like a man shipwrecked upon a desert island, found it necessary to do a bit of everything. He was alone, and a division of labor was impossible, even were it desirable. And so it was that one man alone recorded the economic, the ritual, the technological, the political, and the kinship aspects of a single society. In fact, he found he could only achieve an understanding of some of the more strange and exotic customs by this sort of overview of the whole culture. The fabric of native life seemed to be so intricately woven that Malinowski, for example, could only perceive the meaning of certain fishing patterns among the Trobianders when he had understood certain magical notions. Or take the Andaman Islanders. It was only after Radcliffe-Brown had analyzed their rituals that he could begin to understand the bonds that hold these men together. These early fieldworkers were trying to understand how all the parts fit together to make a working "whole" society—a society which had adapted to and was adapting a local environment for the purpose of life.

This functionalist approach—the view of culture as an interwoven whole—was not new. Armchair anthropologists of an earlier time, such as Maine and Fustel de Coulanges, had this same view of culture. What was new was the act of going out with this point of view and collecting raw data. The results were not just more data on the variety of cultures in the world, but a different sort of data from that picked up by traders and government officials. It was now more than an interest in exotic minutiae torn out of context; these field studies were explorations in the commonplace and familiar, as well as the strikingly different. Customs which had previously been conceived of as strange or unusual were described as parts of the general design of living.

Since the time of the early fieldworkers, the detailed, and often tedious process of recording the social and cultural life of a people has been replicated by anthropologists in a variety of cultures the world over. The range of societies covered is great—from hunting-and-gathering groups like the American Shoshone and South African Bushmen to large scale civilizations such as Japan and India, from the study of nomadic societies such as the Bedouin, to an industrial American town like Yankee City. And the topics which anthropologists focus upon are equally diverse—child-rearing practices, culture change, language, or law, politics, music, and religion. As a result of this unprecedented ethnographic activity we are now beginning to document in detail the range of variation in human societies. We are now beginning to realize what men have been capable of in social and cultural creations.

The anthropologist lives and works in two worlds. When he is in the field he is recording data by observation and interview. In all his studies he investigates patterns of behavior and this much of his work is descriptive (and, as mentioned by Hymes in his discussion of linguistic anthropology, "an adequate ethnographic description is truly a theoretical task"). Beyond this, however, there is the interpretive part of the science—that part which seeks to relate direct observations to a logical framework of concepts and to a body of general statements about human culture. The anthropologist has to keep both the particular and the general in mind at once. His experience with cultures through time and space stimulates him to work at the complementary tasks of recording unique historical events and generalizing about such events. The special perspective of the anthropologist requires him to be aware of time events—for example, the development and diffusion of

certain ideas and material objects, such as tobacco or the alphabet. He also has to be aware of what we might call timeless events—the fact that certain cultural phenomena recur in the same way under special circumstances. For example, in many societies in the world people practice a custom we refer to as the postpartum sex taboo. It is taboo for a husband and wife to have intercourse for a specified period after their child is born. John Whiting has suggested that in societies where this taboo extends into many months or even years it is quite likely that we will find another customary practice, namely that of plural marriage. Another custom which has world-wide distribution is that of male initiation rites, and again the anthropologist is curious as to why some societies have male initiations and what may be associated with them. Whiting also looked into this question and came up with the intriguing hypothesis that in patrilineal, male-dominated societies, where the mother nurses her son for a very long period, we are likely to find very severe male initiation rites. It is important in male-dominated societies to have men that are *men,* and the purpose of male initiation rites is to emphasize this. These rites are designed to make a man out of a boy who has, for so many years of his life, had a much closer identification with his mother than with his father.

In every culture, however simple or complex, we find some kind of family, some kind of political and economic organization, religious beliefs, ways of settling grievances and punishing crimes, aesthetic and recreative expression, material culture, and so on. I have indicated that we study a wide range of societies in order to understand the universal features of human societies, as well as to understand the particular nature of any idea or institution in a society. At this point I would like to mention some observations that have been made about culturally patterned agression and conflict.

Conflict between husbands and wives occurs, in different degrees, in all societies. Sometimes such conflict ends in what we call "divorce," but again this varies with the culture. In working with two societies in Africa the English anthropologist Max Gluckman noticed that among the Zulu of Natal there was a very low incidence of "divorce" and that among the Lozi of Northern Rhodesia there was a high incidence of "divorce"—and he wondered why it should be that some societies are characterized by brittle and others by long-enduring marriage partnerships. He puts forth an interesting hypothesis: namely, that "divorce" rates vary with the type of descent system. A high divorce rate would be expected to occur in matrilineal societies, a low divorce rate in patrilineal societies; and bilateral societies such as ours would be expected to fall somewhere between the highest and the lowest rate. Another anthropologist, Lloyd Fallers, worked with an African group which was patrilineal in descent but not characterized by stable marriage as Gluckman would have predicted. This led Fallers to reformulate the original hypothesis as follows: "Where a woman either through the complete transfer of her childbearing properties, or by other means, is socially absorbed into her husband's lineage, patriliny tends to stabilize marriage; where a wife is not so absorbed [into her husband's lineage group] and thus remains a member of the lineage into which she was born, patriliny tends to divide marriage by dividing the loyalties of the spouses." While such theories do not take cognizance of the total range of variables relevant to marriage stability, they do center our attention on a very pertinent point—namely that an understanding of the context of marriage is crucial to an analysis of marital stability. There are certain conditions where the prognostication for a lasting marriage is not good. We tend to approach the problem of divorce in Western society by looking at case histories of particular couples in conflict, but we would profit by looking also at the relation between the couple and the larger kin and non-kin groups in society. As Gluckman states this, "Social factors and not only personal disharmonies may control divorce rates in Western society." Regardless of whether one is interested in the Zulu or the Lozi, the

theories formulated to explain specific aspects of these and other particular societies will be useful as points of comparison for viewing marriage stability in our own society. The study of divorce is a study in the conflicts between a man's or a woman's interests and allegiances—a study which has broad implications for society, above and beyond an interest in the elementary family.

The anthropologist also argues that the functions of conflict are multiple. Traditionally, the study of conflict has been the study of the disruptive or disintegrative factors in society, but conflict may produce ties that bind as well as those that divide people. Using African data, for example, Gluckman examined the cohesive effects of conflicts of interests. Referring to the Nuer of East Africa, he describes a situation where an individual is, on the one hand, linked with a group of people through the bonds of kinship, and, on the other hand, to another group, which may be an enemy of the first, through bonds of residence. He concludes, "If there are sufficient conflicts of loyalties at work, settlement will be achieved and law and social order maintained." Such a theory does not of course make a case for the cohesive effects of strife or contentious behavior, but rather suggests that conflicts of interest may bring people together.

Conflict may also be a way of maintaining order. Let us take the study of the feud for instance. The feud as an institution has often been described by ethnographers as an important mechanism of social control in societies which lack formal governmental institutions and officers. A classic case is the Ifugao of the Philippines. Another would be the Scottish Highlanders where the feud has historically been viewed as a "lawless" institution. But is it a lawless institution? A close analysis of the feud in context illustrates that in a very real sense the feud was a "legal" institution, whose function was to punish serious transgressions and act as a brake to prevent aggression. Among the Nuer of Africa we could say that the feud was a valuable institution, necessary for maintaining and integrating social groups in a society where the principle of opposition is basic to the social structure.

Research on conflict and aggressive behavior bears serious thought because the implications are so important to modern man and the dilemma of war. Anthropologists are not pessimistic about warfare. We know that destructive behavior is not a necessity for human life, for there have been enough cases recorded of the constructive channeling of human behavior so that warfare was not necessary. Evidence indicates that warfare was unknown during the earlier part of the Neolithic in Europe and the Orient; organized warfare was unknown in aboriginal Australia and in certain parts of the New World. What we have been able to establish is that different types of culture carry with them varying degrees of propensity for war. Groups like the Pueblo Indians of the American Southwest for many centuries rarely engaged in offensive warfare. On the other hand, among the Tupinamba of Brazil warfare was a major activity. We need to look into such cases. The suggestion that severe inhibition of aggression *within* a society such as the Tupinamba "encourages" outlets for aggression by means of warfare is not to be taken lightly.

All the examples previously mentioned of marital conflict, feuds, and societal inhibition of aggression have in the main been concerned with the impact of such behavior on the society at large. Other anthropologists have been concerned with the ways in which a society inculcates in its children certain ideas about aggression—attitudes about aggression are taught to children in all societies. Clyde Kluckhohn and Whiting and Child have explored the general question of what happens when aggression is severely inhibited in early childhood—that is, when children are taught never to express anger by aggressive behavior towards their fellow men. Preliminary findings suggest, for example, that if such feelings can not be expressed between people there will be a high degree of phantasy projection of such feelings onto sorcerers and witches. And this hypothesis, when followed through, leads us into the generally fascinating problem of why some societies practice witchcraft and others do not.

Thus far, I have talked principally about anthropological experience in preliterate societies. Anthropologists, however, have not found it difficult to shift their focus from the small, preliterate society to the modern world, and today this is evidenced by the kinds of research they are doing. We find anthropologists not only in the university, but also in government, in industry, and in hospitals, and their research is not so different in general method and approach from that of their field trips in preliterate societies. Gregory Bateson and his colleagues for example find themselves, as anthropologists, working with schizophrenic patients. Their research in psychotherapy utilizes some ideas very basic in anthropology. Mental illness is viewed as both a cultural and a genetic problem. Several years ago Beaglehole noted that there were strong tendencies among certain Pacific Island groups to particular kinds of mental illness. The Filipinos, for example, tended towards catatonic schizophrenia; among the Hawaiians there was a predominance of paranoia; and manic and depressive states were common among Japanese patients. All these patterns suggest the influence of cultural factors, although there is some evidence that this remains to be clarified. Urban ecologists have found that certain types of mental illness characterize the center of a metropolitan area whereas others are usually found on the periphery, and these findings again suggest the importance of environment. It has also been suggested that mental illness may be communicable, much as other kinds of behavior diffuse from one society to another. Bateson in dealing with schizophrenic patients abandoned the idea that a patient can be treated as an isolate. He and his colleagues investigated the patterns of parent-child interaction which seem to characterize the families of schizophrenics, and they have developed a theory about the kind of interaction which is conducive to the development of schizophrenia. The mental patient is treated simultaneously with his family. Owing in great part to the studies of anthropologists, the patient is no longer viewed as a single thread; if he is to be understood he must be examined in the fabric of his whole cultural *and* genetic heritage.

The main point to remember in all these examples is that what we learn about one society can tell us something about another. Margaret Mead gained insight into American problems of adolescence by investigating the lives of young Samoans. Political movements such as Zionism can best be understood if compared with a variety of similar nativistic movements that have been recorded through time. Similarly the deterrent effects of capital punishment can be evaluated by the study of societies where capital punishment is not used. What we discover in the study of an institution such as the family in any one society makes more intelligible the nature of the family in our own culture, while the comparative view enables us to see mankind as a whole.

The phrase "viewing culture as a whole" is an oft-repeated one in anthropology, and it is often repeated because it has led to some valuable insights as to what makes men tick. Statements such as "people drink too much," may be relatively meaningless unless they are supported by a detailed description of drinking in a particular context. In my own work among the Zapotec Indians of Mexico I recorded the various settings in which drinking took place. In each context drinking meant something in particular: it was considered bad for a man to drink alone, good to drink in company, courteous to drink in the courts of law, improper to drink in the presence of ritual kinsmen unless invited, and so on.

Many years ago Donald Horton demonstrated that the higher the level of anxiety in a society the greater the frequency of alcoholism, and now the interesting question becomes—in what settings does alcoholism increase and with what kinds of anxieties? When I left the Zapotec there was a generally worried atmosphere about what would happen to them now that the rapidly expanding Mexican system of roadways had put them in

closer contact with modern Mexican national culture. They were worried as to how this contact with the non-Zapotec world would affect their mores and customs. Merchants would now be able to come in from the state capitol; there was already an increase in the production of cash crops, and many of them realized that their economy would no longer depend solely upon the fluctuations of climatic conditions, but would also be affected by price conditions of the nation and the world. These people are facing new crises, new anxieties, and alcoholism is on the increase. Will they increase their consumption of alcohol by drinking in groups, or will there be an increase in solitary drinking—drinking which is not traditionally sanctioned—and why?

The anthropologist realizes, and painfully so at times, that few problems involving humans can be defined and solved within the confines of any narrow analysis. Any kind of anthropological research itself is a multilevel investigation. We are aware that cultures which appear to be quite similar in many basic features of form may nevertheless show striking behavioral dissimilarities, and it is necessary for the anthropologist to investigate simultaneously form, content, and the various levels of culture, such as what people do, what they think they do, and what they feel they ought to do. It has been pointed out by anthropologists working in industry, for example, that you can not always find out what will motivate efficient work production simply by asking people—and the reason you often can not is because so much of culture is out of the range of the conscious. This is why an anthropologist doing research in a factory does not only sit in an office and interview workers, but also spends hours working and observing in the production room.

The emphasis that anthropologists have placed upon participant observation cannot be overstressed, especially for those interested in the development of the so-called underdeveloped countries of the world. One of the problems faced by those who plan economic development is that of social distance—those patterns of behavior which separate men. Certainly in many contexts social-distance mechanisms are useful and indeed necessary for maintaining order, role identity, and predictability, but they may also serve as barriers to communication. In many underdeveloped countries today we observe the development of an elite educated class—a class that is striving to utilize modern technical knowledge for the improvement of their peoples' lives. This goal implies change, but the social distance between the educated and the masses of the people often stands in the way of communication and thus in the way of diffusion of ideas and material culture. Participant observation by this educated elite may be useful in breaking down the barriers to communication.

Several themes have been underlined in this description of anthropological exploration: how anthropologists view culture as a whole, how their description of particular societies permits them to generalize for mankind, how anthropological techniques have been applied to modern societies, and how perspectives gained in other societies enable viewing our own with some measure of detachment. Participant observations and more recent techniques developed as part of the ethnoscientific enquiry equip anthropologists to discover both unconscious and conscious levels of culture not easily reported by informants or observed by the anthropologist. Much has been accomplished in less than a half-century of field work, but we have yet only a glimmer of the possibilities for anthropology.

selection 4

Fieldwork in Malta

Jeremy Boissevain

From *Being an Anthropologist, Fieldwork in Eleven Cultures,* George D. Spindler (ed.), Holt, Rinehart and Winston, Inc., 1970, pp. 58–84. Copyright © 1970, Holt, Rinehart and Winston, Inc. By permission of the author, and the publisher and the copyright holder. With minor corrections by the author.

Preface

All anthropological research can be divided into four major phases: (1) the preparation for the field, (2) the actual fieldwork, (3) the analysis and writing up, and, last but not least, (4) a period of introspection and reanalysis after the first major work based on the fieldwork has left the researcher's hands. Personally I consider each of more or less equal importance. The preparation and formulation of the questions by the researcher before he sets out into the field influence the sort of data with which he will return. Even a talented researcher using the most sophisticated research techniques will only find the answers to the questions he asks. On the other hand, even if he has excellent data, unless he submits himself and the data to a rather rigid discipline, he will not be able to digest it. Moreover, once digested, it must then be set out clearly and simply so that the reader who knows little or nothing about the problem and area will be able to understand the exposition.

Phase 1 and especially phase 3 are generally given insufficient importance. Yet in terms of input, these demand an investment of at least three or four times as much time and energy as phase 2. I stress this because in this chapter I focus primarily on phase 2, the actual fieldwork. The reader should remember, however, that as far as I am concerned, all phases are of equal importance. . . .

Full of expectation my wife and I and our two daughters, aged six and four, left England for Malta in our Morris Minor station wagon on Monday, June 27, 1960, camping along the way.

Arrival and First Contacts

We arrived in Malta at dawn on Monday, July 18, 1960 after an overnight trip on one of the expensive and dilapidated little Italian ships that ply between Malta and Syracuse. We were welcomed by Father Charles Vella, and within two hours we were cleared through customs, our car had been unloaded, and we were having breakfast in the Meadowbank Hotel on the Sliema seafront. This was to be our home for the next three weeks.

The next two days were spent . . . seeing to a deluge of official papers. On Wednesday I set out to see if I could find my way to Hal-Farrug. I had never been there before and, like most foreigners living in Malta, as well as a large number of Malta's town-dwelling elite, I did not know my way about the southern villages at all. An entry in my diary for that day reads as follows:

Went for a drive to Farrug. Got lost and passed through Mqabba. This is quite an interesting looking town. It has about the right "look." Then through to Safi, where a group of ten- to thirteen-year-olds surrounded my car and asked me why I wanted to go to Hal-Farrug, because people there were "savages." The children were friendly enough but tough; they hung about the car for quite a bit. They wanted me to come back and talk to them.

This was my first introduction to the good-natured rivalry between villages and the friendly but aggressive curiosity of village children. There is a Maltese proverb that eloquently sums up this character trait: "God protect us from wild bees and village children." After driving about a bit more I found my way to Hal-Farrug. The diary entry continues:

Farrug is a small town. It looked cosy. I stopped at a shop for a box of matches and an orangeade. A friendly lady making fishnet in the shop served me. Several boys dressed only in short trousers and undershirts came in to stare at me. I noticed a sign which said Farrug Stars Football Club.

These were the first impressions jotted down in haste and, as is evident, in not nearly enough detail, because those first impressions are extremely important. I had spent fifteen minutes drinking orangeade, smoking a cigarette, and trying my Maltese out on the lady of the shop. The shop turned out to be the football club in which I was later to spend many evenings. The first impressions of Farrug were very positive.

The day after I finally met Dun Gorg, the parish priest of Farrug, who, at Father Charles Vella's request, had located a house for us. The house belonged to Tereza Abela. It was the ground floor of a house in which her daughter Angela and son-in-law Leonard lived. It consisted of a room that opened onto the street, another behind that, and a small room with a sink, which opened onto a little courtyard at the other side of which was a fourth room which until very recently had been used as a stable. The house was very sparsely furnished and the courtyard was lined with an elaborate system of cages housing chickens and rabbits, and clouds of flies.

The next day I brought my wife along to see it, and we agreed that it had great possibilities. Tereza Abela, who had had some experience renting property she owned in a neighboring town to English Service families, said she would carry out the necessary changes. She promised to paint the stable, arrange for a shower, sink, and toilet, provide beds, a large working table, chairs, and some sort of a sideboard. Carmelo, her eldest son, a skilled electrician at the dockyard, arrived and I was able to discuss a number of technical details with him. Dun Gorg promised to keep an eye on things and assured me that if anyone in the village could, Tereza would see that her boys carried out the work in the fortnight promised. He would see to it that Tereza remained interested in encouraging her boys. We left well pleased at the prospects of finally being able to begin fieldwork in two weeks.

We spent the next twenty days settling down to life in Malta in general, filling in more documents, collecting our trunks, and shopping for the innumerable odds and ends of household equipment that we would need. The logistics of everyday living are in fact a great deal more complicated than those whose life has settled down into a comfortable pattern realize.

Another thing I did was to visit systematically a number of my old contacts with the government. This brought me into the Department of Social Welfare, Department of Information, Central Office of Statistics, University, Department of Agriculture, and law courts. I also made courtesy calls on the Governor and Lieutenant Governor. . . .

Finally the great day arrived. On Saturday, August 6, 1960, at about five in the evening, we moved into our house. Before we knew it, our children were playing happily out on the street with neighboring children, and gazing in awe at the hundreds of goats and sheep streaming back to the houses at sunset. One of the Abela boys came in to ask how things were. He tried, without success, to get the kerosene refrigerator to run. He told us that the music we could hear came from the square. The Saint Martin Band Club was holding a rally to whip up enthusiasm for the coming centenary of their saint. He poked at the refrigerator several more times and then hurried to the square himself.

After tucking the children into their beds in the white-washed stable, which had now become their bedroom, I steeled myself to go to the square. For many months I had been nervously thinking about the moment when I would have to stride across the square in the full gaze of the whole village, and begin my fieldwork. In brief I had a very bad case of stage fright. Unfortunately I had not realized

that there was absolutely nothing to be nervous about, for my fieldwork had in fact begun quite some time before.

A few steps beyond our front door I met Salvu, another of Tereza Abela's sons, with a friend, and together we walked toward the music. The square in front of the Saint Martin's Club was milling with people. Music blared from a loudspeaker stuck in one of the windows. People were clapping and shouting slogans and poems in honor of Saint Martin. Though many were indeed staring at me, I found I did not mind: I was talking to Salvu and his friend. In front of the band club I saw another familiar face, Pietru Cardona, a local school teacher to whom Dun Gorg had introduced me on my first visit. He pulled me into the band club to admire his tape recorder, which was in fact producing the deafening music. Inside I met old Victor Azzopardi, the senior village school teacher, church sacristan and, at the time, treasurer of the Saint Martin Band Club. Though at first reserved, he loosened up at once when I told him I knew Francis Chetcuti, who a few years before had been headmaster in the village. An excited stream of words about band clubs, *festa* music, different types of fireworks, and how you make them kept washing over me. After a bit I left Pietru and walked with Salvu Abela and his friend through the village. Though we attracted comments, they were good natured one. They finally brought me back home. I nodded to Leonard, our upstairs neighbor, who was hiding in the shadow of his doorway listening to a furious quarrel between neighbors a little farther up the street. I learned later that one had hung an enormous picture of Dom Mintoff, the labor leader, over his door. His opposite neighbor objected violently. Fieldwork had begun. The beginning had been painless and pleasant.

Adjustment to Hal-Farrug

Although our adjustment to the way of life of our neighbors proceeded rapidly, it was not always without problems. There were basic household problems and new influences that affected our family customs. Besides these, we of course also faced the problem of learning new roles and modes of behavior.

The house was small, but it was reasonably comfortable. It was certainly much more comfortable than the tent in which we had camped for the three weeks previous to our arrival in Malta. Foolishly, we kept comparing, sometimes rather guiltily, our surroundings with the tents and mud huts which we imagined to be typical of anthropological housing in the field. What we forgot was that these would not have been ordinary mud huts placed at random, but the local equivalent of the town houses and mansions of the elite. Applying this principle to Hal-Farrug, we should have maintained a much higher living standard. The focus on peasants, villages, and slums in the sociological literature on southern Europe in general reflects the researchers' inability to keep up with the local elite. It may be possible to study peasants even if you live in a mansion, but if you live in a peasant house it is not possible to meet as an equal those who live in mansions.

Partly as a result of this error, and our recent camping experience, we did little to improve the comfort of our sparsely furnished quarters. The easy chairs remained those of our camping trip: ground-level folding stools. With a few pounds' worth of screening material I ended the constant invasion of flies that almost drove us to despair during the first forty-eight hours. The flies were now confined to the outside, where they continued to attack relentlessly, quickly spotting the laundry on the line and leaving indelible traces on the finish of our car.

The plumbing performed well for the first three weeks and then rebelled. I discovered this as I was having a shower and the neighbors above flushed their toilet. Suddenly I was ankle deep in rebellion. After this I arranged to have the mini-cesspit that served both our houses emptied weekly. In fact most of our neighbors had sewage troubles and the smell of sewage gas was with us everywhere in the village. Fortunately the village is today connected with the main sewage system of the island.

We, or rather Inga, very soon got used to the main problem of housekeeping: the fact that Maltese rise very early. We were anxious to buy as much as we could in the village in order not only to give the business to our neighbors, but also to establish contact. She soon learned to go shopping early, for most of the meat and fresh vegetables were bought up by the women at 5:00 in the morning on their way back from the first Mass. After her first shopping expedition at 8:30, when all she had been able to find were a few bits of meat and some wilted vegetables, she usually set out just before 7:00. It did not take long before she was shouting at the vegetable vendor just like our neighbors, and disdainfully flinging the produce about on his cart in order to get a good bargain. I . . . think that Maltese vegetable vendors are among the most abused persons in the world. Whenever she had problems concerning shopping she always found a willing escort of women who showed her where she could buy what she wanted.

My new role as a researcher forced us to modify a number of our family customs. I felt obliged to be in the village as much as possible to see what was happening, but I could not always predict when important events would take place. This meant that my coming and going in the family circle was often irregular. Inga very soon got used to seeing me disappear in the evening after I had read a story to the children in their stable, which now smelled sweetly of the esparto-grass stuffing their mattresses. Unlike Maltese women, she did not have the network of relatives in the village whom she could visit while her husband was away, but she quickly made many friends, with whom she visited.

Our children made friends quickly with the children of a large farming family opposite us. They, too, had a lot to learn about customs. They especially had difficulty getting used to not accepting biscuits, sweets, and soft drinks eagerly as soon as they were offered. This is considered greedy. They soon learned to refuse politely several times before being convinced to accept the gift. In a short time too they learned songs in praise of the archbishop, and to make rude noises whenever the name of Dom Mintoff was mentioned. Some of their little playmates were rather conservative.

Another problem we had was what I call the two worlds of Malta: town and country. The way of life and the network of contacts that we were building in the villages were completely alien to our upper-class Maltese friends from the towns. But perhaps "problem" is too strong a word. After we moved to Farrug, we dropped out of the sight of many of the acquaintances we had among the town-dwelling elite. A few friends would come and visit us occasionally. Although they never said so directly, the contrast of our sparsely furnished village house with the sumptuous townhouse in which we had once lived was puzzling to most of our Maltese acquaintances. Most Maltese, and especially the competitive professional classes, are intensely materialistic. It was inconceivable to them that someone should *choose* to live in our present surroundings: a tragedy must have befallen us. We saw less and less of them. Maybe this was just as well. The arrival of doctors, lawyers, and ex-cabinet ministers to see us would have troubled the image we were trying to establish. Nonetheless, our very occasional sorties to a nobleman's reception or a formal luncheon with the governor, highlighted the cleavage between the way of life of the villagers and of the town-dwelling professional classes. Equally instructive were the patronizing and disdainful references to Hal-Farrug and villages like it, and to the people who lived there, by the Anglicized upper-classes we met at thse functions. The women in particular cooed in their English-accented, Italianized Maltese at the quaint, rustic way I spoke their language. Although we went to few such functions, those we attended taught us a great deal.

Bringing a large family into the field obviously creates certain problems of adaptation. A good deal of time and energy is invested in the simple logistics of everyday life. These unquestionably take time away from research and writing. Sometimes the combined pressure of the established roles of father and husband plus the new roles the anthropologist is learning and tentatively acting out becomes a considerable strain. Nonetheless the positive advantages gained from having a family in the field far outweigh these dis-

advantages. To begin with, a family provides an island which is part of another way of life. In Hal-Farrug certainly this prevented me from becoming completely absorbed in local events and helped to maintain a certain objectivity. Second, it provides companionship. Although the researcher can become close to his informants, he is always an outsider. Research can be a lonely business. Third, a family gives the researcher an adult status. In a society in which all adults are expected to marry, those who produce children (our third daughter was born shortly after we left Farrug!) are regarded as more complete persons. This means that you share this status and the experience that this brings with leaders of the community. Finally, through Inga and the children I made a number of extra contacts with neighbors, and gained valuable insights into the world of the women.

In short, though we had some problems of adjustment, none were insurmountable. That they were not was in so small measure due to two factors: the flexibility and willingness of the members of my own family to learn new customs and modify behavior and the extreme helpfulness and patience of the people of Hal-Farrug. Within a month or so after our arrival we were no longer *L-Ingliz* and *L-Ingliza,* the generic nicknames given to all foreigners; we became *Gerri* and *Gerrija.* We thus received personal nicknames derived from my Christian name from our neighbors. There were still, however, many problems of adjustment that I had to solve in my role as participant observer.

Participant Observation

The chief research technique of an anthropologist is very different from that of a sociologist. The sociologist works with informants in a research situation, and then retires from the scene. His contacts are generally short and not repeated over time. He knows his informant only in the role of informant. An anthropologist, on the other hand, must be able to get along with people well, for he remains in contact with his informants over a long period of time. He must play many roles before them: not only that of interviewer, but also that of husband, father, neighbor, friend, patron, client, clique-member, and so on. Many of these are new roles for him. Moreover, he must play these roles, whether old or new, in public. In small communities such as Hal-Farrug, the anthropologist, as the newcomer and representative of a foreign culture, is constantly at the center of the village stage. He is consciously acting. After a bit he is usually acting well and receiving compliments from his audience. This is a very heady mixture. The experience of course varies, but it is something that all anthropologists who have done fieldwork share, and in a certain measure it sets them apart from those who have not.

I enjoy fieldwork. Looking back on the work that I have done in my various occupations, it is the close and prolonged periods of contact with people in the field that stand out as high points in my life. Of these the most important was the first.

All anthropologists, I think, are faced with two conflicting roles as participant observers. In Hal-Farrug I felt this very strongly. On the one hand, I wished to construct as large and wide-ranging a network of contacts as possible. On the other, I needed to pursue specific bits of information from selected informants. Although much of the quality of the information I was able to get depended upon the friendships that I had been able to build, the techniques of building those friendships very often got in the way of the information I tried to collect. This is because informants see themselves not as informants but as friends. For the anthropologist they are both. In retrospect, it seems as though I spent many frustrating hours discussing world news with Pietru Cardona—especially the fate of Patrice Lumumba, for the time was 1960—when I would have preferred discussing the band club rivalry, political factions, and gossip relating to key figures I was studying. My relations with Pietru at this stage were not close enough to get this sort of information through prolonged direct questioning. I had to get it indirectly during many hours spent with him and, of course, others, doing things which interested them. With Pietru I discus-

sed Lumumba, with others it was hunting or catching birds, with yet others it was football and drinking.

Later, after many hours of what one might call informant servicing, I developed a few key informants with whom I could retire in private to discuss matters which they did not want others to know they were telling me. I was able to get this information because of the time and energy invested in playing the role of friend and conversationalist. These, and I come back to this, are time-consuming activities. With experience a researcher can learn to be more economical with his time than I was. This depends in part upon his ability to formulate his problem extremely clearly. In no case can he dispense with investing much of his time playing the role of friend to his informants. The information he collects is directly related to his ability to make and maintain friendships among his informants.

There were other new roles that I had to learn to play. One was that of churchgoer. Although we are not Catholic I was determined to go to Mass regularly to hear what was said, to observe who came and where they sat and so forth. Consequently, at 5:45 A.M. on the Monday morning after our arrival, I went to the second of the two daily Masses. Remembering the Mass of the day before, which I had attended from the pavement outside because the church was so crowded, I arrived early to assure a vantage point. There was no one in the church when I arrived, and I sat on the right hand side of the nave, in the third row from the front. Hardly had I settled down when a horde of tittering girls arrived suddenly and surrounded me. I turned uncomfortably around and saw three nuns seated on the aisle. There appeared to be no one else in the church except those around me. It suddenly became apparent that I was sitting in the place traditionally occupied by the nuns and their numerous little charges. After an embarrassed half hour of being observed closely and giggled at intensely, I bolted. Later that day I met Dun Gorg. He discreetly suggested that I sit in one of the lateral apses where the men sat, because it was the custom for the women in the villages to sit in the central nave. I had learned this the hard way. By then I had decided to spend my mornings sleeping and to confine my church attendance to the crowded and important Sunday Mass. I had learned two valuable lessons: to conserve my energy and time as much as possible, and to try and get a description of how I should behave in a given situation before being confronted by it.

The people of Farrug also had adjustment problems. They had a stranger in their midst who was an enigma. I had a family yet I did not go to work like other men. I seemed to be always about, and I asked so many questions. At the outset I explained to the parish priest that I wanted to study all aspects of life in a typical village for my Ph.D. thesis. Yet this information did not circulate widely. When people asked him what I was doing he would try to explain. By no means did everyone ask him, and not all those who did understood his explanation. It soon became apparent that I was remarkably well informed about matters they thought no nonvillager could know. These were simply things such as village nicknames, where people lived, what they did, how many children they had, where they worked, and so on. I certainly did not make it apparent that I knew other more intimate details. There was one man in particular who was troubled. He had heard about me from other people, but never asked me directly what I was doing. He was convinced I was a spy. The problem he and some of his friends faced, as I learned later from Pietru, was to determine for which country I was spying. Because I was American, had studied in England, had a Swedish wife and one child born in Japan, another in Malta, it was not a straightforward matter. He decided finally that I must be a United Nations spy, and began spreading this information about. Pietru told me what was happening and who was responsible. I made a point of meeting the man in his bar. In the course of an evening's hard drinking, for he had an absolutely phenomenal capacity (which I do not), I convinced him that I enjoyed drinking, that I was a student on a very limited budget, that I was genuinely interested in Maltese villagers, that

spies usually operate among the town folk, that I had to write a thesis for my teachers, and that he could help me a lot by telling me about his own experience as a leader in the Saint Martin Band Club. The following day I had a frightful hangover, for we had been drinking pint glasses containing a mixture of cheap local wine, beer, and lemonade—a grassroots shandy. I never heard any more about spying.

As participant observer I took part in a wide range of activities. I spent a good deal of the day talking to the shopkeepers and to old men sitting on their doorsteps, and in the evening with the younger men in their cafes, clubs, and on their doorsteps. I also went along on excursions, festas, pilgrimages, weddings, picnics, parties, and receptions in the various clubs. We had Dun Gorg in to dinner, and after he left the village I often took his successor to the neighboring airport for a drink, a change of scenery, and private conversation. I attended football matches, went hunting, spent a day clap-netting birds, photographed weddings and baptismal parties, went to the fields with farmers, and made the rounds with vendors. In short I saw a lot of the people of Farrug in the various roles they played.

I also systematically pursued a number of key informants: the parish priest, Pietru, old Victor Azzopardi, the sacristan, his brother Pawlu, the president of the Saint Rocco Band Club, the baker and many others. To get systematic information about political matters it was often necessary to see them in privacy. This presented a problem, for the people of Farrug live very close together, and Malta is overpopulated. Moreover Farrugin are reluctant to invite anyone but their closest relatives into their own houses regularly. Exceptions were the parish priest and the shopkeepers. Fortunately Pietru's unmarried sister ran a bazaar and we could talk there in English, which he spoke well. I often went with single informants on picnics or to festas in other villages. Sometimes I drove them into Valletta with me. Occasionally we would simply go for a drive to be alone. Some came to our house, but this gave rise to speculation among the neighbors and the informants were uneasy. In short, our car, brought to provide transportation, in fact also provided important isolation with key informants.

About a month after arrival I began to establish a routine. I got up at 6:00 or 6:30 every morning. Often I would spend a peaceful hour working on my notes before the rest of the family arose. After breakfast, at about 8:00, I left to pick up our car, which was garaged at Tereza Abela's farm on the edge of the village. Normally I went a roundabout way which took me past the parish church, the parish priest's house, the baker's shop, and Pietru Cardona's. It also took me past the main bus stop. All along the way I talked to people, and I always stopped for a chat with Pietru or his sister in her bazaar. This twenty- to thirty-minute swing through the village usually brought me up to date. I then brought the car to the house and my wife brought our eldest daughter to an English-language school in a neighboring town. In the beginning I studied Maltese in the mornings; later I used them to interview the older men who stayed in the village, or to work in the public library in Valletta. Noon was hectic because either my wife or I would have to drive to pick up our daughter for lunch and then return her an hour later, collecting her again at 3:30. In the afternoon I always stayed in the village to work on my notes, and, if the night before had been particularly grisly, I also took a short nap.

Except between 6:30 and 7:30, when I was at home eating and putting the children to bed, I was constantly busy with informants from 4:00 in the afternoon until the clubs and bars closed at about 10:30 or 11:00. After this I would get to work on my notes, first completing my diary and then writing up detailed notes of interviews and observations made during that day. Often I was too exhausted by 12:00 or 12:30 to continue, and would simply jot down an outline of subject to write up the next day. Sometimes my day's work would end with some scribbled nonsense, an illegible scrawl or an ink blot when I fell asleep over my notes.

An illustration of a more or less average day will perhaps make clearer the rhythm of research. I will not say that it is a typical day, for every day was different. It does, however, illustrate the general attempt to establish and maintain a wide range of links, and to interview certain people more intensively.

Monday, September 19, 1960, started as usual. On the way to pick up the car I learned from Pietru that a number of Requiem Masses were to be held that day in memory of the nineteen-year-old boy electrocuted a year before in one of the quarries surrounding the village. After Inga and Ieneke had left for school, I settled down to study Maltese. After an hour I got fed up and went out to practice it. I went first to the little bazaar of Pietru's sister, where I spent forty-five minutes talking to Pietru's two sisters, his mother, and three customers who came to the shop. I then crossed the street to talk to a farmer, who had come to get a drink in Pietru's cousin's bar. We spent the best part of an hour discussing his farming problems and, of particular importance to me, his reaction to the discussion of the parish priest in church the day before about the financial situation of the Saint Rocco Confraternity. Between 11:00 and 12:00 I worked intensively with the parish priest on my household card system. Dun Gorg liked to display his phenomenal memory and was dictating details of every family in the village: name, nickname, place of birth, age, occupation, band club allegiance and, in passing, choice bits of gossip as well as his personal likes and dislikes.

After lunch, I reviewed the household cards I had prepared with Dun Gorg in the morning, and wrote up the case histories and other information he had provided. (Much later I compared his data to the door-to-door census of my own, and found his to be amazingly accurate.) Then after Inga and Ieneke returned home at 3:45, I took the car to the garage to wash it. Carmelo Abela came home at about 4:30. After his tea he came and gave me a hand with the car. When he started to tell me how he had met his fiancée, I began to wax the car to have an excuse to stay with him. As soon as Carmelo left me for his fiancée, I returned home and wrote up the story of his courtship while the details were still fresh.

That evening at 8:00, I met Pietru accidentally in front of the parish priest's house. We decided to go for a walk outside the village to find some cool air. At about 9:00 we returned and sat in front of the school chatting. Pietru told me the story of his own courtship and the difficult time he had deciding to break his engagement. We also discussed at great length the evil eye; it had given him a fever the day before. At about 10:30 Pietru went home, and I stopped by his aunt's wine shop. Since only the duty policeman was there chatting to Pietru's cousin, and she obviously was anxious to go to bed herself, I left after fifteen minutes. Although I intended to write up my notes fully, when I got home I found that I was too tired. I simply filled in my diary for the day and outlined the topics to write up the following day. I went to bed at about midnight. . . .

Other Research Techniques

Besides the participant observation described in the preceding section, I employed a number of other research techniques to gather information on Hal-Farrug. At the public library I systematically went through years of newspapers and yearbooks in order to piece together the background. The newspapers in particular were a useful source of information. The Maltese have acquired from the British the habit of writing letters to the editor. If a village faction fight grows particularly bitter, the weaker party very often tries to wound its opponents by ridiculing them through a letter to the editor. This then gives rise to a furious polemic in which all sorts of fascinating data are made public. In this way I gathered a number of interesting tips on important clashes in Farrug's political past.

The problem of how much time to devote to archives of various sorts is a problem in countries with a long written history. I can offer no rule of thumb. I also consulted some of the parish archives to get vital statistics on deaths, marriages, baptisms. Through contacts established with CARE, I was able to study the police archives pertaining to the village for the past thirty-five years. In addition, I went through records at the Rationing Office, the Electoral Office, and with Rediffusion, the wired sound-broadcasting company. I also, unsuccessfully, advertised in the press and searched the libraries for diaries. It would obviously take me too far afield to discuss the type of information gleaned from the various sources and its relevance. . . .

In the beginning in Hal-Farrug I made extensive use of my camera to connect names to faces. I photographed many crowd scenes, and later asked informants to identify the persons. One of the most useful pictures in this respect was the portrait of the Saint Martin partisans posing proudly with the mountain of fireworks they prepared for the centenary of their Saint. People would tip me off when interesting things were going to happen, and, if crowds were present, see that I got a ringside seat with a running commentary. Although there was also a keen photographer in the village who earned a bit of extra money with his hobby, we did not really compete. I only charged the cost price on my pictures, which for the most part were scenes in which he was not particularly interested. The camera also was a convenient means of getting me invited to intimate family celebrations, such as betrothal parties, where a regular village photographer would have been an uncomfortably familiar figure. Although once an avid amateur photographer, I soon found that taking really good photographs is incompatible with being a good anthropologist. Both are full time occupations. Moreover the best angles are often far from informants.

Direct interviews of course were one of the chief techniques I used. I had interviews with the various village leaders, association officers, living former village parish priests and police officers, politicians who had canvassed in the village, and many more. Many of these interviews were formal in the sense that I had made appointments for them. Many were also accidental, such as the interviews with Carmelo Abela and Pietru Cardona described above. If I could, I always spent some time before an interview preparing it and thinking through the questions, making sure that I had them firmly in my head. Very often I would jot down key words with a ballpoint on my palm or, more usually, on a page in my pocket notebook. In the course of the interview I would elicit a date or an address which gave me an excuse to open the notebook so that I could jot down trigger words to remind me later of the subjects discussed. Once the notebook was open I could also unobtrusively check the prepared list of questions to make sure that I had covered all the planned subjects. An interview with untrained informants, especially if you are after information he is not too eager to part with, has a way of branching out along unforeseen paths. Later it is surprisingly difficult to remember the different topics discussed.

Genealogies were a help in learning how the villagers were related to each other. I collected ten extensive genealogies which were sufficient to place everyone in the village. Genealogical data I collected on the census provided further information. Because I was not particularly interested in kinship at that time, the genealogical data I have on Hal-Farrug is rather thin. Later, in the summer of 1968, I was to collect a giant genealogy from Pietru Cardona, who has over 400 living relatives of his generation. This, however, belongs to a later period of research.

I conducted the village census in the fourth month. For many days I procrastinated whether it would be worth the effort. Finally I decided it would be, and that I should do the work myself and not try to get someone else to do it. The data I collected related primarily to household composition, occupation, and membership in the various associations. Although I tried to get information on extra sources of cash income and land ownership, this made people suspicious. Since the economic data they then gave was extremely unreliable, I soon stopped asking for them, fearing that it would jeopardize my relations with the villagers. Even our neighbor Leonard, Tereza Abela's son-in-law, did not want me to note down that he supplemented his dock yard policeman's salary by buying and selling eggs and poultry.

It is important to remember that I was in Malta during a time of political crisis (1960–

1961). Questions which were related to politics were difficult to pose. Many persons did not wish to disclose their true political sympathy for many reasons. Those who supported the Labour Party were afraid of being branded as communist heretics by the faithful; some were afraid of losing their jobs; yet others were afraid of generating conflict with family or neighbors. Another sensitive subject I have already mentioned was allegiance to a particular festa faction. For this reason I did not include direct questions relating to political or festa faction affiliation on the census. In this small community it was of course possible to get this information, as well as that on extra sources of income, indirectly.

Once I stopped asking about money, I was welcomed into most of the 244 households. The few exceptions were houses in which mentally disturbed members of the household were confined. The success of the census was in no small measure due to the way in which Dun Frangisk announced from the pulpit that I was going to every household to ask some harmless questions. In fact, in most of the houses where I called, the problem was not reserve but overfriendliness. Many thought of my visit as a social occasion and offered me the glass of whisky that good manners demanded. Moreover many gave me eggs, soft cheeses, and tomatoes. I often had to dash home to keep my pockets from bursting, and once I had raw egg slithering down the inside of my leg. The census took eleven days. By the second day I had developed a confidence and smoothness which made me feel a little silly about the hesitation I had had about carrying out the survey.

On the 8th of January we moved from Farrug to Kortin, where we lived until we left Malta in September. The object of the move was to gather comparative information on a larger village and one that was not divided by band club rivalry. Although I intended to return to Hal-Farrug after three months, the house was no longer available when we wanted to move back. Tereza Abela and her sons had moved into it, leaving her husband, with whom she had quarrelled, to look after the farm. Though I continued to visit Hal-

Farrug regularly to attend a number of the important functions, including many weddings, participant observation in the village was obviously reduced to a minimum. Later a research assistant and I made short comparative studies of the general organization, leadership, and patterns of conflict in twelve other communities. Much later, during the summer of 1967, thanks to the generosity of the Wenner-Gren Foundation for Anthropological Research, I was able to revisit Hal-Farrug to bring myself up to date. Pietru provided me with very valuable assistance, as did a number of others, including the new parish priest. Some of tha data I collected at this time found its way into *Hal-Farrug.*

Processing the Data

One of the most critical phases of fieldwork is processing the voluminous data collected. I received little systematic instruction on this during my graduate work. Though I heard vague descriptions of how anthropologists processed their data, the only "anthropologist's field notebook" I was actually able to touch and look at, and this only after many unsuccessful requests, was one of Malinowski's old field notebooks from the Department's museum. From Paul Stirling I heard how John Barnes kept his notes. Since this seemed an economical method I decided to adopt it myself.

I used a variety of notebooks. To begin with I had a little pocket notebook with a hard cover and a pencil, which I carried with me always. In this I jotted down odd bits of information during interviews, and more detailed outlines of the subjects discussed as soon as informants were out of sight. I also kept a second one in which I systematically put down the meaning of new words I heard; unfortunately I discontinued this after two months. I used a stenographer's notebook for formal interviews when I knew I could write, and for all genealogies, for copying data from the police records, and for rough notes from newspapers and other archives. Finally I had a series of much larger notebooks which I kept under lock and key in our house. Into

these I wrote up in detail interviews and personal observations, some points of which I had usually jotted down in my pocket or stenographer's notebook. The lined pages were numbered consecutively and I ruled in a large margin on the left hand side. The entries were made chronologically. In the margin I wrote the headings under which the entry could be indexed. Following Paul Stirling's advice, I indicated as many possible headings as I could. These headings and subjects were consolidated in three central indexes at the back of each notebook: events and subjects peculiar to Hal-Farrug, names of people, and events and subjects of general importance. Every day I tried to bring this index up to date, cross-referencing where necessary. While in the field I did not allow myself enough time to do this properly.

Besides these notebooks I also kept a daily diary into which I entered appointments and a rather terse summary of persons and places visited during the day. This was a chore which I did not do in great enough detail, but I did do it faithfully. The importance of this diary had rightly been stressed repeatedly at the field seminar in London. It provides a rough structure to the subject matter in the notebooks, as well as a record of how I spent my time, and whom I saw on what occasion. I had separate notebooks for Gozo, where I carried out a certain amount of research, and for the detailed notes which I took from library books. I indexed them all in the same way.

As already indicated, I developed a card system which provided data on household composition, occupation, nicknames, political allegiance, band club affiliation, and place of birth of each member. This card system, set up with the help of the parish priest at the end of the first month in Hal-Farrug, was invaluable, and I constantly drilled myself with the names, addresses, nicknames, and occupations of the village's 1300 inhabitants. Even today I still remember this information, and on return visits recently I have again, I fear, raised the spectre of the spy with it.

Besides notebooks and cards I had a system of folders for various activities, certain persons, genealogies, and subjects such as kinship, godparenthood, church organization, and so on. I placed these upright in a cardboard box. Into these I filed pamphlets, texts written by villagers, sheafs of notes, pictures and newspaper cuttings. I also had a growing collection of government departmental reports, pamphlets, statistical abstracts, and census reports to which I made constant reference in my comparative work.

Fortunately the Colonial Social Science Research Council required its research fellows to make an interim report after the first half year. I did this when I moved to Kortin. I began consolidating my notes on Friday, January 13. A month later I posted the report, a 14,000-word paper on local politics in Hal-Farrug, to the Colonial Office and to Dr. Lucy Mair, my supervisor at the London School of Economics. It had been a busy month. I first worked out the statistical results of the house to house census. This was a particularly time-consuming piece of work. I also indexed my notes, thought through a number of basic problems, and made plans for the rest of my research. I could not, however, work on the report continually: The sewage problem again arose and the plumbing could only be manipulated through the floor of the converted chicken house I was using as my study. There were also many more general problems of settling into a new village. Writing the report forced me to rethink basic problems and look at my material in terms of those problems. In doing so I discovered numerous shortcomings in my material. Moreover, because I now had a written piece, I was able to elicit valuable criticism and comments from my supervisor and her colleagues at the London School of Economics. This feedback was invaluable.

Two months later I again took time off from actual research and retired to a friend's summer house in Saint Paul's Bay for a week. Isolated from family, neighbors, and informants, I again indexed notes, read my material through, took stock of where I was, and where I still had to go. Unfortunately I did not write anything. Finally, I must mention that I had valuable discussions on many aspects of my fieldwork as well as some of my findings with friends and persons outside the villages. Most of these were what could be

called quasiacademics, that is, they were persons who had certain academic interests but who were not even part-time academics. They included a government secretary who was an expert on folklore, employees of the library who knew where the books I needed were placed (many were not cataloged!) and who had done considerable private research for Sunday supplement articles and pamphlets, a priest who was conducting pastoral research, a police sergeant interested in folklore, and many more. These, unlike most at the university, were keenly interested in my research and offered many insights, as well as access to their clipping files and records.

Foolishly, I did not show them my interim report, and thus missed the feedback this would have provided. The reason I did not show it is perhaps partly due to the way my research was sponsored. I was working with funds received from the British Government via the Colonial Social Science Research Council. As political relations between Malta and Britain at the time were very delicate, I felt most awkward about my sponsorship. I therefore did not disclose the exact source of funds unless I was pressed to do so, preferring merely to note that a British institution had sponsored me. Had the true nature of the source come out, I was sure, and still am, that my relations with Malta Labour Party officials would have been much less cordial than they were. Consequently, I had always the slightly embarrassed feeling that I was there under false colors. This of course was foolish, for the area of research and the problems on which I was working were completely those of my own choosing, not those of the British Government. Nonetheless, the feeling persisted, and I was not as forthright about my work as I should have been, and have since become.

Analysis and Writing

We returned to London by air in the middle of September 1961. I took with me my notebooks containing some 1500 pages, some 360,000 words of notes, plus the household cards of Hal-Farrug and Kortin. The rest of my data—pounds of books, papers, surveys, and cards—followed by ship. Fortunately we were able to move into a furnished house. This meant there were few settling in problems and I was able to begin work immediately.

The first task was of course to complete my indexing. I expanded certain sections of the index. Using these new categories I re-read all my notes, indexing as I went along. This task, as I remember it, took about two weeks of intensive, tedious work. After that I began writing. I was determined to deliver my final report to the Colonial Office by the time my research grant ran out in the end of November.

Mondays through Saturdays, I worked flat out from 7:00 in the mornings to about 10:00 at night, with four hours off for meals and playing with the children. On Friday mornings, however, I went to Professor Raymond Firth's seminar at the London School of Economics, where in the course of the year I gave several papers. Since I did not have the resources to continue after the summer, my thesis had to be completed before August 1962. I could not afford the luxury of going to any of the other interesting research seminars at the L.S.E.

The third week in November I presented Dr. Mair with a 25,000-word typescript. She gave it very severe criticism, and I spent the next two weeks rewriting and editing it before I passed it on to the typist. With considerable satisfaction I delivered the required three copies to the Colonial Office around the middle of December. These apparently disappeared into the great maw of the dying colonial apparatus and, as far as I have been able to gather, were never looked at again by anyone. They apparently never reached Malta. A year later I had to lend my personal copy to Sir Maurice Dorman, the new British Governor of Malta!

My supervisor's criticism of the final report, if anything, was even more severe than of the first draft. I took her pungent but most instructive marginal comments to heart and began work on my thesis. The first chapter required a good bit more historical research and I journeyed back and forth to the Colonial Office Library a number of times. That chapter gave me a good bit of trouble, and not surprisingly, it was rejected twice by Lucy Mair. I then worked methodically through each of the nine chapters, revising where necessary after sessions with my supervisor. I finished it the beginning of July, and in August left for a research post in Sicily, returning to London briefly in November for the examination of the thesis. . . .

part 2

Prehistory

Human Society before the Urban Revolution

Robert Redfield

From *The Primitive World and Its Transformations.* Cornell University Press, 1953, pp. 1–23. Copyright 1953, Cornell University. By permission of Mrs. Robert Redfield, the publisher and copyright holder.

What can be said that is general and true about the condition of mankind before civilization? The question is directed to a time from five to six thousand years ago. At that time human populations were to be found on all the world's continents, with the possible exception of Australia. Greenland had not yet been invaded by man, and some of the islands of the Pacific were as yet without human occupants. But there were people in a great many widely scattered parts of the habitable earth, not very many of them in any one place, and not very many of them altogether. No city had yet been built anywhere.

The question is whether anything can be said, with show of reason and evidence, about *all* the human beings that were there then, whether they lived in the arctic or in the tropics, whether they hunted, fished, or farmed, and whatever may have been the color of their skins, the languages they spoke, or the particular beliefs and customs that they had. The question demands a positive characterization of their manner of life. The description should be more than a mere statement of the things that those early men did not have that we today do have. It should say: this is what they did; this is how they felt; this is the way the world looked to them.

The question, so understood, appears to require more than can be provided from trustworthy evidence, but I do not think that it really does. It can be answered from two sources of information. The archaeologists dig up the material things that men of those times made and used, and from these things draw reasonable inferences about their manner of life. And, secondly, the ethnologists tell us a good deal about the ways of life of those people who until recent times have remained uncivilized: the primitive, the preliterate—or, to use the old-fashioned terms—the savage and the barbaric peoples. To learn what precivilized men were like, we may look to the accounts of the remains of ancient camps and settlements unaffected by cities, either because they were there before there were any cities anywhere, or because they stood remote and unreached by ancient cities already arisen. And also we may look to what has been written in great detail about many hundreds of present-day tribes and bands and villages, little communities of the never civilized. I do not assume that these latter people have experienced no changes in the several thousands of years since the first cities were built. The particular thoughts and beliefs of the present-day preliterates have probably changed a good deal during many hundreds of generations. The customs of these people are not "earlier" than is our own civilization, for they have had as long a history as have we. But what I do assert is that the surviving primitive peoples have remained substantially unaffected by civilization. Insofar as the conditions of primitive life remain—in the smallness of the community, and in its isolation and nonliteracy—so, too, the kind of thoughts and beliefs, however changed in specific content, remain of a kind characteristic of primitive society. That there is such a kind is evidenced to us from the fact that we can generalize as to this manner of thought and belief from the surviving primitive peoples, in the face of the very great variety of content of thought and belief which these exhibit. These surviving primitive peoples provide us with instances of that general and primordial kind of human living which it is my immediate purpose to describe.

Now it is fortunate for the present enterprise that these two sources of information, the archaeological and the ethnological, supplement each other. Where the former is weak, the latter is strong; and where the ethnologist may be insufficiently impressed by the influence of technology on the manner of life of a human community, the archaeologist can hardly fail to be impressed. This is what he sees: the material things. Moreover, of the many meanings which are locked in the artifacts that ancient peoples made, it is those meanings which relate to practical action, especially the getting of foods, which communicate themselves most readily to the archaeologist who finds them. A Plains Indian medicine bundle or an Australian totemic design as an archaeological object by itself would convey only a little of the very great deal which the ethnologist who can talk to a

living Indian or Australian can find out that it means. So the archaeologist's view of the manner of life of the precivilized peoples will emphasize the practical aspects of living and the material influences on change. An archaeologist should make a little effort to lean deliberately away from a materialist view of human life and a conception of history in simple terms of economic determinism. His work inclines him toward it. On the other hand, the ethnologist is often in a position where he can find out little or nothing of the history of the people he is studying, as they have written nothing down about it, having no means to do so; and so it may sometimes appear to him that they are to be explained chiefly in terms of the kinds of marriage choices he finds them making when he finds them, or the potlatches they give. In the absence of a history, the way the material conditions of living limited that people here or gave them a chance to develop something there may not be apparent.

Archaeologist and ethnologist, however, do often talk to each other, and indeed in some cases are the same person. So the separation of work, the difference in emphasis, is not so great as I have perhaps made it sound. In the attempt to characterize the precivilized manner of life, I will begin by following Childe, an archaeologist. Professor Childe is interested in the effects on human development of changes in the technology by which food is produced. He makes a separation of importance between that period in human history when men were hunters and fishers only (savagery), and that period when men had learned how to be agriculturalists or animal breeders (barbarism). The change from the one kind of life to the other he calls a revolution, "the food-producing revolution."

The discovery of how to produce food was, of course, of enormous importance in human history, and it is not too much to call it a revolution and to group it, as Childe does, with the "urban revolution," when civilization came into being, and with the industrial revolution of modern times. Yet certain qualifications or additions need to be made. It has been pointed out that the food-producing revolution was the more notable event in that from the condition of food collecting one could not predict that food producing would be achieved, but that when once food production had increased human population and made leisure possible, civilization was bound to come about. And it is also necessary to recognize that some of the changes characteristic of each stage may have taken place, in one community or another, before the revolution in technology that Childe stresses had occurred there. Thus we know that a sedentary village life is possible to a people who know nothing of agriculture or animal husbandry. The fishing Indians of our Northwest coast lived a village life and developed certain aspects of their culture very highly. In prehistoric times there existed on the Scandinavian coast sessile communities, quite comparable with Neolithic farmers in the village character of life, with pottery and the polishing of flint, but without crops or herds. Also, it is not unlikely that with the advent of agriculture there began some of those changes which we are able to see only when cities and writing have made them visible to us. The excavations in Iraq, already mentioned, suggest this possibility. As the changes in technology, so also the changes in the human mind which are the subject of these pages may have well begun before the urban revolution, even before the food-producing revolution.

Nevertheless, within the wide generalizations that I am here attempting, the food-producing revolution and the urban revolution may be considered as two parts of one great transformation. To one interested in changes in human habits and capacities of mind, the urban revolution is the more important part, for it is with the coming of city life that we are able to see novel and transforming attitudes taken toward life and the universe. That these novel attitudes began earlier is likely, and farther on in these pages indications will be drawn from present-day primitive societies that occasional beginnings of these civilized attitudes were to be found in the precivilized societies had we been there to look for them. The question as to the relative importance of Childe's two first

revolutions may be set aside with this statement: the food-producing revolution was perhaps the turning point in the human career, but it was through the urban revolution that the consequences of the turn were realized.

Now let us attempt a characterization of mankind in precivilized times. Let us begin with the simple statement that in the primary condition of mankind the human community was small. As Childe says, writing of the food-collecting period, hunters and vegetable-food collectors usually live in small roving bands. Even the more stable settlement of Pacific coast Indian fishing people, of recent times exceptionally well provided with food, includes hardly more than thirty occupied houses and several hundred people. Nor does the immediate transition to food producing increase substantially the size of the community, now a group of farmer's huts or a center of cattle raising.

On the whole the growth of population was not reflected so much in the enlargement of the settlement unit as in a multiplication of settlements. In ethnography neolithic villages can boast only a few hundred inhabitants. . . . In prehistoric Europe the largest neolithic village yet known, Barkaer in Jutland, comprised fifty-two small, one-roomed dwellings, but sixteen to thirty houses was a more normal figure; so the average local group in neolithic times would average two hundred to four hundred members.

Certain food-producing town centers well on the way to civilization do give indication of larger populations, but hunters' bands or food producers' settlements are alike in general contrast to the far larger community which was the ancient city with its seven thousand to twenty thousand inhabitants. What is here worth emphasizing is that until the rise of civilization mankind lived in communities so small that every adult could, and no doubt did, know everybody else.

These communities were isolated from one another. Again Childe gives us to understand that the change in this regard with the coming of agriculture was a change in some degree, but at first not a radical change.

Throughout both Paleolithic and Neolithic times each little group was largely self-contained and self-supported, as the surviving primitive societies, whether hunters or growers of vegetable or animal food, are largely self-contained and self-supported. The trade that occurred in Paleolithic times was chiefly trade in nonessentials; with Neolithic times the trade intensified and included some staple commodities, such as stone for querns and flint for hand axes. But the trade did not greatly limit the essential separateness of the local community. The isolation of the Neolithic settlement continued into the medieval English village. Villagers of primitives or peasants today are still relatively isolated, and, on the whole, when such people have more than casual association with outsiders, it is with people who are much like themselves, in neighboring bands or settlements that are like their own community.

So we may characterize mankind in its primary condition as living in small and isolated communities. These communities were of course without writing. I do not say more of this absence of literacy and literature; its importance as a criterion of primitive as contrasted with civilized living is familiar. To these qualities others may be added. The precivilized community was composed of one kind of people. If this fact is not to be deduced from the archaeologist's data, it follows from what we know of isolated primitive communities seen today. Small and isolated communities are intimate communities; people come to have the same ways of doing things; they marry with and live almost entirely with others like them in that community.

Next we may say that the members of the precivilized community had a strong sense of group solidarity. No doubt they thought of themselves as naturally belonging together, and so far as they were aware of people different from themselves, they thought their own ways to be better than the ways of others. These things also may be said, not only because they are necessary consequences of the isolation and the smallness of the community, but because we see them to

be true of contemporary primitive communities. Civilized communities are more heterogeneous, and the sense of group solidarity is qualified by the number and variety of kinds of groups to which the individual makes attachment—or by the difficulty of making firm attachments to groups in some urban situations.

Let us follow Professor Childe further in his characterization of precivilized man. We see that now he must make increasing use of reasonable deduction and of the evidence from ethnology. He tells us that in the precivilized community there were no full-time specialists. He asserts this for the reason that in communities with simple hunting or even farming "there simply will not be enough food to go round unless every member of the group contributes to the supply." In the primitive societies of the present day there are rarely full-time specialists. So the assumption is fairly well founded that in the early condition of mankind what men did was customarily different from what women did, but what one man did was much like what another did. There were men with special skills at activities carried on by all men, and there were probably shamans or other part-time practitioners in the spiritual and healing arts. Differences among individuals with respect to the depth of understanding of cosmogonic and religious ideas may have been very considerable; this is a matter to which we shall recur on a later page. But, on the whole, all men shared the same essential knowledge, practiced the same arts of life, had the same interests and similar experiences.

Yet another characteristic of precivilized living may be asserted. Within those early communities the relationships among people were primarily those of personal status. In a small and intimate community all people are known for their individual qualities of personality. Few or no strangers take part in the daily life. So men and women are seen as persons, not as parts of mechanical operations, as city people see so many of those around them. Indeed, this disposition to see what is around one as human and personal like oneself is not, in precivilized or primitive society, limited to people; a great deal of what we call "nature" is more or less so regarded. The cosmos is personal and human-like.

Also in this connection it may be said that the groupings of people within the primitive community is one that depends on status and on role, not on mere practical usefulness. There are fathers, or older people, or shamans, or priests; each such kind of person is accorded prestige. In civilized societies the network of relationships of utility—the numbers and kinds of people who produce goods and services are so great and are at such remote distances—that many of the relationships that keep people provided with what they use are not involved in status at all, for those who use the goods. In primitive societies the status relationships are universal and dominant; the exceptions to be made would be those relatively few that arise out of trade with foreign communities.

Furthermore, in this personal universe where categories of relationships involve status, the forms and groupings of kinship provide the basic classifications. The original human society was one of kinsmen. Childe speaks of the "sentiment of kinship" which in considerable part held the group together. Within the precivilized society, it is safe to assume that relationships were essentially familial. The primary arrangements of personal status and role are those connected with that universally persistent kind of family anthropologists now call "nuclear" and the extensions of this primary kinship into many, possibly even all, of the other relationships within the community. Moreover, the categories of kinship may include elements of nature, as some animals, and supernatural beings. Of course we cannot say just what were the kinship institutions in the thousands of bands and settlements that constituted precivilized society. In his latest book Childe with ingenuity and prudence draws reasonable inferences as to elements of social organization in precivilized societies known only archaeologically. The result suggests the presence in one place of single-family households, in another of large households includ-

ing several or many nuclear families, and a variety of forms of marriage. Nevertheless the very smallness and isolation of the precivilized community everywhere allows us to say that in the early condition of humanity, the community, as well as the cosmos of which its members felt it to be a part, was essentially made up of personal relationships, and that the patterning of these relationships was primarily accomplished by developments derived from the differences of age, sex, and familial connection. Today, among western Australian peoples, "the whole society forms a body of relatives," and the intimate connection between the body of relatives and nature, through the water hole or other center of animal multiplication, and the totemic rites, is familiar to readers of Australian ethnology.

What, essentially, held together this primordial human community? Was it the mutual usefulness to one another of those few hunters or fishers or farmers? To answer, Yes, is to recognize what is obviously true: "Cooperation is essential to secure food and shelter and for defense against foes, human and subhuman." But answer, Yes, is also to suggest a possible misconception. The "identity of economic interests" of which Childe writes in the paragraph in which he so interestingly characterizes the mode of life of man before civilization, is a fact which any of us would have observed had we been there to see the precivilized community, and which is an obvious inference from what we know more directly about it. But this does not mean that in those communities men worked primarily for material wealth. The incentives to work and to exchange labor and goods are, in primitive and precivilized society especially, various and chiefly noneconomic (in the narrow sense). They arise from tradition, from a sense of obligation coming out of one's position in a system of status relationships, especially those of kinship, and from religious considerations and moral motivations of many kinds. The point has been put very convincingly by Karl Polanyi. Let us then add to our characterization of the precivilized society that it was a society in which the economy was one determined by status (as contrasted with the society imagined and in part realized in nineteenth-century Europe and America, in which the economy was determined by the market). In the precivilized or the primitive society "man's economy is, as a rule, submerged in his social relations." Essentially and primarily, man "does not aim at safeguarding his individual interest in the acquisition of material possessions, but rather at ensuring social good-will, social status, social assets. He values possessions primarily as a means to that end." We are talking now of a time before the acquisitive society.

To answer only that the precivilized community was held together by reason of mutual usefulness is to fail to say what it is that most importantly and characteristically holds such a community together. Indeed, Childe sees and states succinctly, in terms which Durkheim caused many of us to use, the difference in this regard between the precivilized settlement and the city. It is not the former, but the earliest cities that "illustrate a first approximation to an organic solidarity based upon functional complementarity and interdependence between all its members such as subsist between the constituent cells of an organism." It is the urban community that rests upon mutual usefulness. The primitive and precivilized communities are held together essentially by common understandings as to the ultimate nature and purpose of life. The precivilized society was like the present-day primitive society in those characteristics—isolation, smallness, homogeneity, persistence in the common effort to make a way of living under relatively stable circumstances—to which we have already attended, and therefore it was like the parallel societies which we can observe today in that its fundamental order was a matter of moral conviction. In both cases the society

exists not so much in the exchange of useful functions as in common understandings as to the ends given. The ends are not stated as matters of doctrine, but are implied by the many acts which make up the living that goes on in the society. Therefore, the morale of a folk society—its power to act consistently over periods of time and to meet crises effectively—is not dependent upon discipline exerted by force or upon devotion to some single principle of action, but to the concurrence and consistency of many or all of the actions and conceptions which make up the whole round of life.

For the homogeneity of such a society is not that homogeneity in which everybody does the same thing at the same time. The people are homogeneous in that they share the same tradition and have the same view of the good life. They do the same kinds of work and they worship and marry and feel shame or pride in the same way and under similar circumstances. But at any one time the members of a primitive community may be doing notably different things: the women looking for edible roots while the men hunt; some men out on a war party while others at home perform a rite for its success. And when there is a familial ceremonial or a magico-religious ritual affecting the whole community, the differences in what is being done may be very great. In the activities to gain a material living, labor, as between man and man or woman and woman, may be divided. But the total specialization of functions, as among people of different sexes and age-or-kinship positions, and as among participants in a rite, may be very considerable. The point to be stressed is that all these activities conduce to a purpose, express a view of man's duty, that all share, and to which each activity or element of institution contributes.

We can safely say these things of the precivilized societies as we can say them of the primitive societies because these things follow from the other characteristics which we have already conceded, and are attested in every very isolated, undisturbed primitive society we observe today. For the same reasons it is possible to add yet other attributes to the characterization. In the most primitive societies of living men into which we may enter and which we can come directly to understand, the controls of each are informal; they rest on the traditional obligations of largely inherited status, and are expressed in talk and gesture and in the patterns of reciprocal action. Political institutions are few and simple, or even entirely absent. The members of these societies "believe in the sacred things; their sense of right and wrong springs from the unconscious roots of social feeling, and is therefore unreasoned, compulsive and strong." People do the kind of things they do, not because somebody just thought up that kind of thing, or because anybody ordered them to do so, but because it seems to the people to flow from the very necessity of existence that they do that kind of thing. The reasons given after the thing is done, in the form of myth and the dress of ceremony, assert the rightness of the choice. Particular things are done as a result of decision as to that particular action, but as to the class of action, tradition is the source and the authority. "The Indians decide now to go on a hunt; but it is not a matter of debate whether one should, from time to time, hunt." So the principles of rightness which underlie the activities are largely tacit. And they are not the subject of much explicit criticism, nor even of very much reflective thought. Institutions are not planned out, nor is their modification a matter of much deliberate choice and action. Legislation, though it may occur, is not the characteristic form of legal action in primitive societies. And what Malinowski refers to as "science" in connection with the primitive peoples is better distinguished as practical knowledge. And these things too may with confidence be attributed to the precivilized societies. Yet, because in them thought and action were largely traditional and uncritical, it does not follow that activities were automatic or empty of meaning. Rather we must suppose that activity with them as with us involved lively and variable subjective states. Ruth Bunzel, studying Pueblo potters, found that the Indian woman who was in fact copying the designs of other potters with only the smallest variation was unaware that she copied, condemned copying as wrong, and had a strong conviction that she was in fact inventive and creative. And as for the meaning of life—that was, so to speak, guaranteed. One did what tradition said one did, making a multitude of interesting and particular

choices. But all of it fell within and was motivated by the common understandings of the little community as to the nature and purpose of life.

The attempt to gather together some of the attributes of that form of human living which prevailed before the first civilizations arose may now be halted. Later we shall examine some of the respects in which it is necessary to qualify this characterization. Enough of the characterization for the needs of these pages has been assembled. There results a picture, very generalized, of the organization of life, social control, and motivation among most of the societies of mankind during most of human history. The point upon which we are to insist, for its importance in considering the topics of the following lectures, is that in this early condition of humanity the essential order of society, the nexus which held people together, was moral. Humanity attained its characteristic, long-enduring nature as a multitude of different but equivalent systems of relationships and institutions each expressive of a view of the good. Each precivilized society was held together by largely undeclared but continually realized ethical conceptions.

Professor Childe unfortunately happened upon a figure of comparison that leads in the direction just opposite to the truth when he wrote that the solidarity of the precivilized community was "really based on the same principles as that of a pack of wolves or a herd of sheep." Even the little glimpses of religion and sense of obligation to do right which are accorded the archaeologist show us that twenty-five thousand years ago the order of society was moral order. That of wolves or sheep is not. Childe's facts prove that this was so and that his comparison of precivilized society with that of animals is misleading. Describing the wall paintings, the personal adornments, the trade in cowrie shells, and the hints these things give of a life of the mind and the spirit among the Western Europeans of the Ice Age, Childe says, "Savagery produced a dazzling culture." It is Childe who uses this adjective for the cultures at the end of the Ice Age that found expression in necklaces of animal teeth, in well-executed realistic paintings of the animals that were hunted, in stone-weighted skeletons of reindeer cast into a German lake, "presumably as an offering to the spirit of the herd or the genius of the land," according to Childe.

The antiquity of the moral order is not fully attested by archaeology. A people's conceptions as to the good are only meagerly represented in the material things that they make. A tribe of western Australia, the Pitjendadjara, today carry on a religious and moral life of great intensity, but they make and use material objects so few and so perishable that were these people exhibited to us only through archaeology, we would barely know that they had existed and we would know nothing of their moral life. As described by Charles P. Mountford in his charming book, these aborigines perform their rites to increase animal and plant food, and they follow a morality of personal relations with dignity and conscience. Mountford says that they make but five tools: a spear, a spear thrower, a wooden carrying dish, a stone slab on which to grind food, and a digging stick. Perhaps this investigator overlooked some of the articles made by these aborigines, but it is certainly true that naked and wandering, with almost none of the material possessions and power which we associate with the development of humanity, they are nevertheless as human as are you and I.

We may suppose that fifty thousand years ago mankind had developed a variety of moral orders, each expressed in some local tradition, and comparable to what we find among aborigines today. Their development required both the organic evolution of human bodily and cerebral nature and also the accumulation of experience by tradition. As the tradition began to accumulate while the organic evolution was still going on, the moral order—and the technical order—began to be established among the apelike men of the early Pleistocene. On the other hand, until bodily and cerebral nature equivalent to that of men living today had been developed, we cannot fairly attribute to those earliest hu-

manoid societies a moral order comparable, let us say, with that of the Australian blackfellow. Even in the case of so relatively late a being as Neanderthal man there was a factor of biological difference which would have limited the development of culture. But by a time seventy-five or fifty thousand years ago, the biological evolution of mankind had reached a point at which the genetic qualities necessary for the development of fully human life had been attained. This reaches the conclusion that for a period of time at least five times as long as the entire period of civilization man has had the capacity for a life governed by such moral orders as we see in primitive societies today. The men who left the paintings of Altamira were fully human and not very different from us. And I follow Eliseo Vivas when he writes:

That does not mean, of course, that they pursued the identical values and were capable of the same theoretical sophistication of which we are capable; it merely means that they probably had the same degree of moral sensibility, though perhaps focused toward different objects than those toward which we, the men of contemporary technological society, focus ours.

In recognizing that every precivilized society of the past fifty or seventy-five millenniums had a moral order to which the technical order was subordinate, I do not say that the religious and ethical systems of these societies were equally complex. Then, as now, there were "thin cultures" and "rich cultures." Childe sees certain of the mesolithic cultures as "thin" in comparison with the cultures that preceded them. It is not, of course, clear that the thinness lay in the moral life. Maybe they had a religious and personal life that is not represented in the archaeology. However this may be in that particular case, we are to recognize that the development of technology had, even in precivilized times, an important influence on the moral life. While the Australians show us how little material culture is needed for the development of a moral order, such a contrast as that between the Haida and the Paiute Indians reminds us that generally speaking a people desperately concerned with getting a living cannot develop a rich moral or esthetic life. The moral order of a hard-pressed people may be itself simple. But I insist that it is there in every case.

One other point is to be made about the moral orders that preceded civilization. Morality has had its developmental history. I shall return to this development in the last chapter. Here I say that when the moralities of primitive or precivilized peoples are judged by men of the present day, some are found to be better than others; and the judgment makes allowances for practical difficulties encountered by the primitive people. In primitive societies known today where the food quest is all absorbing one does not condemn the people for failing to develop much creative art or for failing to show a particularly humane consideration for other people. The Siriono of Bolivia, as recently reported by Allen R. Holmberg, live a harsh and precarious life in a tropical rain forest. They have their moral order—systems of intense inhibition as to sexual relations with certain relatives, ideas as to the rights and duties of relatives to share food, fearful attitudes toward invisible spirits, and so forth. But men's activities "remain on the same monotonous level day after day and year after year, and they are centered largely around the satisfaction of the basic needs of hunger, sex and avoidance of fatigue and pain." Holmberg saw a band of Indians walk out of a camp leaving a woman, sick to death, alone in her hammock. "Even the husband departed without saying good-bye." It is stern necessity that makes for this conduct; children, who can be cared for, are tenderly treated at much expenditure of effort. On the other hand, elsewhere we are reminded of the degree to which respect for personal integrity may develop among primitive food collectors. Among the Yagua, another people living under difficult conditions in the topical forest of South America, although the entire clan lives in a single long house, Fejos tells us that the members of the large household "are able to obtain perfect privacy whenever they wish it

simply by turning their faces to the wall of the house. Whenever a man, woman or child faces the wall, the others regard that individual as if he were no longer present."

I turn now to the distinction between the technical order and the moral order, and from that proceed to contrast precivilized and primitive living with civilized living in terms of this distinction. Technical order and moral order name two contrasting aspects of all human societies. The phrases stand for two distinguishable ways in which the activities of men are co-ordinated. As used by C. H. Cooley and R. E. Park, "the moral order" refers to the organization of human sentiments into judgments as to what is right. Describing how the division of labor puts an organization of society based on occupation and vocational interests in place of an older kind of organization of society, Park contrasts these newer ties, based on common interests, with "forms of association like the neighborhood, which are based on contiguity, personal association, and the common ties of humanity." The division of labor modifies this older moral order. Here we will extend the significance of the phrase, and make it cover all the binding together of men through implicit convictions as to what is right, through explicit ideals, or through similarities of conscience. The moral order is therefore always based on what is peculiarly human— sentiments, morality, conscience—and in the first place arises in the groups where people are intimately associated with one another. The word "values" is a related conception, but the phrase "moral order" points to the nature of the bonds among men, rather than to a category of the content of culture. We may conceive of the moral order as equally present in those societies in which the rules for right conduct among men are supported by supernatural sanctions and in those in which the morality of human conduct is largely independent of the religion (in the sense of belief and cult about the supernatural). "Moral order" includes the binding sentiments of rightness that attend religion, the social solidarity that accompanies religious ritual, the sense of religious seriousness and obligation that strengthens men, and the effects of a belief in invisible beings that embody goodness. The moral order becomes vivid to us when we think of the Australian Arunta assembling, each man to do his part, denying himself food, making the sacred marks or performing the holy dances, that the witchetty-grub may become numerous and the whole band thus continue to find its food. Or of the old Chinese family performing the rituals for the ancestors. Or of the members of the boys' gang refusing, even in the face of threats from the police, to "tell on" a fellow member.

By a corresponding extension of another and more familiar term, all the other forms of co-ordination of activity which appear in human societies may be brought together and contrasted with the moral order under the phrase "the technical order." The bonds that co-ordinate the activities of men in the technical order do not rest on convictions as to the good life; they are not characterized by a foundation in human sentiments; they can exist even without the knowledge of those bound together that they are bound together. The technical order is that order which results from mutual usefulness, from deliberate coercion, or from the mere utilization of the same means. In the technical order men are bound by things, or are themselves things. They are organized by necessity or expediency. Think, if you will, of the orderly way in which automobiles move in response to the traffic light or the policeman's whistle, or think of the flow of goods, services, and money among the people who together produce, distribute, and consume some commodity such as rubber.

Civilization may be thought of as the antithesis of the folk society. It may also, and consistently with the first antithesis, be thought of as that society in which the relations between technical order and moral order take forms radically different from the relationships between the two which prevail in precivilized society.

Civilization (conceived now as one single thing and not—as by Toynbee—as twenty-one different things) may be said to exist to the extent, to the degree, and in the respects in which a society has developed away from the kind of precivilized society which I have been describing. Civilization is, of course, things added to society: cities, writing, public works, the state, the market, and so forth. Another way of looking at it is from the base provided by the folk society. Then we may say that a society is civilized insofar as the community is no longer small, isolated, homogeneous and self-sufficient; as the division of labor is no longer simple; as impersonal relationships come to take the place of personal relationships; as familial connections come to be modified or supplanted by those of political affiliation or contract; and as thinking has become reflective and systematic. I do not mention all of the characteristics of folk societies which I named in foregoing paragraphs; these are enough to suggest the point of view we might adopt. If we do adopt this way of conceiving civilization, we shall think of Toynbee's twenty-one civilizations as different developments away from the folk society. We see then that civilizations do not depart from the nature of the folk society evenly or in the same way. In Chinese civilization the organization of social relationships according to the categories and attitudes of kinship retained its importance while philosophy and the fine arts passed through long histories of development. The Andean civilization developed political and administrative institutions of impressive complexity and far-reaching influence while yet the Indians who developed them were without writing. The Mayan peoples, in contrast, extended their political institutions little beyond that attained by the ordinary tribe while their intellectual specialists carried some parts of mathematics and astronomy to heights that astonish us. In short, the several civilizations start up from their folk bases into specialized developments in which some elements of the folk society are left behind while others are retained. Yet this fact does not destroy the impression that, as a manner of life taken as a whole, civilization is one kind of thing different from the life of the folk society.

The contrast between technical order and

moral order helps us to understand the general kind of thing which is civilization. In the folk society the moral order is great and the technical order is small. In primitive and pre-civilized societies material tools are few and little natural power is used. Neither the formal regulations of the state or church nor the nonmoral ordering of behavior which occurs in the market plays an important part in these societies. It is civilization that develops them.

It is civilization, too, that develops those formal and apparent institutions which both express the moral order and are means toward its realization. The technical order appears not only in tools, power, and an interdependence of people chiefly or wholly impersonal and utilitarian, but also in greater and more varied apparatus for living—apparatus both physical and institutional. Under ten headings Childe has summarized the characteristics of civilized life whether lived at Uruk, Mohenjo-daro, or Uxmal among the Mayans. One, the reappearance of naturalistic art, has a significance not immediately plain, and may be a little doubtful. Of the other nine, six plainly announce the growth of the technical order: (1) the great increase in the size of the settlement (the material equipment for human association becomes far larger); (2) the institution of tribute or taxation with resulting central accumulation of capital; (3) monumental public works; (4) the art of writing; (5) the beginnings of such exact and predictive sciences as arithmetic, geometry, and astronomy; and (6) developed economic institutions making possible a greatly expanded foreign trade. Each of these six suggests the increasing complexity of social organization, and the remaining three criteria explicitly declare features of that social organization which are characteristic of civilization; (7) full-time technical specialists, as in metal working; (8) a privileged ruling class; and (9) the state, or the organization of society on a basis of residence in place of, or on top of, a basis of kinship.

In folk societies the moral order predominates over the technical order. It is not possible, however, simply to reverse this statement and declare that in civilizations the

technical order predominates over the moral. In civilization the technical order certainly becomes great. But we cannot truthfully say that in civilization the moral order becomes small. There are ways in civilization in which the moral order takes on new greatness. In civilization the relations between the two orders are varying and complex.

The great transformations of humanity are only in part reported in terms of the revolutions in technology with resulting increases in the number of people living together. There have also occurred changes in the thinking and valuing of men which may also be called "radical and indeed revolutionary innovations." Like changes in the technical order, these changes in the intellectual and moral habits of men become themselves generative of far-reaching changes in the nature of human living. They do not reveal themselves in events as visible and particular as do material inventions, or even always as increasing complexity in the systems of social relationships. Nor is it perhaps possible to associate the moral transformations with limited periods of time as we can associate technological revolutions with particular spans of years. Yet the attempt to identify some of the transformations in men's minds can be made.

One might begin such an attempt by examining the manner of life of the most primitive people we know today, and perhaps also something that is told us about ancient peoples, for evidence of the appearance of forms of thought, belief, or action which a little knowledge of the history of some civilization shows us became influential in changing human life. We see some far-reaching change in the moral or intellectual life of the Western world, perhaps, and so guided we return to the primitive societies to see if it had a beginning there. So we might come to some understanding of some of the relations in history between the two kinds of orders.

As to the trend of this relationship throughout history, I have one general impression. It is that the moral order begins as something pre-eminent but incapable of changing itself, and becomes perhaps less eminent but more independent. In folk society the moral rules bend, but men cannot make them afresh. In civilization the old moral orders suffer, but new states of mind are developed by which the moral order is, to

some significant degree, taken in charge. The story of the moral order is attainment of some autonomy through much adversity.

selection 6

The Legacy of Sumer

Samuel Noah Kramer

From *The Sumerians.*
University of Chicago Press,
n.d., pp. 269–299. © 1963,
University of Chicago. By
permission of the author, and
the publisher and copyright
holder.

On the assumption that civilization is of some value for man, the long-dead Sumerians might well point with "fingerless" pride to the numerous innovations, inventions, and institutions which they helped to originate. To be sure, it might be said that these would have come to be in any case, Sumerians or no Sumerians. But this hardly seems to the point—the Sumerians were there first, and it seems not unfair to give credit where credit is due. Be that as it may, in this chapter I shall attempt to sketch rather briefly and hesitatingly some of their more palpable and significant contributions to the culture of man. . . .

It was a Semitic people—the Amorites—who put an end to the Sumerians as a political, ethnic, and linguistic entity. To be sure, the conquered conquered the conquerors, and the Amorites, commonly known as Babylonians because their capital was the city of Babylon, took over Sumerian culture and civilization lock, stock, and barrel. Except for the language, the Babylonian educational system, religion, mythology, and literature are almost identical with the Sumerian, excluding, of course, the expected changes and variations due to political developments and the passing of time. And since these Babylonians, in turn, exercised no little influence on their less cultured neighbors, particularly the Assyrians, Hittites, Hurrians, and Canaanites, they, as much as the Sumerians themselves, helped to plant the Sumerian cultural seed everywhere in the ancient Near East. And this brings us to the legacy of Sumer down through the ages, including our own, although in our age this heritage is no longer an active and creative source of cultural growth but a rather melancholy if not altogether uninspiring theme for antiquarian history.

The tracking-down of Sumer's legacy may well begin with the socio-political institution commonly known as the city-state which, in Sumer, developed out of the village and town in the second half of the fourth millennium B.C. and was a flourishing institution throughout the third millennium. The city—with its free citizens and assembly, its nobles and priests, its clients and slaves, its ruling god and his vicar and representative on earth, the king, its farmers, craftsmen, and merchants, its temples, walls, and gates—is found all over the ancient world from the Indus to the western Mediterranean. Some of its specific features may vary from place to place, but by and large it bears a strong resemblance to its early Sumerian prototype, and it seems not unreasonable to conclude that not a few of its elements and counterparts go back to Sumerian roots. It may well be, of course, that the city would have come into being in the ancient world whether Sumer had existed or not. But this is not at all certain; in Egypt, for instance, the city-state never took root, and the same might have happened in other parts of the ancient world.

One of the most characteristic features of the Sumerian city-state throughout the greater part of the third millennium B.C. was written law, beginning with the writing of legal documents such as sales and deeds and culminating in the promulgation of specially prepared law codes. Written legal documents and law codes are found in later periods all over the ancient Near East, and there is little doubt that although these may differ in details they all go back to Sumerian prototypes; even Greece and Rome would probably never have had their written laws had it not been for the Sumerian penchant for keeping a record of their legal transactions.

In the matter of scientific achievement, it is probably in the field of mathematics that the Sumerians made their major contribution to future generations by devising the sexagesimal system of place notation, which may have been the forerunner of the Hindu-Arabic decimal system now in use. Traces of the Sumerian sexagesimal system exist even today in the measurement of the circle and angle by degrees and in some of the weights and measures that were current until relatively recent times.

In the field of technology, the potter's wheel, the wheeled vehicle, and the sailboat are all probably Sumerian inventions. And while metallurgy is certainly not of Sumerian origin, the products of the Sumerian metalworkers were dispersed all over the ancient Near East, and some even reached as far as Hungary and Central Europe.

Architecture was the major art of Sumer from earliest times, in particular the construction of temples with their stone foundations and platforms, niched cellas, painted walls and altars, mosaic-covered columns, and impressive facades; it would not seem unlikely that at least some of these architectural techniques were diffused over the ancient world. Sumerian architects also made use of the dome, vault, and arch, and it is not improbable that the arch first came to Greece and Rome from contact with Babylonia, which had inherited it from Sumer. Near Eastern sculpture, too, particularly the practice of fashioning statues of gods and men, may go back to Sumerian origins, since it was the Sumerian theologians who first conceived of the idea that the statue represented the ruler, or even some other high official, standing before his god in unceasing prayer, as it were, for his life. The Sumerian cylinder seal "rolled" its way all over the ancient world from India to Cyprus and Crete, and there is many a church in Europe today whose capitals are ornamented with conventionalized motifs going back to scenes first imagined and engraved by the Sumerian artist and craftsman.

The achievements of the Sumerians in the areas of religion, education, and literature left a deep impress not only on their neighbors in space and time but on the culture of modern man as well, especially through their influence, indirect though it was, on the ancient Hebrews and the Bible. The extent of the

Hebrew debt to Sumer becomes more apparent from day to day as a result of the gradual piecing together and translation of the Sumerian literary works; for as can now be seen, they have quite a number of features in common with the books of the Bible. This chapter will close, therefore, with a sketch of the Biblical parallels found in Sumerian literature by isolating and analyzing the various beliefs, tenets, themes, motifs, and values which seem to be common to the ancient Hebrews and the much more ancient Sumerians.

The form and content of the Sumerian literary works have been discussed and analyzed in great detail [not included in this text], and no further elaboration is needed at this point. It goes without saying that a written literature so varied, comprehensive, and time-honored as the Sumerian left a deep impress on the literary products of the entire Near East. Particularly was this so since at one time or another practically all the peoples of western Asia—Akkadians, Assyrians, Babylonians, Hittites, Hurrians, Canaanites, and Elamites (to name only those for which positive and direct evidence is available at the moment)—had found it to their interest to borrow the cuneiform script in order to inscribe their own records and writings. The adoption and adaptation of this syllabic and logographic system of writing, which had been developed by the Sumerians to write their own agglutinative and largely monosyllabic tongue, demanded a thorough training in the Sumerian language and literature. To this end, no doubt, learned teachers and scribes were imported from Sumer to the schools of the neighboring lands, while the native scribes traveled to Sumer for special instruction in its more famous academies. The result was a wide dissemination of Sumerian culture and literature. The ideas and ideals of the Sumerians—their cosmology, theology, ethics, and system of education—permeated to a greater or lesser extent the thoughts and writings of all the peoples of the ancient Near East. So, too, did the Sumerian literary forms and themes—their plots, motifs, stylistic devices, and aesthetic techniques. And the Hebrews of Palestine, the land

where the books of the Bible were composed, redacted, and edited, were no exception.

To be sure, even the earliest parts of the Bible, it is generally agreed, were not written down in their present form much earlier than 1000 B.C., whereas most of the Sumerian literary documents were composed about 2000 B.C. or not long afterward. There is, therefore, no question of any contemporary borrowing from the Sumerian literary sources. Sumerian influence penetrated the Bible through the Canaanite, Hurrian, Hittite, and Akkadian literatures—particularly through the latter, since, as is well known, the Akkadian language was used all over Palestine and its environs in the second millennium B.C. as the common language of practically the entire literary world. Akkadian literary works must therefore have been well known to Palestinian men of letters, including the Hebrews, and not a few of these Akkadian literary works can be traced back to Sumerian prototypes, remodeled and transformed over the centuries.

However, there is another possible source of Sumerian influence on the Bible which is far more direct and immediate than that just described. In fact, it may well go back to Father Abraham himself. Most scholars agree that while the Abraham saga as told in the Bible contains much that is legendary and fanciful, it does have an important kernel of truth, including Abraham's birth in Ur of the Chaldees, perhaps about 1700 B.C., and his early life there with his family. Now Ur was one of the most important cities of ancient Sumer; in fact, it was the capital of Sumer at three different periods in its history. It had an impressive *edubba;* and in the joint British-American excavations conducted there between the years 1922 and 1934, quite a number of Sumerian literary documents have been found. Abraham and his forefathers may well have had some acquaintance with Sumerian literary products that had been copied or created in their home town academy. And it is by no means impossible that he and the members of his family brought some of this Sumerian lore and learning with them to Palestine, where they gradually became part of the traditions and sources utilized by the Hebrew men of letters in composing and redacting the books of the Bible.

Be that as it may, here are a number of Biblical parallels from Sumerian literature which unquestionably point to traces of Sumerian influence:

1. *Creation of the Universe.* The Sumerians, like the ancient Hebrews, thought that a primeval sea had existed prior to creation. The universe, according to the Sumerians, consisted of a united heaven and earth engendered in some way in this primeval sea, and it was the air-god, Enlil—perhaps not unlike the *ruachelohim* of Genesis—who separated heaven from earth.

2. *Creation of man.* Man, according to both the Hebrews and the Sumerians, was conceived as having been fashioned of clay and imbued with the "breath of life." The purpose for which he was created was to serve the gods—or Jahweh alone, in the case of the Hebrews—with prayer, supplication, and sacrifices.

3. *Creation techniques.* Creation, according to both Biblical and Sumerian writers, was accomplished primarily in two ways: by divine command and by actual "making" or "fashioning." In either case, the actual creation was preceded by divine planning, though this need not have been explicitly stated.

4. *Paradise.* No Sumerian parallels to the story of the Garden of Eden and the Fall of Man have yet been found. There are, however, several paradise motifs that are significant for comparative purposes, including one that may help to clarify the rib episode in Genesis 2:21–23. Moreover, there is some reason to believe that the very idea of a divine paradise, a garden of the gods, is of Sumerian origin.

5. *The flood.* As has long been recognized, the Biblical and Sumerian versions of the Flood story show numerous obvious and close parallels. Noteworthy, too is the fact that according to at least one Mesopotamian tradition there were ten antediluvian rulers, each with a life span of extraordinary length,

which is reminiscent of some of the Biblical antediluvian patriarchs.

6. *The Cain-Abel motif.* The rivalry motif depicted in the undoubtedly much abbreviated Cain-Abel episode of the Bible was a high favorite with the Sumerian writers and poets.

7. *The Tower of Babel and the dispersion of mankind.* The story of the building of the Tower of Babel originated, no doubt, in an effort to explain the existence of the Mesopotamian ziggurats. To the Hebrews, these towering structures, which could often be seen in a state of ruin and decay, became symbols of man's feeling of insecurity and the not unrelated lust for power which brings upon him humiliation and suffering. It is most unlikely, therefore, that a parallel to this story will be found among the Sumerians, to whom the ziggurat represented a bond between heaven and earth, between god and man. On the other hand, the idea that there was a time when all peoples of the earth "had one language and the same words" and that this happy state was brought to an end by an irate deity may have a parallel in a golden-age passage which is part of the Sumerian epic tale "Enmerkar and the Lord of Aratta."

8. *The Earth and its organization.* The Sumerian myth "Enki and the World Order: The Organization of the Earth and Its Cultural Processes" provides a detailed account of the activities of Enki, the Sumerian god of wisdom, in organizing the earth and in establishing what might be termed law and order on it; this poem has its Biblical echoes in, for example, Deuteronomy 32:7–14 (note especially verse 8) and Psalm 107.

9. *Personal God.* To judge from the covenant between God and Abraham—note, too, the reference to a "god of Nahor" in Genesis 31:53—the ancient Hebrews were familiar with the idea of a personal god. The belief in the existence of a personal god was evolved by the Sumerians at least as early as the middle of the third millennium B.C. According to Sumerian teachers and sages, every adult male and family head had his "personal god," or a kind of good angel whom he looked upon as his divine father.

This personal god was in all probability adopted by the Sumerian paterfamilias as the result of an oracle or a dream or a vision involving a mutual understanding or agreement not unlike the covenant between the Hebrew patriarchs and Jahweh.

To be sure, there could have been nothing mutually exclusive about the covenant between the Sumerian and his tutelary deity, and in this respect, therefore, it differed very significantly from that between Abraham and his god. All that the Sumerian expected of his personal god was that he speak in his behalf and intercede for him in the assembly of the gods whenever the occasion demanded and thus insure for him a long life and good health. In return, he glorified his god with special prayers, supplications, and sacrifices, although at the same time he continued to worship the other deities of the Sumerian pantheon. Nevertheless, as the Sumerian literary document "Man and His God" indicates, there existed a close, intimate, trusting and even tender relationship between the Sumerian and his personal god, one which bears no little resemblance to that between Jahweh and the Hebrew patriarchs and, in later days, between Jahweh and the Hebrew people as a whole.

10. *Law.* That the Biblical laws and the long-known Hammurabi law code show numerous similarities in content, terminology, and even arrangement is recognized by practically all students of the Bible. But the Hammurabi code itself, as has been shown in recent years, is an Akkadian compilation of laws based largely on Sumerian prototypes. In fact, there is good reason to infer that the extraordinary growth and development of legal concepts, practices, precedents, and compilations in the ancient Near East goes back largely to the Sumerians and their rather one-sided emphasis on rivalry and superiority.

11. *Ethics and morals.* The ethical concepts and moral ideals developed by the Sumerians were essentially identical with those of the Hebrews, although they lacked their almost palpable ethical sensitivity and

moral fervor, especially as these qualities are exemplified in the Biblical prophetic literature. Psychologically, the Sumerian was more distant and aloof than the Hebrew—more emotionally restrained, more formal and methodical. He tended to eye his fellow men with some suspicion, misgiving, and even apprehension, which inhibited to no small extent the human warmth, sympathy, and affection so vital to spiritual growth and well-being. And in spite of his high ethical attainments, the Sumerian never reached the lofty conviction that a "pure heart" and "clean hands" were more worthy in the eyes of his god than lengthy prayers, profuse sacrifices, and elaborate ritual.

12. *Divine retribution and national catastrophe.* Jahweh's wrath and the humiliation and destruction of the people that incurs it constitute an often repeated theme in the Biblical books. Usually the national catastrophe comes about through a violent attack by some neighboring people, especially selected as Jahweh's scourge and whip. To this theme the historiographic document "The Curse of Agade" offers a rather interesting parallel: Enlil, the leading deity of the Sumerian pantheon, having been deeply angered by the blasphemous act of a ruler of Agade, lifted his eyes to the mountains and brought down the barbarous and cruel Gutians, who proceeded to destroy not only Agade but almost all of Sumer as well.

13. *The plague motif.* The Sumerian myth "Inanna and Shukalletuda: The Gardener's Mortal Sin" contains a plague motif which parallels to some extent the Biblical plague motif in the Exodus story: in both cases, a deity angered by the misdeeds and obduracy of an individual sends a series of plagues against an entire land and its people.

14. *Suffering and submission: the "Job" motif.* Quite recently, a Sumerian poetic essay which is of rather unusual significance for Biblical comparative studies has become available. Its central theme, human suffering and submission, is identical with that treated so sensitively and poignantly in the Biblical Book of Job. Even the introductory plot is the

same: A man—unnamed in the Sumerian poem—who had been wealthy, wise, righteous, and blessed with friends and kin is overwhelmed one day, for no apparent reason, by sickness, suffering, poverty, betrayal, and hatred. Admittedly, however, the Sumerian essay, which consists of less than one hundred and fifty lines, compares in no way with the Biblical book in breadth, depth, and beauty; it is much closer in mood, temper, and content to the more tearful and plaintive psalms of the Book of Psalms.

15. *Death and the nether world.* The Biblical Sheol, and, for that matter, the Hades of the Greeks, has its counterpart in the Sumerian Kur. Like the Hebrew Sheol, the Kur was the dark, dread abode of the dead. It was a land of no return, from which only exceptionally the shade of a once prominent figure might be called up for questioning. In the Sumerian literary documents, there are several other interesting parallels with Hebrew ideas relating to the nether world: its depiction as the pitiful home of former kings and princes; the raising of the shades of the dead from it; and the imprisonment in it of the god Dumuzi, the Biblical Tammuz, for whom the women of Jerusalem were lamenting as late as the days of the prophet Ezekiel. . . .

selection 7

Perhaps 60 percent of all currently ambulatory American archaeologists are concerned primarily with culture history; this includes most of the establishment and not a few of the younger generation. Another 10 percent, both young and old, belong to what might be called the "process school." Between these two extremes lies a substantial group of archaeologists who aim their fire freely at both history and process. . . .

Most culture historians use a theoretical framework that has been described as "normative" (the term was coined by an ethnologist and recently restressed by an archaeologist). That is, they treat culture as a body of shared ideas, values and beliefs—the "norms" of a human group. Members of a given culture are committed to these norms in different degrees—the norm is really at the middle of a bell-shaped curve of opinions on how to behave. Prehistoric artifacts are viewed as products of these shared ideas, and they too have a "range of variation" that takes the form of a bell-shaped curve.

In the normative framework cultures change as the shared ideas, values and be-

Culture History v. Cultural Process: A Debate in American Archaeology

Kent V. Flannery

From *Scientific American,* Vol. 217, No. 2, 1967, pp. 119–122. Copyright © 1967, Scientific American, Inc. By permission of the author, and the publisher and copyright holder.

liefs change. Change may be temporal (as the ideas alter with time) or geographic (as one moves away from the center of a particular culture area, commitment to certain norms lessens and commitment to others increases). Hence culture historians have always been concerned with constructing "time-space grids"—great charts whose columns show variation through the centuries. Some have focused an incredible amount of attention on refining and detailing these grids; others have been concerned with discovering "the Indian behind the artifact"—reconstructing the "shared idea" or "mental template" that served as a model for the maker of the tool.

While recognizing the usefulness of this framework for classification, the process school argues that it is unsuitable for explaining culture-change situations. Members of the process school view human behavior as a point of overlap (or "articulation") between a vast number of *systems,* each of which encompasses both cultural and noncultural phenomena—often much more of the latter. An Indian group, for example, may participate in a system in which maize is grown on a river floodplain that is slowly being eroded, causing the zone of the best farmland to move upstream. Simultaneously it may participate in a system involving a wild rabbit population whose density fluctuates in a 10-year cycle because of predators or disease. It may also participate in a system of exchange with an Indian group occupying a different kind of area, from which it receives subsistence products at certain predetermined times of the year; and so on. All these systems compete for the time and energy of the individual Indian; the maintenance of his way of life depends on an equilibrium among systems. Culture change comes about through minor variations in one or more systems, which grow, displace or reinforce others and reach equilibrium on a different plane.

The strategy of the process school is therefore to isolate each system and study it as a separate variable. The ultimate goal, of course, is reconstruction of the entire pattern of articulation, along with all related systems, but such complex analysis has so far proved

beyond the powers of the process theorists. Thus far their efforts have not produced grand syntheses. . . but only small-scale descriptions of the detailed workings of a single system. By these methods, however, they hope to explain, rather than merely describe, variations in prehistoric human behavior.

So far the most influential (and controversial) menber of the process school has been Lewis R. Binford. . . . It is Binford's contention that culture historians are at times stopped short of "an explanatory level of analysis" by the normative framework in which they construct their classifications. Efforts to reconstruct the "shared ideas" behind artifact populations cannot go beyond what Binford calls "paleopsychology"—they cannot cope with systemic change. And where Willey says that "archaeology frequently treats more effectively of man in his relationships to his natural environment than of other aspects of culture," Binford would protest that most culture historians have dealt poorly with these very relationships; their model of "norms," which are "inside" culture, and environment, which is "outside," makes it impossible to deal with the countless systems in which man participates, none of which actually reflect a dichotomy between culture and nature. The concept of culture as a "superorganic" phenomenon, helpful for some analytical purposes, is of little utility to the process school.

As a convenient example of the difference in the two approaches, let us examine three different ways in which American archaeologists have treated what they call "diffusion"—the geographic spread of cultural elements. It was once common to interpret the spread of such elements by actual migrations of prehistoric peoples (a view, still common in Near Eastern archaeology, that might be called the "Old Testament effect"). The culture historians attacked this position with arguments that it was not necessary for actual people to travel—just "ideas." In other words, the norms of one culture might be transmitted to another culture over long distances, causing a change in artifact styles, house types and so on. A whole terminology was worked out for this situation by the culture historians: they described cultural "traits" that had a "center of origin" from which they spread outward along "diffusion routes." Along the way they passed through "cultural filters" that screened out certain traits and let others pass through; the mechanics of this process were seen as the "acceptance" or "rejection" of new traits on the part of the group through whose filter they were diffusing. At great distances from the center of origin the traits were present only in attenuated form, having been squeezed through so many filters that they were almost limp.

Since process theorists do not treat a given tool (or "trait") as the end product of a given group's "ideas" about what a tool should look like but rather as one component of a system that also includes many noncultural components, they treat diffusion in different ways. The process theorist is not ultimately concerned with "the Indian behind the artifact" but rather with the system behind both the Indian and the artifact: what other components does the system have, what energy source keeps it going, what mechanisms regulate it and so on? Often the first step is an attempt to discover the role of the trait or implement by determing what it is functionally associated with; some process theorists have run extensive linear-regression analyses or multivariant factor analyses in order to pick up clusters of elements that vary with each other in "nonrandom" way. When such clusterings occur, the analysis postulates a system—tools $X, Y,$ and Z and variables dependent on one another, constituting a functional tool kit that varied nonrandomly with some aspect of the environment, such as fish, wild cereal grains, white-tailed deer and so on. But definition change in one part of a system produces change in other parts; hence the process theorists cannot view artifacts X, Y and Z as products of cultural norms, to be accepted or rejected freely at way stations along diffusion route. When such elements spread, it is because the systems of which they are a part have spread—often at the expense of other systems.

Thus the archaeologist James Deetz recently presented evidence that the spread of a series of pottery designs of the Great Plains reflected not the "acceptance" of new designs by neighboring groups but a breakdown of the matrilocal residence pattern of a society where the women were potters. Design subconsciously selected by the women (and passed on to their daughters) ceased to be restricted to a given village when the matrilocal pattern collapsed and married daughters were no longer bound to reside in their mothers' villages. In that case, although each potter obviously did have a "mental template" in her mind when she made the pot, this did not "explain" the change. That spread of design could only be understood in terms of a system in which designs, containers and certain female descent groups were nonrandomly related components. The members of the process school maintain that this is a more useful explanatory framework, but even they realize that it is only a temporary approach. They are becoming increasingly aware that today's human geographers have ways of studying diffusion that are far more sophisticated and quantitative than anything used by contemporary archaeologists.

One other example of the difference in approach between the culture historian and the process theorist is the way each treats the use of "ethnographic analogy" in archaeological interpretation. The culture historian proposes to analyze and describe a prehistoric behavior pattern, then search the ethnographic literature for what seems to be analogous behavior in a known ethnic group. If the analogy seems close enough, he may propose that the prehistoric behavior served the same purpose as its analogue and then use ethnographic data to "put flesh on the archaeological skeleton."

The process theorist proposes a different procedure. Using the analogous ethnic group, he constructs a behavioral model to "predict" the pattern of archaeological debris left by such a group. This model is then tested against the actual archaeological traces of the prehistoric culture, with the result that a third body of data emerges, namely the differences between the *observed* and the *expected* archaeological pattern. These differences are in some ways analogous to the "residuals" left when the principal factors in a factor analysis have been run, and they may constitute unexpectedly critical data. When the archaeologist sets himself the task of *explaining* the differences between the observed archaeological pattern and the pattern predicted by the ethnographic model, he may come up with process data not obtained through the use of analogy alone.

Willey is certainly alert to the current debate, and although he summarizes the New World in a predominantly culture-history framework, he concludes Volume I with a discussion of the hopes and promises of the process school. These he leaves for the future: "I shall be less concerned with process or a search for cultural 'laws,'" he says, "than with at times attempting to explain why certain cultural traditions developed, or failed to develop." Certainly the process school would argue that he cannot explain, within a culture-history framework, why such traditions developed or failed to develop; yet, as he explicitly states, explanation is not the purpose of this volume but rather history.

Let us hope, as Willey seems to, that there is a place in American archaeology for both approaches. Certainly we can use both the historical synthesis and the detailed analysis of single processes. By no stretch of the imagination do all process theorists propose to reject history, because it is only in the unfolding of long sequences that some processes become visible.

In fact, what does the difference between the two schools really amount to? In terms of the philosophy of science, I believe the process approach results in moving "decisions" about cultural behavior even farther away from the individual. It is part of a trend toward determinism that the culture historians began.

It was once common to hear human history explained in terms of "turning points," of crucial decisions made by "great men." The view proved unacceptable to the culture historians, with their normative framework of shared ideas, values and beliefs. They argued convincingly that this body of shared norms

determined the course of history—not the individual, who was simply a product of his culture. . . ."

Now the process school would like to move crucial decisions still farther from the individual by arguing that systems, once set in motion, are self-regulating to the point where they do not even necessarily allow rejection or acceptance of new traits by a culture. Once a system has moved in a certain direction, it automatically sets up the limited range of possible moves it can make at the next critical turning point. This view is not original with process-school archaeologists—it is borrowed from Ludwig von Bertalanffy's framework for the developing embryo, where systems trigger behavior at critical junctures and, once they have done so, cannot return to their original pattern. The process school argues that there are systems so basic in nature that they can be seen operating in virtually every field—prehistory not excepted. Culture is about as powerless to divert these systems as the individual is to change his culture.

Obviously individuals *do* make decisions, but evidence of these individual decisions cannot be recovered by archaeologists. Accordingly it is more useful for the archaeologist to study and understand the system, whose behavior is detectable over and over again. Obviously this approach is too deterministic for some purposes, but for others it is of great theoretical value.

But then if both historical and processual approaches are useful, why should there be a debate at all? I believe the debate exists because of two basically different attitudes toward science.

The previous generation of archaeologists, who did mostly culture history but also laid the foundations for the process school, were often deathly afraid of being wrong. Many of them felt (and many still feel) that if we will only wait until all the facts are in they will speak for themselves. They spoke in awe of the incompleteness of the archaeological record and of the irresponsibility of speculating on scanty data. Somehow they seemed to feel that if they could get together a few more potsherds, a few more projectile points or a few more architectural details, their conclusions would be unshakable. There has not been, however, any convincing correlation between the quantities of data they amassed and the accuracy of their conclusions.

The process theorists assume that "truth" is just the best current hypothesis, and that *whatever* they believe now will ultimately be proved wrong, either within their lifetime or afterward. Their "theories" are not like children to them, and they suffer less trauma when the theories prove "wrong." Their concern is with presenting developmental models to be tested in the field, and they have noted no consistent relationship between the usefulness of a given model and the absolute quantity of data on which it is based. To be useful a model need only organize a body of disorganized data in such a way that hypotheses can conveniently be tested, accepted, modified or rejected. Thus the process school will continue to present model after model on the basis of returns from the first few precincts, and at least some of the culture historians will continue to accuse them of being "hasty," "premature" and "irresponsible." And the issue will be settled years from now by another generation that will probably not belong to either school. . . .

selection 8

Current Thinking in American Archeology

William A. Longacre

From *Current Directions in Anthropology* (Bulletins of American Anthropological Association), Vol. 3, No. 3, Part 2, Sept. 1970, pp. 126–137. By permission of the author, and the publisher.

The topic for this Institute session is: Current Thinking in American Archeology. Obviously two speakers cannot say everything there is to say about such a vast topic. There is neither time nor adequate background or interest on our parts to explore all the dimensions of current thinking in our discipline.

In a sense, we have been charged to speak for the archeological profession, but this is obviously too great a responsibility. To do this effectively, we should have a panel of about 30 archeologists to cover such an inclusive subject. It would be rash for me to attempt to speak for all my colleagues. Therefore, I must apologize for the selective coverage that I offer, and for any distortions or inaccuracies caused by my ignorance in some of the areas I will discuss. I welcome additions and corrections in the discussion that follows.

I should also point out that I am not aiming my remarks at my archeological colleagues. The Institute Program, as I understand it, is designed to brief colleagues in the other disciplines of anthropology with respect to current method and theory in American archeology.

To do this, I will concentrate on several

major topics, including: (1) the place of archeology within anthropology, (2) certain aspects of logic from the Philosophy of Science, (3) the nature of archeological data and (4) various methodological considerations. Professor Deetz covers other aspects.

Historically, in America archeology has always been considered a part of the larger discipline of anthropology. Its development is inseparably tied to the development of anthropology as a whole. The archeologist deals with past cultures from an anthropological point of view and is concerned with making contributions toward the attainment of the goals of anthropology. As these goals have changed, so has archeology changed. I feel that to understand current archeological method and theory, an understanding of the historical development of both anthropology and archeology is necessary.

In the early decades of the present century, archeology was largely concerned with culture history. Reconstructing the lifeways of past peoples and the changes in these lifeways through time became the absorbing explicit goal of American archeology. The field was strongly influenced by general anthropological theory of the time.

Culture area theory, concepts of trait and trait complex, and the trait inventory approach to describing cultures became the mainstay of American archeology. As in cultural anthropology, descriptions of cultures and studies of diffusion of traits were of great interest. Of great importance then, as now, was the development of techniques that would permit chronological inference.

As the thirties ended, there was a growing sense of dissatisfaction within and outside of archeological circles with the success of archeological contributions evaluated in terms of the interests of general anthropology. Perhaps the best known criticisms were those of Kluckhohn and Taylor. Taylor's detailed criticism was published after the war as a monograph, *A Study of Archaeology.* The focus of these criticisms was that archeology was not doing all it could with respect to contributing to an understanding of the nature of culture and the nature of cultural change.

It is fair to say that these criticisms had very little effect upon the practice of archeology during that period, except perhaps for anger at the somewhat hostile manner in which they were presented.

During the 30s and 40s interesting changes were ongoing in anthropological theory. To the long-standing interests in culture history were added the new concepts of structural-functionalism and its focus on systemics of societies and neo-evolutionary theory, largely through the work of Julian Steward and Leslie White. There was little direct impact of these theoretical breakthroughs on the archeology of that period. The primary concern continued to be with culture history.

In fact, there gradually developed a pattern of divergence in the interests of cultural anthropologists and archeologists that was sometimes hard to reconcile. Archeology students grew increasingly impatient with courses in the details of kinship and cross-cousin marriage, as they could see no relevance to their own interests in prehistory. Likewise, budding cultural anthropologists could see little utility in memorizing sequences of past cultures and tool types in archeology courses.

But the strong bonds of shared interest in the culture history of various regions of the world and the concern with the development of major cultural achievements, such as agriculture and civilization from a comparative point of view, continued. The fifties saw increasing concern with drawing inferences about the organization of society and the behavioral aspects of life in the past, in addition to descriptions of architecture and artifacts. Concepts such as "settlement pattern" and an increasing emphasis on "problem orientation" typified this post-war period. Specific hypothesis testing, such as Braidwood's well-known work on early food production in the Near East, also became more common.

Braidwood reasoned that the beginnings of agriculture took place in that environmental zone of the Near East which contained the wild ancestors of the domesticates. To test this proposition he undertook archeological surveys and excavations in the "Hilly

Flanks" zone, investigating early agricultural villages with the aid of specialists from a variety of natural sciences. The results of these investigations are well known. Recently, an alternative proposition regarding the beginnings of agriculture was advanced, but it has not been fully tested yet.

Concern for culture history continued and was enlarged to include stages and levels of the development of culture with a capital "C." These interests culminated in continental-wide culture histories in terms of major stages, such as Willey and Phillips' well known book, *Method and Theory in American Archaeology,* published in 1958.

During the sixties, there has been continued interest in culture history both in terms of regional histories and a more comparative approach either on a continental or world-wide scope. Descriptions of cultures in terms of traits and concern with diffusion vs invention and other historical questions continue.

But the sixties have also witnessed some interesting changes in method and theory that have had an effect on the practicing of archeology in this country. These changes have largely been due to the impact of a variety of developments in other fields. Currently, we are seeing the results of the influence of neo-evolutionary theory and cultural ecology, as well as modified structural-functionalism, systems theory and statistics.

Important current concepts are those of system and adaptation. Some archeologists are moving away from a concept of culture that sees it as a set of norms or ideals which are internalized and shared. They argue that cultures are composed of highly interrelated subsystems, and it is this highly systemic whole that stands between the biological population and the total enviornment. As such, culture is not shared but participated in differentially, and its various subsystems are subjected to selective pressures that lead to adjustments and changes as well as stability. Thus, the focus is upon processes of cultural stability and change, and the goal is to better understand the nature of culture through comparative analysis.

To be successful, such efforts must obviously deal with organizational and behavioral aspects of past societies as well as the more readily inferred technological, economic and stylistic phenomena. The realization of this has led to a series of important shifts in method and theory in American archeology. One of the more important areas of shift has been in the rigorous employment of the scientific method.

This leads us to the philosophy of science, which is a topic of current debate in archeological circles. There seems to have been a shift in philosophy which is both a shift in emphasis and a change from implicit to highly explicit constructs.

For example, there is a current debate regarding the proper roles of induction and deduction in archeology. This debate, in my opinion, has been necessary, if somewhat overemphasized. It is, after all, difficult to oppose these two logical procedures in considering the scientific method. Both are essential to the carrying out of scientific inquiry, and there is an interplay between them in carrying out research.

Archeologists have always operated within a deductive framework. The problem is that the deductive framework has largely been implicit or even unrecognized by the practitioners. To make matters more complicated, those few archeologists who have attempted to address themselves to the complexities of the philosophy of their own science seemed to say that they were operating inductively. I think we can demonstrate that they, like their colleagues, were really operating within a deductive framework. The claims of induction as the proper way to do archeology have created complex, if not emotional, problems growing out of the current explicit concern with the scientific method.

For example, from the twenties on, we find explicitly stated the equation of the scientific method with cold objectivity combined with the careful gathering of "all" the facts. Once enough facts are in, then they can be interpreted. The idea is summed up in the expression, "the facts will speak for themselves." Objectivity was the goal, the avoidance of predetermined conclusions.

But objectivity is, I argue, a myth. Archeologists then, as now, were operating deductively. Appropriate interests, questions and problems were generated from the particular body of anthropological theory held by the investigator. Perhaps the most important aspect of theory in this regard concerns the nature of culture.

A normative approach sees material remains as reflections of the ideals that form the crux of culture. Changes in the materials reflect changes in the norms as a result of diffusion or invention. The "facts" that were so carefully gathered were only those that the particular body of theory permitted the investigator to recognize. "Facts" can only be perceived when they are brought into focus as a result of the interests of the investigator which, in turn, are structured in terms of theory.

Let me give a quick example. If theoretically one views culture as a set of shared norms, then one can feel relatively secure in the assumption that an archeological site will be fairly homogeneous, at least with respect to the ideal styles of pottery or architectural forms. If the site is stratified, it would be reasonable to expect changes through time in the typical styles of houses and pots, which over a number of sites should permit the establishment of a regional chronology. Thus, except for certain kinds of finer problems, a trench through the site or some test pits should produce an adequate sample to identify the ideal ceramic styles or house forms that typify that particular period or periods. It follows that one can not only get chronological information from such an excavation, but one can also make statements about the nature of the prehistoric culture or cultures involved.

But, consider the different approach to the same site by the investigator who brings quite different questions to the excavation. If he is concerned with the organization of the extinct society that occupied the community or if he is attempting to test a specific hypothesis about changing styles of pottery as a reflection of a shift in post-marital rules of residence through time, the way he digs the site will be quite different. Indeed, the kinds of facts this latter investigator gathers might

well be quite different, and the two investigations would produce great differences in the approach to typology and analysis as well.

The current interest in the scientific method is one portion of a larger concern with developing methods that are more powerful and more efficient in dealing with questions about the nature of culture and cultural processes. One of the central concerns is with developing the means of testing propositions and hypotheses utilizing past cultures, taking advantage of the vast time depth available to the archeologist. Given a body of theory, the investigator views his universe in a particular way, finds certain problems more interesting than others and makes assumptions about the phenomena under study. He then arrives at a series of alternative hypotheses or propositions about a problem that interests him and designs appropriate research to test these hypotheses.

One of the most critical steps in this procedure comes at this point. This is the deduction of test implications that will permit the investigator to test the various hypotheses. It is not impossible to "do" science without this step, but not to do it is at best a terribly inefficient way to test hypotheses. More often than not, the focusing upon test implications will lead to the identification of new "facts" that might be highly relevant to testing and that have never before been perceived. For example, in a recent investigation carried out in the Southwest, James Hill and Richard Hevly were interested in testing hypotheses about possible pueblo room uses. One test implication that they thought of *before excavation* concerned the differential distribution of fossil pollen on room floors. They reasoned that the pollens from storage rooms would be different from those of ceremonial chambers or habitation rooms. This led to the systematic collection of pollen samples from the floors of the excavated rooms and the subsequent comparative study. This test, along with others, enabled the investigators to make strong inferences about pueblo room usage.

It is reasonable to expect that most pueblo room floors have quantities of fossil pollen in

them. The field of palynology has been analyzing fossil pollen for over 50 years. The
failure to utilize pollen as a powerful tool for
arriving at room functions, intrasite dating,
activity localization and other things cannot
be explained by the lack of "pollen facts" in
prehistoric pueblo sites or the lack of techniques to exploit these data. It seems best
explained by the short-circuiting of this highly critical step in the scientific method, the
generation of test implications and the inevitable broadening of the perception of relevant data that can be gathered. It is inconceivable that any investigator can gather "all
the facts," and those that are gathered tend
to be more mute than talkative!

Once the test implications are generated,
then the investigator designs research to test
the various hypotheses of interest. This involves the selection of a site or sites that
seem most likely to be appropriate, and the
particular sampling design if the site cannot
be completely excavated. Also, decisions
about such things as the techniques of excavation and the precision controls that are
exercised for recording the provenience of
artifacts are made at this point.

The kinds of analyses that are planned for
the particular segment of the data that is
collected are also basically determined at this
juncture. There may be some adjustment in
this realm as analysis gets underway, but the
basic decisions are made as a part of the
overall research design.

It is important to recognize the creative
interaction between induction and deduction
that typifies scientific endeavor during the
final stages of carrying out the scientific
method. As data are gathered and analyzed,
new test implications or even alternative hypotheses may be suggested as an intellectual
by-product of this portion of research. This is
an inductive process and is a very important
step in creative research. It is, however, properly carried out within a deductive framework,
and it would be extremely inefficient, at best,
to hope that all hypotheses and their test
implications would blossom forth during
these final stages.

Let us then turn to a consideration of the
nature of archeological data, a topic of considerable interest in current American archeology. From the preceding discussion, it
should be clear that the perception of the
nature of archeological data is in large measure determined by the body of theory that
any particular archeologist holds. The nature
of the data and the potential of those data will
vary, for example, depending upon the view
of the nature of culture.

Let me illustrate that observation with current thoughts about the nature of archeological data. If one adopts the view that culture is
a systemic whole composed of interrelated
subsystems, then it is reasonable to assume
that all material items function in a most
intimate way within the various subsystems of
a cultural system. It follows, therefore, that
the material remains in an archeological site
should be highly structured or patterned directly as a result of the ways in which the
extinct society was organized and the ways in
which the people behaved. Thus, the structured array of archeological data will have
direct relationship to the unobservable organization and behavior of the extinct society.

This, of course, provides the potential link
between what the archeologist digs up in the
way of hearths, potsherds and arrowheads
and such behavioral and organizational phenomena as social and political institutions.
Given this view, our ability to deal with such
indirectly observable things seems more sensitive to the sharpness of our hypotheses and
their test implications than to any sort of
inherent weakness in the nature of archeological data *per se.*

This line of argument is in direct contrast
to the view that (1) the vagaries of preservation are such that only a portion of the original material is preserved in archeological
context, and (2) material items are not too
useful in drawing inferences about very many
aspects of past societies, especially those of
organization and behavior. Thus, archeological data are deficient, first because they represent only a sample of the original range of
material items and second because they cannot reflect things like social organization in
any case.

Because of these conflicting views, we can read in the current archeological literature such statements as ". . .data relevant to most, if not all, the components of past sociocultural systems *are* preserved in the archeological record. . ." or "Even under the best of circumstances we must be content with statements of probability, gross purposes, and flexible performance of tasks, since we will never have complete knowledge of the total cultural context of prehistoric technologies."

The debate over the "real" significance of archeological data and their potential for testing propositions about the past is at present about at the stage of arguments about the number of heavenly messengers that could occupy the head of a pin. With respect to things archeological, I have always preferred good works rather than faith; what we obviously need is increased research that, as a by-product, will test these assumptions about the nature of archeological data. There seem to be two ways of going about this. One is to adopt the former view and assume that all things are reflected in the archeological data and generate hypotheses and their test implications and carry out tests. If the results are positive and logically consistent and if hypotheses that test positively are re-tested with independent data, then, after enough testing, the assumption would seem to be correct. This seems to be the way that most archeologists are tackling the problem.

The second approach would take the archeologist to a context where he could control both the patterned array of material items and the organizational and behavioral aspects of a society at the same time. Control of both sides of the coin, as it were, should permit an assessment of the reflection of such nondirectly observable phenomena as social organization in the structure of variability in material items.

To do this, the archeologist would have to go into an ethnographic situation, and there is a growing interest currently in such research. Such "action archeology" or archeologically-oriented ethnography is badly needed. To date, there have been relatively few such studies. Richard Gould of the Amer-

ican Museum has spent several field seasons among Australian aborigines studying tool making and use. There also have been some recent studies of pottery making peoples that I will return to later in this discussion. A somewhat similar context for carrying out such research lies in the field of historical archeology. If records are adequate, historically documented sites might be used to test a variety of interesting hypotheses. To date, there has been very little exploitation of historical data in such research. One notable exception has been the work directed by my colleague, Professor Deetz, in historical materials from the Plains and California and Colonial period cemeteries in the Northeast.

One thing is becoming clear and that is that the range of variability in archeological data is immense, almost infinite. We have been very selective in exploiting the observable variability in our analyses and have tended to ignore variability rather than focus upon it. There appear to be 3 dimensions of variation: (1) stylistic, (2) technological and (3) variation resulting from the design of the item for its projected use. These 3 categories are not mutually exclusive and variability in all 3 categories seems to be differentially distributed within an archeological site as well as regionally.

Take a ceramic container, for an example. We can make observations of attributes or features which we could categorize as stylistic: color, decoration, lip shape and so on. Likewise, use-oriented features such as size, shape, aperture size, shape of the bottom and porosity might be recorded. Technological properties such as tempering materials, method of construction and types of trace-elements present in the clays could also be observed. Considering the magnitude of such variation and the complexities of measuring the co-variation between and among all observational categories, the potential for test implications for a variety of propositions is astronomical. Recognition of this potential has led to an increasing use of statistical tools in modern archeology.

There is, of course, a long history of the use of statistical techniques in American archeology. The nature of archeological data is quantitative and, as such, is subject to techniques of statistical description and inference. Virtually from the beginning of scientific reporting of archeological data, techniques of statistical description have been utilized.

It is not until relatively recently, however, that more sophisticated statistical techniques have begun to be used involving both techniques of description and inference. The reasons for the increased use of sophisticated statistics in American archeology are difficult to discover, but they probably lie in a combination of factors. These would include among others: (1) test implications requiring the manipulation of quantitative data, (2) the impact of the success of certain statistical techniques in other fields, especially other social sciences, and (3) the availability of equipment capable of quickly and efficiently running the complex calculations involved in many of these techniques.

Statistical techniques are not magical. Their potential for archeological analysis is great and they provide a series of powerful tools for us to use. Statistical techniques equip us with the means for efficiently describing data and measuring co-variation among those data. They also form a useful means of comparing samples for similarity and difference. More often than not, significant patterns that are too subtle to be recognized by inspection are revealed in statistical analyses. For current archeological methodology, two areas of statistical theory are important—sampling and statistical description and inference.

Most archeologists are involved with sampling prehistoric sites; rarely can an entire site be excavated. The archeologist is faced with the problem of drawing a sample that is representative of the population to be sampled. This is true on the higher level of determining which site or sites are to be excavated as well. One of the best discussions of archeological sampling I know of is found in a paper by James Hill.

Statistically valid sampling techniques derived from probability theory, with expert judgment added, form powerful tools for the archeologist to use. They provide a means for more efficiently drawing a sample from whatever prehistoric universe is of interest—a sample that maximizes whatever prior knowledge exists and the "expertise" of the investigator. These techniques are designed to make use of the fund of knowledge and experience that is available and to most efficiently discover new information.

The application of statistically valid sampling techniques offers the best chance of removing unconscious bias on the part of the investigator. Obviously, bias that is unrecognized more often than not will lead to distortion and less representative samples from the archeological universe.

There are two types of statistically valid sampling techniques that have had widest use in the United States. These are: simple random sampling and stratified random sampling. The former technique is useful when nothing is known about a site as a result of archeological investigation or surface indications. It can be a useful device to gather information permitting the partitioning of the population in preparation for a stratified sampling technique. For example, it is a powerful tool for the selection of a surface sample from a site where structural features or other means for differentiating the site from surface remains are lacking. The results might well permit the discovery of patterned distributions of surface materials which would enable the investigator to draw a stratified excavation sample.

The basic method of statistically valid sampling is rooted in probability theory. To be adequate, the sample must reflect accurately the nature of the target population defined in terms of the questions being asked by the investigator. This means the sample must be large enough to have a good chance of being accurate, and it must be proportionally representative of the kinds of individuals available in the population (eg, types of houses, ceremonial structures and trash deposits in a site; types of sites in an areal investigation). The more that is known about a population prior to the drawing of a sample, the greater the chances of selecting a sample that will accurately reflect the population. Sample size is determined through the use of formulae based in probability theory.

Removal of bias on the part of the investigator is achieved by thoroughly mixing the population or each stratum making up a population so that each individual composing the population has an equal chance of being selected. This is generally done by numbering the components of the population from 1 to n and referring to a table of random digits to select the samples.

Stratified random sampling is the application of the simple random sampling technique to each stratum recognizable in the population to be sampled. The more strata that are delimited in the population to be sampled, the higher the probability of an accurate sample. This is why the prior knowledge and experience of the archeologist—his expertise—is so important to the application of statistical sampling.

All of the quantitative techniques of statistical description and inference rest upon the assumption that the samples being described or compared are representative of the populations from which they are drawn. Both our temporal and cultural inferences are made in the assumption that differences and similarities in the samples being utilized are real and not a product of sampling error.

Time does not permit an exhaustive review of all useful statistical techniques in the drawing of temporal and cultural inferences in archeology. Brief remarks are in order, however, primarily to draw attention to the potential of such techniques.

The use of statistics has always been an important aspect of making temporal inferences. Relative dating techniques such as stratigraphy and seriation rely in large part upon the comparison of quantities of various styles of cultural materials. The significance of such comparisons can be assessed by utilizing one of several statistical tests that are available, for example, the Chi-square test.

Rather sophisticated statistical tests are being devised in order to arrange stylistic phenomena into chronological sequence (seriation); interesting fine scale variations over space are being investigated and large scale computer applications are being made.

Statistical aids in the area of cultural inference are legion. In large part they encompass multivariate analyses and techniques for the analysis of variance. These techniques enable the assessment of the degree of association and co-variation of all classes and types of archeological data recovered. It is upon these associations that some of the recent exciting inferences regarding prehistoric societies have been based. These inferences are based upon the assumption that all items found in an archeological site are highly patterned with respect to one another and in their placement in the site itself. This patterning is the result of the loss, breakage, abandonment or disposal of items in a manner that should reflect the localization of specific kinds of activities in certain areas of the site, and the nature of the particular social unit performing the localized activity.

The use of such sophisticated statistical tests to measure associations and co-variation as multiple regression and factor analysis has only recently been possible because of the availability of high-speed data-processing equipment. In a very real sense, the computer revolution has affected American archeology.

The use of the computer has greatly aided the drawing of cultural inferences from archeological data. Recent work with the distribution of stylistic phenomena has permitted inferences regarding the nature of residence, size and composition of social groups, the division of labor and the nature of patterns of inheritance.

Deetz, using both archeological and historical data, was able to demonstrate a correlation between the clustering of stylistic attributes of pottery from a historic Arikara site and the strength of the uxorilocal residence pattern. The supporting historical data indicated that for the duration of the site's occupation, the pattern of co-resident related females resulting from a strong marital residence rule gradually broke down. Deetz demonstrates a contemporaneous lessening in the degree of clustering among attributes of decoration found on the pottery (produced by women). This suggested that females co-resident in one household form a "micro-tradition" of style that is different from other such units and that the nature of residence units might be reflected in the array of stylistic phenomena.

A somewhat similar analysis was undertaken with prehistoric data from a site in the American Southwest. The distribution of 175 design attributes on pottery was analyzed at a Pueblo site dated around AD 1150. The study was undertaken using a multiple regression analysis that measured the co-variation among the design attributes and their provenience at the site. The clustering of the stylistic phenomena taken in conjunction with the architectural pattern of the site and the highly patterned cemetery suggested the presence of at least two residence units made up of related females and in-marrying females and their offspring. These units were maintained for several generations, which indicated that inheritance of some things (rooms, access to a well-defined cemetery and certain ceremonial activity) was in the female line.

A site in the same area dating around AD 1250 was studied by Hill. He employed a factor analysis in his research and was able to suggest both continuity and change in behavioral aspects compared to the earlier site. The size of the residence units had remained constant but they were combined into larger social units. Changes such as this were related by Hill to a changing environment. All of these studies have aided our understanding of the evolution of culture in the Southwest and have permitted generalizations about certain cultural processes.

Lewis and Sally R. Binford have used a factor analysis on data recovered from a variety of Mousterian sites from the Old World to make inferences regarding site functions and the nature of task performances. Freeman and Brown were able to infer functional relationships among types of pottery from a site in the American Southwest using a linear regression technique. Cluster analysis and other multivariate techniques are being used by Cowgill and his colleagues in the analysis of materials from the urban site of Teotihuacan, Mexico. Similarly, cluster analysis is being employed by Culbert in his analysis of Maya pottery from the Peten site of Tikal in Guatemala.

Some of the most exciting uses of sophisticated statistical techniques have concerned the analysis of ceramics to make statements about aspects of organization of society and behavior. Hill has utilized factor analysis to infer residence units in the Southwest and Whallon has used design attributes to attempt to deal with patterns of endogamy and exogamy in New York. Similarly, Leone has tested the hypothesis that increasing economic autonomy produces increasing social autonomy in archeological sites in the Southwest.

Researches such as these have stimulated ethnographic work recently among pottery making peoples, carried out by archeologists in several parts of the world. They also have brought into perspective the use of ethnographic analogy in archeology, now also a matter of current interest.

Ethnographic analogy as a tool for archeological interpretation has long been important in American archeology. It has been especially important in the interpretation of particular artifacts and their method of manufacture. Analogy has also been extended to bolster inference about organizational and behavioral aspects of extinct societies.

The role of ethnographic analogy in interpretation has been called into serious question lately, especially with respect to the interpretation of behavioral and organizational phenomena. If we *base* our interpretations on the ethnographic present, then we are saying we have nothing to learn from the past. It also suggests that we have no way of testing propositions concerning culture using archeological data, that we can only rely upon ethnographically known peoples.

The interpretation of archeological materials using ethnographic analogy can never be satisfactory. There is no way of *testing* hypotheses about the past using ethnographic information. Ethnography, along with other sources, provides a wide range of test impli- cations for the testing of propositions utiliz- ing archeological data. But the important point here is that the testing is done using archeological data. The acceptance or rejec- tion of the hypothesis is based upon the outcome of the test and not upon an argu- ment of plausibility stemming from ethno- graphic analogy.

This is illustrated by the ethnographic work being carried out by certain archeolo- gists among pottery making groups. Some of these workers have stated that the purpose of their investigations is to *evaluate* the work of archeologists like Hill who made infer- ences about prehistoric Pueblo society using tests carried out on ceramics. Hill's work and others like it cannot be evaluated by such studies. Perhaps the more general proposi- tions about reflections of organization and behavior in material items can be tested in carefully designed ethnographic studies, but it seems absurd to attempt to test the results of a specific analysis carried out on archeo- logical materials over 600 years old in such a situation. The way to *evaluate* such studies is to assess the methods and the samples used. To *test* the same hypothesis again would require independent data and a second ex- periment, using an appropriate *archeological* context of the same age and in the same area.

Among the best of the archeologically oriented ethnographic work among pottery making peoples, is current research being conducted by Stanislawski of the University of Oregon. He is working among the Hopi and his results to date are extremely interesting. He is providing alternative hypotheses about the nature of learning the art of pottery mak- ing and actual ceramic production that have never been tested archeologically. His work

should also enlarge our roster of test implica- tions in using ceramics in archeological tests. Hopi pottery making is, of course, intimately tied up in the tourist trade in the Southwest, so some of these new hypotheses might not be too applicable, but they should be tested in any case.

There are many other current problems and interests that should be discussed but, unfortunately, time will not permit. Let me mention some of these in closing to alert you to their existence.

Systems theory has begun to have an im- pact in American archeology, especially those concepts that have proved useful in the field of ecology.

The best discussion of general systems for the archeologist that I know of is in a book, *Analytical Archaeology* by David L Clarke, a young British prehistorian. I should point out that this book is fairly heavy reading and somewhat exasperating because of the lack of an anthropological orientation, but it is most provocative and I recommend it to you.

Cultural ecology, likewise, is of great cur- rent importance. Basic concepts such as adaptation, energy flow, and the general sys- tems theory involved, are being utilized in extremely interesting studies. Cultural an- thropologists such as Rappaport and arche- ologists such as Flannery and Struever are especially concerned with ecology in their current research.

Current research is also being conducted archeologically using hypotheses and test implications derived out of economic theory, demography, cognitive anthropology and even structural studies *à la Levi-Strauss*. Our discipline is enjoying an extremely rich elab- oration currently, a most healthy and exciting period in the history of American archeology.

The Bering Strait Land Bridge

William G. Haag

From *Scientific American,*
Vol. 206, No. 1, 1962, pp.
112–123. Copyright © 1962,
Scientific American, Inc. By
permission of the author, and
the publisher and copyright
holder.

The New World was already an old world to the Indians who were in residence when Europeans took possession of it in the 16th century. But the life story of the human species goes back a million years, and there is no doubt that man came only recently to the Western Hemisphere. None of the thousands of sites of aboriginal habitation uncovered in North and South America has antiquity comparable to that of Old World sites. Man's occupation of the New World may date back several tens of thousands of years, but no one rationally argues that he has been here even 100,000 years.

Speculation as to how man found his way to America was lively at the outset, and the proposed routes boxed the compass. With one or two notable exceptions, however, students of American anthropology soon settled for the plausible idea that the first immigrants came by way of a land bridge that had connected the northeast corner of Asia to the northwest corner of North America across the Bering Strait. Mariners were able to supply the reassuring information that the strait is not only narrow—it is 56 miles wide—but also shallow: a lowering of the sea level there by 100 feet or so would transform the strait into an isthmus. With little else in the way of evidence to sustain the Bering Strait land bridge, anthropologists embraced the idea that man walked dry-shod from Asia to America.

Toward the end of the last century, however, it became apparent that the Western Hemisphere was the New World not only for man but also for a host of animals and plants. Zoologists and botanists showed that numerous subjects of their respective kingdoms must have originated in Asia and spread to America. (There was evidence also for some movement in the other direction.) These findings were neither astonishing nor wholly unexpected. Such spread of populations is not to be envisioned as an exodus or mass migration, even in the case of animals. It is, rather, a spilling into new territory that accompanies increase in numbers, with movement in the direction of least population pressure and most favorable ecological conditions. But the immense traffic in plant and animal forms placed a heavy burden on the Bering Strait land bridge as the anthropologists had envisioned it. Whereas purposeful men could make their way across a narrow bridge . . . the slow diffusion of plants and animals would require an avenue as broad as a continent and available for ages at a stretch. . . .

Sounding of the Bering and Chukchi seas depicts a vast plain that is not deeply submerged. At its widest the plain reaches 1,300 miles north and south, 600 miles wider than the north-south distance across Alaska along the Canadian border. The granitic islands that rise above the water testify that the plain is made of the same rock as the continents.

David M. Hopkins of the U.S. Geological Survey has shown that this great plain sank beneath the seas somewhat more than a million years ago as a result of the downwarping of the crust in the Arctic region that began with the Pleistocene epoch. Before that, Hopkins calculates, most of the area was above sea level throughout most of the 50-million-year duration of the preceding Tertiary period.

The continuity of the land mass of Asia and North America during the Tertiary period helps to solve a major portion of the biologist's problem. The paleontological evidence indicates that numerous mammals, large and small, moved from Asia to America during that time. With the subsidence of the land, however, the flow must have stopped. Nor is there any chance that the land rose up again during the million-year Pleistocene period. It is true that the Pacific region along the Aleutian and Kurile island chains is geologically active. But by comparison the Bering Strait region is rather stable; studies of ancient beach terraces on the islands in the surrounding seas indicate that the vertical movement of the land could not have exceeded 30 feet in the course of the Pleistocene. The smoothness of the Bering Sea floor is another indication of prolonged submergence. Deep layers of marine sediment have smoothed out whatever hills and valleys it acquired when it was dry land and exposed to erosion.

Fossil evidence for the origin and geographic distribution of North American mammals nonetheless shows that numerous animals, large and small, came from Asia during the Pleistocene. Beginning early in the Pleistocene, several genera of rodents arrived; such small mammals breed more rapidly than, say, elephants, and they spread far southward across North America, although not into South America. Later came the larger mammals: the mastodon and mammoth, musk oxen, bison, moose, elk, mountain sheep and goats, camels, foxes, bears, wolves and horses. (The horses flourished and then died out in North America; the genus was not seen again in the New World until the conquistadors brought their animals across the Atlantic.) Evidence from botany as well as from zoology requires a substantial dry-land connection between Asia and North America throughout the Pleistocene.

At this point it is well to remember that the sea level at any given place on the globe depends not only on the height of the land but also on the depth of the ocean. The depth of the ocean in this sense is a question of the volume of water in the ocean. With the Pleistocene began the ice age that has apparently not yet run its course. During this million-year period, for reasons subject to warm debate, at least four great ice sheets have built up, advanced and retreated on the Northern Hemisphere. That the ice can lock up considerable quantities of water on the land is evident even in the present interglacial period. The abrupt melting of the Greenland and Antarctic icecaps would, according to various estimates, raise the present world-wide sea level by as much as 300 feet.

To estimate the volume of water locked up on the land in the great continental glaciers of the Pleistocene one begins with the measurement of the land area covered by the glaciers. The great ice sheets gathered up sand, gravel and larger rubble and, when the ice proceeded to melt, deposited a mantle of this "till" on the exposed ground. From such evidence it is calculated that ice covered 30 per cent of the earth's land area during the glacial maxima of the Pleistocene.

To arrive at the volume of water in the

Last great glaciation, the Wisconsin, at its maximum covered about 30 per cent of the earth's land area. The glaciers (1) and accompanying pack ice (2) locked up vast quantities of sea water, lowering sea level by 460 feet and exposing a 1,300-mile-wide, ice-free land bridge in the region of Bering Strait (3). The broken line marks present-day seacoasts and lake shores.

glaciers, however, one must have some idea of the thickness of the ice as well as the area it covered. The Greenland icecap is more than a mile deep, and in Antarctica the rock lies as much as three miles below the surface of the ice. It is clear that the Pleistocene glaciers could have been thousands of feet thick. Multiplication of the area of the glaciers by thicknesses predicated on various assumptions has shown that the freezing of the water on the land may have reduced the ancient sea level by 125 to 800 feet. Such calculations are supported by evidence from coral atolls in tropical seas. Since the organisms that build these atolls do not live at depths greater than 300 feet, and since the

limy structures of such islands go down several thousand feet, a lowering of the sea level by more than 300 feet is necessary to explain their existence.

By all odds the best evidence for the rise and fall of the ancient sea level is offered by the Mississippi Valley, its delta and the adjoining shores of the Gulf of Mexico. In Pleistocene times about a dozen major streams entered the Gulf. As ice accumulated in the north, lowering the level of the sea, the streams followed the retreating shore line downward. On the steeper gradient the water flowed faster, cutting deeper and straighter valleys. Then, as the ice retreated, the sea rose and again moved inland, reducing the velocity of the streams and making them deposit their burdens of gravel and silt at their mouths and farther inland. Consequently during the glacial minima the rivers built up great flood plains over which they wore meandering courses. Each glacial advance brought a withdrawal of the Gulf and quickened the rivers; each retreat raised the level of the Gulf and forced the rivers to build new flood plains.

Had the earth's crust in this region remained stable, all traces of the preceding flood plain would have been erased by the next cycle of cutting and building. But the rivers, particularly the Mississippi, deposited vast quantities of sediment in their lower valleys, building "crowfoot" deltas like that of the Mississippi today. (Many large rivers, such as the Amazon, have never built such deltas because coastwise currents distribute their sediments far and wide.) The accumulating burden of offshore sediments tilted the platform of the continent, pressing it downward under the Gulf and lifting it inland. In succeeding cycles, therefore, the build-up of the flood plain started farther downstream. . . .

It has been determined that the Wisconsin glacier reached its maximum 40,000 years ago and lowered the sea level by as much as 460 feet. As the glacier grew and the oceans receded, an ever broader highway was revealed at the Bering Strait. With a sea-level fall of only 150 feet, the bridge connecting the two continents must have been nearly 200 miles wide. Because the slope of the sea floor is so gentle, a further fall in the sea level uncovered much larger regions. At 450 feet the entire width of the undersea plain from one edge of the continental shelf to the other must have been exposed, providing a corridor 1,300 miles wide for the flow of biological commerce between the no longer separate continents. During the peak periods of the earlier glaciations the Bering Strait land bridge would have presented much the same appearance.

Because the maximum exposure of the land bridge necessarily coincided with a maximum of glaciation, one might think the bridge would have been blocked by ice. Geological evidence shows, however, that neither the Chukchi Peninsula in Siberia nor the westward-reaching Seward Peninsula of Alaska were glaciated during the Wisconsin period. Even large areas of central Alaska remained ice-free throughout the period. As for the now submerged plain on the floor of the Bering Strait and the adjoining seas, it seems clear that the rocky rubble, found where currents clear away the silt, was "rafted" there by icebergs; no part of this accumulation is attributed to glacial till deposited by the melting of glacial ice on the surface.

Conditions are made the more propitious for life on the bridge by the latest theory on the causes of glaciation. Paradoxically, this demands a warm Arctic Ocean over which winds could become laden with moisture for subsequent precipitation as snow deep in the Hudson Bay area, where the glacier had its center of gravity. Western Alaska would have had little snowfall and no accumulation of ice. This deduction is supported by the finding of trees in the Pleistocene deposits on Seward Peninsula. It is not thought, however, that the land bridge was ever anything but tundra. . . .

Giving full weight to the biological evidence, it seems amply demonstrated that a bridge wider than present-day Alaska joined the Old and New worlds during a large part of the Pleistocene. There is much to suggest that the land surface of this bridge was smooth and unbroken. And it appears that large animals moved freely across it during the 80,000 years of the Wisconsin stage and probably throughout much of the preceding interglacial stage.

Before the end of the Wisconsin period the first men must have crossed the bridge. It seems almost a truism that Asiatic man would have followed the slow spread of Asiatic animals into the New World. The men would most likely have come along the coastal margins and not across the interior that lies under the present-day strait. Their remains are covered, therefore, not only by 300 feet or more of water but also by as much as 100 feet of sediment laid down in the Recent period as the sea encroached on the continental shelf. Archaeologists need not be surprised in the future to discover evidence of man here and there in North America 50,000 years old and even older.

selection 10

During the 19th century several discoveries were made in America suggesting the presence of man during the Ice Age, but the evidence was inconclusive. Two schools of thought developed. One held that evidence of the presence of man in the New World did not extend back much beyond the obvious evidence of the prehistoric Mound Builders, Pueblos, Aztecs, or Incas of no more than 2000 B.C. The other school held that man lived among, and hunted, the giant game animals that became extinct at the end of the Pleistocene.

It became apparent that, if the truth were to be known, the skeletons of late Pleistocene game animals would have to be scientifically excavated by trained observers, to see if any evidence of man could be found. If it could be, the undisturbed association of artifacts with bones of an extinct animal in geological deposits of Pleistocene age could be presented to witnesses from the scientific community for verification. Such was the case in 1926 when paleontologists from the Denver Museum of Natural History discovered fluted stone projectile points in association with skeletons of extinct bison near Folsom, New Mexico. The following year, as more bones and "Folsom points" were found *in situ,* scientists from various parts of the continent witnessed the discovery, and in subsequent years more than 100 sites have been described where artifacts of early man occur *in situ* with bones of either mammoth, camel, extinct horse, or bison.

In the United States today we have an excellent, but by no means complete, understanding of cultural development during the

The Earliest Americans

C. Vance Haynes, Jr.

From *Science,* Vol. 166, 1969, pp. 709–714. Copyright 1969, American Association for the Advancement of Science. By permission of the author, the publisher, and copyright holder.

final phase of the Pleistocene glaciation, known as the Valderan Substage. As for the earlier substages, after 40 years of searching, little positive evidence for earlier occupation of the New World has been found. But, as discussed below, we may be on the threshold of a second breakthrough regarding knowledge of the antiquity of man in America.

Geochronology

At the time of the Folsom discovery it was not possible to estimate the age of the find any more precisely than to say that the association with *Bison antiquus* meant that man was present in America near the end of the Ice Age. Today our understanding of the time range for early man is much more precise because of the study of geological sequences to which archeological finds can be related. Radiocarbon dating has made possible both the precise dating and the accurate correlation of these sequences in widely separated areas.

The study of stratigraphic sequences of loess, till, and lake sediments in the mid-continental area has provided a record of geological time corresponding to the fluctuations of late Pleistocene glaciers, but occurrence of archeological sites within these strata are rare. Most of the stratigraphic record of early man is in the western United States, where erosion and sparse vegetation provide better exposures for the accident of discovery. For convenience of discussion I have subdivided the Paleo-Indian period, or the time of early man, into three hypothetical subperiods (Fig. 1) and have arbitrarily selected the boundaries to correspond to those of the time-stratigraphic subdivisions of the Wisconsinan stage as defined by Frye and others.

The late Paleo-Indian period corresponds to the Valderan substage of between 11,800 and 7000 years ago. The middle Paleo-Indian includes the Twocreekan, Woodfordian, and Farmdalian substages, from 28,000 to 11,800 years ago, and any sites older than the Farmdalian-Altonian boundary (28,000 years

ago) would fall into the early Paleo-Indian period. My discussion follows the reverse order of stratigraphic succession, proceeding from the best understood to the least understood period.

Late Paleo-Indian Period

During Valderan time, continental glacial ice expanded from Canada into the United States for the last time, and its retreat through the Cochrane District of Ontario brought the Valderan substage to a close. During this time early man was well established in the New World, where, since the Folsom discovery, his hunting sites and camps have been found from Tierra del Fuego to Nova Scotia. In the earliest part of this period, between 11,500 and 11,000 years ago, there existed throughout the United States a culture of highly skilled and technologically advanced hunters who used a distinctive fluted projectile point known as the Clovis point for killing mammoths as well as other big game animals. The transition from the use of Clovis points to Folsom points approximately 11,000 years ago coincides with the extinction of mammoths, horses, camels, and several other members of the Pleistocene megafauna (Fig. 2), but species of bison remained and were hunted between 11,000 and 7000 years ago by early man using a variety of projectile point types collectively called Plano points.

This sequence is understood because geologists and archeologists working together in the western United States have mapped sequences of alluvium, reflecting cycles of deposition and erosion, within which the temporal relationships of culture, fossils, and samples for radiocarbon dating could be accurately read and correlated with the glacial chronology.

At the Hell Gap site in eastern Wyoming, archeologists have uncovered an unusually complete sequence of superimposed cultural horizons in which the change in early man's artifact assemblages has been observed through a span of 4 millennia between 11,000 and 7000 years ago. Actual "living floors" for

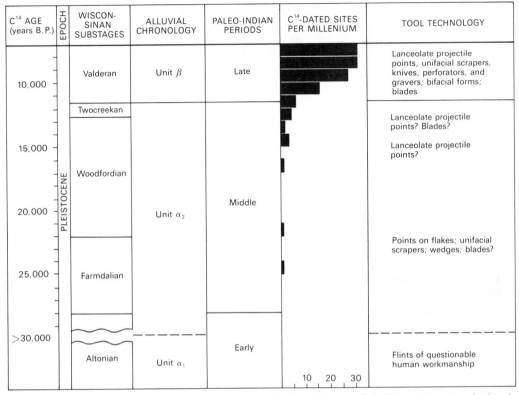

C^{14} AGE (years B.P.)	EPOCH	WISCONSINAN SUBSTAGES	ALLUVIAL CHRONOLOGY	PALEO-INDIAN PERIODS	C^{14}-DATED SITES PER MILLENIUM	TOOL TECHNOLOGY
10,000	PLEISTOCENE	Valderan	Unit β	Late		Lanceolate projectile points, unifacial scrapers, knives, perforators, and gravers; bifacial forms; blades
		Twocreekan				Lanceolate projectile points? Blades?
15,000		Woodfordian		Middle		Lanceolate projectile points?
20,000			Unit α_2			
25,000		Farmdalian				Points on flakes; unifacial scrapers; wedges; blades?
>30,000		Altonian	Unit α_1	Early	10 20 30	Flints of questionable human workmanship

Fig. 1. Chart showing the correlation of geological and archeological events of the Wisconsinan stage in America south of Canada.

Folsom, Agate Basin, Alberta, Cody, and Frederick cultural horizons were uncovered, and thousands of artifacts were found lying where they had been abandoned or lost by early man. The occurrence of discontinuous carbonaceous layers throughout the sequence permitted multiple radiocarbon dating of the entire sequence.

In the eastern United States late Pleistocene alluvial sequences are rare and not so easily mapped, and most late Paleo-Indian sites have been found either on the surface or within the plowed zone where artifacts of all ages are mixed. Because of these factors the temporal relationship of fluted points to archaic eastern types, or of these to the western finds, was not understood. However, in recent years cultural-stratigraphic sequences have been demonstrated in North Carolina and in West Virginia, and a buried site producing fluted points was found in Nova Scotia. Whereas the earliest age for fluted points

in the East is still not known, we now know that the Debert fluted points of Nova Scotia are 10,600 years old and are, therefore, an eastern contemporary of the Folsom type in the West. At the Saint Albans site in West Virginia and the Doerschuck site in North Carolina, archaic artifacts are 8000 to 10,000 years old and hence overlap in time late Paleo-Indian artifacts elsewhere.

The most important find to be made in South America since the discovery of the 10,000-year-old early-man site of Fells Caves in Tierra del Fuego is at Lake Tagua Tagua in central Chili, where an assemblage of stone and bone artifacts has been found in association with bones of extinct game animals in deposits for which an age of 11,380 ± 320 years [a radiocarbon date of 11,380 ± 320 B.P. (GX-1205)] has been obtained. What is significant about this discovery, other than that it dates from early Valderan time, is the fact that it is within a stratigraphic sequence

72

Prehistory

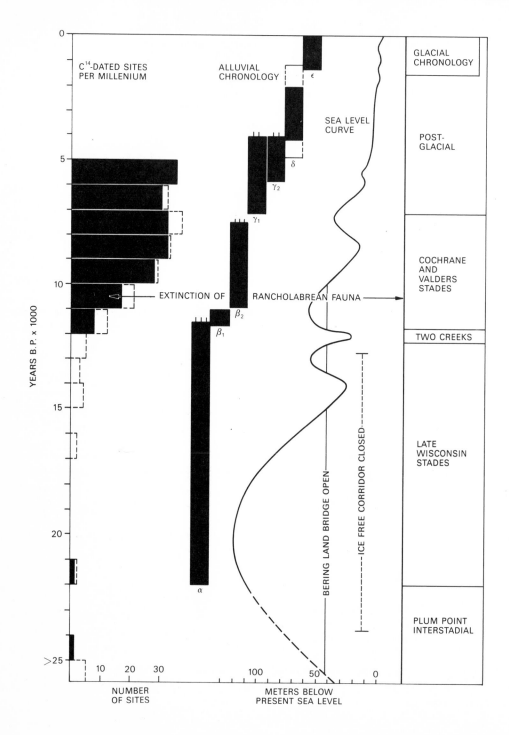

Fig. 2. Chart comparing chronologies of alluvial deposition sea-level fluctuations [after Hopkins], and glaciation to the increase in the number of Paleo-Indian sites with time, as measured by the radiocarbon method.

containing overlying deposits with bones, shells, and artifacts which, taken all together, constitutes compelling evidence in support of the interpretation that the site was a late Pleistocene hunting camp where animals were butchered for food, skins, and other uses. So far, no projectile points have been found at the site but it seems reasonable to expect that some will appear with further excavation.

Recent discoveries in Alaska suggest that different core and blade industries, indicating cultural diversity, had become established there during early Valderan time, but the age of fluted points found on the surface in northern Alaska remains undetermined.

Although there is still much to learn about the temporal relations of various cultures of the late Paleo-Indian period, the trend of investigation today is toward learning more about early man's way of life. Where possible, the precise distribution of artifacts on an ancient surface of occupation is plotted to determine different activity areas. This was done at the Debert site in Nova Scotia, where over 4000 artifacts were discovered *in situ,* making this the largest single-component early-man site yet found east of the Great Plains. The data supported the interpretation that the site was probably a caribou hunting camp visited seasonally by a band of perhaps 40 individuals.

The Murray Springs site in southeastern Arizona, while smaller than Debert, probably has the least disturbed "living floor" of any Clovis site known. The removal by hand of an unusual layer of black organic material laid down very soon after occupation has revealed this floor, in which even the tiniest flake lies exactly where it has lain for 11,200 years. Hemmings and I have mapped the *in situ* position of stone and bone tools and of thousands of waste flakes relative to the positions of butchered carcasses of mammoths, bison, and a horse. . . .

Middle Paleo-Indian Period

The maximum extent of the late Pleistocene glaciation occurred during the Woodfordian substage when practically all of Canada may have lain under a great thickness of ice which effectively blocked the passage of man or animals between Alaska and the coterminous United States. The preceding Farmdalian substage is believed to have been relatively less glacial, but it is not known how much of Canada was ice-free during this time. The end of the Woodfordian substage was the beginning of deglaciation which began 14,000 or 15,000 years ago and proceeded with an alternative series of retreats and diminishing advances through the Valderan substage. A major recession is believed to have occurred during the Twocreekan substage.

It is not known how far the ice borders retreated during Twocreekan time, but it has been suggested that the Cordilleran and Laurentide ice which merged along the eastern front of the Rocky Mountains may have separated during this time, thus making travel between Alaska and central North America possible for the first time in approximately 10,000 years. It has also been suggested that this happened either 13,000 years ago or in late Valderan time.

Twocreekan deposits are rare, because erosion was more prevalent than deposition, but at the type site near Two Creeks, Wisconsin, a deposit of sand contains trees that were killed by rising water of glacial Lake Chicago when advancing Valders ice blocked the outlet and subsequently submerged the trees 11,900 years ago. In the eastern part of the continent no artifacts have been found in Twocreekan deposits.

In the western United States pluvial lakes were at their highest stands during Woodfordian time and earlier, as evidenced by shore features and lacustrine beds dated by the radiocarbon method. In both halves of the continent there have been surface finds of artifacts thought to be temporally related to shore features of lakes of Woodfordian or Twocreekan age, but none have been recovered enclosed in lacustrine deposits where contemporaneity could be clearly demonstrated. The situation is similar for the surface distribution of fluted points in the glaciated mid-continent. Whereas no artifacts have been recovered from within glacial deposits, the surface distribution of fluted points in Michigan and Wisconsin appears to be related to Port Huron and Valders moraines, suggesting that man entered the area between late Woodfordian and early Valderan time.

Until recently the very existence of a middle Paleo-Indian period was subject to challenge on grounds of insufficient evidence, but recent finds in the northwestern United States are more convincing than any others yet made in this country. In a cave beneath a lava butte in south-central Idaho, stone artifacts and cut bone were found in deposits that were subsequently assigned ages of 14,500 to 15,000 years, and a leaf-shaped projectile point found in the deposits is of a type thought by some to have been a developmental predecessor of fluted points; however, I have offered an alternative interpretation of the dating in my comments to Bryan. At Fort Rock Cave in Oregon, a radiocarbon date of 13,200 ± 170 B.P. (GAK-173) was recently obtained for charcoal reportedly associated with a lanceolate projectile point, although the documentation has not yet been published. Again the material was found in a cave or rock shelter in which there was an overlying sequence of archeological strata for which consistent dates had been obtained.

No bones of early man from the middle Paleo-Indian period have as yet been found by the archeologist, but in eastern Washington human bones, stemmed lanceolate projectile points, bone points, and a delicate bone needle were found *in situ* in a stratigraphic sequence for which the geochronology had already been worked out. The estimated age of between 10,800 and 13,000 years makes this find at the Marmes shelter the oldest firmly established date for human skeletal remains in the New World. Current investigations of the site, which include radiocarbon dating, may reveal more precisely whether this occupation was Valderan or earlier. The Midland skull from western Texas is probably at least as old as the Marmes find, but the geochronology of the Scharbauer site is less precisely known.

The existence of sites of pre-Valderan age in South America has been indicated by dates, obtained by the radiocarbon method, between 12,000 and 16,000 years ago, but so far their association with artifacts has been questionable. In Mexico, the discoveries near Puebla and Tlapacoya constitute the strongest evidence yet offered of a middle Paleo-Indian occupation of the New World. At several sites in and around the Valsequillo reservoir near Puebla the occurrence of a developmental sequence of artifacts in association with bones of extinct game animals, all within a thick stratigraphic sequence, lends support to the interpretation that at least the lower parts of the sequence are Woodfordian or older. A radiocarbon date of 21,850 ± 850 B.P. (W-1895) on shell, which commonly yields erroneous dates, suggests a Woodfordian age for part of the sequence. At the Hueyatlaco site a marked uncomformity within the Valsequillo gravels separates upper deposits with bifacially flaked artifacts from lower deposits in which only flake- and blade-type artifacts have been found. . . .

At the Tlapacoya site between Mexico City and Puebla, shore deposits of ancient Lake Chalco surround a volcanic hill around which two sites of early man have been found. Both are in volcanic ash that is interfingered with littoral peat deposits; an age of approximately 24,000 years has been obtained for wood from these deposits. It is believed that at least some obsidian flakes and artifacts were introduced into the deposits by rodents, but a shallow depression containing powdered charcoal which yielded a date of 24,000 ± 4000 B.P. (A-794B) is believed to be an ancient hearth. Bones of late Pleistocene animals occurred in beach gravels around the hearth, and at another site on the opposite side of the hill an obsidian blade was found beneath a large log which yielded a date of 23,150 ± 950 (GX-959), indicating that the site is of Farmdalian age—the only site of that age yet known.

As yet no site from the middle Paleo-Indian period has yielded anywhere near the quantity of artifacts and debitage known for many of the late Paleo-Indian sites, and, with the possible exception of Valsequillo, no cultural stratigraphic sequence has been demonstrated. Although none of the sites are as convincing as the Folsom site was for the late period, it appears to be only a matter of time before a convincing find is made, but, until it is, the existence of a middle Paleo-Indian period must not be considered proven.

Early Paleo-Indian Period

If evidence from the middle period seems scarce, that from the early Paleo-Indian period is practically nonexistent. . . . Recently, at the Calico Hills site, near Yermo, California, very crude flints, reported to be artifacts, have been found in alluvial-fan gravels of Pleistocene age. Because this site exemplifies most of the problems encountered with possible archeological sites thought to be of early Paleo-Indian age, I consider it here in some detail. The ancient alluvial-fan gravels, containing up to 10 percent of chert derived from bedrock which crops out in the Calico Hills 3 miles (3.8 kilometers) to the west, have been intensely weathered to a depth of over 6 meters. This ancient soil has superimposed upon it a calcareous red B-horizon and a vesicular A-horizon in the upper half meter, which indicates a second episode of weathering. The strength of soil-profile development shown by the upper red soil is as great as, or greater than, that of mid-Wisconsinan soils elsewhere in the southwestern United States, and many geologists, including myself, believe that the deposit is no younger than Altonian. The additional factor of 6 meters of rotten gravel below the red soil is convincing evidence that the deposit is of pre-Wisconsinan age (more than 70,000 years old), because such a depth of weathering is not known in Wisconsinan deposits. Some geologic age estimates of between 30,000 and 120,000 years have been made, but an age of 500,000 cannot be precluded.

The origin of what have been called artifacts within the deposits is even less certain, but some authorities, including those conducting the excavations, appear to be absolutely convinced that some of the fragments of chert show flaking that could only have been done by man. Others contend that even the best specimens could have been chipped and flaked naturally, especially in view of the fact that each "artifact" has been selected from literally hundreds or thousands of individual pieces of chert, excavated from gravels which, when fresh, experienced intergranular percussion and pressure at various times during their transportation from outcrops in the Calico Hills. Natural flaking would have been further aided by the igneous-rock cobbles which make up a significant percentage of the rocks and which, when fresh, would have served as natural hammerstones.

Another line of evidence that has been offered in support of the hypothesis that man was present during deposition of the alluvial fan is the occurrence of "artifacts" in anomalous concentrations, one of which is associated with fragments of bone and tusk, but the degree of concentration is dependent upon both the subjective selection of "artifacts" and the relative proportion of these to natural pieces of chert. The variability of this ratio for a representative sample of the fan has not been determined. The occurrence of dispersed fragments of bone and tusk is not unexpected in any Pleistocene gravel; therefore their presence has no bearing on the question of whether or not the flints are artifacts. The main difficulty in the Calico Hills case is that the situation there does not lend itself to definitive solution. The question is whether the flints are of archeological or of geological origin, but, as with "eoliths," the two could be indistinguishable at very early levels and under geological conditions where natural flints are a significant component of the deposit. . . .

Theoretical Considerations

Theories of the initial peopling of the New World are intimately related to sea level and glaciation during the late Pleistocene, because it is generally agreed that man passed from the Old to the New World by way of an emerged Bering platform and thence through central Canada. The vast continental glaciers grew at the expense of water from the oceans, so sea level was lowest when glaciation was greatest. During glaciation the emergence of the Bering platform made Alaska as much a part of the Asian continent as of the North American, and people living in northeastern Asia would naturally have migrated throughout Beringia into Alaska, and eventually through central Canada, once the glaciers there had retreated enough to open an ice-free corridor (Fig. 2).

Because of our lack of precise knowledge of the timing of these events, we do not know whether man could have crossed the Bering land bridge when it first emerged 28,000 to 25,000 years ago and still have had time to pass through Canada before the Laurentide ice merged with Cordilleran ice and blocked the passage. The passage would not have again become open until sometime after deglaciation began—between 14,000 and 8500 years ago. It is possible that the passage may have opened and closed several times in conjunction with the retreats and advances of the ice during deglaciation, and it has been proposed that the first late Wisconsinan migration was a migration of the predecessors of the Clovis hunters during either the Two Creeks retreat or the Bowmanville.

If early man was on the North American continent during the early Paleo-Indian period, he would have had to cross the land bridge during Altonian time or earlier. One current hypothesis is that all early-man developments derived from an early migration and that passage through Canada was not again possible until late Valderan time, when early man may have migrated in the other direction, northward. On the other hand, the very existence of an ice barrier is questioned by some.

The detailed history of an early ice-free corridor through Canada may be very difficult to learn by means of geological investigation because later advances of the ice may have obliterated much of the evidence. On the other hand, the archeological record of early man in central North America may shed light on the history of ice-free corridors. Compelling evidence of man's presence in central

North America before deglaciation began would indicate that man must have traversed Canada in pre-Woodfordian time. The relatively abrupt appearance of a new or different industry may correlate with the opening of an ice-free corridor during deglaciation, as has been suggested for the Clovis-point industry, but this appearance will be recognizable only from a horizon in the geochronological record beyond which positive evidence for the industry will be lacking. Therefore, in order for negative evidence to be significant, it is essential that the presence of industries at an early date be established by only the most compelling evidence. . . .

Summary and Conclusions

The presence of early man south of Canada during Valderan time has been demonstrated repeatedly by discoveries of sites where artifacts, including lanceolate projectile points, have been found in association with bones of extinct animals in geological deposits dated by the radiocarbon technique. During the first millennium of Valderan time, fluted projectile points predominate in archeological horizons throughout much of North America. Evidence for horizons characterized by earlier projectile points is limited to two cave deposits and possibly the Hueyatlaco site in Mexico. The seemingly abrupt appearance of the relatively sophisticated fluted point tradition throughout much of North America during late glacial time has led to the hypothesis that it may have stemmed from a separate migration through central Canada during one of the intraglacial retreats of the ice near the end of deglaciation. According to another hypothesis, all early-man industries derive from a common non-projectile-point industry that had its origin in the Old World but made its way to the New World in early or even pre-Wisconsinan time. It remains to be determined whether either or both of these hypotheses, or parts of them, are valid.

For establishing man's presence, the minimum requirements met for the Folsom site still apply for future excavations. The primary requirement is a human skeleton, or an assemblage of artifacts that are clearly the work of man. Next, this evidence must lie *in situ* within undisturbed geological deposits in order to clearly demonstrate the primary association of artifacts with stratigraphy. Lastly, the minimum age of the site must be demonstrable by primary association with fossils of known age or with material suitable for reliable isotopic age dating. These requirements have now been met repeatedly for the late Paleo-Indian period, but they have not yet been satisfactorily met for the middle Paleo-Indian period, and our knowledge of the early Paleo-Indian period is still hypothetical. In the future, and because of the importance of such data, the evidence must be witnessed and verified *in situ* by several authorities, just as it was at Folsom. This is particularly important in archeology, where, as in no other science, the evidence is partly destroyed in the recovery of data and can be duplicated only by the chance discovery of a similar situation.

selection 11

Archeology as Anthropology: A Case Study

William A. Longacre

From *Science,* Vol. 144, 1964, pp. 1454–1455. Copyright 1964, American Association for the Advancement of Science. By permission of the author, the publisher, and copyright holder.

Recently, certain archeologists have expressed concern over the few contributions that archeology has made to the general field of anthropology. A combination of advances in methodology and the adoption of cultural models which focus on cultural processes has resulted in contributions that go beyond mere taxonomy and inventories of stylistic traits. Many aspects of extinct cultural systems (for example, social organization) are not directly reflected in material objects and are therefore difficult for the prehistorian to interpret. This paper indicates one way in which archeology can elucidate some of the features of social life.

Selected data obtained during the excavation of one prehistoric community in eastern Arizona were used to answer questions concerning aspects of its social system. The purposes of this study were: (i) to augment the cultural history of the upper Little Colorado area and to provide a clearer understanding of the role of the region in the prehistoric Southwest, (ii) to demonstrate the value of combining systematic sampling procedures with traditional as well as new methods of data processing (for example, computer processing), and (iii) to make specific contributions to the growing body of anthropological knowledge and theory (for example, to demonstrate the presence of localized matrilineages in the Southwest by A.D. 1200).

In this report I describe the analysis of one community, the Carter Ranch Site, located in eastern Arizona and occupied approximately from A.D. 1100 to 1250. This area today is semiarid with most of its precipitation occurring during the summer months as torrential storms. Palynological studies, which permit inferences concerning the past climate, indicate that there have been no great climatic changes in the past 3500 years. There is evidence that a minor shift in the rainfall pattern, from one of roughly equal winter-summer precipitation to the present pattern, took place by about A.D. 1000. It was after this shift became pronounced that the Carter Ranch Pueblo was occupied.

By A.D. 1000, the area was covered by a network of small villages (pueblos) consisting of one or two multi-room buildings. By 1250, most of the region was abandoned; very large Pueblo villages were located on two permanent streams in the area. The area was totally abandoned by 1500.

The Carter Ranch Site consisted of 39 dwelling rooms built as a main block with two wings surrounding a plaza which contained two kivas (underground ceremonial structures). A detached Great Kiva (a large ceremonial building built partly aboveground) was situated about 10 meters northwest of the room block. The site was located in a valley containing about 60 sites roughly contemporary with it.

During the course of the occupation of the Carter Ranch Site, ecological pressures became more acute as the shift in rainfall became more pronounced. The cultivation of corn probably became difficult and mutual economic assistance in the form of cooperation between villages would seem to have been advantageous under conditions of such economic stress. The appearance of Great Kivas suggests the development of multi-community patterns of solidarity with a religious mechanism to "cement the ties." In the area's settlement system, the Carter Ranch Site functioned as a ceremonial center and united a number of communities into one sociopolitical sphere.

A series of analyses were undertaken to determine the social system of the community itself. One was a detailed design element analysis of the ceramics from the site. The smallest elements of design, which were defined from more than 6000 sherds, were considered important because they might not have been "in focus" to the potter who might therefore have selected them in an unconscious manner. If there were a system of localized matrilineal descent groups in the village, then ceramic manufacture and decoration would be learned and passed down within the lineage frame, it being assumed that the potters were female as they are today among the western Pueblos. Nonrandom preference for design attributes would reflect this social pattern.

The distribution of 175 design elements was plotted for the site and was found to be nonrandom, certain designs being associated with distinct blocks of rooms. This suggested the presence of localized matrilineal groups. To test this phenomenon further, the frequencies of the design elements were subjected to a multiple regression analysis on the I.B.M. 7094 computer. This analysis showed that there were three groupings of rooms and kivas on the basis of similarities and differences of occurrence of elements of design on the pottery from the floors. Each group of rooms was associated with a kiva. There were two main groups, one each in the southern and northern parts of the village. A small cluster of rooms in the northeastern portion of the village with an associated kiva was similar to the main block of rooms localized in the southern part of the Pueblo. I interpret this as a group which segmented from the lineage in the southern part and began a separate localized lineage in the northeastern portion of the community.

The various kinds of pottery excavated during 1961 were subjected to a regression analysis. Nonrandom groups of ceramics appeared to be correlated with certain rooms, suggesting that specific tasks were carried out in particular types of rooms. Rooms of several different types were repeated in each room block. This probably reflects household units housing an extended family or lineage segment. Nonceramic artifacts obtained during the 1961 and 1962 excavations, and ceramic types from the 1962 excavations, and ceramic types from the 1962 season were subjected to a multiple regression analysis on the I.B.M. 7094. The pottery types were associated with particular types of rooms, exactly as in the previous analysis. Other artifacts were much less confined in distribution. Each dwelling was used for several functions, with an activity or set of related activities prevalent in each room. This is precisely the pattern of room utilization in the modern western Pueblo household.

One group of ceramics was associated with ceremonial units, such as kivas, indicating that a set of stylistically distinct vessels were associated with ritual activities. Vessels of these types were also associated with the burials, suggesting grave-side ritual.

A cemetery of three separate areas was excavated in the midden east of the site. In the northern midden were interments that were oriented east-west, whereas the southern midden had burials oriented north-south. An analysis of design elements on the ceramics in the graves indicated that the burials in the northern section of the midden were associated with the localized descent group in the northern part of the village, and that the southern burial area was associated with the descent group localized in the southern portion of the site. The burials in the center of the midden were mixed, both in terms of their orientation and the occurrence of design elements. Almost all of the ornaments and unusual items that probably reflect differences in status, included as grave goods from the entire sample of burials, were from this central area. Likewise, the burials in the central portion of the midden had twice as many vessels per burial as the burials in other areas of the midden. This central cluster of burials probably represents individuals of relatively high status from all localized social groups in the community, buried in a separate section of the cemetery. The importance of the site as

a ceremonial focal point suggests that high status would have been earned by individuals through participation in ritual activities rather than acquired through inheritance.

The regression analyses of artifacts reflect a rigid division of labor at the site. For example, weaving implements were found with a male burial indicating that weaving was a male activity, and these items were strongly correlated with artifacts used in ritual activities associated with the kivas. This suggests that weaving was a masculine task and was carried out in the kiva, just as it is today in the western Pueblos. The distribution of tools associated with female activities was quite different from that of items associated with male activities. Most tasks were evidently performed by groups organized according to sex.

These analyses permit comparisons to be made between the modern western Pueblos and one portion of their prehistoric background. The presence of localized matrilineages and lineage segments at the Carter Ranch Site demonstrates continuity for this western Pueblo trait for more than 700 years. A similar pattern for the household as the basic local unit can now be documented. Other stable processes are now demonstrable. These include the basic form of the rigid division of labor and particular activities associated with each of the sexes.

Significant differences can be shown as well. One of the most striking is the change in inter-community integration and a related change in the intra-community pattern itself. Communities made up of from one to three localized matrilineages (probably corresponding to single clans as well) were united through the mechanism of centralized ritual. Strong mechanisms for multi-community integration are not present among the modern western Pueblos.

Related to these changes was a change in the nature of the organization of the community itself. Villages up to A.D. 1300 probably were more commonly composed of single localized lineages. The economic advantages accruing to larger aggregates of people in the face of environmental pressures resulted in the establishment of communities of more than a single lineage after 1300. Strong localized lineages are not conducive to a strong village integration when a village consists of several lineages. I would expect the development of integrative ties that crosscut social groups to develop within the village under these circumstances. These would be such things as the development of societies with strong ritual functions, the breakdown of the association of kiva with clan, and the assumption by the kivas of more village-wide significance (for example, by association with

societies). Crosscutting integrative mechanisms such as these would promote community solidarity at the expense of the disruptive lineage strength, and this is the pattern today among the western Pueblos.

These examples serve to document my case for the potential use of this approach in investigations of prehistoric communities. The method and theory incorporated in this study can be used to advantage in testing hypotheses of reconstruction, as well as for providing background to aid in understanding the development of certain sociological phenomena.

selection 12

The Ethno-Archaeology of Hopi Pottery Making

Michael B. Stanislawski

From *Plateau*, Vol. 42, No. 1, Summer 1969. Copyright 1969, Northern Arizona Society of Science and Art, Inc. By permission of the author and the publisher and copyright holder.

Introduction

Last summer my wife and I went to the Hopi Mesas for seven weeks, to begin a study of Hopi pottery making. We did so to collect information on material culture that would be of benefit to both archaeologists and ethnographers; for in order for archaeologists to understand well the artifacts, processes, systems, or social patterns of a prehistoric site, it is necessary to have knowledge of the material culture of local living peoples assumed to be the descendents of prehistoric groups in the area.

Unfortunately, most ethnographers are not now interested in material culture, and thus archaeologists will have to collect such ethnographic information to make their analogies and inferences. Studies published by Raymond H. Thompson on Yucatecan Maya pottery making, and by Richard Gould on the use of stone by aboriginal groups in southwestern Australia, are instances of this archaeological concern. Nathalie Woodbury is now also studying Pueblo pottery in this manner; and Don Lathrap and his students at Illinois are making similar studies of pottery and potters in the Peruvian Montana.

Another stimulus in beginning this project was the fact that several modern archaeologists have postulated a correlation of pottery styles and types with individual lineage units in prehistoric Southwestern sites. Yet we noted that recent ethnographic information concerning this possible correlation of pottery and social units had apparently not been collected. In fact, the social meaning of pottery has not been well studied (particularly concerning the Hopi, Zuni, and other Western Pueblo groups) since the work of Bunzell in the 1920's. However, the Hopi still make a large quantity of pottery in the native, or traditional manner, using native clays, polishing and scraping tools, and native paints and firing methods. It appeared to be an excellent area in which to test some problems of ethno-archaeology.

The specific purposes of our 1968 study were to collect information concerning the traditional tools and techniques of Hopi and Hopi-Tewa pottery making, the modern uses of pottery and potsherds; the methods of teaching pottery making to children and adults, and the social patterns of transmission; and the distribution of pots, potsherds, and pottery types within the Hopi and Tewa communities. In this regard we were also trying to collect Hopi and Tewa linguistic terms referring to pottery and pottery making, in order to understand their own classification of ceramic types.

Preparation and Field Work

We were aided in our study by Edward Dozier of the University of Arizona, who suggested Hopi-Tewa informants and friends we might see. The staff of the Museum of Northern Arizona, Flagstaff, was equally vital in our field work project; for they provided us with their personal knowledge of Hopi culture, and unpublished Hopi data, and also gave us access to the Museum library, field notes, and large collection of Hopi pottery and other ethnographic materials.

We began with a study of the Museum (of Northern Arizona's) large historic pottery collection, and by study and classification of the pottery submitted to the 1968 Hopi Craftsman Exhibition. In both cases we were able to study the groups of pottery made by a single Hopi potter, and thus to get an idea of personal style. We were able to collect other general information concerning working Hopi potters and their output in terms of colors, styles, and vessel shapes, and some of their genealogical relationships, by studying the records of past Hopi Exhibitions (from 1930 to the present); and also by studying the excellent notes of Katharine Bartlett and Margaret Wright. In this way we began to build our genealogies, and were able to start a master list of working Hopi potters, village by village. To my knowledge, there is no current published list of working pottery makers, and no other information concerning the total number of potters now working, or their output. Finally, we were able to photograph every potter's collection submitted, by individual potter. (There were more than 250 pots submitted, by more than 30 individual makers.) We thus have an invaluable permanent record which can be segregated by potter, clan, or lineage unit. We hope to continue this photo collection over the next four or five years, in order to build up a large comparative sample.

In the field, we secured a small Hopi house in the village of Polacca, below First Mesa. We first met Hopi-Tewa potters in Polacca and Hano, but as we got to know individuals they would refer us to their Hopi relatives and friends. We met other potters casually as we walked through the three villages of Walpi, Sichomovi and Hano and were called into houses to see pottery for sale. Eventually, more than a dozen women allowed us to sit with them for up to several hours and watch while they made pottery.

Some Preliminary Results of the 1968 Study

Hopi potter census
We interviewed 28 Hopi and Hopi-Tewa potters this past summer: 16 Tewa and 12 Hopi; and of these, 12 potters (10 Tewa and 2 Hopi) were interviewed most extensively, We began

an indexed card file containing such information as name, village, age, relatives, and major pottery styles, for about 150 working potters, one-third of these being Tewa. We have additional information in our card files on a large number of potters now no longer making pottery, no longer living locally, or deceased; and have relatively good genealogies of most of the Tewa potters, emphasizing, of course, females in the line. Fortunately, Hopi-Tewa clan and lineage structure favors such an emphasis; but even so, it is often difficult to discover a woman's maiden name, for both the Hopi and Tewa do not like to use their own names, nor names of their relatives and neighbors, and all strongly dislike talking about any dead person by name. A 1968 Hopi census, supported by the Tribal Council, may help.

Potters' hall-marks

As part of our genealogy work, we also began to study signature and hall-marks on Hopi pottery. We know of at least 14 women using hall-marks (such as an ear of corn, an antelope, a flower, etc.); apparently such identification marks were encouraged by traders and by the Museum of Northern Arizona staff in the early 1930's, as a means of encouraging sales. It was *not* a native tradition, and never took hold widely. Most Hopi potters still do not identify their pottery, and those that do usually write their name. This again is due to recent encouragement by local traders. The hall-mark, when used, seems to be a symbol of the woman's Hopi-Tewa name (spotted corn, soft feather, etc.) and this name was often taken from that of the father's sister.

Pottery types and styles in production

A third part of the 1968 study was concerned with the classification of Hopi vessels forms in modern production, the decoration colors used (for both design and background), and the painting styles and motifs used. We were especially interested in certain pottery types, such as whiteware and indented or tooled redware, and vessel forms, such as tiles and *po'osivu* kettles. We currently have Hopi show records, records from traders' collections, and interview accounts of many of the

pottery forms made by more than 50 potters. A problem to be tackled next year is to determine why certain potters on First Mesa and Third Mesa continue to make plainware, including Navajo style pottery, while most others do not. Few women now make plainware at all, and the problem of Navajo style pottery is particularly interesting. One Hopi-Tewa potter of First Mesa now makes pitched black water jars and cooking pots for sale to the Navajo, as her mother did, and several women on Third Mesa make pottery somewhat reminiscent of Navajo pottery in form, color and finish. It is interesting to note that at least six women on Third Mesa say they may call the second major Tribal Council meeting to protest this breakdown of village specialization.

Craft Training and Correlation of Social Units

One of the major questions we hope to answer in the coming years is the method of Hopi pottery training, and the association of family unit and pottery style or type. We began to study this problem in 1968 by the collection of genealogies and the observation of teaching in progress. We concentrated on whiteware pottery makers, i.e. those making pottery slipped white on all surfaces before firing, or slipped white on the interior of bowls. At least six women make only white-slipped pottery, but a minimum of 20 more produce occasional pieces of pottery slipped white on both surfaces, or slipped white only on the interior, with a red exterior slip. In both cases, black, or black and red designs are used on the white background. Plain white pottery is rarely if ever produced.

We can now trace the origin of this modern whiteware pottery on the Mesas at least four generations back, and can begin to show how the style was transmitted to others, and to trace its spread. Virtually all of the makers are related by marriage or descent, and learned from one another. However, people of at least five clans are involved, and several more lineages. For one recent generation we know that a daughter of one of the original whiteware makers learned from her mother, taught her sister-in-law from another village on First Mesa, who taught both her own mother and *her* sister-in-law from another mesa. In short, the Hopi and Tewa who are involved in producing this style of pottery may live close together (because of marriage and descent ties) but they come from at least two different Mesas, five different villages, and four or five clans. Production of the same (and very distinct) pottery style does not correlate with homogeneity of clan or lineage background, nor the transmission of learning within a single lineage unit. Nor do all these people live in contiguous or nearby room blocks.

This case does mainly involve the more acculturated Hopi-Tewa potters; and several of the families involved live outside the main villages and thus may be more free in behavior. However, it also does indicate that great caution must be used in inferring lineage or clan relationships by pottery distribution alone.

The learning of the style seems to involve a minimum of instruction or direct order; rather a grandmother, aunt or mother will encourage her relatives to watch and copy her work. Then she will re-mold, or re-paint their attempts, in order to show them the proper result. It is interesting that it is the grandmother or aunt who often does this; mothers of small children seldom make pottery at all, and may not return to the craft until the children are grown or away.

Use and re-use of potsherds
Another interest was the problem of Hopi and Tewa use of potsherds, and how this might affect sherd distribution in the homes and around the village. We found that sherds were not simply discarded garbage, but were used in at least seven ways. They were used as temper for new pottery; as templates from which designs were copied for painting new pottery; in firing, to cover and protect pottery; and also as chinking in building walls and window frame areas, and in ovens (and were considered superior to stones in this use). Sherds of ceremonial clay pipes or cloud-blowers were carefully gathered and placed in local shrines to protect the community;

and potsherds that resulted from a series of unusual firing accidents would be saved, too, for they indicated coming death or tragedy within the family, and had to be guarded in the home. In short, some sherds are sacred, others are used in building activity, and others to help make new pottery. Both modern and prehistoric sherds are collected, stockpiled in the houses, and used in these ways; and this would, of course, markedly affect the quantity and distribution of potsherds within the Hopi village. These factors of use and re-use may well have been the same in the past, and would affect the stratigraphic unit counts and room correlations we make in archaeological studies.

Technology
Finally, we collected information on the technology of Hopi pottery making; for example, on the methods of gathering clay; the clay types used to make different types of pottery; the preparation of clay; the tempering, coiling, scraping, drying, painting, and firing processes, and the uses of the finished pots. We found that fifteenth century clay mines are still used, and that deaths and injuries occur in using them; that some potters are now mixing clays to produce a unique pink background; that stone, sand or potsherd temper is nearly always added to the clay in Hopi and Tewa pottery making in order to make scraping and smoothing easier; and that coal, as well as sheep dung, is frequently used to fire whiteware, and often used to start the fires for redware or yellowware firing. The different background colors used on decorated pottery (red, yellow, white, and pink) are thus partly the result of clay and slip used, and the amount of air supplied and of oxidation during firing, but partly also the result of amount of time left in the fire, the rapidity of cooling, and the type of fuel used in firing.

For the Future

We plan to return to the Hopi Mesas in the summer of 1969, to continue our study, emphasizing methods of learning and transmission of design style. We hope to collect linguistic terms for pottery and pottery making, in order to try to understand the Hopi and Tewa classification (for example, Hopi-Tewa seem to ignore rim form and emphasize gross vessel form and use instead). We hope to be able to contrast Hopi and Hopi-Tewa pottery, and to begin to work with the Third Mesa potters now producing plainware. Finally, we hope eventually to be able to make a master list of all Hopi potters now producing, their major styles, their genealogies, etc., and to be able to distinguish the individual, family, clan, village or mesa pottery types or styles from one another, and thus to suggest the social meaning and correlations of pottery to the Hopi and Hopi-Tewa. This is some of the basic type of information needed by archaeologists in order to make analogies or inferences concerning the past.

part 3

Physical Anthropology

The New Physical Anthropology

Sherwood L. Washburn

From *Transactions of the New York Academy of Sciences,* Series II, Vol. 13, No. 7, 1951, pp. 298–304. By permission of the author and the publisher.

Recently, evolutionary studies have been revitalized and revolutionized by an infusion of genetics into paleontology and systematics. The change is fundamentally one of point of view, which is made possible by an understanding of the way the genetic constitution of populations changes. The new systematics is concerned primarily with process and with the mechanism of evolutionary change, whereas the older point of view was chiefly concerned with sorting the results of evolution. Physical anthropology is now undergoing the same sort of change. Population genetics presents the anthropologist with a clearly formulated, experimentally verified, conceptual scheme. The application of this theory to the primates is the immediate task of physical anthropology.

In the past, physical anthropology has been considered primarily as a technique. Training consisted in learning to take carefully defined measurements and in computing indices and statistics. The methods of observation, measurement, and comparison were essentially the same, whether the object of the study was the description of evolution, races, growth, criminals, constitutional types, or army personnel. Measurements were adjusted for various purposes, but measurement of the outside of the body, classification, and correlation remained the anthropologists' primary tools. The techniques of physical anthropology were applied to a limited group of problems, and any definition or statement of traditional anthropology must include both the metrical methods and the problems for which the methods were used. Further, anthropology was characterized by theories, or rather by a group of attitudes and assumptions.

There has been almost no development of theory in physical anthropology itself, but the dominant attitude may be described as static, with emphasis on classification based on types. Any such characterization is oversimplified, and is intended only to give an indication of the dominant techniques, interests, and attitudes of the physical anthropologist. Except for emphasis on particular animals, physical anthropology shared much with the zoology of the times when it developed. Much of the method was developed before the acceptance of the idea of evolution, and all of it before the science of genetics.

Physical anthropology should change, just as systematic zoology has changed. The difficulties which accompany the necessary modifications can be greatly reduced if their nature is clearly understood. Naturally, in a time of rapid flux there will be numerous doubts and disagreements as to what should be done. This is natural, and what I have to offer is a tentative outline to indicate how parts of the new physical anthropology may differ from the old.

The old physical anthropology was primarily a technique. The common core of the science was measurement of external form with calipers. The new physical anthropology is primarily an area of interest, the desire to understand the process of primate evolution and human variation by the most efficient techniques available.

The process of evolution, as understood by the geneticist, is the same for all mammals. The genetic composition of a population may be described in terms of gene frequencies. The modification of these frequencies results in evolution, which is caused by *selection,* mutations, drift, and migrations. Mutations and migrations introduce new genetic elements into the population. But selection on the phenotype, adapting animals to their environment, is the primary cause of alteration in gene frequencies.

This is essentially a return to Darwinism, but with this important difference: Darwin wrote in a pregenetic era. Therefore, he did not understand the mechanism which makes possible the production of variation and the possibility of selection. Since Darwin's ideas could not be proved in detail by the techniques available in his time, the concept of selection did not become fully effective. Therefore, some pre-evolutionary ideas continued in full force. More Linnaean species were described from types after Darwin than before. The idea of evolution created interest in species, but the species were described in pre-evolutionary terms. Further, it is possible

for people to hold a variety of theories in place of, or in addition to, Darwin's. For example, Lamarckian ideas have continued right down to today. Orthogenesis has been widely believed and irreversibility has been regarded as law.

It has been claimed that evolution should be described in terms of non-adaptive traits, yet this is impossible if evolution is largely due to selection. The first great achievement of the synthesis of genetics, paleontology, and systematics is in clearing away a mass of antiquated theories and attitudes which permeate the writings of the older students of evolution. Further, the new evolutionary theory shows which aspects of past work are worth using, extending, and strengthening. This is possible because much of the mechanism of evolutionary change is now understood, clearly formulated, and *experimentally verified.* The logic of Darwin's great theory could only become fully effective when techniques had been developed to prove that selection was right and that other ideas of evolution were wrong. A change in theory, no matter how popular, is not enough. The new ideas must be implemented by effective techniques.

If a new physical anthropology is to differ effectively from the old, it must be more than the adoption of a little genetic terminology. It must change its ways of doing things to conform with the implications of modern evolutionary theory. For example, races must be based on the study of populations. There is no way to justify the division of a breeding population into a series of racial types. It is not enough to state that races should be based on genetic traits; races which can not be reconciled with genetics should be removed from consideration. If we consider the causes of changes in gene frequency as outlined above, and if we are concerned with the process of evolution, the task of the anthropologist becomes clear. He has nothing to offer on mutation, but can make contributions with regard to migration, drift, and selection.

The migrations of man made possible by culture have vastly confused the genetic picture. Before selection can be investigated, it is necessary to know how long a people has been in an area and under what conditions they have been living. For example, the spread of European people, of Bantu speakers, or of Eskimo, all have changed the distribution of the blood groups. The interpretation of the genetic situation demands an understanding of history. Whether people became adapted to cold by selection or by change in their way of life completely alters the interpretation of the distribution of physical traits. This has been widely recognized by anthropologists, and the solution of this difficulty requires the active collaboration of archaeologists, ethnologists, linguists, and students of the physical man.

Drift is related to population size, and this depends on the way of life. Again, as in the case of migration, the situation in which drift may have taken place cannot be specified by the physical anthropologist alone, but requires the active collaboration of many specialists. The adoption of modern evolutionary theory will force a far closer and more realistic collaboration between the branches of anthropology than ever before.

Although much of the present distribution of races may be explained by migration and although drift probably accounts for some differences, selection must be the explanation of long term evolutionary trends and of many patterned variations as well. Anthropologists have always stressed the importance of adaptation in accounting for the differences between apes and men, and sometimes have used the idea in interpreting racial divergencies. But suggestions of adaptations are not enough. It is easy to guess that a form is adaptive, but the real problem is to determine the precise nature of a particular adaptation. . . . I would like to take this opportunity to present an outline, a beginning, of an analysis of the human body into complexes which may vary independently.

In this work, the guiding principle has been that the major force in evolution is selection of functional complexes. A variety of methods has been used to demonstrate the adaptive complexes. The four major methods

for factoring complexes out of the body are: (1) comparison and evolution; (2) development; (3) variability; and (4) experiment. All these have been used by numerous investigators, but, to the best of my knowledge, they have not been combined into a working system. All must be used to gain an understanding of the human body.

The figure [see page 90] shows the body divided into the major regions, which seem to have had remarkable independence in recent evolutionary history. The complex to attain its present pattern first is that of the arms and thorax. This complex is associated with arm swinging in the trees, the way of life called "brachiation." It is associated with a reduction in the deep back muscles and in the number of lumbar vertebrae and consequent shortening of the trunk and elongation of all parts of the upper extremity, adaptation of the joints and muscles to greater pronation, supination in the forearm, and flexion and abduction at the shoulder. Many changes in the positions of viscera are associated with the shorter trunk. We share this complex with the living gibbons and apes. The bipedal complex was the next to develop and seems to have been fundamentally human in the South African man-apes. The major changes are in the ilium and in the gluteal muscles. Just as in the arm, the change is in a bone-muscle complex, which makes a different way of life possible. The head seems to have attained essentially its present form during the fourth glacial advance, perhaps 50,000 years ago. The brain continued to enlarge until the end of the last interglacial period, and the face decreased in size for some time after that. The great increase in the size of the brain and decrease in the face was after the use of tools.

Evolution, in a sense, has dissected the body for us, and has shown that great changes may occur in arms and trunk, pelvis and legs, and brain case, or face, accompanied by little change in the rest of the body. The first two complexes to change are related to brachiation and bipedal locomotion. The final changes in the head may well be related to changed selection after the use of tools.

To carry the analysis further, it is necessary to deal with one of the areas suggested by this preliminary dividing of the body. Let us consider the face, and especially the lower jaw. The figure [see page 91] shows a lower jaw divided into regions which can be shown to vary independently by all the methods of analysis suggested before. The coronoid process varies with the temporal muscle. The angle of the jaw varies with the masseter and internal pterygoid muscle. The tooth-supporting area varies with the teeth. The main core of the jaw is affected by hormones which do not affect the other parts, as shown in acromegaly. Alizarin dye, which stains the growing bone, reveals the pattern of growth. The split-line technique (Benninghoff) shows the mechanical arrangement.

After making an analysis of this kind, com-

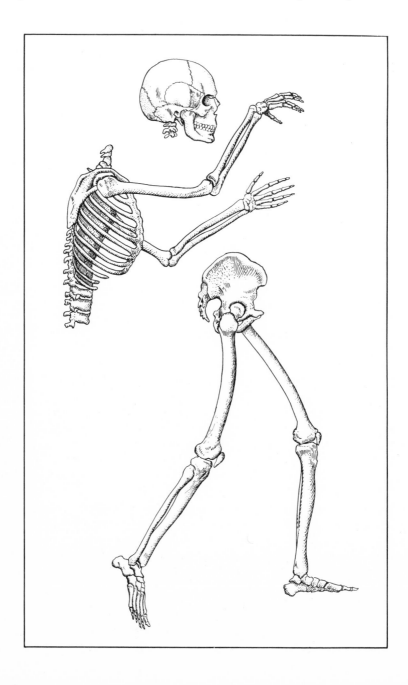

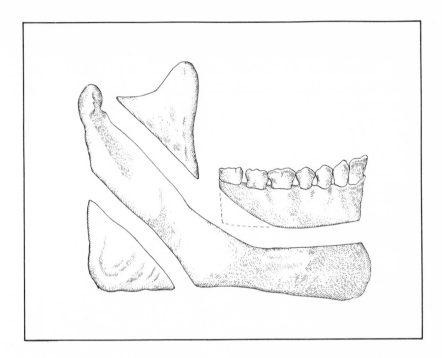

parisons of a different sort are possible. The simple statement, that a trait is or is not there, is replaced by the attempt to understand under what conditions it might be present. For example, if the simian shelf is developed in monkeys and apes when the jaws are long and the anterior teeth large, then the South African man-apes and other fossil men would not be expected to have such a shelf. The dental characters necessary to bring out the expression of the shelf are absent in all except the Piltdown jaw. It can be argued that we have the potential for a simian shelf but that we do not have the necessary tooth and jaw size to make it evident. Trying to understand the process which produces a trait leads us to very different evaluations than does a listing of presence or absence.

In the light of this sort of information, let us look at the skull of an Eocene lemur, *Notharctus*. The jaw is long, in conformity with the length of the teeth. It is low, and there is a large angular region. This region has been described as lemuroid. If this angle has remained there for 50 million years, however, over countless generations of lemurs, it must have more of a function than to mark the jaw as primitive or to help us in identifying lemur

jaws. If the mandible of a remarkably similar modern lemur (genus *Lemur*) is examined, it is found that the internal pterygoid muscle inserts at the end of the angle, but that the masseter muscle inserts only on the lateral side of the ascending ramus, leaving the angle bare of muscle. An internal pterygoid muscle inserting in this position is a protruder of the jaw. The function of the angle of the lemur jaw is to provide insertion for a large, functionally important muscle. The dependence of the angular process on the internal pterygoid and the exact function of the internal pterygoid need to be experimentally verified.

The only point to be stressed now is that the theory that such a process is of adaptive significance, and that it is maintained by selection, leads one to look for a functional complex. If such a process is regarded simply as a taxonomic aid, or as nonfunctional, no guide is available for research or future understanding.

The post-orbital bar of this same lemur again illustrates the advantage of assuming, until it is proved otherwise, that a part is functionally important. Originally, the complete bony ring around the orbit may have been for protection or for some other unknown function. Once the ring is established, however, the skeletal framework for radical modification of the skull is present. The change from the lemur skull, with a wide interorbital region, to the monkey skull, with reduced olfactory mechanism and reduced interorbital space, is mechanically possible because pressure, tension, and buttressing of the sides of the face are provided by the complete ring of bone around the orbits. Structures which probably developed as part of a protective mechanism were pre-adaptive for a reorganization of the face.

Classic Neanderthal man differs from other fossil men in that the angle of the lower jaw is poorly developed, the part of the malar bone associated with the origin of the largest part of the masseter muscle is small, and the lateral part of the brow-ridge is less sharply demarcated. All these differences may be related, and certainly the association of the small angle and malar suggest that the masseter muscle was small compared to the temporal muscle. Differences of this sort should be described in terms of the variation in the groups being compared. Since similar differences may be found in living men, the development of appropriate quantitative descriptive methods is merely a matter of time and technique. The procedure is: (1) diagnose the complex; (2) develop methods appropriate to describe variations in it; and (3) try to discover the genetic background of these variations.

So far, we are still engaged in finding the complexes, but even at this level it is possible to make suggestions about fossil men. Probably some Mongoloid groups will have the highest frequency of the big masseter complex, and some of the Negro groups the lowest. This is merely stating some traditional physical anthropology in a somewhat different way by relating statements about the face to those on the lower jaw and relating both to a large and important muscle. It differs from the traditional in the technique of analysis and avoids speculation of the sort which says that the characteristics of the Mongoloid face are due to adaptation to cold.

In this preliminary analysis of the lower jaw, the attempt has been made to divide a single bone into relatively independent systems and to show that the differences make sense in terms of differing adaptations. Eventually, it may be possible to understand the genetic mechanisms involved. If this type of analysis is at all correct, it is theoretically impossible to make any progress in genetic understanding by taking the traditional measurements on the mandible. They are all complex resultants of the interrelation of two or more of the variables. The measurements average the anatomy in such way that it is as futile to look for the mode of inheritance of the length of the jaw as it is to look for the genes of the cephalic index.

The implications for anthropology of this type of analysis may be made clearer by some comparisons of the skulls of monkeys. If the skulls of adult male and adult female vervets are compared, many differences may be seen. The male skull is larger in all dimensions, particularly those of the face. If, however, an adult female is compared to a juvenile male with the same cranial capacity and the same weight of temporal muscle, all the differences disappear, except that in the size of the canine tooth. What would appear to be a very large number of unrelated differences, if traditional methods were used, are only aspects of one fundamental difference in the size of the face. If a large-faced monkey is compared with a small-faced one, both of the genus *Cercopithecus,* there appear to be many differences. Yet again, if animals of the same cranial capacity and the same temporal muscle size are compared, almost all the measurements are the same. The species difference is in quantity of face, although this appears in many different forms. If these two skulls were fossil men, differing in the same way, and if they were treated by the usual anthropological methods, they would be found to differ in numerous observations, measurements, and indices. Yet one may be transformed into the other by a simple reduction in mass of face (including teeth, bones, muscles). Perhaps many fossils are far less different than we have supposed. The methods used created the number of differences, just as a metrical treatment of these monkeys would make the adults appear very distinct.

The purpose of this paper has been to call attention to the changes which are taking place in physical anthropology. Under the influence of modern genetic theory, the field is changing from the form it assumed in the latter part of the nineteenth century into a part of modern science. The change is essentially one of emphasis. If traditional physical anthropology was 80 per cent measurement and 20 per cent concerned with heredity, process, and anatomy, in the new physical anthropology the proportions may be approximately reversed. I have stressed the impact of genetics on anthropology, but the process need not be all one way. If the form of the human face can be thoroughly analyzed, this will open the way to the understanding of its development and the interpretation of abnor-malities and malocclusion, and may lead to advances in genetics, anatomy, and medicine. Although evolution is fascinating in itself, the understanding of the functional anatomy which may be gained from it is of more than philosophical importance. The kind of systemic anatomy in which bones, muscles, ligaments, etc. are treated separately became obsolete with the publication of the "Origin of Species" in 1859. The anatomy of life, of integrated function, does not know the artificial boundaries which still govern the dissection of a corpse. The new physical anthropology has much to offer to anyone interested in the structure or evolution of man, but this is only a beginning. To build it, we must collaborate with social scientists, geneticists, anatomists, and paleontologists. We need new ideas, new methods, new workers. There is nothing we do today which will not be done better tomorrow.

Physical Anthropology: The Search for General Processes and Principles

Gabriel W. Lasker

From *American Anthropologist,* Vol. 72, 1970, pp. 1–8. By permission of the author, and the publisher.

Description and History Versus Comparison and Experiment

. . . In physical anthropology there is a deep dichotomy between such historical and descriptive studies and the study of the general process of human biology by comparative and experimental methods. . . .

I hope some scholars will continue to pursue the biological history of man. . . . However, I see other problems that seem more relevant. To me this alternative approach can be considered the search for general processes. I see an understanding of process as the key to the application of physical anthropology to medicine, dentistry, public health, and population policy.

There is nothing new about the dichotomy between historical and descriptive studies on the one hand and comparative analytic and experimental studies of process on the other. By 1911 Boas had compared the changes of stature and head form of several different groups in the United States and this study followed an earlier work in which Fishberg demonstrated a difference in stature and probably head form between American-born and European Jews. Fishberg also noted that, until middle age, American Jews have a lower death rate than non-Jews but that after middle age the death rate of Jews is higher. Fauman and Mayer find this still true today but still lack the disease-specific mortality data and analysis of specific variables (whether overeating, smoking, atmospheric contaminants, anxiety, or whatever) that would allow development of general principles through partitioning of the variance.

Changing Contents in the Journals of Physical Anthropology

Simon examined the contents of the *American Journal of Physical Anthropology* from 1918 through 1947 and found 111 articles relating form to function. She noted,

> *The trend in investigations of form and function has been toward more intensive studies of*

small structural units, more adequately controlled. The conclusions drawn from these later studies have changed from sweeping assertions unwarranted by the data, exemplified by broad pronouncements of physical inferiority of a specific race, to the statement of relationships of variables to constants in the formation of [human anatomical] structures. . . .

It seems evident that the problems of form and function have become more and more a matter of careful technical experimentation and analysis. The importance of all variables affecting a structure has been recognized, and experimental methods for understanding their operation devised and put into practice. The most recent articles foreshadow success in dealing with restricted inquiries at the biological level.

But did they? I see little evidence in the subsequent literature. The problem is that inquiries limited to restricted anatomical structures in man require extensive comparative materials. And those restricted to limited materials—say the population of a particular geographic locus—often lack the focus on a manageable problem. Data has often been best collected in this way, of course, but it is the multiplication of comparable data from various such studies that is needed for solution of most problems.

I have compared the general thrust of articles and brief reports on physical anthropology appearing in two journals during two periods of time. There is only a slightly increased trend to what I would call the comparative-analytic approach, but it is by no means new and the increase in emphasis seems modest indeed. It occurs in only one of the two journals. Excluding a small number that are not properly within the scope of physical anthropology, for 1946–1950 I rate thirty-five percent of 173 items to be more properly described as "comparative or experimental." For the period since 1963 I rate forty-two percent of 410 "comparative or experimental" (Table 1). Descriptive and historical articles have decreased correspondingly. Some studies are both historical and comparative and the classification is subjective. Nevertheless, when I rerated all the articles a

second time after several months interlude, the general results were similar. . . .

In the effort to make anthropology more relevant to the world our students will live in, some anthropologists have developed another subdiscipline, urban anthropology. . . . Some [papers] were concerned with the human biological concomitants of increased urbanization of the whole society viewed as a single cultural sequence, others attempted to compare city dwellers with inhabitants of smaller communities. The former considered discreet events of long ago for which controls are generally lacking. The latter called for the study of the biological consequences of differential fertility, morbidity, and mortality and the genetic effects of various social and cultural determinants and applied a strategy that consists of the search for meaningful interrelations between elements in the ecological setting and the genetic constitution of the urban population.

The study of general processes is the study of human beings in particular situations, not for what we can learn about those populations, but for the sake of generalization about mankind anywhere in comparable situations. This is, of course, the purpose of experimental science in general. In anthropology the method usually involves comparative observations rather than experimental manipulation of subjects, but I consider this difference insignificant compared to that which separates these approaches from integrating best guesses in historical studies.

Although the purpose is to generalize about mankind, the ecological setting of the studies is usually of considerable significance. In investigations of man this setting is a sociocultural ecology. Thus when Takahashi wished to relate the frequency of cerebral stroke in Japanese to the winter climate of the various districts, he had to take indoor as well as outdoor temperatures into account since only in those parts of Japan where heating of homes is not customary would one anticipate maximum correlations between outdoor temperatures and biological effects.

For general purposes, then, comparative anthropological studies can be conducted

Table 1.   The number of articles and brief reports on physical anthropology in two U.S. journals

		DESCRIPTIVE OR HISTORICAL	COMPARATIVE OR EXPERIMENTAL	THEORETICAL OR CRITICAL
American Journal of	1946–1950	82	41	9
Physical Anthropology	1964–1968	151	106	26
Human Biology	1946–1950	15	19	7
	1964–1968	55	67	5
Total	1946–1950	97	60	16
	1963–1968	206	173	31

among hunting, food-collecting, and subsistence farming peoples, in peasant and other rural settings, or on cosmopolitan subjects in a variety of more or less urban agglomerations.

The International Biological Project

Individual scholars working in the more traditional societies often face difficulties living and working in the field and take so long acquiring language and cultural know-how that the comparisons tend to be few, or to be complicated by the problems of collating work by different people using somewhat different methods. Nevertheless, organized team efforts like those of the Department of Human Genetics of the University of Michigan among Indians of the South American montaña have been very fruitful. Since for this kind of study cooperating teams are often most efficient in developing data, the Human Adaptability Project of the International Biological Program (IBP) promises successful attack in just such traditional societies on problems of human response to heat, cold, altitude, food shortages, and other conditions on a wide international basis. Since so-called "primitive" peoples are losing both the characteristic conditions of life and modifying their own genetic makeup by admixture from outside, the IBP has placed considerable emphasis on the urgency of these studies. Three major U.S. IBP projects concentrate largely on this set of problems.

First, William S. Laughlin and his colleagues continue their studies of Eskimo and Aleutian populations. They are concerned with such questions as longevity, population density, and physique and, since arctic people are linearly arranged around the northernmost fringes of habitation at all longitudes, they retain the characteristic historical interest in movements and exchanges as well as in the comparative analysis of process.

Secondly, James V. Neel has seized the opportunity to investigate nothing less than "the biology of primitive man, with all its ramifications." Characteristically he and his numerous associates in the Population Genetics of the American Indian Program of IBP set themselves what I call general problems such as the nature and rate of human dispersion and the process of emergence of human diversity. Even the question of diseases faced by transition from Indian to *campesino* or *caboclo* status is couched in terms of processes in the epidemiology of change from "small band" to "large herd."

Thirdly, Paul T. Baker heads an IBP program on the Biology of Human Populations at High Altitude. The method is clearly generalizing and comparative. Cold adaptation of Peruvian Indians is compared with that of peoples of the Arctic, of Tierra del Fuego at the tip of South America, and of Australian Aborigines. Adaptation of Andean Indians to the reduced oxygen tension of the thin air at high altitudes is compared with non-Indians in the Peruvian highlands, with highlanders near sea level and, at least potentially, with similarly adapted people at high altitudes in Tibet and elsewhere and with the experiences in aviation medicine, mountaineering, and the Olympic athletes at the altitude of Mexico City. Suitable comparisons allow differentiation of adaptations of populations genetically selected at various elevations, individuals born there, persons acclimatized subsequently at various ages and for various periods, and those newly arrived at the elevation. All other aspects of the environment are greatly affected by cultural adaptations, but until the recent and limited use of oxygen and other therapies, altitude produced an exposure to hypoxia that was unmodified by man's culture. The contrast between this aspect and cold adaptation is exemplified in the same study designs.

Our interests in the isolated, economically self-sufficient, hunting, and farming communities are not important because they represent a traditional field of physical anthropology nor because as anthropologists we share with social anthropologists some special skills in this class of investigation. The importance lies in the fact that a science of physical anthropology needs a diverse arena for the testing of the generality of its findings about the biological processes in man. These populations lie at one pole in the array of examples of pools of genetic potential and of ecological conditions in which the biological activities play their role. The other extreme is found in urban settings. Generalization must also take these sociocultural conditions and genetic predispositions into account as I have already noted. Newton Morton has listed the genetic problems he thinks are favorable for study in "primitive groups." These include "inbreeding, outbreeding, assortative mating, hybridization between populations, genetic drift and founder's principle" (all taken from a list of problems for research posed by IBP). These are all also susceptible to study in city, national, and continental populations. Morton also lists other problems as "beyond the scope of fruitful genetic study at this time." These include fertility differentials and sex-specific mortality, the implications of which, for population genetics, seem to me among the problems more likely to be solved in an urban setting.

Measurements of Distance in Human Biology

When problems are transferred from the genetic isolate to continental populations, how-

ever, the units of study tend to be not discreet mendelian populations but samples separated by some measure of distance (whether measured as phenotypic differences, differences in gene frequencies, differences in number or recency of shared ancestors, or simple geographic distance measured in kilometers). In fact many of the general problems reside in the comparison of· different conceptions of human biological distance.

Some years ago I proposed an attempt to classify distances of some of these kinds for societies of various levels on a worldwide basis. I was able to make only a few pilot studies of the kind, however. Nevertheless others have also examined these dimensions and we have a few measurements of distance of a variety of types. The worldwide surveys of genetic polymorphic systems, growth, and physique proposed by IBP will further extend knowledge of this kind. In respect to geographic distance, Kücheman, Boyce, and Harrison have shown that, in a traditional town, the locus from which one draws a mate is seldom more than a day's walk round trip (averaging between some four to twelve miles and increasing only slightly for the years from the seventeenth century to about 1860). In some Mexican and Peruvian towns I estimated a mean size of the mating circle (as calculated from the distance between birthplaces of parents) as having a radius of only slightly larger than that even in the mid-twentieth century.

Spuhler and Clark found median distances between place of birth and place of marriage for residents of the city of Ann Arbor, Michigan, to increase from forty miles in 1900 to 110 in 1950 when the circle encompassed a population of some 6.8 million people.

Another way to approach the question is through study of the frequency of surnames. If presence of the same surname is evidence of common origins in a reasonably fixed and large proportion of cases, then the fewer the number of surnames and the more frequent the occurrences of each, the more shared origins. When a maternal and paternal ancestor have the same surname, (as occurs in the offspring of President Franklin Delano Roosevelt and Eleanor Roosevelt) it is called isonymy and it may, under certain assumptions be used to estimate the degree of inbreeding. Furthermore an estimate of the extent of such isonymy to be expected in a population can be calculated from the frequency of occurrence of surnames alone. (Under one set of assumptions it is the sum of the squares of the frequencies of each surname.) By this method I predicted that in the fishing town of San José, Peru, one in seventeen pairs of affinal relatives would be isonymous. I found one in seventeen to be so. By contrast, a four percent sample of surnames of individuals listed in the phone book for the Eastern suburbs of Detroit yields an estimated expected rate of isonymy of one in two thousand-odd. This is about 1/120 as common as in San José, Peru. The difference between the sizes of the areas of the breeding circles of these places is probably somewhat smaller. On the other hand the difference in effective size of these two types of breeding population is more likely of the order of 1200 to 1 rather than 120 to 1 to judge from Spuhler and Clark's data and my own.

These types of comparative data of isonymy and breeding distances can be refined to take assortative mating, the Wahlund effect, into account. Large differences in scale, the biological concomitants of which are now based on scanty and sometimes contradictory evidence, would yield to comparative surveys of this type. The biological effects of human isolate breaking are still poorly understood. They can be resolved however by studies using clearly established techniques. Furthermore whether or not the increase in stature and other changes observed in offspring of village-exogamous mating are due to genetic heterosis, their nature poses a problem worthy of study. . . .

Weiner, the convenor of the Human Adaptability Project of IBP said

The International Biological Programme is thus comparative in its analytical approach, it encompasses vanishing or threatened biotypes and therefore much of the work is a matter of urgency, and being comparative it calls for agreement and standardization on a world scale. Finally, the programme has far reaching practical implications

since it seeks to enhance our understanding of the ecological basis of biological productivity and human welfare. . . .

The Relationship of Physical Anthropology to Specialized Biology

Roberts believes that physical anthropology in the United States is stricken with malaise. He says that by the early post-war years the realization had crystallized that the subject

today is less closely allied to the social, historical and cultural subjects; that the broad study of human population biology that is physical anthropology not only belongs with, but has much to offer, the more specialized biological and medical science; and that physical anthropology, like other biological sciences was rapidly evolving from a descriptive phase of factual accumulation, speculation and hypothesis, to a phase of experiment, the rigorous testing of hypothesis to give theory.

The methods of investigation Roberts advocates are similar to those I favor, but identification with the new biology must be selective and critical. The molecular dimension, like others, will be useful only if the questions are pertinent. One area in which this remains still to be exploited is the question of growth. Among the subfields of physical anthropology, that of human growth has had its share of purely descriptive studies—merely listing the dimensions of children of different ages, for instance. In growth studies the comparative method has been limited to a few studies of the effects of environmental variables such as diet and disease. With the progress of developmental biology the way may soon be open for study of the genetic components of human growth and understanding of the molecules which mediate them. . . .

We now have an opportunity to make saltatory advances in the search for general processes and principles in physical anthropology and to train new cadres for the task. I believe that, even if we have moved slowly in the past, failure of physical anthropology to move in this direction now would relegate the subject to a minor and subsidiary role, as a sort of civilized luxury.

The Human Revolution

Charles F. Hockett
and
Robert Ascher

From *Current Anthropology,* Vol. 5, No. 3, 1964, pp. 135–146. Copyright 1964, Wenner-Gren Foundation for Anthropological Research. By permission of the authors, the publisher, and the copyright holder.

The editor regrets that we cannot reprint here the several pages of interesting *Comment,* nor the authors' *Reply,* that were published in the same issue of *Current Anthropology* with this article. The commentators were Weston La Barre, Frank B. Livingstone, George Gaylord Simpson, George A. Agogino, Ray L. Birdwhistell, Alan Lyle Bryan, J. Desmond Clark, Carleton S. Coon, Earl W. Count, Robert Cresswell, A. Richard Diebold, Jr., Theodosius Dobzhansky, R. Dale Givens, Gordon W. Hewes, Ilse Lehiste, Margaret Mead, Ashley Montagu, Hans G. Mukarovsky, John Pfeiffer, Bernard Pottier, Adolph H. Schultz, Henry Lee Smith, Jr., James L. Swauger, George L. Trager, Eugene Verstraelen, and Roger W. Wescott.

This essay attempts to set forth the story of the emergence of the first humans from their prehuman ancestors. A special feature is that we have tried to incorporate the various steps and stages of the evolution of language into the total picture. . . .

The term "revolution" in our title is not intended to be flamboyant. A revolution is a relatively sudden set of changes that yield a state of affairs from which a return to the situation just before the revolution is virtually impossible. This seems to be the sense of the word intended by V. Gordon Childe when he speaks of the "Neolithic Revolution" and of the "Urban Revolution." But these two revolutions were experienced by our fully human ancestors. The second could not have occurred had it not been for the first. The first could not have taken place had it not been for an even earlier extremely drastic set of changes that turned nonhumans into humans. These drastic changes, as we shall see, may have required a good many millions of years; yet they can validly be regarded as "sudden" in view of the tens of millions of years of mammalian history that preceded them.

For the reconstruction of human evolution we have evidence of two sorts, plus certain firm and many tentative principles of interpretation.

One kind of evidence is the archeological, fossil, and geological record. The fossil record of our own ancestry is still disappointingly sparse for the bulk of the Miocene and Pliocene. It seems unlikely that such records can ever be as complete as we might wish. But techniques of interpretation improve, and we suspect that the archeological record, in particular, holds an as yet unrealized potential.

The second kind of evidence is the directly observable physical structure and ways of life of ourselves and of our nearest nonhuman cousins, the other hominoids of today. Chimpanzees, gorillas, orangutans, gibbons, siamangs, and humans have ultimately a common ancestry not shared with any other living species. We shall refer to their most recent common ancestors as the *proto-hominoids.* Since all the hominoids of today constitute continuations of the proto-hominoids, we can attempt to reconstruct something of the physical structure and of the lifeways of the common ancestors by comparing those of the descendants. Such an effort at reconstruction must at the same time propose realistic courses of development from the ancestral group down to each of the directly observable descendant groups, and must make proper provision for those strains known only through fossils or archeological remains.

The method is very much like the comparative method in historical linguistics—and, as a matter of fact, it was first devised in the latter context, only subsequently transferred to the domain of biological evolution. The term "comparative" appears also in "comparative morphology" (or "comparative anatomy"); we must therefore emphasize that the method of which we are speaking applies not only to gross anatomy but also to the fine-scale phenomena dealt with in biochemistry, and not only to structure but also to behavior.

In any domain of application, a comparative method shares with all other historical methods the fact that it can yield reliable results only insofar as one can be sure of certain key *irreversible* processes. Given information about stages *A* and *B* in the history of a single system, we can posit that stage *A* preceded stage *B* if and only if the change from *A* to *B* is the sort that happens, while a change from *B* to *A* is impossible or highly improbable. In historical linguistics, the requisite irreversibility is afforded by sound change. The philologists of the late 19th century were correct when they characterized sound change as slow, constant, inexorable, and beyond conscious control; for, as we shall see later, it is a necessary by-product of a crucial design feature of all human language, and could not be eliminated save by altering language into something unrecognizable. Whenever sound change leads to the repatterning of the phonological system of a language—and this has happened about 100 times in English between King Alfred's day and our own—the consequences ramify through every part of the language;

soon the results are so scattered, so subtle, and from the point of view of effectiveness of communication so *trivial,* that a return to the state of affairs before the repatterning has, in effect, probability zero.

The situation in biological evolution is much more complicated, with no simple analogue for sound change. Is a particular organ in a particular species (living or fossil) vestigial or incipient? Is the swimming bladder of current teleosts a former lung, or is the lung of lungfishes a one-time swimming bladder? Evolutionists are plagued by such questions. The answers are often obtainable, but not through any simple formula. A new fossil does not automatically resolve the dispute, since one's opinions as to lines and directions of development will affect one's notions as to how the new fossil is to be fitted into the picture.

For the *mechanisms* of change we are in less trouble. We have now a good understanding of genetics, and also of the traditional transmission of lifeways. The latter was once believed to be exclusively human, but this is not so. At least for land mammals and for birds, genetics and tradition work in a constant dialectic complementation, neither being wholly responsible for anything. We are also clearer about a point that used to be quite obscure: the domain (so to speak) within which these two mechanisms operate is not the individual but the community, which has a gene pool, a distribution of phenotypes, and a repository of lifeways, and which, as a functioning unit, faces the problems of survival.

The greatest pitfall in evolutionary thinking stems from the keenness of hindsight. For example, we know that long ago, over a long period of time, our own ancestors abandoned the trees for the ground and developed effective machinery for bipedal locomotion. This seems beyond dispute, because the pre-hominoid primates were arboreal and we ourselves are bipedal ground walkers. But when we ask *why* this change, we must remember that our ancestors of the time were not striving to become human. They were doing what all animals do: trying to stay alive.

Thus, in searching for causes of the

change we must look to conditions pertaining at the time. There are only two possibilities. The conditions at that time may have been such that minor variations in gait and posture had no bearing on survival. We should then class the change that actually did take place as fortuitous. Or, the conditions of life at the time may have positively favored selection for bipedal locomotion and upright posture. If this is what happened, then the change was adaptive. By definition, a change that was neither adaptive nor fortuitous would lead to the extinction of the strain that underwent it, and in the present instance we know that did not happen.

The most powerful antidote for the improper use of keen hindsight is a principle that we shall call "Romer's Rule," after the paleontologist A. S. Romer who has applied it so effectively—without giving it any name—in his own work. We phrase this rule as follows:

> *The initial survival value of a favorable innovation is conservative, in that it renders possible the maintenance of a traditional way of life in the face of changed circumstances.*

Later on, of course, the innovation may allow the exploration of some ecological niche not available to the species before the change; but this is a consequence, not a cause.

One of Romer's examples concerns the evolution of Devonian lungfishes into the earliest amphibians. The invasion of the land was feasible only with strong fins (which in due time became legs). But strong fins were not developed "in order to" invade the land. The climate of the epoch was tempestuous; the water level of the pools in which the lungfishes lived was subject to sudden recessions. There was thus selection for those strains of lungfishes which, when stranded by such a recession, had strong enough fins to *get back to the water.* Only much later did some of their descendants come to stay ashore most of the time.

It is worthy of note that Romer's Rule is not antiteleological. We are permitted to speak in terms of purposeful behavior whenever we are dealing with a system that incorporates negative feedback. Individual organisms, and certain groupings of organisms (the kind we call "communities"), are such systems. There is nothing wrong in asserting that a stranded Devonian lungfish tried his best to get back to the water. We are forced, however, to distinguish carefully between purposes and *consequences,* and we are not allowed to ascribe "purposefulness" to any such vague and long-continuing process as "evolution."

No principle, no matter how universal, answers all questions. Romer's Rule cuts as keenly as any razor ever devised by Occam to expose, excise, and discard unworkable pseudo-explanations. Yet it is applicable, in a sense, only after the fact. For example, in this paper we follow majority opinion and trace man's ancestry back to a point of separation from the ancestors of the great apes, the gibbons, and the siamangs. Having assumed this, we elaborate one of Romer's own suggestions as to how some of the early developments may have come about. Suppose, however, that new fossil finds should convince us that man is actually more closely related to some other group of surviving primates. We should then be confronted by a different set of putative historical facts requiring explanation; but we should evoke the same Rule as we sought that explanation. That Rule does not tell us which line of descent to postulate.

The Proto-Hominoids

From the location, date, and morphology of the fossil dryopithecine *Proconsul* we infer that the proto-hominoids lived in East Africa in the Middle or Lower Miocene or, at the earliest, in the Upper Oligocene. This does not mean that *Proconsul* himself—in any of the strains or species so far identified—was a proto-hominoid; indeed, he is not a good candidate as an ancestor of the gibbons and siamangs, to whom, by definition, the proto-hominoids were ancestral. But *Proconsul* was clearly an *early* hominoid, and at the moment he is the best fossil evidence available for the date and provenience we seek.

The proto-hominoids inherited certain crucial capacities from their totally tree-dwelling ancestors. It is the arboreal pattern that developed the keen accommodative vision characteristic of the higher primates, de-emphasized the sense of smell, turned forelimbs into freely movable arms with manipulative hands, and built brains somewhat larger than the average for land mammals.

The balance of the characterization we are about to give—what Count would call a "biogram" of the proto-hominoids—derives mainly from the comparative method applied to what we know of the hominoids today. . . . We shall not give all the evidence in detail. Furthermore, for the sake of vividness we shall allow some interpolations of a degree of precision that may be unwarranted. The proportion of guesswork in each statement will, we think, be fairly obvious.

Like most of their descendants, the proto-hominoids were hairy. Like all of them, they were tailless. They were smaller than we are, though not so small as present-day gibbons, whose size has decreased as an adaptation to brachiation. They had mobile facial muscles; they had neither mental eminence nor simian shelf (nor mastoid processes); they had large interlocking canines, and could chew only up and down; their tooth pattern was $\frac{2:1:2:3}{2:1:2:3}$. It seems likely that there was little sexual dimorphism, although on this the comparative evidence is conflicting. The chromosome count was somewhere in the forties.

They lived in bands of from ten to thirty, consisting typically of one or a very few adult males plus females and offspring. They had a roughly defined nucleated territoriality: that is, the territory within which the members of a band moved about had only roughly demarcated boundaries, but centered on the specific arboreal sites in which they built their nests. The total population was probably never very great, nor very dense, from the protohominoids all the way down to the first true humans.

They were expert climbers and spent much of their lives in the trees of the tropical or subtropical forests which were their habitat, certainly building their nests in the trees and sleeping there. Like rodents, they climbed up a tree head first; unlike rodents, they climbed down stern first. They slept at night, from dusk to dawn, which in the tropics means nearer to one-half of each twenty-four-hour period than to the one-third characteristic of ourselves in recent times. They were active during the day. Some activities, particularly the constant search for food, led them not only among the trees—in which they may have brachiated, but with no great expertness—but also quite regularly to the ground below. On the ground, they could stand with a semi-upright posture (erect enough to raise their heads above shoulder-high grass to look about), and they could sit with arms free for manipulative motions; they could walk on all fours and could run on their feet, but bipedal walking was infrequent and awkward.

Occasionally they would pick up a stick or stone and use it as a tool. Judging from modern chimpanzees, they may have reshaped such tools slightly, using nothing but their hands and teeth to do so, and may have carried a tool for a short distance for immediate use, thereafter discarding it. They carried other things too, in mouth or hands or both, in connection with nest-building; and at least the females, perhaps on occasion the males, carried infants.

Their diet was largely vegetarian, supplemented by worms and grubs, and sometimes by small mammals or birds that were injured or sick and thus unable to escape. (We might call this "*very* slow game.") They scavenged the remains of the kills of carnivores whenever they could. Unlike all other mammals except the Dalmatian coach hound, their bodies produced no uricase; hence uric acid was not converted into allantoin before secretion in the urine, and had a chance to accumulate in the bloodstream. The structural formula of uric acid is something like that of caffein and, like the latter, it seems to be a mild brain stimulant. Since this type of purine metabolism is shared by all the hominoids, it can hardly explain our own unusual brilliance; but it may help to account for the generally high level of hominoid intelligence as compared with other primates and other mammals.

The males had the pendulous penis typical of the primates. Copulation was effected exclusively with the dorsal approach common to land mammals in general. Gestation required about thirty weeks. The uterus was single-chambered, and twinning was as rare as it is for us today. The placenta was of the single-disc type. The young required and received maternal care for many months. Mammary glands were pectoral; nursing females held infants to the breast in their arms, though doubtless the infant clung to the mother's fur also. The eruption of permanent teeth began perhaps at two and one-half or three. Menarche was at eight or nine years; general growth stopped for both sexes at nine or ten. The females showed a year-round menstrual cycle rather than a rutting season. Inbreeding within the band was the rule. The life-span was potentially about thirty years, but death was largely from accident, disease, or predation, or a combination of these, rather than old age. Corpses were abandoned, as were members of the band too sick, injured, or feeble to keep up with the rest, and were disposed of by predators or scavengers. Adult males were sexually interested in females and "paternally" interested in infants, but without any permanent family bond, and without any jealousy when they were themselves sexually satisfied.

Relations with adjacent bands were normally hostile to neutral, rarely if ever friendly; yet there was surely enough contact to provide for some exchange of genes. Social differentiation within the band turned largely on age and sex, secondarily on physical strength. In case of conflict of interest within the band, the huskiest adult males normally got their way. Collective activities required intragroup coordination, effected by various forms of communication—patterns of body motion, pushing and prodding, changes of body odor, and vocal signals. The conventions of these forms of communication were transmitted in part genetically, but in some part by tradition, acquired by the young through guided participation in the ways of the group. This implies also a certain capacity to learn from experience, and to pass on any new skills thus acquired to other members of the band by teaching and learning, rather than merely by slow genetic selection. But we may assume that usually there was very little new in any one lifetime thus to be learned or passed on.

A kind of activity called *play* is widespread among land mammals, and obviously intensified among primates; we can be sure that the proto-hominoids indulged in it, at least before maturity. It is very hard to characterize play precisely beyond saying that it resembles one or another serious activity without being serious. Play at fighting, observable for example among dogs, goes through much the same gross motions as true fighting but the participants receive no injury. Sexual play has the general contours of courtship, but ends short of coitus, or with mock coitus. We suspect that play is *fun,* for any species that manifests it, and that that is the immediate motive for indulging in it. But play is also genuinely pedagogical, in that the young thereby get needed practice in certain patterns of behavior that are biologically important for adult life.

The proto-hominoids did not have the power of speech. The most that we can validly ascribe to them in this respect is a call system similar to that of modern gibbons. Even this ascription may be stretching the comparative evidence somewhat. It is not hard to assume that a line of continuity from the proto-hominoids to the gibbons should have maintained such a call system essentially unchanged. It is also quite reasonable, as we shall see, to explain the evolution of a call system into language among our ancestors. The difficulty is to account for the apparently less highly developed vocal-auditory signaling of the great apes. Our hypothesis for the proto-hominoids suggests that the communicative behavior of the great apes may be somewhat more subtle and complex than has yet been realized. Be this as it may, we posit a call system for the proto-hominoids because we know no other way to proceed.

The essential design features of a call system are simple. There is a repertory of a half-dozen or so distinct signals, each the appropriate vocal response—or the vocal segment of a more inclusive response—to a recurrent and biologically important type of situation. Among gibbons, one such situation is the discovery of food; another is the detection of danger; a third is friendly interest and the desire for company. A fourth gibbon call apparently does nothing but indicate the whereabouts of the gibbon that emits it: this call keeps the band from spreading out too thin as it moves through the trees. One can guess at other possible situations appropriate for a special call: sexual interest; need for maternal care; pain. Band-to-band differences in calls may help to distinguish friend from alien.

A single call may be varied in intensity, duration, or number of repetitions, to correlate with and give information about the strength of the stimulus which is eliciting it. However, the signals of a call system are *mutually exclusive* in the following sense: the animal, finding himself in a situation, can only respond by one or another of the calls or by silence. He cannot, in principle, emit a signal that has some of the features of one call and some of another. If, for example, he encounters food and danger at the same time, one of these will take precedence: he is constrained to emit either the food call or the danger call, not some mixture of the two.

The technical description of this mutual exclusiveness is to say that the system is *closed.* Language, in sharp contrast, is *open* or *productive:* we freely emit utterances that we have never said nor heard before, and are usually understood, neither speaker nor hearer being aware of the novelty.

A call system differs from language in two other ways, and perhaps in a third. (1) Gibbons do not emit, say, the food call unless they have found food (or, perhaps, are responding to the food call from another gibbon, as they approach for their share of it). Furthermore, the gibbon that finds food does not go back to headquarters and report; he stays by the food as he emits the call. A call system does not have *displacement.* Language does: we speak freely of things that are out of sight or are in the past or future—or

even nonexistent. (2) The utterances of a language consist wholly of arrangements of elementary signaling units called *phonemes* (or *phonological components,* to be exact), which in themselves have no meanings but merely serve to keep meaningful utterances apart. Thus, an utterance has both a structure in terms of these meaningless but differentiating elements, and also a structure in terms of the minimum meaningful elements. This design feature is *duality of patterning.* A call system lacks it, the differences between any two calls being global. (3) Finally, the detailed conventions of any one language are transmitted wholly by the traditional mechanism, though, of course, the capacity to learn a language, and probably the drive to do so, are genetic. On this score we are still in ignorance about gibbons. Regional differences in gibbon calls have been noted, but various balances between tradition and genetics can yield that. We believe it safer to assume that proto-hominoid call systems were passed down from generation to generation largely through the genes, tradition playing a minor role. This assumption is the conservative one—it gives us more to try to explain in later developments than would any alternative.

This completes our characterization of the proto-hominoids, which can now serve as a point of departure for the story of our own evolution.

Out of the trees

Some of the descendants of the proto-hominoids moved out of the trees and became erect bipeds. Romer's description of how this may have begun affords another example of the application of the Rule we ascribe to him.

Geological evidence suggests that at one or more times during the East African Miocene a climatic change gradually thinned out the vegetation, converting continuous tropical forest into open savannah with scattered clumps of trees. As the trees retreated, some bands of hominoids retreated with them, never abandoning their classical arboreal existence; their descendants of today are the gibbons and siamangs. Other bands were caught in isolated groves of slowly diminishing extent. In due time, those bands whose physique made it possible for their members to traverse open country to another grove survived; those that could not do this became extinct. Thus, for those bands, the survival value of the perquisites for safe ground travel was not at all that they could therefore begin a new way of life out of the trees, but that, when necessary, they could make their way to a place where the traditional arboreal way of life could be continued. The hominoids that were successful at this included those ancestral to the great apes and to ourselves.

Sometimes the band forced to try to emigrate from a grove would be the total population of that grove. More typically, we suspect, population pressure within a diminishing grove would force bands into competition over its resources, and the less powerful bands would be displaced. Also, when a migrating band managed to reach another grove, it would often happen that the new grove was already occupied, and once again there would be competition. Thus, in the long run, the trees would be held by the more powerful, while the less powerful would repeatedly have to get along as best they could in the fringes of the forest or in open country. Here is a double selective process. The trees went to the more powerful, provided only that they maintained a minimum ability to traverse open country when necessary: some of these successful ones were ancestral to the great apes of today. Our own ancestors were the failures. We did not abandon the trees because we wanted to, but because we were pushed out.

We are speaking here of displacements and movements of whole bands, not of individual animals. There is one thing that surely accompanied any band whenever it moved: the essential geometry of its territoriality. At any halt, no matter how temporary, whether in the trees, under the trees, or in open country, some specific site became, for the nonce, "home base"—a GHQ, a focus, relative to which each member of the band

oriented himself as he moved about. Headquarters was the safest place to be, if for no other reason than the safety of numbers. In a later epoch—though doubtless earlier than will ever be directly attested by archeology—headquarters among our own ancestors came to be crudely fortified, as by a piled ring of stones; it became the place where things were kept or stored; in due time it became house, village, fort, city. But earliest of all it was *home.* The tradition for this sort of territoriality is much older than the proto-hominoids, and has continued unbroken to the present day.

It is at this point in our story that we must stop referring to our ancestors as "hominoids" and start calling them "hominids." Of course, all hominids are hominoids; but we have now seen the sorting-out of the pre-apes from the pre-humans, and when we wish to speak exclusively of the latter the appropriate term is "hominid."

Carrying

It is no joke to be thrown out of one's ancestral home. If the next grove is only a few miles away, in sight, then one has something to aim for; but sooner or later movements must have taken place without any such visible target. Treeless country holds discomforts and dangers. There may not be much food, at least not of a familiar sort. There may be little available water, for the trees tend to cluster where the water is more abundant. And there are fleet four-footed predators, as well as herbivorous quadrupeds big and strong enough to be dangerous at close quarters. One cannot avoid these other animals altogether, since their presence often signals the location of water, or of food fit also for hominid consumption. The quest for food must be carried on constantly, no matter how pressing may be the drive to find a new grove of trees in which to settle. It is a wonder that any of the waifs of the Miocene savannah survived at all. Enormous numbers of them must have died out.

The trick that made survival possible for

some of them was the trick of *carrying*. The proto-hominoids, as we have seen, probably carried twigs and brush to make nests, and certainly carried infants. Also, they had fine arms and hands usable for carrying as well as for climbing, grasping, and manipulating; and the comparative evidence suggests that they occasionally picked up sticks or stones to use as tools. These are the raw-materials for the kind of carrying to which we now refer. But it takes something else to blend them into the new pattern. In the trees, hands are largely occupied with climbing. The infant-in-arms grabs onto the mother when the latter needs her hands for locomotion. The twig being taken to the nest is transferred to the mouth when the hand cannot at the same time hold it and grasp a tree branch. One puts down one's ad-hoc tool when one has to move.

The conditions for carrying are no better on the ground than in the trees if the hand must revert to the status of a foot. But if bipedal locomotion is at all possible, then the hand is freed for carrying; and the survival value of carrying certain things in turn serves to promote a physical structure adapted to bipedal locomotion.

Two sorts of ground carrying in the hands may have been extremely early; there seems to be no way of determining which came first. One is the carrying of crude weapons; the other is the transportation of scavenged food.

The earliest ground-carrying of weapons may well have been a sort of accident. Imagine an early hominid—perhaps even a pre-hominid hominoid—sitting on the ground and pounding something (a nut, say) with a handy stone. A predator approaches. Our hero jumps up and runs away as best he can on two legs—there are no trees nearby to escape into—but keeps his grasp on the stone for no better reason than that he does not need his hand for anything else. Cornered, he turns, and either strikes out at the predator with the hand that holds the stone, or else throws it. The predator falls or runs off, and whatever in our hero's genes or life experience, or both, has contributed to his

behavior stands a chance of being passed on to others.

The first carrying of scavenged food back to headquarters (instead of consuming it on the spot) may also have been a sort of accident. A scavenging hominoid is eating the remains of a predator's kill where he has found it, and is surprised by the predator who is coming back to make another meal from the same kill. The hominoid runs off towards headquarters, still holding a piece of meat in his hand. In due time, he or his successors develop the habit of carrying the spoils off without waiting for the predator to turn up.

As described, these two early kinds of hand-carrying involve movements of a single animal *within* the band's territory, The carrying-along of things as the whole band moves is another matter, and probably a later development. Surely the earliest carrying of this latter sort was of unshaped weapons of defense. Yet other things might have been taken along. Extra food would be a great rarity, but if some were taken along because no one happened to be hungry as a movement began, it would be important if the band reached a particularly barren region. Water-carrying would have been extremely valuable—primates in general have to drink at least once a day, in contrast to some mammalian species which can store up several days' supply. Short hauls of small quantities of water cupped in the large leaves of tropical plants may have been quite early; large-scale water transport as a whole band moves must have been a gread deal later, since it requires technologically advanced containers.

The side-effects of carrying things in the hands are of incalculable importance. We have already seen that its immediate practical value helped to promote bipedal walking, which in turn selected both for carrying and for an upright posture that renders bipedal walking mechanically more efficient. A less obvious consequence is that carrying made for a kind of behavior that has all the outward earmarks of what we call "memory" and "foresight": one lugs around a heavy stick or stone despite the absence of any immediate need for it, as though one were remembering past experiences in which having it available was important and were planning for possible future encounters of the same kind. Taking scavenged meat back to headquarters without waiting for the predator to return to his kill also looks like foresight. We do not mean to deny the validity of the terms "memory" and "foresight." The point is that the outward earmarks surely came first, and only over a long period of time *produced* the psychological characteristics to which these terms refer.

A third consequence of carrying and of wandering was a change in dietary balance. The first tools to be carried were defensive weapons. Often enough, no doubt, the use of these weapons against a predator, even if successful, would only scare him off. But sometimes the predator would be killed. Why waste the meat? We can also suppose that the wandering Miocene or Pliocene hominids occasionally found themselves in open country where no suitable plant food was available. Herbivorous animals could eat the grass; quadruped predators could eat the grazers; ant the hominids, if they were lucky, could eat the grazers or the predators, or else starve. Thus the hunted became the hunters, and weapons of defense became weapons of offense.

The gradual increase of meat in the diet had important consequences of its own, to which we will turn after noting one further direct consequence of hand-carrying.

The use of the hands for carrying implied that the mouth and teeth, classically used for this by land mammals, birds, and even reptiles, were freed for other activities. It can quite safely be asserted that if primate and hominid evolution had not transferred from mouth to hand first the grasping and manipulating function and then the carrying function, human language as we know it would never have evolved. What were the hominids to do with their mouths, rendered thus relatively idle except when they were eating? The answer is: they chattered.

Remember that the proto-hominoids are assumed in this account to have had a call

system, and that that system would not have been lost by the stage we have now reached. The hunting of dangerous animals is a challenge even with advanced weapons. With primitive weapons there is a great advantage if it can be done collaboratively. But this calls for coordination of the acts of the participants. Their hands hold weapons and are thus unavailable for any complicated semaphor. Their visual attention must be divided between the motions of the quarry and those of the other participants. All this favors an increase in flexibility of vocal-auditory communication.

Other factors also favor such an increase. Meat is a highly efficient and compactly packaged food, as compared with uncultivated plants. A small kill may not go very far, but with collective hunting larger quarry were caught. After such a large kill, there is often more food than can be consumed even by all the direct participants in the hunt. Sharing the food among all the members of the band comes about almost automatically, in that when the hunters themselves are sated they no longer care if the rest take the leavings. Thus the sharing of meat makes for the survival of the whole band. Collective hunting, general food-sharing, and the carrying of an increasing variety of things all press towards a more complex social organization, which is only possible with more flexible communication. These same factors also promote what we vaguely call the "socialization" of the members of the band.

Another development bearing on the quality, if not the degree, of hominid socialization must have taken place during the same period. At some point during the slow morphological shift to efficient upright posture, the frontal approach for copulation must have first become anatomically possible, and it was doubtless immediately exploited. It may even be imagined that, for certain strains of the hominids at certain times, the expansion of the gluteus maximus rendered the dorsal approach so awkward that the invention of the frontal approach had the conservative value required by Romer's Rule. Humans have never shown much tendency to confine themselves to this position for intercourse, but it does seem to be universally known, and is almost exclusively human. Just how this change may have affected hominid lifeways is not clear. Our guess is that it changed, for the adult female, the relative roles of the adult male and of the infant, since after the innovation there is a much closer similarity for her between her reception of an infant and of a lover. This may have helped to spread the "tender emotions" of mammalian mother-infant relations to other interpersonal relationships within the band, ultimately with such further consequences as the Oedipus complex.

Opening of the Call System

We have seen a changing pattern of life that would be well served by a vocal-auditory communicative system of greater complexity and subtlety. Now a call system can become more flexible, within limits, through the development of totally new calls to fit additional types of recurrent situation. But it cannot take the first step towards language as we know it unless something else happens: through a process about to be described, the closed system becomes open.

Let us illustrate the way in which this can come about by describing what may occasionally happen among the gibbons of today—although, to be sure, such an occurrence has never been observed. Suppose a gibbon finds himself in a situation characterized by both the presence of food and the imminence of danger. The factors are closely balanced. Instead of emitting either the clear food call or the unmistakable danger call, he utters a cry that has some of the characteristics of each. Among gibbons such an event is doubtless so rare and unusual that the other members of the band have no way of interpreting it; thus, the consequences are negligible. But if we suppose that the early weapon-carrying hominids had a somewhat richer call system (though still closed), functioning in a somewhat more complex social

order, then we may also assume that this type of event happened occasionally, and that sooner or later the other members of a band responded appropriately, therefore handling an unusually complex situation more efficiently than otherwise. Thus reinforced, the habit of *blending* two old calls to produce a new one would gain ground.

Indeed, we really have to believe that this is what happened, because the phenomenon of blending is the only logically possible way in which a closed system can develop towards an open one. Let us represent the acoustic contours of one inherited call arbitrarily with the sequence of letters *ABCD* and those of another with *EFGH*. All we mean by either of these representations is that each call possesses two or more acoustic properties on which primate ears could focus attention; it does not matter just how many such acoustic properties are involved nor just what they are. Suppose that *ABCD* means "food here," while *EFGH* means "danger coming." Finding both food and danger, the hominid comes out with *ABGH*. If this new call becomes established, then the 2 old calls and the new one are all henceforth *composite,* instead of unanalyzable unitary signals. For, in *ABCD*, the part *AB* now means "food" and the part *CD* means "no danger"; in *EFGH, EF* now means "no food" and *GH* means "danger"; while *ABGH* means "food and danger" because *AB* and *GH* have acquired the meanings just mentioned. One might eventually even get *EFCD*, obviously meaning "no food and no danger."

It must be asked whether this mechanism of blending can really turn a closed system into an open one. The answer is that it can start the transformation (while no other known mechanism can), but that further developments must follow. Consider the matter for a moment in a purely abstract way. Suppose the inital closed system has exactly ten calls, and that each is blended with each of the others. After the blending, there are exactly 100 calls. From one point of view, a repertory of 100 calls—or of 1,000, or of ten million—is just as closed as is a system of 10 calls. A second point of view is more important. Each of the hundred possible calls now consists of 2 parts, and each part recurs in other whole calls. One has the basis for the habit of *building* composite signals out of meaningful parts, whether or not those parts occur alone as whole signals. It is this habit that lies at the center of the openness of human languages. English allows only a finite (though quite large) number of sentences only two words long. But it allows an unlimited number of different sentences because there is no fixed limit on how long a sentence may be.

Surely the opening-up of the closed call system of our ancestors required literally thousands of years, just as all the other developments on which we have touched came about at an extremely leisurely pace. It is irrelevant that the production of a single blend, or the momentary accidental carrying of a stick or stone in the hand, is a brief episode. A potentially crucial type of event can recur numberless times with no visible effect, or with effect on a band that later becomes extinct for unrelated reasons, for every one occurrence that has minuscule but viable consequences. When the opening-up of the formerly closed call system was finally achieved, the revolutionary impact on subsequent developments was as great as that of hand-carrying.

For one thing, the detailed conventions of an open system cannot be transmitted wholly through genes. The young may emit some of the calls instinctively. But they are also exposed to various more or less complex composite calls from their elders, and are obliged to infer the meanings of the parts, and the patterns by which the parts are put together to form the whole signals, from the acoustic resemblances among the calls they hear and from the behavioral contexts in which they are uttered. (To this day, that is how human infants learn their native language.) Thus, the development of an open system puts a premium on any capacity for learning and teaching that a species may have, and selects for an increase in the genetic basis for that capacity.

If the conventions of a system have largely to be learned before the system can be ef-

ficiently used, then much of that learning will eventually be carried on away from the contexts in which the utterances being practiced would be immediately relevant. We recall the general mammalian phenomenon of play. The development of an open, largely traditionally transmitted, vocal-auditory communicative system means that *verbal play* is added to play at fighting, sexual play, and any other older categories. But this, in turn, means that situations are being talked about when they do not exist—that is, it means the addition of displacement to the design features already at hand. Speaking of things which are out of sight or in the past or future is very much like carrying a weapon when there is no immediate need for it. Each of these habits thus reinforces the other.

What was formerly a closed call system has now evolved into an open system, with details transmitted largely by tradition rather than through the genes, and with the property of displacement. Let us call such a system *pre-language*. It was still not true language, because it lacked the duality of patterning of true language. Nothing like pre-language is known for sure in the world today. Any hominid strain that developed its vocal-auditory communication only to this stage has become extinct. If we could hear the pre-language of our forerunners, it would probably not sound like human speech. It would sound much more like animal calls, and only very careful analysis would reveal its language-like properties.

The development of openness, with the various consequences already mentioned, either accompanied or paved the way for some radical developments in tool habits. We imagine that tool *manufacture*—as over against the using and carrying of tools—received its single greatest impetus from this source. If carrying a weapon selects for foresight, shaping a rough weapon into a better one indicates even greater foresight. The manufacturing of a generalized tool—one designed to be carried around for a variety of possible uses—and the development of tools specialized for use in the making of other tools, certainly followed the inception of pre-language. Weapon-making and tool-shaping are further activities at which the young can play, as they learn their communicative system and other adult ways by playing with them.

We must suppose that the detailed conventions of pre-language underwent changes, and became differentiated from one band to another, much more rapidly than had the earlier call system from which it sprang (though perhaps much more slowly than languages change today). Both of these points are implied by the increased relative role of tradition as over against genetics. New blends were not uncommon. They introduced new patterns for combining elements into whole signals, and old patterns became obsolete. Any such innovation of detail spread naturally to all members of the band in which it occurred, but not readily, if at all, from one band to another. If a band fissioned into two bands—this must have happened repeatedly throughout hominoid and hominid history— the "daughter" bands started their independent existence with a single inherited pre-language, but innovations thereafter were independent, so that in course of time the two daughter bands came to have two "mutually unintelligible" pre-languages. This is exactly—except for rate of change—what has happened to true human languages in recent millennia; we must assume that the phenomena of change and of divergence are as old as the emergence of pre-language.

The Inception of Duality

Something else had been happening during prehominid and hominid evolution up to this point. In apes, the glottis lies very close to the velum, and articulatory motions anything like those involved in human language are structurally awkward. The development of upright posture, with the completion of the migration of the face from the end to the ventral side of the head, turns the axis of the oral cavity to a position approximately at right angles to the pharynx, and introduces a marked separation of glottis from velum. Hundreds of genera-

tions of chattering, first in a call system and then in pre-language, increases the innervation of the vocal tract and enriches the cortical representation of that region. The stage is set for the development of the kinds of articulatory motions familiar today.

Now, neither of these changes leads directly and inevitably to duality of patterning. Indeed, the first change is in no sense logically required if duality is to develop; in a way, it was fortuitous, since it was a by-product of changes taking place for a totally different set of selective reasons. In another species with a different earlier history, duality might use some other apparatus. If early primate history had for some reason promoted precision of control of the sphincter, and of the accumulation and discharge of intestinal gas, speech sounds today might be anal spirants. Everything else about the logical design of human language could be exactly as it actually is. The failure to distinguish in this way between the logically possible and the historically actual has led many investigators astray: they infer, for example, that our ancestors could not have had language until the articulatory apparatus had evolved to what it is now. They then interpret fossil jaws in invalid ways—and offer inadequate explanations of why the speech parts should have changed their morphology as they actually have during the Pleistocene.

However, the two changes described above did set the stage in a certain way. The hominids were in a state in which, if duality did develop, the machinery used for it was in all probability going to be the kind of articulatory motions we still use.

We can envisage the development of duality as follows. Pre-language became increasingly complex and flexible, among the successful strains of hominids, because of its many advantages for survival. The constant rubbing-together of whole utterances (by the blending mechanism described earlier) generated an increasingly large stock of minimum meaningful signal elements—the "premorphemes" of pre-language. Lacking duality, however, these pre-morphemes had to be holistically different from one another in their acoustic contours. But the available articulatory-acoustic space became more and more densely packed; some pre-morphemes became so similar to others that keeping them apart, either in production or in detection, was too great a challenge for hominid mouths, ears, and brains. Something had to happen, or the system would collapse of its own weight. Doubtless many overloaded systems did collapse, their users thereafter becoming extinct. In at least one case, there was a brilliantly successful "mutation": pre-morphemes began to be listened to and identified not in terms of their acoustic gestalts but in terms of smaller features of sound that occurred in them in varying arrangements. In pace with this shift in the technique of detection, articulatory motions came to be directed not towards the generation of a suitable acoustic gestalt but towards the sufficiently precise production of the relevant smaller features of sound that identified one pre-morpheme as over against others.

With this change, pre-morphemes became true morphemes, the features of sound involved became phonological components, and pre-language had become true language.

Although brilliant and crucial, this innovation need not have been either as sudden or as difficult as our description may seem to imply. With openness, but as yet without duality, the hearer is already required to pay attention to acoustic detail, rather than merely to one or another convenient symptom of a whole acoustic gestalt, if he is to recognize the constituent pre-morphemes of a composite call and thus react appropriately to the whole call. In a pure call system, the beginning of a call may be distinctive enough to identify the whole call; the rest does not have to be heard. In pre-language, one cannot predict from the beginning of a call how it will continue and end. This clearly paves the way for duality. It is then, in one sense, but a small step to stop regarding acoustic details as *constituting* morphemes and start interpreting them as *identifying* or *representing* morphemes.

Here, as for all the other developments we have mentioned, we must remember Romer's

Rule. The ultimate consequences of the inception of duality have been enormous. But the immediate value of the innovation was conservative. It rendered possible the continued use of a thoroughly familiar type of communicative system in a thoroughly familiar way, in the face of a gradual but potentially embarrassing increase in the complexity of the system.

The emergence of true language from a closed call system, by the steps and stages we have described, should properly be thought of not as a replacement of one sort of communicative system by another, but rather as the growth of a new system within the matrix of the old one. Certain features of the proto-hominoid call system are still found in human vocal-auditory behavior, but as accompaniments to the use of language rather than as part of language. The proto-hominoids could vary the intensity, the pitch, and the duration of a single call. We still do this as we speak sentences in a language: we speak sometimes more loudly, sometimes more softly, sometimes in a higher register and sometimes in a lower, and so on. Also, we use certain grunts and cries *(uh-huh, huh-uh, ow!)* that are not words or morphemes and not part of language. These various *paralinguistic* phenomena, as they are called, have been reworked and modified in many ways by the conditions of life of speaking humans, but their pedigree, like that of communicative body motions, is older than that of language itself.

The phenomenon of sound change, mentioned briefly at the outset of this paper, began immediately upon the transition from pre-language to true language, continues now, and will continue in the future unless our vocal-auditory communication crosses some currently unforeseeable Rubicon. The phonological system of a language has almost as its sole function that of keeping meaningful utterances apart. But a phonological system is a delicately balanced affair, constantly being thrown into slight disbalance by careless articulation or channel noise and constantly repatterning itself in a slightly altered way. It is perfectly possible, in the course of time, for two phonemes to fall together—that is, for the articulatory-acoustic difference between them to disappear. Obviously, this changes the machinery with which morphemes and utterances are distinguished. The interest this holds for us is that it affords an example of the workings of Romer's Rule in a purely cultural context instead of a largely genetic one.

What happens seems to be about as follows. A particular phonemic difference is slowly eaten away by sound change, to the point that it is no longer reliable as a way of keeping utterances apart. This is the "changed circumstances" of Romer's Rule. The speakers of the language develop, by analogy, a way of paraphrasing any utterance that would be potentially ambiguous if uttered in the traditional way. The paraphrase is the "innovation" of the Rule. The value of the paraphrase is that the speakers can thereby continue to speak in largely the same way they learned from their predecessors. The innovation is minor and trivial, but effective in that if the phonemic contrast disappears entirely, ease of communication is in no way impaired. The inevitable and continuous process of sound change never reduces the machinery of a language to zero. A compensation of some sort is developed for every loss of contrast.

Chronology

We have now outlined a plausible evolutionary sequence leading from the proto-hominoids to our earliest truly human ancestors. For we assert that as soon as the hominids had achieved upright posture, bipedal gait, the use of hands for manipulating, for carrying, and for manufacturing generalized tools, and language, they had become men. The human revolution was over. Two important questions remain. How long did the changes take? How long ago were they completed?

It is certain that the changes we have talked about did not begin before the time of the proto-hominoids. But at present we have no way of knowing how much later than that was their inception. Conceivably the hominids of the Middle or Upper Pliocene, though already separated from the pongids, were very little more like modern man than were the proto-hominoids.

On the other hand, we are convinced that all the crucial developments of which we have spoken had been achieved by about one million years ago—that is, by the beginning of the Pleistocene.

The most important evidence for the date just presented is the *subsequent* growth of the brain, attested by the fossil record. The brain of *Australopithecus* is scarcely larger than that of a gorilla. But from about three-quarters of a million years ago to about forty thousand years ago, the brain grew steadily. Part of this increase reflects an overall increase in body size. Allowing for this, there is still something to be explained. Was the increase in relative size fortuitous or adaptive?

It is utterly out of the question that the growth was fortuitous. A large brain is biologically too expensive. It demands a high percentage of the blood supply—12% in modern man, though the brain accounts for only about 2% of the body's volume—and all that blood, in an upright biped, must be pumped uphill. It requires an enlarged skull, which makes for difficulty during parturition, particularly since the development of upright posture resculptures the pelvis very badly for childbirth. This cost cannot be borne unless there are compensations.

We must therefore assume that if a species has actually developed a bigger and more convoluted brain, there was survival value in the change. For our ancestors of a million years ago the survival value of bigger brains is obvious if and only if they had *already* achieved the essence of language and culture. Continued growth would then be advantageous up to a certain maximum, but thereafter unprofitable because it made for excessive difficulties in other respects but yielded no further usable gain in brainpower.

The archeological and fossil record supports our data, or even suggests that we have been too conservative. Until recently, the earliest obviously shaped tools that had been dug up were not quite so ancient, but they implied an earlier period of development that was not directly attested. Now, however, we have the direct evidence of at least crudely shaped stone tools in association with hominid fossils from Bed I at Olduvai, for which a maximum date of one and three-quarter million years ago is seriously proposed. What is more, the Australopithecines show the typically human reduction in the size of the canine teeth, formerly used for cutting and tearing; and this reduction could not have been tolerated had the hominids not developed tools with which to perform such operations.

It might be suggested that, although all other crucial innovations of the human revolution were as early as we have proposed, the inception of duality may have been later. There are two reasons why we think that duality is just as old as the rest.

One side-effect of brain growth is that the top of the head is pushed forward to form a forehead. We do not see why this should in itself entail a recession of the lower part of the face, to yield the essentially flat perpendicular human physiognomy which, with minor variations, now prevails. In terms of the balancing of the head above an upright body, perhaps the recession of the snout and the decrease in its massiveness are useful. If cooking is a sufficiently old art, then perhaps this external predigestion of food at least rendered possible the reduction in size of teeth and jaws. But it seems to us that these factors still leave room for a further influence: that of the habit of talking, in a true language that uses the kinds of articulatory motions that are now universal, requiring precise motions of lips, jaw, tongue, velum, glottis, and pulmonary musculature. If true language can be assumed for our ancestors of a million years ago, then it is old enough to have played a role in the genetically monitored evolutionary changes in what we now call the "organs of speech." And if this is correct, then "organs of speech" is no metaphor but a biologically correct description.

Our other reason for believing that duality of patterning, and the modern type of sound-producing articulatory motions, are very old, turns on time, space, and degrees of uniformity and diversity. The fossil record shows that the human diaspora from East Africa cannot be much more recent than the Middle Pleistocene. This means that several hundred thousand years have been available for a genetic adaptation to a wide variety of climates and topographies. Yet man shows an amazingly small amount of racial diversity— far less, for example, than that of dogs, which has come about in a much shorter span of time. (Of course, the difference in generation span between men and dogs must be taken into account; but when one allows liberally for this the comparison, though less striking, still seems valid.)

There is this same striking lack of diversity in certain features of language. Though we have no fossils, our observations of the languages of today, and of those few attested by written records during the past few millennia, have some relevance. Almost every type of articulation known to function in any language anywhere recurs in various other languages, with no significant pattern of geographical distribution. Phonological systems—as over against individual speech sounds—show much less variety than could easily be invented by any linguist working with pencil and paper. This uniformity precludes the independent invention of duality of patterning, and of modern articulatory motions, in two or more parts of the world. The crucial developments must have taken place once, and then spread. The innovations could have been either recent or ancient, except for an additional fact: in every language, the phonological raw materials are used with remarkable efficiency. This speaks for great antiquity, since we cannot imagine that such efficiency was an instant result of the appearance of the first trace of duality.

True diversity is found in more superficial

aspects of language, and in all those other phases of human life where tradition, rather than genetics, is clearly the major mechanism of change and of adaptation. We are thus led to a familiar conclusion. The human revolution, completed before the diaspora, established a state of affairs in which further change and adaptation could be effected, within broad limits, by tradition rather than genetics. That is why human racial diversity is so slight, and it is why the languages and cultures of all communities, no matter how diverse, are elaborations of a single inherited "common denominator.". . .

selection 16

Adaptive Changes in the Human Body

Carleton S. Coon, Stanley M. Garn, Joseph B. Birdsell

From *Races: A Study of the Race Formation in Man.* Charles C Thomas, 1950, pp. 36–45. By permission of the authors and the publisher.

Within the confines of a given zone of environment it may be some culturally determined factor, like the choice of food grown, or its importation from elsewhere, that determines body size, rather than the unaltered, or unprocessed, attributes of the environment itself.

Dry Heat

One kind of environment, however, appears to produce special effects on all those who live in it for many generations. That is the extreme, the rigorous environment of the hot desert. The famous Tuareg of the Sahara reveal themselves, when shorn of their robes and veils by the anthropologist, to be tall, lean, skinny men, with long arms and legs, short, shallow bodies, narrow hands and feet. The average adult male European who tries to wield a Tuareg sword is unable to compress his hand into the space meant for it on the hilt. The Tuaregs have only been living on the desert for 1300 years, since the introduction of the camel from Asia. Their ancestors were Berbers from the Moroccan Middle Atlas, and facially they still look like Berbers, and they still have a large minority of blue and green iris color, like their mountain kinsmen. But the Middle Atlas Berbers who live in cool forests and grasslands have a normal body build, legs as short and hands and feet as wide as those of a normal European.

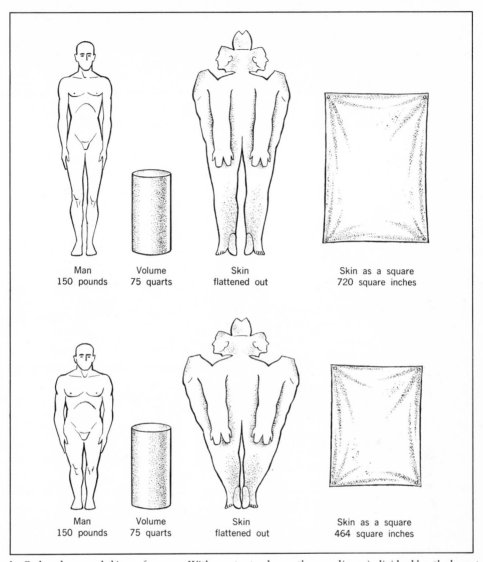

Fig. 1   Body volume and skin surface area. With constant volume, the more linear individual has the largest area.

The Somalis of the desert regions of the Horn of Africa are built very much like the Tuareg; and so are the Australian aborigines who inhabit the desert regions of northern and central Australia. Precise evidence from desert-living American Indians is not at hand, but we understand that long limbs and narrow extremities characterize such peoples as the Seri. Zoologists and paleontologists know that animals that live in deserts tend to have long, slender, light-boned bodies, with the emphasis on length and slenderness of the limbs, while animals that live in lush, moist environments tend to be heavier boned. That this principle should apply to man is not surprising.

All the peoples just mentioned are literally *skinny*. Their skin surface area is great in proportion to their volume and weight. They are not tall; high stature does not necessarily go with this kind of build. The critical factor seems to be for the organism to present the maximum skin surface area in proportion to mass and weight to the external environment,

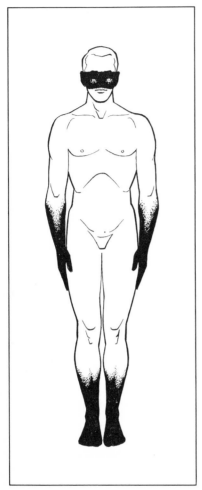

Fig. 2 Critical areas for cold—the extremities, the nose, the eyes, and the middle face.

are forced to live on concentrated low-bulk, high-protein, high-fat and high-sugar diets; for example, in Arabia and the Sahara, milk and milk products, dates, and some grains are the foods of the desert dwellers. Bulky, high-cellulose fruits and vegetables, which do not grow in deserts and are hard to transport, are off their menu. A long-gutted organism, like a gorilla, can operate efficiently on high-bulk, low-concentrated diets. A short-gutted, narrow organism like a weasel requires more concentrated food.

Damp Heat

Peoples who live in moist heat, like the Pygmies and Forest Negroes of Africa, the Indonesians and Melanesians, and the Indians of the Amazon-Orinoco basin, do not exhibit this lanky desert form. Their bodies have less heat and more humidity to cope with. Heat loss cannot, it seems, be increased through an increase of relative surface area, owing to the difficulty of evaporation in a nearly saturated atmosphere. These people show no clear adaptation in body form to their special environment which, it must be remembered, was the original environment in which the ancestors of man lived before their descent from the trees. The living genera of anthropoid apes show a great range of body form in this environment. Their differences in shape seem related to means of locomotion rather than to the factors considered above.

Extreme Cold

Another environment which leaves its mark on people is that of the Arctic. We must remember that human beings were not able to live in climates involving extreme seasonal cold until they had attained a level of technological skill necessary to make warm clothing. Otherwise they could not have left their houses or caves to go hunting in the middle of winter. Here again the time factor is short compared with the time span of human evolution, but still it gives us between 700 and 1000

thus permitting a maximum of cooling surface for evaporation [as shown in the figure on page 115]. Now 50 per cent, more or less, of the body's blood is inside of the legs at any given time. A long, pipe-like leg is an excellent radiator; it exposes much more cooling surface per unit of weight and volume than a short, barrel-like one, which may be more useful in other environments.

Looking at the information which we have at our command, environmental, cultural, and anatomical, for all continents, we can see that there is a three-way correlation between food, body form, and desert living and it is not possible to separate out the independent variables. Suffice it to say that desert dwellers generations. All of the people living around the Arctic Circle, from North Cape to Greenland, are short. They vary from 154 to 164 cm. in stature means, with few absolutely tall individuals. They include people whose ancestors have moved into this region in fairly recent times. In Norway the population of Finnmark is much shorter than that of the more southerly provinces, and the Norwegian settlers themselves are shorter than their relatives farther south. In Siberia the Yakuts, Turkish herdsmen forced north by the expansion of Genghis Khan's empire, are shorter than their kin on the grasslands to the south. It is probable that Russian colonists, several generations on the spot, have lost stature as well. In Greenland we have statistical evidence of the gradual reduction in stature among the colonists from Iceland, up to the time of their extinction. Iceland itself, warmed by the Gulf Stream, does not fall in the stature zone with which we are concerned, although there is evidence that a temporary change of climate during the Middle Ages was accompanied by an equally temporary depression in stature.

The short peoples who live around the Arctic Sea are also uniform in another respect: they are thick set. Their bodies are chunky, their chests thick and wide, their legs short and thick, their fingers and toes short, and their wrists and ankles small and fat-covered. Even so, in Alaska surgeons on ships and in mission stations amputate many frozen toes from Eskimos; this is said to be their commonest operation. In contrast to the inhabitants of overheated deserts, Arctic peoples present the least possible skin surface area to the outside world, in proportion to volume and weight [as shown in the figure on page 115]; and even that surface they keep covered, except for their faces, when outdoors in the cold. They are built to radiate as little heat as possible. As it is, much of the animal fat eaten by an Eskimo or Chukchi is expended in heat loss, for they have almost twice the caloric requirements of people living in our environment. Any eyewitness account written by explorers will mention the enormous quantities of fatty foods which

these people eat. Some of it they store. When they are young and in their prime they tend to be fat-protected as well as muscular. Old age brings a loss of fat under the skin, wrinkling, and general inability to withstand the rigors of the environment. Death comes early; few live to be really old.

Why Arctic peoples are relatively globular is clear enough; *how* they became so is harder to answer. However, we know enough about the physiology of heat loss to venture an explanation. Individuals who exhibit the minimum surface area for their volume are those who have the least prominent surface projections, and the maximum development of visceral protection. This is like insulating the furnace to save heat. Sleep studies have shown that during slumber the temperature of the extremities approaches outside air temperature, while the viscera are maintained near the waking temperature. Short extremities are less likely to cool to a dangerous level than long ones, particularly if the bones and blood vessels are well covered with fat and muscle.

A second possible effect of cold is its influence on the growing organism: through stimulation of the adrenals and their secretion of cortical hormones, and the consequent storing of fat, building of muscle, and early closure of the epiphyses of the long bones. This may help make Arctic peoples short and relatively globular. This effect may be considered as a temporary or phenotypical change which might be altered dramatically by changing the environment of a child at an early age, and leaving the more-than-adequate diet constant.

Arctic-dwelling peoples sometimes go hungry, and many die of starvation. Selection would favor those who could store and utilize fat, as it would those who could escape freezing their extremities. In the siege of Leningrad, women suffered less from starvation than men, presumably because of their greater fat reserves per unit of body weight. Dickerson and Gowen have described a breed of mice which show a hereditary ability to utilize food more efficiently and thus develop "obesity" than other breeds fed on the same diets. Such a capacity, while unpopular in our society, is of unquestioned survival value in others where food is scarce.

Starvation is a powerful force in natural selection, in man as in other animals. This principle is a general one and must apply to other peoples outside the Arctic area who are of interest to anthropologists. Many "primi-tives" grow fat when they are taken off the range and put on reservations. Some who live on deserts and are at the same time exposed to starvation develop concentrations of fat in special areas, especially the buttocks, while the extremities are not affected. This combination is found among the South African Bushmen.

selection 17

Somatic Paths to Culture

J. N. Spuhler

From *The Evolution of Man's Capacity for Culture,* J. N. Spuhler (arr.), Wayne University Press, 1959, pp. 1–12, as reprinted from *Human Biology,* Vol. 31, No. 1, 1959, pp. 1–13. Copyright © 1959, Wayne State University Press. By permission of the author, and the publishers and the copyright holder.

. . . In thinking about human phylogeny, I believe in using all, or nearly all, the hominoid fossils we know about, so long as they are not fragments. To argue that none of the known man-like fossils are in *the* human phylogenetic line seems to me obscurantist. To argue that the fossils we know about are "somewhat near" but not exactly on the main line seems unnecessarily cautious and hedging and may give the unknown greater weight than the known. Perhaps Weidenreich and Heberer went too far in using all known hominid specimens they considered authentic. But I prefer their use of all of them to Wood Jones' use of almost none.

There is not space here to give a review of new developments in human paleontology. In the last few years we have acquired a wealth of new specimens and new ideas and we have also been able to discard some old specimens and ideas with good cause. If additional fossils become available it may be necessary to make major revisions in what I am about to say. By taking an abstract level—the level of the taxonomic genus—I can avoid some undecided issues on the phylogenetic placement of individual specimens. For the moment I am going to assume a human evolutionary sequence of 4 or 5 genera:

1. Leaving out the periods before the Miocene, we start with *Proconsul,* the earliest ape whose skull is known. I assume *Proconsul* had precursors who developed the gener-

al features of a man-like thorax and arms as we know them today, but that these terrestrial apes were not highly specialized as brachiators. There is no reason to suppose that any human ancestors since the Miocene have been arboreal to the extent characteristic of living gibbons, orangutans, or chimpanzees.

2. We don't know what happened in the Pliocene.

3. At least by Early Pleistocene there is *Australopithecus,* now known from dozens of good, or as Broom would say, "beautiful," specimens, and the earliest evidence of man-like animals with bipedal locomotion.

4. By Early Pleistocene times, and lasting into Middle Pleistocene in parts of Asia, we have the genus *Pithecanthropus.* From the neck down they were very like the genus *Homo* and like him they were tool makers, fire users, and hunters. Their brain volume was intermediate between *Australopithecus* and *Homo.*

5. At least by Middle Pleistocene we have the genus *Homo,* represented by such forms as Swanscombe, Fontéchevade, the Neanderthals, and Upper Paleolithic man. Everyone agrees that some, if not all, members of the genus *Homo* have culture.

Now, in the context of this sequence of 4 known genera, and with comparisons from living monkeys and apes, I want to discuss 7 biological topics which are preconditions for the beginning of culture. They are:

1. Accommodative vision,
2. Bipedal locomotion,
3. Manipulation,
4. Carnivorous-omnivorous diet,
5. Cortical control of sexual behavior,
6. Vocal communication,
7. Expansion of the association areas in the cerebral cortex.

Of course, these 7 conditions alone did not make a population of apes lacking culture into a population of men with culture. The evolution of man was not predetermined by a few conditions in a population of Miocene apes. Mutations are the fundamental genetic events in the historical process of the acquisition of the capacity for culture. Mutations are random events that do not point in an orthogenetic direction. But mutations are limited by the structure of the gene which mutates and this structure is determined by the evolutionary forces, especially selection, active in the history of the gene. In this way populations that survive accumulate genes which are favorable in the prevailing environment of the population.

To illustrate the complexity of human evolution since the Miocene as seen at the mutational level, let me do some speculative arithmetic—using figures that have fair justification and are conservative. From the Miocene to now there must have been at least two million generations in the hominoid line. If the total breeding population in successful plyla was 10 thousand, we have 20 billion individuals as real or potential ancestors of modern man. If genes at the average locus mutate at a rate of 1 in 100,000, and if only 1 in 200,000 of these result in new and favorable steps (and that is a low estimate), we still could have about 20 thousand "visible," favorable mutational steps (in all loci) since the Miocene in the hominoid line.

Thus when we talk about 7 conditions we are perhaps oversimplifying the matter. But there is not time for further discussion, even if we knew what to say. And, I should add, the 7 conditions I list do not represent unit mutations, although mutation is the ultimate source of the genetic variation in each condition. Further, the order of listing is not strictly chronological. Evolutionary changes in the 7 conditions were interdependent and roughly synchronous.

1. *Accommodative vision.* Vision has been the primary sense in vertebrates as far back as we know them. It makes possible their great mobility. The most complex vertebrates, birds and mammals, interact with their external environment predominantly *via* their eyes. Under the influence of the arboreal habitat, primate vision was perfected into a lead-

ing sense. Visual behavior is one key difference between the nocturnal, mostly solitary
Prosimians, and the diurnal, more social Anthropoidea. The difference between these two
is perhaps the largest gap in non-human Primate social behavior. With upright, or
sitting-up posture, vision in the Anthropoidea
gained strict control of manipulation—it became super*vision,* a guide and control of fine
manipulation.

The relationship between the evolution of
keen vision and fine manipulation is two-
directional. As Polyak says: "... vision itself
[became] more refined and the intellectual
absorption and mental utilization more complete and lasting, as the skilled movements
became more complex and more efficient."
We will find that this kind of bothway causation with two or more systems evolving simultaneously, where progress in each stimulates
change in the other, is important to the understanding of many topics in this symposium.

Before taking up bipedal locomotion, let
me mention one good thing that came out of
the Piltdown affair. It was the insight given,
for example in Hooton's excellent paper, on
the asymmetrical character of human evolution. Hooton ... was early to stress that different regions of the human body change at
different rates. Many workers today would
follow Washburn's separation of the human
body into three regions distinct in phylogeny,
with arms and thorax the oldest, the bipedal
complex of pelvis and legs later, and the head
and face latest of all to reach their modern
form.

2. *Bipedal locomotion.* Although functional differentiation of the front and hind
limbs started with the first tetrapods where
the front legs reach out and the hind legs
push, *Australopithecus* is the first primate
with upright bipedal locomotion (the tarsiers
are bipedal hoppers). The australopithecine
pelvis, sacrum, and femur resemble modern
man in those features which make his upright
posture possible. There are some features of
full bipedalism not found in *Australopith-*

ecus—these are fully developed in *Pithecanthropus* from Java and Peking. Australopithecine locomotion was certainly more
similar to that of *Pithecanthropus* and *Homo*
than to any of the quadramanus primates. We
must conclude that, by the early Pleistocene,
hominoids were bipedal with free hands
which could be used to handle tools. We will
see that this was a master adaptation that
demanded other adaptations leading to
man's capacity for culture.

3. *Manipulation.* A good start toward precise manipulation is seen in monkeys. When
monkeys sit up their hands are temporarily
free and are used to bring objects close to the
organs of touch, vision, taste, and smell. But
something like a quantum jump is made when
the hands are continually free for such activity as they are in an upright, fully bipedal
hominoid. Then the arms and hands—under
the guidance of binocular vision with good
accommodation—are principal organs for interaction with the immediate physical environment. Getting food, eating, grooming,
fighting, making, using, and carrying tools,
these manipulations, accompanied by a rich
flow of sense data including those from the
more developed proprioceptive arm-and-
hand muscle sense, enlarge the flow of information to the brain which in turn fosters
development of association areas for storage
of past experience with the hands and guides
and initiates new hand movements. The neural delay required when some extra-organic
tool is interposed between stimulus and response probably had much to do with the first
ability to use symbols and the start of language. The co-adaptation of the hands, senses, and association areas in precise manipulation seems a first basis for the subsequent
development of human intelligence.

4. *Carnivorous-omnivorous diet.* Man and
the tarsier are unusual among primates in
being carnivores. Many monkeys are omniv-
ores and take small animals as prey. Man is
unique among living primates in taking large
animals for food and these in large numbers.
Fortunately we have some fossil evidence

on the problem of diet. It is still an open question whether the Australopithecines were hunters or the hunted. But by Middle Pleistocene times the *Pithecanthropus* of Peking were hunters of large mammals as well as gatherers of hackberries and other plant food.

The change to a partially carnivorous diet had extremely broad implications for the social organization of early hominoids. Carnivores get a large supply of calories at each kill. This concentrated food is more easily transported to a central, continually used shelter than is low-calorie plant food, especially before containers were available.

Whoever killed the baboons and bucks associated with the Australopithecines must have been tool carriers as well as tool users. Tool carrying implies a degree of conceptualization not required in the occasional use of tools. Before starting on the hunt there must be a minding which associates the tool with an event which is to occur in the future. This type of mentation has not been observed in captive chimpanzees or monkeys, and certainly not in wild non-human primates. The archaeological record shows it was a consistent part of *Pithecanthropus* behavior by Middle Pleistocene times.

Compact animal protein high in calories is a good basis for food sharing. Of non-human mammals it is only the carnivores that share gathered food. It is unlikely that the long dependency of human children—so important in the acquisition of culture by individuals—could develop in a society without food sharing. And the amount of information which needs to be transduced in a communication system for plant eaters like the gibbons is small compared to that needed in group-hunting of large animals. Gibbons share, by vocal communication, knowledge about the location of food collected and eaten individually on the site; hominoids share in the location, collection, and consumption of food.

5. *Cortical control of sexual behavior.* There seems little danger that modern an-

thropologists will overlook the importance of sex in the evolution of culture. Some of us fail to emphasize that, with regard to the physiology of sexual behavior, man is neither a) completely like most other beasts, nor b) completely different from non-human animals. Here, as in many other biological characters, the apes and man are alike and man and the apes are unlike other mammals. In the majority of mammals sexual behavior is seasonal and the sexual periods correspond to times when the female has high probability of ovulation and conception. In such mammals including the lower primates, copulation is evoked by an increase of gonadal hormones in the body fluids. In such animals we can bring about, or prevent, copulation by gonadectomy and hormonal injections. But in man and the chimpanzee, and probably also in other apes, copulation is strongly under cortical control and is not prevented by gonadectomy.

An important adaptation for culture is the change from built-in nervous pathways to neural connections over association areas (where learning and symboling can be involved) in the physiological control of activities like sleep, play, and sex. Cortical rather than gonadal control of female sexual receptivity may not be essential to the hominoid family (observations on other animals suggest not), but cortical dominance in sexual activity may have contributed to the easy transition of the family from a social unit where sex and reproduction were more important than food economy to a unit where subsistence is the dominant familial function.

6. *Vocal Communication.* Human speech is an overlaid physiological function. It uses a set of body parts of quite diverse primary action. Consider the muscles used in speaking. Most of our coordinated muscular movement involves corrections and adjustments from proprioceptors. But the laryngeal muscles lack proprioceptors, and feedback control of speech comes by way of the ear and the 8th cranial nerve. When we talk, the voice box, tongue, and lips must work together

smoothly and precisely. The 10th nerve controls the adjustment of the vocal cords and the 5th nerve the movement of the lips. Both of these involve branchial muscle while the 12th nerve moves the tongue with somato-motor muscle. The neurological basis of speech is not clear, but it is clear that the only place where the motor organs and steering apparatus of speech are wired together is in the cerebral cortex. Perhaps hand-tool manipulation in group activities like hunting coordinated by vocalization may have helped to make the connections.

Although the larynx is homologous in all primates its position in the throat differs in man. The larynx of quadrupedal primates from the lemur to the chimpanzee is in close to slight contact with the soft palate. This is why chimpanzees cannot make long, resonant sounds. As a consequence of upright posture and flexion of the craniofacial base, the larynx in man is moved down the throat away from contact with the soft palate, and an oral chamber is formed which makes possible resonant human phonation.

This is not to deny a rich variety of vocal production to the chimpanzee and other primates. The position of the larynx, however, is one reason why attempts to teach chimpanzees English have failed. Unfortunately no one has tried seriously to teach a chimpanzee to learn to speak using chimpanzee "phonemes."

7. *Expansion of the cerebral cortex.* Current statements in the anthropological literature regarding the size of man's brain often involve misinterpretations in one or the other of two directions. On one extreme, some investigators stress the fact that, compared with *mammals* in general, especially large mammals, man's brain is unusually large, both absolutely and relatively. For example, a 150 pound man has a three pound brain, while a 150 pound sheep has a one-quarter pound brain, and a 1500 pound cow has a one pound brain. On the other extreme, the stress is put on the conclusion that man's brain is indeed large, but not unexpectedly so. For example, when the log of brain weight

in *primates* is plotted against the log of body weight, the slope of the regression line is steeper than it is among mammals in general (proportional to the 0.79th power of body weight in primates, the 0.66th power in mammals), and on visual inspection the plot shows—as log transformations often do—remarkably little scatter, suggesting that brain weight in modern man is just about what would be predicted given the general regression of brain on body weight in primates and a knowledge of man's body weight alone. But if we take 1345 gm as a brain weight typical for modern man, say of 60 or 70 kg body weight, we find man's brain is significantly larger than the value of 1095 gm of brain for 70 kg of body, predicted by van Bonin's regression formula: log brain weight = 0.79 log body weight − 1.00. A conclusion which avoids both extremes might stress at least two reasons for man's large brain weight: a) about 80% of man's brain weight may be explained because he is a primate of large body size, and b) about 20% of man's brain weight results from an evolutionary increase in the relative size of hominid brains—resulting in a total brain weight which is vast compared with mammals in general, and is significantly large compared with primates in general. One reason we have overstressed the size of man's brain, even among primates, is that the chimpanzee and gorilla have relatively small brains, especially for primates. Similar arguments suggest that the frontal lobes in man, while well developed, are not of extraordinary and unexpected volume compared with other higher primates. . . .

Man is not much different from other primates, especially the apes, in the general sequence of events from conception to birth. After birth, the ontogenetic pattern in man differs markedly from that of all non-human primates but differs in a direction forecast by the general trend of primate evolution. I would guess that this elongation of the life periods after birth is a consequence of physiological adaptation to the acquisition of culture. Culture is a biological adaptation with a nongenetic mode of inheritance depending on symbolic contact rather than fusion of gametes. It has greatly supplemented somatic evolution. In all known human societies, in-dividuals participate in social systems whose members represent more than a single biological family in which all are connected (as the social insects are) by gametes from one parental set. No human family is a self-sufficient system of social action. Symbols rather than gametes make this so. It may be assumed that the genes controlling the growth cycle in man have been changed through selection to man's *human, cultural* environment.

selection 18

The Study of Race

S. L. Washburn

From *American Anthropologist,* Vol. 65, No. 3, Part 1, 1963, pp. 521–531. By permission of the author, and the publisher.

. . . Discussion of the races of man seems to generate endless emotion and confusion. I am under no illusion that this paper can do much to dispel the confusion; it may add to the emotion. The latest information available supports the traditional findings of anthropologists and other social scientists—that there is no scientific basis of any kind for racial discrimination. I think that the way this conclusion has been reached needs to be restated. The continuation of antiquated biological notions in anthropology and the over-simplification of facts weakens the anthropological position. We must realize that great changes have taken place in the study of race over the last 20 years and it is up to us to bring our profession into the forefront of the newer understandings, so that our statements will be authoritative and useful.

This paper will be concerned with three topics—the modern concept of race, the interpretation of racial differences, and the social significances of race. . . .

The races of man are the result of human evolution, of the evolution of our species. The races are open parts of the species, and the species is a closed system. If we look, then, upon long-term human evolution, our first problem must be the species and the things which have caused the evolution of all mankind, not the races, which are the results of local forces and which are minor in terms of the evolution of the whole species. . . .

The evolution of races is due, according to

modern genetics, to mutation, selection, migration, and genetic drift. It is easy to shift from this statement of genetic theory to complications of hemoglobin, blood groups or other technical information. But the point I want to stress is that the primary implication of genetics for anthropology is that it affirms the relation of culture and biology in a far firmer and more important way than ever in our history before. Selection is for reproductive success, and in man reproductive success is primarily determined by the social system and by culture. Effective behavior is the question, not something else.

Drift depends on the size of population, and population size, again, is dependent upon culture, not upon genetic factors as such. Obviously, migration depends on clothes, transportation, economy, and warfare and is reflected in the archeological record. Even mutation rates are now affected by technology.

Genetic theory forces the consideration of culture as the major factor in the evolution of man. It thus reaffirms the fundamental belief of anthropologists that we must study man both as a biological and as a social organism. This is no longer a question of something that might be desirable; it must be done if genetic theory is correct.

We have, then, on the one hand the history of genetic systems, and on the other hand the history of cultural systems, and, finally, the interrelation between these two. There is no evolution in the traditional anthropological sense. What Boas referred to as evolution was orthogenesis—which receives no support from modern genetic theory. What the geneticist sees as evolution is far closer to what Boas called history than to what he called evolution, and some anthropologists are still fighting a nineteenth-century battle in their presentation of evolution. We have, then, the history of cultural systems, which you may call history; and the history of genetic systems, which you may call evolution if you want to, but if you use this word remember that it means selection, migration, drift— it is real history that you are talking about and not some mystic force which constrains man-

kind to evolve according to some orthogenetic principle.

There is, then, no possibility of studying human raciation, the process of race formation, without studying human culture. Archeology is as important in the study of the origin of races as is genetics; all we can do is reconstruct as best we can the long-term past, and this is going to be very difficult. . . .

Genetics shows us that typology must be completely removed from our thinking if we are to progress. For example, let us take the case of the Bushmen. The Bushmen have been described as the result of a mixture between Negro and Mongoloid. Such a statement could only be put in the literature without any possible consideration of migration routes, of numbers of people, of cultures, of any way that such a mixing could actually take place. The fact is that the Bushmen had a substantial record in South Africa and in East Africa and there is no evidence that they ever were anywhere else except in these areas. In other words, they are a race which belongs exactly where they are.

If we are concerned with history let us consider, on the one hand, the ancestors of these Bushmen 15,000 years ago and the area available to them, to their way of life, and, on the other hand, the ancestors of Europeans at the same time in the area available to them, with their way of life. We will find that the area available to the Bushmen was at least twice that available to the Europeans. The Bushmen were living in a land of optimum game; the Europeans were living close to an ice sheet. There were perhaps from three to five times as many Bushmen ancestors as there were European ancestors only 15,000 years ago.

If one were to name a major race, or a primary race, the Bushmen have a far better claim in terms of the archeological record than the Europeans. During the time of glacial advance more than half of the Old World available to man for life was in Africa. The numbers and distributions that we think of as normal and the races whose last results we see today are relics of an earlier and far different time in human history.

There are no three primary races, no three major groups. The idea of three primary races stems from nineteenth-century typology; it is totally misleading to put the black-skinned people of the world together—to put the Australian in the same grouping with the inhabitants of Africa. And there are certainly at least three independent origins of the small, dark people, the Pygmies, and probably more than that. There is no single Pygmy race. . . .

The concept of race is fundamentally changed if we actually look for selection, migration, and study people as they are (who they are, where they are, how many they are); and the majority of anthropological textbooks need substantial revision along these lines.

Since races are open systems which are intergrading, the number of races will depend on the purpose of the classification. This is, I think, a tremendously important point. It is significant that as I was reviewing classifications in preparing this lecture, I found that almost none of them mentioned any purpose for which people were being classified. Race isn't very important biologically. If we are classifying races in order to understand human history, there aren't many human races, and there is very substantial agreement as to what they are. There are from six to nine races, and this difference in number is very largely a matter of definition. These races occupied the major separate geographical areas in the Old World.

If one has no purpose for classification, the number of races can be multiplied almost indefinitely, and it seems to me that the erratically varying number of races is a source of confusion to student, to layman, and to specialist. I think we should require people who propose a classification of races to state in the first place why they wish to divide the human species and to give in detail the important reasons for subdividing our whole species. If important reasons for such classification are given, I think you will find that the number of races is always exceedingly small.

If we consider these six or nine geographical races and the factors which produced them, I think the first thing we want to stress is migration. . . .

Migration has always been important in human history and there is no such thing as human populations which are completely separated from other human populations. And migration necessarily brings in new genes, necessarily reduces the differences between the races. For raciation to take place, then, there must be other factors operating which create difference. Under certain circumstances, in very small populations, differences may be created by genetic drift, or because the founders are for chance reasons very different from other members of the species.

However, the primary factor in the creation of racial differences in the long term is selection. This means that the origin of races must depend on adaptation and that the differences between the races which we see must in times past have been adaptive. I stress the question of time here, because it is perfectly logical to maintain that in time past a shovel-shaped incisor, for example, was more efficient than an incisor of other forms and that selection would have been for this, and at the same time to assert that today this dental difference is of absolutely no social importance. It is important to make this point because people generally take the view that something is always adaptive or never adaptive, and this is a fundamental oversimplification of the facts.

Adaptation is always within a given situation. There is no such thing as a gene which has a particular adaptive value; it has this value only under set circumstances. For example, the sickle-cell gene, if Allison and others are right, protects against malaria. This is adaptive if there is malaria, but if there is not malaria it is not adaptive. The adaptive value of the gene, then, is dependent on the state of medicine and has no absolute value. The same is true of the other characteristics associated with race. . . .

I turn now to a brief statement on the influence of culture upon race. Beginning with agriculture and continuing at an ever-increasing rate, human customs have been interposed between the organism and the environment. The increase of our species from perhaps as few as five million before agriculture to three billion today is the result of new technology, not of biological evolution. The conditions under which the races evolved are mainly gone, and there are new causes of mutation, new kinds of selection, and vast migration. Today the numbers and distribution of the peoples of the world are due primarily to culture. Some people think the new conditions are so different that it is better no longer to use the word race or the word evolution, but I personally think this confuses more than it clarifies.

All this does not mean that evolution has stopped, because the new conditions will change gene frequencies, but the conditions which produced the old races are gone. In this crowded world of civilization and science, the claim has been made repeatedly that one or another of the races is superior to the others. Obviously, this argument cannot be based on the past; because something was useful in times past and was selected for under conditions which are now gone, does not mean that it will be useful in the present or in the future.

The essential point at issue is whether the abilities of large populations are so different that their capacity to participate in modern technical culture is affected. Remember in the first place that no race has evolved to fit the selective pressures of the modern world. Technical civilization is new and the races are old. Remember also that all the species of *Homo* have been adapting to the human way of life for many thousands of years. Tools even antedate our genus, and our human biological adaptation is the result of culture. Man and his capacity for culture have evolved together, as Dr. Dobzhansky has pointed out. All men are adapted to learn language—any language; to perform skillful tasks—a fabulous variety of tasks; to cooperate; to enjoy art; to practice religion, philosophy, and science.

Our species only survives in culture, and, in a profound sense, we are the product of the new selection pressures that came with culture.

Infinitely more is known about the language and culture of all the groups of mankind than is known about the biology of racial differences. We know that the members of every racial group have learned a vast variety of languages and ways of life. The interaction of genes and custom over the millennia has produced a species whose populations can learn to live in an amazing variety of complex cultural ways.

Racism is based on a profound misunderstanding of culture, of learning, and of the biology of the human species. The study of cultures should give a profound respect for the biology of man's capacity to learn. Much of the earlier discussion of racial inferiority centered on the discussion of intelligence; or, to put the matter more accurately, usually on that small part of biological intelligence which is measured by the IQ. In the earlier days of intelligence testing, there was a widespread belief that the tests revealed something which was genetically fixed within a rather narrow range. The whole climate of opinion that fostered this point of view has changed. At that time animals were regarded as primarily instinctive in their behavior, and the genes were supposed to exert their effects in an almost mechanical way, regardless of the environment. All this intellectual climate has changed. Learning has proved to be far more important in the behavior of many animal species, and the action of the complexes of genes is now known to be affected by the environment, as is, to a great degree, the performance that results from them. For example, Harlow has shown that monkeys learn to learn. Monkeys become test wise. They become skillful in the solution of tests—so monkeys in Dr. Harlow's laboratories are spoken of as naive or as experienced in the use of tests. To suppose that humans cannot learn to take tests is to suppose that humans are rather less intelligent than monkeys. . . .

We can generalize this point. All kinds of human performance—whether social, athletic, intellectual—are built on genetic and environmental elements. The level of all kinds of performance can be increased by improving the environmental situation so that every genetic constitution may be developed to its full capacity. Any kind of social discrimination against groups of people, whether these are races, castes, or classes, reduces the achievements of our species, of mankind.

The cost of discrimination is reflected in length of life. The Founding Fathers were wise to join life, liberty, and the pursuit of happiness, because these are intimately linked in the social and cultural system. Just as the restriction of social and economic opportunity reduces intelligence so it reduces length of life.

In 1900 the life expectance of White males in the United States was 48 years, and in that same year the expectance of a Negro male was 32 years; that is a difference of 50 per cent, or 16 years. By 1940 the difference had been reduced to ten years, and by 1958 to six. As the life expectancy of the Whites increased from 48 to 62 to 67 years, that of the Negroes increased from 32 to 52 to 61 years. They died of the same causes, but they died at different rates.

Discrimination, by denying equal social opportunity to the Negro, made his progress lag approximately 20 years behind that of the White. Somebody said to me, "Well, 61, 67, that's only six years." But it depends on whose six years it is. There are about 19 million people in this country sociologically classified as Negroes. If they die according to the death rate given above, approximately 100 million years of life will be lost owing to discrimination.

In 1958 the death rate for Negroes in the first year of life was 52 per thousand and for Whites 26. Thousands of Negro infants died unnecessarily. The social conscience is an extraordinary thing. A lynching stirs the whole community to action, yet only a single life is lost. Discrimination, through denying education, medical care, and economic progress, kills at a far higher rate. A ghetto of hatred kills more surely than a concentration camp, because it kills by accepted custom, and it kills every day in the year.

A few years ago in South Africa, the expectation of life for a Black man was 40 years, but it was 60 at the same time for a White man. At that same time a White woman could expect 25 more years of life than a Black woman. Among the Blacks the women lived no longer than the men. People speak of the greater longevity of women, but this is only because of modern medicine. High birth rates, high infant mortality, high maternal mortality—these are the hallmarks of the history of mankind.

Of course there are biological differences between male and female, but whether a woman is allowed to vote, or the rate that she must die in childbirth, these are a matter of medical knowledge and of custom. Biological difference only expresses itself through the social system.

Who may live longer in the future—Whites or Negroes? There's no way of telling. Who may live longer in the future—males or females? There is no way of telling. These things are dependent on the progress in medical science and on the degree to which this progress is made available to all races and to both sexes.

When environment is important, the only way genetic difference may be determined is by equalizing the environment. If you believe in mankind, then you will want mankind to live on in an enriched environment. No one can tell what may be the ultimate length of life, but we do know that many people could live much longer if given a chance.

Whether we consider intelligence, or length of life, or happiness the genetic potential of a population is only realized in a social system. It is that system which gives life or death to its members, and in so doing changes the gene frequencies. We know of no society which has begun to realize the genetic potential of its members. We are the primitives living by antiquated customs in the midst of scientific progress. Races are products of the past. They are relics of times and conditions which have long ceased to exist.

Racism is equally a relic supported by no phase of modern science. We may not know how to interpret the form of the Mongoloid face, or why Rh^0 is of high incidence in Africa, but we do know the benefits of education and of economic progress. We know the price of discrimination is death, frustration, and hatred. We know that the roots of happiness lie in the biology of the whole species and that the potential of the species can only be realized in a culture, in a social system. It is knowledge and the social system which give life or take it away, and in so doing change the gene frequencies and continue the million-year-old interaction of culture and biology. Human biology finds its realization in a culturally determined way of life, and the infinite variety of genetic combinations can only express themselves efficiently in a free and open society.

part 4

Primates

Field Studies of Old World Monkeys and Apes

S. L. Washburn,
Phyllis C. Jay, and
Jane B. Lancaster

From *Science,* Vol. 150, 1965. pp. 1541–1547. Copyright 1965, American Association for the Advancement of Science. By permission of the authors, the publisher, and copyright holder.

For many years there has been interest in the evolutionary roots of human behavior, and discussions of human evolution frequently include theories on the origin of human customs. In view of the old and widespread interest in the behavior of our nearest relatives, it is surprising how little systematic information was collected until very recently. . . .

The increased interest in primates, and particularly in the behavior of free-ranging primates, has given rise to several symposiums, and results of the new studies have been published almost as soon as they have been completed . . .

. . . Here we wish to direct attention to the nature of the recent field studies and to a few of their major contributions. Perhaps their greatest contribution is a demonstration that close, accurate observation for hundreds of hours is possible. Prior to Schaller's field work, reported in 1963, it was by no means clear that this kind of observation of gorillas would be possible; previous investigators had conducted very fragmentary observations, and Emlen and Schaller deserve great credit for the planning and execution of their study. A field study of the chimpanzee that seemed adequate in the 1930's now seems totally inadequate, when compared to Goodall's results. Today a field study is planned to yield something of the order of 1000 hours of observations, and the observer is expected to be close to the animals and to recognize individuals. A few years ago observations of this length and quality were thought unnecessary, if not impossible.

The importance of studies in which groups are visited repeatedly and animals are recognized individually may be illustrated by the problems they make it possible to study. For example, during one season of the year chimpanzees "fish" for termites by breaking off sticks or stiff grasses and sticking the prepared implement into a termite hole, and this whole complex of nest examination, tool preparation, and fishing is learned by the young chimpanzee. It can be seen at only one time of the year and can be appreciated only by an observer whose presence no longer disturbs the animals. Habituation to the observer is a slow and difficult process. Goodall reports that after 8 months of observations she could approach to no closer than 50 meters of the chimpanzees and then only when they were in thick cover or up a tree; by 14 months she was able to get within 10 to 15 meters of them. The problem of tool use in nonhuman primates has been reviewed by Hall, but the essential point here is that the amount of throwing and object manipulation in the monkeys (Cercopithecidae) was greatly exaggerated in travelers' tales, which were uncritically accepted, and it took years of observation in a favorable locality to reveal the complexity of this kind of behavior in the chimpanzee.

Predation

Another example of the value of continued observations is in the study of deliberate hunting by baboons. In three seasons of field work and more than 1500 hours of observation DeVore had seen baboons catch and eat small mammals, but apparently almost by chance, when the baboon virtually stepped on something like a newborn antelope and then killed it. But in 1965 DeVore saw repeated incidents of baboons surrounding, hunting, and killing small mammals.

The whole matter of predation on primates has been difficult to study. Rare events, such as an attack by an eagle may be very important in the survival of primates, but such attacks are seldom observed, because the presence of the human observer disturbs either the predator or the prey. We think that the present de-emphasis of the importance of predation on primates arises from these difficulties of observation and from the fact that even today most studies of free-ranging primates are made in areas where predators have been reduced or eliminated by man. Most predators are active by night, and there is still no adequate study of the nocturnal behavior of any monkey or ape. Predation probably can best be measured by studying the predators rather than the prey.

Recognition of individual animals is nec-

essary for the study of many problems, from the first stages of the analysis of a social system to observations of social continuity or constancy of group membership; such observations are exceedingly difficult under most field conditions. For example, understanding of the dominance system implies repeated recognition of a number of animals under sufficiently various conditions so that the patterns of interaction become clear. Again, to be sure that a group has lost or gained a member, the observer must know the whole composition of the group.

Long-continued observations have proved to be important in many unexpected ways. For example, rhesus monkeys have been observed in several of their many very different habitats, and it has been found that young rhesus play more in cities than in some kinds of forest and play in the forest more at some seasons than at others. These differences are due in part to the amount of time which must be spent in getting food; the same forest troop may play more when fruits are available and hunger may be rapidly satisfied than at times of the year when the diet is composed of tiny seeds which take a long time to pick. Extracting the small seeds of sheesham pods during the months when rhesus troops spend most of their time in the sheesham trees takes many hours of the day. What might easily have been described in a short-term study as a species-specific difference of considerable magnitude turns out to be the result of seasonal and local variations in food source. It is essential to sample behavior in several habitats to gain an understanding of the flexibility of the built-in behavior pattern of a species, flexibility which precludes the need for development of new forms of genetically determined behavior to cope successfully with different habitats.

The long-term study in which many groups of a species are observed in different, contrasting localities, and in which at least some groups are known so well that most of the individuals can be recognized, will correct many false notions and will make valid generalizations possible. Although so far there have been only a few major investigations of this sort, some important generalizations seem possible.

Environment and Social Behavior

Nowhere is the extent to which the behavior of a species is adaptable and responsive to local conditions more apparent than among groups of rhesus living in India. Rhesus occur naturally in such diverse environments as cities, villages, roadsides, cultivated fields, and many types of forest ranging to altitudes of over 2400 meters. Contact with man varies in these habitats from constant and close to rare and incidental.

Where rhesus groups are subjected to pressures of trapping, harassment, and high incidence of infectious disease, groups are tense and aggression is high. These pressures are found in areas where there is most contact and interaction with man, such as in cities and at places of pilgrimage. The animals are in generally poor physical condition, and numerous old and new wounds are evidence of a high rate of intragroup fighting. Tension among groups occupying adjacent areas of land is similarly high where there is insufficient space for normal movement and behavior, and where there may be intense competition for a limited supply of food and water. This is in sharp contrast to those groups living away from man where normal spacing among groups can be effected by the means evolved by the species. In the latter environments, such as forests, the rhesus are in excellent physical condition and what aggressive behavior occurs functions to maintain stable social groups and relationships among the members of the group; wounds are substantially fewer, and disease appears to be rare.

There has been considerable controversy in discussions of the relationships among social groups of the same species as to whether or not the geographical area occupied by a group should be called a territory or a home range. The point we wish to emphasize is that, within one species, populations living in different habitats may act quite differently toward neighboring groups. Populations may be capable of a wide variety of behavior patterns ranging from exclusive occupation of an area which may be defended against neighboring groups to a peaceful coexistence with conspecifics in which wide overlap in home ranges is tolerated. Because local populations of a species may maintain their ranges in different ways it is necessary to investigate all variations in group spacing in diverse habitats before attempting to describe characteristic behavior patterns for any species.

Not unexpectedly, population and group composition reflect these differences in habitat and stress. Groups living on the Gangetic plains, where trapping, harassment, and disease are important factors, are smaller, and the proportion of young members is also significantly smaller. The long-term effects of pressures on different rhesus populations in northern and central India are now being investigated by a team of anthropologists of the National Center for Primate Biology.

A city presents a very different set of challenges to a rhesus group than does a forest. Often there are no trees to sleep in; living space must be shared with man and his domestic animals. Food is not available in the form common to other habitats, and monkeys may have to depend on their skill in stealing food from man. Often the food has been prepared by man for his own consumption, or it consists of fruits and vegetables pilfered from houses, shops, and streets. Garbage is picked through and edible portions are consumed. It is essential that the monkeys learn to differentiate between those humans who represent a real threat to their safety and those who are safe to approach. They must react quickly and learn to manipulate doors, gates, and other elements of the physical environment unique to their urban habitat. This is a tremendously different setting from that in which most rhesus live. City rhesus are more manipulative, more active, and often more aggressive than are forest rhesus. Clearly, the same species develops quite different learned habits in different environments.

Annual Reproductive Cycle

The belief, which has been widely maintained, that there is no breeding season in monkeys and apes gave rise to the theory that the persistence throughout the year of groups, or highly organized troops, was due to continuous sexual attraction. The evidence for a breeding season has been reviewed by Lancaster and Lee who found that in many species of monkeys there is a well-marked breeding season. For example, Mizuhara has presented data on 545 births of Japanese macaques of Takasakiyama. There were on the average approximately 90 births per year over six consecutive years. The average length of the birth season was 125 days, but it varied from 95 to 176 days. The majority of the births occurred in June and July. Copulations were most frequent in November to March and were not observed during the birth season, and in spite of this the highly organized group continues as a social unit throughout the year.

The birth season has been studied in other groups of Japanese macaques, and in general the situation is similar. There is no doubt that both mating and birth seasons are highly restricted in the Japanese macaque. The birth season is spring and summer, but its onset and duration vary considerably. If observations were limited and combined for the whole species, as they were in early studies, the birth season would appear to be much longer than in fact it is for an individual group, and it is the events within the local group, not averages of events for the species, that bear upon the role of sexual attraction in holding primate society together.

Under very different climatic conditions, in India, rhesus macaques also have a birth season, but copulations were observed in all months of the year, although probably not with equal frequency. Among rhesus on a small island off Puerto Rico births occur from January to June, and copulations are restricted to July–January. These data confirm the point that a birth season will be more sharply defined in a local group than in a species as a whole. There is a mating season among rhesus introduced on the island, but only a peak of mating in the same species in their native India. It is clear that survey data drawn from many groups over a wide area must be used with caution when the aim is to interpret the behavior of a single group. Since the birth season is an adaptation to local conditions, there is no reason to expect it to be the same over the entire geographical distribution of a species, and under laboratory conditions rhesus macaques breed throughout the year.

No data comparable to those for the macaques exist for other primates, and, since accurate determination of mating and birth seasons requires that reasonable numbers of animals be observed in all months of the year and that groups be observed in different localities, really adequate data exist for only the Japanese macaque. However, Lancaster and Lee were able to assemble data on 14 species of monkeys and apes. They found that probably the most common situation is a birth peak, a time of year at which births tend to be concentrated, rather than sharply limited mating and birth seasons. This is highly adaptive for widely distributed species, for it allows the majority of births to occur at the optimum time for each locality while maintaining a widely variable basic pattern. The birth season may be a more effective adaptation to extreme climatic conditions. There may be a birth peak in the chimpanzee, and there may be none in the mountain gorilla, but, since we have no more data than are necessary to clarify the reproductive pattern in a single species of macaque, we can conclude only that, while birth seasons are not present in either gorillas or chimpanzees, a peak is possible in chimpanzees, at least for those living near Lake Tanganyika.

Prior to the recent investigations there was a great deal of information on primate reproduction, and yet as late as 1960 it was still possible to maintain that there were no breeding seasons in primates and that this was the basis of primate society. Until recently the question of seasonality was raised without reference to a birth season as distinguished from a birthpeak, or to a limited mating season as distinguished from matings throughout the year with a high frequency in a particular period.

Frequency of Mating

Obviously many more studies are needed, and one of the intriguing problems is the role of potency. Not only does the frequency of mating vary through the year, but also there appear to be enormous differences in potency between species that are reproducing at a normal rate. In nearly 500 hours of observation of gorillas, Schaller saw only two matings, fewer than might be seen in a troop of baboons in almost any single morning. The redtail monkey (*Cercopithecus ascanius*) mates rarely, but the closely related vervet (*Cercopithecus aethiops*) does so frequently. To a considerable extent the observed differences are correlated with structure, such as size of testes, and all these species seem to be reproducing at an adequate and normal rate. There is no evidence that langurs (*Presbytis entellus*) are less successful breeders than rhesus, but the langurs copulate less frequently.

Now that more adequate data are becoming available, the social functions of sexual behavior should be reinvestigated. The dismissal of the theory that sexual attraction is *the* basis of primate society should open the way for a more careful study of the multiple functions of sexual behavior. The great differences among the primate species should provide data to prove or disprove new theories. In passing it might be noted that the human mating system without estrous cycles in the female and without marked seasonal variations is unique.

Systems of Mating

Mating systems, like the presence or absence of seasonality in breeding and the frequency of copulation, are extremely variable in monkeys and apes. Eventually the relation of these variations to species adaptations will be understandable; at present it is most important to note that monkeys do not necessarily live either in harems or in promiscuous hordes as was once assumed. Restrictive mating patterns such as the stable and exclusive pair-bond formed between adult gibbons and the harem system of the Hamadryas baboon are comparatively rare. The most common mating pattern of monkeys and apes is promiscuity more or less influenced by dominance relationships. In species in which dominance relations are not constantly at issue, such as langurs, chimpanzees, or bonnet macaques, matings appear to be relatively promiscuous and are often based on the personal inclination of the estrous female. When dominance relationships are constantly at issue, as in baboons, Japanese macaques, and rhesus macaques, sex often becomes one of the prerogatives of dominant rank. In such species dominant males tend to do a larger share of the mating than do more subordinate animals, but it is only in unusual situations that subordinate animals are barred from the mating system altogether. Mating systems probably support the general adaptation of the species to its environment. In most baboons and macaques the tendency for a few males to do much of the mating may be partly a by-product of natural selection for a hierarchy of adult males which dominates the troop so that in a dangerous terrestrial habitat external dangers will be met in an orderly way. Selection is not only for a male which can impregnate many females but it may also have favored a dominance-oriented social organization in which sexual activity has become one of the expressions of that dominance.

Dominance Relationships

Long-term field studies of monkeys and apes in their natural habitats have emphasized that social relationships within a group are patterned and organized in very complex ways. There is no single "monkey pattern" or "ape pattern"; rather, there is great variability, both among different species and among different populations of the same species, in the organization and expression of social relationships. A difference in the relative dominance of individuals is one of the most common modes of social organization in monkey and ape societies. Dominance is not synonymous with aggression, and the way dominance is expressed varies greatly between species. In the gorilla, for example, dominance is most often expressed by extremely attenuated gestures and signals; a gentle nudge from the dominant male is more than enough to elicit a submissive response from a subordinate, whereas, in baboons, chases, fights, and biting can be daily occurrences. In many primates there is a tendency for the major age-sex classes to be ranked in a dominance order; for example, in baboons, macaques, and gorillas, adult males as a class are usually dominant over adult females, and females are dominant over young. This may not always be true, for in several species of macaques some females may outrank some adult males, although groups dominated by a female (such as the Minoo-B troop of Japanese macaques) are extremely rare. Dominance relationships may be quite unstructured, as in the chimpanzee, where dominance is expressed in interactions between individuals but where these relationships are not organized into any sort of hierarchy. A much more common situation is one in which dominance relations, among males at least, are organized into linear hierarchies that are quite stable over time, as in baboons, langurs, and macaques. Sometimes these dominance hierarchies are complicated by alliances among several males who back each other up very effectively or even by an alliance between a male and a female. Although dominance varies widely among monkeys and apes both in its form and function, it is certainly one of the most important axes of social organization to be found in primate societies.

Genealogical Relationships

Recognition of individual animals and repeated studies of the same groups have opened the way to the appreciation of other long-continuing social relationships in monkeys and apes which cannot be interpreted in terms of dominance alone. Long-term studies of free-ranging animals have been made on only two species of nonhuman primates, Japanese macaques, which have been studied since 1950 by members of the Japan Monkey Center, and Indian rhesus macaques living free on Cayo Santiago, Puerto Rico, the island colony established by Carpenter in 1938. In these studies when the genealogy of the animals has been known, it has been obvious that genetic relationships play a major role in determining the course and nature of social interactions. It becomes clear that bonds between mother and infant may persist into adult life to form a nucleus from which many other social bonds ramify. When the genealogy of individual animals is known, members of commonly observed subgroupings, such as a cluster of four or five animals grooming or resting together, are likely to be uterine kin. For example, members of a subgroup composed of several adult animals, both male and female, as well as juveniles and infants, may all be offspring of the same female. These relations continue to be very important in adult life not only in relaxed affectional relationships but also in dominance interactions. Sade saw a female rhesus divert the attack of a dominant male from her adult son and saw another adult female protect her juvenile half-sisters (paternity is not determinable in most monkey societies). There is a very high frequency of grooming between related animals, and many animals never seek grooming partners outside of their own genealogies.

It should be stressed that there is no information leading us to believe that these animals are either recognizing genetic relationships or responding to any sort of abstract concept of family. Rather these social relationships are determined by the necessarily close association of mother with newborn infant, which is extended through time and generations and which ramifies into close associations among siblings. We believe that this pattern of enduring social relations between a mother and her offspring will be found in other species of primates. Because of their dramatic character, the importance of dominance and aggression has been greatly exaggerated compared to that of continuing, positive, affectional relations between related animals as expressed by their sitting or feeding together, touching, and grooming. Much of this behavior can be observed easily in the field, but the extent to which it is in fact an expression of social genealogies has been demonstrated only in the studies cited above.

Positive, affectional relations are not limited to relatives. Male Japanese macaques may take care of young by forming special protective relationships with particular infants, but whether these males have any special relationship to the infants as either father or brother is uncertain, and the mating system is such that paternity cannot be known either to the observer or to the monkeys. MacRoberts has recorded a very high frequency of care of infants by males in the Gibraltar macaque. In addition, he has demonstrated that these positive protective relations are very beneficial to the juvenile. Two juveniles which had no such close relationship were forced to be peripheral, were at a great disadvantage in feeding, and were groomed much less than other juveniles in the group.

The status of the adult can be conferred on closely associated young (frequently an offspring when the adult is female), and for this reason the young of dominant animals are more likely to be dominant. This inheritance of rank has been discussed by Imanishi for the Japanese macaque and by Koford for the rhesus. Sons of very dominant females seem to have a great advantage over other males both because their mothers are able to back them up successfully in social interactions and because they stay with their mothers near the other dominant animals at the center of the group. They may never go through the stage of being socially and physically peripheral to the group which is typical for young males of these species. A male cannot simply "inherit" high rank; he must also win this position through his own abilities, but his chances of so doing are greatly increased if he has had these early experiences of associating with and being supported by very dominant animals.

There could hardly be a greater contrast than that between the emerging picture of an orderly society, based heavily on affectionate or cooperative social actions and structured by stable dominance relationships, and the old notion of an unruly horde of monkeys dominated by a tyrant. The 19th-century social evolutionists attributed less order to the societies of primitive man than is now known to exist in the societies of monkeys and apes living today.

Communication

Research on the communication systems of monkeys and apes through 1962 has been most ably summarized and interpreted by Marler. Most of the data represent work by field observers who were primarily interested in social structure, and the signals, and their meanings, used to implement and facilitate social interactions were more or less taken for granted. Only in the last year or so have communication systems themselves been the object of careful study and analysis. Marler has emphasized both the extraordinary complexity of the communication systems of primates and the heavy dependence of these systems on composite signals. Most frequently it is not a single signal that passes between two animals but a signal complex composed of auditory, visual, tactile, and, more rarely, olfactory signals.

Communication in some monkey species is based on a system of intergrading signals, whereas in others much more use is made of highly discrete signals. For example, most vervet sounds described by Struhsaker are of the discrete type, there being some 36 different sounds that are comparatively distinct both to the human ear and when analyzed by a sound spectrograph. In contrast, Rowell and Hinde have analyzed the sounds of the rhesus monkey and found that of 13 harsh noises, 9 belonged to a single intergrading subsystem expressing agonistic emotions.

As more and more study is done on primates it will probably be shown that their communication systems tend to be of mixed form in that both graded and discrete signals are used depending on the relative efficiency of one or the other form in serving a specific function. In concert this use of both discrete and inter grading signals and of composites from several sensory modes produces a rich potential for the expression of very slight but significant changes in the intensity and nature of mood in the signaling animal. Marler has emphasized that, except for calls warning of danger, the communication system is little applied to events outside the group. Communication systems in monkeys and apes are highly evolved in their capacity to express motivation of individuals and to facilitate social relationships. Without this ability to express mood, monkeys and apes would not be able to engage in the subtle and complicated social interactions that are a major feature of their adaptations.

Social Learning

Harlow and Harlow's experiments show the importance of learning in the development of social life; however, monkeys and apes are so constituted that, except in the laboratory, social learning is inevitable. They adapt by their social life, and the group provides the context of affection, protection, and stability in which learning occurs. No one factor can explain the importance of social behavior, because society is a major adaptive mechanism with many functions, but one of the most important of these functions is the provision of a rich and protected social context in which young mature. Field observations, although mainly observations of the results of learning rather than of the process itself, provide necessary clues as to the nature of the integration of relevant developmental and social factors. These factors can then be estimated and defined for subsequent intensive controlled research in a laboratory or colony.

It has become clear that, although learning has great importance in the normal develop-

ment of nearly all phases of primate behavior, it is not a generalized ability; animals are able to learn some things with great ease and other things only with the greatest difficulty. Learning is part of the adaptive pattern of a species and can be understood only when it is seen as the process of acquiring skills and attitudes that are of evolutionary significance to a species when living in the environment to which it is adapted.

There are important biological limitations which vary from species to species and which do not reflect differences in intelligence so much as differences in specializations. For example. Goodall has observed young chimpanzees learning to fish for termites both by their observation of older chimpanzees and by practice. It takes time for the chimpanzee to become proficient with these tools, and many mistakes are made. Chimpanzees are not the only primates that like termites, and Goodall has observed baboons sitting near chimpanzees watching and waiting while the latter are getting termites. The baboons are just as eager as the chimpanzees to eat termites but are unable to learn how to fish for termites for themselves.

It is likely that there are important variables among groups of a single species that make it possible for the acquisition of new patterns of behavior or the expression of basic learned species patterns to vary from group to group and from one habitat to another. For example, the nature of the integration and operation of a social unit vary in the extent to which it depends on the personalities of individuals in the group—this is another dimension of our understanding of how social behavior may affect species survival. Particularly aggressive adult males can make the behavior of their groups relative to that of adjacent groups with less assertive males substantially different. For example, a group with very aggressive males can control a larger geographic area than is occupied by a group with much less aggressive males. The tenor of life within a group may be tenser or more relaxed depending on personalities of adults in the group.

Imprinting has traditionally been distinguished from other learning processes by the fact that in imprinting the young animal will learn to follow, to be social, without an external or immediate reward. However, among monkeys and apes, simply being with other animals is a reward, and learning is reinforced by the affectional, attentive, supportive social context of the group. Butler was the first to use the sight of another monkey as a reward in psychological experiments. The field worker sees sick and practically disabled animals making great efforts to stay with their group. Among ground-living forms, animals that have lost or broken limbs or are so sick that they collapse as soon as the group stops moving, all walk along as the troop moves. Instances of wounded rhesus macaques' moving into langur groups after the rhesus have left or been forced out of their own group have been recorded. Clearly, it is essential for the young monkey or ape to mature in a social setting in which it learns appropriate skills and relationships during early years and in which it continues to learn during adulthood. "Where the individual primate is, in temporary isolation, learning a task without reference to any other member of its species, the learning is not normal."

Future Primate Studies

At present many long-term studies are in process and major films are being edited (Goodall on chimpanzee and DeVore on baboon). There will be about twice as many major accounts available in 2 years as there are now. Since it is now clear that detailed descriptive studies of undisturbed free-ranging primates can be made, and since available data show that there are substantial differences in the behavior of the different species, more species should be investigated. So far studies have concentrated for the most part on the larger ground-living forms which are easier to study. There is no study of *Cercocebus,* little on *Colobus,* and nothing on the numerous langurs (*Presbytis*) of southeast Asia. New World monkeys have been investigated very little, and there are numerous genera that have not been the subjects of a major field study. Also, since local variation is important, forms such as the chimpanzee and gorilla should be studied in more and contrasting localities.

Once the general characteristics of the behaviors of several species are known, then interest can shift to topics such as detailed ecology, birth, infant behavior, peer groups, affectionate behaviors, sex, or dominance, to mention only a few. The behavior of a whole species is a large problem, and description has to be at a very general level when the goal is a first general statement. A problem-oriented study permits choice of species and elaboration of techniques. A further advantage of the problem-oriented approach is that it allows the close coordination of the field work with experimental work in the laboratory. Fortunately, no division has developed between those doing the field work and those involved in the experimental analysis of behavior. Many scientists have done both controlled experiments and field studies. The interplay between naturalistic observation and controlled experiment is the essential key to the understanding of behavior. The character of the natural adaptation of the species and the dimensions of the society can be determined only in the field. Many topics, such as geographic range, food, predation, group size, aggression, and the like, can be seen only under field conditions. But the mechanisms of the observed behavior can be determined only in the laboratory, and this is the more complicated task. The relation of a field study to scientific understanding is like the relation of the observation that a man walks or runs to the whole analysis of locomotion. The field worker lists what the animals eat, but this gives no understanding of nutrition. The kinds of interactions may be charted in the field, but their interpretation requires the laboratory. Field workers saw hours devoted to play, but it was Harlow's experiments that showed how essential this activity was to the development of behavior. As the field studies develop it is to be hoped that they will maintain a close relation to controlled experiment. It is most fortunate that the present studies are being carried on by anthropologists, psychologists, and zoologists. An understanding of behavior is most likely to come from the bringing together of the methods and interests of many sciences, and we hope that the field studies remain a part of general behavorial science and do not become independent as workers and problems become more and more numerous.

Even now, in their preliminary state, the field studies can offer some conclusions that might be pondered by students in the multiplicity of departments now dividing up the study of human behavior. Behavior is profoundly influenced by the biology of the species, and problems of perception, emotion, aggression, and many others cannot be di-

vorced from the biology of the actors in the social system. Early learning is important, and an understanding of the preschool years is essential to an understanding of behavior. Play is tremendously important, and a species that wastes the emotions and energies of its young by divorcing play from education has forfeited its evolutionary heritage—the biological motivation of learning. Social behavior is relatively simple compared to the biological mechanisms that make the behavior possible. Ultimately a science of human behavior must include both biological and social factors, and there is no more reason to separate the study of human behavior into many compartments than there would be to separate the field studies from the intellectual enrichment coming from the laboratory.

selection 20

Social Deprivation in Monkeys

Harry F. Harlow
and
Margaret Kuenne Harlow

From *Scientific American,*
Vol. 207, No. 5, 1962, pp.
137–146. Copyright © 1962,
Scientific American, Inc. By
permission of the authors, and
the publisher and copyright
holder.

In *An Outline of Psychoanalysis,* published posthumously in 1940, Sigmund Freud was able to refer to "the common assertion that the child is psychologically the father of the man and that the events of his first years are of paramount importance for his whole subsequent life." It was, of course, Freud's own historic investigations, begun a half-century before, that first elucidated the role of infantile experiences in the development of the personality and its disorders. The "central experience of this period of childhood," he found, is the infant's relation to his mother. Freud's ideas have now shaped the thinking of two generations of psychologists, psychiatrists and psychoanalysts. Much evidence in support of his deep insights has been accumulated, particularly from clinical studies of the mentally ill. Contemporary writers stress inadequate or inconsistent mothering as a basic cause of later disorders such as withdrawal, hostility, anxiety, sexual maladjustment, alcoholism and, significantly, inadequate maternal behavior!

The evidence from clinical studies for this or any other view of human personality development is qualified, however, by an inherent defect. These studies are necessarily retrospective: they start with the disorder and work backward in time, retracing the experiences of the individual as he and his relatives and associates recall them. Inevitably details are lost or distorted, and the story is often so confounded as to require a generous exercise of intuition on the part of the investigator. Nor does evidence obtained in this manner exclude other possible causes of personality disorder. Against arguments in favor of a biochemical or neurological causation of mental illness, for example, there is no way to show that the patient began life with full potentiality for normal development. Given the decisive influence ascribed to the mother-infant relation, there may be a tendency in the reconstruction of the past to overlook or suppress evidence for the influence of other significant early relations, such as the bonds of interaction with other children. Little attention has been given, in fact, to child-to-child relations in the study of personality development. Yet it can be supposed that these play a significant part in determining the peer relations and the sexual role of the adult. Plainly there is a need to study the development of personality forward in time from infancy. Ideally the study should be conducted under controlled laboratory conditions so that the effects of single variables or combinations of variables can be traced.

Acceding to the moral and physical impossibility of conducting such an investigation with human subjects, we have been observing the development of social behavior in large numbers of rhesus monkeys at the Primate Laboratory of the University of Wisconsin. Apart from this primate's kinship to man, it offers a reasonable experimental substitute because it undergoes a relatively long period of development analogous to that of the human child and involving intimate attachment to its mother and social interaction with its age-mates. With these animals we have been able to observe the consequences of the deprivation of all social contact for various lengths of time. We have also raised them without mothers but in the company of age-mates and with mothers but without age-mates.

We have thereby been able to make some estimate of the contribution of each of these primary affectional systems to the integrated adult personality. Our observations sustain the significance of the maternal relation, particularly in facilitating the interaction of the infant with other infants. But at the same time we have found compelling evidence that opportunity for infant-infant interaction under optimal conditions may fully compensate for lack of mothering, at least in so far as infant-infant social and heterosexual relations are concerned. It seems possible—even likely—that the infant-mother affectional system is dispensable, whereas the infant-infant system is the *sine qua non* for later adjustment in all spheres of monkey life. In line with the "paramount importance" that Freud assigned to experience in the first years of life, our experiments indicate that there is a critical period somewhere between the third and sixth months of life during which social deprivation, particularly deprivation of the company of its peers, irreversibly blights the animal's capacity for social adjustment.

Our investigations of the emotional development of our subjects grew out of the effort to produce and maintain a colony of sturdy, disease-free young animals for use in various research programs. By separating them from their mothers a few hours after birth and placing them in a more fully controlled regimen of nurture and physical care we were able both to achieve a higher rate of survival and to remove the animals for testing without maternal protest. Only later did we realize that our monkeys were emotionally disturbed as well as sturdy and disease-free. Some of our researches are therefore retrospective. Others are in part exploratory, representing attempts to set up new experimental situations or to find new techniques for measurement. Most are incomplete because investigations of social and behavioral development are long-term. In a sense, they can never end, because the problems of one generation must be traced into the next.

Having separated the infant from its mother, our procedure was to keep it alone in a bare wire cage in a large room with other infants so housed. Thus each little monkey could see and hear others of its kind, although it could not make direct physical contact with them. The 56 animals raised in this manner now range in age from five to eight years. As a group they exhibit abnormalities of behavior rarely seen in animals born in the wild and brought to the laboratory as preadolescents or adolescents, even after the latter have been housed in individual cages for many years. The laboratory-born monkeys sit in their cages and stare fixedly into space, circle their cages in a repetitive stereotype manner and clasp their heads in their hands or arms and rock for long periods of time. They often develop compulsive habits, such as pinching precisely the same patch of skin on the chest between the same fingers hundreds of times a day; occasionally such behavior may become punitive and the animal may chew and tear at its body until it bleeds. Often the approach of a human being becomes the stimulus to self-aggression. This behavior constitutes a complete breakdown and reversal of the normal defensive response; a monkey born in the wild will direct such threats and aggression at the approaching person, not at itself. Similar symptoms of emotional pathology are observed in deprived children in orphanages and in withdrawn adolescents and adults in mental hospitals.

William A. Mason, now at the Yerkes Laboratories of Primate Biology, compared the behavior of six of these animals, which were then two years old and had been housed all their lives in individual cages, with a matched group of rhesus monkeys that had been captured in the wild during their first year of life and housed together in captivity for a while before being individually housed in the laboratory. The most striking difference was that all the animals that had been born in the wild—and not one of the laboratory-born animals—displayed normal sex behavior. That the laboratory-born animals were not lacking in sex drive was indicated by the fact that the males frequently approached the females and the females displayed part of the pattern of sexual presentation. But they did not orient themselves correctly and they did not succeed in mating. Moreover, the monkeys born in the wild had apparently learned to live with others in a stable hierarchy of dominance, or "pecking order"; consequently in the pairing test they fought one another less and engaged more often in social grooming. They would also release a companion from a locked cage more frequently than did the laboratory-born animals, which usually ignored their caged partner's plight.

The severity of the affliction that grips these monkeys raised in the partial isolation of individual wire cages has become more apparent as they have grown older. They pay little or no attention to animals in neighboring cages; those caged with companions sit in opposite corners with only rare interaction. No heterosexual behavior has ever been observed between male and female cage-mates, even between those that have lived together for as long as seven years. When efforts have been made to bring about matings, by pairing animals during the female's estrus, they have sometimes fought so viciously that they have had to be parted. Attempts to mate the socially deprived animals with sexually adequate and experienced monkeys from the breeding colony have been similarly frustrated.

In the summer of 1960 we undertook to devise a group-psychotherapy situation for 19 of these animals—nine males and 10 females—by using them to stock the monkey island in the municipal zoo in Madison, Wis. This was their first experience outside the laboratory, and they had much to learn in order to survive. They had to learn to drink water from an open trough instead of from a tube in the wall of a cage, to compete for food in a communal feeding situation, to huddle together or find shelter from inclement weather, to climb rocks and avoid the water surrounding the island. Most difficult of all, they had to learn to live together. Within the first few days they made all the necessary physical adjustments. The three casualties—a male that drowned and two females that were injured, and had to be returned to the laboratory—resulted from the stress of social adjustment. Fighting was severe at first; it decreased as effective dominance relations were established and friendship pairs formed. Grooming appeared in normal style and with almost normal frequency. A limited amount of sex behavior was observed, but it was infantile in form, with inadequate posturing by both females and males. In the hope of promoting therapy along this line we introduced our largest, strongest and most effective breeding-colony male to the island around the middle of summer. He immediately established himself at the head of the dominance order. But in spite of his considerable persistence and patience he did not succeed in starting a single pregnancy.

Back in the laboratory these animals ceased to groom and fought more frequently. In pairings with breeding-colony monkeys, not one male has achieved a normal mount or intromission and only one female has become pregnant. After two years we have had to conclude that the island experience was of no lasting value.

As the effects of the separation of these monkeys from their mothers in infancy were first becoming apparent in 1957 we were prompted to undertake a study of the mother-infant affectional bond. To each of one group of four animals separated from their mothers at birth we furnished a surrogate mother: a welded wire cylindrical form with the nipple of the feeding bottle protruding from its "breast" and with a wooden head surmounting it. The majority of the animals, 60 in all, were raised with cozier surrogate mothers covered by terry cloth. In connection with certain experiments some of these individuals have had both a bare-wire and a cloth-covered mother. The infants developed a strong attachment to the cloth mothers and little or none to the wire mothers, regardless of which one provided milk. In fright-inducing situations the infants showed that they derived a strong sense of security from the presence of their cloth mothers. Even after two years of separation they exhibit a persistent attachment to the effigies.

In almost all other respects, however, the behavior of these monkeys at ages ranging from three to five years is indistinguishable from that of monkeys raised in bare wire cages with no source of contact comfort other than a gauze diaper pad. They are without question socially and sexually aberrant. No normal sex behavior has been observed in the living cages of any of the animals that have been housed with a companion of the opposite sex. In exposure to monkeys from the breeding colony not one male and only one female has shown normal mating behavior and only four females have been successfully impregnated. Compared with the cage-raised monkeys, the surrogate-raised animals seem to be less aggressive, whether toward themselves or other monkeys. But they are also younger on the average, and their better dispositions can be attributed to their lesser age.

Thus the nourishment and contact comfort provided by the nursing cloth-covered mother in infancy does not produce a normal adolescent or adult. The surrogate cannot cradle the baby or communicate monkey sounds and gestures. It cannot punish for misbehavior or attempt to break the infant's bodily attachment before it becomes a fixation. The entire group of animals separated from their mothers at birth and raised in individual wire cages, with or without surrogate, must be written off as potential breeding stock. Apparently their early social deprivation permanently impairs their ability to form effective relations with other monkeys whether the opportunity was offered to them in the second six months of life or in the second to the fifth year of life.

One may correctly assume that total social isolation, compared with the partial isolation in which these subjects were reared, would produce even more devastating effects on later personality development. Such disastrous effects have been reported in the rare cases of children who have been liberated after months or years of lonely confinement in a darkened room. We have submitted a few monkeys to total isolation. Our purpose was to establish the maximum of social deprivation that would allow survival and also to determine whether or not there is a critical period in which social deprivation may have irreversible effects.

In our first study a male and female were housed alone from birth for a period of two years, each one in its own cubicle with solid walls. Their behavior could be observed through one-way vision screens and tested by remote control. The animals adapted to solid food slowly, but they had normal weight and good coats when they were removed from the isolation boxes at the end of two years. Throughout this period neither animal had seen any living being other than itself.

They responded to their liberation by the crouching posture with which monkeys typically react to extreme threat. When placed together, each one crouched and made no further response to the other. Paired with younger monkeys from the group raised in partial isolation, they froze or fled when approached and made no effort to defend themselves from aggressive assaults. After another two years, in which they were kept together in a single large cage in the colony room, they showed the same abnormal fear of the sight or sound of other monkeys.

We are now engaged in studying the effects of six months of total social isolation. The first pair of monkeys, both males, has been out of isolation for eight months. They are housed, each monkey in its own cage, in racks with other monkeys of their age that were raised in the partial isolation of individual wire cages. For 20 minutes a day, five days a week they are tested with a pair of these monkeys in the "playroom" of the laboratory. This room we designed to stimulate the young monkeys to a maximum of activity. It was not until the 12th and 27th week respectively that the two totally deprived monkeys began to move and climb about. They now circulate freely but not as actively as the control animals. Although frequently attacked by the controls, neither one has attempted to defend itself or fight back; they either accept abuse or flee. One must be characterized as extremely disturbed and almost devoid of social behavior. The other resembles a normal two-month-old rhesus infant in its play and social behavior, and the indications are that it will never be able to make mature contacts with its peers.

A considerably more hopeful prognosis is indicated for two groups of four monkeys raised in total isolation for the much shorter period of 80 days. In their cubicles these animals had the contact comfort of a cloth-covered surrogate. They were deficient in social behavior during the first test periods in the playroom.But they made rapid gains; now, eight months later, we rate them as "almost normal" in play, defense and sex behavior. At least seven of the eight seem to bear no permanent scars as the result of early isolation.

Our first few experiments in the total isolation of these animals would thus appear to have bracketed what may be the critical period of development during which social experience is necessary for normal behavior in later life. We have additional experiments in progress, involving a second pair that will have been isolated for six months and a first pair that will have been isolated for a full year. The indications are that six months of isolation will render the animals permanently inadequate. Since the rhesus monkey is more mature than the human infant at birth and grows four times more rapidly, this is equivalent to two or three years for the human child. On the other hand, there is reason to believe that the effects of shorter periods of early isolation, perhaps 60 to 90 days or even more, are clearly reversible. This would be equivalent to about six months in the development of the human infant. The time probably varies with the individual and with the experiences to which it is exposed once it is removed from isolation. Beyond a brief period of neonatal grace, however, the evidence suggests that every additional week or month of social deprivation increasingly imperils social development in the rhesus monkey. Case studies of children reared in impersonal institutions or in homes with indifferent mothers or nurses show a frightening comparability. The child may remain relatively unharmed through the first six months of life. But from this time on the damage is progressive and cumulative. By one year of age he may sustain enduring emotional scars and by two years many children have reached the point of no return.

In all of these experiments in partial and total isolation, whether unwitting or deliberate, our animals were deprived of the company of their peers as well as of their mothers. We accordingly undertook a series of experiments designed to distinguish and compare the roles of mother-infant and infant-infant relations in the maturation of rhesus monkey behavior. Our most privileged subjects are two groups of four monkeys each, now two years old, that were raised with their mothers during the first 18 and 21 months respectively and with peers from the first weeks. Each mother-infant pair occupied a large cage that gave the infant access to one cell of a four-unit playpen. By removing the screens between the playpens we enabled the infants to play together in pairs or as foursomes during scheduled observation periods each day. In parallel with these two groups we raised another group of four in a playpen setup without their mothers but with a terry cloth surrogate in each home cage.

From the time the mothers let them leave their home cages, after 20 or 30 days, the mothered infants entered into more lively and consistent relations with one another than did the four motherless ones. Their behavior evolved more rapidly through the sequence of increasingly complex play patterns that reflects the maturation and learning of the infant monkey and is observed in a community of normal infants. The older they grew and the more complex the play platterns became, the greater became the observable difference between the mothered and the motherless monkeys. Now, at the end of the second year, the 12 animals are living together in one playpen setup, with each original group occupying one living cage and its

adjoining playpen. All are observed in daily interaction without the dividing panels. The early differences between them have all but disappeared. Seven of the eight mothered animals engage in normal sexual activity and assume correct posture. The deviant is a male, and this animal was the social reject in its all-male group of four. Of the two motherless males, one has recently achieved full adult sexual posture and the other is approaching it. The two motherless females appear normal, but it remains to be seen whether or not their maternal behavior will reflect their lack of mothering.

Observation of infants with their mothers suggests reasons for the differences in the early social and sexual behavior of these playpen groups. From early in life on the infant monkey shows a strong tendency to imitate its mother; this responding to another monkey's behavior carries over to interaction with its peers. It is apparent also that sexual activity is stimulated by the mother's grooming of the infant. Finally, as the mother begins occasionally to reject its offspring in the third or fourth month, the infant is propelled into closer relations with its peers. These observations underlie the self-evident fact that the mother-infant relation plays a positive role in the normal development of the infant-infant and heterosexual relations of the young monkey.

That the mother-infant relation can also play a disruptive role was demonstrated in another experiment. Four females that had been raised in the partial isolation of individual wire cages—and successfully impregnated in spite of the inadequacy of their sexual behavior—delivered infants within three weeks of one another. This made it possible to set up a playpen group composed of these "motherless" mothers and their infants. The maternal behavior of all four mothers was completely abnormal, ranging from indifference to outright abuse. Whereas it usually requires more than one person to separate an infant from its mother, these mothers paid no attention when their infants were removed from the cages for the hand-feeding necessitated by the mothers' refusal to nurse. Two of the mothers did eventually permit fairly frequent nursing, but their apparently closer maternal relations were accompanied by more violent abuse. The infants were persistent in seeking contact with their mothers and climbed on their backs when they were repulsed at the breast. In play with one another during the first six months, the infants were close to the normally mothered animals in maturity of play, but they played less. In sexual activity, however, they were far more precocious. During the eight months since they have been separated from their mothers, they have exhibited more aggression and day-to-day variability in their behavior than have the members of other playpen groups. The two male offspring of the most most abusive mothers have become disinterested in the female and occupy the subordinate position in all activities.

More study of more babies from motherless mothers is needed to determine whether or not the interrelations that characterize this pilot group will characterize others of the same composition. There is no question about the motherless mothers themselves. The aberration of their maternal behavior would have ensured the early demise of their infants outside the laboratory. As for the infants, the extremes of sexuality and aggressiveness observed in their behavior evoke all too vivid parallels in the behavior of disturbed human children and adolescents in psychiatric clinics and institutions for delinquents.

Another pilot experiment has shown that even normal mothering is not enough to produce socially adequate offspring. We isolated two infants in the exclusive company of their mothers to the age of seven months and then brought the mother-infant pairs together in a playpen unit. The female infant took full advantage of the play apparatus provided, but in three months the male was never seen to leave its home cage, and its mother would not permit the female to come within arm's reach. Social interaction of the infants was limited to an occasional exchange of tentative threats. For the past two months they have been separated from their mothers, housed in in-dividual cages and brought together in the playroom for 15 minutes each day. In this normally stimulating environment they have so far shown no disposition to play together. Next to the infants that have been raised in total isolation, these are the most retarded of the infants tested in the playroom.

It is to the play-exciting stimulus of the playroom that we owe the unexpected outcome of our most suggestive experiment. The room is a relatively spacious one, with an eight-foot ceiling and 40 square feet of floor space. It is equipped with movable and stationary toys and a wealth of climbing devices, including an artificial tree, a ladder and a burlap-covered climbing ramp that leads to a platform. Our purpose in constructing the playroom was to provide the monkeys with opportunities to move about in the three-dimensional world to which, as arboreal animals, they are much more highly adapted than man. To assess the effects of different histories of early social experience we customarily turn the animals loose in the room in groups of four for regularly scheduled periods of observation each day.

The opportunities afforded by the playroom were most fully exploited by two groups of four infants that otherwise spent their days housed alone in their cages with a cloth surrogate. In terms of "mothering," therefore, these monkeys were most closely comparable to the four that were raised with surrogates in the playpen situation. These animals were released in the playroom for 20 minutes a day from the first month of life through the 11th, in the case of one group, and through the second year in the case of the other. In contrast with all the groups observed in the playroom, therefore, they did their "growing up" in this environment. Even though their exposure to the room and to one another was limited to 20 minutes a day, they enacted with great spirit the entire growth pattern of rhesus-monkey play behavior.

They began by exploring the room and each other. Gradually over the next two or three months they developed a game of rough-and-tumble play, with jumping, scuffling, wrestling, hair-pulling and a little nipping, but with no real damage, and then an associated game of flight and pursuit in which the participants are alternately the threateners and the threatened. While these group activities evolved, so did the capacity for individual play exploits, with the animals running, leaping, swinging and climbing, heedless of one another and apparently caught up in the sheer joy of action. As their skill and strength grew, their social play involved shorter but brisker episodes of free-for-all action, with longer chases between bouts. Subsequently they developed an even more complex pattern of violent activity, performed with blinding speed and integrating all objects, animate and inanimate, in the room. Along with social play, and possibly as a result or by-product, they began to exhibit sexual posturing—immature and fleeting in the first six months and more frequent and adult in form by the end of the year. The differences in play activity that distinguish males and females became evident in the first two or three months, with the females threatening and initiating rough contact far less frequently than the males and withdrawing from threats and approaches far more frequently.

Thus in spite of the relatively limited opportunity for contact afforded by their daily schedule, all the individuals in these two groups developed effective infant-infant play relations. Those observed into the second year have shown the full repertory of adult sexual behavior. At the same chronological age these motherless monkeys have attained as full a maturity in these respects as the infants raised with their mothers in the playpen.

Another group of four motherless animals raised together in a single large cage from the age of two weeks is yielding similar evidence of the effectiveness of the infant-infant affectional bond. During their first two months these animals spent much of their time clinging together, each animal clutching the back of the one just ahead of it in "choo-choo" fashion. They moved about as a group of three or four; when one of them broke away, it was soon clutched by another to form the nucleus of a new line. In the playroom the choo-choo linkage gave way to individual exploratory expeditions. During periods of observation, whether in their home cage or in the playroom, these animals have consistently scored lower in play activity than the most playful groups. We think this is explained, however, by the fact that they were able to spread their play over a 24-hour period. At the age of one year they live amicably together. In sex behavior they are more mature than the mother-raised playpen babies. No member of the group shows any sign of damage by mother-deprivation.

Our observations of the three groups of motherless infants raised in close association with one another therefore indicate that opportunity for optimal infant-infant interaction may compensate for lack of mothering. This is true at least in so far as infant-infant and sexual relations are concerned. Whether or not maternal behavior or later social adjustment will be affected remains to be seen.

Of course research on nonhuman animals, even monkeys, will never resolve the baffling complex roles of various kinds of early experience in the development of human personality. It is clear, however, that important theoretical and practical questions in this realm of interest can be resolved by the use of monkeys. The close behavioral resemblance of our disturbed infants to disturbed human beings gives us the confidence that we are working with significant variables and the hope that we can point the way to reducing the toll of psychosocial trauma in human society.

A Comparison of the Ecology and Behavior of Monkeys and Apes

Irven DeVore

From *Classification and Human Evolution.* Viking Fund Publications in Anthropology, No. 7, pp. 301–319. Copyright © 1963, Wenner-Gren Foundation for Anthropological Research, later transferred to Aldine Publishing Company. By permission of the author, the publisher, and the copyright holder.

Comparisons of nonhuman primates have traditionally contrasted the behavior patterns of New World and Old World monkeys. The Platyrrhines of the New World are said to live in loosely organized social groups in which individuals are rarely aggressive and dominance behavior almost absent. The social group of the Old World Catarrhines is described as more rigidly organized by social hierarchies, based on dominance-oriented behavior and frequent fighting among adult males. To the extent that this distinction is valid, the behavioral differences being compared are not those between New and Old World monkeys, but between arboreal and terrestrial species. The only systematic field studies of New World monkeys have been on the howler monkey, *Alouatta palliata,* and Carpenter's brief observations on spider monkeys, *Ateles geoffroyi.* Both of these species are highly specialized, morphologically and behaviorally, for living in the tall trees of the South American jungle. They are seldom seen in the lower branches of trees and almost never come to the ground. On the other hand, behavioral studies of Old World monkeys, principally those of Zuckerman and Carpenter, had until recently included only species in the baboon-macaque group. In both morphology and behavior the baboon-macaques are more terrestrially adapted than any other monkey or ape.

Comparisons between monkey and ape behavior have also been difficult, since Carpenter's gibbon study is the only long term study of an ape that has previously been available. This Asiatic brachiator is as highly specialized for arboreal life as the baboon-macaques are for life on the ground. If the monkeys and apes are arranged along a continuum with those that are terrestrially adapted at one pole and those with specialized arboreal adaptations at the other (Fig. 1), it is clear that long-term naturalistic observations have been confined almost entirely to species lying at the two extremes and that little has been known of the majority of species falling somewhere in between. The species shown in Figure 1 are those for which some field data are available, and the intention is to suggest only the broad outlines of adapta-

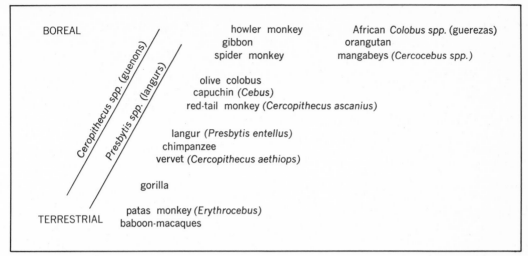

Fig. 1   Schematic representation of selected species of monkeys and apes along a continuum of relative adaptation to terrestrial or arboreal life.

tion to life on the ground or in the trees.

Napier has discussed the habitats of monkeys in detail. In brief, spider monkeys, howler monkeys, gibbons, orangutans, and most species of colobus and mangabeys live in the higher levels of mature, tropical forests. The olive colobus lives by preference in the lower forest level, seldom higher than twenty feet from the ground, yet not descending to the ground; South American capuchin and African red-tail monkeys, though primarily tree dwellers, may also come to the ground to feed. Langurs, vervets, *Cercopithecus l'hoesti,* and chimpanzees seem equally at home on the ground or in trees; and gorillas, patas monkeys, baboons, and macaques are clearly adapted to terrestrial life. Field studies of nonhuman primates are expanding at a rapid rate, with more than fifty workers currently engaged in field research, and in a few years it will be possible to refine greatly the provisional conclusions discussed here. In the following pages the available evidence on home range, intergroup relations, population density, and social behavior is reviewed with respect to adaptation and taxonomy.

Home Range

The size of the area which an organized group of animals customarily occupies, its "home range," varies widely among the primates. Current studies have revealed a high correlation between the size of home range and the degree to which a species is adapted to life on the ground—the more terrestrial the species, the larger its home range (Table 1). Arboreal gibbons occupy a range of only about one tenth of a square mile, and a group of howler monkeys range over about one half of a square mile or less of forest. Since the average gibbon group numbers only four and howler groups average about seventeen, the amount of range needed to support an equivalent amount of body weight in each species is comparable. These home ranges are small, however, by comparison to the home ranges of langur groups, *Presbytis entellus,* studied by Jay (unpub. ms.). Langurs, which frequently feed on the forest floor and raid open fields, range over an average area of three square miles in a year—even though their average group size (twenty-five) is much the same as howler monkeys.

Terrestrial species like the mountain gorilla and the baboon occupy much larger home ranges. Schaller and Emlen found that gorillas in the Virunga Volcanoes region of Albert National Park, Congo, have an average group size of seventeen, and customarily travel over an area of from ten to fifteen square miles during a year. An average troop of forty baboons, living on the East African

Table 1 Summary of available data on group size, population density, and home range for monkeys, apes, wolves, and human hunting groups living in relatively arid, open country

SPECIES	GROUPS		SAMPLE		POPULATION DENSITY, INDIV. PER SQ. MILE	GROUP RANGE, SQ. MILES	SOURCE
	MEAN	EXTREME	POPU-LATION	NO. OF GROUPS			
Orangutan	3	2–5	28	10			Schaller 1961
Gibbon	4	2–6	93	21	11	.1	Carpenter 1940
Black & white colobus	13			1		.06	Ullrich 1961
Olive colobus	12	6–20					Booth 1957
Spider	12	3–17	181	19			Carpenter 1935
Cebidae	15?	5–30					Carpenter 1958
Howler							
1933 census	17	4–35	489	28	82	.5	Carpenter 1934
1951 census	8	2–17	239	30	40		Collias & Southwick 1952
1959 census	18.5	3–45	814	44	136		Carpenter 1962
Langur	25	5–120	665	29	12	3	Jay unpub. ms.
Mountain gorilla							
(Virunga Volcanoes)	17	5–30	169	10	3	10–15	Schaller 1963
Macaca mulata							
temples	42	16–78	629	15			Southwick 1961a
forest	50+	32–68	334	7			Southwick 1961b
M. radiata	32		65	2			Nolte 1955
M. assamensis	19		38	2			Carpenter 1958
Baboon							
Nairobi Park	42	12–87	374	9	10	15	DeVore & Washburn
Amboseli	80	13–185	1203	15			(in press)
Human							Shapera 1930; D.
bushman	20				.03	440–1250	Clark pers. comm.
aborigine	35				.08	100–750	Steward 1936
Wolf	12	9–25+				260–1900	Stebler 1944; Murie 1944

savanna in the Royal Nairobi National Park, covers an area of about fifteen square miles during a year. In general, it is clear that a terrestrial adaptation implies a larger annual range; a baboon troop's range is 150 times as large as that of a gibbon group. Even if these figures are corrected to allow for the greater combined body weight of the individuals in a baboon troop, the baboon home range is still at least five times as large as that of gibbons. It is frequently stated that the habitat of arboreal monkeys is actually three-dimensional, and that a vertical dimension must be added

to horizontal distances traveled before the true size of a group's range can be accurately determined. Many arboreal species, however, seldom come to the ground, or even to the lower levels of the forest. Howler monkeys are largely confined to the upper levels of primary forest, avoiding secondary growth and scrub forest; gibbons ordinarily stay just beneath the uppermost forest canopy; and most species of African colobus monkeys appear to stay above the shrub layer of primary forest. Limited to arboreal pathways through the forest, such species are far less free to exploit an area completely than are primates that do not hesitate to descend to the ground. In effect these arboreal species occupy a two-dimensional area above the forest floor. Some species which exploit both the arboreal and terrestrial areas of their range with facility, such as South American capuchin monkeys, Indian langurs, some African *Cercopithecus spp.,* and probably chimpanzees, may be accurately described as living in a "three-dimensional range." Even terrestrial species such as baboons and macaques spend much of their lives in trees, returning to them to sleep each evening and feeding frequently in them at certain seasons.

The ability to exploit both forested and open savanna habitats has had distinct advantages for the baboon-macaque group, enabling it to spread throughout the Old World tropics with very little speciation. Similarly, the most ground-living Indian langur, *Presbytis entellus,* and the most ground-living *Cercopithecus* monkey, *C. aethiops,* have wider distributions than the other species in their respective genera. In this sense the home range of an organized group of monkeys can be said to be proportional to the geographic distribution of the species. However, this is not always true. The gelada baboon, *Theropithecus gelada,* and the gorilla are geographically restricted, while the gibbon is found throughout Southern Asia. Adaptation of the species to local conditions, the interference of human activities, and competition from other species may explain these contrary examples. Even so, the terrestrial gorilla represents a single, widely separated species while gibbons are divided into a number of well-defined species.

The ability to cross natural barriers and occupy a diversity of environments is reflected in both the size of a group's home range and the amount of speciation that has occurred within its geographic range. This is particularly true when man is considered with the other primates. Speech, tools, and an emphasis on hunting have so altered man's adaptation that direct comparisons are difficult, but if hunter-gatherers living in savanna country with a stone-age technology are

selected for comparison, an immense increase in the size of the home range is apparent. Although detailed studies are lacking, the home ranges of two African bushman groups were estimated as 440 and 1250 square miles. An average bushman band would number only about 20, or half the size of a baboon troop with a home range of 15 square miles. In Australia, depending on the food resources in a particular area, a band of aborigines has a home range of between 100 and 750 square miles; an average band numbers about 35. Many hunter-gatherer ranges average 100 to 150 square miles, and even the smallest are much larger than the biggest home ranges described for non-human primates. The land area it is necessary for human hunters to control is more comparable to that of group-living predators than it is to that of monkeys and apes. The home range of wolf packs, for example, is between 260 and 1900 square miles. Consistent hunting rapidly depletes the available game in a small area, and in the course of human evolution an immense increase in the size of home range would have had to develop concomitantly with the development of hunting.

Core Area and Territoriality

Within the home range of some animal groups is a locus of intensive occupation, or several such loci separated from each other by areas that are infrequently traversed. These loci, which have been called "core areas," are connected by traditional pathways. A core area for a baboon or langur troop, for example, includes sleeping trees, water, refuge sites, and food sources. Troops of baboons or langurs concentrate their activities in one core area for several days or weeks, then shift to another. Most of a baboon troop's home range is seldom entered except during troop movement from one of these core areas to another; a troop in Nairobi Park with a home range of just over fifteen square miles primarily occupied only three core areas whose combined size was only three square miles. Except that baboon range and core areas are larger, this description would apply equally well to langurs or, for that matter, to the coati groups, *Nasua narica,* studied by Kaufmann.

The home ranges of neighboring baboon troops overlap extensively, but the *core areas* of a troop very rarely overlap with those of another troop. The distinction between a group's home range and the core areas within that range becomes important when the question of territorial defense is considered. Carpenter's review of territoriality in vertebrates concludes that "... on the basis of available data territoriality is as characteristic of primates' behavior as it is of other vertebrates." His description of "territory" in another review, however, confirms to what has here been described as "home range," following the distinction between "home range" and "territory" (as a defended part of the home range) made by Burt and others. Groups of baboons, langurs, and gorillas are frequently in intimate contact with neighboring groups of the same species; yet intergroup aggression was not observed in langurs, tension between baboon troops is rare, and gorilla males only occasionally show aggression toward a strange group. Clearly, no definite areal boundaries are defended against groups of conspecifics in these three species. On the other hand, organized groups of these species occupy distinct home ranges, and the fact that a strange baboon troop, for example, is rarely in the core area of another troop indicates that there are spacing mechanisms which ordinarily separate organized groups from each other. Different groups are kept apart, however, not so much by overt aggression and fighting at territorial boundaries, as by the daily routine of a monkey group in its own range, by the rigid social boundaries of organized groups in many monkey species, and, in some species, by loud vocalizations.

Intimate knowledge of the area encompassed in a group's home range is demonstrably advantageous to the group's survival. Knowledge of escape routes from predators, safe refuge sites and sleeping trees, and potential food sources combine to channel a group's activities into daily routines and seasonally patterned movements within a circumscribed area. Beyond the limits of a group's usual range lie unknown dangers and undiscovered food sources, and a baboon troop at the edge of its home range is nervous and ill at ease.

Organization of Primate Groups

In addition to the spacing effect of relatively discrete home ranges, most monkeys and some apes live in organized groups which do not easily admit strangers. Gibbons, howler monkeys, langurs, baboons, and macaques all live in such "closed societies." Although Carpenter described numerous instances of individuals moving from one group to another in his study of the rhesus colony transplanted to Cayo Santiago, Altmann's later study revealed that almost no individuals changed troops during a two-year period. In retrospect it seems likely that when Carpenter first studied the rhesus colony the six heterosexual groups he described were composed of comparative strangers, and that organized troops had not yet had a chance to stabilize. During Altmann's study approximately the same number of animals were divided into two highly stable troops with almost no individuals' changing troop membership—despite the crowded conditions on the island, where natural spacing mechanisms probably could not operate normally.

Studies by the Japan Monkey Center on Japanese macaques, *Macaca fuscata,* confirm the fact that macaque societies are closed groups. During more than 1400 hours of observations on more than twenty-five baboon troops, only two individuals changed to new troops. Jay found that langur troops were similarly conservative, but among langurs individual males or small groups of males may live apart from organized troops. Not all monkey and ape groups have such impermeable social boundaries. Some gorilla groups, for example, can be described as somewhat open or "fluid."

Although different gorilla groups vary considerably in the extent to which they accept individuals into the group, some of them have a high turn-over of adult males. During a twelve-month study period, some dominant adult males remained with a group of females and young throughout, but other adult males frequently left one group, and either led a solitary existence or joined another group. Males who join a group have access to sexually receptive females, and group-living males usually make little or no attempt to repel them. This "relaxed attitude" toward non-group members is reflected in intergroup relations. Schaller and Emlen report that "seven different groups were seen in one small section of forest during the period of study." In contrast, it is doubtful if any adult male baboon or macaque can join a new troop without some fighting with the dominant males of the troop.

At present there are not enough detailed studies of the social behavior of monkeys and apes to determine whether organized groups in most species are relatively closed, as in baboons, or relatively open, as in gorillas. A recent study of hamadryas baboons in Ethiopia by Kummer and Kurt, for example, revealed an altogether different kind of group structure. The hamadryas were organized into small groups of from one to four, rarely as many as nine, females and their offspring accompanying only one adult male. These "one-male groups" aggregated into sleeping parties each night which numbered as many as 750 individuals, but during the day the small, one-male units foraged independently, and membership in them remained constant during the observation period, while the number of individuals gathering at sleeping places fluctuated constantly. Kortlandt's observations of chimpanzees indicate still a different group structure, with anywhere from one to thirty individuals gathered together at one time.

Intergroup Vocalizations

Loud vocalizations seem to aid in spacing groups of some species. Carpenter has sug-gested that "vocal battles" often substitute for physical aggression in howler monkeys and gibbons. Jay found that langurs also give resounding "whoops" which carry long distances and tend to keep langur troops apart; Ullrich found the same is true of black and white colobus. Since these loud cries invariably begin at dawn, when no other group is in sight, and often continue as the group leaves its sleeping place and moves to a feeding area, it seems likely that such vocalizations serve more often to identify the *location* of the troop than to issue a challenge to neighboring troops. Altmann's following observations of howling monkeys support this view:

> The morning roar, despite its spectacular auditory aspects, was not accompanied by any comparable burst of physical activity. While giving the vocalization, the male stood on four feet or sat. Occasionally, he fed between roars . . . . The vocalizations that are given by the males at sunrise are essentially the same as those that are given during territorial disputes, suggesting that these morning howls serve as a "proclamation" of an occupied area.

By advertising its position the troop reduces the likelihood that it will meet a neighboring troop. Such location cries can thereby function as spacing mechanisms, but usually without the directly combative connotation which "vocal battle" suggests. When a gibbon or howler group approaches another group, loud vocalizations increase. Two groups of gibbons, however, will mingle without aggression after the period of vocalizing has passed, and Jay saw langur troops frequently come together without aggression.

Loud vocalizations of the sort found in gibbons, howlers, colobus and langurs are conspicuously absent in baboons and macaques. The situation on the African savanna, where visibility frequently extends for hundreds or even thousands of yards, is very different from the very limited visibility of dense forests. Baboon ranges are large in Nairobi Park, and troops seldom come near each other. Adjustments in the direction of troop movement can easily be made by sight alone. Even when baboon troops do come together, as they frequently did in that part of the Amboseli Reserve where food and water sources were restricted, no intergroup aggression was observed. In view of the relatively high degree of dominant and aggressive behavior typical of baboons, the fact that intertroop relations are pacific may seem contradictory. If defense of territory is not thought of as fundamental in the behavior pattern of primates, however, the peaceful coexistence of neighboring troops is not inconsistent with a high level of agonistic and dominance behavior between individuals within the group.

Loud vocalizations, as a means of keeping groups apart when they are not in visual contact, are also absent in the gorilla. When two groups come together, or in the presence of man, adult males may give dramatic intimidation gestures (abrupt charges, chest beating, etc.) While some of these gestures may be accompanied by loud vocalizations, their impact is primarily visual. As in the baboons and macaques, visual communication tends to substitute for loud vocalizations, and it is suggested that methods of intergroup communication correlate with the degree to which a species is arboreal or terrestrial. Vocal expression as a spacing mechanism is very important in gibbons and howler monkeys, less important among langurs, and virtually absent in the gorilla, the baboons, and the macaques. It is also reasonable to suppose that vocalizations are more important in intragroup behavior in arboreal species, where foliage interferes with coordination of group activity, than they ordinarily are in terrestrial species. Baboon studies to date have concentrated on troops living in open areas, where troop members are usually in constant visual contact. If baboons become separated from the troop, however, contact is reestablished by vocalizations, and when the troop is feeding in dense vegetation soft vocalizations (e.g., low grunting) are apparently more frequent, and may serve to maintain contact between troop members. Many baboons live in forests and a study of these forest-living baboons could definitely

determine whether vocal behavior is more frequent in this habitat than it is on the open plains.

Population Density

Pitelka has pointed out that the fundamental importance of territoriality lies not in the behavior, such as overt defense, by which an area becomes identified with an individual or group, but in the degree to which the area is used exclusively; that is, functionally, a territory is primarily an ecological, not a behavioral, phenomenon. Recent field studies indicate that if territoriality can be ascribed to most monkeys and apes it is in this more general, functional meaning of the term only. As a means of distributing the population in an available habitat, the core area of a nonhuman primate group's home range may serve the same function as literal, territorial defense does in some vertebrate species. At the human, hunter-gatherer level this is much less true. Although a hunting band may have core areas, around water holes for example, the band tends to consider most or all of its home range an exclusive possession. Human hunting activities require the use of large areas, and the hunting range is usually protected from unwarranted use by strangers. One of the important differences between home ranges which overlap and the exclusive possession of a range is reflected in the population density of the species. Although a howler monkey group ranges over about .5 of a square mile, the 28 troops counted in 1933 could not have exclusively possessed more than an average .2 of a square mile per group; in 1959 the average per group could have been no higher than .136 of a square mile. In Kenya, about 50 per cent of a baboon troop's home range overlaps with that of adjacent troops, and a troop would seldom possess more than one square mile of its range exclusively. One result of this extensive overlapping is that the population density of the nonhuman primates is far higher than would be expected from a description of home range sizes alone (Table 1).

The population density of howler monkeys

on Barro Colorado Island in 1959 was 136 individuals per square mile. Terrestrial species like baboons and gorillas have much lower population densities (10 and 3 per square mile), but they are nevertheless far more densely populated than many hunter-gatherers, who average only .03 to .08 per square mile in savanna country. That hunting man, like other large, group-living carnivores, will inevitably have a lower population density than the other primates can be illustrated by the numbers of lions in Nairobi Park. This area of approximately 40 square miles supports a baboon population of nearly 400, but it supports an average of only 14 lions (extremes: 4–30—i.e., 4 to 30 lions).

In summary, all monkeys studied to date live in organized groups whose membership is conservative and from which strangers are repelled. These groups occupy home ranges which may overlap extensively with those of neighboring groups, but which contain core areas where neighboring groups seldom penetrate. Rather than territorial defense of definite boundaries, monkey groups are spaced by daily routine, tradition, membership in a discrete social group, and the location of adjacent groups. Among the apes these same generalizations would seem to hold for gibbons, but they are much less true of gorillas, and, probably orangutans and chimpanzees. The trend toward increasing size of the home range, however, from the very small range of arboreal species to moderately large ranges in terrestrial species, would appear to be true of all monkeys and apes. Means of identifying the position of adjacent groups shifts from loud vocalizations in arboreal species to visual signals in terrestrial ones. Man exemplifies his terrestrial adaptation in his enormously increased home range, his lower population density, and in his reliance on vision in the identification of neighboring groups.

Group Size

Mention has already been made of the average size of the social group in several species of primates; available data on group size are summarized in Table 1. When the size of the social group is compared to the degree of arboreal or terrestrial adaptation of the species, a trend toward larger groups in the terrestrial species is apparent, in both Old and New World monkeys and among the apes. Although there are no adequate data for the orangutan, the largest group ever reported is five, and the average size of a gibbon troop is four. Schaller found that the average gorilla group was seventeen, temporarily as large as thirty, and Kortlandt saw as many as thirty chimpanzees together in his study area. The average size of monkey troops varies from 20 or less in the olive colobus, spider, howler, and *Cebidae* group to an average of 25 (but as large as 120) in langurs, and an average of from 40 to 80 in the baboons and macaques (with some troops as large as 200). Present observations suggest three central grouping tendencies in monkeys and apes: five or less for the gibbon and orangutan; from twelve to twenty in arboreal monkeys and the gorilla; and fifty or more in baboons and macaques. This small sample may be misleading, but it is clear at present that, in addition to having a larger home range and lower population density, terrestrial monkeys and apes live in larger organized groups.

Sexual Dimorphism and Dominance

Field studies of monkeys indicate that dominance behavior, especially of the adult male, is both more frequent and more intense in ground-living monkeys than in other species. This increase in dominance behavior is accompanied by an increase in sexual dimorphism, particularly in those morphological features which equip the adult male for effective fighting—larger body size, heavier temporal muscles, larger canine teeth, etc. If the apes are compared with respect to sexual dimorphism, there is a clear trend toward increasing sexual dimorphism from the arboreal gibbon, where the sexes are practically indistinguishable, to the chimpanzee, in which the male is appreciably more robust, to the gorilla, where sexual dimorphism is greatest. Only the orangutan is an exception. The trend toward increased sexual dimorphism in terrestrial species of monkeys is also apparent. Some male characteristics, such as the hyoid bone in howler monkeys and the nose of the proboscis monkey, are more pronounced in arboreal species, but morphological adaptations for *fighting* and *defense* are clearly correlated with adaptation to the ground. The various baboons and macaques all illustrate this tendency. Among *Cercopithecus* species sexual dimorphism is pronounced in *C. aethiops* and the patas monkey (a species closely related to *Cercopithecus*) and decreases in the more arboreal forms.

The trend toward increased fighting ability in the male of terrestrial species is primarily an adaptation for defense of the group. Zuckerman's account of baboon behavior would indicate that the acquisition and defense of "harems," and concomitant fighting among the males, places a high premium on aggressiveness and fighting ability in intragroup behavior. Behavioral observations on confined animals can be very misleading, however, and no field study of baboons has found that sexual jealousy or fighting is frequent in free-ranging troops. Observations of many baboon troops in close association indicate that intertroop agression is very rare and that males do not try to defend an area from encroachment by another troop (although baboons were seen trying to keep vervet monkeys away from a fruit tree). The fact that hundreds of hamadryas may gather at one sleeping site would indicate that interindividual tolerance is high in this baboon species as well. The intergroup fighting of rhesus which Carpenter observed on Cayo Santiago was probably aggravated by unsettled conditions on the island. One index of these conditions is that more infants were killed than were born during his period of study.

Life on the ground exposes a species to far more predators than does life in the trees. Not only are there fewer potential predators in the trees, but also escape is relatively easy. By going beneath the canopy (to escape raptorial birds) or moving across small branches to an adjacent tree (to escape from felines),

arboreal species can easily avoid most predators except man. The ultimate safety of all nonhuman primates is in trees, and even the ground-living baboons and macaques will take refuge in trees or on cliffs at the approach of a predator (except man, from whom they escape by running).

Much of the day, however, baboons may be as far as a mile from safe refuge, and on the open plains a troop's only protection is the fighting ability of its adult males. The structure of the baboon troop, particularly when the animals are moving across an open area, surrounds the weaker females and juveniles with adult males. At the approach of a predator, the adult males are quickly interposed between the troop and the source of danger. The structure of a Japanese macaque troop is apparently identical, even though no predators have threatened the Takasakiyama group in many years. The ecological basis for sexual dimorphism in baboons has been described elsewhere. Because only the adult males are morphologically adapted for defense, a baboon troop has twice the reproductive capacity it would have, for the same number of individuals, if males and females were equally large. Adaptation for defense is accompanied by increased agonistic behavior within the troop, but intratroop *fighting* is rare. Stable dominance hierarchies minimize aggression among adults, and male baboons and macaques actively interfere in fights among females and juveniles.

Field studies of other monkeys indicate that intragroup aggressive and agonistic behavior decrease by the degree to which a species is adapted to arboreal life. Among langurs, where sexual dimorphism is less pronounced, females may threaten or attack adult males—behavior that is unparalleled in the baboon-macaques. Langurs are usually in or under trees, where escape is rapid and the need for males to defend the group is much less important. The same argument, with suitable qualifications, holds for the other, more arboreal monkeys. The sexes in the olive colobus, for example, are almost identical in size and form; this species is never seen on the ground. This does not imply that the male in other primary species has no protective role. Male colobus, vervets, and howlers have been seen taking direct action against potential predators, and the male in many species is prominent in giving defiant cries and/or alarm calls. With the possible exception of the gibbon, some measure of increased defensive action by adult males is a widespread primate pattern. The evidence does suggest, however, that increased predation pressure on the ground leads to increased morphological specialization in the male with accompanying changes in the behavior of individuals and the social organization of the troop. Although troops of arboreal monkeys may be widely scattered during feeding, a baboon or macaque troop is relatively compact. Some males may live apart from organized groups, either solitarily or in unisexual groups, in less terrestrial species (e.g., langurs), but we discovered no healthy baboons living outside a troop. Dominant adult males are the focal point for the other troop members in baboons, macaques, and gorillas. When the males eat, the troop eats; when the males move, the others follow. Compared to other monkey species: the baboon-macaques are most dominance-oriented; troop members are more dependent upon adult males and actively seek them out; and the social boundary of the troop is strong.

Behavior and Taxonomy

Species-specific behavior has been valuable in the classification of some vertebrate species, notably the distinct song patterns in birds. Spectrographic analyses of primate vocalizations will undoubtedly reveal specic differences in communication patterns, but these are only now being undertaken. Studies of social behavior in monkeys and apes have only begun, and no observations have yet been made in sufficient detail to permit close comparisons. Some general comparisons can be made, however, from studies recently completed.

The African baboons and the Asiatic macaques are very similar in both morphology and general adaptation. Both groups have forty-two chromosomes and their distribution does not overlap, suggesting that they are members of a single radiation of monkeys. Baboons, including drill, mandrill, hamadryas, and savanna forms (but excluding gelada) are probably all species within one genus, *Papio*. Comparisons between the social behavior of East African baboons and macaques (rhesus and Japanese macaques) have been made elsewhere. At all levels of behavior, from discrete gestures and vocalizations to over-all social structure, baboons and macaques are very much alike. Both groups have an elaborate, and comparable, repertoire of aggressive gestures. In social interactions, the same behavioral sequences occur: an animal who is threatened may redirect the aggression to a third party, or may "enlist the support" of a third party against the aggressor. If support is successfully enlisted, two or more animals then simultaneously threaten the original aggressor. Relations between the adults and the young of both groups are similar.

Play patterns in juvenile groups and the ontogeny of behavior follow the same course. Relationships within the adult dominance hierarchies, and the social structure of the troop are comparable. Some details of gesture and vocalization are certainly distinct, and there is a striking difference, for example, in the form and duration of copulation. Copulation in rhesus monkeys usually involves a series of mounts before ejaculation, as does copulation in the South African baboons ("chacma") studies by Hall, while a single mounting of only a few seconds' duration is typical of East African baboons. Details of gesture and vocalization during copulation also vary between the three groups. On the other hand, most of the behavioral repertoire seems so similar that an infant baboon raised in a macaque troop, or vice versa, would probably have little difficulty in leading the adult life of its adopted group. Behavioral observations clearly confirm the evidence of morphological similarity in this widespread group of monkeys. No other primate, except man, has spread so far with as little morphological change as the baboon-macaque group. With man, these monkeys share the ability to travel long distances, cross water, and live in a wide range of environmental conditions.

On the basis of the present, random studies of monkeys and apes, generalizations regarding trends in behavior must remain speculative, particularly since the majority of the studies are concentrated in the baboon-macaque group. Much more useful statements with regard to the adaptive significance of different behavioral and morphological patterns will be possible when field studies of several species within one genus have been undertaken. The *Cercopithecus* group presents a wide range of ecological adaptations, from swamp-adapted species like *C. talapoin,* through the many forest forms, the savanna-living *C. aethiops.* Forms closely related to the *Cercopithecus* group, Allen's swamp monkey, patas, and gelada, would further extend the basis of comparison. A study of patas or gelada monkeys would be particularly useful for cross-generic comparison with baboon and macaque behavior. Although Ullrich has made initial observations, no long term study of an African colobus species is yet available for comparison to Jay's study of Indian langurs. Booth's report that olive colobus do not ascend to the upper levels of forests even when these are not occupied by black colobus and red colobus indicates that even brief field observations of the behavior of sympatric primate species would be an immense aid in settling some of the persistent questions in primate taxonomy.

Summary

Field studies of monkeys and apes suggest a close correlation between ecological adaptation and the morphology and behavior of the species. All terrestrial forms occupy a larger home range, and, in monkeys, the geographic distribution of the species increases according to the degree of terrestrial adaptation. Many arboreal species use loud vocalizations in spacing troops; ground-living forms depend more on visual cues. A marked decrease in population density accompanies terrestrial adaptation. Man is part of this continuum, illustrating the extreme of terrestrial adaptation.

Morphological adaptation of the male for defense of the group is more prominent in ground-living species (except man, whose use of tools has removed the selective pressure for this kind of sexual dimorphism), and least prominent in most species that do not come to the ground. The dependence of the other troop members creates a male-focal social organization in terrestrial species. Dominance behavior is much more prominent in terrestrial monkeys, but actual fighting is rare. Terrestrial life and large adult males have not been accompanied by a comparable increase in dominance behavior in the gorilla, however, indicating that defense is more important than intragroup aggression in the development of sexual dimorphism in terrestrial primates. Man's way of life has preserved the division between the male and female roles in adult primate life, but cultural traditions have replaced biological differences in the reinforcement of this distinction.

Baboon Ecology and Human Evolution

Irven DeVore and S. L. Washburn

The ecology of baboons is of particular interest to the student of human evolution. Aside from man, these monkeys are the most successful ground-living primates, and their way of life gives some insight into the problems which confronted early man. We have been concerned with an attempt to reconstruct the evolution of human behavior by comparing the social behavior and ecology of baboons with that of living hunter-gatherer groups, and applying these comparisons to the archaeological evidence. The following description of baboon behavior and ecology is based on field data collected during 200 hours of observation by Washburn in the game reserves of Southern Rhodesia in 1955, and on more than 1200 hours of observations by both of us in Kenya game reserves during 1959. . . .

From *African Ecology and Human Evolution*. Viking Fund Publications in Anthropology, No. 36, pp. 335–367. Copyright © 1963, Wenner-Gren Foundation for Anthropological Research, later transferred to Aldine Publishing Company. By permission of the authors, the publisher, and the copyright holder.

Classification

The African baboons are very similar to the Asiatic ground monkeys, the macaques. Both groups have forty-two chromosomes, and their distribution does not overlap. The newborn are usually black, changing to brown. Skulls, teeth, and general physical structures are much the same. In social life and basic habits the two groups are very similar. In contrast to all other monkeys (both New and Old World), the macaques and baboons do most of their feeding on the ground. They can cross rivers and may live in dry areas, moving far from trees. Compared to other monkeys they are more aggressive and dominance-oriented, and their average troop size is considerably larger than any other species yet studied. These characteristics have enabled the baboon-macaques to occupy a much larger area than that of any other group of monkeys. It is an area very comparable to that utilized by *Homo* before the time of the last glaciation. Ground living, ability to cross water, an eclectic, varied diet, the protective troop, and aggressive males permitted the baboon-macaques to occupy this vast area with a minimum of speciation. The contrast in the number of species between ground-living and tree-living monkeys emphasizes this point. There are more species in the genus *Cercopithecus* in the African forests than among all the baboon-macaques from Cape Town to Gibraltar to Japan. There are more species of langurs in Southeast Asia alone than species of *Cercopithecus*. Further, the most ground-living of the langurs *(Presbytis entellus)* has the widest distribution, and the same is true for the most ground-living vervet *(C. aethiops)*. The taxonomic contrast between tree and ground monkeys is clearly seen in Ceylon where the island is occupied by one macaque, one dry country langur, and four forest forms. Apparently in Ceylon the rivers have been a major factor in isolating the langurs, but they do not form barriers for the macaques. The general relation between ecology and taxonomy in the monkeys appears clear: the more ground-living, the less speciation. There are many more adaptive niches in the forests than in the drier regions.

The men of the Middle Pleistocene, genus *Homo,* occupied the same range as the baboon-macaques but without speciation. Their way of life (based on tools, intelligence, walking, and hunting) was sufficiently more adaptable and effective so that a single species could occupy an area which ground monkeys could occupy only by evolving into at least a dozen species. This comparison gives some measure of the effectiveness of the human way of life, even at the level of Pekin and Ternifine man. Obviously, there is nothing to be gained by being dogmatic about the number of species of Middle Pleistocene men. Perhaps when many more specimens have been found it will be convenient to recognize two or three species, but the general form of this argument will still hold. There is no suggestion that any of the known fossil men (genus *Homo*) differ in size or form as much as a chacma baboon and a drill, or a crab-eating macaque and a pit-tail macaque. Even in its most primitive form the human way of life radically alters the relation of the organisms to the environment. As early as Middle Pleistocene times man could migrate over three continents without major morphological adaptation.

Australopithecus may have occupied an adaptive position midway in effectiveness between the ground monkeys and early *Homo*. Small-brained, bipedal toolmakers probably occupied larger areas than baboons, and without speciation. It is most unlikely that the East African and South African forms of *Australopithecus* are more than racially distinct. Robinson's suggestion that the jaws from Java called "Meganthropus" are closely allied to the australopithecoid from Swartkrans supports the notion that *Australopithecus* was already able to disperse widely with minimum biological change. The presence of small and large Australopithecoids in South Africa at the same time suggests that their adaptation was much less effective than that of *Homo*. It may be possible to reconstruct more of this stage in human evolution with a more thorough study of the ecology of baboons, and by contrasting their mode of adaptation to that of man. With this hope in mind we will now consider the ecology of baboons in East Africa. . . .

Troop Structure

Baboons are intensely social, and membership in a troop is a prerequisite for survival. Most of a baboon's life is spent within a few feet of other baboons. Baboon troops are closed social systems, individuals very rarely change to a new troop, and the troop regards any strange baboon with suspicion and hostility.

Within the troop, subgroups are based on age, sex, personal preferences, and dominance. When a troop is resting or feeding quietly, most of the adult members gather into small clusters, grooming each other or just sitting. Juveniles gather into groups of the same age and spend the day in these "play groups," eating, resting, and playing together. The most dominant adult males occupy the center of the troop, with the mothers and their young infants gathered around them, and the groups of young juveniles playing close by. These dominant males, and the small black infants near them, seem to be greatly attractive to the other troop members. During quiet periods the other troop members approach the adult males and the mothers, grooming them or sitting beside them. It is unnecessary for male baboons to herd the troop together; their presence alone insures that the other troop members will not be far away.

Around this nucleus of adult males, mothers, and young juveniles are the more peripheral members of the troop—the less dominant adult males, older juveniles, and pregnant or estrus females. Estrus females and their consorts usually stay at the periphery of the troop. Although the juvenile play groups will not wander far from the troop's center, peripheral adults may leave the troop for short periods. While the center of the troop moves slowly along, the adult and older juvenile (subadult) males and adult females sometimes move rapidly ahead to a new feeding spot. This may separate them from the rest of the troop by a quarter of a mile or more, and they may not rejoin the troop for thirty minutes or an hour. Although peripheral adult males may make such a side trip alone, or in small groups, others troop members will not leave the troop unless accompanied by the males. Healthy "solitary males" observed during the early part of our study later proved to be troop members who had left the troop for a short while.

A baboon troop that is in or under trees seems to have no particular organization, but when the troop moves out into the open plains a clear order of progression appears. Out in front of the troop move the boldest troop members—the less dominant adult males and the older juvenile males. Following them are other members of the troop's periphery, pregnant and estrus adult females and juveniles. Next, in the center, comes the nucleus of dominant adult males, females with infants, and young juveniles. The rear of the troop is a mirror image of its front, with adults and older juveniles following the nucleus and more adult males at the end. This order of progression is invariably followed when the troop is moving rapidly from one feeding area to another during the day, and to

its sleeping trees at dusk. A troop which is coming toward trees from the open plains approaches with particular caution. The tall trees in which baboons sleep are found only where the water table is near the surface, usually along a river or beside a pond. Vegetation is usually dense at the base of these trees, and it is in this undergrowth that predators often spend the day. The arrangement of the troop members when they are moving insures maximum protection for the infants and juveniles in the center of the troop. An approaching predator would first encounter the adult males on the troop's periphery, and then the adult males in the center, before it could reach defenseless troop members in the center.

Because they are in front of the troop by twenty to forty yards, the peripheral adult males are usually the first troop members to encounter a predator and give alarm calls. If a predator is sighted, all the adult males actively defend the troop. On one occasion we saw two dogs run up behind a troop, barking. The females and juveniles hurried ahead, but the males continued walking slowly. After a moment an irregular group of some twenty adult males was between the dogs and the rest of the troop. When a male turned on the dogs, they ran off. On another day we saw three cheetahs approach a troop of baboons. A single adult male stepped toward the cheetahs, gave a loud, defiant bark, and displayed his canine teeth; the cheetahs trotted away. If baboons come upon predators while en route to their sleeping trees, the troop stops and waits while the males in the center move ahead and find an alternate route (the young juveniles and mothers with infants stay behind with the peripheral adult males). Eventually the dominant males return, the original order of progression is re-established, and the troop proceeds along the new route. These behavior patterns assure that the females and young are protected in the troop's center.

The ultimate safety of a baboon troop is in the trees. When the troop is away from the trees, the adult males are very important in troop defense. We saw baboons near such predators as cheetahs, dogs, hyenas, and jackals, and usually the baboons seemed unconcerned—the other animals kept well away. Lions, however, will put a baboon troop to flight. From the safety of trees baboons bark and threaten lions but make no resistance to them on the ground. The behavior of baboons when near trees contrasts strikingly with their behavior on the open plains. If the troop is under trees, it will feed on the ground within thirty yards of predators, including lions.

Ecology and Sex Differences

The role of the adult male baboons as defenders of the troop has been described. This behavior is vital to the survival of the troop, and especially to the survival of the most helpless animals—females with new babies, small juveniles, and temporarily sick or injured individuals. Selection has favored the evolution of males which weigh more than twice as much as females, and the advantage to the troop of these large animals is clear, but it is not obvious why it is advantageous for the females to be small. The answer to the degree of sex differences appears to be that this is the optimum distribution of the biomass of the species. If the average adult male weighs approximately 75 pounds and the average adult female 30 pounds, each adult male requires more than twice the food of a female. If the food supply is a major factor in limiting the number of baboons, and if survival is more likely if there are many individuals, and if the roles of male and female are different—then selection will favor a sex difference in average body size which allows the largest number of animals compatible with the different social roles in the troop.

If selection favors males averaging 75 pounds, then it will favor females which are as much smaller as is compatible with their social roles. Since the females must travel the same distances, carry young, engage in sexual and competitive activities, there are limits to the degree of sexual differentiation, but the adaptive value of the difference is clear. For example, a troop of 36 baboons composed of

6 adult males and 12 adult females and their young (18 juveniles and infants) has a biomass of some 1,000 pounds. If the females also weighed 75 pounds each, 6 adult males and 6 adult females would alone total 900 pounds and have only one-half the reproductive potential of 6 adult males and 12 adult females. Because this would halve the number of young, it would greatly reduce the troop's chances of survival. Our data are not sufficiently detailed to analyze the actual distribution of biomass in the troops we observed, but our observations are compatible with the limited data on weights and the numbers of adult animals we saw. Viewing sexual differentiation in size as a function of the optimum distribution of biomass of the troop offers a way of understanding sexual dimorphism fundamentally different from the view which considers only sexual selection, dominance, and intratroop factors. Obviously, all factors should be considered. Adaptation is a complex process and results in compromises between the different selective pressures, but a distribution of biomass which doubles the reproductive potential of a species is so important that other factors may be mimimized.

The importance of sex difference in body size is reinforced by social behavior and the structure of the troop. As described earlier, some subadult and adult males are peripheral in the structure of the troop. They tend to be first, or last, when the troop moves. They are the most exposed to predators and are, biologically, the most expendable members of the troop. Interadult male antagonism results in a social order which both protects females and young and reduces feeding competition with females and young. Without altruism, the dominance behavior of a small number of males keeps a feeding space available to subordinate animals.

Juvenile play prepares the adults for their differential roles. Older juvenile females do not engage in the serious mock fighting which characterizes the play of older juvenile males. In this "play" the males learn to fight, and by the time the canine teeth have erupted and the temporal muscles grown to adult size they have had years of fighting practice. Play, social arrangement, and structural sexual dimorphism all supplement each other, producing a pattern in which the females and young are relatively more protected than the large males. Sexual differentiation must be seen as a part of this whole complex social pattern which leads to the survival of troops of baboons. . . .

Vegetable Foods

The diet of baboons living in the savanna of Nairobi Park can be divided into: the vegetable foods which provide forage for them throughout the year, seasonal fruits, insects, and the live animals which they occasionally catch and eat. Grass is the baboon's single most important food. In ten months of observations, not a single day passed in which baboons were not observed eating grass, and for many weeks during the dry season, grasses composed an estimated 90 per cent of their diet. The portion of the grass eaten varies with the season. When the tassels contain seeds, these are "harvested" by pulling the tassel through the closed palm or clenched teeth. Most often, however, baboons pull up the grass shoots in order to eat the thick, lower stem at the base of culm. Before eating the shoot, the dirt in the root system is carefully brushed away, and the roots themselves bitten off and discarded. By the middle of the dry season, when grass shoots are rare, baboons concentrate on digging up rhizomes—the thick, rootlike runners of the grasses which lie from two to four inches beneath the surface. Even after many weeks or months without rain, these rhizomes are still juicy, providing baboons with considerable water. The ability of baboons to shift to subsurface rhizomes and roots when surface vegetation is dry and sparse is one of their most important adaptations to the grasslands. It enables them to feed in an area which has been denuded of surface vegetation by the many ungulates with whom they share this habitat, and to find sufficient forage during long dry seasons. Digging these rhizomes out of the hard, dry soil with the fingers is a laborious task, and in the dry

season baboons spend longer hours getting their food than they do during the rest of the year. The use of a simple digging stick or sharp stone would enormously increase their efficiency in extracting this food from the ground, but no baboon was even seen trying to use a tool in this way or any other way.

There are numerous plants on the Nairobi plains which have large, tuberous roots or bulbs, and the baboons are very adept at finding the tiny stem or leaf which indicates that such a root lies below. It may take as long as twenty minutes for a baboon to uncover a large root, and require a hole as large as 25 inches long, 8 inches wide, and 15 inches deep. Where the water table is high, along the rivers in Nairobi Park and around the water holes at Amboseli Reserve, the lush grasses attract many animal species, including baboons. Not only is the grass more plentiful here during the dry season, but also the earth is softer and more easily dug and many water plants are found which grow nowhere else in the area. Baboons spend the majority of their time feeding in the grass near the water, but they will also wade into the shallow water to eat such plants as rushes and the buds of water lilies.

The baboon's usual diet is further extended by the various bushes, flowering plants, and shrubs of the savanna. In Nairobi Park they were seen eating the berries, buds, blossoms, and seed pods of such plants. Another very important source of food throughout the year is provided by the acacia trees. Probably the buds, blossoms, and beanlike seed pods of all acacias are eaten, but those of the fever trees (*A. xanthophloea*) are particularly important. Not only is this species used almost exclusively as sleeping trees, but when they are in the height of their bloom the baboons also usually feed in them for one or more hours before starting their morning round, returning in the afternoon for another heavy feeding period at dusk. Out on the plains the ant galls on the short whistling-thorn trees (*A. drepanolobium*) are constantly plucked for the ants inside, and extrusions of its sap are eaten as well. Some edible portion—bud, flower, seed pod, sap—of one of the types of acacia tree will be available within a troop's range at almost any time of year, and acacias are second only to grasses in the quantity of food they provide for Nairobi Park baboons. In addition to the plants and trees which provide forage for baboons all year, certain seasonal foods may constitute the bulk of their diet for short periods. The most important source of these seasonal foods in Nairobi Park are fig trees. When large fig trees are in fruit, the baboons may also use them as sleeping trees.

The most important food sources in the park are the grasses, acacia, and fig trees, but despite the frequency with which they feed in these trees, baboons were never seen eating tree leaves. On the southeastern slope of Mt. Kilimanjaro, baboons were observed feeding on the forest floor, while vervets (*Cercopithecus aethiops* and *C. mitis*) fed in the lower adjacent trees. Leaf-eating *Colobus* monkeys occupied the canopy of the same forest. Their ability to find food both on the open plain and in the trees is a distinct advantage for the baboons. Although they compete with a wide variety of ungulates for their food on the plains at Nairobi Park, their only close competitors in the trees are the vervets. Vervets and baboons are commonly seen feeding in adjoining trees in the park and occasionally they occupy the same tree—the baboons on the lower branches and the vervets in the canopy.

In addition to the staple diet, other vegetable foods were frequently eaten when they were available. These included "kei-apples," croton nuts, sisal plants, mushrooms, and the produce of native gardens (potatoes, yams, bananas, beans, maize, peanuts, sugar cane, etc.) Since almost all cultivated plants in this area have been imported from the New World, it is clear that baboons are very eclectic in their food habits.

Insects

Baboons eat many types of insects when they can find them, but the climate of Nairobi Park with its dry season, its hot days and cool nights does not support a very heavy insect population. The most common insect eaten in the park is the ant living in the galls of the *Acacia drepanolobium* trees. The amount of ants eaten in this way, however, is very small compared to the grasses and plants eaten during the same feeding period. If the troop is walking slowly through an area strewn with large stones, some of these may be turned over and the ground beneath them examined carefully. Under such stones an occasional beetle, slug, or cricket will be found and is quickly eaten. Rarely, an ant nest is uncovered, and the baboon bends over and licks up the contents of the nest from the earth, licking additional ants from its hands and arms afterward. But the baboons' attitude toward insects is one of mild interest, and no troop was ever seen moving from its pathway to systematically turn over the stones in an area.

Besides the ants in acacia galls, a baboon most frequently eats the grasshoppers which it finds on the branches of the bushes or blades of grass where it is feeding. Young baboons are seldom able to capture grasshoppers, but an adult will move the hand cautiously and deliberately to within one or two feet of the insect, then grasp it very quickly in a movement which is usually successful. Not all insects encountered are eaten. When a rock is overturned, some beetles and centipedes are ignored while others are carefully selected. Too few instances were observed to be able to say whether such selection was by individual preference, or whether these insects were avoided by all baboons in the park.

Although insect food is minor in the overall baboon diet, a very heavy infestation of "army worm" caterpillars in the park showed that for short periods insects can become the baboons' most important food. Beginning in early April, during the rainy season, army worms appeared in the park in large numbers. For about ten days the baboons ate little else. Feeding on the worms in a small area were: three baboon troops, totaling 188 animals; several troops of vervet monkeys, perhaps 75 in all; and a group of about 300 Marabou stork (*Leptoptilos crumeniferus*).

The different baboon troops fed very near each other, and the other animals, without incident. All were gorging themselves on the caterpillars; several baboons were timed picking up 100 army worms per minute, and continuing at this rate for from 10 to 15 minutes without a break. The eating of insects, in addition to the extensive inventory of vegetable foods, further increases the dietary adaptability of the baboon.

Live Animals

On six, perhaps seven, occasions during the twelve months of study in Kenya and the Rhodesias, we saw baboons eating freshly killed animals. Twice they caught and ate half-grown African hares (*Lepus capensis crawshayi*). On the first occasion the male in possession of the hare was being harried not only by two more dominant males in this troop, but by a pair of tawny eagles (*Aquila repax raptor*) as well. The male in possession eluded his harassers and managed to consume most of the hare, the eagles retrieving scraps of viscera and skin. In his haste the baboon dropped the rib cage and a foreleg of the hare, with most of the flesh still attached, *but these pieces were ignored* by the other two baboons chasing him, despite their desire to obtain his catch.

Two or three times baboons were seen eating fledgling birds of some ground-nesting species, probably the crowned plover (*Stephanibyx coronatus*). On several occasions they chased fledglings some yards through the grass without catching them. We never saw baboons finding and eating eggs, but when offered a dozen guinea fowl eggs, they ate these without hesitation. Entire eggs were stuffed into the cheek pouches and the shell broken by the hand pressing the cheek against the teeth and jaws. More significant than the few instances of baboons' eating fledglings are the numerous times when baboons were seen feeding across a plain covered by bird nests without discovering the contents of a single nest. The same animals which are able to detect an under-ground root from only a tiny dried shoot on the surface will walk beside a bird nest six inches in diameter without noticing it. Furthermore, four species of weaver bird inhabit the park, and their nests are frequently clustered in the acacia branches where the baboons are eating, but no baboon was ever seen investigating such a nest, much less eating its contents. The baboon's attitude toward food is clearly vegetarian. It is common to see a baboon troop completely mingled with a flock of guinea fowl without incident. The only eggs or fledglings which they seem to recognize as food are those which are literally stepped on as the troop searches for vegetable foods on the plains.

On December 14, near the close of the study, two very young Thomson gazelle (*Gazella t. thomsonii*) were caught and eaten by the adult males of a troop. The actual capture of the second gazelle was seen. An adult male baboon grabbed it, brought it above his head, and slammed it to the ground. He immediately tore into the stomach of the gazelle and began eating. Beginning with the most dominant males, five of the six adult males in the troop participated in eating this gazelle, and two hours later only skin, teeth and large bones remained. The viscera were eaten first, followed by the flesh, and finally the thin brain case was bitten open and the contents carefully scooped out with the fingers—bits of skull being pulled through the teeth and licked clean. The incisors, not the canines, were used in biting and tearing at the flesh.

These two Thomson's gazelle were apparently only a few days old, and were hiding in the grass some 150 yards from the herd of 38 with which they were no doubt associated. After the baboon troop moved on, two females from the herd of gazelle (of 35 females, 2 young, and one adult male) came over and paced nervously around the remains of the carcasses. It seems reasonable to assume that the discovery of these two young gazelle took place under circumstances very similar to those involved in the eating of the young hares, that is, that they were discovered accidentally in the grass. In fact, after the first gazelle had been found, and four of the males were pressing its possessor closely, the males passed within five yards of an African hare sitting in plain view. They clearly saw the hare but did not even walk over toward it.

All these cases of flesh eating have one thing in common—they involve the eating of immature animals whose defense is to hide "frozen" in the grass, and in each case their discovery by the baboons seemed fortuitous. Nothing resembling a systematic search of an area or the stalking of prey was ever observed, nor was fresh meat eaten except when it was found alive or taken up immediately by a waiting baboon. Since baboons avoid lion kills when they are away from trees and other carrion is not eaten, the lack of interest shown by the male in the portion of hare which had been dropped (described above) may be due to their avoidance of carrion. It is also possible that baboons do not recognize as edible any meat which is not alive and easily caught. In either case it seems clear that their attitude toward other animals is not that of a predator, nor do the scores of other species with which they live peacefully so regard them.

The final instance of meat eating was observed in Amboseli Reserve. While watching baboons in an open area, we heard loud screeches and chattering in a tree where baboons and vervets had been feeding peacefully for the previous hour. When we approached the tree we saw an adult male baboon walking through the branches with a juvenile vervet dangling from his mouth, and the vervet troop had left the tree. The baboon consumed most of the vervet, carrying the carcass in his mouth as he walked toward the troop's sleeping tree at dusk. This observation is in striking contrast to the many occasions when the two types of monkey were seen feeding peacefully together. During a brief aggressive interaction between the two species in Nairobi Park, DeVore saw an angry male baboon put a troop of vervets to rapid flight, and this case of meat eating may have been the incidental result of such a situation in the tree at Amboseli. Although Washburn saw baboons chase vervets quite frequently

near Victoria Falls, he only once saw a baboon catch one. This was held in the mouth by the female who caught it. She was apparently bewildered by the situation and soon released it unharmed. In much the same way one of the fledglings DeVore saw eaten was actually caught by a juvenile baboon, which seemed puzzled by the object and quickly relinquished it to an adult male (who promptly ate it).

In summary, baboons may be described as very inefficient predators. Meat eating, to judge by the bewildered state of the female baboon who caught a vervet and of the young juvenile who caught a bird, would appear to be learned by each generation, and meat never becomes an important source of food for the whole troop. Only one baboon other than adult males (an adult female) participated in the eating of meat in any of the instances observed during the study. Accounts of meat-eating in captive baboons are contradictory. Kenya baboons kept near Nairobi Park ate meat readily, but Bolwig found that his captives refused it. In South Africa, where most reports of carnivorous baboons have originated, baboons are only now being systematically studied, and we feel that the importance of meat in the baboon diet has been considerably overstressed. The usual reason given for the habit of meat-eating in South African baboons is that the hardship of drought creates the conditions under which it flourishes, but when the two Thomson's gazelle were eaten in December the park was well into the rainy season, and the vegetable foods baboons ordinarily eat were more abundant than at any other time of year.

It would seem more reasonable to us, on the present evidence, to assume that meat has been a consistent but very minor part of the baboon diet throughout their evolutionary history. In localities where sources of animal protein can be obtained without danger, baboons apparently include these in their regular diet. At Murchison Falls, baboons are often seen digging out and eating crocodile eggs. Hall's description of the foods eaten by baboons along the coast of South Africa is very similar to the inventory of vegetable and insect foods discussed here, except that the South African baboons also eat marine foods such as mussels, crabs, and sand hoppers found along the beach. But baboons are ill fitted anatomically to be carnivores, and too great a dependence on meat eating could have been detrimental to their wide exploitation of the vegetable foods they depend upon today. By their utilization of a wide variety of plant and tree products, baboons have been able to spread over the African continent, and, together with the macaques, to cover most of the tropical Old World.

In the evolution of the human species, meat-eating played a very different role. We have suggested that the earliest hominids may have been living on a diet very like that of the baboons, that is, vegetable foods supplemented by an occasional small animal. The freedom to carry a simple digging implement in the hands would greatly enhance this adaptation. During the dry season in Africa, human hunter-gatherers are also very dependent on the subsurface roots and tubers sought by baboons. A digging stick greatly improves the humans' chance for survival during this period of food shortage, and it may be that the presence of baboon skeletons at Olorgesaille indicates the result of competition between baboons and humans over a limited food supply. It would be an easy step from killing baboons to protect a source of vegetable foods, to killing them for meat.

Scavenging

Scavenging has been regarded as an important phase in the evolution of man's carnivorous habits. It seems reasonable that a primate liking eggs, nesting birds, insects, and an occasional small mammal might add to this diet and develop more carnivorous tastes and habits by gleaning meat from kills. This theory seemed reasonable, and we made a particular effort to examine kills and to observe the relations of the baboons to them. Although we saw over a dozen recent kills (including gnu, giraffe, zebra, waterbuck, impala, Grant's gazelle, warthog, Masai cattle,

and goat) and have thorough records on some, we were primarily looking at baboons. The subject of scavenging is so important, especially in the interpretation of the deposits in which *Australopithecus* is found, that a much more comprehensive study is needed. However, here are our tentative conclusions.

The scavenging theory is not supported by the evidence, and primates with habits similar to those of baboons could get meat by hunting far more easily than by scavenging. There are several reasons for this. The first is that most kills are made at night and are rapidly and thoroughly eaten. When the hyenas leave at dawn, the vultures locate the remains and clean the last meat from the bones. Some kills are made by day. We saw the remains of a gnu which a pride of ten lions finished in an hour. A pride of four lions (two not fully grown) killed a gnu one afternoon and ate almost all of it in one night. The vultures finished the rest, and the bones were undisturbed for three days. Many bones disappeared on the fourth night. Similarly, we saw two lions eat a warthog, three lions eat a Grant's gazelle, and five cheetahs kill and eat an impala. Only the meat of very large animals is left for long, and Africa is well supplied with highly efficient scavengers which leave little meat to tempt a primate.

Actually there are far fewer kills than might be expected from discussions of scavenging. In the part of the Amboseli Reserve which we studied intensively there were on the order of 100 baboons to one lion. The lions move over large areas, and the chances of a troop coming on a "kill" are very few. We saw a troop around a kill left from the previous night only once in Amboseli. It had been largely eaten, and the baboons appeared to take no interest in it. During nine months of observation in Nairobi Park, baboons were seen to pass near four kills and paid no attention to the few scraps of meat left on them. A Grant's gazelle carcass, presumably a leopard kill, hung in a fig tree where baboons ate and slept, but the baboons apparently ignored it. In addition, they did not attempt to eat fresh carrion when this was found. A further complicating factor is that when there is much meat left, the lions usually stay nearby, and the neighborhood of the kill is very dangerous.

In summary, the chances of a kill within the range of a baboon troop are very small; little meat is likely to be left; and the vicinity of the kill is dangerous. Most of the killing and eating is at night, and primates have neither the sense of smell of the hyenas nor the eyes of the vultures to locate the kill. As noted earlier, the baboons seem uninterested in dead animals. A slight increase in predatory activity against young animals would yield a far greater reward than scavenging, would be much less dangerous, and would represent a smaller change in habit. The use of a stick or stone for digging would increase the baboons' food supply more than any other simple invention. Perhaps in *Australopithecus* we see a form which had such a tool to exploit vegetable foods and which also used this tool as a weapon. If tools were being used at all, their use in the deliberate killing of small animals would be only a small change from the behavior observed in baboons. Once man had become a skilled tool-user in these ways, he could extend tool use to the hunting of large animals, to defense, and to driving carnivores from their kills. Scavenging may have become a source of meat when man had became sufficiently skilled to take the meat away from carnivores, but the hunting of small animals and defenseless young is much more likely to lie at the root of the human hunting habit.

Discussion

In this paper we have tried to stress those aspects of baboon ecology which are of the greatest help in understanding human evolution. Obviously, man is not descended from a baboon, and the behavior of our ancestors may have been very different from that of living baboons. But we think that in a general way the problems faced by the baboon troop may be very similar to those which confronted our ancestors. At the least, comparison of human behavior with that of baboons emphasizes the differences. At the

most, such a comparison may give new insights. Many topics have been summarized above, and in this discussion we will call attention only to a few major points.

The size of baboon troops may exceed that of hunter-gatherers, and their population density far exceeds that of primitive man. The human group differs in being exogamous, so that many local groups form the breeding population. We believe that this radically different breeding structure has exerted a profound effect on the later phases of human evolution and has long been a factor in preventing speciation in man.

The social structure of the baboon troop is important to the survival of the species. Survival depends on the adult males being constantly close to the other troop members. Roles in the troop are divided between the sexes, but these are in the context of a compact troop. With man, the hunters leave the local group, sometimes for days, and then return to their home base. Such a pattern is radically different from anything known in monkeys or apes. Hunting with tools basically changed the social structure of the band, the interrelations of bands, the size and utilization of range, and the relation of man to other animals.

Diet has already been discussed and we will not repeat here, except to point out that our opinion of the importance of scavenging has changed through observation of the actual situation at the kills. It is not enough to speculate that scavenging might have been important. One must estimate how much meat is actually available to a vegetarian, and how dangerous it is to get meat by scavenging.

Finally, we would stress that survival is a complex process, and that all the factors which lead to reproductive success must ultimately be considered. Varied diet, social structure, and anatomy, all are important, but their meaning only becomes clear as they are seen making possible the behavior of a population. Sex differences, peripheral animals, and range—each of these has meaning only in terms of the survival of groups. With the coming of man, every major category is fundamentally altered and evolution begins to be dominated by new selection pressures. Some measure of how different the new directions are may be gained from the study of the ecology of baboons.

selection 23

This paper directs attention to the theoretical importance of recent discoveries and observations—especially those in primate field studies—to the interpretation of the fossil record. It is intended not as a review but simply as a discussion of the implications of recent developments.

On the Evolution of Tool-Using Behavior

Jane B. Lancaster

Time and the New Methods of Dating

From *American Anthropologist,* Vol. 70, 1968, pp. 56–64. By permission of the author, and the publisher.

The estimate of the amount of time occupied by the Pleistocene has steadily increased. In 1932 Keith thought that the Pleistocene might have lasted 200,000 years and the Pliocene an additional 250,000. Then for a long time the Pleistocene was estimated at one million years and the Pliocene ten times that long. According to that view, the Pleistocene was divided into two approximately equal parts: the first 500,000 years contained at least some very simple tool traditions, but these were of uncertain date and duration; the second 500,000 years spanned three glacials and contained all the tools of the Acheulian and later toolmaking traditions. With the advent of potassium-argon dating, now partly supported by the fission-track method, radiometric dates rather than relative estimates could be given for these two parts of the Pleistocene. The dates and duration of the last part of the Pleistocene have not been greatly altered but the early part has been radically extended in time. The new radiometric dating suggests well over two million years ago as a probable date for the Pliocene-Pleistocene boundary, but keeps

Table 1.   Chronology of the Pleistocene

Upper	Third Interglacial (Eemian)	100,000 B.P.	
Middle	Second Interglacial (Holstein)	255,000 B.P. or more	
	First Interglacial (Cromerian)	700,000–500,000 B.P.	Acheulian and later traditions
		1,000,000 B.P.	
Lower			
	Villafranchian	2,000,000 B.P.	Oldowan tools
	(Early Villafranchian?)	3,000,000–2,500,000 B.P. ???	

700,000–500,000 B.P. as likely for the onset on the First Interglacial period (Table 1). Two million years ago, according to Evernden and Curtis, is a minimal estimate for the start of the Pleistocene and it may well have begun more than three million years ago. Estimates of the extent of the Lower Pleistocene, especially of the earliest part, the Villafranchian, have been the most radically affected by radiometric dating. The Villafranchian, which was once considered a relatively brief period preliminary to the major events and time spans of the Pleistocene, is now seen as lasting perhaps 2.5 million years and comprising three quarters of the total length of the Pleistocene.

While the radiometric chronology of the late Tertiary and Pleistocene stratigraphic unit is not finally settled, it is very clear that the time spans involved in the early stages of the Pleistocene have been seriously underestimated in the past. Geophysical age determinations indicate the need for a radical revision in our conception of the rate of development of tool-using abilities and techniques and in our understanding of the interrelation of tool types to the biology of their makers. At Olduvai Gorge, chopping tools, trimmed and utilized flakes, polyhedral "flaked" stones, and other utilized stones are found near the base of Bed I in layers dated between 1.9 and 1.75 million years. From these same stratigraphic levels fossils of two distinct hominid forms have been recovered. Regardless of the ultimate classification of the hominid forms found in Bed I, there are none with large brains. Tobias' most generous estimate for the cranial capacity of the

juvenile parietal fragments is still only 725 cc. His more conservative estimate is 670 cc.

The Oldowan industries from Bed I are at present the oldest radiometrically dated stone artifacts, but they need not necessarily represent the very beginning of stone flaking traditions, which we can expect to extend to perhaps a quarter to a half million years earlier. At Olduvai these industries persisted into the time of deposition of the lower part of Bed II, while in upper Bed II early handaxe industries occur. The age of the transition from Oldowan to Acheulian has not been directly determined at Olduvai but archeological and faunal correlations can be made with other strata for which geophysical data indicate an age of between 700,000 and 500,000 B.P. The elementary stone techniques and poorly standardized tool-making tradition of the Oldowan appear in East Africa to have lasted at least one million years and quite probably for more than double that time with little change or advance in their manufacture or in the biology of their makers. We can assign a time span for Oldowan tools from probably earlier than 2,000,000 B.P. up to 500,000 B.P., the time when the first handaxe cultures and the remains of larger-brained men classified as *Homo erectus* began to appear. The only possible makers of the Oldowan tools are small-brained forms (*Australopithecus,* in the broad sense).

There is reason to think that Oldowan tools were used for much longer than the 1.5 million years that passed between the lowest levels of Bed I and the beginning of the European First Interglacial period. Tools similar to the Oldowan may also date from the same or an earlier period at other African sites, such as Laetolil, Omo, Kanam, Ain Hanech, and elsewhere. Furthermore, the small incisors and canines of *Australopithecus* suggest that members of this genus had been using tools for a very long period of time and that the use of tools had almost entirely relieved their dentition of the functions of food getting and self protection. An estimate of two million years of tool use prior to hand-axe cultures and *Homo erectus* is undoubtedly conservative. This would mean that the stage of human evolution in which small-brained men used pebble tools and walked bipedally lasted at least four times as long as have all the subsequent stages. The early part of the evolution of stone tools and of man must have proceeded at a rate very different from the later stages and advances must have come very much more slowly.

To summarize to this point, the archeological discoveries from Bed I in Olduvai Gorge and the advent of new dating techniques have radically altered our conceptions of the duration of the early, primitive stages of tool using and tool making. The natural assumption has always been that tool use was so highly adaptive that once it had been firmly established as part of the normal behavior of the species the pace of evolution quickened immediately. Advances were assumed to have come in rapid succession as the brain, tool-making techniques, and cultural traditions interacted in a mutually stimulating feedback relationship. Events of the past, however, apparently did *not* move this rapidly, at least not in the beginning.

Tool Use by the African Apes

In the same years that discoveries at Olduvai Gorge and advances in the techniques of radiometric dating were being made, field workers were making new efforts to study the behavior of contemporary monkeys and apes in their natural habitats. Most of these modern field studies report very little object-manipulation in nonhuman primates except that directly involved in feeding activity. In feeding, nonhuman primates will turn over rocks, probe fingers into holes, and pull off bark or shells in search of food, but even here they are only manipulating objects and not using tools. In contrast to the findings of field workers on other primate species, Goodall has found that tool use in the chimpanzee is an important behavior pattern. Goodall over a period of six years has observed the behavior of a single population of approximately 60 free-ranging chimpanzees in the Gombe Stream Reserve in Tanzania. There can be little doubt now that tool-using performances by chimpanzees excel those reported for all other animals except man in both variety and complexity. They are also very close to man in many other measures: anatomy of the body, serum proteins, chromosome number and form, and dentition. Therefore it is not surprising that chimpanzees are closest to man in some aspects of behavior as well.

It may well be that further observations on the behavior of gorillas in the wild will produce evidence of tool-using behavior paralleling the performances of the chimpanzees. Schaller with 500 hours of observation of the behavior of the mountain gorilla reported that he never saw gorillas use or show interest in objects except vegetation for nest building and for throwing in aggressive display. The aggressive display of the gorilla is a highly stereotyped sequence of behavior patterns that usually includes the throwing and tossing of vegetation just before a running charge. Many of the same elements, including the throwing of vegetation followed by a charge, constitute the most essential parts of the chimpanzee aggressive display. At least in the one context both species show a strong tendency to manipulate and throw objects. It should be noted that what appear to be species differences in behavior between chimpanzees and gorillas may in part merely reflect Goodall's unique long-term observations; in the first year of her study she only saw one kind of tool use, termiting. Moreover, there may have been important ecological differences between the two study areas.

Schaller worked in a region of lush evergreen vegetation of herbs and vines, where rocks, sticks, and other hard objects were rare. Food plants were abundant and everywhere at hand. The feeding pattern of the gorillas was simply a leisurely grazing through the lush vegetation. In contrast, the Gombe Stream Reserve includes valleys of dense gallery forests and higher points of open woodland and grassy slopes where wood and stone are readily available materials. Food items are often seasonal, concentrated, and hard to get. The chimpanzees make an effort to locate and to gather their food; this is exactly the sort of situation where tool use in food getting might be likely to appear. Finally, the behavior of young gorillas in captivity is very similar to that of young chimpanzees in their interest in and manipulation of objects. In captivity both chimpanzees and gorillas spontaneously learn to throw dirt and food with considerable accuracy at visitors.

Goodall's most remarkable observations of chimpanzee tool use are of the use of twigs and grass blades for "fishing" ants or termites out of their nests. She has collected more than 1000 of these tools and on over a hundred occasions has observed actual termiting. Chimpanzees are very efficient in getting the termites. The animal takes a piece of twig and puts it in the termite hole where the insects seize the end of the stick with their mandibles. The chimpanzee then takes it from the hole and leisurely eats the termites that are clinging to the tip. Not only do the chimpanzees use these twigs very effectively as tools but they also will frequently improve the bit of twig or grass before using it. The animal will break off a piece of vine or a twig and prepare it by stripping away any side branch or leaf that might get in the way and by breaking it to the appropriate length, which differs by a foot or more for anting as opposed to termiting. There is much individual variation in the skill and care with which a tool is made. Some animals will take nearly anything at hand; others will search carefully for just the right piece and then spend some time in preparing it. A few prepare a little pile

of stems before starting to termite and some make the twig even before a nest is found. Goodall saw one male carry a termiting twig in his mouth for more than half a mile while he went from nest to nest looking for one that was ready to work.

The actual grip used to hold the twig for termiting is standardized among adults who hold it between the thumb and the side of the bent index finger. Infants who have not fully mastered the adult technique may grip the tool using only four fingers and not using the thumb at all. Chimpanzees are ambidextrous in their termiting; all animals can use either hand although there may be some individual preference for one hand over the other. This absence of handedness may be indicative of the limitations that the chimpanzee's brain places on its ability to develop highly skilled tool use. By human standards these termiting movements and other kinds of tool-using behavior in chimpanzees always appear clumsy, like the use of tools by a human child. Tool use is learned by the chimpanzee, improves with practice, but never develops the deftness either of human skill or of highly stereotyped innate motor patterns.

Goodall was fortunate enough to observe a one-and-a-half-year-old female in the process of learning how to use the termiting twig. The infant's technique was imperfect. She made tools that were too short to more than just enter the hole; the longest was only two inches whereas the adults always use 6- to 12-inch twigs. The infant's motor patterns were imperfectly coordinated and sometimes she would jerk the twig out of the hole so quickly that the termites were knocked off. Her attention span was very short as well; she would termite for a few minutes and then break off to play. In contrast, adults often work with great concentration for more than an hour without stopping. Goodall also observed that young animals try to termite out of season in what may have been a form of play activity. She is convinced that much of the ability to termite is learned by young animals by observing the adult technique and then practicing it. She often saw infants intently watching an adult termiting and then, when the adult had moved off leaving the twig or grass blade by the nest, the infant would pick up the abandoned tool and try termiting too.

Chimpanzees are not the only primates that like termites, and Goodall has seen baboons near chimpanzees while they are at work. Baboons are eager to eat termites, but they have never been observed trying to fish for termites themselves. The baboons do occasionally watch the chimpanzees termiting but not as intently as do young chimpanzees who will peer at working adults for minutes at a time.

Termiting is a seasonal activity, coming just before the termites begin their nuptial flights, which occur about eight times for each termite heap over a period of four months or more during the rainy season. During most of the year the termites are protected by a concrete-like shell that covers their nests, but for the flights the workers tunnel out to the surface. After each flight, the holes are sealed over until the next. Chimpanzees are able to scratch off the thin covering at the end of the tunnel and thus, by using the fishing technique, are able to eat termites throughout the entire season. Birds, monkeys, and other animals can feast on the termites only during the actual flights. The simple technique of fishing for termites assures the chimpanzees of a protein-rich diet for several months out of every year without competition from other species, and the inability of the baboons to imitate the chimpanzee behavior robs them of the extra protein.

Termiting is only one example of tool use by chimpanzees. Goodall saw them make sponges for dipping water out of crevices and boles of trees that were too small to let them put their faces down to the water. They would take a handful of leaves, chew them slightly, dip the wad into the water and then suck it. Goodall tried the same thing and found it seven to eight times more efficient than the technique used by many nonhuman primates of dipping the hand or fingers into water and letting the water drip into the mouth. Besides using leaves as sponges for drinking water,

chimpanzees use them to wipe water or dirt from the body or sticky substances from the fingers. This use of objects to groom the body is more unusual than it seems. Although some species of bird are known to rub ants in their feathers as a part of grooming and elephants sometimes use objects to scratch themselves, man is the only animal reported to habitually use objects in grooming.

One other way in which chimpanzees use objects as tools is in aggressive display. This behavior is particularly interesting because it suggests that tools for defense may have been developed just as early in man's history as tools for foodgetting. Random throwing of objects—anything that comes to hand such as stones, sticks or other vegetation—is a common element in the excited displays of many primates, and chimpanzees are no exception. They tend to throw things when meeting other groups after a separation or when being annoyed by baboons. Sometimes an animal will even take some care in aiming the object; instead of just tossing it into the air, he will throw it toward the animal at which the display is aimed. Goodall saw chimpanzees aim and throw stones, both overhand and underhand, at baboons and at humans as part of such a sequence of aggressive display. This behavior pattern is significant because, as Washburn has pointed out, it suggests the possible first steps in the evolution of weapons. If an animal is displaying to intimidate an aggressor, object throwing as a part of that display is effective whether he hits the other animal or not. If the total display is not intimidating enough, the chimpanzee is still able to flee or to fight with his canines. It is easy to imagine how the ability to develop skill in aimed throwing of sticks and rocks could gradually evolve until it became so effective that the creature need no longer rely on his canines. Only then would the selective pressure on large canines be relaxed and a behavior pattern, defense with weapons, could ultimately replace the behavioral and morphological pattern of defense by fighting with canines.

These examples of tool use in chimpanzees, when taken together, provide a good starting place for answering questions about how and why tools were used by man's earliest ancestors. It is true that some birds and other mammals use tools, but in any one tool-using species there is likely to be only one kind of tool. There is no nonprimate that uses such disparate objects as termiting twigs, leaf sponges, and stone projectiles. And, conversely, in the chimpanzee there is no single, highly evolved, stereotyped sequence of movements of the sort common in other vertebrate tool users such as the deft twist of a cactus spine used by finches to dig grubs from bark or even the much more complex but still relatively stereotyped patterns of nest building found in many mammals. In the chimpanzee there is a far more generalized tendency to manipulate objects and to use them in many different situations. And, if Goodall is correct, these different ways to use tools constitute a tradition based on biology but transmitted from adults to young by observational learning and practice.

Chimpanzees use tools in an impressive number of different situations, when they are compared with the rest of the animal kingdom in this respect. By far the most common types of tool use in vertebrates are in feeding behavior or in preparation of nests or dens. The use of objects in self-grooming is almost unknown in animals and in aggressive display it has been observed only in monkeys, apes, and man. Goodall's single population of chimpanzees performed more complex kinds of tool use, and in a wider variety of situations, than has been observed for any other animal; that is true even though tool use is a very small part of their behavior repertoire and is a comparatively rare event. This small group of apes over a period of a few years was seen to use tools in agonistic display, in aimed throwing, in a variety of food-getting situations, in drinking, and in self-grooming. Perhaps the making of nests or sleeping platforms should be included in this list too, since it is very similar to these other forms of tool use in that objects are manipulated and modified to perform some important activity better—in this case the nest is a tool for sleeping.

Chimpanzee Learning of Tool-Using Traditions

It would be interesting to know why chimpanzees seem to be able to learn the use of objects more readily than do many other primates. There are important biological limitations on learning abilities that vary from species to species and do not reflect differences in intelligence so much as differences in specialization. Hall has argued that in themselves tool-using performances give no indication of relative intelligence. A finch that uses a cactus spine to extract grubs is no more intelligent than other finches; the species has simply evolved a behavioral pattern to aid in its feeding. Nevertheless, chimpanzees do have large brains and the great apes have a much longer maturation period than do other nonhuman primates; certainly both these characteristics are related to greater learning abilities.

Undoubtedly there are many factors that contribute to the ontogeny of such an important adaptive pattern as the use of objects as tools. Schiller and more recently Chance have emphasized the importance of certain motor patterns occurring in the tool-using performances of captive chimpanzees that appear to be largely determined by heredity and that require only the opportunity for play for their perfection. For example, the tendency to manipulate sticks, to lick the ends, and to poke them into any available hole are responses that occur over and over again in captive chimpanzees. These responses are not necessarily organized into the efficient use of sticks to probe for objects but they probably form the basis of complex motor patterns such as termiting.

Certain kinds of human-like tool use such as overhand and underhand throwing are easier for an ape than for a monkey. The anatomy of the shoulder girdle of man and the apes enables them to throw or toss objects using powerful movements, something which is much more awkward and difficult for a quadrupedal monkey. In contrast, differences between chimpanzees and monkeys in manipulative abilities of the hands are based not so much on anatomical differences in the forelimbs as on the brain and the ability to learn different kinds of object manipulations. The hands of monkeys and apes are equally suited to picking up a stick and making poking or scratching movements with it but differences in the brain make these much more likely behavior patterns for the chimpanzee.

Another factor, one that may be just as important in tool use as genetic tendencies toward motor patterns, is the degree to which chimpanzees can learn by observing the activities of other animals. Hall has emphasized that observational learning is rarer in nonhuman primates than one might expect and that the ability to learn in this way varies tremendously according to the task to be learned and the context in which this learning takes place. Monkeys and apes seem to have greater abilities in this direction than do most other mammals, and Hall has suggested that these abilities are most often demonstrated when the animals are in the relaxed, protected atmosphere of a social group formed of animals linked by close affectional bonds. This is a situation that is common in the natural environment of monkeys and apes, but it is rarely duplicated in the laboratory. Monkeys and apes learn emotional attitudes, such as fear of particular objects of situations, with great ease from other group members as might be expected in animals for which group life is an important adaptive mechanism.

Other, more complex kinds of observational learning in monkeys and apes are much more rare. Frequently the activities of one animal will stimulate another animal to do the same thing, but this sort of social facilitation is often merely a matter of a focusing of the attention of the second animal on a stimulus that then elicits a parallel response. For example, Hall reported an experiment in which a young baboon, raised in captivity, was released near a wild troop. The young animal had been fed the diet of a pet and was unfamiliar with the wild foods of the area in which it was released. It learned how to dig for bulbs and roots by watching the other animals closely and then going over and digging beside them, but, as Hall emphasized, it did not learn how to dig, but rather where and for what to dig. The ability to mimic a novel motor pattern demonstrated by another animal has not conclusively been shown for any nonhuman primate except the chimpanzee. Studies of captive chimpanzees point toward their considerable abilities in all the forms of observational learning mentioned above, ranging from the simpler kinds of attention focusing to something that must be genuine imitation of novel motor patterns. It is likely, then, that both these factors—the existence of simple hereditary motor acts that form the basis of more complex motor patterns of tool use and the ease with which one chimpanzee can learn by observing the activities of another chimpanzee—play important roles in the development of tool-using traditions within local populations of chimpanzees.

Tool-using behavior by chimpanzees is remarkable in the multiplicity of forms it takes, but it is very different from human use of tools in degree if not in kind. Chimpanzees, like men, both use and make tools, but man's brain is highly evolved and highly specialized to learn many different skilled uses of objects. For a species to depend on tool use as a way of life—for obtaining food and for defense—such tool use must be skillful. A spear has to be thrown just as skillfully as a baboon wields its canines in fighting, or the behavior pattern could never replace the morphological pattern in agonistic situations. Skill is a matter of evolutionary changes in the brain that do not fossilize. There are really only two indirect lines of evidence of skill from the past: (1) relative brain size of the tool makers and (2) the tools themselves, in the techniques by which they were made and in the complexity and specializations of the tool assemblages.

The specializations of modern man's brain that allow him to learn many different skilled uses of tools may have come relatively late in the history of tool use, perhaps not until *Homo erectus,* when the rate of change in tool traditions became so rapid and when a major increase in cranial capacity occurred. The slow pace of evolution in tools and in their makers before that time may well reflect a lack of ability to use them skillfully.

The tool-using behavior of chimpanzees suggests the kind of ape ancestor that might be postulated for the origin of the hominid line—an ape that used tools for many different reasons and in many different ways, no matter how insignificant the tool, like leaf sponges, or how undramatic, like termiting twigs, or inefficient, like a clumsily swung stick. The more kinds of tools this ape used the more likely his ancestral role, because it would have been the accumulated influence of many reasons for using tools and many ways of using them that would have taken selective pressure off the specific situation, the specific tool, and the specific movement. Selective pressure was put on a hand that could use many tools skillfully and on a brain capable of learning these skills. Natural selection would then have acted upon a broader category of behavior, one involving the brain, the hand, many objects, and a wide variety of social and ecological situations and problems. The evolution of skilled tool using marks a major change from the kind of tool use that is incidental to the life of a chimpanzee to the kind that is absolutely essential for survival of the human individual.

Problems of Interpretation in the Evolution of Tool Use

Chimpanzee tool-using behavior raises the question of how many millions of years of this sort of casual tool use and object manipulation by apes has existed. It also raises the problem of whether the ancestors of chimpanzees and man used tools before their separation or whether tool use evolved independently in the two species. Any recon-

struction of evolutionary events can be guarded against the possibility of parallelism and convergence only by an evaluation of the degree of similarity between two species in as many different and unrelated systems as possible. The greater the number of similarities that can be found, in as many unrelated biological systems as possible, the higher the chances that one is dealing with true genetic affinities between species and not superficial similarities due to parallel evolution. A large number of such similarities between two species also suggests a shallow time depth of separation in which minor and random differences have not had a chance to accumulate.

Anatomical affinities between man and the apes have long been recognized both in dentition and in the anatomy of the shoulder girdle. Washburn noted that similarities between man and apes in the shoulder girdle involve fine details in a series of highly specialized modifications of the shoulder, elbow, and wrist joints. The full complement of these modifications was not present in the apes of the Miocene and may not have been established until the Miocene-Pliocene border, perhaps 13 million years ago. Washburn argued that man is likely to have separated from the African apes sometime in the early Pliocene, perhaps several million years after the establishment of a modern shoulder girdle in the family Pongidae.

The number of similarities between man and the great apes is extremely impressive. Besides the affinities in dentition and the anatomy of the shoulder girdle mentioned above, man is closer to the great apes than to any other animal in susceptibility to special kinds of viral disease, in blood groups, and in the glands of the axilla, the form of the hair follicles, the chemicals found at the ends of nerves, and many other details of the skin.

The African apes are often specifically cited as being the most similar to man and the orangutan has never been mentioned as being closer to man than are the African apes. In respect to chromosome number and form, the chimpanzee is almost identical to man with only one extra set of arocentric chromosomes. Dunn compared the internal parasites of man and apes and found that man and the African apes shared in common a much greater number of species of parasites, especially the host-specific ones, than do the Asiatic apes and man. Man living in the tropical forests of Southeast Asia shares many more species of helminths with African apes than with the Asiatic apes who are living in the same forest. Thus even when sharing his habitat with the Asiatic apes, man carries the internal parasites of the African apes. Goodman came to the conclusion that man and the African apes are so similar in their serum proteins that *Pan* and *Gorilla* should be classified in the Hominidae, whereas *Pongo* should be left in the Pongidae. Other workers on primate hemoglobins agree on the close affinities between man and the African apes as opposed to the Asiatic apes but do not take such an extreme taxonomic position. Sarich in a quantitative assessment of differences among the apes and man in serum albumins and gamma globulin found that man was very similar to the African apes and much less closely related to the Asiatic apes. The order of magnitude of these differences suggested a separation between man and the African apes going back perhaps 8 million years and a common ancestor for all modern apes and man coming from the Miocene-Pliocene border. There is no reason to think that all the different biological systems mentioned above are either genetically or functionally linked. Thus, an evolutionary change in one of these systems should not necessarily involve corresponding changes in the others. So many similarities between these systems can only be interpreted as reflecting close genetic relationships between man and the African apes, a relationship in which the time of separation is small enough that minor or random differences have not had a chance to accumulate.

The lack of divergence in many different systems strongly supports the idea of an end of the Miocene or early Pliocene (but no earlier) division between man and the African apes, somewhere on the order of 10 million years ago. If this is so, then it may be worth considering the possibility that casual, unskilled tool use might have been typical of many species of apes during the Pliocene. It should be remembered that the late Miocene and early Pliocene represent a time when apes were abundant, diverse, and widely spread over much of the Old World. Fossil apes have been found in Europe, Africa, India, and China—a much larger geographical distribution than that of the modern apes, which live only in restricted areas of Africa and Southeast Asia. The number of different forms of apes was also much greater than today. From a single site, Ruisinga Island in Lake Victoria, there are at least two species from the genus *Dryopithecus* as well as one or more species of gibbonlike apes. The modern apes are only remnants, survivors of a time when the family was highly successful and diverse. Table 2 suggests that a kind of unskilled ape tool use continued without

Table 2 *Chronology of the evolution of tool-using behavior*

GEOLOGICAL TIME DIVISIONS	RADIOMETRIC AGE ESTIMATES	TOOL-USING SPECIES OF PRIMATES	TYPES OF TOOL-USING TRADITIONS
	700,000–500,000 B.P.	*Homo erectus* (1 species only)	Hand axe and later traditions
Pleistocene			
	2,000,000 B.P.	*Australopithecus* (more than 1 species)	Oldowan industries
Pliocene		Pongid and Hominid (many species)	Unskilled, ape tool use (hypothetical)
	13,000,000 B.P.		

major changes for millions of years and has continued down to the present in one or more of the surviving, descendant species of ape.

The onset of the Pleistocene witnessed the emergence of perhaps one or more forms of bipedal hominid that, although possessing relatively small brains, had come to rely on tool use for much of their food getting and defense. Clearly, specializations in the hand and especially the thumb, the reduction in the canines and incisors, and bipedalism, all point toward the importance of tools to their way of life. Both the small brains and the tools themselves suggest a lack of skill in the way these tools were made and used. These hominids of the Early Pleistocene should not be thought of as merely forms transitional to man. They were highly successful, judging by their wide geographic distribution, and they lasted without major changes in either anatomy or tool traditions for a long time, perhaps 2.5 million years. Then, about half a million years ago, a rapid rate of evolutionary development in brain size and complexity of tool assemblages seems to have begun. This later period is associated with the emergence of a single species of tool user, *Homo erectus,* dominating much of the Old World. Remnant species of ape also survived but with quite restricted geographic distribution. Perhaps a new efficiency in the skilled use of tools effectively closed the niche to competition. It probably left no room within the broad niche created by tools for separate species to develop specialized applications. Any possibility for different kinds of tool users—perhaps an open savanna, a woodland, and a forest form (a possibility that may have been realized in *Australopithecus* during the Early Pleistocene)—disappeared and a single species of Hominid, using various tool traditions, spread across the Old World. The increase of efficiency and skill with which tools were used, a trend that probably began in the early Pliocene, may well have been associated with a gradual decrease in the number of primate species able to command a portion of the niche open to tool users. At an early, inefficient stage many species may have tried using tools with variable degrees of success but, as skill and efficiency increased, the competition between tool-using species also increased and the possibility of many forms sharing the niche disappeared.

Summary

Our conceptions of the conditions under which tools first evolved have been radically altered by recent archeological discoveries, new methods of dating, and primate field studies. All point toward a single conclusion—that in itself tool use does not cause a major change in the history of a species. Man is not the only primate to use tools and probably many species of ape have in time past used tools to some degree. The new radiometric dating by potassium-argon and fission-track methods indicates that the Early Pleistocene lasted for at least 2.5 million years and that during that time small-brained men used simple tools with little change or advance. The rapid acceleration of cultural advances, once traditionally thought to be a natural consequence of tools of any sort, came late in the history of tool use and was probably associated with specializations in the human brain that allowed the skilled use of many different kinds of tools. This evolutionary advance occurred in only one genus and species, *Homo erectus,* that preempted the entire niche once open to a number of different kinds of tool users. As Oakley argued some years ago, it is the skill with which man uses his tools that best reflects man's specializations for a human way of life.

part 5

Primitive Technology

The Making of Stone Implements

Kenneth P. Oakley

From *Man the Tool-maker.* British Museum (Natural History), London, 1950, pp. 23–29. By permission of the author and the publisher.

Before describing the succession of Stone Age industries in relation to man's evolutionary development, which is the central theme of this guide, it is useful to consider the various ways in which stone can be worked into tools and weapons. The simplest way of producing a stone which will cut (the primary type of artifact) is simply to break it in half and to use the resulting fresh sharp edge; but to produce a stone tool which is even slightly more specialized, one of two courses must be followed. The lump of stone, whether pebble, nodule or angular fragment, can be brought to the desired shape by flaking, or knapping. The flakes removed from the lump are then primarily waste-products, while the core of the lump becomes the implement. Such is a *core-tool.* Alternatively, flakes struck from the lump can be used as implements, with or without further trimming (known as dressing, retouch or secondary work). In this case the core is the source of *flake-tools,* and will serve to yield flakes until too small, when it is discarded as waste. Before a core will yield flakes of the required shape it may have to be prepared, and in the course of this preliminary work a number of waste flakes are produced. In practice, too, the flakes removed in the production of a core-tool may be selected subsequently for use as implements. The simple classification into core-tool industries and flake-tool industries is further complicated by the possibility that large flakes may be selected to serve as cores. Moreover, even in a flake-tool industry, discarded cores would be used as occasional tools.

Industries producing long parallel-sided flakes are distinguished as *blade-tool* industries. (It is difficult to produce blades in rocks other than flint, chert or obsidian.)

There are several methods of flaking stone, each probably used at some time or other during the Stone Age. Flaking by direct blows with a hammerstone (or other tool for striking) has been the method most widely used, but even this is subject to considerable variation. The stone to be flaked can be held in the hand [as shown in the accompanying figure], or rested on a block, or held against the knee. If, while it is being struck, the stone

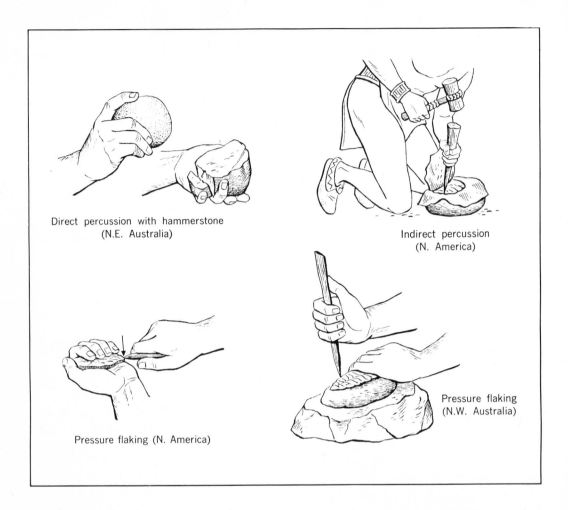

Direct percussion with hammerstone
(N.E. Australia)

Indirect percussion
(N. America)

Pressure flaking (N. America)

Pressure flaking
(N.W. Australia)

is rested on a slab of rock (a technique reminiscent of the simple method of cracking nuts with a pebble), the resulting flakes are liable to show a bulb of percussion at both ends, owing to rebound from the anvil. This so-called biopolar technique was practiced by Pekin Man. The normal primitive method of knapping, however, is to hold the lump of stone to be flaked in the hand, and to strike it repeatedly at selected spots with a pebble of suitable size. Each blow is delivered obliquely downwards near the edge of some conveniently placed flattish area (the striking platform), usually the scar of a flake previously struck off. Whether the flakes are short and thick, producing step-like bites along the edge of the piece of stone, or whether they are thin and extensive, skimming the surface, depends largely on the placing of the blows

and on the angle at which they are delivered. The run of the flake can be controlled by preparation of the face of the core, and also by pressure of the finger. When a piece of stone is held in the hand and struck at the edge by blows directed obliquely downwards, the flakes come off the *lower* surface, against which the fingers or palm are easily pressed. In the shaping of a core-tool such as a hand-axe, which requires to be trimmed equally on two sides, it is turned over from time to time as the paring proceeds.

Experiments by the French master mason, Léon Coutier, have shown that flint and similar rocks can be flaked by direct blows with a stone or bar of hardwood. This "wood-technique" is an effective way of reproducing the smooth skimming flake-scars which form the surfaces of the finer palaeoliths. However, similar flake-scars, with subdued or soft bulbs of percussion, can be produced also by a cylindrical or soft hammerstone, especially if used in conjunction with skillful finger control.

Probably one of the most primitive methods of producing flakes for use as tools is to dash or swing the core against the edge of a larger stone, or anvil. This "block-on-block" technique is liable to produce thick flakes (and deep flake-scars on the core) as in coarse flaking by a hammerstone, but with more protuberant cones and bulbs of percussion, and with a wider flaking angle (the angle between the striking-platform and the surface of the bulb of percussion), Flakes belonging to the primitive Palaeolithic flake industry known as Clactonian show these features.

A common attitude of a stone knapper is a sitting or squatting one, and in the production of flake-tools by percussion with a hammerstone the core is generally held on the left thigh or knee. The knapper starts as a rule with a lump of stone far larger than the core or tool required. Experiments have shown that the preliminary trimming down and the production of large primary flakes are most easily accomplished with a hammerstone weighing about 3 lb., whereas for the subsequent dressing of flakes a hammerstone weighing 2 or 3 oz. gives the best results. . . .

Stone Age knappers relied wholly on craftsman's skill, and when they required flakes of standard type or long blades, they had to take great care in the preparation of the core. Studies of the flaking techniques employed by primitive peoples in recent times show that there are many different ways of producing the same results. The American Indians used various methods of indirect percussion. To produce blades, for instance, a wooden or bone punch was interposed between the hammerstone and the core. Owing to the reduction of shatter, flakes can be split off thus with greater precision than when the hammerstone is used directly. The Aztecs of Mexico and a few North American Indians produced long blades by what is called impulsive pressure. The core was stuck in the ground and gripped by the feet of the flaker,

who either stood or sat, and grasped a wooden staff, which had a cross-piece for resting against the chest, and a spike of horn or hardwood at the other end which was set on the prepared edge of the core. The flaker would thrust forward with his chest, thus using the leverage of the body to split a flake from the core. According to one seventeenth century observer, a Mexican flaker, using this method, could produce as many as 100 knife blades of obsidian in an hour.

Much has been learned about the more primitive flaking techniques by studying the methods of Australian aborigines. As a general rule the shaping of a core-tool takes only a few minutes, but the preparation of a core for the production of flake- or blade-tools is sometimes a lengthy proceeding. Moreover, a number of artifacts are rejected before completion. It has been stated that in North Queensland, for example, a native requiring a new knife will visit a traditional quarry and will perhaps strike as many as 300 flakes before he obtains what he considers to be a suitable blade. The rejects and waste-flakes are left on the working "floor," while the single satisfactory blade is taken away, mounted in a handle of resin and used until it is broken. The dressing, or secondary working of a stone tool to make the edge straighter or more serviceable, or to re-edge it when it has been blunted by use, is usually done by rapping it on a pebble, or with a piece of bone or hardwood. Some of the tribes, especially in the Kimberley region of Western Australia, dress spearheads by pressure-flaking.

According to first-hand accounts of the fashioning of a spearhead by this method, a flake of stone (or glass, or porcelain) is taken and its edges chipped with a hammerstone into a roughly symmetrical leaf form. The margins are then rasped with a piece of sandstone, which breaks away small chips so that a narrow platform or bevel is formed on each side of the edge. The completion of the spearhead by pressure-flaking requires much patience and skill. The native squats on one heel, with the other leg stretched out, and with an anvil stone on the ground between his legs. In his left hand he holds the unfinished spearhead on a cushion of paperbark, placed on top of the anvil stone. In his right hand he holds a pointed stick (or piece of kangaroo bone), in such a way that the sharpened end is close to the wrist and points towards his body. After adjusting the point of the stick against the bevel of the far edge of the flake, he brings the weight of his body to bear on his right arm, and at the same time levers his wrist downwards and outwards. A chip snaps off the lower surface of the flake, while the "jar" of the downward thrust is absorbed by the cushion. The process is repeated time after time, as he works along the edge towards the butt; then the flake is reversed and the same method applied to the other side. A skillful flaker can make a spearhead of bottle-glass in about ten minutes.

selection 25

The First Tipi

Alice Marriott

From *The Ten Grandmothers.* University of Oklahoma Press, 1948, pp. 64–71. By permission of the author and the publisher.

It wasn't really very different, Spear Girl* thought, being married and not being married. You worked just about as hard, and the great difference that you had expected—not having your mother boss you—hadn't happened at all. They were all at home in the old tipi: her mother and sister, and Hunting Horse and herself, and they just went on doing the same old things the same old way. It wasn't much fun.

Bow Girl came and sat beside her, to pack the pounded meat into rawhide cases. They were quiet for a long time, because, being sisters, they didn't need to talk with their voices. After a while their uncle came and sat down with them.

"Where is your husband, niece?" he asked Spear Girl.

"At Sitting Bear's camp. They are making a feast for the Herders Society because that is Young Sitting Bear's society."

"That is your husband's, too."

"Yes, it is his."

Their uncle took out his pipe. It was old, a little short section of the big leg-bone of a deer. He didn't smoke it in the evenings, when all the men gathered around, smoking, because he had a big red pipe that he liked to show off with. But when he really wanted to think, he got out the little old bone pipe.

*This chapter is from the life story of the young Kiowa Indian woman, Spear Girl.

"Your husband goes to society meetings as if he were not married."

"He likes to be with other young men, uncle."

"That's all right. Men like to be with each other part of the time. But part of the time they should be with their wives, too."

"My husband is with me a lot when he isn't working."

"He would be with you more if you had your own tipi."

Spear Girl felt ashamed. They were poor, and they had always been poor, because, until she married, they had no man to work for them all the time. Her uncle was rich, and he helped a lot, but that didn't take the place of someone working all the time. She didn't like to say so to her uncle, because he was good and generous, and helped them more than he was obliged to, as it was.

He shook out his pipe, now, and turned to face her directly. "I've been thinking a lot. Hunting Horse has nobody to help him get started. You have your mother and sister, and that's all. Somebody has to help you two. I guess I'd better do it."

Spear Girl just sat and stared at him. It was like her uncle, but still she hadn't expected it. She didn't even thank him. She just stopped pounding down the dried meat and sat and stared, and Bow Girl stared, too.

"I don't want to give you everything to get you started." Her uncle was putting his pipe away now, because his thinking was over. "I'll give you what you need to make things out of. We won't make a give-away out of it, or have any ceremony. But you'll have what you need to work with. You two will have to do the working yourselves." Then he got up and walked off, and Spear Girl and Bow Girl just watched him go.

It was very late when Hunting Horse got home. The Herders Society members had danced a long time, and then they had eaten a big feast, and he was tired. He just flopped down and started breathing deep, and Spear Girl knew there was no use trying to tell him anything then.

She waked early, with her skin prickling all over, wondering what it was that was going to happen that was so big and good and exciting. Then she remembered. This was the day that they were to get their things to start living with. She punched Hunting Horse in the ribs with her elbow, and he grunted and turned over, and started breathing again. For a minute she started to get angry with him, but the day was too good to spoil, so she got up quietly. She dressed and combed her hair. For a minute she thought about painting her face, and then decided that since it wasn't like getting regular wedding presents, she would look foolish if she did it. Instead, she went out and helped her mother get breakfast.

They had all had breakfast, even Hunting Horse, and the newness had rubbed off the day and most of the excitement was gone, when she saw her uncle coming across the camp. He was leading a horse, piled high with all sorts of things, and behind him came his two wives, each of them leading a horse with a big load. They stopped in front of the tipi.

"There you are, sister."

"Get down, brother."

Her uncle tied the horse, and stepped back into the shade beside the tipi. His wives tied their horses, and began to unload them. Spear Girl started to help them, but her mother called her back.

"You don't unload your own wedding presents, daughter."

She wanted very much to see what they were. But she would have to wait until every single thing was off all three horses before she could look. She got a dipper of water for her uncle, and he drank the water and handed the dipper back to her.

"I'm glad you like to use gourd dippers, niece. I have brought plenty of gourds for you to make them out of."

Well, that was fine. The gourds had got all sun-scorched that summer, and there weren't enough to make dippers for everybody. Even people who had got tin cups from the traders still kept some gourds around, and used old-time dippers for themselves. They just got the tin cups out when they had company and wanted to show off. Spear Girl knew how to make good dippers.

"Thank you, uncle," she said.

"There is everything there that you need to work with," her uncle said. "We have brought hides for a tipi, and willows for beds, and robes and deerskins to make bedding out of. All the hides are dried and rolled up. You'll have to tan them and cut them yourself, but there are a lot there. How many buffalo hides are there?" he asked his first wife.

"Thirty-two," she answered. "Enough for a big tipi. We have logs for tipi-poles over at our camp. Your husband will have to trim them down and bring them over himself."

Spear Girl wasn't paying much attention to the tipi-poles. She was thinking about the cover. Thirty-two hides were a lot, when they had to be tanned, and she had never cut or sewn a tipi-cover. Not very many people tried to cut their own. There were some women who were good at it, and they did that kind of work for everybody. But they wouldn't do the tanning.

Her mother was looking off across the camp, as if there were something she wanted to see on the other side. "My daughter's husband hasn't much to do," she said. "I guess he can start work on the tipi-poles right away."

Spear Girl heard that, and it turned her mind away from the tipi-cover. Her mother shouldn't speak like that, even about her son-in-law. It made her feel queer, and without looking at Hunting Horse she knew it made him feel queer, too. But he didn't say anything. He took his axe and started across to her uncle's tipi.

Everything was all unloaded now. It made a big pile in front of the tipi. People were coming up to see what was happening.

"That's a lot of hides," said Grass Woman. "Who's going to tan all those hides?" Spear Girl straightened up and stopped thinking about what a lot of work it was going to be.

"I am," she answered. "I want to tan the hides for my own tipi."

Bow Girl was standing beside her. "I'm going to help my sister," she added. "We always do everything together."

Nobody said anything, but Spear Girl felt better. The people around her felt better towards her. They must have been afraid she was going to let her mother do all the tanning.

Bow Girl brought water to her uncle's two wives. "That was hot work for you, all that loading and unloading," she told them, and her aunts said, "Yes, it was hot work, all right. Now you can get to work and get hot, too."

That was all right. You ought to get hot, working on your own home. Spear Girl didn't mind it. Grass Woman spoke again. She always had something to say. "That many hides takes a lot of brains for tanning. A hide needs all its own brains to tan itself. I have some brains. My man killed three buffalo this month, and I dried the brains and saved them. I'm going to make rawhide. I don't need them. You can have them."

Spear Girl was feeling better all the time. The newness seemed to be coming back to the day. "Thank you for the brains," she told Grass Woman.

"I have brains, too." That was Pond Woman. "I don't need them. Four buffalo brains."

It was like a give-away, then. It seemed as if every woman in camp had been saving brains. They all wanted to give some away, and they all gave them to Spear Girl. Grass Woman and Pond Woman got their brains, and then the others went for theirs, too. Spear Girl stood and watched flat cakes of dried brains pile up beside the buffalo hides, and felt more and more excited. It was going to be all right. Now she could get to work right away, without waiting for Hunting Horse to finish the poles and then go buffalo hunting and bring her back the brains, one at a time. This way they would finish their work on the tipi almost at the same time. That was right, too. They ought to work together, making their own home.

She said "thank you" to everybody, and when all had seen all the hides and the gourds and the willows for the beds, they went off to their own tipis, and Spear Girl could begin to put things away.

That was harder. There was just the one tipi for four of them, and they had it full already. While she was trying to bring in all the things that rain could spoil, her mother was sitting inside the tipi thinking. Spear Girl felt a little strange about her mother. Everybody else had given her things and had been encouraging, and wanted to see her get ahead, but her mother had hardly spoken all morning. Spear Girl didn't like it. It tied up a knot in her insides. She knew, suddenly, how her mother had felt the night that Spear Girl ran away with Hunting Horse, but knowing didn't make her feel any better now.

Finally her mother got up and came outside the tipi. Spear Girl and Bow Girl had everything picked up or covered up, and the camp looked nice again, with everything where it ought to be. Her mother looked at it all for a moment, with her eyes as if she didn't see.

"That's all right," she said, then. "I guess everything's the way it ought to be."

She was talking about the way the camp looked, but she was talking about something else, too. Spear Girl didn't exactly understand, but she knew that what her mother said went deep; down under the neatness and rightness of having everything where it ought to be.

Her mother sat down beside the tipi, with her legs folded sideways under her.

"I've been thinking a lot," she said. "I think I ought to do something for you, too."

"You don't have to," Spear Girl told her.

"I have the right to," said her mother. "I need to do something. That way I show respect for my daughter and the man she married. If I don't show respect for them, soon nobody's going to respect them. They'll just give things because they're sorry. That's not right. Nobody ought to have people feeling sorry for her."

"That's right," said Spear Girl. "That's what my uncle has said, lots of times."

"I can't do much," her mother went on. "We never did have much. But we have some things. What I'm going to do, I'm going to have the woman come to cut out your tipi. Then I'm going to have more women come to help sew. Lots of women. We'll give them a feast, just the women. That way, your tipi will be made right, just like everybody else's. But you got to tan your hides yourself. Just your sister can help you."

Spear Girl felt better than she ever had in her life, but what was odd about it was that feeling good made her cry. It was good crying, and she didn't mind it, but it was strange to cry just when you felt better than you ever had before. She turned to ask her mother about it, and her mother was crying too, but she was smiling at the same time.

"That's all right, daughter," she said, "You're just a young girl yet. You don't understand things. But feeling good just does make you cry sometimes. You'll know about it all when you get more grown up." She stopped crying and smiled all over. "When you get a home of your own." she added. That was funny, too, because while Spear Girl and Bow Girl talked without words more than they talked with them, neither of them had ever been able to do it with their mother before.

It was a lot of work, getting ready to cut and sew the tipi. Spear Girl and Bow Girl worked and worked with the hides. They wanted them all smooth, scraped down to the same thickness all over, and white; and it took them a long time to get thirty-two hides just the way they ought to be.

All the time that they were working with the hides, Hunting Horse was away all day. One day he worked on the tipi-poles, and the next day he went hunting. Their mother needed a lot of meat for the feast, and as he was the man of the family, it was up to him to get it.

When everything was all ready, Spear Girl laid the hides out smooth, one on top of the other. Everything they had was full of pounded meat, some of it pounded with berries, and some of it plain; and her mother had borrowed extra kettles from their uncle's wives. Even then, there weren't enough to cook in, and she had cooked some of the meat over coals, on sticks, and some of it she had boiled the old-time way, in the skin of a buffalo's stomach. Bow Girl thought that was very funny. "Just like men eating out on a war party," she said, and giggled.

Spear Girl dressed. She put on her best white buckskin dress, with beadwork instead of painting on it; and she braided her hair and painted the parting red, and put a red circle on each cheek. It was too bad to dress all up like that just to sew hides, but as everybody did it, she had to do it, too. Stepping carefully, so as not to get grass stains on her high white moccasins, she went over to Navajo's Eye Woman's tipi to tell her to come and start cutting the cover.

Navajo's Eye Woman knew she was coming and was all dressed up in her best clothes waiting for her. "Get down," she said. Spear Girl sat down beside her and drank the water Navajo's Eye Woman gave her in a tin cup. All her gourd dippers were ready, she remembered. She'd made them by the firelight in the tipi, when it was too dark to tan outdoors.

Navajo's Eye Woman listened to Spear Girl's invitation without saying anything. Then she put her robe around her, got up, and led the way out of the tipi. She had worked so much with hides that many people called her Hide Woman, even if that wasn't her name, and she was bent all over and walked with a stick, from stooping over so much, scraping. Spear Girl hoped she wasn't stooping herself, from tanning thirty-two hides, and straightened up as stiff as she could, following Navajo's Eye Woman back to the old tipi.

Navajo's Eye Woman looked over all the hides very carefully. She turned them over from one side to the other, and she felt over the whole surface to make sure they were all even. Spear Girl was glad they had worked so hard with them. She would have hated to have Navajo's Eye Woman find a poor one. Finally Navajo's Eye Woman finished.

"Spread them all out smooth on the grass," she said. "They are all good. I can use every one."

Spear Girl and Bow Girl tried not to show how proud they felt, spreading the hides out flat on the grass. While they were doing it, Navajo's Eye Woman gave each woman a handful of sinew thread, and she asked each one if she had her awl. Every woman did, and Navajo's Eye Woman nodded. "That's good," she told them. "Bad luck if somebody forgets her awl."

Then she walked around and looked at all the hides carefully, to make sure she got the right one to start with. When she had picked it, she moved it off to itself, took her knife from its sheath at her belt, and began to cut. She cut the ears at the top of the tipi first, and

gave them to the two oldest women to sew, because they were the hardest part.

Spear Girl and Bow Girl were the last to get their sewing. It was just part of the bottom, next to the ground, because they were the youngest there, and that was the easiest part, but they worked hard, because they wanted it to be as right as all the rest of the cover.

They all sewed all day. None of the men came near them. Most of the men were in Sitting Bear's camp talking, because all the women were working on the tipi-cover, and there wasn't anything much for the men to do, or anybody around to tell them to do it.

There was a clear space between the rim of the sun and the ground when they finished, but not a wide one. All the pieces were sewed together, smooth and even, and Spear Girl wondered if she would be able afterwards to remember what woman worked on what piece; the work all looked so much alike. Navajo's Eye Woman looked around for her, and Spear Girl got up and went over to the old woman.

"Where are the poles for this tipi?" asked Navajo's Eye Woman.

Spear Girl stood up straight. She and Hunting Horse had made their plan that morning, early, before anybody else was awake. Now she stood up and faced toward Sitting Bear's tipi, and raised her arm straight up in the air.

Hunting Horse saw her. He had his horses all ready, all three of them. Two of them were loaded with tipi-poles, but the other one had presents on it, the best they had, out of the things Spear Girl's uncle had given them. A buffalo-hide robe with the hair on, a deerskin tanned white, a heavy smoked buckskin, bags of paints, and a gourd dipper—all women's things, that Spear Girl had made herself. Women's things to give to the woman who made the biggest woman's thing.

Hunting Horse led the horses up to the group of women. He dropped the lines, and let the pack-horses stand with the tipi-poles, while he gave the other horse's lines to Spear Girl. She led the horse to Navajo's Eye Woman, and Hunting Horse stood on the edge of the group of women to watch her.

"My husband and I want you to have these things," Spear Girl said, politely.

"That is good. That is kind," Navajo's Eye Woman said. She took the lines, and tied the horse to a tree behind her. "Thank you."

Spear Girl's mother began to set up the tipi-poles. Her brother's two wives came to help her, and they got the job done quickly. You could still see half of the red sun above the red earth.

Navajo's Eye Woman went and stood between the door-posts and raised her arms and prayed. She prayed for long life and good health for the people who would live in that tipi, and she prayed thankfully for the buffalo and the hides that made the tipi. Then she dropped her arms, and some of the women raised the tipi-cover and spread it over the poles. It just fitted.

They had the feast in the new tipi, after Spear Girl had lighted her first fire with coals from her mother's. All the women sat inside in the firelight while the dark grew around the outside, and their shadows grew bigger and bigger on the new white walls. Then they took what food was left—all a big lot of it—and tied it up in bundles to take home and make a feast for their husbands. Each one, as she went out, said, "Thank you for feasting," and every time Spear Girl replied, "Thank you for working."

When everybody else had gone, Bow Girl came and stood beside her, and they looked around at the new, clean, white walls. "I know what you're thinking," said Bow Girl, at last. "You're thinking that now when Hunting Horse comes home, you can put the beds in and have everything ready to start living here."

And that was odd, because Spear Girl wasn't thinking that at all. She was wondering if her mother ever had felt just the way she did right then. Now being married was beginning to feel really different.

How the Bemba Make Their Living

Max Gluckman

From *How the Bemba Make Their Living: An Appreciation of Richards' "Land, Labour and Diet in Northern Rhodesia."* Rhodes-Livingstone Institute Journal, June, 1945, pp. 55–67. By permission of the author and the publisher.

Central Africa is dominantly poor. Over vast areas it has barren soils, the rainfall and water supplies are uncertain, and its people and stock are riddled with disease. Hunger and sickness are the common lot of the African. In this, they are typical of the inhabitants of most Colonies where there is a high incidence of such deficiency diseases as beriberi, pellagra, anemia, nightblindness, tropical ulcer, dental caries, and a high rate of tuberculosis and pulmonary infections in general. Besides these deficiency diseases, the population suffers from a very high infection of malaria, hookworm, bilharzia, venereal disease, leprosy, etc. Many tribes are unable to keep cattle because of lack of pastoral country and the presence of tsetse fly, and where the fly is absent tickborne and other diseases, as well as seasonal shrinkings of pasturage, make stockraising hazardous.

Most Central African peasants have to struggle with hard natural difficulties to maintain themselves at all. The problem of raising their standard of living is evidently an immensely difficult one to solve, considering these alone. In addition, we have to deal with human beings, whose health and energy are low because of tropical heat, malnutrition and disease, and whose habits of custom and belief have been conditioned by a cultural tradition which maintained a precarious balance between life and death. Ignorance and traditional knowledge set limits to the use of potential resources. This balance has been upset by the arrival of Europeans. . . .

The Bemba live in a well-watered bushed plateau and are "men of the trees." To grow their main crop, finger millet, on the poor soils of their plateau home they pollard trees over 8–13 acres, and pile and burn the branches to provide an acre's seed bed. This garden is commonly used for 4–5 years, on a single rotation; but every year they open up new gardens. For the Bemba, rich land is land with many trees, since these ultimately provide his main food-supply. In addition, huts, granaries, fences, beds, stools, drums, canoes, string and the nets and snares made of it, magical substances for curing disease, for increasing the durability of the season's crops, for all purposes, are made from trees. The Bemba, in a tsetse area, have no cattle, and their tools are simple: an axe, a hoe, a spear and a bow. With his axe the Bemba can do much: in a few minutes he makes chairs and tables for the touring European, he strips bark to tie his loads, he shapes poles to build his huts. As he walks through what seems to us to be miles of monotonous bush, his eyes are always on the trees, noting that here grows this species or that, suitable for some specialized profane or ritual use. He watches trees to see where bees are hiving, where caterpillar grubs are swarming, etc. The Bemba live in, with, and by, their trees. This concentration of interest is reflected in their mythology and ritual. The most important national ceremonies performed each year are at the tree-cutting season, when the chiefs pray to their ancestral-spirits to provide plenty of food and to watch over the safety of the young men who swarm up to the tops of the highest trees to cut off the branches, and shout in triumph as these crash to the ground. Richards suggests that the Bemba's pride in their agility and daring in pollarding has heightened their tendency to neglect soil differences, covered by the ash seed-bed, and to take only a minor interest in their subsidiary gardens made in hoed mounds. "The Bemba consider their own system of clearing the bush as characteristic, and therefore superior to that of other tribes. The method of shearing the trees of their branches is exceedingly skillful. It is the man's task *par excellence* in the whole economic routine. The Bemba are daring climbers. . . . No tree is considered too high or too dangerous to climb" (p. 289).* "In this form of cultivation the people's emotions seem entirely centered round one process—a particular method of tree-cutting which is their pride and delight, and closely associated with an elaborate form of ritual" (p. 300). When Richards described the merits of the English system of agriculture, she heard one young man behind her "observe to his friend with a snort of derision,

*This page reference, and all subsequent ones, refer to pages in Richards' book which is the subject of Gluckman's comments here.

'Hm! Afraid to climb, I suppose.' " This form of agriculture has been constantly discouraged by Government officials, since the early days of the British South Africa Company, though agricultural research has recently impressed that it is well-suited to local conditions. "In 1907, a definite order prohibiting tree-cutting was promulgated, with the result that the people grew practically no millet, and in at least one district they had to be fed by Government for fear they should starve. The effort was then abandoned. It is true that these orders were issued to the Natives without any suggestion, apparently, as to an alternative method of cultivation. The research at present (1938–9) undertaken may result in the necessary discovery. But it is doubtful whether any system of 'cultivating on the ground' will have—at any rate for some years—the glamour of the old, and it seems likely, ironically enough, that those very factors which were formerly important incentives to production—the cultural emphasis on the value of tree-cutting and the religious rites associated with it—will act at the present day as barriers in the way of change" (p. 300).

This concentration of interest and prideful emotion on tree-cutting may partly explain why the Bemba do not use the richer soils of *ifipya* sites, tall grass-bush country, which the ecological survey says could be opened up profitably. In fact, the Bemba speak of "bad *ifipya.*" But in addition the Bemba, to use the sites, would have to change his staple diet, probably to kaffir corn or cassava, and according to his dietetic theories cassava does not give energy as millet does (this is correct). In addition, the Bemba likes to feel the heavy millet porridge inside him; he "probably becomes accustomed to a particular sensation of tension inside. To the European this would amount almost to a pain but it is evident that the Bemba want to feel full in just this particular way, and do not feel satisfied unless they have reached this state." Cassava and maize flours are softer and "melt quicker inside." Richards describes how from infancy Bemba are conditioned to and desire this heavy porridge and how they miss it in the towns. This porridge is fed as gruel even to month-old babies, for the Bemba do not clearly see that mother's milk nourishes; the breast gives only comfort. The plight of a Bemba child born in town and sent to his relatives in the country is pitiful, because the porridge "was tasteless, but also because it was rough and gave him pain." However, the same may be said of every tribe and its staple food: Lubale cassava-eaters complain of stomach-ache when on a mealie meal diet, and Lozi maize- and sorghum-eaters dislike too much of the heavier millet porridge or the lighter cassava-meal.

A meal to the Bemba is millet-porridge. This has to be "eased" down by a relish, rarely meat or fish, usually vegetable. Essential though the relish is, it is millet porridge, eaten in heavy, quickly-cooked lumps, which is the Bemba's "daily bread." In proverb and folktale the work *ubwali* stands for food itself. When discussing his kinship obligations a Native will say, "how can a man refuse to help his mother's brother who has given him *ubwali* all these years?" or, "Is he not her son? How should she refuse him *ubwali?*" In fact, he uses the word as we do "bread" in such phrases as "daily bread" or "working for our bread and butter," but more constantly, and really with better reason.

"In Bemba ceremonial *ubwali* stands for food and indirectly for ordinary daily intercourse." It figures in important national ritual, in female initiation, at marriages, and is abstained from by those who become possessed by spirits. Thus physiologically and emotionally the Bemba are conditioned to eat this millet, and are likely to oppose a change in staple, though in the towns they have to eat other food.

Bemba physiological and emotional concentration on this one food runs throughout Richards' account. In this tsetse area, where fish are obtained perennially only in the Bangweulu region on the far east and along the Chambeshi River which cuts diagonally across the kingdom, and where there is a single season of rain on predominantly poor soils, the people rely on this one main crop. Even of it they produce only sufficient for about nine months of the year, and the other

three are distinguished as "hunger months." At the end of the rainy months they regularly expect a shortage, whether it is severe or not. "When the scarcity becomes marked the whole appearance of village life is changed. For adults meals are reduced from two to one a day, and beer is rarely if ever brewed. Children who seem to munch extras all day long in the plentiful season (April–October) are reduced to a single dish late in the day. In one bad year I saw cases of elderly people who ate nothing during the course of a day, and though this is not common, most adult Natives can remember occasions when they went two days without food, and 'sat in the hut and drank water and took snuff'" (pp. 35–36). Little wonder that when the harvest is reaped Bemba use "magic of durability" to increase the strength of the crops and counter witches who would steal its goodness, for "nothing but supernatural aid can carry a woman safely through the hazards of catering." She has to cater for an unknown number of eaters and the demands of relatives, and she lacks accurate methods of measurement: there is no incentive to have big numbers or standards of measurement, for the Bemba have neither cattle nor exchange. Also "the purely possessive attitude to property with all its concomitant virtues, such as thrift, foresight, or self-reliance, are not inculcated in the Bemba child and would probably unfit him for life in his society." Nevertheless, there is a golden mean between the stingy housekeeper and the inefficient housekeeper described graphically as "a fool in the rainy season" (pp. 200–201). . . .

Richards' comparative tables of calories per day show:

Bemba village diet	Typical European or American diet	Government scale	Rhokana Corporation proposed scale
1706	3000	4313	3663

This figure for the Bemba is averaged over a period, and obscures not only the great seasonal variation in intake (in Richards' samples the lowest intake was 286 calories per day in one family in the hunger months, the highest 3164 in another family in the hot season), but also an enormous variation in daily intake. One of the best analyses in the book is that of the Bemba housewife's catering problems. She lacks exact methods of measurement, she has to fit in garden-work, gathering firewood and the long process of preparing food, and she does not know how many mouths she will have to feed at each meal. Relatives may suddenly arrive, or, if she is the village headman's wife, she may suddenly have to feed passing travelers. Even before cooking, it takes hours to pound and grind the hard millet. Her solution is to prepare on the average the same quantity of food, whether five or fifteen are to eat it: and one day her food fills people from a distance, the next day her own dependents may eat elsewhere. . . . If the housewife is the center of several households, she has to provide several baskets of food, but none goes to the boys of nine and over, who have to hang around eating-groups waiting for scraps, and who live in perpetual hunger. . . .

The Bemba accept hunger as part of the regular course of life. "The physical effects of a seasonal shortage of food on the health of people, infant mortality and growth rate of their children has not yet been investigated, but from a sociological point of view there are other effects to be considered besides the lowering of energy due to actual underfeeding which the Natives themselves recognize and describe. In a society in which people regularly expect to be hungry annually, and in which traditions and proverbs accustom them to expect such a period of privation, their whole attitude towards economic effort is affected. In some primitive tribes [as, for example, the Trobrianders of Melanesia] it is considered shameful for an individual or a whole community to go hungry. It is something unexpected, and to be resisted with energy. [Indeed these tribes direct their effort to the accumulation of surplus plenty and its public competitive display, consumption, or distribution.] Among the Bemba scarcity is within the ordinary run of experience, and

accepted as such. This fact has a subtle but very powerful effect on their ideas of wealth and their incentives to work." These ideas and incentives, as will be seen, are rooted in the social organization.

The Bemba's monotonous diet produces cravings and sudden responses to unexpected plenty. Salt was in small supply, and in the old days natural salt from the Mpika pans (one Paramount Chief abandoned his throne to return to the Mpika chieftainship for salt) was one of the few goods traded about the country, and was given as tribute to the chiefs who rewarded with it their faithful followers. To some extent this was still done when Richards was there. The people recognize the craving for salt as most pronounced. Richards describes how at a village in the hunger-season "some children, who had been living for some weeks chiefly on gourds, picked up grains of salt from the floor of my tent with moistened fingers. Their avid faces were striking." Salt figures in folktales, in proverbs, and in ceremonial, and nowadays stands for the wealth of European goods. Two old women said they came to live near the administrative center at Kasama, where they could shop easily: "We came to lick a little of the White man's salt." Salt is still used for barter. The Bemba have a similar craving for meat, and lovingly store small shreds of dried flesh in their huts, and eat the most rotted flesh: so short is meat an educated Bemba "defended the use of putrefying meat by saying, 'Yes, it will give me diarrhoea, but that will be better than throwing the meat away.'" The "attitude to meat shows in a striking fashion the way in which a physiological craving easily accounted for in an area of pronounced shortage of animal protein and salt, becomes associated with all sorts of social and psychological desires. Meat is not only good to eat but it is so rare as to make a break in the daily monotony of food and life. It is a sudden unexpected stroke of good fortune and therefore means that the spirits are on the mortals' side. It means plenty and the royal way of living at the chief's court. It is an occasion for a feast." Therefore when a village obtains a sudden supply of meat it reacts in a way that is quite out of keeping with the purely physiological value of the accession of diet. "It is probably their excitement at the sudden change of diet, their pleasure at the sight of so much food in one community, and their relief at the unexpected appearance of relish got without the usual effort and calculation of ways and means that causes . . . dramatic outbursts of energy."

"For instance, at Kasaka village (September 1933) I shot a large roan antelope which was divided among twenty-two adults and forty-seven children in a community where there had not been much meat available recently. There was probably more than 2 lb. of meat a head on this occasion. Now meat takes some hours to digest, but the energy (or *amaka, i.e.* strength) which the Native claimed that the food gave him was shown not only before the food was digested, but before it was cooked! During the division of the animal the excitement was tense. Men and women gathered round shouting and talking. Before the meal there was a buzz of expectation. Women ground extra flour with enthusiasm, 'Because we have so much meat to eat with it.' Everyone sang at their work. Young men ran skylarking round the village, like a set of English schoolboys in a playground. Directly after the meal, the women gathered near me talking in loud voices. They kept describing with ecstasy how full they felt. 'Our stomachs are rammed tight' *(Munda uauma ndi! ndi! ndi!),* said one with enthusiasm, showing with a gesture a closed fist ramming down material hard. 'Yes,' said another, 'we shall all fall asleep at once *(ukulalafye nku!),* not toss or wake at night as we usually do.' A mother, pointing to a baby of two sprawling, legs wide, replete by the fire, exclaimed, 'Yes look at him, he is so full he cannot sit up straight.' Others pulled down their cloths from their breasts to display their bellies with delight, and indeed there seemed to be quite a visible swelling of the stomach. Part of the excitement seemed connected with the fact that there was not only enough meat for that day, but that it would last till the morrow. The food was so ample that all usual rules of courtesy were put aside. 'There is so

much meat that you need not wait for an invitation to join a group of your friends round a basket,' said a young woman, 'you can just swoop down like a vulture and snatch what you want and no one will care.' An old couple sitting together on the veranda of their hut, repeated with quiet satisfaction over and over again, 'Yes, and there is just as much left for tomorrow.' Another old lady cried light-heartedly, hitting her stomach, 'I have been turned into a young girl, my heart is so light.'

"In a hour or so men and women gathered on the village square and burst into spontaneous dancing of a type I had never seen in ordinary life. Young men charged arm in arm up and down in lines singing Bemba and European songs. They imitated mission drilling and play-acting. Young girls played singing games amid screams of laughter. Drums beat, and the older women and babies clapped and shouted. It was like some wild Dionysiac rabble, and indeed these people might have been taken for drunkards, except that they were better tempered, more energetic, and showed more initiative in inventing new games. The next day, they went to work early, declaring that their arms were strong. The excitement on this particular occasion was admittedly unusual, but I have described it as an example of the extreme delight of the Bemba in the sight of meat, and of meat such profusion that it could be used for once in an utterly reckless way. . . ."

I pass now to examine the relation of these facts to Bemba social organization. This part of the argument has more than academic importance. We have seen that owing to the seasonal variation in amount of food available, and specific diet deficiencies, the Bemba in their home environment lack the energy for sustained effort to break out of the circle of dearth, and that this is emphasized by the psychological effects of recurrent hunger. The effect of these conditions on incentives and ability to produce more is obvious; but these incentives, or as Richards says "rather lack of incentives," are further conditioned by the whole economic and social setting of food production and consumption, and finally have been deleteriously affected by modern changes.

In two publications in the Rhodes-Livingstone Institute series of papers I have argued, with the support of other sociologists, that a dominant economic condition in primitive life is that there is very little variation in standard of living between individuals. This theme also runs through Richards' analysis. We meet it early in her book (at p. 34): "All Bemba individuals can be reckoned as eating, roughly speaking, the same type and quantity of food. Class distinctions practically do not exist in this respect. Chiefs certainly have a much more regular supply of food than commoners and drink very much more beer. In fact they often subsist entirely on the latter to the complete exclusion of solids. Their wives, children, and courtiers also eat on the average more than the ordinary family, so much so that Natives describe especially lavish hospitality as 'housekeeping after the fashion of the capital.' But the difference is one of certainty of supply rather than of greatly increased consumption per day, and a small class of individuals only is affected. Otherwise the rich man and his poorer neighbors eat very much the same throughout the year."

The Bemba, with no cattle, have practically no material possessions and this emphasizes their egalitarian standard of living. There were no material possessions to accumulate, and "the Bemba method of storage allows them to keep their staple crop for a period of about a year, but it is hardly efficient enough to make it possible to accumulate for longer periods" (p. 90). Therefore they could not have stored food beyond one season and in addition "actual possession of great quantities of foodstuffs does not seem to have been a particularly cherished ambition for the Bemba. They valued a reputation for giving, not for having, and the distribution of food brought by villagers as a tribute or levied as toll on the conquered peoples was a measure of wealth. . . . I never heard a chief boast to another about the size of his granaries, but often about the amount of food brought to him and distributed by him. . . . The Bemba

say, 'We will shake the tree until it gives up its fruit,' that is to say we will nag the man until he divides his supplies. If a chief attempted to dry meat and keep it for subsequent division his followers would sit and stare at it and talk about it until he was forced to give them some" (p. 214). The ambition of the Bemba, from the chief down, was to be a host, not a hoarder—and though distribution of food gave a man the service of others, this service only produced food to distribute. Hungry men had the right to "steal from the tribute garden of a chief" (p. 261), and "close relatives of the family may step into a garden and help themselves if really hungry" to maize, sweet potatoes, and cassava, but not gourds or pumpkin. Children especially "grub up roots from the garden of any near relative on either side of the family, saying indignantly if questioned, 'No, we are not stealing, this is our place here'" (p. 186). Visiting relatives must be fed, and during the hunger months men go to where there is food. When a community has been raided by locusts or elephants, "the householder will move himself and his family to live with other kinsmen in an area where food is less scarce." With transport difficulties and lack of exchange "it is simpler for the needy individuals to move to a district of plenty than for the food itself to be transferred to them. Hospitality of this sort is commonly practised in the hunger seasons when families go all over the country 'looking for porridge,' or 'running from hunger'—the rather dramatic Bemba phrase to describe the custom of paying long visits to better off relatives" (p. 109).

From birth the child is conditioned to share his food with his fellows. Bemba "mothers who are such lax disciplinarians in other respects, speak quite sharply to their children on this issue. I have seen a woman seize a lump of pumpkin out of a baby's hand and say in most vehement protest: 'You give some to your friends, you child, you! You sit and eat alone! That is bad what you do'" (p. 197). The child learns that there are certain relatives who have a right to expect goods from him, and an obligation to help him. "Food is something over which his older

brothers and sisters have definite rights. . . .
He is taught that they may pounce on any
delicacy that he may be eating." Richards
contrasts this system under which rights of
precedence are impressed with ours, where
the rule is "give it to Baby first." Where the
Bemba child is taught to share, our children,
growing up in a society where individual
initiative is on the whole encouraged, are
taught to take a pride in their personal possessions.

The Bemba beliefs are supernaturally
sanctioned: the wrath of a person who dies
feeling that his rights have been denied him,
is feared, and charges of sorcery are levied
against the person who by persistent efforts
produces more than he ought to have, in his
station. "Fear of the accusation of pride or
that reputation for personal ambition, which
is so often associated with charges of witchcraft" limits disputes over land, with the
young usually giving way lest they be called
sorcerers (pp. 271–272), and while "an occasional stroke of good luck is not resented
. . . to be permanently more prosperous
than the rest of the village would almost
lead to accusations of sorcery" (p. 215).

On the whole, ambitions are still the same,
but the desire for European goods produces
inequalities in standards of living, a commoner can possess more clothes than an
aristocrat—witchcraft charges increase. "We
are dealing with an economic system in
which the accumulation of large quantities of
any type of material goods was neither very
possible nor considered desirable. The accumulation of food was not an end in itself for
the chief or notable, but rather a means to
enable him to build up a large following of
people which was to him the highest aim in
life. His economic assets consisted in rights
over food produced by others as well as in the
cultivation of millet himself. For the commoner, the possession of excessive food supplies was definitely considered unsuitable,
and people were afraid to admit they had
such a store. In short the surplus crop was
not a Bemba ideal. Under modern conditions
the desire for European goods, and in particular clothes, leads the people to squander

even their available food supplies on objects
which have become more important to them"
(p. 218). These dominant economic conditions form the background for the whole
analysis.

We can now return, for the moment, to the
problem of incentives to production. In these
economic conditions it is difficult for the
Bemba woman to budget, for her food is not
only for the use of her own family, but has
also to feed an indefinite number of relatives
in a system of mutual help. "The economic
conditions under which she lives necessitate
reciprocal sharing of foodstuffs, rather than
their accumulation, and extend the individual's responsibility outside her own household. Plainly, therefore, it does not pay a
Bemba woman to have much more grain than
her fellows. She would merely have to distribute it, and during the recent locust
scourge the villagers whose gardens escaped
destruction complained that they were not
really better off than their fellows for 'our
people come and live with us or beg us for
baskets of millet'" (pp. 201–202).

Though there is this tremendous stress on
sharing and hospitality, and the Bemba
woman has to maintain a delicate adjustment
between the rights of her relatives by blood
and marriage and her own needs in her crops,
it is wrong to describe the system as purely
communistic or communal. The basis is highly individualistic. The Bemba had little difficulty in getting land to work and cut their
gardens where they pleased, though naturally
near their villages. But once a man has cut his
garden it is his and not even a chief will
interfere with him: "it would not pay him to do
so," since the more his subjects the more the
food produced in his country and the more
the tribute he gets. "In fact, in the case of a
new garden the Natives seem to believe that
there is some particularly close connection of
an almost magical nature, between the owner
and the patch of ground he has just cleared of
bush. Although a man can lend his garden to
another in the second or third year, or even
sell the crops on it, he should do neither of
these things in the case of the first year
patch" (p. 185). Despite this sharing, individu-

al ownership of field crops, of bush-goods, caterpillar swarms, hives of wild bees, of meat and fish, "is very clearly defined among the Bemba" (p. 188). The "system of food consumption is determined by rules of individual ownership subject to the claims of elder relatives" (p. 195). . . .

Richards thus shows clearly that in the Bemba economic situation, with its conceptions of wealth, of the purposes for which food should be used, of the values attached to hospitality and to kinship, etc., there is a definite bias against individuals increasing their production. We thus come to one of the "balances" which experts always stress and the dangers of upsetting which they seem always to emphasize. Richards makes a careful, detailed analysis of the actual distribution of food and performance of labor tasks as she observed them in a typical village and she concludes that the establishing of isolated individual families, in which this "lack of incentives" might theoretically be overcome, would be unwise without provision to meet the new difficulties that would be created. For her analysis shows clearly "how the addition of each additional supporting household strengthens the position of the whole family" (p. 171), and a comparison with modern villagers near European centers shows that "the families in these communities are at present in an intermediate position—they do not have to share their supplies as do their fellows in the bush, yet they are much worse off during the hunger months, since they cannot rely on their kinsmen for support. Although it appears that most Africans must ultimately adopt the European system of economy, the encouragement of the single family household, before a system of trade has been established, might well lead to disaster" (p. 153). It must be recognized that joint housekeeping makes for greater security in a society with no system of exchange or purchase of food. To be attached to a "big house" is to share its fortunes—to have the chance of delicacies like beer and meat as often as possible, and to be certain of support in case of a shortage. A comparison between conditions in a modern village where the kinship groups are smaller makes this clear. Where the unit of consumption is only one or two households the people may be better off at good seasons of the year but practically destitute in a bad one.

"Joint cooking also eases the housewife's labor very largely." Richards by analyzing household tasks shows how difficult it is for a woman to fit in the lengthy process of cooking, how grinding and pounding go more quickly in company, and how where there are several women in a team some find relish and bring wood and water while another cooks. The isolated housewife cannot do this, and Richards' notes on typical families show this clearly (p. 132).

Richards traces food, the clearing of land, cooking, storing, and learning of household craft, through these economic conditions in a meticulous analysis, enlivened with the observations of a witty and sympathetic mind. The Bemba stand out as individuals, like Namukonda, "an incisive personality. She was a good organizer, who met each domestic emergency with calm decision and who kept her large family in wholesome awe of her sharp tongue. Her withering comments on the follies of the present generation were a constant delight to me. They were uttered with a shrug, a lifted eyebrow, and a glance of understanding as though between two adults alone in a nursery of tiresome children" (p. 171). We feel the dismay in the family of a young woman who refused to live with her hot-tempered husband and could not persuade her brother to provide his fourteen-year-old daughter as a substitute according to the old Bemba custom. "The injured husband retired to his own family's village to await events. After a few weeks a file of six women with empty baskets on their heads appeared from that direction. The wife's relatives stood aghast at the doors of their huts muttering, 'Yangwe. They have come to take the grain.' They could only watch while the husband's kinswomen lifted the roof of the granary, emptied its contents, and left with their baskets full, after a brisk exchange of obscene abuse between both parties" (p. 190). We sympathize with the lot of a wife, one of six sisters, who lived happily with them in her village through the years of her husband's service to her father, but who when he gained the right to move to his own village could not bear "the contrast between the cheerful female group in her own village and her relative isolation in her husband's community." She ran away three times, and ulti-

mately was divorced (p. 131). We see the modern chief struggling to maintain his court and status with income tremendously reduced, yet who knows all that is going on [in] his country, so that when a Bisa chief comes to ask for his daughter's hand he can send messengers to get beer and food at villages where he knows they will be found.

What Hunters Do for a Living, or, How to Make Out on Scarce Resources

Richard B. Lee

From *Man the Hunter,*
Richard B. Lee and Irven Devore (eds.), pp. 30–48. Copyright © 1968, Wenner-Gren Foundation for Anthropological Research, Aldine Publishing Company. By permission of the author, the publisher and the copyright holder.

The current anthropological view of hunter-gatherer subsistence rests on two questionable assumptions. First is the notion that these peoples are primarily dependent on the hunting of game animals, and second is the assumption that their way of life is generally a precarious and arduous struggle for existence.

Recent data on living hunter-gatherers show a radically different picture. We have learned that in many societies, plant and marine resources are far more important than are game animals in the diet. More important, it is becoming clear that, with a few conspicuous exceptions, the hunter-gatherer subsistence base is at least routine and reliable and at best surprisingly abundant. Anthropologists have consistently tended to underestimate the viability of even those "marginal isolates" of hunting peoples that have been available to ethnographers. . . .

Bushman Subsistence

The !Kung Bushmen of Botswana are an apt case for analysis. They inhabit the semi-arid northwest region of the Kalahari Desert. With only six to nine inches of rainfall per year, this is, by any account, a marginal environment for human habitation. In fact, it is precisely the unattractiveness of their homeland that has kept the !Kung isolated from extensive contact with their agricultural and pastoral neighbors.

Field work was carried out in the Dobe area, a line of eight permanent waterholes near the South-West Africa border and 125 miles south of the Okavango River. The population of the Dobe area consists of 466 Bushmen, including 379 permanent residents living in independent camps or associated with Bantu cattle posts, as well as 87 seasonal visitors. The Bushmen share the area with some 340 Bantu pastoralists largely of the Herero and Tswana tribes. The ethnographic present refers to the period of field work: October, 1963–January, 1965

The Bushmen living in independent camps lack firearms, livestock, and agriculture. Apart from occasional visits to the Herero for milk, these !Kung are entirely dependent upon hunting and gathering for their subsistence. Politically they are under the nominal authority of the Tswana headman, although they pay no taxes and receive very few government services. European presence amounts to one overnight government patrol every six to eight weeks. Although Dobe-area !Kung have had some contact with outsiders since the 1880's, the majority of them continue to hunt and gather because there is no viable alternative locally available to them.

Each of the fourteen independent camps is associated with one of the permanent waterholes. During the dry season (May–October) the entire population is clustered around these wells. . . . Two wells had no camp resident and one large well supported five camps. The number of camps at each well and the size of each camp changed frequently during the course of the year. The "camp" is an open aggregate of cooperating persons which changes in size and composition from day to day. Therefore, I have avoided the term "band" in describing the !Kung Bushman living groups.

Each waterhole has a hinterland lying within a six-mile radius which is regularly exploited for vegetable and animal foods. These areas are not territories in the zoological sense, since they are not defended against outsiders. Rather they constitute the resources that lie within a convenient walking distance of a waterhole. The camp is a self-sufficient subsistence unit. The members move out each day to hunt and gather, and return in the evening to pool the collected foods in such a way that every person present receives an equitable share. Trade in foodstuffs between camps is minimal; personnel do move freely from camp to camp, however. The net effect is of a population constantly in motion. On the average, an individual spends a third of his time living only with close relatives, a third visiting other camps, and a third entertaining visitors from other camps.

Because of the strong emphasis on sharing, and the frequency of movement, surplus accumulation of storable plant foods and dried meat is kept to a minimum. There is rarely more than two or three days' supply of food on hand in a camp at any time. The result of this lack of surplus is that a constant subsistence effort must be maintained throughout the year. Unlike agriculturists who work hard during the planting and harvesting seasons and undergo "seasonal unemployment" for several months, the Bushmen hunter-gatherers collect food every third or fourth day throughout the year.

Vegetable foods comprise from 60–80 per cent of the total diet by weight, and collecting involves two or three days of work per woman per week. The men also collect plants and small animals but their major contribution to the diet is the hunting of medium and large game. The men are conscientious but not particularly successful hunters; although men's and women's work input is roughly equivalent in terms of man-day effort, the women provide two to three times as much food by weight as the men. . . .

For the greater part of the year, food is locally abundant and easily collected. It is only during the end of the dry season in September and October, when desirable foods have been eaten out in the immediate vicinity of the waterholes that the people have to plan longer hikes of 10–15 miles and carry their own water to those areas where the mongongo nut is still available. The important point is that food is a constant, but distance required to reach food is a variable; it is short in the summer, fall, and early winter, and reaches its maximum in the spring.

This analysis attempts to provide quantitative measures of subsistence status including data on the following topics: abundance and variety of resources, diet selectivity, range size and population density, the composition of the work force, the ratio of work to leisure time, and the caloric and protein levels in the diet. The value of quantitative data is that they can be used comparatively and also may be useful in archeological reconstruction. In addition, one can avoid the pitfalls of subjective and qualitative impressions; for example, statements about food "anxiety" have proven to be difficult to generalize across cultures.

Abundance and variety of resources
It is impossible to define "abundance" of resources absolutely. However, one index of *relative* abundance is whether or not a population exhausts all the food available from a given area. By this criterion, the habitat of the Dobe-area Bushmen is abundant in naturally occurring foods. By far the most important food is the mongongo (mangetti) nut *Ricinodendron rautaneni* Schinz). Although tens of thousands of pounds of these nuts are harvested and eaten each year, thousands more rot on the ground each year for want of picking.

The mongongo nut, because of its abundance and reliability, alone accounts for 50 per cent of the vegetable diet by weight. In this respect it resembles a cultivated staple crop such as maize or rice. Nutritionally it is even more remarkable, for it contains five times the calories and ten times the proteins per cooked unit of the cereal crops. The average daily per-capita consumption of 300 nuts yields about 1,260 calories and 56 grams of protein. This modest portion, weighing only about 7.5 ounces, contains the caloric equivalent of 2.5 pounds of cooked rice and the protein equivalent of 14 ounces of lean beef.

Furthermore the mongongo nut is drought resistant and it will still be abundant in the dry years when cultivated crops may fail. The extremely hard outer shell protects the inner

kernel from rot and allows the nuts to be harvested for up to twelve months after they have fallen to the ground. A diet based on mongongo nuts is in fact more reliable than one based on cultivated foods, and it is not surprising, therefore, that when a Bushman was asked why he hadn't taken to agriculture he replied: "Why should we plant, when there are so many mongongo nuts in the world?"

Apart from the mongongo, the Bushmen have available 84 other species of edible food plants, including 29 species of fruits, berries, and melons and 30 species of roots and bulbs. The existence of this variety allows for a wide range of alternatives in subsistence strategy. During the summer months the Bushmen have no problem other than to choose among the tastiest and most easily collected foods. Many species, which are quite edible but less attractive, are bypassed, so that gathering never exhausts *all* the available plant foods of an area. During the dry season the diet becomes much more eclectic and the many species of roots, bulbs, and edible resins make an important contribution. It is this broad base that provides an essential margin of safety during the end of the dry season when the mongongo nut forests are difficult to reach. In addition, it is likely that these rarely utilized species provide important nutritional and mineral trace elements that may be lacking in the more popular foods.

Diet selectivity
If the Bushmen were living close to the "starvation" level, then one would expect them to exploit every available source of nutrition. That their life is well above this level is indicated by the data in Table 1. Here all the edible plant species are arranged in classes according to the frequency with which they were observed to be eaten. It should be noted, that although there are some 85 species available, about 90 per cent of the vegetable diet by weight is drawn from only 23 species. In other words, 75 per cent of the listed species provide only 10 per cent of the food value.

In their meat-eating habits, the Bushmen show a similar selectivity. Of the 223 local

Table 1 !Kung Bushman plant foods

| | PART EATEN | | | | | | | | TOTALS (PERCENTAGES) | | |
Food class	Fruit and nut	Bean and root	Fruit and stalk	Root, bulb	Fruit, berry, melon	Resin	Leaves	Seed, bean	Total number of species in class	Estimated contribution by weight to vegetable diet	Estimated contribution of each species
I. PRIMARY Eaten daily throughout year (mongongo nut)	1	—	—	—	—	—	—	—	1	c.50	c.50*
II. MAJOR Eaten daily in season	1	1	1	1	4	—	—	—	8	c.25	c.3 †
III. MINOR Eaten several times per week in season	—	—	—	7	3	2	2	—	14	c.15	c.1
IV. SUPPLEMENTARY Eaten when classes I–III locally unavailable	—	—	—	9	12	10	1	—	32	c.7	c.0.2
V. RARE Eaten several times per year	—	—	—	9	4	—	—	—	13	c.3	c.0.1 ‡
VI. PROBLEMATIC Edible but not observed to be eaten	—	—	—	4	6	4	1	2	17	nil	nil
TOTAL SPECIES	2	1	1	30	29	16	4	2	85	100	—

* 1 species constitutes 50 per cent of the vegetable diet by weight.
† 23 species constitute 90 per cent of the vegetable diet by weight.
‡ 62 species constitute the remaining 10 per cent of the diet.

species of animals known and named by the Bushmen, 54 species are classified as edible, and of these only 17 species were hunted on a regular basis. Only a handful of the dozens of edible species of small mammals, birds, reptiles, and insects that occur locally are regarded as food. Such animals as rodents, snakes, lizards, termites, and grasshoppers, which in the literature are included in the Bushman dietary, are despised by the Bushmen of the Dobe area.

Range size and population density
The necessity to travel long distances, the high frequency of moves, and the maintenance of populations at low densities are also

features commonly associated with the hunting and gathering way of life. Density estimates for hunters in western North America and Australia have ranged from 3 persons/square mile to as low as 1 person/100 square miles. In 1963–65, the resident and visiting Bushmen were observed to utilize an area of about 1,000 square miles during the course of the annual round for an effective population density of 41 persons/100 square miles. Within this area, however, the amount of ground covered by members of an individual camp was surprisingly small. A day's round-trip of twelve miles serves to define a "core" area six miles in radius surrounding each water point. By fanning out in all directions from their well, the members of a camp can gain access to the food resources of well over 100 square miles of territory within a two-hour hike. Except for a few weeks each year, areas lying beyond this six-mile radius are rarely utilized, even though they are no less rich in plants and game than are the core areas.

Although the Bushmen move their camps frequently (five or six times a year) they do not move them very far. A rainy season camp in the nut forests is rarely more than ten or twelve miles from the home waterhole, and often new campsites are occupied only a few hundred yards away from the previous one. By these criteria, the Bushmen do not lead a free-ranging nomadic way of life. For example, they do not undertake long marches of 30 to 100 miles to get food, since this task can be readily fulfilled within a day's walk of home base. When such long marches do occur they are invariably for visiting, trading, and marriage arrangements, and should not be confused with the normal routine of subsistence.

Demographic factors
Another indicator of the harshness of a way of life is the age at which people die. Ever since Hobbes characterized life in the state of nature as "nasty, brutish and short," the assumption has been that hunting and gathering is so rigorous that members of such societies are rapidly worn out and meet an early death. Silberbauer, for example, says of the Gwi Bushmen of the central Kalahari that

"life expectancy . . . is difficult to calculate, but I do not believe that many live beyond 45." And Coon has said . . .

The practice of abandoning the hopelessly ill and aged has been observed in many parts of the world. It is always done by people living in poor environments where it is necessary to move about frequently to obtain food, where food is scarce, and transportation difficult. . . . Among peoples who are forced to live in this way the oldest generation, the generation of individuals who have passed their physical peak is reduced in numbers and influence. There is no body of elders to hand on tradition and control the affairs of younger men and women, and no formal system of age grading.

The !Kung Bushmen of the Dobe area flatly contradict this view. In a total population of 466, no fewer than 46 individuals (17 men and 29 women) were determined to be over 60 years of age, a proportion that compares favorably to the percentage of elderly in industralized populations.

The aged hold a respected position in Bushman society and are the effective leaders of the camps. Senilicide is extremely rare. Long after their productive years have passed, the old people are fed and cared for by their children and grandchildren. The blind, the senile, and the crippled are respected for the special ritual and technical skills they possess. For instance, the four elders at !gose waterhole were totally or partially blind, but this handicap did not prevent their active participation in decision-making and ritual curing.

Another significant feature of the composition of the work force is the late assumption of adult responsibility by the adolescents. Young people are not expected to provide food regularly until they are married. Girls typically marry between the ages of 15 and 20, and boys about five years later, so that it is not unusual to find healthy, active teenagers visiting from camp to camp while their older relatives provide food for them.

As a result, the people in the age group 20–60 support a surprisingly large percentage of non-productive young and old people.

About 40 per cent of the population in camps contribute little to the food supplies. This allocation of work to young and middle-aged adults allows for a relatively carefree childhood and adolescence and a relatively unstrenuous old age.

Leisure and work

Another important index of ease or difficulty of subsistence is the amount of time devoted to the food quest. Hunting has usually been regarded by social scientists as a way of life in which merely keeping alive is so formidable a task that members of such societies lack the leisure time necessary to "build culture." The !Kung Bushmen would appear to conform to the rule, for as Lorna Marshall says:

> It is vividly apparent that among the !Kung Bushmen, ethos, or "the spirit which actuates manners and customs," is survival. Their time and energies are almost wholly given to this task, for life in their environment requires that they spend their days mainly in procuring food.

It is certainly true that getting food is the most important single activity in Bushman life. However this statement would apply equally well to small-scale agricultural and pastoral societies too. How much time is *actually* devoted to the food quest is fortunately an empirical question. And an analysis of the work effort of the Dobe Bushmen shows some unexpected results. From July 6 to August 2, 1964, I recorded all the daily activities of the Bushmen living at the Dobe waterhole. Because of the coming and going of visitors, the camp population fluctuated in size day by day, from a low of 23 to a high of 40, with a mean of 31.8 persons. Each day some of the adult members of the camp went out to hunt and/or gather while others stayed home or went visiting. The daily recording of all personnel on hand made it possible to calculate the number of man-days of work as a percentage of total number of man-days of consumption.

Although the Bushmen do not organize their activities on the basis of a seven-day week, I have divided the data this way to make

them more intelligible. The work-week was calculated to show how many days out of seven each adult spent in subsistence activities (Table 2, Column 7). Week II has been eliminated from the totals since the investigator contributed food. In week I, the people spent an average of 2.3 days in subsistence activities, in week III, 1.9 days, and week IV, 3.2 days. In all, the adults of the Dobe camp worked about two and a half days a week. Since the average working day was about six hours long, the fact emerges that !Kung Bushmen of Dobe, despite their harsh environment, devote from twelve to nineteen hours a week to getting food. Even the hardest working individual in the camp, a man named ≠ oma who went out hunting on sixteen of the 28 days, spent a maximum of 32 hours a week in the food quest.

Because the Bushmen do not amass a surplus of foods, there are no seasons of exceptionally intensive activities such as planting and harvesting, and no seasons of unemployment. The level of work observed is an accurate reflection of the effort required to meet the immediate caloric needs of the group. This work diary covers the mid-winter dry season, a period when food is neither at its most plentiful nor at its scarcest levels, and the diary documents the transition from better to worse conditions. During the fourth week the gatherers were making overnight trips to camps in the mongongo nut forests seven to ten miles distant from the waterhole. These longer trips account for the rise in the level of work, from twelve or thirteen to nineteen hours per week.

If food getting occupies such a small proportion of a Bushman's waking hours, then how *do* people allocate their time? A woman gathers on one day enough food to feed her family for three days, and spends the rest of her time resting in camp, doing embroidery, visiting other camps, or entertaining visitors from other camps. For each day at home, kitchen routines, such as cooking, nut cracking, collecting firewood, and fetching water, occupy one to three hours of her time. This rhythm of steady work and steady leisure is maintained throughout the year.

Table 2   Summary of Dobe work diary

WEEK	(1) MEAN GROUP SIZE	(2) ADULT-DAYS	(3) CHILD-DAYS	(4) TOTAL MAN-DAYS OF CONSUMPTION	(5) MAN-DAYS OF WORK	(6) MEAT (LBS.)	(7) AVERAGE WORK WEEK/ADULT	(8) INDEX OF SUBSISTENCE EFFORT
I	25.6	114	65	179	37	104	2.3	0.21
(July 6–12)	(23–29)							
II	28.3	125	73	198	22	80	1.2	0.11
(July 13–19)	(23–27)							
III	34.3	156	84	240	42	177	1.9	0.18
(July 20–26)	(29–40)							
IV	35.6	167	82	249	77	129	3.2	0.31
(July 27–Aug. 2)	(32–40)							
4-wk. Total	30.9	562	304	866	178	490	2.2	0.21
Adjusted Total*	31.8	437	231	668	156	410	2.5	0.23

* See text.

Key: Column 1: Mean group size $= \dfrac{\textit{total man-days of consumption}}{7}$.

Column 7: Work week = the number of work days per adult per week.

Column 8: Index of subsistence effort $= \dfrac{\textit{man-days of work}}{\textit{man-days of consumption}}$ *(e.g., in Week I, the value of "S" = 0.21, i.e., 21 days*

of work/100 days of consumption or 1 work day produces food for 5 consumption days).

The hunters tend to work more frequently than the women, but their schedule is uneven. It is not unusual for a man to hunt avidly for a week and then do no hunting at all for two or three weeks. Since hunting is an unpredictable business and subject to magical control, hunters sometimes experience a run of bad luck and stop hunting for a month or longer. During these periods, visiting, entertaining, and especially dancing are the primary activities of men. (Unlike the Hadza, gambling is only a minor leisure activity.)

The trance-dance is the focus of Bushman ritual life; over 50 per cent of the men have trained as trance-performers and regularly enter trance during the course of the all-night dances. At some camps, trance-dances occur as frequently as two or three times a week and those who have entered trances the night before rarely go out hunting the following day. . . . In a camp with five or more hunters, there are usually two or three who are actively hunting and several others who are inactive. The net effect is to phase the hunting and

non-hunting so that a fairly steady supply of meat is brought into a camp.

Caloric returns

Is the modest work effort of the Bushmen sufficient to provide the calories necessary to maintain the health of the population? Or have the !Kung, in common with some agricultural peoples, adjusted to a permanently substandard nutritional level?

During my field work I did not encounter any cases of kwashiorkor, the most common nutritional disease in the children of African agricultural societies. However, without medical examinations, it is impossible to exclude the possibility that subclinical signs of malnutrition existed.

Another measure of nutritional adequacy is the average consumption of calories and proteins per person per day. The estimate for the Bushmen is based on observations of the weights of foods of known composition that were brought into Dobe camp on each day of the study period. The per-capita figure is obtained by dividing the total weight of foodstuffs by the total number of persons in the camp. . . . During the study period 410 pounds of meat were brought in by the hunters of the Dobe camp, for a daily share of nine ounces of meat per person. About 700 pounds of vegetable foods were gathered and consumed during the same period. Table 3 sets out the calories and proteins available per capita in the !Kung Bushman dietary from meat, mongongo nuts, and other vegetable sources.

This output of 2,140 calories and 93.1 grams of protein per person per day may be compared with the Recommended Daily Allowances (RDA) for persons of the small size and stature but vigorous activity regime of the !Kung Bushmen. The RDA for Bushmen can be estimated at 1,975 calories and 60 grams of protein per person per day. Thus it is apparent that food output exceeds energy requirements by 165 calories and 33 grams of protein. One can tentatively conclude that even a modest subsistence effort of two or three days work per week is enough to provide an adequate diet for the !Kung Bushmen.

The Security of Bushman Life

I have attempted to evaluate the subsistence base of one contemporary hunter-gatherer society living in a marginal environment. The !Kung Bushmen have available to them some relatively abundant high-quality foods, and they do not have to walk very far or work very hard to get them. Furthermore this modest work effort provides sufficient calories to support not only the active adults, but also a large number of middle-aged and elderly people. The Bushmen do not have to press their youngsters into the service of the food quest, nor do they have to dispose of the oldsters after they have ceased to be productive.

The evidence presented assumes an added significance because this security of life was observed during the third year of one of the most severe droughts in South Africa's history. Most of the 576,000 people of Botswana are pastoralists and agriculturalists. After the crops had failed three years in succession and over 100,000 head of cattle had died on the range for lack of water, the World Food Program of the United Nations instituted a famine relief program which has grown to include 180,000 people, over 30 per cent of the population. This program did not touch the Dobe area in the isolated northwest corner of the country and the Herero and Tswana women there were able to feed their families only by joining the Bushman women to forage for wild foods. Thus the natural plant resources of the Dobe area were carrying a higher proportion of population than would be the case in years when the Bantu harvested crops. Yet this added pressure on the land did not seem to adversely affect the Bushmen.

In one sense it was unfortunate that the period of my field work happened to coincide with the drought, since I was unable to witness a "typical" annual subsistence cycle. However, in another sense, the coincidence was a lucky one, for the drought put the

Table 3 Caloric and protein levels in the !Kung Bushman dietary, July–August, 1964

CLASS OF FOOD	PERCENTAGE CONTRIBUTION TO DIET BY WEIGHT	PER CAPITA CONSUMPTION WEIGHT IN GRAMS	PROTEIN IN GRAMS	CALORIES PER PERSON PER DAY	PERCENTAGE CALORIC CONTRIBUTION OF MEAT AND VEGETABLES
Meat	37	230	34.5	690	33
Mongongo nuts	33	210	56.7	1,260	
Other vegetable					67
foods	30	190	1.9	190	
Total					
All Sources	100	630	93.1	2,140	100

Bushmen and their subsistence system to the acid test and, in terms of adaptation to scarce resources, they passed with flying colors. One can postulate that their subsistence base would be even more substantial during years of higher rainfall.

What are the crucial factors that make this way of life possible? I suggest that the primary factor is the Bushmen's strong emphasis on vegetable food sources. Although hunting involves a great deal of effort and prestige, plant foods provide from 60–80 per cent of the annual diet by weight. Meat has come to be regarded as a special treat; when available, it is welcomed as a break from the routine of vegetable foods, but it is never depended upon as a staple. No one ever goes hungry when hunting fails.

The reason for this emphasis is not hard to find. Vegetable foods are abundant, sedentary, and predictable. They grow in the same place year after year, and the gatherer is guaranteed a day's return of food for a day's expenditure of energy. Game animals, by contrast, are scarce, mobile, unpredictable, and difficult to catch. A hunter has no guarantee of success and may in fact go for days or weeks without killing a large mammal. During the study period, there were eleven men in the Dobe camp, of whom four did no hunting at all. The seven active men spent a total of 78 man-days hunting, and this work input yielded eighteen animals killed, or one kill for every four man-days of hunting. The probability of any one hunter making a kill on a given day was 0.23. By contrast, the probability of a woman finding plant food on a given day was 1.00. In other words, hunting and gathering are not equally felicitous subsistence alternatives.

Consider the productivity per man-hour of the two kinds of subsistence activities. One man-hour of hunting produces about 100 edible calories, and of gathering, 240 calories. Gathering is thus seen to be 2.4 times more productive than hunting. In short, hunting is a *high-risk, low-return* subsistence activity, while gathering is a *low-risk, high-return* subsistence activity.

It is not at all contradictory that the hunt-ing complex holds a central place in the Bushman ethos and that meat is valued more highly than vegetable foods. Analogously, steak is valued more highly than potatoes in the food preferences of our own society. In both situations the meat is more "costly" than the vegetable food. In the Bushman case, the cost of food can be measured in terms of time and energy expended. By this standard, 1,000 calories of meat "costs" ten man-hours, while the "cost" of 1,000 calories of vegetable foods is only four man-hours. Further, it is to be expected that the less predictable, more expensive food source would have a greater accretion of myth and ritual built up around it than would the routine staples of life, which rarely if ever fail.

Eskimo-Bushman comparisons

Were the Bushmen to be deprived of their vegetable food sources, their life would become much more arduous and precarious. This lack of plant foods, in fact, is precisely the situation among the Netsilik Eskimo, reported by Balikci. The Netsilik and other Central Arctic peoples are perhaps unique in the almost total absence of vegetable foods in their diet. This factor, in combination with the great cyclical variation in the numbers and distribution of Arctic fauna, makes Eskimo life the most precarious human adaptation on earth. In effect, *the kinds of animals that are "luxury goods" to many hunters and gatherers, are to the Eskimos, the absolute necessities of life.* However, even this view should not be exaggerated, since most of the Eskimos in historic times have lived south of the Arctic Circle and many of the Eskimos at all latitudes have depended primarily on fishing, which is a much more reliable source of food than is the hunting of land and sea mammals.

What Hunters Do for a Living: A Comparative Study

I have discussed how the !Kung Bushmen are able to manage on the scarce resources of their inhospitable environment. The essence of their successful strategy seems to be that while they depend primarily on the more stable and abundant food sources (vegetables in their case), they are nevertheless willing to devote considerable energy to the less reliable and more highly valued food sources such as medium and large mammals. The steady but modest input of work by the women provides the former, and the more intensive labors of the men provide the latter. It would be theoretically possible for the Bushmen to survive entirely on vegetable foods, but life would be boring indeed without the excitement of meat feasts. The totality of their subsistence activities thus represents an outcome of two individual goals; the first is the desire to live well with adequate leisure time, and the second is the desire to enjoy the rewards, both social and nutritional, afforded by the killing of game. In short, *the Bushmen of the Dobe area eat as much vegetable food as they need, and as much meat as they can.*

It seems reasonable that a similar kind of subsistence strategy would be characteristic of hunters and gatherers in general. Wherever two or more kinds of natural foods are available, one would predict that the population exploiting them would emphasize the more reliable source. We would also expect, however, that the people would not neglect the alternative means of subsistence. The general view offered here is that gathering activities, for plants and shellfish, should be the most productive of food for hunting and gathering man, followed by fishing, where this source is available. The hunting of mammals is the least reliable source of food and should be generally less important than either gathering or fishing. . . .

Conclusions

Three points ought to be stressed. First, life in the state of nature is not necessarily nasty, brutish, and short. The Dobe-area Bushmen live well today on wild plants and meat, in spite of the fact that they are confined to the least productive portion of the range in which Bushman peoples were formerly found. It is likely that an even more substantial subsistence base would have been characteristic of these hunters and gatherers in the past, when they had the pick of African habitats to choose from.

Second, the basis of Bushman diet is derived from sources other than meat. This emphasis makes good ecological sense to the !Kung Bushmen and appears to be a common feature among hunters and gatherers in general. Since a 30 to 40 per cent input of meat is such a consistent target for modern hunters in a variety of habitats, is it not reasonable to postulate a similar percentage for prehistoric hunters? Certainly the absence of plant remains on archeological sites is by itself not sufficient evidence for the absence of gathering. Recently-abandoned Bushman campsites show a similar absence of vegetable remains, although this paper has clearly shown that plant foods comprise over 60 per cent of the actual diet.

Finally, one gets the impression that hunting societies have been chosen by ethnologists to illustrate a dominant theme, such as the extreme importance of environment in the molding of certain cultures. Such a theme can be best exemplified by cases in which the technology is simple and/or the environment is harsh. This emphasis on the dramatic may have been pedagogically useful, but unfortunately it has led to the assumption that a precarious hunting subsistence base was characteristic of all cultures in the Pleistocene. This view of both modern and ancient hunters ought to be reconsidered. Specifically I am suggesting a shift in focus away from the dramatic and unusual cases, and toward a consideration of hunting and gathering as a persistent and well-adapted way of life.

part 6

Primitive Society

Bontok Social Organization

Felix M. Keesing

From *Some Notes on Bontok Social Organization, Northern Philippines.* American Anthropologist, Vol. 51, No. 4, 1949, pp. 578–601. By permission of the author and the publisher.

The Bontok comprise one of approximately ten ethnic groups into which the "Igorot" (mountain peoples) of the Cordillera Central in North Luzon have been classified. Estimates of the total number in the Bontok group range from about 30,000 to 40,000. They live in 32 villages scattered over wild steep country where the headwaters of the Chico river bisect this great mountain mass. Here, at about the three to five thousand foot level, the malarial forests of the lowlands are replaced by scrub and grass, with occasional stands of pine and oak. Wherever water for irrigation, and soil and rock for building agricultural terraces, can be brought together in sufficient amount, even though enormous labor is involved, a settlement is likely to be established. A close correlation exists between the size of each village and the flow of water which it controls in its ancestral streams. The annual cycle of agricultural production, so ably recorded by Jenks, dominates Bontok life: a drama in which supernatural forces must conjoin with human activity for successful consummation.

The inaccessibility and poverty of this section of the mountain country, its sparseness of population, and the warlike character of its peoples caused the Spanish conquerors of the Philippines to leave it practically untouched for three centuries. Initiating a more active policy from 1860 on, they exercised a precarious control with the aid of garrisons, cutting trails, collecting tribute, enforcing peace, and putting down frequent "revolts." After 1902, when Americans established a special protective type of government for the "non-Christian" peoples of Mountain Province, a group of American and Filipino administrators were able to develop an equilibrium of relationships among Bontok villages and between the Bontok and their neighbors through a series of "peace pacts" for which leading elders were made responsible. Head-taking became an occasional occurrence only, quickly dealt with by constabulary units mainly enlisted locally. Regional and local self-government was fostered, and welfare measures advanced. Protestant and Catholic missions also started work. . . .

Bontok villages are sometimes spoken of in the literature as "towns" or *pueblos.* The Bontok language itself appears to have no generic word for such a community unit, so that the people have adopted the term *ili* from Iloko speech, that is, the language of the coastal Ilocano which has long since become the *lingua franca* of the mountain region. As suggested by the demographic data given above, the average number of people to a Bontok village appears to be somewhat under a thousand. As of 1933, however, there was a range of variation from over 2,000 in the capital, Bontoc, not including a considerable immigrant fringe, to perhaps 300 in small villages high up in poor country.

The village sites have undoubtedly been occupied for centuries, as shown by the extensive group of step-like terraces which surround each. The names of a number of them appear in the records of the first Spanish explorers. Every topographic feature has ancestral associations, while all types of land have their precise definitions of ownership and use. No one lives outside the village, and no system of scattered farming is possible short of a revolution in social organization and belief, of which there are scanty signs.

Each village is zoned into a number of units which are referred to in the literature by such names as "sections," "wards," or "precincts." Out of an elaborate terminology connected with such a unit, the most comprehensive Bontok name for it is *ato,* a term made familiar through Jenks' work. The number of *ato* sections varies from community to community, and in villages actually analyzed with local informants a range showed from as few as six to as many as eighteen.

Each *ato* has a permanent name and its boundaries are clearly defined geographically—though to the eye of the stranger there may be little if any indication as to its limits since the thatched dwellings, stone house platforms, granaries, pigpens, and other structures, including low stone dividing walls and walks, appear to be continuous over the hillside. The ceremonial center of an *ato* is a stone platform of varying shape, having a paved top ringed with large stones for sitting or leaning, a fireplace, one or more carved or pointed posts for displaying heads of slain enemies, and a low rectangular hut at the back end. This platform and the hut provide a formal and informal "clubhouse" for the males of the households attached to the *ato* section; it is ordinarily taboo to females, other than very young children in their fathers' care who sometimes may be there. The older men assemble there in "council" *(intugtukan)* to deliberate on matters of justice, politics and other *ato* concerns. Formerly ceremonies of war and headhunting were consummated at this center, and it was and may still be the repository of skulls; at the time of the writer's visit the *ato* was still thought of as dominantly connected with this type of activity. Rituals including animal sacrifices appropriate to the *ato* are conducted upon the platform, often accompanied by dancing in a space adjacent to it. At night the stones, often mat covered, together with wooden planks in the hut, are a sleeping place for unmarried boys and youths, and for divorced or widowed men of the households. The *ato* group also forms a unit for particular types of economic activity, especially of a ceremonial nature, calling for co-operation among members. Its adherents refer to themselves as *sinpangato,* literally "united with (the group) belonging to the *ato*." . . .

The unity of the village is perhaps most clearly seen in an elaborate system of community rituals (*kanyau*) connected variously with the annual cycle of agriculture, safety from storms, epidemics or fires in the village, droughts affecting the water supply, and other matters of common welfare. These, organized and conducted by recognized experts or priests who variously hold their positions by hereditary right or by nomination according to the nature of the activity, involve common religious holidays (*tengao*), hog sacrifices at sacred groves (*papatay*) on the outskirts of the village, consultation of omens, and other ritual procedures. Above all, the villagers are held together by an elaborate network of kinship connections and neighborly associations, by the needs until recently of common defense, and by the sense of identity so real in a little community with a common tradition and the intimacies of daily contact and gossip. The identity of the village is expressed in the term *sinpangili,* "the united community." . . .

Writers on Bontok also feature as the other characteristic institution the *olag* or girls' house. Each *ato* section has usually one or possibly two low huts of thatch, mud and stones, often built alongside a pig-pit, to which the girls of its constituent households go at night to sleep. A small *ato,* however, may be at times without an *olag,* so that the girls of its households use one in an adjacent *ato.* In other words it is a usual, but not a permanent and inevitable part of the *ato* organization.

The *olag* huts are a nightly gathering place, not only for the unmarried girls and unattached women, but also for unmarried youths and more occasionally unattached older men. Boys and young men are likely to go from their *ato* structures in congenial parties, visiting one *olag* after another, crooning, joking, teasing, and engaging in sex play with the girls. Those who have developed liaisons may, with full public sanction, sleep with their current partners in the hut. Nearly all Bontok marriages are the product of experimental pairing in the *olag,* the test of congeniality usually being that a child is on the way—hence the term "trial marriage" found in the literature. It is necessary, however, clearly to distinguish personal sex play and experimentation under these conditions from marriage proper, as the latter involves public ceremonies, rights and obligations that involve not only the couple, but also their kin groups.

How do these institutions really "function" in the total context of Bontok life? What relation do they have to other elements of the culture such as the household and wider kinship units already mentioned in passing? Is the *ato* membership based on local contiguity, kinship, or the needs of economic, political or other forms of co-operation? What kinship and other considerations regulate the contacts of young people in the *olag?* Such questions as these have not been given

adequate consideration in writings to date. Within the limits of the writer's own field notes, supplemented by other source materials available, the following is a tentative analysis.

The Bontok household can provide the most useful starting point. Its essential nucleus is an "individual family" of husband, wife, and children, almost always monogamous. It has, however, a somewhat elastic membership in terms of the different activities centered around the house—sleeping, eating, doing chores, conducting rituals, and so on. Unattached older relatives, for example, may come for meals, and young men courting the daughters may join in household work. Such a house group is called *pangafong,* literally "(those) belonging to the house." Terms for marriage, too, usually translate as variants of "becoming a householder," *e.g., iafongko,* "marry," *paafongek,* "perform wedding ceremony." An *ato* section will have from about ten to fifty such households within its boundaries.

The better class of Bontok house (*faoy*) is a substantial pyramidal structure on piles, described by Coke as like a "sharply pointed haystack." The ground space beneath has sections for husking rice, cooking, and storage. There is also a box-like compartment (*angan*) in which the husband and wife sleep, together with very young children. Under the eaves, the house has a second story room more less walled in, and a loft used as a storehouse for *palay* (rice on the stalk), and other goods. A far less pretentious structure (*katufong*), rectangular shaped and on the ground, is used by very poor families and sometimes by widows. A feature of a marriage settlement is nearly always the provision of a house by one or other of the relationship groups concerned, customarily the bridegroom's kinsmen in accordance with a dominant principle of patrilocal *ato* residence. The building of a new house consumes much time, labor and wealth, and its erection is an affair in which many kinsmen and neighbors take part, not to mention ancestral and other spirits which are ritually invoked. At particular times in the yearly cycle of activities, and on special occasions such as births, marriages, cases of sickness and deaths, it becomes a gathering place for appropriate groupings of kinsmen and friends.

During much of the day, the house may be deserted. The men and boys, if not away from the village, are usually at the *ato* platforms. The women and girls are likely to be in the fields, often leaving the young children to the care of their somewhat older siblings, to the fathers if they are handy, or to old men and women of the kin group. Females who remain at home because of taboos, childbirth, or to rest from the exacting agricultural tasks gather to work or gossip under their own house eaves or those of relatives and friends. For the two daily meals, or at least for the evening meal, the whole household normally assembles. Perhaps the family pigs should receive mention, too, for in their well-constructed stone pits near the house they are in a real sense members of the group; fed by the girls with leafage gathered after much hard climbing, eating up all the household rubbish including human excreta, providing in turn fertilizer for the fields, and coming at last to a distinguished end in the course of some all-important ritual sacrifice and feast. When darkness falls over the village, the stone pathways that traverse it are alight with moving pine torches as old people, boys and girls go from the households to their sleeping places, and amorous youths commence their visiting. Behind them are left the husband, wife and very young children who will crawl into the sleeping box, stoke up the embers of a fire within, and shut tight the door to keep out the chill mountain air and its wandering ghosts.

Such a household is the main unit for everyday economic, social and religious life. As part of a Bontok marriage, a series of consultations take place between the kin groups involved, as a result of which the couple receive agricultural land and other property to be held in common so long as they remain together. Unmarried persons rarely own important property of their own, so that such arrangements exercise a strong stabilizing force upon the household life. In case of divorce, which can take place by

mutual consent or by pressure brought to bear by one or the other set of relatives—the usual cause being infertility or the repeated death of children—there are elaborate legal prescriptions as to the disposal of such common property. Both husband and wife may also accumulate property separately in their own names through inheritance, gift, manufacture, or in other ways. A woman's rights, and back of them the related rights of her kin group, are meticulously observed.

What is the working relation of the household unit, as pictured here, to the *ato* unit? Normally the households which lie spatially within the *ato* boundaries provide its membership as a social, political and ceremonial grouping. Since *ato* affiliation is based typically on a patrilineal principle, and marriage on the patrilocal principle as noted above, males ordinarily adhere throughout life to the *ato* sections of their fathers' lines. Informants, in speaking of this, usually expressed it by reference to the grandparent generation: "I keep on in the *ato* of my (paternal) grandfather."

As with so much of Bontok usage, however, individuals are not compelled to adhere strictly to the norm, but have latitude to make personal choices. Cases occur when men live within an *ato* section other than that of their male ancestors, as where a newly married youth may stay for a time with his wife's people, or even transfer his allegiance to that *ato* group because of circumstances involved in the marriage settlement, or because of quarrels or personal tastes. A decision to shift is particularly likely to occur at marriage where the wife's relatives are of higher status or possess more rice lands. Again, in cases where a new *ato* has been founded near the village, those initiating such a move have drawn in various kinsmen and perhaps friends. Jenks says in his study that the *ato* "formally releases and adopts men who change their residence from one to another," and refers to a ceremonial feast to mark such adoption. Informants stated that this would be a minor ritual only, though a small animal sacrifice would be in order. Primarily, it was stated, a man signifies his change of allegiance by his "public words," together with his absence from the rituals and enterprises of his former *ato* and his presence at those of the new *ato*.

Allowing for these exceptions, the extent of which could not be ascertained precisely, ancestral tradition and public opinion nevertheless operate strongly to keep a man in the *ato* of his male progenitors. The boys growing up within each *ato* group become steeped in its special lore, and develop rights and duties in relation to it. A term *pangatona*, "*ato* comrades," expresses the warm relation especially between age mates in the group. To leave one's *ato*, or to be absent unnecessarily from its ceremonial activities, would mean risking not only the weakening of important social ties, but also incurring the displeasure of the ancestors and of family and *ato* spirits. An older man would rarely if ever shift to a new *ato*. Even if a young man moves, as through circumstances connected with his marriage, it is said that his sons tend to return to the *ato* of their grandfather.

The *ato* may therefore be visualized as comprising, in ideal terms, both a territorial and a social unit made up of a set of patrilineal and patrilocal households. It provides the main focus for political organization, and also involves important religious, ceremonial, economic, and other ties. Until the last two generations, it has been notably associated with war and head-hunting activities.

The steps that lead to marriage and the formation of the household bring into focus cusomary relationships between the sexes, including the role of the *olag* or girl's house. Principles of sexual segregation operate strongly in Bontok public behavior, and boys and girls tend to work and play apart from each other from their earliest years. Siblings of opposite sex meet within the home during the day, yet restraints are fostered that from the age of perhaps nine or ten become a definite rule of avoidance. This "brother-sister taboo" extends equally to step-children and adopted children. There are also restraints in conversation and in other behavior regarding sex matters between all males and females who are close relatives.

Young people of opposite sex have two main opportunities for getting together: on ceremonial occasions, many of which include dancing, and in the *olag* or girls' house. Even in the dance formations, however, the sexes characteristically line up apart. The *olag* affords the principal place where informal and intimate associations between unmarried and unattached persons of opposite sex can occur. The boys, as has been noted, visit the *olag* huts, and as sexual maturity is reached by boys and girls their casual sex play tends to give place to more serious and permanent liaisons. In the adolescent years, the young people are likely to make *olag* sexual adventures their principal preoccupation. Older unattached men may also visit the *olags*, but married men rarely do so; an elderly Don Juan would be considered rather ridiculous, as a man is expected to have had his playboy days in youth.

Because the girls belonging to the households of each *ato* normally spend their nights in the *olag* of that *ato*, the boys of those households are likely to have sisters, first cousins, or other close female relatives there. The rules of avoidance referred to above tend, therefore, to force boys to go to other *ato* units for their sexual contacts, either in their own village or nowadays even in other villages. If one desires to bring in the word, this operates to provide a kind of informal *ato* "exogamy." On the other hand, there is no explicit prohibition of sex contacts or of marriage between members of any *ato* group as such, other than as regards close relatives, although Jenks gives a table of Bontok marriages forbidden a man thus: mother or step-mother or their sisters, daughter, step-daughter, adopted daughter, sister, brother's widow, and first cousins by blood and adoption. Especially in larger *ato* groups, liaisons seems not infrequent, and these would be facilitated in the rare cases where an *ato* has more than one *olag*. Again, if a boy and girl in the same *ato* are eager to effect a liaison their fellows may help them, either by close female relatives shifting out temporarily to another *olag*, or else by the girl making such a shift. The pattern can be described as an avoidance of close relatives, which often extends on account of *olag* customs to cover approximately the immediate *ato* of the youth or man, and in a similar way to other *ato* groups where there are close female relatives in the *olag.*

The norm of youthful conduct could be stated thus. A boy cannot enter an *olag* in which there are immediate relatives such as his sister or stepsister. He either stays behind in the *olag* to which his amorous party has just been, or passes ahead to the one next on the visiting list. Should he have a somewhat less close female relative, such as a first cousin, aunt, or niece, he may enter, but should "hold back" instead of joining in the fun. Such rules are the more effective in that boys and girls rarely have opportunities for close association outside the *olag,* and public opinion frowns on sex intimacies elsewhere. Sex experiences are so much a matter of mutual interest and co-operation among the boys' and girls' groups, that the deviant would meet with ridicule if not ostracism.

Bontok marriage has two facets. The first is that of choice and compatibility. The great majority of first unions take place within approximately the same age-groups as the result of *olag* romances and experimentation, regulated by the above rules. Subsequent marriages, which are not infrequent because of the death of one of the partners or else of divorce, often cross age lines, especially through older men taking unmarried girls as wives. Genuine attachments often come from *olag* alliances, but the most frequent test of compatibility is that a child is forthcoming. A girl is therefore approved only if she has one lover at a time, ensuring, as the Bontok say, that paternity can be recognized.

The other facet to marriage is where the kin groups concerned, together with the ancestors and supernatural forces, have their say. This takes the form of a complex set of observances, varying with the class status and seniority of the parties, and including performance of symbolic services towards the prospective parents-in-law, consultations within and between the relatives, the reading of omens through animal sacrifices and other means, successfully maintaining a sacred fire during a ritual period and in other ways getting the sanction of the unseen world, and

fianlly the passing of property by the two groups to the couple. Should the marriage be cancelled through family disapproval or bad auguries, an appropriate settlement is made. A pregnant girl may be given a rice field in trust for her expected child, or else some *carabao* (water buffalo). Neither she nor the child would suffer any social stigma. Possibly because women have to work under such trying environmental conditions as in the wet rice fields, and also because there is high infant mortality, children are all too few; the infant would therefore be readily adopted into the kin group of its mother, while the girl would perhaps even be the more sought after for having proved her fertility.

A consummated marriage links the two households concerned and the kin groups back of them with a series of mutual and reciprocal associations, privileges and responsibilities. These are especially elaborate where they involve persons and kin groups of the aristocratic class. Parents-in-law play a role of great importance, receiving every respect and in turn standing by to assist in all difficulties. Again, a husband and wife have relations of propriety and respect towards their brothers- and sisters-in-law, especially the eldest ones. The wife's kin keep an eye on the husband to see that his wife and children are well treated, and vice versa.

A marriage has at first a somewhat tentative character, and the relationships created between "in-laws" are correspondingly tentative. Subsequent participation in ceremonial and other activities, and above all the arrival of children on the scene, "build up" the marriage and cement affinal ties. In relation to the children, the kin groups of the husband and wife become in turn conjoined into a single kin group, which will stand back of such children as they grow up and in turn are married. Each marriage, especially if fertile, thus initiates fresh alignments of kin within the community. Each man, too, is the focal point for a network of lineal and affinal relationships extending not only within his own *ato* but also into the *atos* of his mother, his parents' sisters, his wife, his parents-in-law, his married sisters, his sisters-in-law, his daughters-in-law, and so on. A woman has corresponding ramifications of kinship. These linkages as indicated may even extend to other villages, especially in modern times and in the case of aristocratic lines.

This leads to broader consideration of the principles of kinship which operate beyond the household grouping. The written and photographic materials presented by Jenks show tantalizing glimpses of kin ties at work—groups of relatives building a house, mourning and burying the dead, dividing property among heirs, conducting feasts and animal sacrifices and so on. But apart from a few very general references and a meager list of kinship terms, he fails to trace the many ways in which kinship is actively exercised in interpersonal relationships pertaining to economic, social, political, ceremonial and other activities both within and outside the *ato* units.

An individual in such a close-set community constantly sees in the daily round persons who stand in various relationships to him, and may speak respectfully, stop to gossip, pass a joke, share a task, step aside modestly, or otherwise actively exercise prescribed or permitted kin behaviors. More formally, he is likely to take part relatively frequently in gatherings of kinsmen at his own house or those of others. As noted earlier, even certain types of political and judicial activity may be handled by elders of the kin instead of in the *ato* "councils"; for example, property disputes among relatives or troubles between different kin groups. Weddings and funerals are among the many other occasions in the social round which bring kinsmen together, and also their ramifications such as ceremonies to overcome sterility in a childless couple or holding memorial sacrifices for an illustrious ancestor. Again, bad luck or illness calls for rituals at which relatives come together. Assemblies of kinsmen will be organized and directed by the senior elders present in the group.

The size and membership of such kin gatherings, including the extent to which they involve both lineal and affinal relatives, vary with the occasion, and generally according to the class status and seniority of the persons upon whom the occasion is focused. The Bontok do not have any precise delimitation of such larger kinship associations that would justify speaking of an "extended family" system over and above the household. Terms used to refer to kinsmen *in extenso* are very general. The one by which the identity of a group sharing common descent is expressed in the large is *pangapo,* literally "having unity with the same elders (ancestors)." A consanguineal group looked at from the viewpoint of youth may be called *sinpangapo, i.e.,* belonging to the parent and other ascendant generations; similarly from the viewpoint of age it would be *sinpanganak, i.e.,* belonging to the descendant generations. *Anak* is a classificatory kinship term more strictly for those one generation below that of the speaker. *Apo* is used as a respectful term for elders and those of high rank, and may also be given the more specific connotation of kinsman, living and dead, above the parental generation.

A detailed analysis of the Bontok kinship structure has never been made. Most of its formal terminology is extant in the vocabularies published by Jenks, Clapp, Scheerer, and Seidenadel. Usually, however, terms are translated with little reference to the social context in which they are used, as for example, the marked classificatory character of nearly all terms of reference. Kroeber's important general study of Philippine kinship brings out, however, the major features of this as of other "Malayan type" systems, including marked bilateral emphasis; the merging of collateral with lineal kin; the use of reciprocal terminology; the primary importance of the generation principle; the strong classificatory tendency; and the rarity of sex differentiation in general terms of reference.

Space does not permit full analysis of how these principles work out as regards Bontok kinship structure. It may be noted, however, that the terminology of kinship reference is compounded for the most part from a few basic terms by the use of prefixes, suffixes, and descriptive addenda, including *ay lalaki* to indicate "male" and *ay fafai* to indicate "female." The following are the main terms: grandparent generation and above, *apo;* grandparent, more specifically, *ikid;* father, *ama:* other males of parental generation, *alitau:* mother, *ina;* own sibling, *itad;* child generation and below, *anak;* spouse, *asawa;* parent-in-law, *katukangan;* brother-, sister-in-law, *kasud.* Illustrating further the reciprocal character of kinship terminology, the following are examples of terms indicating relationships to one another: sibling, *agi;* spouses, *sinasawa;* "in-laws" generally, *aliwid;* brothers-in-law, *sinkasud;* brothers-in-law and sisters-in-law, *sininget;* grandparents and grandchildren, *sinpangapo.*

The markedly bilateral character of Bontok kinship has already been stressed in discussing marriage. Though a selective stress to the patrilineal side is discernible, as in the norm of *ato* affiliation, in succession among the aristocracy and sometimes in choosing personal names, an individual takes status and receives property by way of both parental kin groups. In household ceremonies, all ascendant generations on both sides, living and dead, will be honored.

The range of effective kinship appears to be rather elastic. In general, memories of specific genealogical data do not appear to go far back, perhaps at the most for seven or eight generations in the direct male line, and for the average person not more than two or three generations beyond the living. Members of aristocratic kin groups appear the more meticulous in this respect for the obvious reason to be shown that ancestry is of so much greater importance to them. Outstanding personalities, too, especially great warrior heroes of the past, are immortalized in the lore and story of kin and *ato* groups, and their lines of descendants may be kept, as Jenks says, "carefully in memory." Among the living, kin reckoning tends to be significant in close lines only. Usually little importance is attached to collateral ties beyond first cousins. Relationships in more distant lines may, however, be remembered and exercised if they are socially useful; that is, if they involve

links to important kin groups and outstanding individuals, especially those of aristocratic status.

Three additional principles of Bontok social structure, already seen above to some extent as importantly at work in defining status, may be discussed more systematically here: age and generation, seniority among siblings, and rank and class distinctions.

The Bontok child learns from earliest years to obey those of the generations above him within the kin, and to respect older age in general. This principle holds throughout life, and as each individual becomes older there is a corresponding shift from being directed and dictated to by a circle of seniors, toward having rights and responsibilities as regards an enlarging circle of juniors. Correspondingly strong social bonds tend to exist between age-mates, even though no formal age-grade system is involved. Within the hierarchy of generations are included the remembered dead as well as the living, for Bontok religion has as an important element a cult of ancestral spirits *(anito)* who are supposed to continue living around the village margins.

A clear distinction is made between siblings according to their order of birth. The terms *pangolo,* "head" or "senior," *yunan,* "older," *anodi (anochi),* "younger," and *yugtan,* "the last" are not only conversationally prominent, but express a hierarchy of privilege and responsibility. In some respects distinctions of generation and primogeniture transcend distinctions of sex, and this shows especially where the eldest survivor of a kin group or among siblings is a female. Except in the distinctively male functions, as in the *ato* affairs, the eldest women members of a kin group exercise important authority, and this is enhanced if a woman is the eldest among siblings in the senior line. An examination of the *ato* "council" described by Jenks shows it to be essentially a gathering of the male elders from the constituent *ato* households, deriving their right to a voice in *ato* affairs primarily from their age and seniority.

Jenks speaks of such an *ato* "council" as

"thoroughly democratic." Informants with which the writer discussed this matter and the distribution of authority within kin groups, indicated that underlying the out-wardly free-and-easy discussion of problems a marked difference exists in the extent to which participating elders have an effective say. Though "all old people are consulted," an old man "must have influence in the com-munity" for his voice to count strongly. An unimportant or "poor" person, no matter how old "doesn't have much say." In earlier times, one of the major ways in which an individual became influential was to be an outstanding warrior and taker of heads—and, of course, to survive to older age. The other major way, still current, is to be a member of what has been called at a number of points an aristocracy. . . .

At the top of the social scale in Bontok is a class known as *kadangyan (kachangyan),* or nowadays sometimes by the general name used in the mountain region for such an elite, and of *Iloko* origin: *baknang.* The main basis from which *kadangyan* status is derived is hereditary rank, or more strictly descent through senior lines within the class; second-arily it is possession of wealth and perform-ance of major *kanyau* (ritual) observances, involving animal sacrifices and public feasts. In its narrower sense the term *kadangyan* is applied to the current titleholder or head in the senior family line, whose succession at the death of his father has been validated by required *kanyau* ceremonies. More widely it is extended to cover the household and im-mediate kin lines, so that people speak of the *kadangyan* as a class. Faculo and others spoke somewhat vaguely of three grades of *kadangyan* status. At the top were those counted *pangolo* ("head," or "first") or "royal" as Faculo translated it, and estimated by him at about 10 per cent of the *kadangyan* group; next came those classed as *misned* ("second"), and comprising about 15 per cent; and finally those *yugtan* ("last"), com-prising about 75 per cent. It seems more realistic, however, to look at differentiations in *kadangyan* status not in terms of distinct

subclasses, but rather as expressing degrees to which different households and their heads are linked more or less closely to senior *kadangyan* lines.

The individuals and kin groups counting themselves as more or less of *kadangyan* status were estimated by some as perhaps a quarter of the total population. Others re-garded this figure as too high. Clearly it would require a detailed social "census" to make this matter definite, and in any case it would undoubtedly vary by villages. Below this group are the main body of the villagers who hold lands of their own, a kind of middle or commoner class. The households in this group may nevertheless have links through blood and marriage with *kadangyan* lines, which as indicated earlier they find it useful to remember and exercise. Probably few of them would not count themselves as of *kadangyan* derivation in some minor degree. In each generation the descendants in junior *kadangyan* lines (*i.e.,* the offspring of younger sons and daughters in the senior lines) tend to shift downward into this middle group.

At the bottom of the social scale are a class of people in a state of peonage, because of debts and other obligations to their richer fellows. They own little or no rice lands or livestock, and work on a share-cropping or tenancy basis, usually in the service of the top *kadangyan.* The traditional rates of interest and of crop division here as in so many other sections of east and south Asia make escape from this group, once in it, almost impossible so that the obligations tend to carry over indefinitely from generation to generation. The usual name for such people is *pusi* (often translated "poor," and said to be of Spanish derivation); another appellation is *kokitak* ("to be least, last, poorest"). Just as with the *kadangyan* group, this status interpenetrates with the main middle class group by way of blood and marriage ties, and so it is relative to the particular kin connections of the individu-al and household concerned. Links may even join between *kadangyan* and *pusi* groups through marriages of past or present, though this is more rare.

"The Bontok," Faculo writes, "feel that wealth, influence, and dignity do not count without children to inherit and to care for the parents. Life to them is a matter of succession." He describes the absorption of the Bontok with marriage and death ceremonies, with emphasis upon marked contrasts existing between the types for those of high and low class status. "Each class," he says, "has its own marriage and burial customs." These differ to some extent in kind as well as in degree, an example being that outstanding *kadangyan* may be buried in special places away from those of lesser status. He, as well as other informants, described additional rituals emphasized in the *kadangyan* class, including "wedding anniversary feasts " held every three or four years to consolidate their marriages and make them fertile, and mourning ceremonies held periodically to honor their dead ancestors. In 1932, just before the writer reached the Bontok area, a wedding feast held at Dalican village involved the slaughter of 41 carabaos, along with numerous pigs.

Marriage operates as a major factor shaping the status of individuals within this class structure, and fosters counter tendencies of rigidity and mobility. Every marriage creates some new alignment of status. Each child in turn gets an ascribed status according to the position of his father and mother and their lines of kin within the class hierarchy.

At the top, the superior status of the senior *kadangyan* lines is maintained and reinforced through strategic marital alliances. It is quite usual for a *kadangyan* to betroth his children even in infancy, especially eldest sons and daughters, rather than waiting for *olag* liaisons to develop. In some cases those of the highest level marry within close degrees of relationship to maintain status and retain land and other property within their group. They may also marry across village lines, especially under modern conditions of peace, so as to link together lines of the highest status for mutual advantage. A betrothal arrangement made for an eldest son or daughter is likely to be insisted on. With younger children, however, earlier betrothals may be broken in favor of mates of their own choice. Even so, the *kadangyan* class discriminate against those of their members who marry beneath them. This was shown at the time of the writer's visit when an educated young man of high birth married a girl schoolteacher equally educated but of low class origin. His kinsmen refused to accept her into their circle: "She is just poor," they said.

Correspondingly at the bottom of the scale the tendency is for persons of the *pusi* group to marry among themselves for want of other partners. Granting the free-and-easy sex relations of the *olag* system, youths and girls are well aware, both by way of admonitions of kinsmen and their own ambitions to have rice fields and other possessions come to them via the marriage settlement, that the class status of a prospective lover should be taken into account. Faculo, recording in his manuscript on marriage customs the specific case of an *olag* attachment between a youth Kala and a girl Udchao, tells how "Kala's parents, satisfied of the prestige, means and standing of Udchao's parents, called a man from the neighborhood to act as a message-bearer, [and] sent to Udchao's parents to ask if they would agree to the marriage proposal." As a norm it would appear that unions, to be acceptable to the kin groups concerned, should take place within approximately the same class level, especially so in the case of eldest sons and daughters. But many exceptions occur, disrupting any tendency toward sharp class differentiation.

As might be expected in such a hard physical environment, aristocracy has become closely associated with wealth and economic dominance, a tendency which furthermore has been stimulated by the increasing penetration of the modern commercial economy in recent years. Asked as to the origin of the *kadangyan,* informants referred to stories telling how "in olden times rich people had a chance to buy the lands of the poor" and so consolidate their position. The leading *kadangyan* usually own the bulk of rice lands and claim rights over unoccupied lands; they are also likely to have the most hogs, and perhaps large water buffalo herds. A circle of poorer people are always in debt to them, and hence are partially or wholly their tenants and laborers. Over against this, however, the aristocrats carry responsibilities as financiers, storers of food, and organizers of community work. Tradition also demands of them the giving of elaborate feasts and sacrifices on varied ceremonial occasions, these participated in by a wide circle of the community, and even (at least nowadays) by invited guests from other Bontok villages. In this way, they exercise a function of village leadership which Jenks failed to record. In reality they accumulate prestige and, if their services are well performed, popularity, rather than much permanent wealth other than in land.

At times, individuals of *kadangyan* rank have become pauperized. This does not affect their hereditary standing in any immediate way, though it would tend to be impaired if prolonged, especially over several generations, as animal sacrifices believed necessary to bulwark social and supernatural status could probably not be performed. In modern times a few poorer people have risen to wealth and high position through commercial activities or as government officials and employees. While this gives them a status in terms of the new set of values inevitably filtering into the mountains today, and perhaps allows them to make strategic marriages, they remain in the eyes of conservatives—that is, of almost everyone—lowly. The persistence of the class system has become a source of personal difficulty among a small group of educated young people who have come under the influence of democratic American ideas, and at the time the writer was in the area there was presage of growing disturbance. Meantime, as in the past, wealth and other personal factors have remained subordinate to rank by birth.

The *kadangyan* households seem to be scattered fairly evenly through the *ato* sections. Though their houses are not markedly differentiated in construction from those of others, more elaborate material possessions such as rice granaries, a greater number of

pig pens, and ceremonial porcelain jars of high value are usually an index to their status. Within *ato* councils as well as kin groupings, the voice of the *kadangyan* tends to carry a dominant weight. This is especially so now that the old men having fame as fighters and takers of heads are dying off. Such personal exploits gave even low-ranking persons an important place in the public eye, for war was essentially a man's career. With peace and commerce, however, the prestige and influence of the *kadangyan* tends to be enhanced, the more so as the government has generally used people of this class as local officials in the villages. An informant said, "The *kandangyan* now have all the real power."

Both the *ato* and the *olag* systems are also undergoing inevitable changes in modern times. The cessation of headhunting, and the transfer of political and judicial affairs increasingly to the government officials, have tended to thin out the *ato* activities considerably. The *olag* has been a main point of attack for missions and schools as being "immoral." While so far the institutions seem visibly little impaired among the Bontok, a study of their working, and of the attitudes of numbers of younger people toward them, revealed a trend toward disintegration. Already among the neighboring Lepanto, this is well under way. In all Lepanto villages one *ato* has tended to emerge to importance as the center to which officials come, and the others have correspondingly lessened in significance, especially as the people become Christianized and their ritual functions thin out. Again in some villages the girls' house system appears practically at an end.

No attempt has yet been made in the literature relating to such mountain peoples as the Bontok to analyze their cultures from the newer viewpoints of "personality" or "character structure." A number of observers, however, have offered broad characterizations, including Bontok officials in their reports. There is general agreement that the Bontok are the most "aggressive," "pugnacious," "stubborn," "proud," "conservative" and "unrepressed" of the mountain groups; as one writer put it, where members of other groups acting as carriers would stop outside or merely come inside the door, the Bontok would stride unconcernedly into your bedroom. A Bontok man usually looks a person deliberately in the eye, and gives an impression of self-confidence, even superiority, and of being good-humored and relaxed while yet having a very positive attitude to life; women, however, are likely to be more shy in the presence of strangers. Even Bontok conservatism has a certain resiliency, the people having adapted their usages freely where new experience fitted in with their own values. Of the former headhunting, Jenks writes, "(It is) his most-enjoyed and highly prized recreation."

Bontok "personality" ("character") formation offers tempting vistas for analysis: the baby usually slung precariously on the hip of mother or older sister, or being cared for by father or the elders; the traumatic shift from parents and the home sleeping box to the *ato* or *olag;* the little disciplined childhood mainly among age mates; the *kanyau* sacrifices to meet all insecurities; the steep barren habitat and precarious livelihood. A striking feature here is that most of these patterns are shared closely with neighboring ethnic groups, especially the Lepanto. Yet the end results are far from the same, as noted in the previous paragraph.

A search for the key to the distinctive aspects of Bontok character is likely to lead back in part to Bontok history. The Bontok know well that in the eyes of neighbors they have long been feared as the most dangerous and expert fighters in the region, always threatening, always likely to be on top, and their self-evaluations reflect this knowledge.

Again, habitat factors may be involved. The Bontok country is in general the steepest and least hospitable zone of the mountains, and floods from the Chico river and its tributaries periodically wash out sections of the rice terraces, calling for adaptability and toughness of fiber as well as the labor of reconstruction. Again, as implied in a report written in 1931 by a Bontok official which states, "It is the things learned in (the *ato* and *olag*) that renders them so hostile to change," more would have to be known specifically of the role of these institutions in conditioning the distinctive Bontok character.

Summarizing this sketch of Bontok social organization, the household is seen as the basic economic and social unit, taking form typically out of *olag* attachments. Households are aligned, normally on patrilineal and patrilocal principles, into *ato* sections. These are territorial-social groupings having their own traditions and varied political, economic, ceremonial and other functions, particularly connected formerly with war and headhunting. Avoiding Jenks' unduly *ato*-centric focus, it can be seen that the households are also linked by wider kinship ties, lineal and affinal, which transcend *ato* lines, and in which age and generation, seniority, and class status are important principles of organization. The class system is based particularly on degree of relationship to the *kadangyan,* or hereditary aristocrat, whose position is based on succession and inheritance from senior lines, and validated by possession of wealth and by ritual activities. Though political and judicial authority tends to center in the *ato* units, the village as a whole has a real identity, fostered by common interests and ideology, the extensive network of kinship, and a round of common social and religious activities.

Kinship Systems

A. M. Hocart

From *The Life-giving Myth, and Other Essays,* Grove Press, n.d., pp. 173–179. By permission of the publisher.

When we explore a new language, we infer the meaning of words from the objects to which they are applied. The first object gives us a preliminary definition. That may chance to be right, but further experience may compel us to revise it. Thus I may first hear the word "table" used of a list of facts in a book, and so translate it "page." By degrees I shall learn better.

This caution is generally borne in mind by students of literary languages, but it is too often lost sight of in the study of non-literary languages. Many investigators never get beyond the first use of the word that happens to come their way . . . [As an example,] an investigator heard the Uganda word *obuko* applied to palsy. He entered it in his dictionary as "palsy." It really refers to marriage rules, to a breach of which palsy is the consequence.

One of the most flagrant cases is the translation of the so-called classificatory kinship terms. The person most commonly called *tama* in Melanesia, the one most in evidence, is a man's father. He is the man who will be named if you ask, "Who is your *tama?*" So *tama* has been duly set down as "father." The same has been done with other kinship terms in Melanesia and elsewhere. It was soon noticed, however, that other men besides the father are called *tama.* By all rules the first translation should have been dropped, and a new one found to cover all the different *tamas,* and thus express the essence of *tama*-ship. Unfortunately, no single word can do so, and it has remained in the literature of the South Seas as "father," with the proviso that it is "extended" to cover father's brother, father's father's brothers' sons, and so on. Ever since we have been racking our brains to explain how Melanesians can call their uncles, and even remote cousins, "fathers."

The effect on theory has been disastrous. The order in which we have learned the uses of *tama* and similar words has been confused with the order of development in actual history. Because we first took it to mean father we slip unwittingly into the assumption that it meant father originally.

This fallacy has now received official expression in the term "kinship extensions."

That expression implies that the meaning father is primary and that all other uses result from extending the term to an ever-widening circle of kinsmen.

It is curious that this doctrine, which is historical since it describes a process of development in the past, is championed most stoutly by those who are forever gibing at origins, evolutions, historical reconstruction. This is a historical reconstruction, or what is?

The only way of proving that a process has taken place in the past is by recognized historical methods: either produce documents or resort to the comparative method. It is perhaps fortunate in this case that we have little documentary evidence and so must rely on the much more reliable comparative method.

Before we can apply it we must get our facts right. To that end let us forget all we have ever been told about the meaning of classificatory terms and rediscover the language, taking Fijian as an example. Evidently *tama* cannot mean father since it includes cousins to the *n*th degree, even cousins too young to have children; in fact, a man is born a *tama*. We notice, however, that all those cousins have one thing in common: they are once removed; in other words, they are of the generation next to Ego, and, to be more precise, of the one immediately before. Not all the members of this generation, however, are *tama*. There are two sides to that generation, the father's and the mother's; only those on the father's side are *tama*. That is evidently the meaning of *tama*, so our final definition will run:

tama = all males of the previous generation on the father's side. Repeating the process, we go on:
vungo = all males of the generation immediately above and below Ego on the mother's side;
tavale = all males of the same generation on the mother's side.

And so on. When our list is complete we find that all the terms fall into two sets, one set belonging to the father's side, the other to the mother's. Each term refers to a particular generation within one side. In short, these terms do not express consanguinity, as we have unfortunately been accustomed by Morgan to believe, but they fix the place of any relative according to generation and side. If I call a man *tuaka* it is clear that he is of my generation on my father's side, and senior to me; a *wati* is a woman of my generation on the side from which my mother comes.

This last term affords an excellent illustration how a particular use is mistaken for the true one, and the true one comes to be looked upon as an improper one. A Fijian introduces his wife as *wati*, so the word is noted as "*wife.*" When it is found there are hundreds of *watis* who are not his wives, the first translation is not abandoned, but all other uses are explained as extensions: these women, it is explained, are called wives because he might marry any of them if the family so decided; they are wives by anticipation, "potential wives." Upon this muddled lexicography has been built up a whole edifice of primitive promiscuity.

Exactly the same usage exists in Arabic. Arabic-speaking husbands can often be heard addressing their wives as *bint 'amm;* but they also call their paternal uncles' daughters *bint 'amm.* We do not translate "wife," "potential wife," because we know that *bint* is daughter, and *'amm* is paternal uncle; therefore *bint 'amm* means "cousin on the father's side." When a man marries his cousin, as it is best to do, he goes on calling her "cousin" as he has been accustomed to since childhood. The Fijian and the Ashanti do exactly the same.

We can remember the time when an English youth would refer jocosely to his father as "The Governor." No one has ever suggested that this was primary and that the word has been extended to colonial administrators.

All our difficulties spring from a preconceived idea that kinship terms everywhere try to express the same thing as they do in Aryan and Semitic languages, and that in those languages they show the place on the family tree. The result is that in a certain African language the term *nana* is rendered father's father, father's father's brother, and so on through thirty-four European relationships, and then it does not exhaust all the possiblities. And what is the outcome of all this painstaking? We have a list of cases, but we have not got the meaning. It is as if a dictionary under "hot" told us "the sun is hot, pepper is hot, A's temper is hot, the discussion is hot," and left it at that. If we go to the trouble of extracting the meaning of *nana* from the cases we find it simply means "any relative two generations above or below."

At this point we may be asked what evidence have we that the people themselves understand kinship terms in this sense. The same evidence as we have for the meaning of any word, what is common to the cases in which it is used.

As regards the Chinese system we have more, we have the definite statement of a Chinaman. H. Y. Feng produces documentary evidence that the Chinese system was once a cross-cousin system, and so it is akin to the Fijian. As in cross-cousin systems, the kinsfolk are still divided into two: those of the same patronymic, and those of another. These sides he chooses to call "sibs." Besides this vertical division, there is a horizontal one into generations. "These two factors, sib and generation," he sums up, "not only pervade the whole system but regulate marriage." A man marries a woman of another patronym of the first generation.

The hill tribes of Viti Levu, Fiji, indicate very clearly what their kinship terms mean to them. Every hillsman assumes all other hillsmen to be his kinsmen. He is not concerned how near or how far related a stranger may be; he does not search the pedigrees to find out how they are related. All he wants to know is their respective generations. That is easy, because the whole population is divided into two alternate generations called *tako* and *lavo*. If both are *tako* or both *lavo* they are of the same generation, and then the senior is *tuka,* and junior *tadhi,* terms which have unfortunately been translated (by myself among others), as elder and younger brother. Evidently they mean nothing of the kind, since a man's grandfather is his *tuka* as well as his elder brother. The words simply mean "of the same one of the two generations, on the same

side, senior," or "junior," as the case may be. If one man is *tako,* the other *lavo,* then they are related as *tama* and *luve*—that is as one generation to the other. In the case of relatives who are known, and whose side is therefore known, two sets of terms exist, just as in all cross-cousin systems. The line and the generation is what the Fijian looks for in his kinship system, not propinquity.

Why should he be so interested in the generation and so little in the nearness of kin? Because nearness is of little importance in public affairs; generation and line are all important. If a chief, chieftain, or priest dies it is not the next of kin that succeeds, as with us, but the next senior of his generation, no matter how distant; if the deceased was the last of his generation, then it goes to the most senior of the next. A Lauan expresses the rule thus: "X was not made chief, because his *tama* was living." We are not rendering the meaning at all by translating *tama* "father," because X's father was dead. What is meant is that X could not succeed because there was still a member of the previous generation on his father's side to come before him.

We now understand why members of the same generation and side are so carefully distinguished as senior and junior (commonly rendered "elder brother and young brother, classificatory"). The order of seniority is all important. With us only one of a group of brothers has to have his status made clear in royal and titled families; so among such families he bears a special title "heir" which singles him out; the rest are lumped together as brothers, for their seniority is normally of little importance, since they drop out of the succession. It is only when the holder has no issue that the seniority of his younger brothers need be remembered.

It is not the whole of a generation that succeeds, but only those in the male line. Therefore the female line has to be distinguished from the male by special terms. Since the female line is completely excluded, seniority does not come into consideration at all in their case, so no distinction is made between senior and junior. Generation, line, and seniority decide not only succession, but everyday behavior. The duties in the ritual are fixed in the same way.

In short, what we seek most is the next of kin, and so we run up and down the family tree. The Fijians (and the Australian aborigines, and the rest) do not, because there is no point in doing so. All they want is such information as will enable them to place each man on the correct side in the right generation. An inquiry proceeds thus: "How are you related?" "Of the same side and generation." "Why?" "Because our fathers were of the same side and generation." Or else: "We belong to successive generations on opposite sides, because he is of my mother's side and generation."

selection 30

Brother-Sister Avoidance among the Trobriand Islanders

Bronislaw Malinowski

From *The Sexual Life of Savages in North-western Melanesia.* Halcyon House, 1929, pp. 519–524. By permission of the author's estate.

The relation between brother and sister is denoted by the term *luguta.* This term means "sister" when uttered by a male, and "brother" when spoken by a female. In its wider meaning it designates a person of the oposite sex and of the forbidden class, that is, of the same sub-clan or clan as Ego. In its widest and metaphorical sense it is used for any tabooed person or thing. As a metaphor the word "sister" *(luguta)* is frequently used in magical formulae when such things as a blight or a disease are to be exorcized.

The term *luguta* is used only with regard to the tabooed relationship, since children of the same parents and of the same sex use different kinship designations *(tuwagu, bwadagu)* to describe each other; *tuwagu* meaning "my elder brother" (man-speaking) and "my elder sister" (woman speaking); and *bwadagu* "my younger brother" (man speaking) and "my younger sister" (woman speaking).

Round the word *luguta* a new order of ideas and moral rules begins to grow up at an early stage of the individual's life history. The child, accustomed to little or no interference with most of its whims or wishes, receives a real shock when suddenly it is roughly handled, seriously reprimanded and punished whenever it makes any friendly, affectionate, or even playful advances to the other small being constantly about in the same household. Above all, the child experiences an emotional shock when it becomes aware of the expression of horror and anguish on the faces of its elders when they correct it. This emotional contagion, this perception of moral reactions in the social environment is perhaps the most powerful factor in a native community by which norms and values are imposed on an individual's character.

The circumstantial arrangements and set customs which preclude any possibility of intimate contact between brother and sister are also, of course, very important. Brother and sister are definitely forbidden to take part at the same time in any childish sexual games, or even in any form of play. And this is not only a rule laid down by elders, but it is also a convention rigorously observed by the children themselves.

We know already that when a boy grows up and when there is a sister of his living in the parental house, he has to sleep in the bachelors' hut *(bukumatula)*. In her love affairs, the girl must most rigorously avoid any possibility of being seen by the brother. When, on certain occasions, brothers and sister have to appear in the same company— when they travel in the same canoe, for instance, or participate in a domestic meeting—a rigidity of behavior and a sobriety in conversation falls upon all those present. No cheerful company, no festive entertainment, therefore, is allowed to include brother and sister, since their simultaneous presence would throw a blight on pleasure and would chill gaiety.

Although, in a matrilineal society, the brother is the guardian of his sister, although she has to bend down when he approaches, to obey his commands and to regard him as the head of the family, he never has any concern in his sister's love affairs, nor in her prospective marriage. After she is married, however, he becomes the head of her family in more than a metaphorical sense. He is called by his sister's children *kadagu* (my maternal uncle), and as such exercises great influence, especially over the boys.

The careful avoidance by a man of any knowledge about his sister's amorous prospects is, I am certain, not only an ideal but also a fact. I was over and over again assured that no man has the slightest inkling as to whom his sister is going to marry, although this is the common knowledge of everyone else. And I know that nothing remotely touching upon the subject would be uttered within earshot of him. I was told that if a man came by chance upon his sister and her sweetheart while they were making love, all three would have to commit *lo'u* (suicide by jumping from a coco-nut palm). This is obviously an exaggeration which expresses the ideal and not the reality: if such a mishap occurred the brother would most likely pretend to himself, and to them, that the had seen nothing, and would discreetly disappear. But I know that considerable care is taken to preclude any such possibility, and no one would dream of mentioning the subject in the presence of the brother.

Brother and sister thus grow up in a strange sort of domestic proximity: in close contact, and yet without any personal or intimate communication; near to each other in space, near by rules of kinship and common interest; and yet, as regards personality, always hidden and mysterious. They must not even look at each other, they must never exchange any light remarks, never share their feelings and ideas. And as age advances and the other sex becomes more and more associated with love-making, the brother and sister taboo becomes increasingly stringent. Thus, to repeat, the sister remains for her brother the center of all that is sexually forbidden—its very symbol; the prototype of all unlawful sexual tendencies within the same generation and the foundation of prohibited degrees of kinship and relationship, though the taboo loses force as its application is extended.

The nearest female of the previous generation, the mother, is also surrounded by taboo, which is colored, however, by a somewhat different emotional reaction. Incest with her is regarded with real horror, but both the mechanism by which this taboo is brought home and the way in which it is regarded are essentially distinct from the brother-sister taboo. The mother stands in a close bodily relation to her child in its earliest years, and from this position she recedes, though only gradually, as he grows up. As we know, weaning takes place late, and children, both male and female, are allowed to cuddle in their mother's arms and to embrace her whenever they like.

When a small boy begins his playful sexual approaches to small girls, this does not in any way disturb his relationship to the mother, nor has he to keep any special secrecy on the subject. He does not, by preference, discuss these matters with his parents, but there is no taboo against his doing so. When he is older and carries on more serious intrigues, he might, in certain circumstances, even be allowed to sleep with his sweetheart in his parents' house. Thus the relation to the mother and the sexual relation are kept distinct and allowed to run side by side. The ideas and feelings centering round sex on the one hand, and maternal tenderness on the other, are differentiated naturally and easily, without being separated by a rigid taboo.

Again, since normal erotic impulses find an easy outlet, tenderness towards the mother and bodily attachment to her are naturally drained of their stronger sensuous elements. Incestuous inclinations towards the mother are regarded as highly reprehensible, as unnatural and immoral, but there is not the same feeling of horror and fear as towards brother-and-sister incest. When speaking with the natives of maternal incest, the inquirer finds neither the rigid suspense nor the emotional reactions which are alway evoked by any allusion to brother and sister relations. They would discuss the possibility without being shocked, but it was clear that they regarded incest with the mother as almost impossible. I would not affirm that such incest has never occurred, but certainly I have obtained no concrete data, and the very fact that no case survives in memory or in tradition shows that the natives take relatively little interest in it. . . .

The Teachings of My Father

Crashing Thunder

From *Crashing Thunder: The Autobiography of an American Indian,* Paul Radin, D. Appleton and Co., 1926, pp. 56–73. By permission of the publisher.

My father used to keep up the old habit of teaching us the customs of the Winnebago. He would wake us up early in the morning and, seated around the fireplace, speak to us. The girls would be taught separately. Now this is what my father told me:

I

My son, when you grow up, see to it that you are of some benefit to your fellow men. There is only one way in which you can aid them and that is by fasting. Our grandfather, the Fire, he who stands at all times in the center of our dwelling, sends forth all kinds of blessings. Be sure that you make an attempt to obtain his.

My son, do you remember to have our grandfathers, the war chiefs, bless you. See to it that they have compassion upon you. Then some day as you travel along the road of life, you will know what to do and encounter no obstacles. Without any effort will you then be able to gain the prize you desire. The honor will be yours to glory in, yours without exertion. All the disposable war-blessings belong to our grandfathers, the war-controllers, and if reverently you fast and thirst yourself to death, then these will be bestowed upon you. Yet if you do not wear out your feet in frequent journeyings to and fro, if you do not blacken your face with charcoal, it will be all for naught that you inflict this suffering upon yourself. Not without constant effort are these blessings procurable. Try to have one of the spirits created by Earthmaker take pity on you. Whatever he says will come about. If you do not posess one of the spirits from whom to obtain strength and power, you will be of no consequence socially and those around you will show you little respect. Indeed they will jeer at you.

My son, it is not good to die in the village; in your homes. Above all, do not let women journey to the spirit land ahead of you. It is not done. To prevent this from happening do we speak to our sons and encourage them to fast. Some day in life you will find yourself traveling along a road filled with obstacles and then you will wish you had fasted. When such an event confronts you, that you may not find it necessary to reproach yourself, I cousel you to fast. If you have not obtained any knowledge from the spirits, why it may happen that some day, in later life, warriors will be returning from the warpath and as they distribute the war prizes to their sisters, your own sisters will stand there empty-handed envying the rest. [Among the Winnebago a man's sisters, especially his elder sisters, were very highly respected and all war prizes, such as wampum-belts, wampum necklaces, etc., were always given to them whenever a man returned from a successful war-party in which he had secured some honor. These war honors were of various kinds. The greatest was considered to be the feat of having struck the body of a dead enemy first.] But if you obtain blessings from the war-controllers, your sisters will be happy. How proud they will be to receive the prizes, to wear them, and to dance the victory dance! Your sisters too will be strengthened thereby and you will be content and happy.

Now all this it would be well for you to obtain. Try to be a leader of men. To become one, however, is very difficult, the old people used to say. It may happen that you merely pretend to be a leader of men, that you are but a mere warrior in the ranks and yet take it upon yourself to lead a war-party and thus cause a needless waste of life, that you do what is called "throwing away a life." That is the most shameful of all acts. The relatives of the person whom you have thus sacrificed would then have the right to make you suffer, to torture you with burning embers. And then your relatives would have to stand by, sad and humiliated. Not with the blessing of one, not with the blessings of twenty spirits, can you go on the warpath. For that the blessings of all the spirits are necessary—those on this earth, those under it and those who lie pinned through it, the Island Weights; those in the waters and those on the side of the earth, the winds, all four of them. You need the blessings of the spirit who dispenses life from one side of his body and death from the other, the blessings of the Sun, the Moon, the Daylight, and the Earth. All these Earthmaker has make controllers of war and by all these must you be blessed in order to lead a war-party.

My son, if you cast off your dress for many people, that is, if you give to the needy, your people will be benefited by your deeds. It is good thus to be honored by many people. And even more will they honor you if you return victorious from the warpath with one of the four limbs, that is, one of the four war honors. But if you obtain two, or three, or perhaps even four limbs, then all the greater will be the honor. Then whenever a war feast is given you will receive part of the deer that is boiled, either part of its body or part of the head. [The meat of a deer at such a feast is given only to great warriors. The head is regarded as the choicest piece.] When on some other occasion, such as the Four Nights' Wake, you are called upon to recount your war exploits in behalf of the departed souls, be careful, however, not to claim more than you actually accomplished. If you do, you will cause the soul of the man in whose behalf you are telling it, to stumble in his journey to spirit land. [According to Winnebago belief the soul of a deceased individual in his journey to spirit land must cross a very slippery, swinging bridge and it is thought that if, during the wake following the man's burial, any of the invited warriors exaggerate their achievements the unfortunate soul will not be able to cross this bridge and will stumble and fall into the abyss of fire over which it is thrown.] If you tell a falsehood then and exaggerate, you will die before your time, for the spirits, the war-controllers, will hear you. It is indeed a sacred duty to tell the truth on such an occasion. Tell less than you did. The old men say it is wiser.

My son, it is good to die on the warpath. If you die on the warpath, you will not lose consciousness at death. You will be able to do what you please with your soul and it will always remain in a happy condition. If afterwards you wish to become reincarnated as human being, you may do so, or you may take the form of those-who-walk-upon-the-light, the birds, or the form of any animal you please, in short. All these benefits will you obtain if you die on the warpath.

II

My son, if you cannot obtain war-blessings, fast at least for position in life. If you fast then, when you get married you will get along well. You will then not have to worry about your having children and your life will be a happy one. If you fast and have the spirits bless you with all that concerns the happiness of your home, then throughout life you will never be in need of anything. Fast for the food you are to receive. If you fast frequently enough for these things then someday when your children ask for food they will be able to obtain a piece of deer meat without difficulty; they may indeed be able to obtain a piece of moose meat. It lies within your power to prevent your children from ever going hungry.

Now again, my son, let me enjoin you. Do not abuse your wife. Women are sacred. If you make your wife suffer, then you will die in a short time. Our grandmother Earth is a woman, and in abusing your wife you are abusing her. Most certainly will you be abusing your grandmother if you act thus. Since after all it is she who is taking care of us, by your action you will be practically killing yourself.

When you have your home, see to it that whoever enters your lodge obtains something to eat, no matter how little you yourself may have. Such food will be a source of death to you if withheld. If you are stingy about giving food, some one might kill you in consequence; some one may poison you. If you ever hear of a stranger passing through your country and you want to see him, prepare food for him and have him brought to you. In this manner you will be doing good and it is always good to do good, it is said.

If you see a helpless old person, help him if you have anything at all. If you happen to possess a home take him there, and feed him, for he may suddenly make uncomplimentary

remarks about you. You will be strengthened thereby. Or perhaps when he comes, he may bring with him under his arms a medicine bundle, something he cherishes very much and which he will offer you. If it is a bulb-medicine keep it to protect your house. Your home will never then be molested by anything evil and nothing evil will enter your house, neither bad spirits, ghosts, disease, nor unhappiness. Now such will be your life if you do as I tell you. Witches will keep away from you. Thus by fasting will you benefit yourself and your fellow men.

You know that Earthmaker created all the spirits, those that live above the earth, those who live on the earth, those who live under the earth, those who live in the water—all these he created and placed in control of powers. Even the minor spirits Earthmaker placed in control of something. In this fashion he created them and after that, he created us and because we were created last and no further powers were left, he could not put us in control of anything. Then, however, did Earthmaker create a weed and this he placed us in control of. He further told us that none of the spirits he had created would have the power to take this weed away from us without giving us something in exchange. He told us that if we offered him a pipeful of this weed, which we call tobacco, he too would grant us whatever we asked for. Now it so happened that all the spirits came to long for this weed as intensely as they longed for anything in creation and for that reason if, at any time, with tobacco in our hands we make our prayer to the spirits, they will take pity upon us and bestow upon us the blessings which Earthmaker gave them. Indeed so it is, for Earthmaker created it thus.

Fast, my son. If you are blessed by the spirits and then blow your breath upon people who are ill, they will become well. Thus will you help your fellow men. If you can cure any of your fellow men of disease, then you will be of even more than ordinary help to them. If you can draw disease from out the body, people will greatly respect you. If then you happen to be without work, all that you need for your support they will give you. For as long a time as you live they will do this for you. After your death people will speak about your deeds for all time. During your lifetime they will say, "Yes, he really has power."

If you are not able to fast, do at least try to obtain some power from those individuals, who know the virtues and powers of certain plants. It is sad enough, of course, if you will have to admit to yourself that you could not obtain blessings during fasting; but if you could not, at least try to have those who possess the plants I have mentioned, take pity on you. If they take pity on you, they will present you with one of the good plants that give life to man. Now it will not suffice for you to possess merely one plant. You should try to obtain all those plants that grow among the hairy covering of our grandmother, the Earth—all those that give us life—until you have a complete medicine bundle. Then will you truly have reason to feel encouraged.

Some of the medicine men, the shamans, were blessed by the waterspirits. [Waterspirits are mythical animals generally described as having the shape of a lynx or wild-cat and provided with long tails that completely encircle their bodies. Their gifts to man are ambivalent and it depends upon the man whether he cares to make good or bad medicines from their bodies. Their so-called "bones" generally consist of semi- or completely fossilized objects.] If you wish to obtain really powerful blessings and gain the power of curing many people, you will have to fast a long time and sincerely. If four, or say ten, of the truly powerful spirits bless you, then some day when you have children and anything happens to one of them, you will not have to look around for a medicine man, but all you will have to do will be to look into your own medicine bundle. Search there and you will undoubtedly be able to find the medicines necessary for curing your children. Indeed after a while you will be called upon to cure your fellow men. Then you can open your medicine bundle without embarrassment, for you will have the knowledge necessary for treating the sick. You will know where the disease is lodged and your treatment will be successful, for it was only

after the greatest efforts on your part that you succeeded in obtaining the requisite blessings. If you declare to the patient that he will live, then he will live. If you make proper offerings to the medicine and speak to your medicine in the proper manner, it will exert all the power it possesses to cure the patient. Now you must make good offerings to these medicines; you must give many feasts in their honor and then if, in addition, you address them as if they were human beings, they assuredly will help you and do what you ask. You may accordingly accept the payments offered to you by your patients in good conscience and your children will wear these payments in the form of wampum necklaces and thus gain renewed strength. They will be well and happy. These are the reasons why I want you to be extremely careful in your attitude. Medicines are good for all purposes; that is why they were given to us. Earthmaker gave them to us so that we could cure ourselves from disease.

If any one tries to obtain these staffs of life, these medicines and inflicts sufferings upon himself in acquiring them, then assuredly will our grandmother Earth have cognizance of it. She knows all that you have lost in obtaining them and in the long run what you have lost, will be returned to you. You made your offerings for the future and it is good for people to look forward to their future.

Say, you wish to obtain the paint medicine. For that you would have to put yourself in the most abject condition before the spirits. If you smear yourself with your paint medicine it will irresistibly attract the enemy; it will paralyze him, deprive him of all power of movement and utterly overpower him. Keep it in your home and then you will never be in want of riches. People will give you their most valued possessions owing to the influence of this paint medicine. The paint medicine is made from the blood of the waterspirits and that is why it is so holy. People obtain it by fasting and thirsting themselves to death and then receiving a blessing from the waterspirit. Earthmaker placed the waterspirits in possession of these powers so that they could then, in turn, bestow them on us.

Some people succeeded in obtaining a medicine that will enable a person to outdistance another in running. It might perhaps be well for you to learn something about this. There are medicines to be used in courting; medicines to prevent married people from separating; medicines for getting rich; medicines for causing people to become crazy. Should you, for instance, wish to make a person feel very sad at heart, then you can poison him with this last-named medicine and even make him crazy. It is also possible to make a woman who has refused you become a harlot, for this medicine will make her fall in love with every man she sees. Indeed any kind of medicine you desire can you obtain from certain individuals. Some are acquainted with medicines that put one to sleep, others with those that keep one awake and give one insomnia. Some have medicines enabling one to overcome the viciousness of dogs who are put to watch over women; others again have medicines that make people single out the possessor in a crowd. Everyone will look at him and consider him a great man. There are medicines to prevent people from getting tired when walking and medicines to cause a dog fight to take place. In short there are medicines for everything.

Every one must take care of himself and try to obtain that knowledge which will enable him to live in comfort and happiness. Try therefore to learn about the things you will need. If you know them, then as you travel along in life, you will not have to go to the expense of buying them from others, but you will have your own medicines. If you act in this way and if, in addition, you fast properly, you will never be caught off guard in life. Should you possess a home, it will look beautiful and you will never be in want. That is why I know you will never regret this that I am telling you. So you shall travel on your journey through life, along the virtuous road taken by all your fellow men, and your actions and behavior will never become the butt of your neighbor's sarcasm.

Help yourself as you travel along the road of life. The earth has many narrow passages scattered over it. If you have something with which to strengthen yourself, then when you get to these narrow turns you will be able to pass through them safely and your fellow men will respect you. See to it that people like you. Be on friendly terms with every one and then every one will like you. You will be happy and prosperous.

Never do any wrong to your children. Whatever your children ask of you, do it for them. If you act thus people will then say that you are good natured.

If any one in the village loses a friend through death, should you at all be wealthy, cover the expenses of the funeral of the deceased, if you can. Help the mourners likewise in defraying the expenses of feeding the departed. If you act thus, you will do well. All the people you have helped will then really know what kind of a man you are. For the good you do people will love you.

It is not good to win at gambling. You may possibly become rich thereby but that is no life to lead. If you are blessed with luck in cards, if you are blessed with luck at gambling, you will perhaps win things and have plenty of wealth, but none of your children will live.

Now if you do all that I have told you, you will lead a happy and prosperous life. That is why we Winnebago preach to a child we love so that it should never become acquainted with the things that are not right, and never do anything wrong. Then if, in later life, a person does anything wrong, he will do it with a clear knowledge of the consequences of his actions.

III

My son, when you get married, do not make an idol of the woman you marry; do not worship her. If you worship a woman she will insist upon greater and greater worship as times goes on. This is what the old people used to say. They always preached against those men who hearken too strongly to the words of women; who are the slaves of women. Now it may happen that a man has received many warnings as to his behavior in this regard and that he pays no attention to them. It may go so far that when he is asked to attend a war-bundle feast he will refuse to go. [The war-bundle feast was the great war ceremony of the Winnebago. It was given by all those individuals who possessed a war-bundle and since theoretically there was only one war-bundle in each clan, the basis of the organization of the ceremony was the clan. The ceremony consisted largely of prayers, songs and speeches in honor of the spirits more definitely associated with war. For each of these spirits, a buckskin decorated with the symbol sacred to the spirit was prepared and then at the most dramatic moment of the ceremony these buckskins were thrown out of the ceremonial lodge and it was believed that the spirits came down in person to fetch them. The war-bundle feast was specifically a man's ceremony.] It may be that when he is married he will listen to the voice of his wife and refuse to go on a warpath. He might as well have been brought up as a girl. Men who are real men perform the deeds of men, but such a man will never perform a real man's deed. If he should actually attend a war-bundle feast he will be given the leanest piece of meat, only given to a man of no account. Why should any one run the risk of being thus jeered at? Now when a really brave man attends a war-bundle feast he is given a deer's head. This other man gets a lean piece! It will dry up in his throat, so humiliated and disgraced will he feel. After a while he will not be allowed to go to any feast; his wife will not let him. He will listen to the voice of his wife. His relatives will scold him, his sisters will think nothing of him. They will tell people never to go to visit him. Finally when he has become a real slave of his wife he will even hit his relatives if she asks him to. It is for these reasons that I warn you not to listen to women. You will be considered different from others. It is not good.

Remember this too, that women cannot be watched. If you try to watch them and are jealous about them, then your female relatives will also be jealous of them. Finally when your jealousy has developed to the highest pitch, your wife will leave you and run away

with some one else. You have allowed her to see by your actions that you worship a woman, and one alone, and, in addition, you have been watching her all the time. Because of this incessant annoyance she will run away from you. If you think that your wife is the only one to love, you have humbled yourself and she will be taken from you. You have likewise made the woman suffer; you have made her unhappy. The whole world will hear about it. No other woman will want to marry you and you will have the reputation of being a bad man.

Now you may act in the following way: You see people starting on a warpath and you join them knowing that it is an honor to die on the warpath. But you will join them because you feel unhappy at your wife's flight. Now this is not the proper way to act. You are throwing away your life; you are causing the leader of the war-party to throw away a life. If you want to go on the warpath, do not go because your wife has been taken away from you, go because you feel courageous enough to do so.

It is on the warpath that a man has fun! Do not go, however, unless you have fasted adequately. You must fast for each specific warpath. If you do not and yet join a war-party, then in the midst of the fight, a bullet will come your way and kill you. That will happen because you did not fast. If you have performed any deeds of valor, recount them to your sisters and to your sister's children. Those in charge of war-bundles are good to listen to in such matters. Those to whom such people give advice will eat an excellent dish; they will have the honor of sitting near a great warrior in the middle of the lodge.

These are the things of which the old people spoke and this also is the advice I give you. I myself never asked for these things, but my father did. Your grandfather did. He asked for the information relating to the manner in which people are to behave. Never, when you are older, should you allow yourself to get in the predicament of not knowing what is the right thing to do. Ask for this instruction, my son. It is not a matter requiring a few moments; it is something that must be thoroughly learned. You, too, must learn it.

Rank, Wealth, and Kinship in Northwest Coast Society

Philip Drucker

From *American Anthropologist,* Vol. 41, No. 1, 1939, pp. 55–65. By permission of the author and the publisher.

Northwest Coast society was organized on no idealistic premises of the equality of man. Each individual had his place in the arbitrarily calibrated social structure of his community. However, the casual designation so often encountered of this social pattern of ranked statuses as a "class" or "caste" system with nobles, commoners, and slaves, is a crude over-simplification, except as regards the division of society into freemen and slaves. It will be the aim of this paper first to show that there were no social classes among the freemen, but rather an unbroken series of graduated statuses, and second, to investigate the principles underlying this gradation of rank.

For a working definition of a social class we may take the dictionary formulation: "Class: A group of persons, things, qualities, or activities having common characteristics or attributes"; or, "a group of individuals ranked together as possessing common characteristics or as having the same status." Thus, the fundamental requirement of a class, socially speaking, is the sharing by its members of some trait or traits which set them off as a distinct entity within their society. This common attribute, we may expect, will direct specific attitudes and behavior by them and toward them as a group. Where such attributes distinctive of social *groups* were lacking, we are not justified in speaking of a class system.

If we survey Northwest Coast society as a whole, we find that two great social classes existed everywhere: freemen and slaves. The distinguishing criterion, condition of servitude (whether by capture, birth, or debt does not matter here) placed every individual in one or the other group. As a member of his group he enjoyed certain rights or was subject to certain disabilities—depending on which group he was in—and by virtue of his membership was the object of esteem or scorn, and was entitled to scorn or esteem those of the other class. That slaves were sometimes treated with kindness and given certain concessions made no difference in their class membership; they were still slaves, and as such belonged in a sphere apart from the free.

As a matter of fact, the slaves had so little societal importance in the area that they scarcely need be considered in problems relating to the social structure. "Society," in the native view, consisted of the freemen of a particular group. Slaves, like the natives' dogs, or better still, like canoes and sea-otter skins and blankets, were elements of the social configuration but had no active part to play in group life. Their participation was purely passive, like that of a stage-prop carried on and off the boards by the real actors. Their principal significance was to serve as foils for the high and mighty, impressing the inequality of status on native consciousness.

If we seek groupings among the freemen comparable to the division into free and slaves we fail utterly to find them. I do not, of course, mean that all freemen were equals among themselves; but there was no class of nobility set off distinct from a class of "commoners," much less a three- or four-fold class system. We search in vain for any diagnostic traits defining groups within the society of freemen. There were individuals reckoned high and there were those considered lowly, true enough, Those of high rank abstained from menial tasks such as fetching wood and water, they wore costly ornaments and finer garb, and strutted in the spotlight on every ritual occasion. But these were not class prerogatives. They were not restricted to a certain group; there was no point in the social scale above which they were permitted and below which prohibited.

To compare the role of the highest ranking member of a Northwest Coast social group with that of the lowliest member gives an impression of a remarkably vast difference in cultural participation. The significant point is that the difference lay in extent of participation, not kind. One less high than the highest in rank, participated less fully in ostentatious activities. A person a grade above the lowest participated in these a bit more than the one on the bottom rung. And thus the manifestations of statuses of high and low degree shaded into each other.

What actually occurred was that each society consisted not of two or more social classes, but of a complete series of statuses graded relatively, one for each individual of the group. No two individuals were precisely equal in rank, in fact, equivalences would pose insuperable difficulties. This is brought out most clearly in the potlatch. Barnett's keen analysis has brought out the prime function of the potlatch in validating status; all I want to do here is to point out the mechanics of the procedure. In the distribution of the potlatch gifts, it was manifestly necessary to give them out one by one, else a mad scramble would result. Invariably the giving was in order of rank. The highest ranking individual of the recipient group was named first, and given his allotted share; then the second highest, and so on down the line. This order of giving was, from southeast Alaska to the mouth of the Columbia, the most important expression of the concept of rank. For two recipients to be of equal status would throw the whole affair out of gear, obviously, for neither would submit to being called after the other. An event in recent Nootkan history reveals the difficulties involved in such a situation.

"During the latter half of the last century, apparently about eighty years ago, the Tlupana Arm tribe, consisting of several local groups who wintered at o'is, moved down to Friendly Cove, joining the Moachat ('Nootka'). The head man of o'is stood first in the tribe; he had married a close kinswoman of the Moachat chief, and because of his relationship the latter offered him and his tribe a place at Friendly Cove. (The Tlupana Arm groups had been seriously reduced in numbers both through wars and the usual historic-period causes.) In addition, the Moachat chief 'shared' his potlatch-seat with his kinsman. For a time, when one potlatched the joint tribe, he had to give simultaneously to the Moachat and Tlupana first chiefs, and by analogy, to both second chiefs, and so on down the line. This was extremely confusing; both names and both gifts had to be called out simultaneously. No one was satisfied. Finally the Moachat chief in second place gave a potlatch at which he gave to all the Moachat chiefs, from first to last, then began with the

Tlupana Arm chiefs. The first chief of the Moachat then tried to establish another order: himself and the Tlupana first chief; the second of Moachat, then the second of Tlupana; the third of Moachat, then the third of Tlupana, etc.

"This did not meet with favor; the Moachat second chief was really receiving third, the third fifth, and so on. Nor would the Moachat chiefs approve of a plan to give simultaneously to both first chiefs, then to all the Moachat chiefs and after them the Tlupana men. They insisted on following the lead of the second chief, each giving to his own first chief (Moachat) and his fellows first, then to the Tlupana chiefs. The Moachat chiefs were rich, and did most of the potlatching; whether the Tlupana chiefs desisted because of poverty or from tact I do not know. There came to be considerable feeling over the situation. Finally the first chief of Tlupana potlatched, announcing that henceforth he would receive after the Moachat chiefs (and of course his subordinates received after him), so everything was settled. The whole difficulty was, in the informant's view, that the Moachat first chief 'had been trying to violate all the rules of the potlatch' in interfering with the established order of receiving."

In short, there were no classes of statuses in Northwest Coast society. Each individual had his own particular status in the graduated series from high to low; each person's status had its own attributes which were not quite like those of anyone else. To insist upon the use of the term "class system" for Northwest Coast society means that we must say that each individual was in a class by himself.

Before undertaking an analysis of the factors contributing to rank, it will be necessary to define briefly the social units within which rank was regulated. First of all, a survey of the source material indicates very clearly that the primary social unit was the local group, a group of people sharing rights to the utilization of economically important places and occupying a common village. Even among the Northern Nootkans, Southern Kwakiutl, and some Coast Tsimshian, where confederacies of these local groups formed larger

units at the winter villages, the smaller divisions retained their economic autonomy and moreover manifested it in rituals, for the local groups were the usual participating units.

When we come to examine the constitution of the typical local group of the area, a more striking fact appears: everywhere this social division was no more and no less than an extended family (slaves of course excluded) and was so considered by its members. The individual of highest rank in the social unit was related to the lowliest, distantly, it is true, but nevertheless related. So ties of blood as well as common residence and common economic resources welded the group together.

Now while the economic resources— fishing, hunting, and gathering grounds— pertained to the local group as a whole, titularly they belonged to individuals. We have to do here with two overlapping and apparently not well differentiated concepts of property-right. Characteristically, a man is said to have "owned" an economically important tract. This "ownership" was expressed by his "giving permission," as natives usually put it, to his fellows to exploit the locality each season. At the same time fellow-members of his local group—his relatives—had an inalienable right to exploit the tract. The present writer time and again has heard statements by informants from northwest California to Tlingit country to the effect that a certain man "owned" a particular place, for example, a fishing-site, and that his permission was required before other members of his society could use it. Nonetheless no instance was ever heard of an "owner" refusing to give the necessary permission. Such a thing is inconceivable to the natives. The situation is perfectly clear to the Indians, if not to us. Actually, individual ownership in these cases does not mean exclusive right of use, but a sort of stewardship, and the right to *direct* the exploitation of the economic tract by the local group. The latter it was who held exclusive right.

"Nootkan custom illustrated the nature of such rights very clearly. Almost every inch of Nootkan territory, the rarely visited mountainous back-country, the rich long-shore fishing and hunting grounds, and the sea as far out as the eye could reach, was 'owned' by someone or other. An owner's right consisted in the right to the first yield of his place each season—the first catch or two of salmon, the first picking of salmon-berries, etc. When the season came the owner called on his group to aid him in building the weir or picking the berries, then he used the yield of the first harvest for a feast given to his group, at which he stated his hereditary right (or custodianship) to the place, then bade the people to avail themselves of its products. Any and all of them might do so. (Outsiders were prohibited from exploiting these owned places, except where they could claim kinship to the owner, *i.e.,* for the time identify themselves with his local group.) The essence of the individual 'ownership,' was thus simply a recognition of the custodian's right."

The individual "ownership" or stewardship of economic areas was regarded as highly important, giving, as it did, a measure of authority to the incumbent of the position—political authority of a sort, and thus prestige. The rights were inherited according to local rules of inheritance (by the sister's son among Tlingit, Haida, Tsimshian, and Xaisla; by the son elsewhere in the area), so that it came about that in every Northwest Coast society economic wealth was in the hands of the direct descendants of a single line. Due to a disinclination to divide these holdings equally among a group of brothers, the bulk of the economic tracts of a local group was under the custodianship of a single individual at any one time: the eldest heir of the past "owner." This was as true in northwest California as in the regions north of the Columbia where the principle of primogeniture was so explicitly phrased. Thus, the economic possessions of a Northwest Coast society were chiefly in the custody of, or nominally "owned" by, a line of eldest sons of eldest sons (or the matrilineal counterpart of such a line). By virtue of their stewardship these men were elevated to prominence. Directing utilization of the natural resources as they did, they were the acknowledged heads of the groups—the heads of the extended families.

The extended family heads are the individuals referred to commonly as the "chiefs." The close relatives of the chiefs were not lacking in prestige, however, not only because they were intimately associated with the head of the social group, but in addition they customarily held various minor properties, in lands and other things as well. They were ranked according to their nearness to the chief. In the course of a few generations, as the secondary lines of descent diverged more and more from the direct line, and as patrimonies dwindled, descendants of the chief's brothers could claim but a low rank. Nonetheless by virtue of their kinship to the head of the village they retained certain rights and privileges. The rights of utilization of economic tracts by all members may be reckoned an expression of this recognition of blood-relationship, as was, in the north, the right to receive at potlatches even though in a low place. The significance of these last-named facts is that status in its minimum terms—membership in society—was derived from kinship and expressed in terms of wealth. . . .

In peripheral northwestern California, where we might expect to find areal patterns expressed in simplest terms, we find that rank was determined primarily by possession of wealth. The reckoning of status according to one's mother's bride-price savors of the hereditary principle, but the cultural accent was on wealth-holding rather than on blood. Nevertheless social position in this region was hereditary, for the simple reason that the status-giving fortunes were inherited, not earned anew each generation. It must be owned that these statuses were only loosely seriated within the group; the elaborate gradation found in the north was unknown. The outstanding figure in each local society was the head of an extended family who by virtue of his capital directed many activities. His custodianship of economically important sites made him preeminent in matters relating to the food quest; his capital of token goods gave him a voice in ritual affairs, for he had to equip the dancers in the wealth display performances, and in the social life, where he contributed to marriage payments and weregild. Next to this proud figure stood close kinsmen, brothers, cousins, and the like, who basked in reflected glory, as they, according to nearness of kinship, could draw on the resources of the head of the group when necessary. Grading into this group were lesser men who depended on what scraps of riches they might possess, the amount of bride-price paid for their mothers, and their favor in the eyes of their "big friend." (These are not, of course, categories representing distinct social classes, for they shaded imperceptibly into each other.)

From the Columbia to the Straits of Georgia the basis of status was the same as in the south—hereditary wealth—although the fact of heredity was stressed more and more as one proceeds northward. Similarly, more precise systems of ranking within each society are suggested, as we enter the domain of the potlatch where order of precedence becomes a matter of great concern.

It was in the societies north of the Salishan-Wakashan linguistic boundary, however, that the concept of formal status had its most luxuriant growth. The principles underlying this gradation may be brought out most clearly if we begin with a type individual to see how he attained his place in his social system. The first thing that set our individual off from his fellows was his name. Names, on the northern coasts, were very definitely hereditary property, and what is more, each name carried with it a particular social evaluation based on its traditional origin and the honor or disrepute of its bearer subsequently. That is to say, the names themselves were ranked from high to low. Each name had a particular status associated with it, a status which was expressed on formal occasions of feasting and potlatching, where the order of receiving was determined by the sequence of the names. So firmly rooted was this association of name and rank that the process of assuming a particular status, social, political, or ritual, consisted in taking (or having bestowed upon one) a certain name. The Kwaki-

utl, among whom the system of naming reached its most profuse elaboration, had separate names for feasts, for potlatches, and for their secret society performances. A personal name was thus a key to its bearer's status and embodied all the rights, economic and ceremonial, to which he was entitled.

Our friend, then, by taking his real name, defined at a blow his formal status in his society. To assume his name and status two things were requisite. First of all, he had to have a right to the name in question, usually through heredity, though in some regions transfers outside of the direct line of descent might be made: in a repayment of a bride-price, for example, or the name might be captured in war, or seized if a debt was not paid. The sole purpose of the interminable discourses at naming ceremonies was to declare the right of the claimant, through heredity or other legitimate transfer, to the name in question.

The second requisite for name-taking was that it be done formally and publicly, accompanied by a distribution of goods, that is to say, a potlatch. Not only was the name itself considered wealth, and connoted wealth, but wealth in token goods was mandatory for assuming it. If our type individual was heir of the head of his social group, there was, of course, no problem. But were his name of lesser status, he would be unable to potlatch in his own right. This is one of the most significant features of the Northwest Coast wealth system; the national wealth of each society was definitely limited, and there was no way in which a poor man could make a fortune for himself—at least, not in the days before European trade inflated and completely altered the financial system. Formerly, the token wealth of the entire group was concentrated in the hands of the head of the unit just as was the custodianship of economic rights. Not only did he have a certain right to surplus products (those beyond the needs of subsistence) of the lands in his trust, but members of his group gave him the fruits of their industry: canoes, blankets, furs. The head of the group was, in a sense, custodian of the token wealth of the family just as he was custodian of the economic resources. Barnett has pointed out this significant fact in connection with the potlatch: the entire group of the nominal giver united to support the affair out of motives of group loyalty and in return for the patronage and social favors bestowed by the head of the group. It was in this patronage that we find the means by which those of lower rank assumed whatever status they had right to. Names of lower rank were formally bestowed by the chief on those who had the right to them during the course of a potlatch. Among the Nootkans (and perhaps among other groups) the correlation between the group assistance and the chief's patronage was made obvious, for it was etiquette for the chief, in announcing the new name and rank of a member of his group, to tell how much property the latter (or the latter's parents) had contributed to the total amount to be given out. Nothing is clearer than the intimate relationship between hereditary status and wealth in the northern region. Not only were the hereditary fixed rankings in

society based on economic wealth, and themselves considered a form of wealth, but material wealth was necessary for their formal assumption.

In fine, throughout the Northwest Coast, possession of riches was the basis of social gradation. This wealth was inheritable, and thus status was hereditary. The northern and southern regions differed only in whether overt emphasis was put on wealth-holding or inheritance of wealth. In the south, possession counted for most; the fact that wealth was inherited was little stressed. In the north, the fact of inheritance dominated native consciousness, but wealth was an inevitable concomitant of high rank. Wealth and birth everywhere were absolutely inseparable factors in the determination of status. Whatever schismatic tendencies such a system of social inequality theoretically might have had were negated by the unbroken graduation of statuses from high to low, and the bonds of blood kinship which linked the head of each social unit with his humblest subordinate.

The Role
of a Fijian Chief

Clellan S. Ford

From *American Sociological Review,* Vol. 3, 1938, pp. 542–550. By permission of the author and the publisher.

The chief is the leader of his people. He organizes the activities in his district, directing work in the gardens, in house building, and in fishing. He receives in return the best produce of the land. The labor of the men in the district is at his command, though by tradition the chief is liberal, and most of the supplies which he exacts return ultimately to the subjects by whose labor they were produced. No decision of importance in the district may be reached without his approval. Funeral services, for example, may not begin until he has given the word. Visitors must present themselves to the chief before they undertake to carry out the purpose of their visit. At any ceremonial function the chief receives the first bowl of *kava* and determines the order in which others are served. The chief is also the arbiter of disputes within the district. When any trouble arises, the persons involved must be brought before him. He is expected to be fair, judging carefully according to the dictates of custom. He holds the power of life and death over his subjects. Offenses against the chief are not tolerated; it is here that stresses and strains in the status relationship are most clearly apparent. Treason is severely punished. In the old days, for a person to step out of his role as subject and attempt to assume the status of a chief was tantamount to committing suicide. The penalty for plotting against a chief was inevitably death. The examples given in the literature reveal that the subject doomed to execution made little or no effort to avoid his punishment. When discussing this point with a member of the community I was told: "Whatever the chief says shall be carried out. He knows what is best for us. Who would want to destroy the Tui? . . . he is the leader of our community and no one could take his place. If he were not here, we would be lost." This power, now prohibited by the British, is the traditional heritage of a Fijian chief.

Except for the examples referred to, the picture thus far presented has been abstracted from behavior; we have not seen chiefs and their subjects actually living their roles. The formal description of a role necessarily involves a selection of certain aspects of the total behavior and is not always done with eyes open to the exact meaning of the descriptive terms employed, with the result that depth and content of the relationship often disappear. The above statement of the relationship between chief and subject leaves the impression that behavior accords rigidly with the description. The individuals occupying the statuses and roles seem little more than puppets. The personality of the individual is completely lacking.

The actual role of a real person gives a very different picture. When my wife and I arrived at Naviti, I was accepted as an American chief sanctioned by the British government. Our relationship to the chief was formally and rigidly defined. He treated us with respect coupled with an aloofness which was at first disturbing. Since he would be responsible for our treatment, we did our best to break down this barrier of formality and reserve. Although the language handicap, which only gradually was overcome, retarded our efforts, constant association and interest in the things he enjoyed soon led the chief to accept us as something more than mere representatives from another country. After seven months of closest association, spending most of our waking hours in his company, eating with him, and participating in his activities, we became firm friends. The affection which developed between us makes it difficult not to color accounts of his behavior, but I have attempted to give an objective description.

Ratu Kama is a typical Fijian chief in appearance and carries himself with dignity. He is a large, powerful man with broad shoulders, narrow hips, and rather small feet and hands. His piercing eyes, strong chin, and intelligent forehead distinguish a handsome face which, though genial, can be very stern. Despite his fifty odd years, he is in good physical condition and can walk fifteen to twenty miles a day over rugged hills without apparent discomfort. Customarily retiring at midnight, he is at work in the gardens every morning before five. His crowning glory is a mass of bushy black hair about six inches long encircling his head. This he keeps

scrupulously clean and well groomed, washing it daily, anointing it with coconut oil, and combing it to perfection. Once a month it is dyed to prevent the appearance of a single white hair. He bathes at least once a day, carefully manicures his finger and toe nails, and keeps his skin in condition through frequent oil massages. His reasons for this extreme cleanliness and care are twofold. First, he attributes the tropical ulcers and boils so prevalent among Fijians to lack of cleanly habits. Second, he relates the prevalence of colds and pneumonia among the natives to their negligence in the use of oil. In the old days, he says, the natives used to remove their barkcloth when it had become wet. Oil served instead of clothing on wet and rainy days. Now that clothing has supplanted bark-cloth, the Fijian no longer uses coconut oil to keep him warm and dry, and, morever, he seldom changes his cloth *sulu* when it becomes damp. Many now become sick, the chief maintains, because the Fijian physique is not accustomed to this treatment.

Chief Kama enjoys his food immensely, especially when it is highly spiced with chili peppers, and he is extremely proud of the amount he can consume at one meal, regarding the ability to eat great quantities of yam, pork, and fish as an estimable accomplishment. He drinks *kava* to excess and chews or smokes tobacco constantly. He is extremely voluble and seems to enjoy shouting his orders and bellowing his jokes. His best loved pastime is to sit in a meeting house drinking *kava,* smoking a banana leaf cigar, joking and laughing heartily with the men who gather around him. Whenever he has finished overseeing work in the gardens or the building of a house, for example, he takes time off to meet the men informally.

On certain occasions he manifests in striking manner his zest for pleasure and social enjoyment. On his fifty-first birthday he seemed afraid lest he lose a precious minute or two of the festive occasion. Before midnight he was supervising preparations for his birthday feast. He superintended the building of a huge earth oven, the heating of the stones, the slaughtering of the pigs, the special wrapping of a hundred or more yams and other vegetables and fish, and the all important preparation of fancy arrowroot and coconut puddings. When these were cooked, about six o'clock in the morning, he directed the men to make a bundle of all this food, so that it could be suspended from two poles and carried by the village youths. Throughout the preparations, his attitude seemed one of suppressed excitement and anticipation, somewhat like that prevailing among ourselves on Christmas Eve. At the same time he was insistent that everything be done in the traditional manner. The emphasis on custom was reflected in the elaborate adornment of the villagers, who bedecked themselves in brightly colored strips of pandanus leaf, powdered their hair with sandalwood, and painted their faces as though for a victory feast.

We formed a procession, with the food and its bearers following behind, to march several miles to a neighboring town. The shell trumpets of our party announced our approach, and we were met on the outskirts of the village by an escort of two men, one brandishing a spear and the other carrying a club. With due form, we entered the meeting house to attend the *kava* ceremony. The chief, fully attired in *tapa,* his face painted, and his body glistening with coconut oil, seated himself at the far end of the meeting house and at once became grave. Quietly he stated that the ceremony was to be carried out in all details as the *kava* rites had been conducted in the past. Nothing must disturb the majesty of the ceremony. After the mixing of the *kava* had begun, not a sound was heard in the meeting house except the swish and drip of the strainer in the bowl. At intervals old men seated behind the bowl accompanied the movements of the mixer with a weird, high-pitched chorus. The chief looked on with an immobile face, while everyone else scarcely dared to move. After some twenty minutes the mixing was complete, and a cupbearer danced down with a bowl of *kava* for the chief. When all had been served and the ceremony was over, Ratu Kama quickly relaxed and became almost maniacal with joy. He

supervised the feast and spread special mats for each person to sit on. These mats were his presents to the people. He laughed and joked with the men who ate with us and insisted that everyone eat as much as possible. After more than two hours of feasting, he watched formal dances by the women of the village, cheering them on; he danced with the girls, sang, slapped the men on their backs, and did his best to make this a joyous occasion for everyone. During the entire afternoon he acted like a child whose birthday party seems the most important thing in the world. After dark we walked back to our village, went to his house, and drank *kava* until late evening. He was still his happy, jolly birthday self. Suddenly drumbeats sounded, signifying that envoys from an island nearby had arrived. At once he became the cold, stern man who had officiated at the *kava* ceremony in the morning, and for several hours he carried on a dignified conference with the messengers. It seemed impossible that the next morning he could do anything but sleep, yet he was up at five to superintend the gardening. He seemed to be compensating for his good time of the day before, driven by conscience to perform his customary duties.

One of the most significant roles of a Fijian chief is to direct the food gathering activities of his village. One night Chief Kama called the men together and announced that next day we were to go fishing. This called for extensive preparations. Early in the morning the men began to make the *rau*, or fish barrier, and to prepare their spears, while the women mended their nets. When the tide had turned, we went to a place on the reefs selected by the chief. One man took an end of the *rau* and waded out into the water. Another, picking up the vine about ten feet away from the first, followed him out, and so on until, with forty of fifty men carrying the vine barrier, it was transported out on the reef and arranged in a huge circle. The chief stood on the shore shouting directions. The men had to go precisely where he indicated. Once when a carrier stumbled with the vine the chief reproved him, saying: "Get up, you crazy fellow; are you an old, old woman who can't walk?'' When the circle was finally completed, the chief waded out so that he could better give his orders. He made the men stand motionless until he thought the tide suitable and then ordered them to close in on the fish. The men at one end carried the vine clockwise and those at the other counterclockwise, thus making the circle smaller and at the same time doubling the vine and increasing the effectiveness of the barrier. They closed in slowly and more slowly until the circle was about twenty feet in diameter. The chief then ordered the women to crowd around the edge of the vine with their nets and told the men to prepare their spears. Apparently the hard work was over; now it was going to be good sport. Hitherto the chief had been very matter of fact, spending much time judging the wind and tide and studying the contours of the reef. His was the responsibility for a good catch and he took it seriously. No one questioned his decisions nor did he seek advice. Now his attitude changed. He began to spend most of his time joking with the men and teasing the women. He would poke a woman in the seat and laugh heartily, as he saw a big fish leap out of the water, saying: "That is the fish I am going to spear. Shall I give it to you?" It is the chief's privilege to spear the first fish, and it is a matter of pride with him to score a hit on the first throw and also spear the largest fish in the pool. Chief Kama did not seem much concerned. After briefly scanning the water, he poised his spear and flung it almost half way across the enclosure, transfixing a huge forty-pound fish. Recovering his spear and raising his catch aloft, he gave a shout and cried: "That's the way to do it!" thus giving the signal for the men to spear the fish and the women to catch them in their nets. He then turned to us and became very solicitous. He showed me how to poise a spear, throw it, and judge where the fish would be by the time the spear hit the water. He pointed out the various species, telling us which were poisonous, where in the body of the fish the poison was located, and how by careful cleaning one could remove the harmful substance. Now and then he broke off to laugh and joke with the others, entering into the sport with infectious enthusiasm.

The behavior of Ratu Kama during this day of fishing typifies the way he leads his people in food gathering and industrial activities. He always couples extreme enthusiasm with an insistence that everything be done correctly. Part of the time, he is a reserved, commanding leader whose instructions are promptly and accurately carried out, but at other times he delights in becoming one of the group, acts as though he had no responsibilities, and allows the men to joke at his expense as though he had no authority to maintain. On the day in question, there were times when all appeared to stand on the same level; deference to the chief was suspended so that a casual observer could not have distinguished him from his subjects. By his enthusiastic participation, he made the occasion a lark for the men and women of the village; a day of fishing with the chief is regarded by all the people as one of the best days in their lives. His concern for us was typical. Whenever we were present, no matter how busy or excited he was, he found time to explain things to us as if he thought no one else could do so.

Another incident will illustrate the way in which Chief Kama plays the role of judge and arbiter of disputes. Early one morning I was awakened by loud shouts. The chief was outside my house entreating me to come quickly and help him. One of the women of the village had been severely hurt. During the night the roof of her house had leaked and the water had dripped through to the mats which she used for a bed, but her husband continued to sleep soundly through the rain. Intensely annoyed, she seized a large cane knife, the only iron instrument at her disposal, rudely awakened her husband and threatened to kill him. However, according to her story, she carefully held the blade with blunt edge toward him. Dazed from sleep, he thought she was really planning to make an end of him and fled for his life. She chased him around the room, shrieking and calling him names. Finally, as she aimed a blow at his head, he seized a mat from the floor and held it up as a shield. On striking the mat, the knife flew out of her hand and rebounded upon her head, cutting a long gash. She immediately set up such a shriek that the whole village congregated and the chief was called. After I had been summoned and had bandaged the poor woman's head, the chief called a meeting in which he attempted to get to the bottom of the trouble. The husband claimed that he could get no one to help him repair the house and that he was unable to do it alone. He also asserted that his wife spent all of her time making mats, that she seldom cooked for him, and that she neglected the duties of a good housewife. The chief listened with great seriousness and seemed quite disturbed. His problem in such a situation is to clear up the trouble and make peace within the village. This he could have done very easily by ordering the men of the community either to build a new house or to patch the roof of the old one and by fining the man and his wife for causing so much trouble. Kama, however, does not take things so lightly. He was determined to get at the root of the matter and to remove, if possible, whatever causes for trouble might exist. Hence, showing no regard for the pain which the woman was apparently suffering, he summoned her to the meeting. She insisted that her husband was a lazy good-for-nothing, that he spent all his time drinking *kava* and neglected his gardens, that he had made no attempt to repair the house, and that he did none of the things which a good husband should do. As the meeting continued, with first the husband speaking and then the wife, the chief found that he had reached an impasse; each, it seemed, had valid cause for complaint. He then called upon the other members of the village for their testimony. It transpired that the woman thought herself a bit too good for her husband and that he resented this. With this information out in the open, the chief induced the couple to admit to each other that this was one of the main reasons for their quarreling. He ordered the woman thenceforth to be a better housewife to her spouse. The husband he sent off to the gardens to work, warning him that should any future trouble arise between them through his fault, he would be exiled from the village. He then took from his own house a whale's tooth and presented it to the men of the village, asking them please to repair the house completely,

thus eliminating further complaint from that source.

Justice having been dispensed, a mighty weight seemed to fall from the chief's shoulders. He ordered *kava* to be mixed, and as the sun came up he sat and drank with the men, laughing and jesting about the night's experience. He even ordered a feast to be held that day. Everyone attended.

The way he played his part in this incident exemplifies his behavior in similar cases. He always takes his position seriously and is not satisfied until he has been the kind, just father of his people and has settled the dispute as completely as possible. Instead of being vexed, he tries to impress his points in a kindly manner. The proclamation of a feast and his evident good humor were his ways of obliterating the unhappy after effects of such an episode and indicating to the offenders that the incident was closed. The attitude of Chief Kama in cases of this sort contrasts sharply with that of another district chief with whom we had a brief acquaintance. Chief S___ plays the role of judge in a quite different fashion, of which only the most obvious points of contrast can be presented here. In the first place, he is a much smaller man physically than Chief Kama, a fact which may have had something to do with his attitude. On the occasion when we were in his village some trouble had arisen among his subjects. In dealing with the offenders, he was extremely angry and disagreeable. He fined the man and wife who had been quarreling and harangued them at length. He further punished them by forbidding the woman to take part in the formal dance that afternoon and by not permitting the man to attend the *kava* ceremony. Even then he did not allow the village to forget the incident. His surly countenance was a continual reminder of his anger, and his acid remarks made the rest of the day very unpleasant for his subjects.

A Fijian chief is expected to display extreme tact. This does not apply, however, to those instances when he is justified in being angry. Most Fijian chiefs, therefore, exhibit their tact principally in dealing with other chiefs. In their dealings with common people, where the relationship is formally one of command and obedience, adroitness is not customary. In this respect, Chief Kama varied from the norm. Very seldom did he neglect to use tact when handling either men or women. If the situation could not be handled in any other way, he made a joke of it and made his point indirectly. He never used his position to exhibit anger or vexation as did Chief S____.

In his relationship with us, his use of tact was elaborated because we were considered chiefs from another land. One example will suffice to show how he would reprimand us. During our first few months in Naviti, we knew little of Fijian customs. We therefore unwittingly did a number of things which violated native ideas of propriety, but he never would correct us. Many times we asked, "Are we doing the things expected of us?" but he always made some joke or other about a chief from American not being able to do anything wrong, and let it pass. One day, however, as we were talking about the white officials of the British government, with a twinkle in his eye he proceeded to tell us various things certain officials had done in violation of Fijian custom. Everything he mentioned either my wife or myself had done inadvertently in our ignorance of the native folkways. To make certain I was right in my surmise that he was telling us indirectly what we should not do, I said that we had done a number of these very things and that no one had said anything to us about them. Slapping me on the back, he said that we were newcomers to Fiji and would require a long time to learn how to act in true Fijian fashion but that, since we were interested in the people's habits, we would soon learn.

Briefly reviewing these incidents, what can we say about the way Chief Kama plays his social role? First of all, it is apparent that he is a real chief. He maintains his position of authority with little difficulty, feels secure in his position, and has no anxiety over the possibility of losing his status. Not afraid to be liked by his people as an individual, he is able to descend to their level on occasion and to have a good time. When something occurs which makes it necessary for him to reassume his position of authority, there comes an instantaneous and automatic change in his demeanor to which his subjects immediately respond. He gives the impression of a mature person who has worked out his adjustment in life to the point where he is able to accomplish the things expected of him with a minimum of anxiety and fear. He is effective in his social role. On each occasion when he has fulfilled his duty, there is apparently a release of energy which he expends in ways enjoyable both to him and to the members of his village. Furthermore, he seldom takes advantage of his position to inflict pent up aggression on his subjects, and one of his main techniques binding the people to him is his elaborated and extended use of tactfulness. His authority in reality is based as much upon the good will of his subjects as upon the traditional heritage of power which he holds by right of birth. Within a formal system of status based upon fear, Chief Kama has developed a status relationship founded primarily upon affection. This is a variation within the social patterning directly in contrast to the behavior of Chief S____, whose insecurity was so evident.

Ibo Law

Charles K. Meek

From *Essays Presented to C. G. Seligman.* London: Kegan Paul, Trench, Trubner & Co., Ltd., 1934, pp. 209–226. By permission of the author and the publisher.

In the space allowed for this paper it will only be possible to refer to a few of those concepts of the Ibo which may be conveniently described as "legal," more particularly as it will be necessary to include an account of the social and religious organization, with which the whole of the legal system is closely interwoven. For Ibo law is not a well-defined institution by itself, but is rather the expression, when such is called for, of the innumerable latent rules governing all the tribal institutions.

The Ibo-speaking peoples number about 3,185,000 people, and are centered mainly in the Onitsha, Owerri, Benin, and Ogoja Provinces of Nigeria. It is with the North-Western groups inhabiting the political divisions of Onitsha Province, known as Nsukka and Awgu, that this paper is principally concerned. . . .

The Ibo consist of a number of sub-tribes such as the Awhawzara and Awhawfia. But these terms are primarily geographical, and the most striking feature of Ibo society as a whole is the absence of any strong tribal or sub-tribal organization. In the Nsukka and Awgu divisions there is no higher social or political unit than the "village-area," *i.e.,* the group of villages united by the possession of a common name and territory, the belief in descent from a common ancestor, the sharing of common customs and cults, and sometimes of a common *chi* or soul.

The village-area may thus constitute a clan (but there is no clan exogamy). But it is frequently a local rather than a kinship grouping; for, though the component villages may vaguely claim a common ancestor, it can often be proved that there was no original relationship, and in many cases, indeed, no relationship is claimed. Such unity as they possess is due to economic and political circumstances and to intermarriage.

A village-area is known as an *obodo* or *mba* or *ala,* and includes a number of subdivisions known as *ṅkporo* or *ogbwe.* The *ṅkporo* in turn is subdivided into smaller groups or hamlets known as *ónuma* or *nchi.* The hamlet may coincide with the single kinship grouping known as *umunna* or may embrace sev-

eral *umunna*. An *umunna* may be composed
of a single group of related families, each of
which consists of such close relatives as a
man and his wife, brothers or first cousins
and their wives and children; or it may consist
of two or more related groups of such families. Where the *umunna* consists of a single
group of related families it may, for the purposes of this article, be described as an
"extended-family," and where it consists of
two or more groups of related families it may
be described as a "kindred."

The *umunna* is the basic social unit. Where
it consists of a single extended-family it is
invariably an exogamous unit. (The exception
is the Ache district in which marriage with
close consanguineous relatives, *e.g.,* first
cousins, is permissible.) Where it embraces a
number of related extended-families it may or
may not be an exogamous unit. Intermarriage
between related extended-families is sometimes allowed and sometimes forbidden. The
exogamous unit may therefore be as small as
a dozen people or as large as five or six
hundred. A large *umunna* differs little from a
small clan (unless we are to regard exogamy
as a *sine qua non* of clanship). Descent is
reckoned patrilineally.

With regard to the religious conceptions of
the people it may be said shortly that the Ibo
believe in the existence of a Supreme Spirit
known as Chuku. In his creative aspect
Chuku is described as Chineke or Chukwoke
or Chi Okike. He sends rain, makes the crops
grow, and is the source from which men
derive their *chi* or soul. He is sometimes
equated with and sometimes regarded as the
father of Anyanu (the Sun). He is also the
father of Igwe (the Sky), Amadi Ọha (Lightning), and Ale (the Earth-deity). Sacrifices are
not usually offered to Chuku, but he is
regarded as the ultimate recipient of all sacrifices. In the Nsukka Division every householder offers regular sacrifice to Anyaṅu (the
Sun), but in the Awgu Division there are no
sun-shrines, though a man may occasionally
hang up a chicken in a piece of cleft bamboo
with a prayer to Anyaṅu that he will receive it
and convey it to Chuku. Incidentally the peoples of Awka are known to those Awgu as
"the children of the Sun."

The most important deity in the religious
and social life of the people is Ale or Ala or
Ane, the Earth-deity. Ale is regarded as the
owner of men, whether alive or dead. The cult
of ancestors is therefore closely associated
with Ale, who is queen of the Underworld (but
is also sometimes regarded as a male deity).
Ale is the source of human morality, and is in
consequence the principal legal sanction.
Homicide, kidnapping, poisoning, stealing
farm-products, adultery, giving birth to twins
or abnormal children, are all offenses against
Ale, and must be purged by sacrifice to her.
Laws are made in her name, and by her oaths
are sworn. Ale is, in fact, the unseen president
of the community, and no group is complete
which has not its shrine and priest of Ale.

Under the control of Ale are numerous
godlings or spirits, of whom the most important is Njoku, the giver and protector of
yams. The ancestors of the people also live
under the control and act as the agents of Ale.
They profoundly influence the lives of their
descendants. They are the guardians of
morality, and regard any departure from custom as a breach of morality. It is for this
reason that priests of cults and heads of
families, who are the living representatives of
the ancestors, have frequently eschewed association with the new-fangled laws of the
Government.

The head of each family-group, or *okpara*
as he is called, owes his authority (or such
authority as he possesses) largely to the fact
that he is the representative and mouthpiece
of the family ancestors, symbolized by the
sacred stick known as *ọfọ*. This stick, which is
a section of a branch of a species of tree
believed to have been set aside by Chuku as a
symbol and guarantee of truth, is inherited
and carefully preserved by all heads of families.

All priests of cults have an *ọfọ,* which is the
recognized means of communication with the
deity or spirit of the cult. But it represents
also the ancestors who formerly ministered to
the cult. It is the symbol of authority of the
living priests, and the guarantee and means
of transmission of his "Holy Orders." And just
as the priest himself tends to become identified with the god he serves, so the *ọfọ* be-

comes identified with the deity or spirit in whose service it is used. In many groups _ofọs_ are even specifically identified with the god or spirit of Truth and Justice. Oaths are sworn on _ofọs_ and no _ofọ_-holder would swear falsely by his _ofọ,_ unless he had become a renegade.

There is a final aspect of ancestor-worship which is of prime importance in the administration of justice, _viz.,_ the societies (secret from women) in which the ancestors or ancestral leaders are [im] personated by maskers known as Mọ. These societies act as policemen of the community, and are used particularly as a means of disciplining the female members of the community. The Mọ might, on their own initiative, drive an adulterous woman out of the kindred, and banish anyone suspected of practicing witchcraft, or compel him or her to submit to the ordeal of drinking sasswood.

With this brief summary we may now proceed to give some details of the manner in which law functions among the Ibo, and as law begins within the family-group or _umunna,_ we shall consider first the mode by which the _umunna_ is governed.

An _umunna_ is composed of groups of compounds, each of which contains one or several small or biological families closely related to each other. Each of these families is in most respects an economic unit, as each farms and trades on its own account. But each compound or household recognizes its senior member as its moral and political controller. Similarly, each group of households constituting a distinct extended-family within the _umunna,_ is subject to the control of the various heads of households, presided over by the _okpara_ or senior householder, who holds the family _ofọ,_ and represents the family in all its external relations. Where the _umunna_ contains a number of extended-families, the control is vested in the whole body of elders, presided over by the head of the senior extended-family, who is the holder of the senior _ofọ._ The authority of the _okpara_ is based on the fact that he is regarded as living in close association with the ancestors, and is thus the chief repository of custom. He has charge of the shrine of the founder of the

umunna, to whom he offers regular sacrifice once a year on behalf of the whole kindred, and irregular sacrifice on behalf of individuals who may be directed by the diviner to offer sacrifice. He can bring any recalcitrant member to heel by the mere threat of invoking his _ofọ_ against that man. To insult him is to insult the ancestors, who are regarded as ever present in his _ofọ._ One guilty of such an offense would be brought before him and the other elders, and ordered to hand over a chicken, some kola-nuts, and a pot of palm-wine, that sacrifice might be offered to the ancestors, lest in their anger they should kill the offender. The advice of the senior elder cannot usually be disregarded, unless he is so old and decrepit that another has to act on his behalf. He takes immediate steps to stop inter-family fights, and, assisted by the other elders, investigates all disputes, warning those who have misbehaved themselves that if they repeat their conduct they need not look to him for assistance. If the matter were serious, such as theft from a fellow-member of the kindred, he would warn the thief that a repetition of his offense would lead to his expulsion from the village, or being sold as a slave to the Aro (who are itinerant traders and slave dealers). He might even, with the concurrence of the other elders of the kindred, order him to be tied hand and foot and placed on a platform over a smoking fire for two days without food or drink. He might threaten to drive out of the family-group any young man who had shown himself to be lazy and taken no steps to obtain a wife. (But in a first offense, a recalcitrant son is brought to book by his own father or the head of the small family-group.) He [the _okpara_] might order a member of the family-group who owed a debt to a fellow-member, or to a member of another family-group, to pay the debt forthwith, under the penalty of having a taboo (a knotted palm-leaf) placed on his property. He might, in association with the other elders, inflict a severe fine on anyone committing adultery with the wife of a kinsman, and order the poisoning of one who had committed incest. He could, in former days, call on the father of twins or abnormal children to rid the kindred immediately of the "abominable thing." When gifts, fees, or sacrificial foods are divided he, as the holder of the senior ọfọ, takes the first share, and when meetings are held to settle disputes he announces the decision, holding the ọfọ in his right hand and quoting precedents for the decision.

The head of a kindred, or family-group, is not, however, an autocrat, unless he happens to be a man of outstanding personality. If he is weak and untrustworthy he has little influence, and his functions may, by common consent, be delegated to any suitable person. Even a young successful man may be accorded the position of leadership. One who has obtained a public office or title may overshadow the senior elder, and in some communities, if there is a priest of Ale in the kindred, he may, even if he is a comparatively young man, be accorded the position of principal authority. Furthermore, if the kindred is large, there is usually considerable jealousy between the various extended-families composing the kindred, and each extended-family endeavors, for its own honor, to settle quietly any case of delinquency on the part of one of its members, without bringing it to the notice of the head official of the kindred. The authority of the head of the kindred is also qualified by the fact that he cannot act solely on his own initiative. In all important matters he is bound to consult and seek the support of the other elders and important persons of the kindred.

A well-known feature of the legal system is the collective responsibility of the family-group for the conduct of its members. The stock example of this is in cases of murder or manslaughter. Immediate retaliation was made by the kin of the murdered man on any member of the murderer's kin, and the property of the nearest relatives of the murderer was pillaged. In consequence of this rule the murderer was expected *by his own family* to commit suicide immediately, in order to save the whole family from attack and their property from spoliation. If the murderer failed to do this the whole of his kin had to seek refuge in flight.

When the anger of the murdered man's kin had subsided, the kin of the murderer could return, on condition that the murderer *or some other member of his family* committed suicide. Details will be given on this subject later, and it need only be remarked here that, in consequence of this rule of collective responsibility, the elders of a kindred constantly warned their young men to keep control over their feelings and avoid the use of lethal weapons. Further, as murder was considered an offense against Ale (the Earth-deity), the crime, if committed against a fellow-member of the same family, was not one which could be palliated or settled privately by the family itself. The whole community took action against the murderer, and his own brother might be the first to set fire to his house. Even if a man killed his brother accidentally, he had to fly and remain away for a period of one month. He was then permitted to return; but at the first festival of Ale he had to take a goat, fowl, new basket, cloth, and some yams to the shrine of Ale where he knelt down and said, "Ale, I bring these gifts to you. I did not kill my brother by design. I went out hunting like the rest, and killed him by an accident. Ale spare my life." The various articles brought were left at the shrine. The animals were not sacrificed. The goat became sacred and taboo, and was allowed to wander about unharmed. Indeed, it was given the right of way on the road. If it bore young ones they also became taboo, being known as "Ewu Ale." The goat was in fact a scapegoat, for it was stated that the "evil" which had moved the man to kill his fellow had passed into the goat, and that if anyone ate the flesh of that goat the inherent "evil" would cause his death. It is to be noticed that in a case of this kind (*i.e.*, of a man killing a member of his own extended-family or kindred) no blood-money was payable, on the ground that it would be heinous to derive profit from the death of a "brother."

The collective responsibility of the kinship group is shown also in numerous other ways. Thus (at Oduma), if a man had been summoned by the elders of the town to answer some charge, and refused to attend, the elders would send young men to bring him by force. If they could not find him they would capture any member of the accused's extended-family and keep him a prisoner until the accused appeared. This would induce the elders of the accused's extended-family to bring pressure on the parents of the accused to produce him or disclose his whereabouts. If the accused had run away to some distant town, the members of his extended-family would be called on to pay the penalty of the accused's offense. Similarly in cases of debt, if the creditor could not induce the debtor to repay the loan, he would go to the compound of any of the accused's relatives who happened to be absent on their farms, and capture goats or any other articles equivalent to or in excess of the amount of the debt. Later in the day he would send word to the owner of the property informing him of the reasons of his action. The owner in turn would bring pressure on the debtor to pay the sum he owed. If the creditor belonged to another village he might, if sufficiently adroit, appropriate property from anyone in the creditor's village, the elders of which would then force the debtor to pay. These regulations did not, of course, imply that there was any collective ownership of property or that a person was held morally responsible for the sins of his relatives. They were simply an obvious method of obtaining redress through those who were in a position to bring pressure. Nevertheless they served to maintain the kinship solidarity.

Just as the *umunna* is the basis of the social system, so the mode by which it is governed is the pattern of the mode of government of each larger group, whether it be an ọnuma (hamlet), ṅkporo (village), or abodo (village-area). It is government by the body of elders presided over by the senior elder. It was never government by a single individual, though a single individual might exercise a position of leadership, either on account of some special office or exceptional influence or affluence.

In using the term "government" it is not to be supposed that public notice was taken of every case which was a breach of customary law. The governing body only concerned itself with cases which were (a) an offense

against religion (or, as the Ibo would say, "abominable") and so would bring disaster on the community unless the steps prescribed by custom were taken, or (b) which were likely to break up the solidarity of the *umunna, ọnuma, ṅkporo,* or *abodo.* A man might steal from another and, if caught red-handed, be sold into slavery by the owner of the stolen property, without reference to the elders or any one else. Or a creditor might recover his debt by appropriating a goat or other property belonging to the debtor, or a member of his kinship or local group. Or again two parties to a dispute might refer their dispute not to the whole council of the group, but to certain arbitrators chosen by each side.

The term "government," moreover, was government only in a very qualified sense, for even in cases where the group solidarity was endangered the central council of elders might be powerless to intervene. The body of elders was a body of mediators and referees rather than of prosecutors and judges, and the community was a republic in the true sense of that term, *i.e.,* a corporation in which government was the concern of all.

Instances may now be given to illustrate the composition of the councils, and the methods of procedure. Firstly, as regards the personnel of the village or village-area courts or councils, though all the elders (heads of extended-families) are members of the council and are nominally on an equal footing, there are particular personages or classes to whom special reference must be made. These are (a) the senior elder or holder of the senior ọfọ; (b) the announcers of decisions; (c) the holders of "staves of judgment," *i.e.,* a special class of judges or arbitrators found in certain communities; (d) rich or influential men who had attained a special position as arbitrators; (e) titled persons.

As regards the most senior elder, he generally acted as president of the council, to the extent that he opened the proceedings by a prayer to the gods and ancestors to be present at their deliberations, to enable them to arrive at a right decision, and punish any elder who attempted to pervert justice and any witness who gave false evidence. (The head of the senior family in the town is frequently known as the *Onyishi,* and in some communities, before he is given this formal title, he is made to swear that he will not adjudicate in secret, take sides in disputes, appropriate communal or other property by force, or apply public moneys to his own purposes.)

It may be noted, incidentally, that it was permissible for either party to a case to demand the withdrawal of any elder, on the ground that that elder was a hereditary enemy of his family. There was thus a system of challenging "jurors." Moreover, the general body of elders could by common consent call on any of their number who was known to be a bad character to withdraw from the proceedings.

The announcers of decisions were always prominent personages at councils or trials. They had usually to be men of good address and to have a sound knowledge of the customary procedure. They were commonly the holders of the senior *ofo,* but if the holder of the senior *ofo* was not a good speaker he had to delegate one of the family-group to act as his deputy. In some communities the duty of announcing decisions was not assigned to any particular person or office. Any good speaker would be called upon to perform this duty. But in other communities certain families had a special right of announcing decisions, and in some cases these families acted as principal arbiters in all disputes.

A man of outstanding wealth might in any group attain for himself a measure of chieftainship, if he was able and generous. With him rested the decision whether the group should go to war or not, for he could provide the powder and firearms. In this way he attained control over the younger age-grades, which readily placed themselves at his service for any purpose. He might even call on them to work on his farms. By rendering services to all who came to him for help he was constantly adding to the number of his free-born followers, and by demanding a major portion of captives taken in war (in return for providing powder and firearms) he

was constantly adding to the number of his slaves. It is easy to understand, therefore, how a rich, generous man could become the principal judge and center of authority. His presence would be called for in every important case, and few would care to oppose his views.

Finally, we come to the groups of titled people who, as being the richest men in the community, took the most prominent part in its control. They included in their ranks the heads of the most important extended-families. They were in some communities the principal judges and principal executive officers, and enjoyed numerous privileges. Thus at Inyi those holding titles took the most important part in all judicial matters. Breaches of customary law were reported to the senior titleholder in the *ñkporo* or quarter and he, together with other holders of the title, would go to the offender's house and capture or kill one of his goats, pending further investigation of the case. If the offense was small the loss of the goat might be considered a sufficient punishment, but if it was serious the holders of titles might order the man to be sold and divide the proceeds among themselves. If the culprit had taken refuge in the house of the priest of Ale, the holders of titles would capture and sell a boy or girl from his family. Fines were imposed on anyone who insulted a member of the order, and it is said that people were afraid even of offending a person whose brother was the holder of a title.

Among the Isu Ochi the holders of titles enjoyed numerous privileges. They inflicted heavy fines on anyone who assaulted one of their order, and if the offender was unable to pay the fine he was sold into slavery. Even to abuse the holder of a title was an offense, and it was an offense also for any non-titled person to enter the house of a titled person after dark. One who committed adultery with the wife of a titled man was sold into slavery (whereas in ordinary cases there was no official penalty unless the adultery had taken place in the husband's house, in which case the adulterer was fined). Creditors could distrain the property of debtors, but they could not do so if the debtor was the holder of a title. The holders of titles, besides taking a principal part in trials, acted as guardians of orphans and of their property, a rule which was found to be necessary, as the relatives of orphaned children had sometimes sold the children into slavery.

The holders of titles were distinguished by a spear or iron staff. Their influence has now in many areas completely disappeared, as, with the advent of the Government, they could no longer enjoy their former privileges.

In the Nsukka Division the control of the village was vested mainly in the titled personages known as Asogwa, who employed the minor titled officials known as Ndishi Iwu as their executive officers. In most villages the Ndishi Iwu used the cults of Qmabe or Qdo as the legal sanction, and, if any person broke a law or refused to obey an order of the council, the Iwu would proceed to his house with a masker of the cult and place a knotted palm-leaf in the roof, thereby interdicting the owner from touching anything until the taboo had been removed. In some localities the Ndishi Iwu were also the principal judges, but in others the principal judges were the holders of the Qzo title or that known as "Eze." In a few villages, the Eze or Ezes of the village had attained a position which almost amounted to chieftainship, but this was due to the influence of the Igala tribe. For among the Ibo the indigenous form of government is essentially of a democratic or conciliar character.

We may now give some examples of the legal procedure, and it is hardly necessary to remark that in order to understand Ibo legal procedure we must divest ourselves of many English legal conceptions, such as the rigid distinction between "civil" and "criminal" cases, or the idea that public notice had to be taken of every offense. Even in cases of "sin" no public action might be necessary, as the sinner might automatically punish himself in the manner prescribed by custom. Or, again, a criminal might be automatically punished by his own family or by the person against whom he had committed a crime. If a criminal was caught *flagrante delicto* in the presence of witnesses there was no necessity as a rule

for any form of trial. Trials occurred in doubtful cases, and if, after the hearing of evidence, the matter still remained doubtful, it was decided by an oath or an ordeal. It must be remembered also that there was no hard and fast code. The community reacted in various ways according to the circumstances of the case. The elders who tried cases had to consider the social position of the accused, the attitude and strength of his kindred, whether he was a useful member of society or not, and so on. Decisions were in fact judicious rather than judicial.

To commit murder was an offense against Ale, and it was the concern of the whole community to see that the steps prescribed by custom were carried out. If the murderer hanged himself forthwith (which he frequently did, either from remorse at having killed one of Ale's children, or in order to save his family from attack and the loss of their property, or because he was expected to do so) his brother was (at Owelle) required to offer sacrifice to Ale before burying the body of the murderer. He took eight yams and one chicken to the priest of Ale who, standing before the symbol of the cult, spoke as follows, "Ale, this chicken and these yams have been given to you by the brother of the man who killed your child and then hanged himself. He beseeches you to accept this atonement and to refrain from pursuing the brothers and children of the murderer. He who killed a fellow-man has also killed himself. Let his crime therefore follow him to the next world." It will be observed from this rite that the family of the murderer was considered as sharing in the responsibility of the crime unless it took steps to dissociate itself from the murder. It had to provide a cow, goat, fowl, two yards of cloth, and a keg of powder for the funeral rites of the murdered man.

If the murderer did not immediately hang himself but took refuge in flight, his family had also to fly, for the kin of the murdered man (including maternal relatives) immediately made a raid on the compounds and property of the kin of the murderer. In this raid any members of the local group might join. The compounds of the murderer's family were burned to the ground, their yams were uprooted, and their palms cut down. All property found might be appropriated, but in some communities it was taboo for the patrilineal relatives of the murdered man to keep any of the raided property, on the ground that this would be "eating blood-money." But relatives in the female line might do so, as their Ale was not concerned with the death of men in other local groups.

The family of the murderer remained in exile for a period of at least one month, when they might be invited by the elders of their town to return, the consent of the kin of the murdered man having first been obtained. The murderer himself continued to remain in exile. In some communities (*e.g.,* at Oduma) the following rite was performed before the return of the exiled family. The senior *ada* or sister of each of the kindreds concerned went together to the compounds of the exiled family and swept them out thoroughly. They then took a cock and a hen, tied them together with a palm-leaf, and walked round the compounds, saying, "Ale, do not permit such a thing to occur again. Ale, be not angry with us." They then collected the sweepings of the compound and threw them and the two fowls into the "bush of evil." This rite of purification is known as *Eza fu ntu ochu, i.e.,* "The sweeping-out of the ashes of murder."

On the return of the exiled family a public meeting would be held to inquire into the matter and decide what atonement must be made by the murderer's kin. This meeting might be held in the compound of the priest of Ale, but the priest usually took no part in the discussions, from fear of making some mistake for which Ale would punish him. In some towns meetings connected with a murder were always held in an open space clear of all houses, lest the pollution of the murder should infect the houses. The proceedings were conducted principally by the elders or, in certain communities, by particular individuals who had special authority to deal with cases of homicide. These would consider all the circumstances of the case, and elicit whether the homicide was accidental or deliberate, and, if the latter, whether there

were any extenuating circumstances. If it appeared that the homicide had been accidental, the manslayer might be allowed to return after twenty-eight days, and on his return would be required to offer sacrifice to Ale. But in some communities there was no difference in the penalty for accidental homicide and murder, owing to the belief that if a man killed another by what we should term an accident he must at some previous time have committed an act abominable to Ale. If there were extenuating circumstances he might be permitted to produce a substitute to be publicly killed. The substitute might be some notorious thief of whom the community wished to be rid, and the killing was carried out by a man hired from another town for the purpose, as it was considered an offense against Ale to slay a fellow-townsman, even if that townsman had been guilty of murder. Sometime later the murderer was required to go through the form of dedicating a person to the service of Ale, as a substitute for the man he had killed. He went to another town and hired a man for this purpose. He took this hireling, together with a tortoise, an *aiagere* fowl, a piece of *ofo* wood, a pottery plate, and a pot, to the shrine of the priest of Ale. The hireling was stripped naked and the priest spoke as follows, "Ale, this man has been brought to you as a substitute for your son who was killed." The murderer added, "Please, Ale, let me go free and be not wrathful with me again." The hireling then knelt before the shrine. He did not apparently remain permanently as an *osu* or slave of Ale, but was allowed to return to his own town. (Persons permanently dedicated to the gods are known as *osu*. They are despised, and no free person will marry an *osu*. They are also feared, being regarded as dynamized by the god. If they committed theft, they were not prosecuted, lest the anger of the god should be incurred. Even at the present time some Court members are afraid of trying an *osu* on any charge.)

Whether there were extenuating circumstances or not, the murderer might in some communities be called on to hang himself if he re-appeared in the town. Or he might be required to produce some member of his family-group to hang himself in his stead. (It was not uncommon, *e.g.*, at Nengwe, for the brother of a murderer to hang himself as a substitute, on the ground that the murderer was a better man than himself.) But if a substitute hanged himself, the murderer (at Owelle) had to make atonement by the following rite. He summoned the priest of Ale to his house and presented him with a white chicken and a yam. The priest roasted the yam and, holding the chicken and yam in his hand, said, "Ale, I am giving this fowl to you to appease your wrath against this man. Ale, I am going to give this man a yam to eat, and I beseech you that you will refrain from taking his life when he partakes of anything which has been touched by a man of Owelle." The murderer was then given the yam to eat. The fowl was appropriated by the priest.

It may be noted in conclusion that no person who had been guilty of homicide and had been allowed to return home was permitted to take part in any festival of Ale. During such a festival he had either to absent himself from the town or else sit on a platform, as contact of his person with the ground was regarded as a pollution of the Earth-deity. No one would eat in the company of a murderer, and a murderer's wife abandoned him.

The procedure in cases of theft varied according to the nature of the article stolen, and according to whether the theft had been committed within or without the kinship group. But the procedure in one town might differ considerably from that in another.

If a man stole any article of property from a member of his own kinship group the owner of the property might merely warn the thief and take no further steps. Or he might report the theft to the elders, who would warn the thief and possibly order him to be tied up for several days without food. If the thief had committed similar thefts before, the elders might direct that he should be sold as a slave to the Aro.

In many localities, if a man stole an article from a member either of his own kinship or local group, he was merely subjected to ridicule and contempt. When people met him on the road they would say, *Uu!* "Thief!" (For some offenses a culprit might be sung through the town by one of the age-grades.) If he was the holder of a title he would no longer be accorded any share of dues received. Even if he repeated his offense he might not (in some groups) be sold, on the ground that in former times an epidemic had invaded the group as a consequence of selling a close kinsman.

But one caught red-handed stealing from a member of another local group or quarter was usually accorded different treatment—he was sold automatically by the owner of the stolen property. Under certain circumstances he was allowed to redeem himself. For if on some previous occasion a man of the thief's kindred had caught a man of the other kindred in the act of stealing his property, and had refrained from selling him, then it was incumbent on the victim's kindred in the present case to act with similar generosity.

Space does not permit any detailed account of the legal procedure in offenses such as assault, adultery, the use of black magic, or other "abominable" acts. It may, however, be noted that, while adultery within the kinship group was an "abomination" which necessitated public condemnation and a ritual purification, adultery outside the kinship group was a private injury with which the general public had usually no concern. But an adulterer was liable to be assaulted by the injured husband, and this might lead to a state of war between two groups. Or, if the adulterer refused to pay compensation to the husband, the members of the latter's group might violate women belonging to the adulterer's group, as opportunity occurred, until public peace became so endangered that the elders of the whole village-area found it necessary to intervene.

Twins, children born with teeth, children born with hand or foot first, cripples, and children who cut the upper before the lower teeth, were destroyed or handed over to Aro traders. A child who was unable to walk before he had reached the age of three was regarded as having committed an offense against Ale in his former life, and was destroyed or sold. A girl who donned a cloth like a male, or menstruated before she had taken to wearing a cloth, was also handed over to Aro traders. Her relatives and friends would wail on hearing the news, and four days after the girl's departure her mother would shave her head; for an evil thing had fallen on her head and had to be removed.

Disputes about land were, and still are, a common source of fighting, which may continue for a considerable time before the matter is finally threshed out in an assembly of elders. In olden days land disputes between individuals of the same group were commonly referred to one of the companies of warriors or head-getters, to whom the winner of the case paid a fee. This privilege of the warriors was considered an inducement to young men to acquit themselves bravely in battle.

The decisions of judges were not always tamely accepted. An unsuccessful litigant might dispute the decision and call on the judges to swear finally on their ofos that their decision was in accordance with precedent; or he might leave the assembly shouting out that he would not abide by the decision. In such a case the elders would proceed to his house on the following day, and on arrival would keep tapping the ground with their staves. This would usually cause the man serious alarm, and he would ask them to desist, promising to carry out their behests. But as the conduct of such a one had been an insult to Ale and the ancestors, he would be called on to perform a rite known as *Imfo jo Ale,* or "The appeasing of the Anger of Ale."

Meetings held to decide disputes frequently ended in an uproar or a fight, and the dispute might drag on for years. In other cases the evidence might be so inconclusive that the elders would direct the disputants to take their case to some distant oracle, such as the so-called "Long Juju" at Aro Chuku. In such cases the loser of the suit might be sold into slavery by the priests of the oracle, or if allowed to return home would have to pay heavy damages to the winner.

Laws were passed in an assembly of all the elders of the town, and were sometimes given

formal validity by a sacrifice to Ale or some other deity. Thus, if it became apparent that market brawls were becoming frequent and likely to lead to murder and intra-kindred or intra-quarter fighting, the elders of the town might meet together and decide that, if anyone in future engaged in fighting in the market, he should be heavily fined. Having arrived at this decision they would buy a goat and take it to the priest of Ale, who, holding the goat by a rope, would say, "Ale, the elders of the town have brought this goat to you in order to inform you of their wishes touching the market. They say that it is not their desire that fights should occur in the market, lest this should lead to loss of life. Ale, it is not your desire that men should kill one another, as we are your children. They declare that if anyone breaks this rule he shall pay a fine of fourteen currency rods, and they ask you, Ale, to enforce this law by dealing with anyone who refuses to pay this fine. Ale, when the elders call upon you (to assist them in dealing with a law-breaker) do you answer their call (by bringing misfortune upon him)." He would then turn to the elders and say, "Is not this your wish?" They would all reply, "Ale, this is our wish." The priest would then kill the goat, and as he put the knife to the goat's throat would say, "Take the life of this goat and spare our lives." The flesh of the goat would be cooked and divided, and morsels of the heart, liver, and kidneys would be deposited by the priest on the cultus-symbol.

The elders would then go home, and each would inform the members of his kindred of the passing of the law. If anyone subsequently broke the law he would be arrested by young men and handed over to the head of his kindred, who would be instructed to collect the fine and bring it to the market on the following market-day. On that day the elders would walk round the market beating their matchets and saying, "Fellow-townsmen, come and take what is yours." The head of the culprit's kindred would then hand the fourteen rods to the senior elder, who would say, "Fellow-townsmen, you have seen that the fine has been paid." They would reply, "We have. Let it be handed over to the keeper of fines." The rods would then be handed to a man delegated by the elders to receive fines and hold them until they were required for some general sacrifice. The culprit would be escorted by the elders and Ale priests to the shrine of Ale. He would hand a pot of palm-wine to the priest and then squat down before the cultus-symbol. The priest would pour a little of the wine into a buffalo-horn and pass the horn round the culprit's head, saying, "Ale, I and the elders of the town have brought this man before you to tell you that he has paid his fine for 'breaking' your market. He has brought this wine to appease your wrath. Pursue him not. A man's child may offend his father, but he is forgiven when he repents." He would then pour the libation, and the remainder of the wine would be drunk by all present, the culprit included.

The legal sanction was not always Ale. When a law was made the elders might call on the priest of any cult to bring some material object from the shrine. The priests and elders would then say, "We have made such and such a law. If anyone breaks this law may this spirit kill that person." The priest would then strike the ground with the object. If the law was broken the punishment might be left to the spirits. But the law-breaker would fore-stall punishment by going to the priest, who would perform sacrifice on the man's behalf, saying, "So-and-so admits that he has gone against you and he comes now to redeem himself."

In some cases rules would be made without any religious sanction. Thus the elders might announce in the market that wood was not to be cut in a certain area under the penalty of a fine of one goat. If a man was reported for breaking this rule, the elders would send young men to catch a goat from his kindred or local group. If the accused redeemed the goat the money obtained was divided out among the elders and the matter ended. But if he did not redeem it, the goat would be sold or killed, and if the accused lost his case he would be called on to pay two goats to the owner of the goat. If the accused won his case, his accuser had to pay the cost of the two goats. If the accused was a woman,

her fine was payable by her husband or son. But in some towns her fine was payable by her parents through the person who had acted as middleman when her marriage had been arranged.

Other instances of legislation were (a) that no one should visit a neighboring town during an epidemic, and (b) that women should not visit the market of an unfriendly town. The elders might post young men on the roads to see that the rules were observed, and the young men were authorized to confiscate the property of anyone who attempted to break the rules. Rules might also be made forbidding the cutting of sticks (to be used for training yam tendrils) before a certain date.

In some cases an age-grade or group of age-grades might take the initiative in making rules. Thus, if it became apparent that stealing was on the increase, a group of age-grades might meet and decide that the penalties for stealing must be increased, and their decision would be announced to and accepted by the elders. Or an age-grade group might meet to fix the local price of palm-wine, or standardize the rate of the bride-price or rents chargeable for land.

This paper may be concluded by a few remarks on the changes in legal conceptions and practice which have occurred as a result of British Administration and direct contact with Western civilization.

When the British Government assumed the administration of the country, district Native Courts were established. This was a necessary step toward bringing the country under proper control and putting an end to practices which were considered inhuman or incompatible with modern civilization. The Native Courts were encouraged to administer native law as far as possible, but as most of the old legal sanctions now became illegal the native law administered in the Native Courts became a shadow of its former self. The elders, moreover, of the kindred, village, and village-area were deprived of their judicial functions and in consequence lost much of their authority. The Native Courts in fact acted as a disruptive agent on the social structure.

Recently, however, the Government, after close examination of the ancient system, has sought to restore the power of the elders by encouraging them to settle minor cases locally, and by giving formal recognition to the village-area councils. There is a general policy of decentralization, and the old district courts are being replaced, wherever possible, by "clan" courts. The personnel of the Native Courts has been enlarged so as to include as far as possible all the most important elders of each local group. A complete return, however, to the old system, by which each village-area, or even village, recognized no higher authority than itself, would be impracticable, and distasteful also to the people, who demand a higher form of central authority than formerly existed, having acquired a wider sense of solidarity. Nor is there any general desire for a complete return to the old forms of legal procedure, even were this permissible. For the younger generation has lost faith in many of the old legal sanctions, as a result of the rapid spread of Christianity. It is said with truth that the younger people no longer obey their elders as before, and the blame for this is often laid at the door of the Government. But the real reasons are religious and economic. Children who have become Christians are often compelled to disagree with their pagan parents, and to refuse to take part in practices which they have been taught to regard as heathen. Many of them, moreover, leave their homes for long periods in search of work, and live lives of freedom from the numerous restraints imposed in their own homes. Such tend to degenerate in character, and when they return home they find it difficult to resume their former life, more especially as they have acquired new wants which cannot be satisfied in their parent village.

But the extraordinary natural adaptability of the Ibo should enable them to surmount most of the difficulties of the present period of transition.

Natchez Burial Customs

Le Page du Pratz

From John R. Swanton's translation of portions of *Histoire de la Louisiane,* 3 vols., 1758, Paris, by Le Page du Pratz, in Indian Tribes of the Lower Mississippi Valley and Adjacent Coast of the Gulf of Mexico. *Bureau of American Ethnology Bulletin* 43, 1911, pp. 144–149. By permission of the translator and the publisher.

This is the death of the Tattooed-serpent, my particular friend and the friend of all the French. He was great war chief of the Natchez Nation and brother of the great Sun, who allowed him an absolute authority over the entire nation. . . .

We entered his [the great Sun's] house, where he said aloud, *Ouitiguitlatagoup,* he is quite dead. Then he seated himself and bent over, resting his head on his hands. The instant he said that his brother was dead his wife, who was present, uttered loud cries. This was a signal of sadness for the entire nation, which was awaiting the outcome of this malady, which could not fail to be fatal to them as soon as the Tattooed-serpent should be dead. Then one heard groans and lamentations on all sides. The most doleful cries were made to resound under the neighboring trees. Almost immediately two consecutive discharges of guns were heard to warn all the villages, which replied a few moments afterwards.

I will spare the reader many scenes which would only sadden him, and I will report of the funeral honors which were rendered to the Tattooed-serpent only those which are extraordinary and of which Europeans have no knowledge.

A short time after these discharges the speaker (*porte-parole*) entered and began to weep. The great Sun raised his head and looked at his favorite wife, to whom he made a sign that we did not understand, until she had thrown a vessel of water on the fire, which was entirely extinguished by it. Then the speaker, or chancellor, of the great chief howled in salutation to his sovereign and went out. As soon as he was outside of the cabin he uttered a fearful cry, which was instantly repeated by all the people of the villages.

The fire extinguished in our presence and the redoubled cries of the entire nation made me fear, with reason, for the great Sun and even for ourselves, for who could guess the consequences of the despair in which we saw all plunged?

The great Sun being always bent over and his eyes closed, I approached a common Sun and asked him what the extinguished fire and the doleful cries signified. He replied that it was the signal to extinguish all the fires, and that it made all the Natchez tremble with reason, because the extinction of the fires was not done on account of the death of the Tattooed-serpent.

I understood by these words that the sovereign wished to die. . . .

He [the Tattooed-serpent] was on his bed of state, dressed in his finest clothing, his face painted with vermilion, moccasined as if to go on a journey, and wearing his crown of white feathers mingled with red. His arms had been tied to his bed. These consisted of a double-barreled gun, a pistol, a bow, a quiver full of arrows, and a war club. Around the bed were all the calumets of peace which he had received during his life, and near by had been planted a large pole, peeled and painted red, from which hung a chain of reddened cane splints, composed of 46 links or rings, to indicate the number of enemies he had killed. I do not at all pretend in reporting this fact to guarantee the number of the exploits of this man.

All his people were around him. Food was served to him at his accustomed hours, as if he had been living, and his retainer [or head servant—loué], seeing that he did not touch it, said to him, "You no longer wish, then, to take what we present you? Are these things no more to your taste? Why is it, then, that you rebuff us and our services do not please you any more? Ah! you do not speak as usual. Without doubt you are dead. Yes; it is done. You are going to the country of the spirits, and you are leaving us forever." Then he uttered the death cry, which was repeated by all those in the cabin. They replied in the village, and from voice to voice the same cry passed in an instant into the other villages of the nation, who all together made the air reverberate with their doleful cries.

The company in the cabin was composed of the favorite wife of the defunct, of a second wife, whom he kept in another village, to visit when his favorite wife was pregnant, his chancellor, his doctor, his head servant (loué), his pipe bearer, and some old women,

all of whom were going to be strangled at his burial.

To the number of the victims there joined herself a Noble woman, whom the friendship that she had for the Tattooed-serpent led to join him in the country of the spirits. The French called her La Glorieuse, because of her majestic bearing and her proud air and because she was intimate only with distinguished Frenchmen. I regretted her so much the more that, possessing a deep knowledge of simples, she had saved the lives of many of our sick, and I myself had drawn good lessons from her. These things filling us with sadness, the favorite wife, who perceived it, rose from her place, came to us with a smiling air, and spoke to us in these terms, "French chiefs and nobles, I see that you regret my husband's death very much. It is true that his death is very grievous, as well for the French as for our nation, because he carried both in his heart. His ears were always full of the words of the French chiefs. He has always traveled by the same road as the French, and he loved them more than himself. But what does it matter? He is in the country of the spirits, and in two days I will go to join him and will tell him that I have seen your hearts shake at the sight on his dead body. Do not grieve. We will be friends for a much longer time in the country of the spirits than in this, because one does not die there again. It is always fine weather, one is never hungry, because nothing is wanting to live better than in this country. Men do not make war there any more, because they make only one nation. I am going and leave my children without any father or mother. When you see them, Frenchmen, remember that you have loved the father and that you ought not to repulse the children of the one who has always been the true friend of the French." After this speech she went back to her place. . . .

[After the Frenchmen had prevailed upon the great Sun not to kill himself], the fire of the great Sun being relighted, the signal was given to relight all the others. . . .

A few moments afterwards the young Sun came to tell me that orders had been given (as he had promised, although feignedly) to have only those die who were in the cabin of the deceased, because they were his food; that besides there would be put to death a bad woman, if she had not already been killed, and an infant which had already been strangled by its father and mother, a forfeit which purchased their lives at the death of the great Sun, ennobled them, and raised them from the grade of Stinkards.

A few moments later the grand master of ceremonies appeared at the door of the dead man's house with the ornaments which were proper to his rank. . . . He uttered two words and the people in the cabin came out. These persons were the favorite wife and his other wife, his chancellor, his doctor, his head servant, his pipe bearer, and some old women. Each of these victims was accompanied by eight male relations, who were going to put him to death. One bore the war club raised as if to strike, and often he seemed to do so, another carried the mat on which to seat him, a third carried the cord for strangling him, another the skin, the fifth a dish in which were five or six balls of pounded tobacco to make him swallow in order to stupefy him. Another bore a little earthen bottle holding about a pint, in order to make him drink some mouthfuls of water in order to swallow the pellets more easily. Two others followed to aid in drawing the cord at each side.

A very small number of men suffices to strangle a person, but since this action withdraws them from the rank of Stinkards, puts them in the class of Honored men, and thus exempts them from dying with the Suns, many more would present themselves if the number were not fixed to eight persons only. All these persons whom I have just described walk in this order, two by two, after their relations. The victims have their hair daubed with red and in the hand the shell of a river mussel which is about 7 inches long by 3 or 4 broad. By that they are distinguished from their followers, who on those days have red feathers in their hair. The day of the death they have their hands reddened, as being prepared to give death.

Arrived in the open space the mats of the foremost are placed nearest the temple, the favorite to the right and the other wife to the left of the road, the others afterward according to their rank, 6 to 7 feet apart on the two sides of the road, the breadth of which between them is at least 30 feet. The persons who are going to die are made to sit down on their mats, then all together make the death cry behind them. The relatives dance the death dance and the victims on their mats dance in time also without leaving their places. After this dance the entire group returns to the cabin in the same order. This is a rehearsal of the tragedy which is going to be played the day of the funeral procession. It is done twice a day.

Everything was tranquil enough that day on the part of the great chief, who went to the temple after he had been shown the head of the bad woman. He ordered that her body be eaten by beasts without being buried, to carry the head to his brother, and then to throw it into the cypress swamp 2 leagues from his body.

The same day at sunrise, while we were engaged in restraining the great chief, a man named Ette-actal had been brought, escorted by 30 warriors. We all knew him because he had lived with M. de Bienville, commandant-general, with whom he had taken refuge. He had married a female Sun who had died, and according to the laws of his nation he ought to die with her. But this law not being to his taste, as soon as he had seen her in the agony [of death] he fled secretly toward the landing, took some provisions, descended night and day in a little dugout and went to place himself under the protection of Monsieur, the commandant of the capital, and offered himself to him as his hunter and one of his slaves. His service was accepted. The Natchez even promised his master that he had nothing to fear because, the ceremony being completed and he not having been found in that time, he was no longer a lawful prize. This native, thus reassured, went from time to time to see his relatives and friends, and nothing had ever been said to him. But this last time, the great Sun having learned from the French that M. de Bienville had been recalled to France, considered that the letters of reprieve of Ette-actal were abrogated by the absence of his protector. Thus he judged it suitable to make him pay his debt to the Tattooed-serpent in the capacity of a relation to his wife, and it was for this reason that they brought him.

When this man saw himself in the cabin of the great chief of war, in the number of victims who were going to be sacrificed to his manes, he was moved with the liveliest grief to see himself taken this time without hope of safety and began to weep very bitterly. The favorite wife having perceived this, said to him, "Are you not a warrior?" "Yes," said he, "I am one." "Nevertheless you weep," she replied, "your life is then dear to you? If it is so, then it is not good that you come with us. Go away with the women."

He replied, "Certainly life is dear to me. I have no children. It is well that I travel some time longer on the earth until the death of the great Sun and die with him." "Go away, I tell you," said she, "it is not good that you come with us and that your heart remain behind you on the earth. Once more, take yourself away from here, and let me see you no more."

Ette-actal had brought a little sack in which were the small utensils necessary for the ceremony, but without disturbing himself about them he left all, and, satisfied to have still time to himself before the death of the great Sun, he took to flight at the last word of the favorite and disappeared like a flash. But in the afternoon three old women were brought, two of whom were his relations, who, being extremely aged and wearied of life, offered themselves to pay his debt. Although these two women were so old that for many years they had totally lost the use of their limbs, their hair was no grayer than is commonly that of women of 50 in France. They appeared, besides, to bear themselves well.

The generosity of these two women purchased the life of the warrior, Ette-actal, and acquired for him the rank of Honored man. His condition having become much better and his life being thus assured, he became insolent, and profiting by the instructions

which he had received from the French, he made use of it to deceive his countrymen.

The third old woman that they had brought had not been able to use her legs for at least fifteen years, without, however, experiencing any other difficulty in any part of the body. Her face was calm and her hair entirely white, a thing which I had never seen among the natives, and in spite of her great age, which surpassed a century, her skin was not too much wrinkled. All of these three old women were dispatched to the evening rehearsal, one to the door of the Tattooed-serpent and the two others to the square. . . .

The day of the funeral procession having arrived, we went to the house of the great Sun. The favorite wife, who knew that we were there, came with her company to bid us adieu. She had the Suns of both sexes and their children called, to whom she then addressed these words:

"It is very grievous that your father is dead. As for me, I am going with him to the country of the spirits, and he waits only for us in order to set out. It is also well since he is dead that I am no longer able to walk on the earth. For you who are young it is good that you walk a long time without design [i.e., without duplicity] and with a straight heart. I leave you grain and my coffers, the keys [?] of which I here give you. Do not speak any evil of the French. Walk with them. Walk there as your father and I have walked, without design. Speak of them as he and I have spoken. Do nothing contrary to the friendship of the French. Never lie to them. They will give you food and the other things of which you have need, and if they give you nothing, return without murmuring. They were friends of your father, so love them all and never refuse to see them even when they will not receive you well.

"And you French chiefs," she added, turning toward us, "always be friends of the Natchez; trade with them, do not be too stingy with your goods, and do not repel what they bring you, but treat them with gentleness." Then having observed that one of our party was affected to tears by the spectacle, she said to him, "Do not weep. I know that my husband and I were great friends of the

French, because we also loved you much, although I have never eaten with them, because I am a woman. But I am able to eat with them now, because I am going to the country of the spirits. Let them, then, bring us food to eat, so that I may eat with the French chiefs."

Immediately some dishes were brought, we seated ourselves, and we took the meal with her. She then rose, and followed by her company, she returned to the cabin of her husband with a firmness altogether surprising.

I have reported these speeches and the bearing of this favorite, who could be only of the common people, being the wife of a Sun, in order to show the skill with which she preserved the friendship of the French for her children, how much intelligence this nation has, and that it is not at all that which one ordinarily understands by the word savage, which the majority of people bestow on it very unsuitably.

I have said elsewhere that the temple, the house of the great chief, and that of the Tattooed-serpent were on the square; that that of the great Sun was built on a mound of earth carried to a height of about 8 feet. It was on this mound that we placed ourselves at the side of the dwelling of the great Sun, who had shut himself in in order to see nothing. His wife, who was also there, was able to hear us, but we had no fear that she would reveal what we might say against such a cruel custom. This law did not please her enough for her to find fault with those who spoke ill of it. As for the great Sun, he was on the other side and was not able to hear our remarks. From this place, without disturbing the ceremony, we were able to see everything, even into the interior of the temple, the door of which faced us.

At the appointed hour the master of ceremonies arrived, adorned with red feathers in a half crown on his head. He had his red baton, in the shape of a cross, at the end of which hung a cluster of black feathers. He had all the upper portion of his body reddened, with the exception of his arms, in order to let it be seen that he did not dip his hands in the blood. His belt, which girded him above his hips, was ornamented with feathers, of which one row was black and the following was red, and afterward alternately as far as the knees. His legs were of their natural color.

He entered the house of the great Sun in this dress to ask him, without doubt, for permission to start the funeral procession. We were not able to hear what the reply was made to him, because this sovereign ordinarily spoke in a very low although serious tone. But we heard very distinctly the salutation which the master of ceremonies afterward made him, who went out instantly to proclaim the departure of the funeral procession. . . .

As soon as the master of ceremonies went to the door of the deceased he saluted him, without entering, with a great *hou*. Then he made the death cry, to which the people on the square replied in the same manner. The entire nation did the same thing and the echoes repeated it from afar. The body of the strangled infant was near the door by which the body of the dead man was to be brought out. Its father and its mother were behind it, leaning against the wall, their feet on some Spanish moss, esteeming themselves unworthy to walk on the earth until the body of the deceased had passed over it. As soon as the body appeared they laid their infant down, then raised it when it was outside, in order to expose it at each circle which it [the body] made until it had reached the temple.

The Tattooed-serpent, having come out of his cabin in his state bed, as I have pictured it, was placed on a litter with two poles, which four men carried. Another pole was placed underneath toward the middle and crosswise, which two other men held, in order to sustain the body. These six men who carried it were guardians of the temple.

The grand master of ceremonies walked first, after him the oldest of the war chiefs, who bore the pole from which hung the cane links. He held this pole in one hand and in the other a war calumet, a mark of the dignity of the deceased. Then came the body, after which marched the procession of those who were going to die at his burial. Together they circled the house from which they had come out three times. At the third turn they took the road to the temple, and then the relatives of the victims placed themselves in the order which I have described for the rehearsal, but they walked very slowly, because they were going straight to the temple, while the body circled about as it advanced. . . . At each circuit made by the body the man of whom I have spoken threw his child in front of it in order that the body should pass over. He took it up again by one foot to do the same at the other circuits.

Finally the body reached the temple, and the victims put themselves in their places as determined in the rehearsals. The mats were stretched out. They seated themselves there. The death cry was uttered. The pellets of tobacco were given to them and a little water to drink after each one. After they had all

been taken [each victim's] head was covered with a skin on which the cord was placed around the neck, two men held it in order that it should not be dragged away [to one side] by the stronger party, and the cord, which had a running knot, was held at each end by three men, who drew with all their strength from the two opposite sides. They are so skillful in this operation that it is impossible to describe it as promptly as it is done.

The body of the Tattooed-serpent was placed in a great trench to the right of the temple in the interior. His two wives were buried in the same trench. La Glorieuse was buried in front of the temple to the right and the chancellor on the left. The others were carried into the temples of their own villages in order to be interred there. After this ceremony the cabin of the deceased was burned, according to custom.

The Vision Quest and the Guardian Spirit

George A. Pettitt

From *Primitive Education in North America.* University of California Publications in American Archaeology and Ethnology, Vol. 43, No. 1, 1946, pp. 87–94. By permission of the author and the publisher.

The wide distribution and relatively intensive development of the vision quest and the guardian-spirit concept in North America have led to the recognition of these traits as two important cultural characteristics of this area, and the vision pattern has been cited as the unifying religious fact among primitive tribes of the continent.

It is not my purpose to discuss these practices as discrete entities, for that has been done at some length by Ruth Benedict. Instead, I will indicate the relationship of these practices to educational procedures, and suggest, from an analysis of the functioning of the vision quest and the guardian-spirit concept in the process of intellectual and emotional development of the individual, that there is a fundamental kinship or social equivalence between these and other primitive practices involving the idea of supernaturally derived power. Incidentally, some light will be thrown on the essential nature of the psychic experiences supposedly involved in the vision.

In discussions of the vision quest and the guardian-spirit complex, it is usual to cite the Thompson Indians of the Plateau region of western Canada as the people who have accepted or developed the greatest number of traits which are typical of the complex wherever it is found on the continent. The Thompson Indians are said to present the type picture of vision questing and the acquisition of a guardian spirit. Therefore, the salient features of Thompson Indian practices are outlined below.

According to Teit, boys when old enough to dream of an arrow, a canoe, or a woman began an intensive search for a guardian spirit. This happened, usually, between the ages of twelve and sixteen. More will be said about the age of beginning the vision quest later, but it is important to recall that earlier reference has been made to the daily cold baths which many Indian boys were obliged to take, to food taboos, and to physical tests of one kind or another which enlivened the youngster's life from the time he was able to walk and run until he became a man. The beginning of the vision quest was perhaps a climax to these practices, rather than the introduction of a new discipline. The Thompson Indians are typical in this respect. They were given to annual, midwinter ceremonial whippings, also, in which the object was to frighten boys too young to be whipped, and encourage the stoicism of those old enough to volunteer for the ordeal. This, too, may be classed as a preliminary of the vision quest. But when a boy's dreams became propitious, regardless of chronological age, his vision quest began in earnest. As a ceremonial beginning he was required to run, with bow and arrows in his hands, until bathed in perspiration and on the point of exhaustion, when he was made to plunge in cold water. This was repeated four times a day for four days. The importance of the quest on which he was about to start was stressed by a coat of red paint on his face, a cedar bark or skin headband, ornaments of deer hoof tied to knees and ankles, and a skin apron symbolically decorated to indicate the life occupation for which he was most desirous of gaining supernatural power. The boy was, in other words, the center of public attention in this as in other aspects of primitive education. He was probably envied by his younger friends, and admired by the elders of the camp, and the pride engendered undoubtedly would help him to survive the not inconsiderable ordeals through which he had to pass. Although his first four days were consumed in running and bathing, the first four nights were given to dancing, singing, and praying, with little or no sleep, around a fire on some nearby mountain peak. At dawn the boy solemnly drew his bow and discharged an arrow into the sky.

Having acted out the prologue, the boy then began to work in earnest. He went on lonely pilgrimages into the mountains, staying away from home and eating nothing for from four to eight days on end. It was a common practice to schedule these pilgrimages in winter, so that the boy would not be tempted by berries and roots. During these vigils the boy usually took nothing with him but a fire drill and a sleeping mat. He intensified the effect of his fasting by taking herbal concoctions with a purgative action, and by poking long twigs down his throat until he vomited. He also heated rocks, threw water over them, and sweated himself thoroughly, perhaps whipping his body with nettles at the same time. Then he would plunge into a mountain stream, following which he would gather the warm rocks from the sweat bath, start across country throwing the rocks as far as he could, running to pick them up, and throwing them again, to insure himself against disease, ill fortune, and laziness. To vary the monotony he might set up a small target at a considerable distance and shoot at it with an arrow. If he missed he would pick up the arrow, run about four miles, and then try his skill again. If he continually missed he might run all night. If he was unable to hit the target before dawn he knew that his greatest talents would not be exhibited as hunter. But if he shot some small animal and gave it to some old person to eat, that would improve his chances.

The boy continued this exhausting regime until he had a dream of some animal or bird which would be his protector through life, and received the inspiration for a spirit song with which to call his protector and secure power in all he might attempt. Often a father, if possessed of great power himself, would give his boy some amulet symbolic of his own guardian spirit, to dream over. It was believed that this was an effective way of encouraging the same or another guardian spirit to take pity on the boy. When the boy believed that he had an important dream, one that he did not quite understand, and which gave him a queer feeling, he would mention it to his father, and discuss the interpretation. If the conviction came to him that he had received a spirit-inspired dream or vision, he prepared a medicine bag of the skin of the spirit animal, and filled it with other objects which in the course of his quest had for some reason taken on significance. These were the tangible symbols of his power. If the spirit was that of a bird he gathered feathers from that bird and tied them to his hair. Then he polished his spirit song as suggested by his vigil or perhaps by remarks dropped by his father, and worked out a design symbolic of his power with which he decorated rocks in lonely parts of the mountains.

The more this and similar stories of Indian vision quests are studied the less satisfactory does it seem to classify the acquisition of a guardian spirit, as most writers do, in the category of religious education. There are too many other factors involved. As indicated earlier in this study, it is impossible to do justice to primitive pedagogy if educational practices are arbitrarily divided into religious and nonreligious. The Indians of North America had no specifically named, conceptual category equivalent to our generalization "religious." They undoubtedly could have differentiated between the natural and the supernatural if they wished, but they apparently saw no reason for so doing; and if a classificatory system which they did not use is applied to their practices, the result is to confuse the issue. To discuss primitive religious education seems to be as futile in reaching a complete understanding of primitive pedagogy as would be a treatise on the moving parts of an engine as distinct from the stationary parts in reaching an understanding of the mechanics of the device.

There is no doubt that religious concepts are involved in the vision quest and in the idea of a guardian spirit. But they were not used in the modern sense of escaping from things of the flesh. Rather, they were utilized in a practical attempt to give greater assurance of achieving comforts of the flesh. Morals and ethics were linked with religious practices and beliefs, but not so much through fear of the hereafter as through a desire to establish a reciprocal trade arrangement with the supernatural whereby success in the daily routine could be achieved. There was little implication of worshiping supernatural beings for what they had done in the past, or might do after death. Greater stress was laid on the immediate future, and gratitude entered the picture strongly only if we define it as a lively anticipation of favors yet to come. Rasmussen relates an experience among the Eskimo which clearly illustrates this attitude. In September, 1907, he visited a group of Eskimo living in pristine paganism untouched by Christianity. In June, 1908, he visited the same group and discovered much to his surprise that, to the last man, they had been converted to a curious version of Christianity. Their former religious practices had dropped into the background. The reason for this sudden change, apparently, was a visit by a partly Christianized Eskimo hunter from a distant area. The garbled Christian prayers this man utilized as hunting charms seemed to be far more efficacious in attracting caribou; so the group dropped old practices and adopted the new. Later, when the prayers failed to work as well as expected, they advanced the theory that the white man's prayers, like his guns, wear out with use, and presumably they went back to their traditional beliefs.

As Radin states: "Can we, without further analysis, calmly assume that fear is the primordial emotion with which men began? The answer must be definitely in the affirmative, but not in the sense claimed by most ethnological theorists. They are fond of treating it as an instinct (fear of the dark, fear of the unknown, fear of the strange.). But psychology aside, what does the documentary evidence we now possess for primitive cultures tell us? The answer is clear. Primitive man is afraid of one thing, of the uncertainties of the struggle for life." It may be added that the fear was not entirely of death, but rather of failing to live successfully.

It is not necessary to elaborate on the nature of primitive religion. The point to be made is merely that in the vision quest and the acquisition of a guardian spirit the objective was not to produce a disciple of a religious faith, but to produce an independent, self-confident, and self-reliant personality, buoyed up by an inner conviction of his ability to meet any and all situations. The painful ordeals through which the individual achieved a guardian spirit had a significance of their own, apart from increasing the susceptibility of the individual to a psychic experience. They strengthened his character, and supplied him with experience in withstanding physical suffering, which was probably just as important in giving him self-assurance as was the conviction that a supernatural being had extended a sheltering arm. That the individual's social and economic well-being was the objective is attested by evidence of many kinds. That a conviction of power was the goal is clear when we take into consideration all the other ways in which this goal was sought, through conferring power-freighted names, and through associating with and studying under men and women reputed to have power.

It is pertinent to note that among the previously cited Thompson Indians, where the vision quest was a dominant feature of a boy's training, and to a certain extent of a girl's as well, twin children were excused from the ordeal because they were believed to be born with more than ordinary spiritual power derived from "Grizzly Bear." Apparently their obvious advantage over their age mates in the ownership of a twin brother or sister, plus special ceremonies for them, and special rituals that they had to observe, were sufficient to give them the inner conviction of self-sufficiency and of supernatural affiliation without long vigils. The way in which this inner conviction worked can be illustrated by a statement from the life of John Tanner among the Ojibwa. He explains that his foster mother, as a young girl, had been blessed with a dream in which she saw an aged, white-haired woman walking with two canes. She had a conviction that this was herself and that it meant that come what would, she would live a long, long time. Tanner concludes: "In all her subsequent life, this excellent woman retained the confident assurance that she would live to extreme old age, and often, in times of the greatest distress from hunger, and of apparent danger from other causes, she cheered her family . . . and roused them to exertion by infusing some part of her confident reliance upon the protection of a superior and invisible Power."

Because the vision quest and the acquisition of a guardian spirit are commonly given their greatest overt expression as boys and girls approach maturity, this complex is often spoken of as a puberty-linked phenomenon. Actually, however, as has been intimated in the discussion of the Thompson Indians, the process of acquiring and maintaining power started in early childhood, and continued through maturity. The beginning of the quest has also been ascribed to individual initiative and imitation. The facts run contrary to this conclusion. The acquisition of power was not left to the individual's imitative faculties, at least as a general practice. It was urged upon him with an insistence inversely proportional to the amount of supernatural power he was believed to have inherited from famous forebears, or obtained as a gift from famous elders, or acquired from propinquity to powerful individuals, in connection with the name he bore, or ceremonies gone through, or personal property such as amulets, or articles of dress or use, or songs and prayers and rituals. In other words, the vision was just one of a number of ways, though the most important, perhaps, of obtaining an inner conviction of self-sufficiency, both as one personality among many in the social group, and as a seeker after long life and comfort in the theater of nature. Lowie finds that a Crow boy at the time of his vision quest did not need any prompting. We may suspect that this is so because the prompting had taken place earlier, for human beings are not born with the desire to go on a vision quest. Elsewhere Lowie stresses his point, that the Crow youth is conditioned to the vital importance of a vision from infancy up.

In the autobiography of Crashing Thunder, the Winnebago, it is pointed out that from earliest childhood, boys were encouraged to blacken their faces and to practice fasting in order some day to be able to obtain a vision. Among the Omaha, "small boys seven to eight years of age and upwards were sent out together in the early morning with faces covered with clay by their parents to one of a few selected spots. This happened every fine spring morning. . . . They were technically fasting as they went out before breakfast." Ohiyessa, the Sioux, states that his grandmother started him on the trail to the Great Mystery at the age of eight. Maximilian reports for the Hidatsa: "There have been instances of fathers subjecting their children, only six or seven years of age, to these tortures. We ourselves saw one suspended by the muscles of the back, after having been compelled to fast four days." For the Parry Island Ojibwa it is said: "The Ojibwa held that the Great Spirit, or his intermediaries, the *manides,* imparted [knowledge, power, or ability, the indispensables to success and happiness] in visions to each individual at the earliest possible age, that is to say, as soon as the soul and shadow were sufficiently awake to understand and appreciate them. Consequently, they carefully trained their children to make them receptive to these 'blessings.' They encouraged the children to dream, and to remember their dreams. Every morning, even now, Pegahmagabow lies beside his two boys seven and nine years old, respectively, and asks them what dreams have come to them during the night."

When Pegahmagabow himself was about seven years old his parents made him swallow gunpowder to awaken his soul and shadow. Many boys are given charcoal and other substances for the same purpose, and are made to fast. These fasts become progressively longer until the moment has come when the child is psychologically ripe, either before, during, or after adolescence, and then solitary vigils are added to the fasting. Landes confirms these data for the Ojibwa of western Ontario, stating that boys of four to five years are already under siege by their relatives, and are being urged not to rest content with the protection of their name-power, but to fast in preparation for a vision. A boy's face is blackened so that all will know he is fasting and encourage him. If a little fellow fasts all day he is rewarded by choice bits of meat in the evening. From this time until puberty there is a constant harping on "dreaming for power." The parents arrange a schedule of fasting, graduated to the child's age and strength and to their own fanaticism on the subject. He is greeted in the morning with the question, "Which will you eat, bread or charcoal?" If he chooses bread he is cuffed and asked again.

Farther east, among the Delaware, Harrington reports: "Parents were especially anxious, of course, that their sons should have supernatural aid, hence, when a boy reached the age of about twelve years, they would frequently pretend to abuse him, and would drive him, fasting, out into the forest to shift as best he might, in the hope that some *manî'te* would take pity on the suffering child and grant him some power or blessing that would be his dependence through life." Sometimes Delaware boys were taken out on vigils by their fathers, and were given daily doses of some drug to cause vomiting. By practice, they were occasionally able to go for twelve days on end eating only one bit of meat as large as the little finger each evening.

To the west, in the Plateau area, the Nez Percé boy "began his preparation for spiritual attainment almost in infancy. The child, either boy or girl, when less than ten years of age, was told by the father or the mother that it was time to have . . . spiritual power." The boys were sent on progressively longer vigils to mountains as far as twelve miles away from camp, to fast and to keep a fire blazing all night. Among the interior Salish, "children, especially boys, were sent at frequent intervals to solitary places, in order that one or another of these spirits might take pity on them. These journeys were begun early in life, among some tribes even at the age of five years." The first trip might be to the sweat house. Gradually the trips were lengthened, and to make sure that the child carried out instructions some task would be set, such as finding and bringing in an object previously left at the appointed place by the anxious relatives of the youngster.

The practice of arranging some task in order to check on the child's fulfillment of instructions, was quite common among the border tribes of the Northwest Coast area. For the Wishram, Spier and Sapir report: "A child began to train, that is, prepare for a spirit experience, when still quite young, six to twelve years old 'when he can talk plainly.' He was sent out at night . . . [to] finish an appointed task at the designated spot. This was always stereotyped; piling up rocks, pulling up young oak or fir trees, or making withes of the saplings. The task was accommodated to the child's strength."

Additional citations could be given to confirm the fact that children were carefully trained for the vision quest from an early age, but those already given are representative, and sufficient to indicate that such practices were at least quite general if not absolutely universal. The training given was not exclusively religious in nature, even though its eventual purpose was to stimulate what might be termed a "religious thrill"—a pervading sense of having witnessed or experienced some mystery. Incidentally, the children were hardened to fasting, to cold and exposure, to pain, and to loneliness at night in isolated spots frequented by prowling animals. The general effect, obviously, even aside from a successful vision, was to build the kind of character that the Indians admired.

Further evidence stresses the fact that the underlying idea of the quest for power and a guardian spirit was less the acquisition of religious tenets than the acquisition of an inner conviction of individual self-sufficiency, in which the supernatural played an important part because the ultimate authority for everything lay in that realm. Among the Dakota and Pawnee, for example, guardian spirits were obtained directly only by shamans. The lay individual merely had one assigned to him. The Crow, Arapaho, Hidatsa, Winnebago, Blackfoot, and other Indians might purchase power as a commodity, as well as find it for themselves. Among the Hidatsa, Crow, Arapaho, Pawnee, Arikara, Omaha, and the Central Algonkian, the power might be inherited and had only to be confirmed by an inner conviction of its potency in order to be used. This idea occurs also in the Northwest. We cannot be dogmatic on the subject of religious training among the North American Indians. All I desire to show is that the classifying of the vision quest and the acquisition of a guardian spirit as purely religious, in the modern conception of religion as a spiritual concern divorced from practical or intellectual activities, is a mistake. The object of the training and of the experience was success in life. Conversely, success in life was a substitute for intensive courting of the supernatural. The person who could get power, an inner conviction, without following the normal procedure, was not universally looked down upon, but was con-

sidered fortunate. The average layman worried about the spiritual only if he lacked an inner conviction of his own capability and luck.

Among the Ojibwa, according to Jenness: "Any Indian who through industry and good judgment is more successful than his neighbors rouses their suspicion that he possesses an unfair advantage; that his prosperity is due not to his natural talents and diligence, but to his acquisition of some powerful medicine which he carefully secretes from his fellowmen."

From the histories of Blackfoot ceremonial-bundle owners it is clear that the son of successful parents may procrastinate in his quest for power, whereas the young nobody is precociously assiduous. In the biographies of twenty-three Plains Indians it is clear that six never made a successful vision quest, but some of the six got along without it, apparently because they achieved a conviction of power in other ways. Wissler states there is often an implication that a man did not know he had dreamed power until he accomplished something worthwhile, then he decided that he must have done so. The same implication is found in the story of an Oto recorded by Whitman. Littlerump, a Crow, confessed to Lowie: "All who had visions were well-to-do. I was to be poor, that is why I had no visions." This confession is highly informative, for, among the Crow, a man could seek to have someone's power transferred to him if he could not get any of his own. The conclusion is that Littlerump was a man of little capability, and that this proved he had never been able to establish permanent contact with the supernaturals who doled out good fortune. He might have been very religious, and probably tried to be. The story of Hillside, another Crow, is also informative. He had been given very powerful medicine as a boy. But his first war parties were flagrant failures, and he lost his conviction of power in a wave of fear when he barely escaped from the last one with his life. While running away he decided he really did not have any medicine power. Then he fell to the ground exhausted, and had a dream, not of his own medicine but of his brother's. Thus he knew that he just had the wrong medicine, and when this vital mistake was rectified he immediately became successful.

In California, the same concept of power acquisition as a practical aid to success occurs. Kroeber says of the Yurok: "A wealthy man exhorts his sons to accost visitors in a quiet and friendly manner and invite them to their house; thus they will have friends. A poor man, on the other hand instructs his son not in policy but in means to acquire strength. He tells him where to bathe at night; then a being will draw him under the water and speak to him, and he will come away with powerful physique and courage." The important point in the Yurok curriculum for the training of the ideal, wealthy man was "concentration." Boys were told to concentrate on gaining wealth and to avoid thinking about anything else, especially women. Thus they became wealthy, and, naturally, along the way they must have acquired supernatural approval.

Similar statements to the effect that poor boys had to seek power, and that a successful man knew he had power, and that certain people obtained power at birth, or inherited it, or received it by gift, are frequent in the Northwest area. The clearest statement noted in any field report is that for the Wishram: "Since the measure of success was held to be directly dependent on the extent of power, and this was held to vary from one individual to another, we cannot but conclude that the actual causal sequence was the reverse: those who were successful credited themselves with unusual spirit power."

Additional insight into the educational significance of the vision quest and the acquisition of a guardian spirit is to be obtained from a study of the nature of the vision supposedly obtained by these primitive ascetics, on the one hand, and by an analysis of what takes place of a similar character in tribal groups lacking the vision–guardian-spirit complex, on the other.

The Logic of African Science and Witchcraft

Max Gluckman

From *The Logic of African Science and Witchcraft: An Appreciation of Evans-Pritchard's "Witchcraft Oracles and Magic among the Azande" of the Sudan*. Rhodes-Livingston Institute Journal, June 1944, pp. 61–71. By permission of the author and publisher.

I have selected this book for the first appreciation in our journal, because it is one of the most notable contributions to the scientific understanding of African problems. Though the researches on which it is based were made in the Sudan, the general argument applies to all African tribes who believe in witchcraft, oracles or divination, and magic. The author describes clearly the functioning of witchcraft and magic in a book that is fascinating to the specialist, and is also written so simply and vividly that every layman who begins it will not be able to leave it till he has followed the argument to its close. For an understanding of the behavior of Africans, and, as will be seen, of ourselves where we do not act on scientifically valid grouds, it is a work which everyone should read. Since the book explains to us not only customs of the Sudan Azande, but also the basis of such wide fields of human behavior, I shall here set out the general lessons which it teaches, and then touch on the differences between the Azande and our own peoples. However, as Evans-Pritchard does not consider in detail aspects of Azande behavior other than what he calls the mystical, I begin by referring to these.

The title of this review poses the question: is there a fundamental difference between African and European logic, and if so, is it due to physical differences, or to psychological ones related to the different social conditions in which Africans and Europeans live? Without entering into the arguments for and against, I may say that the consensus of scientific opinion is that there is no proof of any great difference between the brains of various races. If there are any differences, they are altogether insufficient to account for the great differences between cultures and modes of thought, and above all, they cannot account for the rapid spurts in cultural development which some countries achieved in very short time. That is, if we have to explain London and an African village, we cannot do so by bodily differences between Londoners and Africans: we must investigate their history and struggles, especially their contacts with other peoples, and other social factors.

For if an African were brought up from birth by a Londoner, he would be a Londoner. We know that shipwrecked European children were distinguishable from their African foster-people only by their color.

Therefore, if the mind of the African differs from the European's, it is because he has grown up in a different society, where from birth his behavior and ideas are molded by those of his parents and fellows. If he inherits a "mind," he inherits it socially, and not physically.

Most Europeans are handicapped in judging Africans' intelligence, for they deal with them only as employees, working in unfamiliar ways. The sociologist is fortunate in having to act and converse with them in their own ideas and idiom, and most find that once one has grasped their idiom, they are intelligent and logical companions. They are also knowledgeable companions, for every African knows much about his own laws, politics, history, art, medicine, so that conversation with them often becomes general and philosophical.

First, the African has a wide technical knowledge which is accurate and scientific. For example, the Lozi people live in a large plain on the Zambezi which is flooded each year, and to make a living, they have to take into account soils, vegetation, the time of the flood's coming and its depth, rainfall and temperature, in order to decide where to make their gardens and when to plant them. Some gardens they build up above the waters, other places they drain. Government experts describe this Lozi agriculture as remarkable, and say that they can suggest no improvements in it unless they first experiment. The Lozi have twenty-two recorded methods of catching fish with nets, dams, traps, and weapons, and to use these they have to smelt and work iron, make string and rope from roots and bark, and know the movements of fish with the rise and fall of the flood.

They are also keen and penetrating lawyers. Their laws and procedure differ from ours, but within their framework they reason clearly, distinguishing the issues involved, and applying old laws precisely to new situations. Nevertheless, a European often cannot grasp the logic which underlies the course of argument and the decision in a case tried by African judges. This is because the background of African cases is different from our own. Very many African lawsuits are between relatives; this is largely so because Africans count their ties with very distant relatives, very much further than we do. When one relative sues another though he may come to court over a certain thing on which a case rests, what he wants investigated may not be that single dispute, but the whole behavior of this relative to him. Where our lawyers concern themselves only with the thing that the present quarrel is about, the African judges go into the rights and wrongs of the litigants' behavior to each other over a long period. Leakey says that when a Kikuyu pledges land against a loan of stock, if the pledgee works and improves the land he gets back only the stock he loaned; if he holds the land without working it, and it reverts to bush, he gets additional stock. The Kikuyu argue in the opposite way to us, but logically, that in improving the land the pledgee has got profit out of it, and this is his interest. He therefore is not entitled to compensation for his improvements or interest on the stock he lent to the pledgor.

In political debate the African is advanced and intelligent. Africans, like ourselves, are vexed in this war by rising prices, and I heard some Lozi indunas discuss the delicate problem of fixing the price of fish. Here are some of the economic arguments they raised. All distinguished clearly the rights of producers and consumers, saying that they themselves were both, since they fished and bought fish. One said that supplies of fish varied with the month and the state of the flood, and when fish were scarcer prices inevitably rose; he appreciated what we call the law of supply and demand. Another argued that if the fisherman needed money badly, he would accept little money, while the buyer, if staging a feast, would pay a lot. A third pointed out that with the prices of store-goods rising, the price of fish must rise; he saw the spiral of rising prices. On the other hand, another induna countered, fish are cheap and essential and a small rise would be accepted by the buyers; that is, the principle of marginal utility. Another, who came from a distant place near Livingstone, said that prices must vary with locality, for fish at Mongu were cheap because money was scarce, while at Sesheke fish were dear because money was plentiful. Thus he realized that money is a commodity, like other goods, affected by supply and demand. Some indunas pointed to the difficulty of enforcing a fixed price, with the people crowding into a "black market." Some said that the fisherman must not be allowed to profit at the general expense of the community; others were on his side, the fisherman had to make or buy his nets and work in cold waters from morning to night, and therefore he was entitled to a good price. Finally, the head of the Council said that they must check the rise in price, and as the government they must exert the power to check breaches of the law.

I have emphasized the African's intelligence, in technological and administrative matters, within his own culture. In these realms he reasons much as we do, though within much narrower ranges of facts, and of course without testing his theories by scientific experiment. This ability to reason clearly also appears where he works with beliefs and ideas that are different from ours, notably those about witchcraft and magic, a system of ideas which our civilization abandoned some 150 years ago. Many Europeans, particularly peasants, still hold them. That these beliefs subsisted till so recently in educated Europe and America, shows that they are not innate in Africans, but are part of their culture, as they were of ours. Anyone who follows Evans-Pritchard's exposition of the intellectual aspect of Zande magic and witchcraft will be fascinated by their logical skill. At the beginning of his book, Evans-Pritchard stresses that he is excluding their technological knowledge, examples of which, for the Lozi, I have given above.

The fundamental point is that the African is born into a society which believes in witch-craft and therefore the very texture of his thinking, from childhood on, is woven of magical and mystical ideas. More important still, since magic and witchcraft are lived, far more than they are reasoned about, his daily actions are conditioned by these beliefs, till at every turn he is confronted by the threat of witchcraft and meets it with divination and magic. The weight of tradition, the actions and behavior of his elders, the support which chiefs give to the system, all impress on the African the truth of the system, and since he cannot measure it against any other system, he is continually caught in the web of its making. Evans-Pritchard stresses too, that the African does not go about his business in constant terror of witchcraft nor does he approach it with an awesome fear of the supernatural; when he finds it is working against him he is angry against the witch for playing a dirty trick on him.

These points emerge from a brief analysis of the essential characteristics of the system of witchcraft-divination-magic beliefs and behavior. The Azande, like many other Central African tribes, believe witchcraft to be a physical condition of the intestines (as found in a corpse, it is probably a passing state of digestion), which enables the soul of the witch to go out at night and harm his fellows. There is also sorcery (which is more commonly believed in in Southern Africa) which is the use of magical substances for anti-social purposes. A man may have witchcraft in his body, and yet not use it; his witchcraft may be "cool." Africans are not interested in witchcraft as such, but in the particular witch who is bewitching them at a certain moment. They do not get the idea that they are being bewitched and are therefore going to suffer some misfortune, such as to fall ill and die. What happens is that they suffer misfortune, and after it has occurred blame it on a witch; and if it is a misfortune past and done with, they find out who the witch is and get him to withdraw his evil influence or tackle it with magic. Therefore Evans-Pritchard says he knows of no Zande who would die in terror of witchcraft, and this is confirmed by other trained observers.

The problem which the African answers with his belief in witchcraft is this, "Why misfortune to me?" He knows that there are diseases which make people ill; he knows that hippos upset dugouts and drown people. But he asks himself, "Why should I be ill and not other people?" The man whose son has drowned when a hippo upset his dugout, in effect says, "My son frequently traveled by dugout on the river where there are always hippo, why on this one occasion should the hippo have attacked and drowned him?" This he answers, "Because we were bewitched." He knows full well that his son was crossing the river to visit his mother's family, and that the hippo, irritable because it had a calf, was migrating upstream when it met the dugout. We say that it was providence or ill-luck which brought the hippo and the son together so that the son died, as we do when a man crossing the road from one shop to another is run over by a car; when the African says it is witchcraft that caused these deaths, he is explaining a coincidence which science leaves unexplained, except as the intersection of two series of events. The African is fully aware that his son drowned because his lungs filled with water; but he argues that it was a witch, or a sorcerer by his medicines, who brought together the paths of dugout and an angry mother-hippo to kill the son. The Azande explain it by a hunting simile. The first man who hits a buck shares the meat with the man who puts the second spear in it. "Hence if a man is killed by an elephant Azande say that the elephant is the first spear (existing in its own right) and witchcraft is the second spear and that together they killed the man. If a man spears another in war the slayer is the first spear and witchcraft is the second spear and together they killed him."

Witchcraft thus explains why, but not how, misfortunes happen to you. A sociologist in the Union gives an illuminating illustration. The child of a well-educated African teacher died of typhus, and the teacher said that the child was killed by a witch. The sociologist remonstrated that typhus was caused by an infected louse. The teacher replied, "I know that it was a louse from a person ill with typhus which gave my child typhus, and that he died of typhus, but why did the louse go to my child and not to the other children with whom he was playing?" Scientists may explain why some unhappy people attract lice more than others do, but largely it is chance that puts one child, and not another, in the path of an infected louse; we say providence, bad luck, chance; the African says, witchcraft.

Africans thus immediately they suffer misfortune think that a witch has been working against them. Every kind of accident or of ill may be ascribed to witchcraft. But this does not mean that the African does not recognize lack of skill and moral lapses. For an unskilled potter to say that his pots broke in firing because he was bewitched, would not convince his fellows if he had left pebbles in the clay; but the skilled potter who had followed all the rules of his craft would be supported in saying this. It would not be a sound defense for a criminal to plead that he did wrong because he was bewitched to do so, for it is not believed that witchcraft makes a man lie, steal, betray his chief, or commit adultery.

This is how witchcraft works as a theory of causes. The African goes further. Witchcraft does not harm people haphazardly, for the witch wants to hurt people he hates, has quarreled with, of whom he is envious. So that when a man falls ill, or his crops fail (for on good soil crops should not fail), he says that someone who envied him his many children, the favor of his chief, or his good employment by Europeans and his fine clothes, therefore hated him and has used medicines or evil power to do him ill. Witchcraft is thus a moral theory for witches are bad people, hating, grudging, envious, spiteful. A witch does not just attack his fellows, he attacks those whom he has reason to hate. There is a clear distinction between the man who has witchcraft in him but is a good man and does not use it against his fellows, the man who wants to do others harm but has not the power of witchcraft or cannot get the evil medicines of sorcery, and the witch himself—the man who has the power to bewitch and uses that power. Since people are only interested in whether their fellows are witches when they suffer misfortunes, they seek among their enemies for those who may have this power. They think of someone with whom they have quarreled, and suspect him of the evil deed. We find thus that witchcraft as a theory of causes of misfortunes is related to personal relations between the sufferer and his fellows, and to a theory of moral judgments as to what is good and bad.

When a man suffers a misfortune which he cannot remedy, such as the breaking of his pots in firing, he may just accept it, as witchcraft, just as we would say, "Bad luck." But when witchcraft is making him ill and may cause him to die, when it is blighting his crop, or when by divination he finds that it is threatening him in the future, he does not sit down hopelessly under it. He has to scotch its evil working. This he does by using medicines against it, which will stop the witchcraft and possibly kill the witch, or by calling in a diviner to find out who is the witch so that he can be put out of business, or persuaded to remove his witchcraft. The diviner does not seek for the witch haphazardly. Most methods of divination allow one of two possible answers, yes or no, to a stated question. For example, the Axande give a "poison" (of course they do not know it is a poison) with strychnine properties to fowls which die or do not die to say "yes" or "no" to a question of the form, "Is A the witch who is harming me?" Thus a man, seeking for the witch among the people he thinks wish him ill, must eventually get the answer "yes" to one of them. This particular oracle is out of human control; others, including witch doctors, are less trusted by the Azande as being subject to human manipulation. But even the Zande witch doctor, though he works on his knowledge of local gossip, does not often deliberately cheat. He may seek, or be asked by his client to seek, for the witch among say four names. These are the names of enemies of the client, and though the witch doctor may choose from these, or others whom he knows wish his client ill, by unconscious selection, there is a moment when by bodily sensation

he knows that the medicines, which give him his divining power, say, "It is A who is the witch, not B." Or the diviner will indicate someone generally without specifying a name—e.g., "one of your wives," "an old woman"—and the client will fix on some definite person, among his neighbors, who is thus described and whom therefore he thinks has reason to wish him ill. Charges of witchcraft thus reflect personal relations and quarrels. Often a man accuses not someone who hates him, or who is envious of him, but someone whom he hates or envies. The African knows this, and may stress it when he is not involved in the case or when he is the accused, but he forgets it when he is making the accusation. In Zululand a man accused his brother of having bewitched him because he was jealous of him. An old diviner, aware of psychological projection, told me, "Of course, it is obvious that it is the complainant who hates his brother, though he thinks it is his brother who hates him." But that diviner believed firmly in his own power to detect witchcraft. . . .

The theory of witchcraft is thus seen to be reasonable and logical, even if it is not true. Since it explains the intersection of two chains of events by the enmity of people with evil power, it works in fields our modern science leaves unexplained. Thus the African cannot see that the system is untrue and moreover he has to reason with the system as we do with our scientific beliefs. Wherever the system might conflict with reality its beliefs are vague, and deal with transcendent non-observable facts; the witch works at night with his soul, the soul of the poison oracle (which is not personified, but has consciousness) finds out the witchcraft. The theory is a complete whole, in which every part buttresses every other part. Illness proves that a witch is at work, he is discovered by divination, he is persuaded to withdraw his witchcraft. Even though he may feel himself that he is not the real witch, he will at least show that he intends no harm to the sick man. Or he is attacked with magic. It is difficult for the African to find a flaw in the system. Skepticism exists, and is not socially repressed, and Evans-Pritchard writes that the "absence of formal and coercive doctrine permit Azande to state that many, even most, witch doctors, are frauds. No opposition being offered to such statements they leave the main belief in the prophetic and therapeutic powers of witch doctors unimpaired. Indeed, skepticism in included in the pattern of belief in witch doctors. Faith and skepticism are alike traditional. Skepticism explains failures of witch doctors, and being directed toward particular witch doctors even tends to support faith in others." Even the witch doctor who works by sleight of hand believes that there are doctors who have the magic to make this unnecessary. "In this web of belief every strand depends upon every other strand, and a Zande cannot get out of its meshes because this is the only world he knows. The web is not an external structure in which he is enclosed. It is the texture of his thought and he cannot think that his thought is wrong. Nevertheless, his beliefs are not absolutely set but are variable and fluctuating to allow for different situations and to permit empirical observation and even doubts." Within this web, the African may reason as logically as we do within the web of scientific thought. If your house, which you have protected with lightning-conductors, is nevertheless struck by lightning you say that the workman was bad, the wires poor, or there was a break in the wiring. If the African has had his village protected with medicines against storms and it is struck by lightning, he says the magician was bad, his medicine poor, or a taboo was broken. This method of reasoning, within a system, is remarkably illustrated in a book which the Nazis published. It consisted of a collection of anti-Hitler cartoons from the newspapers of the whole world, and contained many by Low. The cartoons did not show the German people what the decent world thought of Hitler, but proved to them that if other governments allowed the god Hitler to be thus attacked, these other countries must be vile and hostile to Germany, as Hitler maintained. So the African's mind in his system, works as the European's mind does.

I have given other examples in my article on *The Difficulties, Limitations and Achievements of Social Anthropology* [in this same issue of the Rhodes-Livingstone Institute Journal] to show how Evans-Pritchard's analysis of witchcraft illuminates the working of human thought in other spheres. For instance, he makes this comparison. The Azande as we have seen exclude witchcraft as a cause of moral lapses. "As in our own society a scientific theory of causation, if not excluded, is deemed irrelevant in questions of moral and legal responsibility, so in Zande society the doctrine of witchcraft, if not excluded is deemed irrelevant in the same situations. We accept scientific explanations of the causes of diseases, and even of the causes of insanity, but we deny them in crime and sin because here they militate against law and morals which are axiomatic. The Zande accepts a mystical explanation of the causes of misfortune, sickness, and death, but he does not allow this explanation if it conflicts with social exigencies expressed in law and morals."

I make one final point here, in answer to the oft-made statement that witchcraft charges are based on cheating. Evans-Pritchard emphasizes that the patient, who wishes to abolish the witchcraft harming him, above all people does not wish to cheat, for what good is it to him if he detects the wrong person as witch? But he does accuse his personal enemies.

When the African, with these beliefs, comes to deal with Europeans, there are many ways in which they affect his behavior so that it seems incomprehensible to us. For example, he queries, "It is true that the White doctors are very good in treating disease, but while they cure the disease they don't treat the witchcraft which caused the disease, and that will continue to do harm." Evans-Pritchard shows that the Zande's oracles are "his guide and councillor," whom he consults about every enterprise. Evans-Pritchard himself lived thus, and found it as good a way as any other of ordering his affairs. But because of it, Europeans often cannot understand Azande behavior: why a Zande will suddenly move from his home to shelter in the bush (because of witchcraft), why a homestead will suddenly be moved (because of witchcraft attacking them in that spot), and so on. Frequently his guests suddenly departed without bidding him farewell, and he was angry till he realized that the oracles had told them that witchcraft was threatening them. "I found that when a Zande acted toward me in a manner that we would call rude and untrustworthy his actions were often to be accounted for by obedience to oracles. Usually I have found Azande courteous and reliable according to English standards, but sometimes their behavior is unintelligible till their mystical notions are taken into account. Often Azande are tortuous in their dealing with one another, but they do not consider a man blameworthy for being secretive or acting contrary to his declared intentions. On the contrary they praise his prudence for taking account of witchcraft at every step. . . . With the European it is different. We only know that a Zande has said he will do something and has done nothing or has done something different, and we naturally blame the man for lying and being untrustworthy, for the European does not appreciate that Azande have to take into account mystical forces of which he knows nothing." Evans-Pritchard gave a feast to which a prince promised to come; he sent to tell that he would not come. Suddenly he arrived. He arranged to stay the night; in the night he disappeared. He had been told that witchcraft threatened him, and it was a great compliment to the sociologist that he attended the feast; his wayward actions were to deceive the witches. I myself had a favored informant in my employ who kept replying to my summonses, that he would come; but stayed away until I moved my home. He had been threatened with witchcraft at the one spot, not the other. For notions of place and time in witchcraft thought vary from ours; witchcraft may threaten a man now from the future, so the future is in the present, and has to be avoided by not adopting a line of action which was contemplated, as going on a journey; or a man will decide to build his homestead on a

certain spot, by eliminating other spots where witchcraft will threaten him, though he has not yet built on them.

There is a second way in which witchcraft behavior may affect Africans when we deal with them. Under these beliefs, people who produced good crops while their neighbors' harvests were meager; who had large healthy families while all around was illness; whose herds and fishing prospered exceedingly; these fortunate people were sometimes believed to make good by magic and witchcraft at the expense of their fellows. We have seen in a quotation above that they believed themselves open to attack from witches. The Zande "knows that if he becomes rich the poor will hate him, that if he rises in social position his inferiors will be jealous of his authority, that if he is handsome the less favored will envy his looks, that if he is talented as a hunter, a singer, a fighter, or a rhetorician, he will earn the malice of those less gifted, and that if he enjoys the regard of his prince and of his neighbors he will be detested for his prestige and popularity." These are the motives that lead to witchcraft. Such beliefs were only possible in a society with nowhere to sell surplus goods, with no luxuries so that there was no heavy pressure on any member to produce more than he required for his own needs. Africans have come from a society with these beliefs into our economic system where they are expected to work long and hard, trying to outdo their fellows, and perhaps the beliefs deter them in this struggle and affect their efficiency. I know Africans who blame their misfortunes on witches envious of their higher wages, or their fine would-be European-style houses. It is possible that fear of witchcraft prevents Africans developing what skill and capacity they have, in their work for Europeans, though this fear would be unimportant in comparison with other factors preventing their development, such as disease and social barriers.

I have given part of the argument of Evans-Pritchard's book to set out the main framework of magic-witchcraft thought. I hope I have shown how skillfully the argument is set out. In my short review I am unable to do more than indicate its unlimited riches of delight, which make reading and rereading it an unfailing fascination. Everyone who is interested in human problems in this region should own the book. But I must warn the layman that in applying its conclusions to our own tribes, he must do so with care. The central argument applies absolutely, but there are certain important differences. Among the Azande, witchcraft was not a crime but a delict, for which compensation was paid only on a death. In many Southern African tribes witchcraft is a crime, and the state punished witches by killing them. Also in Southern Africa sorcery (the deliberate use of evil magic) was believed to be at work, rather than witchcraft (causing ill by inherent evil power plus malice). This produces important changes in the whole system, which can be traced. . . .

In quoting Evans-Pritchard to show how beliefs in witchcraft affect Africans' behavior and thought, I have emphasized that often their minds work in the same logical patterns as ours do, though the material with which they think is different, so that it is clear that if they were given the same education and cultural background as we have, they would think with the same materials and in the same way as we do. But it is not only beliefs in witchcraft that differentiate the African's ideas from ours. His whole way of life is different from ours, he is considered to be inferior, and he is certainly on the whole abjectly poor. A Bechuana chief, lecturing to a University audience, said that the coming of Western civilization to his people had put a square bed into a round hut. Where the African behaves differently from us, we must remember that he comes from a round hut, usually without a square bed, into our homes with their comparative wealth of furniture, that he comes from a simple axe and hoe to our complicated machinery. In his hut, close to the ground, of the earth earthy, full of flies and without taps or washbasins, with only a basket of meal and some dried fish in it, he cannot have the same standards of efficiency and cleanliness as we have. Even if he, for example, grasps the connection of disease with dirt and insects, he cannot avoid them. Therefore, when he works for Europeans, and when he is away from his work, he is living by two different sets of standards, not with a different mind. These are weighty explanations of his vagaries, not only his preknowledge of mystical forces in the future; changes in his way of life, as well as the operation of economic forces in our highly productive system, are tending to break down his system of thought. Further, Wilson has indicated that the personal animosities, which are the basis of witchcraft charges, can lie only in a small-scale primitive society where social relationships are highly personal, and not in the modern world system where men's lives are affected by large-scale impersonal organizations. Therefore, new forces will break down the closed mystical system of Africa. . . .

One Hundred Per Cent American

Ralph Linton

From *The American Mercury*, Vol. 40, 1937, pp. 427–429. By permission of the author and the publisher.

There can be no question about the average American's Americanism or his desire to preserve this precious heritage at all costs. Nevertheless, some insidious foreign ideas have already wormed their way into his civilization without his realizing what was going on. Thus dawn finds the unsuspecting patriot garbed in pajamas, a garment of East Indian origin; lying in a bed built on a pattern which originated in either Persia or Asia Minor. He is muffled to the ears in un-American materials: cotton, first domesticated in India; linen, domesticated in the Near East; wool from an animal native to Asia Minor; or silk whose uses were first discovered by the Chinese. All these substances have been transformed into cloth by methods invented in Southwestern Asia. If the weather is cold enough he may even be sleeping under an eiderdown quilt invented in Scandanavia.

On awakening he glances at the clock, a medieval European invention, uses one potent Latin work in abbreviated form, rises in haste, and goes to the bathroom. Here, if he stops to think about it, he must feel himself in the presence of a great American institution; he will have heard stories of both the quality and frequency of foreign plumbing and will know that in no other country does the average man perform his ablutions in the midst of such splendor. But the insidious foreign influence pursues him even here. Glass was invented by the ancient Egyptians, the use of glazed tiles for floors and walls in the Near East, porcelain in China, and the art of enameling on metal by Mediterranean artisans of the Bronze Age. Even his bathtub and toilet are but slightly modified copies of Roman originals. The only purely American contribution to the ensemble is the steam radiator, against which our patriot very briefly and unintentionally places his posterior.

In this bathroom the American washes with soap invented by the ancient Gauls. Next he cleans his teeth, a subversive European practice which did not invade America until the latter part of the eighteenth century. He then shaves, a masochistic rite first developed by the heathen priests of ancient Egypt and Sumer. The process is made less of a penance by the fact that his razor is of steel, an iron-carbon alloy discovered in either India or Turkestan. Lastly, he dries himself on a Turkish towel.

Returning to the bedroom, the unconscious victim of un-American practices removes his clothes from a chair, invented in the Near East, and proceeds to dress. He puts on close-fitting tailored garments whose form derives from the skin clothing of the ancient nomads of the Asiatic steppes and fastens them with buttons whose prototypes appeared in Europe at the close of the Stone Age. This costume is appropriate enough for outdoor exercise in a cold climate, but is quite unsuited to American summers, steam-heated houses, and Pullmans. Nevertheless, foreign ideas and habits hold the unfortunate man in thrall even when common sense tells him that the authentically American costume of gee string and moccasins would be far more comfortable. He puts on his feet stiff coverings made from hide prepared by a process invented in ancient Egypt and cut to a pattern which can be traced back to ancient Greece, and makes sure that they are properly polished, also a Greek idea. Lastly, he ties about his neck a strip of bright-colored cloth which is a vestigial survival of the shoulder shawls worn by seventeenth-century Croats. He gives himself a final appraisal in the mirror, an old Mediterranean invention, and goes downstairs to breakfast.

Here a whole new series of foreign things confronts him. His food and drink are placed before him in pottery vessels, the popular name of which—china—is sufficient evidence of their origin. His fork is a medieval Italian invention and his spoon a copy of a Roman original. He will usually begin the meal with coffee, an Abyssinian plant first discovered by the Arabs. The American is quite likely to need it to dispel the morning-after effects of overindulgence in fermented drinks, invented in the Near East; or distilled ones, invented by the alchemists of medieval Europe. Whereas the Arabs took their coffee straight, he will probably sweeten it with sugar, discovered in India; and dilute it with cream, both the domestication of cattle and the technique of milking having originated in Asia Minor.

If our patriot is old-fashioned enough to adhere to the so-called American breakfast, his coffee will be accompanied by an orange, domesticated in the Mediterranean region, a cantaloupe domesticated in Persia, or grapes domesticated in Asia Minor. He will follow this with a bowl of cereal made from grain domesticated in the Near East and prepared by methods also invented there. From this he will go on to waffles, a Scandinavian invention, with plenty of butter, originally a Near-Eastern cosmetic. As a side dish he may have the egg of a bird domesticated in Southeastern Asia or strips of the flesh of an animal domesticated in the same region, which have been salted and smoked by a process invented in Northern Europe.

Breakfast over, he places upon his head a molded piece of felt, invented by the nomads of Eastern Asia, and, if it looks like rain, puts on outer shoes of rubber, discovered by the ancient Mexicans, and takes an umbrella, invented in India. He then sprints for his train—the train, not the sprinting, being an English invention. At the station he pauses for a moment to buy a newspaper, paying for it with coins invented in ancient Lydia. Once on board he settles back to inhale the fumes of a cigarette invented in Mexico, or a cigar invented in Brazil. Meanwhile, he reads the news of the day, imprinted characters invented by the ancient Semites by a process invented in Germany upon a material invented in China. As he scans the latest editorial pointing out the dire results to our institutions of accepting foreign ideas, he will not fail to thank a Hebrew God in an Indo-European language that he is a one hundred per cent (decimal system invented by the Greeks) American (from Americus Vespucci, Italian geographer).

Body Ritual among the Nacirema

Horace Miner

From *American Anthropologist,* Vol. 58, No. 3, 1956, pp. 503–507. By permission of the author and the publisher.

The anthropologist has become so familiar with the diversity of ways in which different peoples behave in similar situations that he is not apt to be surprised by even the most exotic customs. In fact, if all of the logically possible combinations of behavior have not been found somewhere in the world, he is apt to suspect that they must be present in some yet undescribed tribe. This point has, in fact, been expressed with respect to clan organization by Murdock. In this light, the magical beliefs and practices of the Nacirema present such unusual aspects that it seems desirable to describe them as an example of the extremes to which human behavior can go.

Professor Linton first brought the ritual of the Nacirema to the attention of anthropologists twenty years ago, but the culture of this people is still very poorly understood. They are a North American group living in the territory between the Canadian Cree, the Yaqui and Tarahumare of Mexico, and the Carib and Arawak of the Antilles. Little is known of their origin, although tradition states that they came from the east. . . .

Nacirema culture is characterized by a highly developed market economy which has evolved in a rich natural habitat. While much of the people's time is devoted to economic pursuits, a large part of the fruits of these labors and a considerable portion of the day are spent in ritual activity. The focus of this activity is the human body, the appearance and health of which loom as a dominant concern in the ethos of the people. While such a concern is certainly not unusual, its ceremonial aspects and associated philosophy are unique.

The fundamental belief underlying the whole system appears to be that the human body is ugly and that its natural tendency is to debility and disease. Incarcerated in such a body, man's only hope is to avert these characteristics through the use of the powerful influences of ritual and ceremony. Every household has one or more shrines devoted to this purpose. The more powerful individuals in the society have several shrines in their houses and, in fact, the opulence of a house is often referred to in terms of the number of such ritual centers it possesses. Most houses are of wattle and daub construction, but the shrine rooms of the more wealthy are walled with stone. Poorer families imitate the rich by applying pottery plaques to their shrine walls.

While each family has at least one such shrine, the rituals associated with it are not family ceremonies but are private and secret. The rites are normally only discussed with children, and then only during the period when they are being initiated into these mysteries. I was able, however, to establish sufficient rapport with the natives to examine these shrines and to have the rituals described to me.

The focal point of the shrine is a box or chest which is built into the wall. In this chest are kept the many charms and magical potions without which no native believes he could live. These preparations are secured from a variety of specialized practitioners. The most powerful of these are the medicine men, whose assistance must be rewarded with substantial gifts. However, the medicine men do not provide the curative potions for their clients, but decide what the ingredients should be and then write them down in an ancient and secret language. This writing is understood only by the medicine men and by the herbalists who, for another gift, provide the required charm.

The charm is not disposed of after it has served its purpose, but is placed in the charm-box of the household shrine. As these magical materials are specific for certain ills, and the real or imagined maladies of the people are many, the charm-box is usually full to overflowing. The magical packets are so numerous that people forget what their purposes were and fear to use them again. While the natives are very vague on this point, we can only assume that the idea in retaining all the old magical materials is that their presence in the charm-box, before which the body rituals are conducted, will in some way protect the worshipper.

Beneath the charm-box is a small font. Each day every member of the family, in succession, enters the shrine room, bows his head before the charm-box, mingles different sorts of holy water in the font, and proceeds with a brief rite of ablution. The holy waters are secured from the Water Temple of the community, where the priests conduct elaborate ceremonies to make the liquid ritually pure.

In the hierarchy of magical practitioners, and below the medicine men in prestige, are specialists whose designation is best translated "holy-mouth-men." The Nacirema have an almost pathological horror of and fascination with the mouth, the condition of which is believed to have a supernatural influence on all social relationships. Were it not for the rituals of the mouth, they believe that their teeth would fall out, their gums bleed, their jaws shrink, their friends desert them, and their lovers reject them. They also believe that a strong relationship exists between oral and moral characteristics. For example, there is a ritual ablution of the mouth for children which is supposed to improve their moral fiber.

The daily body ritual performed by everyone includes a mouth-rite. Despite the fact that these people are so punctilious about care of the mouth, this rite involves a practice which strikes the uninitiated stranger as revolting. It was reported to me that the ritual consists of inserting a small bundle of hog hairs into the mouth, along with certain magical powders, and then moving the bundle in a highly formalized series of gestures.

In addition to the private mouth-rite, the people seek out a holy-mouth-man once or twice a year. These practitioners have an impressive set of paraphernalia, consisting of a variety of augers, awls, probes, and prods. The use of these objects in the exorcism of the evils of the mouth involves almost unbelievable torture of the client. The holy-mouth-man opens the client's mouth and, using the above mentioned tools, enlarges any holes which decay may have created in the teeth. Magical materials are put into these holes. If there are no naturally occurring holes in the teeth, large sections of one or more teeth are gouged out so that the supernatural substance can be applied. In the client's view, the purpose of these ministrations is to arrest decay and to draw friends.

The extremely sacred and traditional character of the rite is evident in the fact that the natives return to the holy-mouth-man year after year, despite the fact that their teeth continue to decay.

It is to be hoped that, when a thorough study of the Nacirema is made, there will be careful inquiry into the personality structure of these people. One has but to watch the gleam in the eye of a holy-mouth-man, as he jabs an awl into an exposed nerve, to suspect that a certain amount of sadism is involved. If this can be established, a very interesting pattern emerges, for most of the population shows definite masochistic tendencies. It was to these that Professor Linton referred in discussing a distinctive part of the daily body ritual which is performed only by men. This part of the rite involves scraping and lacerating the surface of the face with a sharp instrument. Special women's rites are performed only four times during each lunar month, but what they lack in frequency is made up in barbarity. As part of this ceremony, women bake their heads in small ovens for about an hour. The theoretically interesting point is that what seems to be a preponderantly masochistic people have developed sadistic specialists.

The medicine men have an imposing temple, or *latipso*, in every community of any size. The more elaborate ceremonies required to treat very sick patients can only be performed at this temple. These ceremonies involve not only the thaumaturge but a permanent group of vestal maidens who move sedately about the temple chambers in distinctive costume and headdress.

The *latipso* ceremonies are so harsh that it is phenomenal that a fair proportion of the really sick natives who enter the temple ever recover. Small children whose indoctrination is still incomplete have been known to resist attempts to take them to the temple because "that is where you go to die." Despite this fact, sick adults are not only willing but eager to undergo the protracted ritual purification, if they can afford to do so. No matter how ill the supplicant or how grave the emergency, the guardians of many temples will not admit a client if he cannot give a rich gift to the custodian. Even after one has gained admission and survived the ceremonies, the guardians will not permit the neophyte to leave until he makes still another gift.

The supplicant entering the temple is first stripped of all his or her clothes. In everyday life the Nacirema avoids exposure of his body and its natural functions. Bathing and excretory acts are performed only in the secrecy of the household shrine, where they are ritualized as part of the body-rites. Psychological shock results from the fact that body secrecy is suddenly lost upon entry into the *latipso*. A man, whose own wife has never seen him in an excretory act, suddenly finds himself naked and assisted by a vestal maiden while he performs his natural functions into a sacred vessel. This sort of ceremonial treatment is necessitated by the fact that the excreta are used by a diviner to ascertain the course and nature of the client's sickness. Female clients, on the other hand, find their naked bodies are subjected to the scrutiny, manipulation and prodding of the medicine men.

Few supplicants in the temple are well enough to do anything but lie on their hard beds. The daily ceremonies, like the rites of the holy-mouth-men, involve discomfort and torture. With ritual precision, the vestals awaken their miserable charges each dawn and roll them about on their beds of pain while performing ablutions, in the formal movements of which the maidens are highly trained. At other times they insert magic wands in the supplicant's mouth or force him to eat substances which are supposed to be healing. From time to time the medicine men come to their clients and jab magically treated needles into their flesh. The fact that these temple ceremonies may not cure, and may even kill the neophyte, in no way decreases the people's faith in the medicine men.

There remains one other kind of practitioner, known as a "listener." This witch-doctor has the power to exorcise the devils that lodge in the heads of people who have been bewitched. The Nacirema believe that parents bewitch their own children. Mothers are particularly suspected of putting a curse on children while teaching them the secret body rituals. The counter-magic of the witch-doctor is unusual in its lack of ritual. The patient simply tells the "listener" all his troubles and fears, beginning with the earliest difficulties he can remember. The memory displayed by the Nacirema in these exorcism sessions is truly remarkable. It is not uncommon for the patient to bemoan the rejection he felt upon being weaned as a babe, and a few individuals even see their troubles going back to the traumatic effects of their own birth.

In conclusion, mention must be made of certain practices which have their base in native esthetics but which depend upon the pervasive aversion to the natural body and its functions. There are ritual fasts to make fat people thin and ceremonial feasts to make thin people fat. Still other rites are used to make women's breasts larger if they are small, and smaller if they are large. General dissatisfaction with breast shape is symbolized in the fact that the ideal form is virtually outside the range of human variation. A few women afflicted with almost inhuman hyper-mammary development are so idolized that they make a handsome living by simply going from village to village and permitting the natives to stare at them for a fee.

Reference has already been made to the fact that excretory functions are ritualized, routinized, and relegated to secrecy. Natural reproductive functions are similarly distorted. Intercourse is taboo as a topic and scheduled as an act. Efforts are made to avoid pregnancy by the use of magical materials or by limiting intercourse to certain phases of the moon. Conception is actually very infrequent. When pregnant, women dress so as to hide their condition. Parturition takes place in secret, without friends or relatives to assist, and the majority of women do not nurse their infants.

Our review of the ritual life of the Nacirema has certainly shown them to be a magic-ridden people. It is hard to understand how they have managed to exist so long under the burdens which they have imposed upon themselves. But even such exotic customs as these take on real meaning when they are viewed with the insight provided by Malinowski when he wrote:

"Looking from far and above, from our high places of safety in the developed civilization, it is easy to see all the crudity and irrelevance of magic. But without its power and guidance early man could not have mastered his practical difficulties as he has done, nor could man have advanced to the higher stages of civilization."

part 7

Language

Being and Value in a Primitive Culture

Dorothy Lee

From *The Journal of Philosophy*, Vol. 46, No. 13, 1949, pp. 401–415. By permission of the author and the publisher.

Anthropologists have realized in recent years that people of other cultures than our own not only act differently, but that they have a different basis for their behavior. They act upon different premises; they perceive reality differently, and codify it differently. In this codification, language is largely instrumental. It incorporates the premises of the culture, and codifies reality in such a way that it presents it as absolute to the members of each culture. Other aspects of behavior also express, if not as clearly, the specific phrasing of reality which each culture makes for itself. Therefore, through an intensive analysis of language, ceremonial and everyday behavior, myths and magical formulas, it is possible to arrive at the philosophic basis of a culture, and to see to some extent how reality appears to its members.

I present in the following pages such an analysis: a study of being and value in the culture of the Trobriand Islanders of the Archipelago stretching between New Guinea and the Solomon Islands. This society has been described at length by Bronislaw Malinowski, whose works have furnished the data for this study.

The Trobrianders are concerned with being, and being alone. Change and becoming are foreign to their thinking. An object or event is grasped and evaluated in terms of itself alone, that is, irrespective of other beings. The Trobriander can describe being for the benefit of the ethnographer; otherwise, he usually refers to it by a word, one word only. All being, to be significant, must be Trobriand being, and therefore experienced at the appropriate time as a matter of course by the members of each Trobriand community; to describe it would be redundant. Being is never defined, in our sense of the word. Definition presents an object in terms of *what it is like* and *what it is unlike,* that is, in terms of its distinguishing characteristics. The Trobriander is interested only in *what it is.* And each event or being is grasped timelessly; in our terms, it contains its past, present, and future, but these distinctions are nonexistent for the Trobriander. There is, however, one sense in which being is not self-contained. To be, it must be part of an ordained pattern; this aspect will be elaborated below.

Being is discrete and self-contained; it has no attributes outside of itself. Its qualities are identical with it and without them it is not itself. It has no predicate; it is itself. To say a word representing an object or act is to imply the existence of this, and all the qualities it incorporates. If I were to go with a Trobriander to a garden where the *taytu,* a species of yam, had just been harvested, I would come back and tell you, "There are good *taytu* there; just the right degree of ripeness, large and perfectly shaped; not a blight to be seen, not one rotten spot; nicely rounded at the tips, with no spiky points; all first-run harvesting, no second gleanings." The Trobriander would come back and say *"Taytu";* and he would have said all that I did and more. Even the phrase "There are *taytu"* would represent a tautology, since existence is implied in being, is, in fact an ingredient of being to the Trobriander. And all the attributes, even if he could find words for them at hand in his own language, would have been tautological, since the concept of *taytu* contains them all. In fact, if one of these were absent, the object would not have been a *taytu.* Such a tuber, if it is not at the proper harvesting ripeness, is not a *taytu.* If it is unripe, it is a *bwanawa;* if overripe, spent, it is not a spent *taytu* but something else, a *yowana.* If it is blighted it is a *nukunokuna.* If it has a rotten patch, it is a *taboula;* if misshapen, it is an *usasu;* if perfect in shape but small, it is a *yagogu.* If the tuber, whatever its shape or condition, is a post-harvest gleaning, it is an *ulumadala.* When the spent tuber, the *yowana,* sends its shoots underground, as we would put it, it is not a *yowana* with shoots, but a *silisata.* When new tubers have formed on these shoots, it is not a *silisata* but a *gadena.* An object cannot change an attribute and retain its identity. Some range of growth or modification within being is probably allowed, otherwise speech would be impossible; but I doubt whether they are conscious of it. As soon as such change, if we may introduce one of our concepts here, is of-

ficially recognized, the object ceases to be itself.

As being is identical with the object, there is no word for *to be;* as being is changeless, there is no word meaning *to become.* Becoming involves temporality, but Trobriand being has no reference to time. With us, change in time is a value, and place in a developmental sequence is necessary for evaluation. We cannot respond with approval or disapproval, unless we know that a thing is getting bigger or better or surer. If I am told that Robert Smith is an instructor at $3000, I cannot respond to this adequately, unless I know that he is just out of graduate school, or that he used to be a professor at the age of forty, but now, at sixty, he has been demoted to this position. Our language is full of terms such as the one I have just used—demotion—giving us tools for the evaluation of being in terms of place in a climactic historical sequence. By dint of constant vigilance, we can refrain from using these terms; but we have no choice when it comes to placing events in time. Our language codifies reality in such a way as to predispose us to view events in terms of temporality. Even if I decide to use such expressions as "it be" or "it flow," I have achieved nothing, since you who hear me automatically make these acceptable to yourself by translating them into "it is" and "it flows," merely putting me down as uneducated. Whenever I make an assertion, I have to give it temporal limits, in reference to past, present, or future, or at any rate I have to imply temporality. Trobriand verbs are timeless, making no temporal distinctions. A Trobriander can, if he chooses, refer to an act as completed, but that, it seems to me, is an aspect of the act, not a temporal reference. History and mythical reality are not "the past" to the Trobriander. They are forever present, participating in all current being, giving meaning to all his activities and all existence. A Trobriander will speak of the garden which his mother's brother planted, or the one which the mythical Tudava planted, in exactly the same terms with which he will refer to the garden which he himself is planting now; and it will give him satisfaction to do so.

Being is apprehended as a whole, not in terms of attributes. This is something very difficult for members of our culture to achieve; we rarely value sheer being in itself, except perhaps when we are "blindly" in love. Even mothers are often incapable of valuing their children in this way, demanding instead attributes and achievements before they will respond with love. I watched a college student once in a predicament created by this inability to react to being itself. Faced with a vivid, gurgling infant in the presence of its mother, she felt it necessary to react but had no basis for doing so. She tried hard to discover attributes to guide her, asking, "Does she talk?" "Does she creep?" hoping for something on which to base approval; and, finally, having received a negative answer to all her questions, she remained dumb and immobilized. The Trobriander does not say, "how bright" or "how big"; his equivalent in this situation would have been "how baby."

Being is evaluated discretely, in terms of itself alone, not in comparison with others. This, again, is foreign to our thinking, except perhaps in the sphere of art. To return to Robert Smith, if you tell me that he is an instructor at $3000 a year, I can respond to this with approbation, commiseration, etc., only if I know what the rank and pay of other men instructors are apt to be. To evaluate, I have to compare this being with other beings of its kind. To be good, being has to be as good as, if not better than. For the Trobriander, being is good only as itself.

Now our own language makes it easy, though not imperative, to compare beings at every turn. It provides us with a large number of comparatives, through morphology and vocabulary. Our speech is studded with terms such as better, bigger, inferior, average, compared to, normal, equal, in relation to, etc., showing that we constantly are passing judgment according to a comparative standard. The Trobriander has no such means, unless we accept his rarely used words "it-sames" and "it-differents" as comparative. The magic formulas given by Malinowski are full of similes, as only in this way can they be made comprehensible to his readers. But in Trobri-

and, these are all metaphors. Where Malinowski's translation reads, for example, "thy shoots are as quick as the eyes of the black ant," the Trobriand text reads, "no thine eye, thine eye black-ant." When Malinowski says, "I am your senior," the Trobriand text reads, "old man I."

We can see this emphasis on *being* alone when we analyze the Trobriand sentence. Here we find that the words are presented discretely, without elements to show the relation of one word to the other. A verb contains its subject, a noun contains its "predicate" as well as its other attributes. The few words which Malinowski translated as adjectives are either nouns—a big-one, or verbs—it-goods. The language does not even express an object-to-object relationship, as ours does, for example, when it relates grammatical subject to the object which is acted upon. In English, we express this relationship through word order; when we say, for example, "Mary ate the pie," or, "John kicked Mary," we clearly distinguished the actor from the one acted upon, by order of precedence, and we can not avoid making the distinction. The Trobriander, on the other hand, merely expresses act and participants; *i-wo-ye tau* "it-beat-man" means either that the man is beating someone or that someone is beating the man. Such a phrase usually refers either to a known situation, which needs no elucidation, or is told within a context which makes its meaning clear. If, however, the Trobriander for some reason feels that he must specify, he can do so, but he does not do so as a matter of course, as we do, since his language does not predispose or constrain him to do so.

To be, an object must be true to itself, not in terms of its relationship with other beings. To be good, it must be the same always. Sameness is a value to the Trobrianders. Trobriand being never came into existence; it has always been, exactly as now, above ground in "historic" times, below ground in mythical times. At some time the ancestress of each group emerged from a specific hole, bringing with her all the customs, skills, and beliefs of that group, their patterns of behavior, the details of their magic, their pedigreed yams. This "past" is immanent in all Trobriand being. Instead of description in terms of attributes, the Trobriander gives an account of historical or mythical past, presenting essence. In all his undertakings, this "past" is present, giving to them validity and value. Wherever he goes, his surroundings have meaning for him; every waterhole, rock, or cleft is imbued with mythical significance. Myth and history, as intrinsic to being, enhance value. For example, the Trobrianders have certain important valuables which constitute the gifts in the *kula,* an endless circular series of ceremonial gift-givings which occupies, with the preparation involved, perhaps half the life of Trobriand men. These objects have value, but no "utility"; they are "ornaments" which can not be used to adorn the "owner"; and they can be possessed only a few months by each recipient. Giving-in-itself, that is, nonpurposive giving, is good; through participation in this gift-giving pattern the *kula* valuables are good. Each valuable is named and its personal history known. In this lies much of its value; giver and recipient, and the village of the "owner," get satisfaction out of the recounting of the specific *kula* acts of which the article was a part, going from named giver to named recipient. Chronology and historical sequence are irrelevant; the history is important not as development but as the ingredient of being.

The Trobriander has no word for history. When he wants to distinguish between different kinds of occasions, he will say, for example, "Molubabeba in-child-his," that is, "in the childhood of Molubabeba," not a previous phase of *this* time, but a different kind of time. For him, history is an unordered repository of anecdote; he is not interested in chronological sequence. For example, Malinowski recorded an account of a famine which was given with complete disregard to chronology; an effect which is achieved only deliberately by our sophisticated writers. If we rearrange the clusters of statements so that they represent for us a historical sequence, we have to give them in the following order; one, four, three, two, five.

For us, chronological sequence is of vital importance, largely because we are interested not so much in the event itself, but rather in its place within a *related* series of events; we look for its antecedents and its consequences. We are concerned with the causal or telic relationship between events or acts. To the Trobriander, events do not fall of themselves into a pattern of causal relationships, as they do for us. I am not here concerned with the question of whether causality is given, or is read into existence. Whichever may be the case, we in our culture automatically see and seek relationships, not essence, and express relationship mainly in terms of cause or purpose. The maddeningly persistent question of our young children is "why," because this is the question implicit in most of our ordinary statements and other behavior, to be answered either in causal or telic terms, since cause and purpose are equally dynamic for us, and are identified in our use of "why." (This does not mean that Trobriand parents are relieved from such questions; they are probably constantly asked "what." According to Margaret Mead this is what the Manus children are continually asking adults.) Esthetically, as well as practically, cause and purpose are both important to us; cause gives us a satisfying explanation and purpose ennobles or gives meaning to the act. We teach the importance of purposive action to infants, directly and indirectly by act and speech. We teach it in the schoolroom, in sports, in politics, in moral precept. The unreflective scientist takes causation for granted, the orthodox historian studies history to discover the causes for events. To the Trobriander, on the other hand, being or event remains discrete, sufficient unto itself, true and of value as itself, judged and motivated and understood in terms of itself alone. In the face of this apprehension of being, concepts such as causation and purpose appear irrelevant; I have introduced them here only because they are so basic to our thinking that we accept them as given in experience, and their presence is assumed by us in all cultures, as a matter of course. (This absence of causal concepts, as well as of a comparative standard, seemed at first so striking to me that I wrote a paper describing Trobriand thought in terms of what it was not, as non-causal and noncomparative. It now seems to me that I was viewing the Trobrianders then through the eyes of my own culture, relationally, seeing them according to what they were unlike, and so stressing the absence of concepts which have no relevance to their thought. . . . The paper in question is A Primitive System of Values. *Philosophy of Science,* Vol. 7, No. 3, 1940, pp. 355–378.) In the language of the Trobrianders, there are no terms such as because, so as to, cause, reason, effect, purpose, to this end, so that, why. This does not mean that the Trobrianders are incapable of explaining a sequence in terms of cause and effect, but rather that this relationship is of no significance. In the texts given by Malinowski *for (pela)* occurs occasionally, in such a context that it is possible to translate it as *because,* as Malinowski does, and it sounds natural that one should do so, and, once or twice, "what-thing-for" is used in such a position that we can take it to mean "for what purpose." It is significant that *pela* is verbal, meaning *to jump,* not a connecting link but a leap to another. I shall not go here into the discussion of the meaning of the doubtful *pela;* I do not think it is an expression of causality, but even if it is, it occurs extremely rarely and does not contradict the conclusion that, for the Trobriander, events do not automatically fall into the mold of causality or teleology. Malinowski's frequent "why" evoked from the Trobrianders either confused and self-contradictory answers, or the usual "It was ordained of old"—not an explanation but a description of value, tautological but necessary for the ignorant ethnographer.

We ask here, how is influence or motivation or effect phrased among the Trobrianders? How is magical action understood, for example? The answer is, it is understood in exactly these terms, as action, not cause. The magician does not *cause* certain things to be; he *does* them. As the gardener with his material implements burns the brush, breaks the clods, etc., so the garden magician with his various formulas "awakens the sprout,"

"drives up the shoots overground," "throws the headgear of the *taytu,*" "makes several branches," "pushes the *taytu* tubers into the soil," according to Trobriand account. This is not influence, nor the force of magic; rather it is "to magic." Malinowski, in presenting accounts of magic, uses purposive phraseology, since in this way only can his readers understand magic. But where he gives in translation, "The *okwala* rite is made so that *taytu* might really grow, so that it might ripen," the Trobriand has actually said: "okwala, it-grow truly, it-ripen"; just a number of events. It so happens, in the example, that the sequence in the account corresponds to the actual order of fact; but quite often there is not even such correspondence. And in the acts themselves there is often not even the sequence into which we could at least read causality. For example, when the Trobriander wants to fell a tree he first exorcizes the *tokway,* the tree-dwelling spirit, reciting a spell which gets the *tokway* down. After that he gives the *tokway* some food. If the food was offered first, on the ground, or at least promised, we could see this as a causal inducement. Actually, the *tokway* has no alternative and no freedom of choice at all; he is brought down by the spell. The offering of the food itself is merely part of the established procedure, and is not causally related to the exorcism.

It follows that the Trobriander performs acts because of the activity itself, not for its effects; that he values objects because they are good, not good for; in fact, objects and activities that are good for, are of no value to him. Take, for example, his yams and his yam gardening. To Malinowski, who spent many months with them, dependent upon them socially as well as materially, gardening meant yam gardening, and food meant yams. It was only after he had occupied himself with his Trobriander material for about fifteen years and written several books on the subject, that he realized that taro was an ancient and substantial item of food, much easier to grow than yams, less demanding of care and good soil, perhaps almost as important as yams from the point of view of sheer material nourishment. But taro is only good for; it is only good for food, or, less than that, for stopping hunger; and it is grown for such use. Therefore it was of no value or importance to the Trobriander, and escaped Malinowski's notice. Yams, on the other hand, incorporate the social good. They are good in themselves, and participate daily in good situations, as free, nonutile gifts.

A man gardens yams with the expenditure of much care and effort, with physical and magical skills, putting in long, hot hours of work. He gardens as many plots as he is capable of—not as many as his neighbors, or as many as he "needs." About half of these he sets aside as the *urigubu* plots. These he harvests with pride, exhibiting beautiful heaps of *taytu*. Then he sends this harvest, by festively arrayed youths and maidens, not to his yam house, but to the hamlet of his sister's husband. In this man's garden the *taytu* are heaped again, and it is this man now who exhibits them with pride as the gift. Finally, his yam house is put in order, and magic is performed in it. Ideally, the magic makes the *taytu* rot uneaten in the yam house; it fills the owners with nausea at the thought of eating the *taytu*; it gives them, instead, an urge to go to the bush and eat what grows there. This keeps the *taytu* free of purpose; ideally, they are not food. *Taytu* are constantly being given and received as gifts, in a system of free giving without what we call ulterior motives; not for altruism, not in barter or exchange for. Most of the gift *taytu* are usually eaten eventually, but only incidentally. In the *urigubu* gardens of the man who grew them, have remained all the tubers which are not *taytu*; the ones which are misshapen, or unduly small or blighted in some way. These go to the gardener's not-good yam house. They are merely to be eaten, and we do not hear of them again. The *taytu*, however, have a very important place in the everyday, as well as the ceremonial, life of the people. *Taytu* are not, like the taro, good for. *Taytu* have value, not use; value lies in being, not in relationship.

The pariahs among the Trobrianders are the people who barter. There is one such

unfortunate district of highly skilled manufacturers who have no adequate soil for the growing of *taytu*. They barter manufactured articles, spending their time in this not-good occupation, but more than that, they are lacking in the growing of *taytu* and in pure gift-giving, that is, in good. They are greatly despised by the agricultural villages. The coastal villages also cannot grow many yams, and acquire more through what seems to us an exchange of fish for yams. However, this has been patterned along gift-giving lines, and escapes the purposiveness of barter. A man of a specific interior village will have a life-long gift-partner in a fishing village. Whenever he wants to, he arrives at the fishing village with some baskets of yams, and leaves them as a gift at a specific spot. This precipitates a pattern of events which ends in his returning home with a gift of fish. He cannot go to *any* village with his *taytu*, or to *any* man within this village; the gift to anyone else would have no meaning, neither would it induce anyone else to go fishing. His *taytu* were not pay or inducement, but the opening step in a specific patterned procedure involving a specific individual.

Here another aspect of Trobriand being is involved. I have spoken of being as discrete, and apprehended as itself alone. I must now qualify this statement. Being has no independent existence. It is itself only as part of an established pattern. To members of our culture, being is defined by its attributes, relationships, and functions; temporally in terms of becoming, spatially in terms of its relationships. For the Trobrianders, being is defined by a fixed place in an established pattern. It is perhaps too much to ask my readers to believe that one element in a pattern can be and is perceived only in terms of its specific position within the pattern itself, and without reference to any other element; that in fact a pattern is conceived as something other than a system of relationships. Nevertheless, I believe such to be the case among the Trobrianders. Being is not seen in terms of its relationships to a plurality of elements in the pattern, but rather as a fixed point in a single, changeless whole.

Only in this place can being be itself; only as it fills its place is it desired or valued. Being is good and true in terms of pattern. Gift-giving, for example, is good only within a patterned Trobriand situation. It is neither virtuous nor altruistic; both these terms involve meaningless relational concepts. In Trobriand gift-giving, the need of the recipient, or the effect upon him, is not involved. I doubt whether the Trobrianders could be persuaded to send yams to the starving Bikinians; and even if they did send yams, their act would not have value. The harvest gift to the sister's husband is not an act of altruism. The giver is concerned only with fulfilling his role, his place in a specific Trobriand pattern. If he gave taro to his sister's husband, the gift would not have been good; if he gave the yams to his own brother, his act would not have been good. What is good in this situation is the *urigubu*. To be good, this gift must be *urigubu;* to be true, that is, to be *urigubu,* it must be (*a*) a gift of *taytu;* (*b*) from man to sister's husband; (*c*) at harvest time. Both the good and the true are defined by place in pattern. *Taytu* figure as gifts upon different occasions, between different individuals. In each case the gift is named and valued differently. When *taytu* are given to a friend at the launching of a canoe, they follow a different procedure, and are *kabigodoya;* when they are a harvest gift to a specialist, they are a *karibudaboda.* *Taytu,* then, are *urigubu, kabigodoya, karibudaboda,* according to their place in different patterns; and each gift derives different being, and different value in accordance to the pattern in which it has place. I should explain here that in each case the *taytu* remain *taytu* though they participate in different situations; it is the gift which is different according to its place in a different pattern.

This conception of being and value gave the early pearl traders much trouble. They found out soon that money or the things they offered were no inducement to work. They noticed, however, that the Trobrianders set great store by certain large blades made of stone. At first, they had these imitated carelessly, but found that the natives did not want them; then they had them made of slate in Europe, but these also were rejected by the Trobrianders. Finally they had the native stone quarried and sent to Parisian craftsmen; but these beautiful blades also were rejected. These things, of course, could not be valued, since they were not truly Trobriand, had not been made "as ordained of old"; but more than that, they could not be an inducement, and could have no meaning, since they were external to the pattern. When the Trobrianders were finally persuaded to dive for pay, it was only the natives of those villages which had always dived for oysters who were persuaded; those of the other coastal villages, where diving had not been ordained of old, would not dive. And the natives of the appropriate villages did so grudgingly. To the disgust of the pearl traders, they would leave their diving and go off fishing for the day, as soon as a number of baskets of yams made their appearance on the beach, even though the traders offered them twenty times as many yams. The natives would work for extraneous inducement as long as there was no good undertaking to indulge in; but when their gift-partners arrived with yams, they initiated a patterned situation which had meaning for the natives.

You will say, "But is not this an inducement or cause?" I think it is not. By themselves, the few baskets of yams on the beach are just a few baskets of yams. Offered by the trader they would have had no meaning. Brought from a different Trobriand village, they would have effected nothing; and when they come from the appropriate village, it is only the partners of the specific givers who go off fishing as a matter of course. Given from anyone to anyone, the *taytu* are of no value. I think the yams are not an inducement to action. The giving of them, however, starts a pattern; once the gift has taken place, the pattern becomes evident and the recipient is presented with a role which holds value for him; to get satisfaction from it, to be a good Trobriander, he must fill it. By us, the two acts, the receiving of the yams and the procuring of the fish, are seen in relationship; and this relationship is seen as dynamic; one act influences the other, or causes the other.

To the Trobriander, what is dynamic is the validity and value derived from the pattern. The coastal villager goes fishing because (this is my own word) he gets satisfaction from fulfilling his role in the pattern.

The appearance of the baskets of yams is not a cause, but it does precipitate a pattern. The Trobrianders have their own equivalent for cause, in terms of their concept of pattern. For this they use the term *u'ula,* a word very commonly used, for what we would call a variety of meanings. It stands for the trunk of a tree below the branches, for the base of a pole, or the bottom of a structure; it means the organizer of an expedition or the initiator of any undertaking; it refers to the first part of a magical formula. The *u'ula* is sometimes contemporaneous with the rest of the objector pattern, sometimes not. To the Trobriander, I think, it indicates place, not temporality. Realized or not, the pattern is always there; the pole has a bottom, the spell has a beginning; and this pattern is known as a whole, not as a temporal process. Once made evident through the *u'ula,* the total must be realized. To this extent, and in our terms only, can we understand *u'ula* to be the equivalent of *cause;* the *u'ula* is dynamic but only in reference to the pattern, not toward the next event. The *u'ula* precipitates the next event but only incidentally, because it precipitates the patterned procedure, through its place in the pattern; it so happens that the next event is a part of this pattern.

This is how we can understand the "actual" and mythical behavior of the Trobrianders. For example, when an *uvalaku,* a *kula* expedition of a special kind, has been organized to sail to distant tribes where the Trobrianders will receive as gifts certain necklaces from specific partners, the chief gives a *kayguya'u,* a great ceremonial distribution of food. This is an act very serious in its implications, and performed after much consultation and deliberation; because, once this *kayguya'u* is given, the expedition must be carried out to its end, however unfavorable the winds, or the conditions within the village. Once the pattern has been initiated, has been given evidence, the whole must be realized, or, to put it differently, the whole is inevitably there; I am floundering here because my language cannot reproduce the Trobriand identity of the concepts underlying *has been, must be,* and *is.* Knowing the pattern, the Trobriander knows how to act to the end of the pattern. Conversely, the *kayguya'u* is an *u'ula,* has meaning, and can even be said to be itself, only by virtue of its place in the *uvalaku* pattern. Outside of it, it is just another food-distribution, initiating nothing, unless it is something else as part of another pattern.

For us, not only purpose, but previous action, is used as a basis or guide for determining what to do next. For the Trobriander, who does not see acts in relation, pattern is the guide; though actually it does not "lead" him to a decision, since his act is predetermined by the pattern. There is a sequence in one of the myths which exemplifies this. Toweyre kills his brother who has been acting in an un-Trobriand fashion, working for individual ends. This act of Toweyre is not part of a Trobriand pattern; however, this does not mean that he now has to come to an independent decision on how to act on the basis of murdering his brother. A brother's death itself initiates a pattern. As the next of kin (in Trobriand society, a man's children and his father are not his kin), Toweyre goes back to the village and instructs his dead brother's children to prepare the body for the funeral, and he himself arranges for the appropriate food distribution, the *sagali.*

Within the pattern the Trobriander feels safe and acts with assurance. Away from home, he likes to reproduce known previous order, even physically. When a food distribution, a *sagali,* is given to which many different hamlets from a distance are invited, the geographic location of these hamlets is reproduced on the beach. (I am afraid it is impossible for me to show conclusively that this is not an interest in relative position.) Again, in one of the myths is given a description of a shipwreck, a dreadful event since it plunges the sailors into witch-infested waters. The crew of the large canoe drift ashore clinging to the outrigger, onto which they have jumped from their places in the canoe. As they reach shore, they are in great danger from flying witches; in the face of it, they walk in exactly the order in which they have drifted ashore; when they sit waiting for night to come and hide them from the witches, they maintain this order; in this order they finally march to their village where they are medicated magically to free them from danger. Now they are safe again, and the order need not be maintained. Again, it is impossible for us not to see here the order of lineal relationship; but I do not think that it appears as relational to the Trobrianders.

For members of our culture, value lies ideally in change, in moving away from the established pattern; and safety is ensured through scientific prediction, not exact experience. We hopefully expect next year to be better, brighter, different; if, as we hope, it brings change, we can safely meet it with the use of logic and science. Our advertisers thrive on this value of the different, the not-experienced; our industries have long depended on our love for new models. The Trobriander, on the contrary, expects and wants next year to be the same as this year and as the year before his culture emerged from underground. Advertising is nonsense for the Trobriander, because the new is not good and the old is known and valued, so to talk about it persuasively is nonsense. In repetition of the experienced, in sameness, he finds, not boredom, but satisfaction as well as safety. Members of our culture go into unchartered seas fearlessly, depending on compass and the science of navigation; they explore new lands eagerly. The Trobrianders go into *known* waters; they recount the *kula* myths, and then go from known landmark to known landmark, myth-imbued and full of history; they do not even set their course by the stars or the sun. They repeat old journeyings, their own or those of mythical or historical *kula* figures.

Something must be said here about individual and pattern; how does an individual Trobriander enter a pattern? There are various ways in which he does so and we in our culture would distinguish them according to the principle of whether he enters automatically, or whether he does so by act of will. By virtue of being born, an individual enters certain patterns of behavior in terms of certain people, those, for example, who are his relatives by blood or affinity. Here he has no choice; the pattern happens to him through the accident of his birth. Again, when his sister marries, or his wife dies, or his *kula* partner arrives, this precipitates a pattern of activities involving his participation, where he has no choice, unless, of course, he is ready to be un-Trobriand. There are certain patterns, however, where he does have freedom of choice; here, whether the pattern is to be precipitated or not, devolves on an act of will of his own. This is the only point where he does have freedom; once he initiates the pattern, he must follow an established procedure. However, I think the concept of freedom of choice is incommensurate with Trobriand value or behavior, and, in fact, a false measure. For us, to act as we want to act necessarily involves freedom of choice, but for the Trobriander the concept is meaningless. I think the Trobriander has no more and no less freedom when he initiates than when he continues an ordained pattern. In each case, he acts as he wants to, because the act, and the pattern which validates it, holds satisfaction for him; he acts in this way because he is Trobriand, and the pattern is Trobriand. To be Trobriand is to be good. "Act of will" and "freedom of choice" are irrelevant as principles of classification or evaluation.

Then comes the question of whether all beings are part of a pattern, and its corollary: is all being good? Is any being good apart from pattern? I do not think that all being is good; rather, that the good, or value, is found in being, but not in all being. There is much giving going on daily, but it is not good giving; it may be merely desultory giving from husband to wife or a man to his brother—gift situations which are not part of any gift pattern. Much of the unpatterned everyday behavior is not good; eating is not good, nor is love-magic, or love-making. On the other hand, some being is good apart from the pattern in which it participates. Such are the *vaygu'a* with which the pearl traders failed so miserably; such also is the *taytu.* In each case, the history of these is a pattern in itself. The *taytu,* for example, is planted and grown according to an ordained pattern. Each part of the procedure is inaugurated by a garden magician, and no member of the gardening group can act independently, can choose to leave his scrub not burned or have it burned at a different time, or set fire to it himself rather than wait for the magician to do the initial firing. At one time the resident magistrate ignorantly set fire to the scrub himself and thus initiated a year of drought. On the other hand, taro is not good; but none of the activities concerned with it are patterned. The gardener in this case proceeds as he likes, and incorporates whatever magic he chooses into the process. Ultimately, then, it is pattern that bestows value; but good being may incorporate its own pattern. Whether this is a difference between good being (*taytu* or *kula* givings) and not-good being (taro and gifts to one's brother) or whether it is rather a difference between being and mere existence, I am not qualified to say.

Is the Trobriander truly blind to relationship? Does he never respond to external motivation? The gardening of the Trobriander certainly can be seen as work toward the end of growing yams. Obviously—to us— when a man gives the harvest gift, this act brings giver and receiver into relation; how can the Trobriander fail to see this relation? We would say that it is impossible to have pattern without having elements in relation to one another. These objections are inherent to our own codification of reality. We make them because it is impossible for members of our culture to apprehend being without relationships. We can see motivation only as coming from outside, in relationship, and would therefore say that where we have acts there must be motivation, and where there is motivation relationships must be recognized. Again, we are accustomed to equate change with the dynamic, sameness with the static; and to put these pairs in opposition. So it is hard for us to see that sameness itself can be dynamic, as it is for the Trobriander, who does not need "motivation" for his acts, since their very sameness holds value, so that they "motivate" themselves.

These objections raise a further, and a more basic, question: is the Trobriander blind to relationships, or are there no relationships? Do we who base our behavior on relationships read these relationships into reality, or are they given? Which codification is true to reality? I would say that the two are not mutually exclusive. They represent different facets of reality and different meaningful phrasings for each culture. The fact that each culture has chosen to base itself on only one aspect does not mean that the other is false. Our peculiar codification makes us blind to other aspects of reality, or makes these meaningless when presented. But one codification does not exhaust reality; neither, if it were false, would a society, I believe, be able to survive with it at its base. The Trobrianders, according to our view of life, should be bored automatons. Actually they act as they want to act, poised and sure, in activities which hold meaning and satisfaction. Whether they are given or read into reality by us, temporality, causation, teleology, and relationship in general have neither meaning nor relevance for Trobriand behavior; but Trobriand behavior is nevertheless good because it is concerned with being; and being, in its appropriate pattern, incorporates value and truth.

The Aztec Writing System

Charles E. Dibble

This hitherto unpublished paper is used by permission of the author. Illustrations are by David E. Reiser.

The Aztecs were highly skilled in the art of writing. As in many cultures, literacy was not the province of all but rather of a select few. An Aztec native trained and skilled in the art of recording the thoughts and events of the Aztecs was known as a *Tlacuilo.*

The art was often transmitted from father to son, the wisdom and skill of these select families being highly respected and appraised by the rulers. The reading of the codices was taught in the colleges where the priests initiated the novice in the ways of interpreting and deciphering the religious writings.

The materials utilized to provide a writing surface varied—the most common materials being deerskin, fiber paper and woven cotton cloth. A thin layer of chalk was often spread on the material to assure a smoother and whiter writing surface. The colors most commonly employed were shades of white, black, blue, red, green, yellow, and brown. The colors were essentially plant and mineral pigments, luster and brilliance being supplied with oils, resins, and gums. Sometimes the figures were painted on both sides of a large sheet. Sometimes the codex formed a roll; more often the codex was in the form of a strip about twelve inches wide and several feet long, which strip was folded as a scenic post card.

The order and manner of reading varied from codex to codex. Some were read from bottom to top, others from right to left or left to right and still others from top to buttom. Once the manner of reading is established it follows through consistently on the succeeding pages.

The content of codices was as varied as the topics they desired to record. The documents are generally referred to as

mythological, historical, genealogical, geographical, religious, tribute lists, maps, and almanacs.

Various stages in the development of writing were utilized side side in the Aztec documents.

Many of the hieroglyphic recordings were pictographic, *i.e.,* the picture tells the story. Thus a temple in flames tells us of the destruction of a sanctuary by fire. Other portions of the same codices reveal recordings which are ideographic, *i.e.,* the important thing is the idea, abstract or concrete, which the picture calls forth rather than the picture itself. Two persons from different tribes in battle dress and poised for conflict express the idea of two tribes at war rather than two persons.

Cholula (Chololan) was an aboriginal religious center near present-day Puebla, Mexico. The name means "Place of the Flight," because the city was on the road transversed by the mythological Quetzalcoatl in his flight to the East. *Choloa* is the Aztec verb for flee, run or jump. But, the deer is an animal which flees, runs and jumps. Thus the Aztec writers indicated the city of Cholula ideographically

 by painting the two front feet of the deer. Also, much of the Aztec writing was syllabic or alphabetic, *i.e.,* the picture told no story; called forth no idea, but indicated a syllable or a single sound. The Aztec flag (*pantli*) could be used, not to recall a flag but the syllable "pan." The word for teeth was *tlantli;* so teeth could be pictured to indicate the syllable "tlan." Water (*atl*) was frequently utilized by the *Tlacuilo* when he desired to express the sound "a."

Thus the town "Apan" was indicated by combining water (*atl*) and flag (*pantli*).

"Atlan" was expressed by representing water (*atl*) and teeth (*tlantli*).

The Aztec numbering system was vigesimal. In our decimal system $10 \times 1 = 10$; $10 \times 10 = 100$; $10 \times 100 = 1,000$; $10 \times 1000 = 10,000$; etc. In the vigesimal system progression is by 20s: $20 \times 1 = 20$; $20 \times 20 = 400$; $20 \times 400 = 8,000$; $20 \times 8000 = 160,000$, etc.

The Aztecs expressed numbers up to nineteen with dots. 1 was one dot⊙; 3 was three dots ⊙⊙⊙; 6 was six dots ⊙⊙⊙⊙⊙; 19 was nineteen dots ⊙⊙⊙⊙⊙⊙⊙⊙⊙⊙⊙⊙⊙⊙⊙⊙⊙⊙⊙; Twenty was expressed

with a flag

Forty was expressed with two flags $(2 \times 20 = 40)$.

Three hundred and eighty was indicated with nineteen flags $(19 \times 20 = 380)$.

The sign for 400 resembled a pine tree.

 Eight hundred would be indicated with two pine trees $(2 \times 400 = 800)$,

The next unit, 8,000, was shown by a pouch for holding copal.

By combining these signs any number could be recorded; 8,859 would require one copal pouch (8,000),
two pine trees
$(2 \times 400 = 800)$.

two flags $(2 \times 20 = 40)$,

⊙⊙⊙⊙
⊙⊙⊙⊙⊙
⊙⊙⊙⊙⊙
⊙⊙⊙⊙⊙   and nineteen dots.

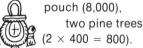

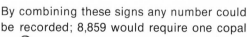

Important in Aztec hieroglyphic interpretation is their calendar system, because, without an accurate chronology, the historic material is rendered confused and almost valueless. They named their years after four objects, which also served as names of days. The first year was Rabbit (*Tochtli*);

the second year was Cane (*Acatl*);

the third was Flint Knife (*Tecpatl*);

and the fourth year was House (*Calli*). The four always occurred in this order, and the sequence was never broken. However, to further differentiate the years, numerical coefficients from 1 to 13 were attached to the four "year bearers." Once the sequence of 1 to 13 was attached to the sequence of four the combination was never interrupted. By mathematical calcula-

tion it is apparent that the same year sign will have the same numerical coefficient in 4 × 13 = 52 years.

This period of 52 years occasioned by the reoccurrence of the same year sign with the same numerical coefficient constituted the Aztec cycle. The completion of each cycle was the cause for festivity, celebration and the creation of a new sacred fire.

In the writing and interpreting of codices, certain conventionalized representations occurred with such frequency that a listing of them facilitates immeasurably the process of decipherment:

Women are recognized by posture,

hair dress,

 and a garment known as *huipil*.

Man is distinguished by posture,

hair dress,

and the breech cloth (*maxtli*).

A mummy bundle seated on a mat-covered throne means the death of a ruler.

Old age was shown by wrinkles on the face.

A living person seated on the same mat-covered throne tells us who has been the successor.

A baby in a cradle-basket expresses birth.

Warfare is expressed by a shield and flag (symbols of war),

Marriage is expressed by the husband facing the wife and the children of the couple appear below them.

or by means of two warriors in combat,

People were named after animals, birds, plants, and natural phenomena.

The name glyph was attached to the nape of the neck.

or by one warrior holding a prisoner by the hair of the head.

Migration, or movement of a person, is told by footprints, the direction of the footprints indicating the direction of travel.

A series of hieroglyphs can, of course, be combined to frame a full sentence. For example,

Often, when the individual's name was of secondary importance and his tribal affinity was of paramount concern, the tribal hieroglyph was attached to the neck.

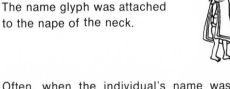

A servant is pictured speaking with his emperor, Maxtla. The hieroglyphs in their order are: deer's feet (the deer being an animal which flees, his feet are used to express the verb "to flee"—*choloa*—see hieroglyph for *choloa* on page 300; Tlacateotzin (person); Texcoco (city); Nezahualcoyotl (person); canoe. The series is to be deciphered as: "Tlacateotzin fled, or is fleeing, with Nezahualcoyotl to or toward Texcoco in a canoe."

A second combination gives a more complex thought.

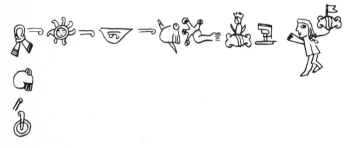

The historian, Ixtilxochitl, explains its meaning:

"The tyrant has ordered the taking of Chimalpopoca's life and the life of Tlacateotzin of Tlatelolco, that there should be neither king nor ruler of the Mexican and Aculhua nations, and that all should be subject to the domination of the court of the Tepaneca Monarch."

Deciphering the hieroglyphs of the series in their order, we conclude definitely that they give the content of the quotation. In order they are: skull (take the life of—an ideographic expression of death); Maxtla (name hieroglyph of the tyrant); Tlacateotzin (name hieroglyph of person); Tlatelolco (name hieroglyph of the city); skull with arrow (there should be neither king nor ruler); Aculhua (name hieroglyph of tribe or nation); house (be under the domain of the court of the monarch); and the last hieroglyph represents a Tepaneca warrior, indicating rule and domination.

By Their Speech Shall Ye Know Them

Clyde Kluckhohn
and
Dorothea Leighton

From the *Tongue of the People.* In *The Navaho,* Harvard University Press, 1948, pp. 197–208. Copyright 1946 by the President and Fellows of Harvard College. By permission of the author, the publisher, and the copyright holders.

Any language is more than an instrument for the conveying of ideas, more even than an instrument for working upon the feelings of others and for self-expression. Every language is also a means of categorizing experience. What people think and feel, and how they report what they think and feel, is determined, to be sure, by their individual physiological state, by their personal history, and by what actually happens in the outside world. But it is also determined by a factor which is often overlooked; namely, the pattern of linguistic habits which people have acquired as members of a particular society. The events of the "real" world are never felt or reported as a machine would do it. There is a selection process and an interpretation in the very act of response. Some features of the external situation are highlighted; others are ignored or not fully discriminated.

Every people has its own characteristic classes in which individuals pigeonhole their experiences. These classes are established primarily by the language through the types of objects, processes, or qualities which receive special emphasis in the vocabulary and equally, though more subtly, through the types of differentiation or activity which are distinguished in grammatical forms. The language says, as it were, "Notice this," "Always consider this separate from that," "Such and such things belong together." Since persons are trained from infancy to respond in these ways they take such discriminations for granted, as part of the inescapable stuff of life. But when we see two people with different social traditions respond in different ways to what appear to the outsider to be identical stimulus-situations, we realize that experience is much less a "given," an absolute, than we thought. Every language has an effect upon what the people who use it see, what they feel, how they think, what they can talk about.

As pointed out in the section on grammar, [not given here] the language of The People delights in sharply defined categories. It likes, so to speak, to file things away in neat little packages. It favors always the concrete and particular, with little scope for abstractions. It directs attention to some features of every situation, such as the minute distinctions as to direction and type of activity. It ignores others to which English gives a place. Navaho focuses interest upon doing—upon verbs as opposed to nouns or adjectives.

Striking examples of the categories which mark the Navaho language are the variations in many of its verb stems according to the types of their subjects or objects. As has been illustrated above, the verb stem used often depends upon whether its subject (or object) is in the long-object class (such as a pencil, a stick, or a pipe), the granular-mass class (such as sugar and salt), the things-bundled-up class (such as hay and bundles of clothing), the animate-object class, and many others.

It must not be thought that such classification is a conscious process every time a Navaho opens his mouth to speak. It would, of course, paralyze speech if one had to think, when about to say a verb, "Now I must remember to specify whether the object is definite or indefinite; whether it is something round, long, fluid, or something else." Fortunately this is no more necessary in Navaho than in English. The Navaho child simply learns that if he is talking about dropping baseballs or eggs or stones he uses a word different from the word he would use if he spoke of dropping a knife or a pencil or a stick, just as the English-speaking child learns to use different words (herd, flock, crowd) in mentioning a group of cows, sheep, or people.

The important point is that striking divergences in manner of thinking are crystalized in and perpetuated by the forms of Navaho grammar. Take the example of a commonplace physical event: rain. Whites can and do report their perception of this event in a variety of ways: "It has started to rain," "It is raining," "It has stopped raining." The People can, of course, convey these same ideas—but they cannot convey them without finer specifications. To give only a few instances of the sorts of discrimination the Navaho must make before he reports his expe-

rience: he uses one verb form if he himself is aware of the actual inception of the rain storm, another if he has reason to believe that rain has been falling for some time in his locality before the occurrence struck his attention. One form must be employed if rain is general round about within the range of vision; another if, though it is raining round about, the storm is plainly on the move. Similarly, the Navaho must invariably distinguish between the ceasing of rainfall (generally) and the stopping of rain in a particular vicinity because the rain clouds have been driven off by wind. The People take the consistent noticing and reporting of such differences (which are usually irrelevant from the white point of view) as much for granted as the rising of the sun.

Navaho is an excessively literal language, little given to abstractions and to the fluidity of meaning that is so characteristic of English. The inner classification gives a concreteness, a specificity, to all expression. Most things can be expressed in Navaho with great exactness by manipulating the wide choice of stems in accord with the multitudinous alternatives offered by fusing prefixes and other separable elements in an almost unlimited number of ways. Indeed Navaho is almost overneat, overprecise. There is very little "give" in the language. It rather reminds one of a Bach fugue, in which everything is ordered in scrupulous symmetry.

The general nature of the difference between Navaho thought and English thought —both as manifested in the language and also as forced by the very nature of the linguistic forms into such patterns—is that Navaho thought is prevailingly so much more specific, so much more concrete. The ideas expressed by the English verb "to go" provide a nice example. To Germans the English language seems a little sloppy because the same word is used regardless of whether the one who goes walks or is transported by a train or other agency, whereas in German these two types of motion are always sharply distinguished in the two verbs *gehen* and *fahren*. But Navaho does much more along this line. For example, when one is talking about travel by horse, the speed of the animal may be expressed by the verb form chosen. The following all mean "I went by horseback."

łį́į́ shił níyá,	(at a walk or at unspecified speed).
łį́į́ shił yíldloozh,	(at a trot).
łį́į́ shił neeltą́ą́,	(at a gallop).
łį́į́ shił yílghod,	(at a run).

When a Navaho says that he went somewhere he never fails to specify whether it was afoot, astride, by wagon, auto, train, or airplane. This is done partly by using different verb stems which indicate whether the traveler moved under his own steam or was transported, partly by naming the actual means. Thus, "he went to town" would become:

kintahgóó 'ííyá,	He went to town afoot or in a nonspecific way.
kintahgóó bił 'i'ííbą́ą́z,	He went to town by wagon.
kintahgóó bił 'o'oot'a',	He went to town by airplane.
kintahgóó bił'i'íí'ééł,	He went to town by boat.
kintahgóó bił'o'ooldloozh,	He went to town by horseback at a trot.
kintahgóó bił'o'ooldghod,	He went to town by horseback at a run (or perhaps by car or train).
kintahgóó bił'i'nooltą́ą́,	He went to town by horseback at a gallop.

Moreover, the Navaho language insists upon another type of splitting up of the generic idea of "going" to which German is as indifferent as English. The Navaho always differentiates between starting to go, going along, arriving at, returning from a point, etc., etc. For instance, he makes a choice between:

kintahgi níyá,	He arrived at town.
kintahgóó 'ííyá,	He went to town and is still there.
kintahgóó naayá,	He went to town but is now back where he started.

Let us take a few more examples. The Navaho interpreter, even though his behavior or side comments may make it perfectly apparent that he feels there is a difference, will translate both *háájíísh 'ííyá* and *háágósh 'ííyá* as "where did he go." If you say to him, "The Navaho sounds different in the two cases and there must be some difference in English meaning," the interpreter is likely to reply, "Yes, there is a difference all right, but you just can't express it in English." Now this is not literally true. Almost anything which can be said in Navaho can be said in English and vice versa, though a translation which gets everything in may take the form of a long paraphrase which sounds strained and artificial in the second language. In the case of the examples given above, the nearest equivalents are probably: "in what direction did he leave" and "for what destination did he leave."

In English one might ask, "Where did he go" and the usual answer would be something like, "He went to Gallup." But in Navaho one would have to select one of eight or ten possible forms which, if rendered exactly into English, would come out something like this: "He started off for Gallup," "He left to go as far as Gallup," "He left by way of Gallup," "He left, being bound for Gallup (for a brief visit)," "He left, being bound for Gallup (for an extended stay)," etc.

The People are likewise particular about other differentiations, similar to some of those discussed earlier in this chapter:

kin góne yah 'iikai,	We went into the house (in a group).
kin gone' yah ahiikai,	We went into the house (one after another).
or:	
chizh kin góne yah'íínil,	I carried the wood into the house (in one trip).
chizh kin góne yah 'akénil,	I carried the wood into the house (in several trips).

It is not, of course, that these distinctions *cannot* be made in English but that they *are not* made consistently. They seem of importance to English-speakers only under special circumstances, whereas constant precision is a regular feature of Navaho thought and expression about movement.

The nature of their language forces The People to notice and to report many other distinctions in physical events which the nature of the English language allows speakers to neglect in most cases, even though their senses are just as able as those of the Navaho to register the smaller details of what goes on in the external world. For example, suppose a Navaho range rider and a white supervisor see that the wire fence surrounding a demonstration area is broken. The supervisor will probably write in his notebook only: "The fence is broken." But if the range rider reports the occurrence to his friends he must say either *béésh 'alc'ast'i* or *béésh' ald'aat'i;* the first would specify that the damage has been caused by some person, the second that the agency was nonhuman. Further, he must choose between one of these statements and an alternative pair—the verb form selected depending on whether the fence was of one or several strands of wire.

Two languages may classify items of experience differently. The class corresponding to one word and one thought in Language A may be regarded by Language B as two or more classes corresponding to two or more words and thoughts. For instance, where in English one word "rough" (more pedantically, "rough-surfaced") may equally well be used to describe a road, a rock, and the business surface of a file, Navaho finds a need for three different words which may not be used interchangeably (see Figure 1). While the general tendency is for Navaho to make finer and more concrete distinctions, this is not invariably the case. The same stem is used for "rip," "light beam," and "echo," ideas which seem diverse to white people. One word is used to designate a medicine bundle with all its contents, the skin quiver in which the contents are wrapped, the contents as a whole, and some of the distinct items of the contents. Sometimes the point is not that the images of Navahos are less fluid and more delimited but rather just that the external world is dissected along different lines. For example, *digóón* may be used to describe both a pimply face and a nodule-covered rock. In English a complexion might be termed "rough" or "coarse" but a rock would never, except facetiously, be described as "pimply." Navaho differentiates two types of "rough rock"—the kind which is rough in the manner in which a file is rough, and the kind which is nodule-encrusted. In these cases (see Figure 2) the difference between the Navaho and the English ways of seeing the world cannot be disposed of merely by saying that Navaho is more precise. The variation rests in the features which the two languages see as essential. Cases can even be given where Navaho is notably less precise: Navaho gets along with a single word for flint, metal, knife, and certain other objects of metal (see Figure 3). This, to be sure, is due to the historical accident that, after European contact, metal in general and knives in particular largely took the place of flint. But in the last analysis most linguistic differentiations, like other sorts of cultural selectivity, rest upon the historical experience of the people.

How the Navaho and English languages dissect nature differently perhaps comes out most clearly when we contrast verbal statements. Take a simple event such as a person dropping something. The different "isolates of meaning" (thoughts) used in reporting this identical experience will be quite different in Navaho and in English (see Figure 4). The

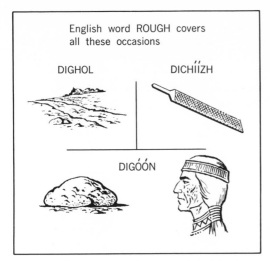

Fig. 1 *In this case, Navaho distinguishes more kinds of roughness than does English.*

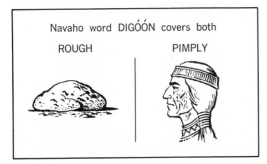

Fig. 2 *Here, English will generally use two different words rather than the same one for both conditions.*

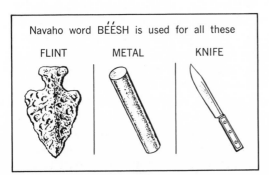

Fig. 3 *These are all one sort in the Navaho view— mostly because metals and knives came to them at the same time to take the place of flint.*

ENGLISH specifies
1. Subject: *I*
2. Type of action: *drop*
3. Time of action: while speaking or just before

NAVAHO specifies
1. Subject: *sh*
2. Direction of action: downward— *Naa*
3. Definite or indefinite object: (verb form)
4. Type of object: (verb stem) here a bulky, roundish, hard object—*Naa*
5. Amount of control of subject over process:

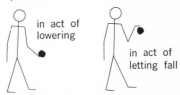

in act of lowering

in act of letting fall

6. From area of the hand: *-lak'ee*

Naash'aah lak'ee (I am in the act of lowering the definite, bulky roundish, hard object from my hand.)

Naashne' lak'ee (I am in the act of letting the definite, bulky, roundish, hard object fall from my hand.)

Fig. 4 *"I drop it."*

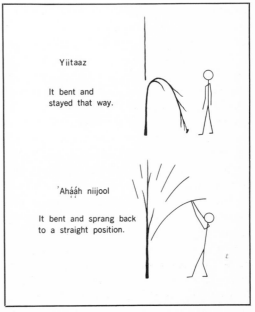

Yiitaaz

It bent and stayed that way.

'Aháah niijool

It bent and sprang back to a straight position.

Fig. 5 *"It bent."*

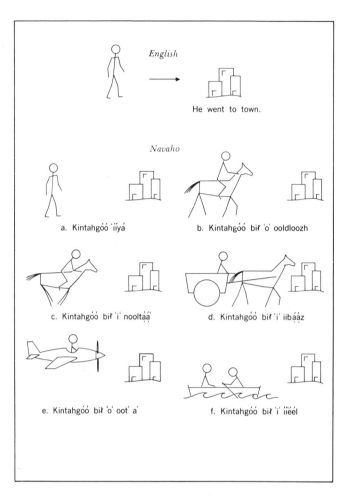

Fig. 6   "He went to town."
The verb here implies means of locomotion *because, for example, b. and c. would be used mostly for a horse, d. for something that rolls, e. for something that flies. In b. and c.,* speed of locomotion *is also indicated.*

only two elements which are the same are "I" and "sh," both of which specify who does the dropping. A single image "drop" in English requires two complementary images (*naa* and *'aah*) in Navaho. English stops with what from the Navaho point of view is a very vague statement—"I drop it." The Navaho must specify four particulars which the English leaves either unsettled or to inference from context:

1. The form must make clear whether "it" is definite or just "something."

2. The verb stem used will vary depending upon whether the object is round, or long, or fluid, or animate, etc., etc.

3. Whether the act is in progress, or just about to start, or just about to stop or habitually carried on or repeatedly carried on must be rigorously specified. In English, "I drop it" can mean once or can mean that it is customarily done (e.g., in describing the process of getting water from my well by a bucket). All the other possibilities are also left by English to the imagination.

4. The extent to which the agent controls the fall must be indicated: *naash'aah* means "I am in the act of lowering the round object" but *naashne'* means "I am in the act of letting the round object fall."

To make the analysis absolutely complete, it

must be pointed out that there is one respect in which the English is here a bit more exact. "I drop it" implies definitely (with the exception of the use of the "historical present") that the action occurs as the speaker talks or just an instant before, while the two Navaho verbs given above could, in certain circumstances, refer either to past or to future time. In other words, Navaho is more interested in the type of action (momentaneous, progressing, continuing, customary, etc.) than in establishing sequences in time as related to the moving present of the speaker.

Many other sorts of difference could be described, some of which are illustrated [in Figs. 5 to 7]. A full technical treatment would require a whole book to itself. The widest implications have been beautifully phrased by one of the great linguists of recent times, Edward Sapir:

Language is not merely a more or less systematic inventory of the various items of experience which seem relevant to the individual, as is so often naively assumed, but is also a self-contained, creative symbolic organization, which not only refers to experience largely acquired without its help but actually defines experience for us by reason of its formal completeness and because of our unconscious projection of its implicit expectations into the field of experience. In this respect language is very much like a mathematical system which, also, records experience in the truest sense of the word, only in its crudest beginnings, but, as time goes on, becomes elaborated into a self-contained conceptual system which previsages all possible experience in accordance with certain accepted formal limitations. . . . [Meanings are] not so much discovered in experience as imposed upon it, because of the tyrannical hold that linguistic form has upon our orientation in the world. Inasmuch as languages

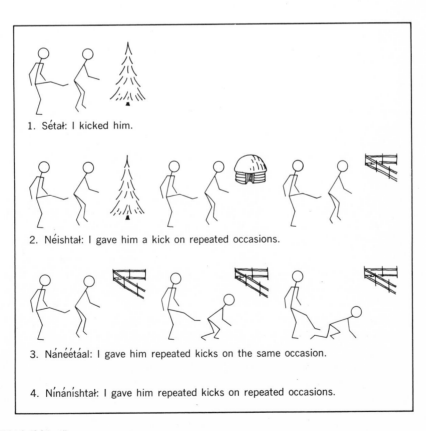

1. Sétał: I kicked him.

2. Néishtał: I gave him a kick on repeated occasions.

3. Náneétáal: I gave him repeated kicks on the same occasion.

4. Nínáníshtał: I gave him repeated kicks on repeated occasions.

Fig. 7   "I kicked him."

differ very widely in their systematization of funda-mental concepts, they tend to be only loosely equiv-alent to each other as symbolic devices and are, as a matter of fact, incommensurable in the sense in which two systems of points in a plane are, on the whole, incommensurable to each other, if they are

plotted out with reference to differing systems of coordinates . . . .

In many ways the Navaho classifications come closer to a freshly objective view of the nature of events than do those of such languages as English or Latin. . . .

part 8

Society and Culture

The Symbol: The Origin and Basis of Human Behavior

Leslie A. White

From *Etc.: A Review of General Semantics,* Vol. 1, 1944, pp. 229–237. By permission of the author and the publisher.

I

In July, 1939, a celebration was held at Leland Stanford University to commemorate the hundredth anniversary of the discovery that the cell is the basic unit of all living tissue. Today we are beginning to realize and to appreciate the fact that the symbol is the basic unit of all human behavior and civilization.

All human behavior originates in the use of symbols. It was the symbol which transformed our anthropoid ancestors into men and made them human. All civilizations have been generated, and are perpetuated, only by the use of symbols. It is the symbol which transforms an infant of *Homo sapiens* into a human being; deaf mutes who grow up without the use of symbols are not human beings. All human behavior consists of, or is dependent upon, the use of symbols. Human behavior is symbolic behavior; symbolic behavior is human behavior. The symbol is the universe of humanity.

II

The great Darwin declared that "there is no fundamental difference between man and the higher mammals in their mental faculties," that the difference between them consists "solely in his [man's] almost infinitely larger power of associating together the most diversified sounds and ideas." Thus the difference between the mind of man and that of other mammals is merely one of degree, and it is not "fundamental."

Essentially the same views are held by many present day students of human behavior. Professor Ralph Linton, an anthropologist, writes: "The differences between men and animals in all these [behavior] respects are enormous, but they seem to be differences in quantity rather than in quality." "Human and animal behavior can be shown to have so much in common," Professor Linton observes, "that the gap [between them] ceases to be of great importance." Dr. Alexander Goldenweiser, likewise an anthropologist, believes that "in point of sheer psychology, mind as such, man is after all no more than a talented animal" and "the difference between the mentality here displayed [by a horse and a chimpanzee] and that of man is merely one of degree."

That there are numerous and impressive similarities between the behavior of man and that of apes is fairly obvious; it is quite possible that even chimpanzees in zoos have noted and appreciated them. Fairly apparent, too, are man's behavioral similarities to many other kinds of animals. Almost as obvious, but not easy to define, is a difference in behavior which distinguishes man from all other living creatures. I say "obvious" because it is quite apparent to the common man that the nonhuman animals with which he is familiar do not and cannot enter, and participate in, the world in which he, as a human being, lives. It is impossible for a dog, horse, bird, or even an ape, ever to have *any* understanding of the meaning of the sign of the cross to a Christian, or of the fact that black (white among the Chinese) is the color of mourning. But when the scholar attempts to *define* the mental difference between animal and man he sometimes encounters difficulties which he cannot surmount and, therefore, ends up by saying that the difference is merely one of degree: man has a bigger mind, "larger power of association," wider range of activities, etc.

There is a *fundamental* difference between the mind of man and the mind of nonman. This difference is one of kind, not one of degree. And the gap between the two types is of the greatest importance—at least to the science of comparative behavior. Man uses symbols; no other creature does. A creature either uses symbols or he does not; there are no intermediate stages.

III

A symbol is a thing the value or meaning of which is bestowed upon it by those who use it. I say "thing" because a symbol may have

any kind of physical form; it may have the form of a material object, a color, a sound, an odor, a motion of an object, a taste.

The meaning, or value, of a symbol is in no instance derived from or determined by properties intrinsic in its physical form: the color appropriate to mourning may be yellow, green, or any other color; purple need not be the color of royalty; among the Manchu rulers of China it was yellow. The meaning of the word "see" is not intrinsic in its phonetic (or pictorial) properties. "Biting one's thumb at" someone [used by Shakespeare in *Romeo and Juliet*] might mean anything. The meanings of symbols are derived from and determined by the organisms who use them; meaning is bestowed by human organisms upon physical forms which thereupon become symbols.

All symbols must have a physical form otherwise they could not enter our experience. But the meaning of a symbol cannot be perceived by the senses. One cannot tell by looking at an *x* in an algebraic equation what it stands for; one cannot ascertain with the ears alone the symbolic value of the phonetic compound *si;* one cannot tell merely by weighing a pig how much gold he will exchange for; one cannot tell from the wave length of a color whether it stands for courage or cowardice, "stop" or "go"; nor can one discover the spirit in a fetish by any amount of physical or chemical examination. The meaning of a symbol can be communicated only by symbolic means, usually by articulate speech.

But a thing which in one context is a symbol is, in another context, not a symbol but a sign. Thus, a word is a symbol only when one is concerned with the distinction between its meaning and its physical form. This distinction *must* be made when one bestows value upon a sound-combination or when a previously bestowed value is discovered for the first time; it *may* be made at other times for certain purposes. But after value has been bestowed upon, or discovered in, a word, its meaning becomes identified, in use, with its physical form. The word then functions as a sign rather than a symbol. (A *sign* is a physical form whose function is to indicate some other thing—object, quality, or event. The meaning of a sign may be intrinsic, inseparable from its physical form and nature, as in the case of the height of a column of mercury as an indication of temperature; or it may be merely identified with its physical form, as in the case of a hurricane signal displayed by a weather bureau. But in either case, the meaning of the sign is perceived by the senses.) . . . This fact that a thing may be both symbol (in one context) and nonsymbol (in another context) has led to some confusion and misunderstanding.

Thus Darwin says, "That which distinguishes man from the lower animals is not the understanding of articulate sounds, for as everyone knows, dogs understand many words and sentences."

It is perfectly true, of course, that dogs, apes, horses, birds, and perhaps creatures even lower in the evolutionary scale, can be taught to respond in a specific way to a vocal command. But it does not follow that no difference exists between the meaning of "words and sentences" to a man and to a dog. Words are both signs and symbols to man; they are merely signs to a dog. Let us analyze the situation of vocal stimulus and response.

A dog can be taught to roll over at the command "Roll over!" A man can be taught to stop at the command "Halt!" The fact that a dog can be taught to roll over in Chinese, or that he can be taught to "go fetch" at the command "roll over" (and, of course, the same is true for a man) shows that there is no necessary and invariable relationship between a particular sound combination and a specific reaction to it. The dog or the man can be taught to respond in a certain manner, to *any* arbitrarily selected combination of sounds, for example, a group of nonsense syllables, coined for the occasion. On the other hand, any one of a great number and variety of responses may become evocable by a given stimulus. Thus, so far as the *origin* of the relationship between vocal stimulus and response is concerned, the nature of the relationship, *i.e.,* the meaning of the stimulus, is

not determined by properties intrinsic in the stimulus.

But, once the relationship has been established between vocal stimulus and response, the meaning of the stimulus becomes *identified with the sounds;* it is then *as if* the meaning were intrinsic in the sounds themselves. Thus, "halt" does not have the same meaning as "hilt" or "malt." A dog may be conditioned to respond in a certain way to a sound of a given wave length. Sufficiently alter the pitch of the sound and the response will cease to be forthcoming. The meaning of the stimulus has become identified with its physical form; its value is perceived with the senses.

Thus we see that in establishing a relationship between a stimulus and a response the properties intrinsic in the stimulus do not determine the nature of the response. But, *after the relationship has been established* the meaning of the stimulus is *as if* it were *inherent* in its physical form. It does not make any difference what phonetic combination we select to evoke the response of terminating self-locomotion. We may teach a dog, horse, or man to stop at any vocal command we care to choose or devise. But once the relationship has been established between sound and response, the meaning of the stimulus becomes identified with its physical form and is, therefore, perceivable with the senses.

So far we have discovered no difference between the dog and the man; they appear to be exactly alike. And so they are as far as we have gone. But we have not told the whole story yet. No difference between dog and man is discoverable so far as learning to respond appropriately to a vocal stimulus is concerned. But we must not let an impressive similarity conceal an important difference. A porpoise is not yet a fish.

The man differs from the dog—and all the other creatures—in that *he can and does play an active role in determining what value the vocal stimulus is to have, and the dog cannot.* As John Locke aptly put it, "All sounds [*i.e.,* in language] . . . have their signification from the arbitrary imposition of men." The dog does not and cannot play an active part in determining the value of the vocal stimulus.

Whether he is to roll over or go fetch at a given stimulus, or whether the stimulus for roll over be one combination of sounds or another is a matter in which the dog has nothing whatever to "say." He plays a purely passive role and can do nothing else. He learns the meaning of a vocal command just as his salivary glands may learn to respond to the sound of a bell. But man plays an active role and thus becomes a creator: Let x equal three pounds of coal and it does equal three pounds of coal: let removal of the hat in a house of worship indicate respect and it becomes so. This creative faculty, that of freely, actively, and arbitrarily bestowing value upon things, is one of the most commonplace as well as *the* most important characteristic of man. Children employ it freely in their play: "Let's pretend that this rock is a wolf."

The difference between the behavior of man and other animals, then, is that the lower animals may receive new values, may acquire new meanings, but they cannot create and bestow them. Only man can do this. To use a crude analogy, lower animals are like a person who has only the receiving apparatus for wireless messages; he can receive messages but he cannot send them. Man can do both. And this difference is one of kind, not of degree; a creature can either "arbitrarily impose signification," to use Locke's phrase, can either create and bestow values, or he cannot. There are no intermediate stages. (Professor Linton speaks of "the faintest foreshadowings of language . . . at the animal level," but precisely what these "faintest foreshadowings" are he does not say.) This difference may appear slight, but, as a carpenter once told William James in discussing differences between men, "it's very important." All *human* existence depends upon it and it alone.

The confusion regarding the nature of words and their significance to men and the lower animals is not hard to understand. It arises, first of all, from a failure to distinguish between the two quite different contexts in which words function. The statements, "The meaning of a word cannot be perceived with the senses," and " The meaning of a word can be perceived with the senses," though contradictory, are nevertheless equally true. (What we have to say here would, of course, apply equally well to gestures—*e.g.,* the "sign of the cross," a salute—a color, a material object, etc.) In the *symbol* context the meaning cannot be perceived with the senses; in the *sign* context it can. This is confusing enough. But the situation has been made worse by using the words "symbol" and "sign" to label, not the *different contexts,* but *one and the same thing:* the word. Thus a word is a symbol *and* a sign, two different things. It is like saying that a vase is a *doli* and a *kana*—two different things—because it may function in two contexts, esthetic and commercial. (Like a word, the value of a vase may be perceived by the senses or be imperceptible to them depending upon the context in which it is regarded. In an esthetic context its value is perceived with the senses. In the commercial context this is impossible; we must be *told* its value—in terms of price.)

That which is a *symbol* in the context of origination becomes a *sign* in use thereafter. Things may be either signs or symbols to man; they can be only signs to other creatures.

IV

Very little indeed is known of the organic basis of the symbolic faculty; we know next to nothing of the neurology of symbolizing. And very few scientists—anatomists, neurologists, physical anthropologists—appear to be interested in the problem. Some, in fact, seem to be unaware of the existence of such a problem. The duty and task of giving an account of the organic basis of symbolizing does not fall within the province of the sociologist or the cultural anthropologist. On the contrary, he should scrupulously exclude it as irrelevant to his problems and interests; to introduce it would bring only confusion. It is enough for the sociologist or cultural anthropologist to take the ability to use symbols, possessed by man alone, as given. The use to which he puts this fact is in no way affected by his, or even the anatomist's, inability to describe the symbolic process in neurological terms. However it is well for the social scientist to be acquainted with the little that neurologists and anatomists do know about the structural basis of "symboling." We, therefore, review briefly the chief relevant facts here.

The anatomist has not been able to discover why men can use symbols and apes cannot. So far as is known the only difference between the brain of man and the brain of an ape is a quantitative one: ". . . man has no new kinds of brain cells or brain cell connections." Nor does man, as distinguished from other animals, possess a specialized "symbol-mechanism." The so-called speech areas of the brain should not be identified with symbolizing. These areas are associated with the muscles of the tongue, larynx, etc. But symbolizing is not dependent upon these organs. One may symbolize with the fingers, the feet, or with any part of the body that can be moved at will. (The misconception that speech is dependent upon the so-called [but miscalled] organs of speech, and, furthermore, that man alone has organs suitable for speech, is not uncommon even today. Thus Professor L. L. Bernard lists "The fourth great organic asset of man is his vocal apparatus, also characteristic of him alone."

The great apes have the mechanism necessary for the production of articulate sounds: "It seemingly is well established that the motor mechanism of voice in this ape [chimpanzee] is adequate not only to the production of a considerable variety of sounds, but also to definite articulations similar to those of man." Also: "All of the anthropoid apes are vocally and muscularly equipped so that they could have an articular language if they possessed the requisite intelligence."

Furthermore, the mere production of articulate sounds would not be symbolizing any more than the mere "understanding of words and sentences" is. John Locke made this clear two and a half centuries ago: "Man, therefore had by nature his organs so fashioned, as to be *fit to frame articulate sounds,* which we call words. But this was not enough to produce language; for parrots, and several

other birds, will be taught to make articulate sounds distinct enough, which yet, by no means, are capable of language. Besides articulate sounds, therefore, it was further necessary, that he should be *able to use these sounds as signs of internal conceptions;* and to make them stand as marks for the ideas within his own mind, whereby they might be made known to others. . . ."

And J. F. Blumenbach, a century later, declared, . . . "That speech is the work of reason alone, appears from this, that other animals, although they have nearly the same organs of voice as man, are entirely destitute of it" [quoted, Yerkes and Yerkes, 1929, p. 23]).

To be sure, the symbolic faculty was brought into existence by the natural processes of organic evolution. And we may reasonably believe that the focal point, if not the locus, of this faculty is in the brain, especially the forebrain. Man's brain is much larger than that of an ape, both absolutely and relatively. (Man's brain is about two and one-half times as large as that of a gorilla. "The human brain is about 1/50 of the entire body weight, while that of a gorilla varies from 1/150 to 1/200 part of that weight.") And the forebrain especially is large in man as compared with ape. Now in many situations we know that quantitative changes give rise to qualitative differences. Water is transformed into steam by additional quantities of heat. Additional power and speed lift the taxiing airplane from the ground and transform terrestrial locomotion into flight. The difference between wood alcohol and grain alcohol is a qualitative expression of a quantitative difference in the proportions of carbon and hydrogen. Thus a marked growth in size of the brain in man may have brought forth a *new kind* of function.

V

All culture (civilization) depends upon the symbol. It was the exercise of the symbolic faculty that brought culture into existence and it is the use of symbols that makes the perpetuation of culture possible. Without the symbol there would be no culture, and man would be merely an animal, not a human being.

Articulate speech is the most important form of symbolic expression. Remove speech from culture and what would remain? Let us see.

Without articulate speech we would have no *human* social organization. Families we might have, but this form of organization is not peculiar to man; it is not *per se, human.* But we would have no prohibitions of incest, no rules prescribing exogamy and endogamy, polygamy or monogamy. How could marriage with a cross cousin be prescribed, marriage with a parallel cousin proscribed, without articulate speech? How could rules which prohibit plural mates possessed simultaneously but permit them if possessed one at a time, exist without speech?

Without speech we would have no political, economic, ecclesiastic, or military organization; no codes of etiquette or ethics; no laws; no science, theology, or literature; no games or music, except on an ape level. Rituals and ceremonial paraphernalia would be meaningless without articulate speech. Indeed, without articulate speech we would be all but toolless; we would have only the occasional and insignificant use of the tool such as we find today among the higher apes, for it was articulate speech that transformed the nonprogressive tool-using of the ape into the progressive, cumulative tool-using of man, the human being.

In short, without symbolic communication in some form, we would have no culture. "In the Word was the beginning" of culture—and its perpetuation also. ("On the whole, however, it would seem that language and culture rest, in a way which is not fully understood, on the same set of faculties. . . ." It is hoped that this essay will make this matter more "fully understood.")

To be sure, with all this culture man is still an animal and strives for the same ends that all other living creatures strive for: the preservation of the individual and the perpetuation of the race. In concrete terms these ends are food, shelter from the elements, defense from enemies, health, and offspring. The fact that man strives for these ends just as all other animals do has, no doubt, led many to declare that there is "no fundamental difference between the behavior of man and of other creatures." But man does differ, not in *ends* but in *means.* Man's means are cultural means: culture is simply the human animal's way of living. And, since these means, culture, are dependent upon a faculty possessed by man alone, the ability to use symbols, the difference between the behavior of man and of all other creatures is not merely great, but basic and fundamental.

VI

The behavior of man is of two distinct kinds: symbolic and nonsymbolic. Man yawns, stretches, coughs, scratches himself, cries out in pain, shrinks with fear, "bristles" with anger, and so on. Nonsymbolic behavior of this sort is not peculiar to man; he shares it not only with other primates but with many other animal species as well. But man communicates with his fellows with articulate speech, uses amulets, confesses sins, makes laws, observes codes of etiquette, explains his dreams, classifies his relatives in designated categories, and so on. This kind of behavior is unique; only man is capable of it; it is peculiar to man because it consists of, or is dependent upon, the use of symbols. The nonsymbolic behavior of man is the behavior of man the animal; the symbolic behavior is that of man the human being.

It is the symbol which has transformed man from a mere animal to a human animal. (It is for this reason that observations and experiments with apes, rats, etc., can tell us nothing about human behavior. They can tell us how ape-like or rat-like man is, but they throw no light upon human behavior because the behavior of apes, rats, etc., is nonsymbolic.

The title of the late George A. Dorsey's best seller, *Why We Behave Like Human Beings,* was misleading for the same reason. This interesting book told us much about vertebrate, mammalian, primate, and even man-animal behavior, but virtually nothing about symbolic, *i.e.*, human behavior. But we are glad to add, in justice to Dorsey, that his chapter on the function of speech in culture in *Man's Own Show: Civilization*, is probably the best discussion of this subject that we know of in anthropological literature.)

As it was the symbol that made mankind human, so it is with each member of the race. A baby is not a human being so far as his behavior is concerned. Until the infant acquires speech there is nothing to distinguish his behavior qualitatively from that of a young ape.

The baby becomes a human being when and as he learns to use symbols. Only by means of speech can the baby enter and take part in the human affairs of mankind. The questions we asked previously may be repeated now. How is the growing child to know of such things as families, etiquette, morals, law, science, philosophy, religion, commerce, and so on, without speech? The rare cases of children who grew up without symbols because of deafness and blindness, such as those of Laura Bridgman, Helen Keller and Marie Heurtin, are instructive. Until they "got the idea" of symbolic communication they were not human beings, but animals; they did not participate in behavior which is peculiar to human beings. They were *in* human society as dogs are, but they were not *of* human society. And, although the present writer is exceedingly skeptical of the reports of the so-called "wolf-children," "feral men," etc., we may note that they are described, almost without exception, as without speech, "beastly," and "inhuman." (In their fascinating account of their experiment with a baby chimpanzee, kept for nine months in their home and treated as their

infant son was treated, Professor and Mrs. Kellogg speak of the "humanization" of the little ape: "She may thus be said to have become 'more humanized' than the human subject. . . ."

This is misleading. What the experiment showed so strikingly was *how like an ape a child of Homo sapiens is before he learns to talk.* The boy even employed the ape's "food bark"! The experiment also demonstrated the ape's utter inability to learn to talk, which means an inability to become humanized at all.)

VII

Summary. The natural processes of organic evolution brought into existence in man, and man alone, a new and distinctive ability: the ability to use symbols. The most important form of symbolic expression is articulate speech. Articulate speech means communication of ideas; communication means preservation—tradition—and preservation means accumulation and progress. The emergence of the organic faculty of symbol-using has resulted in the genesis of a new order of phenomena: a superorganic, or cultural, order. All civilizations are born of, and are perpetuated by, the use of symbols. A culture, or civilization, is but a particular kind of form (symbolic) which the biologic, life-perpetuating activities of a particular animal, man, assume.

Human behavior is symbolic behavior; if it is not symbolic, it is not human. The infant of the genus *homo* becomes a human being only as he is introduced into and participates in that supraorganic order of phenomena which is culture. And the key to this world and the means of participation in it is the symbol.

Diffusionism and Darwinism

Erik K. Reed

From *Brief Communications.*
American Anthropologist,
Vol. 63, No. 2, Part 1, 1961,
pp. 375–377. By permission of
the author and the publisher.

Among the important points which seem to me to have been missed, overlooked, or distorted in recent—and not so recent—discussions of evolutionism in archeology-anthropology (e.g., papers by various authors in the Anthropological Society of Washington symposium volume, *Evolution and Anthropology: A Centennial Appraisal,* Washington, D. C., 1959; publications by Julian Steward and by Leslie White) is this: The concept of unilinear and uniform progress through certain stages, and consequent expectations and attempts to find the same identical stages in different parts of the world, with the concomitant notion of psychic unity of mankind applied to specific details and utilized to explain close correspondences in culture—all this may be *called* evolutionism, as it has been, but it certainly is not, or was not, Darwinism. Neither the fact of biological evolution nor the theory which best explains it, that of variation and selection, requires or in any way suggests unilinear world-wide progression through uniform stages.

Actually, the extreme diffusionists probably are closer to corresponding with biological evolution. The rise of a new species, and hence also the appearance of a new genus or larger taxon, occurs initially within a subdivision or population of a previously existing species. and takes place gradually by increase and spread of variations, with or without disappearance of the previous form as such. The essence of transformation by variation and selection, in fact, is precisely that no species, or other grouping of living individuals, plant or animal, is ever abruptly and completely changed to a different and new form. Surely no biologist would ever have said that all cultural sequences—that is, all men—must pass or have passed through similar levels of development quite separately, independent but parallel. That would be like claiming that all fishes are going to become amphibians eventually, or that all Eocene horses changed simultaneously from having four toes on their front feet to three toes when they learned of the imminent arrival of Oligocene times.

The diffusionist view of cultural change is almost identical with normal biological evolution: a variation arises within an existing form (and uniquely, appearing only once; at a definite, if generally unknown, time and place) and, if it is a favorable variation (acceptance by other people would here represent or constitute survival value), it spreads.

Attacks on "unilinear evolutionism" have been largely unnecessary or misdirected, consequently. And few of the founders of evolutionism in anthropology ever said, either, that all men have to pass through all stages in the proper order. Tylor, for example, simply pointed out that advanced civilizations are "results of gradual development from an earlier, simpler, and ruder state of life. No stage of civilization comes into existence spontaneously, but grows or is developed out of the stage before it"—which is manifestly self-evident to the point of truism. And similarly, Morgan asserted that "savagery preceded barbarism . . . as barbarism is known to have preceded civilization." In these and other statements by these men and others, at least those few of Tylor's caliber, I see neither teleology and orthogenesis nor insistence on widespread uniformity. Boas was, I judge, attacking only minor and incidental misconceptions of evolution in advising that "we renounce the vain endeavor to construct a uniform systematic history of the evolution of culture."

In a paper entitled "Conflict and Congruence in Anthropological Theory," the situation is cogently summarized by Linton C. Freeman:

> In E. B. Tylor's work we find evolution in its purest form; it includes not only the search for diachronic relationships, but the use of evaluative criteria as well. Tylor lived and wrote in a period and place where the dominant theme of the culture was progress . . . if we reinterpret Tylor's stress upon evolutionary stages, we find that he has suggested a characteristic relationship among his variables. He has proposed, for example, that a change in settlement pattern will be accompanied by a change in occupational specialization. . . . In short, Tylor has proposed a specific interrelationship among a set of societal variables.

Mr. Freeman then points out that the struc-

tural-functionalists are simply making the same statement but from a purely synchronic point of view.

There has been, admittedly, such misuses and misconceptions as Boas was rightly criticizing. The idea that a nomadic pastoral stage was required in the central basis or general and theoretical sequence and should be interpolated between hunters-gatherers and sedentary agriculturalists was based on logic, not evidence, and had to be discarded; but at least it was, after all, logical and simply happened to be wrong. The idea that all of the same cultural periods, all of the same stone-working stages and other successive technological developments, should be expected and found in the same order, in every area, likewise is not theoretically unreasonable, but obviously had to be qualified considerably. And it can be a diffusionist concept rather than automatically and necessarily leading inevitably to the idea of psychic unity and parallel independent development; but using it with diffusion—variation and radiation—in mind, the absence of certain stages, and of many important specific traits, in various areas is much more readily acceptable.

The concept or phrase "multilinear evolution" is a perfectly acceptable one for a sort of quick descriptive summary reference to what has gone on; but I am not sure that it adds very much—evolution is multilinear. The histories of, say, Galápagos finches on separate islands are different; those of, say, Old World primates and South American monkeys differ far more widely. The histories of separate cultures in various parts of the world are, naturally, different. But the tremendous complexity of the history of human culture and the enormous number of its variations do not obviate, though they quite evidently obscure, the simple basic fact, recognized from Tylor and before to Leslie White, that the more complex forms follow and are based on and essentially derived from simpler ones, in culture as among living things.

The theory of succession in social organization from promiscuity through matrilineal organization followed by patriarchy and polygyny to bilateral monogamy is not acceptable; but the statement that social stratification and specialization occur with advanced complex technology presumably would be. Urban civilizations not only came later in time than unspecialized villages, they develop out of them. Sedentary agricultural societies followed and grew out of less sedentary groups dependent entirely on wild foods. This does not mean that all food-collectors must in time become agriculturalists, or that they must necessarily have polished stone or pottery before they can become sedentary and agricultural, or bronze before iron, or else, that they must inevitably acquire or develop bronze and pottery shortly after they have become farmers grouped in villages.

But neither does this flexibility mean that there are no regularities, no continuous line or trends in human history, no cultural evolution, and no sense to it all.

selection 45

Peasant Society and the Image of Limited Good

George M. Foster

From *American Anthropologist,* Vol. 67, 1965, pp. 293–310. By permission of the author, and the publisher.

The members of every society share a common cognitive orientation which is, in effect, an unverbalized, implicit expression of their understanding of the "rules of the game" of living imposed upon them by their social, natural, and supernatural universes. A cognitive orientation provides the members of the society it characterizes with basic premises and sets of assumptions normally neither recognized nor questioned which structure and guide behavior in much the same way grammatical rules unrecognized by most people structure and guide their linguistic forms. All normative behavior of the members of a group is a function of their particular way of looking at their total environment, their unconscious acceptance of the "rules of the game" implicit in their cognitive orientation. . . .

In speaking of a cognitive orientation—the terms "cognitive view," "world view," "world view perspective," "basic assumptions," "implicit premises," and perhaps "ethos" may be used as synonyms—I am as an anthropologist concerned with two levels of problems: (1) the nature of the cognitive orientation itself which I see as something "psychologically real," and the ways in which and the degree to which it can be known; and (2) the economical representation of this cognitive orientation by means of models or integrating principles which account for observed behavior, and which permit prediction of behavior yet unnoted or unperformed. Such a model or principle is, as Kluckhohn has often pointed out, an inferential construct or an analytic abstraction derived from observed behavior.

A model or integrating principle is not the cognitive orientation itself, but for purposes of analysis the two cannot be separated. A well-constructed model is, of course, not really descriptive of behavior at all (as is, for example, the term "ethos" as used by Gillin to describe contemporary Latin American culture). A good model is heuristic and explanatory, not descriptive, and it has predictive value. It encourages an analyst to search for behavior patterns, and relationships between patterns, which he may not yet have recognized, simply because logically—if the model is sound—it is reasonable to expect to find them. By the same token, a sound model should make it possible to predict how people are going to behave when faced with certain alternatives. A model therefore has at least two important functions: it is conducive to better field work, and it has practical utility as a guide to policy and action in developmental programs. . . .

How does an anthropologist fathom the cognitive orientation of the group he studies, to find patterns that will permit building a model or stating an integrating principle? Componential analysis and other formal semantic methods have recently been much in vogue, and these techniques unquestionably can tell us a great deal. But the degree of dissension among anthropologists who use these methods suggests that they are not a single royal road to "God's truth." I suspect there will always remain a considerable element of ethnological art in the processes whereby we come to have some understanding of a cognitive orientation. However we organize our thought processes, we are engaging in an exercise in structural analysis in which overt behavior (and the simpler patterns into which this behavior is readily seen to fall) is viewed somewhat as a reflection or representation of a wider reality which our sensory apparatus can never directly perceive. Or, we can view the search for a cogni-

tive view as an exercise in triangulation. Of each trait and pattern the question is asked, "Of what implicit assumption might this behavior be a logical function?" When enough questions have been asked, the answers will be found to point in a common direction. The model emerges from the point where the lines of answers intersect. Obviously, an anthropologist well acquainted with a particular culture cannot merely apply simple rules of analysis and automatically produce a model for, or even a description of, a world view. In effect, we are dealing with a pyramidal structure: low-level regularities and coherences relating overt behavior forms are fitted into higher-level patterns which in turn may be found to fall into place at a still higher level of integration. Thus, a model of a social structure, sound in itself, will be found to be simply one expression of a structural regularity which will have analogues in religion and economic activities.

Since all normative behavior of the members of a group is a function of its particular cognitive orientation, both in an abstract philosophical sense and in the view of an individual himself, all behavior is "rational" and sense-making. "Irrational" behavior can be spoken of only in the context of a cognitive view which did not give rise to that behavior. Thus, in a rapidly changing world, in which peasant and primitive peoples are pulled into the social and economic context of whole nations, some of their behavior may appear irrational to others because the social, economic, and natural universe that in fact controls the conditions of their life is other than that revealed to them—however subconsciously—by a traditional world view. . . .

In this paper I am concerned with the nature of the cognitive orientation of peasants, and with interpreting and relating peasant behavior as described by anthropologists to this orientation. I am also concerned with the implications of this orientation and related behavior to the problem of the peasant's participation in the economic growth of the country to which he may belong. Specifically, I will outline what I believe to be the dominant theme in the cognitive orientation of classic peasant societies, show how characteristic peasant behavior seems to flow from this orientation, and attempt to show that this behavior—however incompatible with national economic growth—is not only highly rational in the context of the cognition that determines it, but that for the maintenance of peasant society in its classic form, it is indispensable. The kinds of behavior that have been suggested as adversely influencing economic growth are, among many, the "luck" syndrome, a "fatalistic" outlook, inter- and intra-familial quarrels, difficulties in cooperation, extraordinary ritual expenses by poor people and the problems these expenses pose for capital accumulation, and the apparent lack of what the psychologist McClelland has called "need for Achievement." I will suggest that peasant participation in national development can be hastened not by stimulating a psychological process, the need for achievement, but by creating economic and other opportunities that will encourage the peasant to abandon his traditional and increasingly unrealistic cognitive orientation for a new one that reflects the realities of the modern world.

The model of cognitive orientation that seems to me best to account for peasant behavior is the "Image of Limited Good." By "Image of Limited Good" I mean that broad areas of peasant behavior are patterned in such fashion as to suggest that peasants view their social, economic, and natural universes—their total environment—as one in which all of the desired things in life such as land, wealth, health, friendship and love, manliness and honor, respect and status, power and influence, security and safety, *exist in finite quantity* and *are always in short supply,* as far as the peasant is concerned. Not only do these and all other "good things" exist in finite and limited quantities, but in addition *there is no way directly within peasant power to increase the available quantities.* It is as if the obvious fact of land shortage in a densely populated area applied to all other desired things: not enough to go around. "Good," like land, is seen as inherent in nature, there to be divided and redivided, if necessary, but not to be augmented.

For purposes of analysis, and at this stage of the argument, I am considering a peasant community to be a closed system. Except in a special—but extremely important—way, a peasant sees his existence as determined and limited by the natural and social resources of his village and his immediate area. Consequently, there is a primary corollary to The Image of Limited Good: if "Good" exists in limited amounts which cannot be expanded, and if the system is closed, it follows that *an individual or a family can improve a position only at the expense of others.* Hence an apparent relative improvement in someone's position with respect to any "Good" is viewed as a threat to the entire community. Someone is being despoiled, whether he sees it or not. And since there is often uncertainty as to who is losing—obviously it may be ego—*any* significant improvement is perceived, not as a threat to an individual or a family alone, but as a threat to *all* individuals and families.

This model was first worked out on the basis of a wide variety of field data from Tzintzuntzan, Michoacán, Mexico: family behavior, exchange patterns, cooperation, religious activities, court claims, disputes, material culture, folklore, language, and many other bits and pieces. At no point has an informant even remotely suggested that this is his vision of his universe. Yet each Tzintzuntzeno organizes his behavior in a fashion entirely rational when it is viewed as a function of this principle which he cannot enunciate.

The model of Limited Good, when "fed back" to behavior in Tzintzuntzan, proved remarkably productive in revealing hitherto unsuspected structural regularities linking economic behavior with social relations, friendship, love and jealousy patterns, health beliefs, concepts of honor and masculinity, *egoísmo* manifestations—even folklore. Not only were structural regularities revealed in Tzintzuntzan, but much peasant behavior known to me from other field work, and reported in the literature, seemed also to be a function of this cognitive orientation. This has led me to offer the kinds of data I have utilized in formulating this model, and to explain the interpretations that seem to me to follow from it, as characterizing in considerable degree classic peasant societies, in the hope that the model will be tested against other extensive bodies of data. I believe, obviously, that if the Image of Limited Good is examined as a high-level integrating principle characterizing peasant communities, we will find within our individual societies unsuspected structural regularities and, on a cross-cultural level, basic patterns that will be most helpful in constructing the typology of peasant society. The data I present in support of this thesis are illustrative, and are not based on an exhaustive survey of peasant literature.

In the following pages I will offer evidence under four headings that seems to me to conform to the model I have suggested. I will then discuss the implications of this evidence.

1. When the peasant views his economic world as one in which Limited Good prevails, and he can progress only at the expense of another, he is usually very near the truth. Peasant economies, as pointed out by many authors, are not productive. In the average village there *is* only a finite amount of wealth produced, and no amount of extra hard work will significantly change the figure. In most of the peasant world land has been limited for a long, long time, and only in a few places have young farmers in a growing community been able to hive off from the parent village to start on a level of equality with their parents and grandparents. Customarily land is not only limited, but it has become increasingly limited, by population expansion and soil deterioration. Peasant productive techniques have remained largely unchanged for hundreds, and even thousands, of years; at best, in farming, this means the Mediterranean plow drawn by oxen, supplemented by human-powered hand tools. Handicraft techniques in weaving, pottery-making, wood-working and building likewise have changed little over the years.

In fact, it seems accurate to say that the average peasant sees little or no relationship between work and production techniques on the one hand, and the acquisition of wealth on the other. Rather, wealth is seen by villagers in the same light as land: present, circumscribed by absolute limits, and having no relationship to work. One works to eat, but not to create wealth. Wealth, like land, is something that is inherent in nature. It can be divided up and passed around in various ways, but, within the framework of the villagers' traditional world, it does not grow. Time and tradition have determined the shares each family and individual hold; these shares are not static, since obviously they do shift. But the reason for the relative position of each villager is known at any given time, and any significant change calls for explanation.

2. The evidence that friendship, love, and affection are seen as strictly limited in peasant society is strong. Every anthropologist in a peasant village soon realizes the narrow path he must walk to avoid showing excessive favor or friendship toward some families, thereby alienating others who will feel deprived, and hence reluctant to help him in his work. Once I brought a close friend from Tzintzuntzan, working as a bracero in a nearby town, to my Berkeley home. When safely away from the camp he told me his brother was also there. Why did he not tell me, so I could have invited him? My friend replied, in effect, that he was experiencing a coveted "good" and he did not want to risk diluting the satisfaction by sharing it with another.

Adams reports how a social worker in a Guatemalan village unwittingly prejudiced her work by making more friends in one barrio than in the other, thereby progressively alienating herself from potential friends whose help she needed. In much of Latin America the institutionalized best friend, particularly among post-adolescents, variously known as the *amigo carnal,* or the *cuello* or *camaradería* constitutes both recognition of the fact that true friendship is a scarce commodity, and serves as insurance against being left without any of it. The jealousies and feelings of deprivation felt by one partner when the other leaves or threatens to leave sometimes lead to violence.

Widespread peasant definitions of sibling

rivalry suggest that a mother's ability to love her children is viewed as limited by the amount of love she possesses. In Mexico when a mother again becomes pregnant and weans her nursing child, the child often becomes *chípil*. It fusses, cries, clings to her skirt, and is inconsolable. The child is said to be *celoso*, jealous of its unborn sibling whose presence it recognizes and whom it perceives as a threat, already depriving him of maternal love and affection. . . .

In parts of Guatemala chipe is a term used to express a husband's jealousy of his pregnant wife, for temporary loss of sexual services and for the attention to be given to the baby. Tepoztlán husbands also suffer from *chipilez*, becoming sleepy and not wanting to work. Oscar Lewis says a husband can be cured by wearing a strip of his wife's skirt around his neck. In Tonalá, Jalisco, Mexico, husbands often are jealous of their adolescent sons and angry with their wives because of the affection the latter show their offspring. A wife's love and affection are seen as limited; to the extent the son receives what appears to be an excessive amount, the husband is deprived. . . .

3. It is a truism to peasants that health is a "good" that exists in limited quantities. Peasant folk medicine does not provide the protection that scientific medicine gives those who have access to it, and malnutrition frequently aggravates conditions stemming from lack of sanitation, hygiene, and immunization. In peasant societies preoccupation with health and illness is general, and constitutes a major topic of interest, speculation, and discussion. Perhaps the best objective evidence that health is viewed within the framework of Limited Good is the widespread attitude toward blood which is, to use Adams' expression, seen as "non-regenerative." For obvious reasons, blood is equated with life, and good blood, and lots of it, means health. Loss of blood—if it is seen as something that cannot be renewed—is thus seen as a threat to health, a permanent loss resulting in weakness for as long as an individual lives. Although best described for Guatemala, the belief that blood is non-regenerative is widespread in Latin America. This belief, frequently unverbalized, may be one of the reasons it is so difficult to persuade Latin Americans to give blood transfusions: by giving blood so that someone can have more, the donor will have less. . . .

4. Oft-noted peasant sensitiveness to real or imagined insults to personal honor, and violent reactions to challenges which cast doubt on a man's masculinity, appear to be a function of the belief that honor and manliness exist in limited quantities, and that consequently not everyone can enjoy a full measure. In rural Mexico, among braceros who have worked in the United States, American ethnologists have often been asked, "In the United States it's the wife who commands, no?" Masculinity and domestic control appear to be viewed much like other desirable things: there is only so much, and the person who has it deprives another. Mexican men find it difficult to believe that a husband and wife can share domestic responsibilities and decision making, without the husband being deprived of his *machismo.* Many believe a wife, however good, must be beaten from time to time, simply so she will not lose sight of a God-decreed familial hierarchy. They are astonished and shocked to learn that an American wife-beater can be jailed; this seems an incredibly unwarranted intrusion of the State into God's plans for the family.

The essence of machismo is valor, and *un hombre muy valiente,* i.e., a *macho,* is one who is strong and tough, generally fair, not a bully, but who never dodges a fight, and who always wins. Above all, a macho inspires respect. One achieves machismo, it is clear, by depriving others of access to it.

In Greece *philotimo,* a "love of honor," equates closely with Mexican machismo. A man who is physically sound, lithe, strong, and agile has philotimo. If he can converse well, show wit, and act in other ways that facilitate sociability and establish ascendency, he enhances his philotimo. One attacks another male through his philotimo, by shaming or ridiculing him, by showing how he lacks the necessary attributes for a man. Consequently, avoiding ridicule becomes a major concern, a primary defense mechanism among rural Greek males. In a culture shot through with envy and competitiveness, there is the ever-present danger of attack, so a man must be prepared to respond to a jeer or insult with a swift retort, an angry challenge, or a knife thrust. "Philotimo can be enhanced at the expense of another. It has a see-saw characteristic; one's own goes up as another's declines . . . the Greek, in order to maintain and increase his sense of worth, must be prepared each moment to assert his superiority over friend and foe alike. It is an interpersonal combat fraught with anxiety, uncertainty, and aggressive potentials. As one proverb describes it, 'When one Greek meets another, they immediately despise each other.'"

If, in fact, peasants see their universe as one in which the good things in life are in limited and unexpandable quantities, and hence personal gain must be at the expense of others, we must assume that social institutions, personal behavior, values, and personality will all display patterns that can be viewed as functions of this cognitive orientation. Preferred behavior, it may be argued, will be that which is seen by the peasant as maximizing his security, by preserving his relative position in the traditional order of things. People who see themselves in "threatened" circumstances, which the Image of Limited Good implies, react normally in one of two ways: maximum cooperation and sometimes communism, burying individual differences and placing sanctions against individualism; or extreme individualism.

Peasant societies seem always to choose the second alternative. The reasons are not clear, but two factors may bear on the problem. Cooperation requires leadership. This may be delegated democratically by the members of a group itself; it may be assumed by a strong man from within the group; or it may be imposed by forces lying outside the group. Peasant societies—for reasons that should be clear in the following analysis—are

unable by their very nature to delegate authority, and assumption of authority by a strong man is, at best, temporary, and not a structural solution to a problem. The truncated political nature of peasant societies, with real power lying outside the community, seems effectively to discourage local assumption and exercise of power, except as an agent of these outside forces. By the very nature of peasant society, seen as a structural part of a larger society, local development of leadership which might make possible cooperation is effectively prevented by the rulers of the political unit of which a particular peasant community is an element, who see such action as a potential threat to themselves.

Again, economic activities in peasant societies require only limited cooperation. Peasant families typically can, as family units, produce most of their food, farm without extra help, build their houses, weave cloth for their clothes, carry their own produce to market and sell it—in short, take care of themselves with a degree of independence impossible in an industrial society, and difficult in hunting-fishing-gathering societies. Peasants, of course, usually do not live with the degree of independence here suggested, but it is more nearly possible than in any other type of society.

Whatever the reasons, peasants are individualistic, and it logically follows from the Image of Limited Good that each minimal social unit (often the nuclear family and, in many situations, a single individual) sees itself in perpetual, unrelenting struggle with its fellows for possession of or control over what it considers to be its share of scarce values. This is a position that calls for extreme caution and reserve, a reluctance to reveal true strength or position. It encourages suspicion and mutual distrust, since things will not necessarily be what they seem to be, and it also encourages a male self image as a valiant person, one who commands respect, since he will be less attractive as a target than a weakling. A great deal of peasant behavior, I believe, is exactly what we would predict from these circumstances. . . .

Since an individual or family that makes

significant economic progress or acquires a disproportionate amount of some other "good" is seen to do so at the expense of others, such a change is viewed as a threat to the stability of the community. Peasant culture is provided with two principal mechanisms with which to maintain the essential stability:

1. An agreed-upon, socially acceptable, preferred norm of behavior for its people and

2. A "club" and a "carrot," in the form of sanctions and rewards, to ensure that real behavior approximates this norm.

The agreed-upon norm that promotes maximum community stability is behavior that tends to maintain the status quo in relationships. The individual or family that acquires more than its share of a "good," and particularly an economic "good," is, as we have seen, viewed as a threat to the community at large. Individuals and families which are seen to or are thought to progress violate the preferred norm of behavior, thereby stimulating cultural mechanisms that redress the imbalance. Individuals or families that lose something, that fall behind, are seen as a threat in a different fashion; their envy, jealousy, or anger may result in overt or hidden aggression toward more fortunate people.

The self-correcting mechanisms that guard the community balance operate on three levels, viz:

Individual and family behavior. At this level I am concerned with the steps taken by *individuals* to maintain their positions in the system, and the ways in which they try to avoid both sanctions and exploitation by fellow villagers.

Informal and usually unorganized group behavior. At this level I am concerned with the steps taken by the *community,* the sanctions that are invoked when it is felt someone is violating the agreed-upon norm of behavior. Negative sanctions are the "club."

Institutionalized behavior. At this level I am

concerned with the "carrot": major community expressions of cultural forms which neutralize achieved imbalances. Each of these forms will be examined in turn.

On the individual-family level, two rules give guidance to preferred behavior. These can be stated as:

Do not reveal evidence of material or other improvement in your relative position, lest you invite sanctions; should you display improvement, take action necessary to neutralize the consequences.

Do not allow yourself to fall behind your rightful place, lest you and your family suffer.

A family deals with the problem of real or suspected improvement in its relative position by a combination of two devices. First, it attempts to conceal evidence that might lead to this conclusion, and it denies the veracity of suggestions to this effect. Second, it meets the charge head on, admits an improvement in relative position, but shows it has no intention of using this position to the detriment of the village by neutralizing it through ritual expenditures, thereby restoring the status quo.

Accounts of peasant communities stress that in traditional villages people do not compete for prestige with material symbols such as dress, housing, or food, nor do they compete for authority by seeking leadership roles. In peasant villages one notes a strong desire to look and act like everyone else, to be inconspicuous in position and behavior. This theme is well summed up in the Wisers' paragraph on the importance of dilapidated walls suggesting poverty as a part of a family's defense.

Also much remarked is the peasant's reluctance to accept leadership roles. He feels—for good reason—that his motives will be suspect and that he will be subject to the criticism of neighbors. By seeking, or even accepting, an authority position, the ideal man ceases to be ideal. A "good" man therefore usually shuns community responsibilities (other than of a ritual nature); by so doing he protects his reputation. Needless to say, this aspect of socially approved behavior heavily penalizes a peasant community in the modern world by depriving it of the leadership which is now essential to its development.

The mechanism invoked to minimize the danger of loss of relative position appears to center in the machismo-philotimo complex. A tough, strong man whose fearlessness in the face of danger, and whose skill in protecting himself and his family is recognized, does not invite exploitation. A "valiant" individual can command the "respect" so much sought after in many peasant societies, and he can strive toward security with the goal in mind (however illusory) of being able to live—as is said in Tzintzuntzan—*sin compromisos* ("without obligations" to, or dependency on, others). A picture of the ideal peasant begins to emerge: a man who works to feed and clothe his family, who fulfills his community and ceremonial obligations, who minds his own business, who does not seek to be outstanding, but who knows how to protect his rights. Since a macho, a strong man, discourages exploitation, it is clear that this personality characteristic has a basic function in peasant society. Not surprisingly, defense of this valuable self-image may, by the standards of other societies, assume pathological proportions, for it is seen as a basic weapon in the struggle for life.

The ideal man must avoid the appearance of presumption, lest this be interpreted as trying to take something that belongs to another. In tracing the diffusion of new pottery-making techniques in Tzintzuntzan I found that no one would admit he had learned the technique from a neighbor. The inevitable reply to my question was *Me puse a pensar* ("I dreamed it up all by myself"), accompanied by a knowing look and a tapping of the temple with the forefinger. Reluctance to give credit to others, common in Mexico, is often described as due to *egoísmo,* an egotistical conceited quality. Yet if egoísmo, as exemplified by unwillingness to admit profiting by a neighbor's new pottery knowledge, is seen as

a function of an image of Limited Good, it is clear that a potter *must* deny that the idea is other than his own. To confess that he "borrowed" an idea is to confess that he has taken something not rightfully his, that he is consciously upsetting the community balance and the self image he tries so hard to maintain. Similarly, in trying to determine how compadrazgo (godparenthood) ties are initiated, I found no informant who admitted he had asked a friend to serve; he always was asked by another. Informants appear to fear that admission of asking may be interpreted as presuming or imposing on another, trying to get something to which they may not be entitled.

A complementary pattern is manifest in the general absence of compliments in peasant communities; rarely is a person heard to admire the performance of another, and when admiration is expressed by, say, an anthropologist, the person admired probably will try to deny there is any reason to compliment him. Reluctance of villagers to compliment each other again looks, at first glance, like egoísmo. But in the context of the Limited Good model, it is seen that such behavior is proper. The person who compliments is, in fact, guilty of aggression; he is telling someone to his face that he is rising above the dead level that spells security for all, and he is suggesting that he may be confronted with sanctions. . . .

The ideal man strives for moderation and equality in his behavior. Should he attempt to better his comparative standing, thereby threatening village stability, the informal and usually unorganized sanctions appear. This is the "club," and it takes the form of gossip, slander, backbiting, character-assassination, witchcraft or the threat of witchcraft, and sometimes actual physical aggression. These negative sanctions usually represent no formal community decision, but they are at least as effective as if authorized by law. Concern with public opinion is one of the most striking characteristics of peasant communities.

Negative sanctions, while usually informal, can be institutionalized. In peasant Spain, especially in the north, the charivari (*cen-*

cerrada) represents such an instance. When an older man marries a much younger woman—usually a second marriage for the groom—marriageable youths serenade the couple with cowbells (*cencerros*) and other noisemakers, parade straw-stuffed manikins representing them through the streets, incense the manikins with foul-smelling substances, and shout obscenities. It seems clear that this symbolizes the resentment of youths, who have not yet had even one wife, against the inequalities represented by an older man who has already enjoyed marriage, who takes a young bride from the available pool, thereby further limiting the supply for the youths. By institutionalizing.the sanctions the youths are permitted a degree of freedom and abuse not otherwise possible.

Attempted changes in the balance of a peasant village are discouraged by the methods just described; *achieved* imbalance is neutralized, and the balance restored, on an institutional level. A person who improves his position is encouraged—by use of the carrot—to restore the balance through conspicuous consumption in the form of ritual extravagance. In Latin America he is pressured into sponsoring a costly fiesta by serving as *mayordomo*. His reward is prestige, which is viewed as harmless. Prestige cannot be dangerous since it is traded for dangerous wealth; the mayordomo has, in fact, been "disarmed," shorn of his weapons, and reduced to a state of impotence. There is good reason why peasant fiestas consume so much wealth in fireworks, candles, music, and food; and why, in peasant communities the rites of baptism, marriage, and death may involve relatively huge expenditures. These practices are a redistributive mechanism which permits a person or family that potentially threatens community stability gracefully to restore the status quo, thereby returning itself to a state of acceptability. Wolf, speaking specifically of the "closed" Indian peasant community of Mexico as it emerged after the Conquest, puts it this way: "the system takes from those who have, in order to make all men have-nots. By liquidating the surpluses, it makes all men rich in sacred experience but poor in earthly

goods. Since it levels differences of wealth, it also inhibits the growth of class distinctions based on wealth. . . . In engineering parlance, it acts as a feedback, returning a system that is beginning to oscillate to its original course."

I have said that in a society ruled by the Image of Limited Good there is no way, save at the expense of others, that an individual can get ahead. This is true in a closed system, which peasant communities approximate. But even a traditional peasant village, in another sense, has access to other systems, and an individual can achieve economic success by tapping sources of wealth that are recognized to exist outside the village system. Such success, though envied, is not seen as a direct threat to community stability, for no one within the community has lost anything. Still, such success must be explained. In today's transitional peasant communities, seasonal emigration for wage labor is the most available way in which one can tap outside wealth. Hundreds of thousands of Mexican peasants have come to the United States as braceros in recent years and many, through their earnings, have pumped significant amounts of capital into their communities. Braceros generally are not criticized or attacked for acquisition of this wealth; it is clear that their good fortune is not at the direct expense of others within the village. . . .

These examples, however, are but modern variants of a much older pattern in which luck and fate—points of contact with an open system—are viewed as the only socially acceptable ways in which an individual can acquire more "good" than he previously has had. In traditional (not transitional) peasant communities an otherwise inexplicable increase in wealth is often seen as due to the discovery of treasure which may be the result of fate or of such positive action as making a pact with the Devil. Recently I have analyzed treasure tales in Tzintzuntzan and have found without exception they are attached to named individuals who, within living memory, have suddenly begun to live beyond their means. The usual evidence is that they suddenly opened stores, in spite of their known previous poverty. Erasmus has recorded this interpretation among Sonora villagers, Wagley finds it in an Amazon small town, and Friedmann reports it in southern Italy. Clearly, the role of treasure tales in communities like these is to account for wealth that can be explained in no other manner.

The common peasant concern with finding wealthy and powerful patrons who can help them is also pertinent in this context. Since such patrons usually are outside the village, they are not part of the closed system. Their aid, and material help, like bracero earnings or buried treasure, are seen as coming from beyond the village. Hence, although the lucky villager with a helpful patron may be envied, the advantages he receives from his patron are not seen as depriving other villagers of something rightfully theirs. In Tzintzuntzan a villager who obtains a "good" in this fashion makes it a first order of business to advertise his luck and the source thereof, so there can be no doubt as to his basic morality; this behavior is just the opposite of usual behavior, which is to conceal good fortune.

Treasure tales and concern with patrons, in turn, are but one expression of a wider view: that any kind of success and progress is due to fate, the favor of deities, to luck, but not to hard work, energy, and thrift. . . .

In the traditional peasant society hard work and thrift are moral qualities of only the slightest functional value. Given the limitations on land and technology, additional hard work in village productive enterprises simply does not produce a significant increment in income. It is pointless to talk of thrift in a subsistence economy in which most producers are at the economic margin; there is usually nothing to be thrifty about. As Fei and Chang point out, "In a village where the farms are small and wealth is accumulated slowly, there are very few ways for a landless man to become a landowner, or for a petty owner to become a large landowner. . . . It is not going too far to say that in agriculture there is no way really to get ahead. . . . To become rich one must leave agriculture." And again, "The basic truth is that enrichment through the

exploitation of land, using the traditional technology, is not a practical method for accumulating wealth." And, as Ammar says about Egypt, "It would be very difficult with the fellah's simple tools and the sweat involved in his work, to convince him that his lot could be improved by more work."

It is apparent that a peasant's cognitive orientation, and the forms of behavior that stem therefrom, are intimately related to the problems of economic growth in developing countries. Heavy ritual expenditures, for example, are essential to the maintenance of the equilibrium that spells safety in the minds of traditional villagers. Capital accumulation, which might be stimulated if costly ritual could be simplified, is just what the villager wants to prevent, since he sees it as a community threat rather than a precondition to economic improvement.

In national developmental programs much community-level action in agriculture, health and education is cast in the form of cooperative undertakings. Yet it is abundantly clear that traditional peasant societies are cooperative only in the sense of honoring reciprocal obligations, rather than in the sense of understanding total community welfare, and that mutual suspicion seriously limits cooperative approaches to village problems. The image of Limited Good model makes clear the peasant logic underlying reluctance to participate in joint ventures. If the "good" in life is seen as finite and non-expandable, and if apart from luck an individual can progress only at the expense of others, what does one stand to gain from a cooperative project? At best an honorable man lays himself open to the charge—and well-known consequences—of utilizing the venture to exploit friends and neighbors; at worst he risks his own defenses, since someone more skillful or less ethical than he may take advantage of the situation.

The Anglo-Saxon virtues of hard work and thrift seen as leading to economic success are meaningless in peasant society. Horatio Alger not only is not praiseworthy, but he emerges as a positive fool, a clod who not knowing the score labors blindly against hopeless conditions. The gambler, instead, is more properly laudable, worthy of emulation and adulation. If fate is the only way in which success can be obtained, the prudent and thoughtful man is the one who seeks ways in which to maximize his luck-position. He looks for the places in which good fortune is most apt to strike, and tries to be there. This, I think, explains the interest in lotteries in underdeveloped countries. They offer the only way in which the average man can place himself in a luck-position. The man who goes without lunch, and fails to buy shoes for his children in order to buy a weekly ticket, is not a ne'er-do-well; he is the Horatio Alger of his society who is doing what he feels is most likely to advance his position. He is, in modern parlance, buying a "growth stock." The odds are against him, but it is the *only* way he knows in which to work toward success.

Modern lotteries are very much functional equivalents of buried treasure tales in peasant societies, and at least in Tzintzuntzan the correlation is clearly understood. One elderly informant, when asked why no one had found buried treasure in recent years, remarked that this was indeed true but that "Today we Mexicans have the lottery instead." Hence, the "luck" syndrome in underdeveloped countries is not primarily a deterrent to economic progress, as it is sometimes seen from the vantage point of a developed country, but rather it represents a realistic approach to the near-hopeless problem of making significant individual progress. . . .

For the above reasons, I believe most strongly that the primary task in development is . . . to try to change the peasants' view of his social and economic universe, away from an Image of Limited Good toward that of expanding opportunity in an open system, *so*

that he can feel safe in displaying initiative. The brakes on change are less psychological than social. Show the peasant that initiative is profitable, and that it will not be met by negative sanctions, and he acquires it in short order.

This is, of course, what is happening in the world today. Those who have known peasant villages over a period of years have seen how the old sanctions begin to lose their power. Local entrepreneurs arise in response to the increasing opportunities of expanding national economies, and emulative urges, with the city as the model, appear among these people. The successful small entrepreneurs begin to see that the ideal of equality is inimical to their personal interests, and presently they neither seek to conceal their well being nor to distribute their wealth through traditional patterns of ritual extravagance. . . . The problem of the new countries is to create economic and social conditions in which this latent energy and talent is not quickly brought up against absolute limits, so that it is nipped in the bud. . . .

Viewed in the light of Limited Good peasant societies are not conservative and backward, brakes on national economic progress, because of economic irrationality nor because of the absence of psychological characteristics in adequate quantities. They are conservative because individual progress is seen as—and in the context of the traditional society in fact is—the supreme threat to community stability, and all cultural forms *must* conspire to discourage changes in the status quo. Only by being conservative can peasant societies continue to exist as peasant societies. But change cognitive orientation through changing access to opportunity, and the peasant will do very well indeed. . . .

The Social Consequence of a Change in Subsistence Economy

Ralph Linton

From the *Tanala of Madagascar.* In Abram Kardiner (ed.), *The Individual and His Society,* Columbia University Press, 1939, pp. 282–290. By permission of the author and the publisher.

The culture ... described is that of the Tanala of the dry rice cultivation. Wet rice cultivation, which introduced so many elements in social change that the whole culture was eventually altered, was borrowed from their Betsileo neighbors to the east. It was at first an adjunct to dry rice carried on by individual families. Before the new method was introduced on a large scale, there were already rice swamps of permanent tenure, which never reverted to the village for reassignment. But land favorable for this use was very limited, because of natural factors. Thus there gradually emerged a group of landowners, and with the process came a breakdown in the joint family organization. The cohesiveness of this older unit was maintained by economic interdependence and the need for cooperation. But an irrigated rice field could be tended by a single family, and its head need not recognize any claim to share it with anyone who had not contributed to its produce.

This group of permanent rice sites formed the nucleus of a permanent village, because the land could not be exhausted as was the land exploited by the dry method. As land suitable for wet rice near the village was presently all taken up, the landless households had to move farther and farther away into the jungle. So far away would they be that they could not return the same day. These distant fields also became household rather than joint family affairs.

The moving of the older unit from one land site to another had kept the joint family intact. But now single landless households were forced to move, while there were in the same unit landowners who had a capital investment and no incentive to move. The migrant groups were thus cross-sections of the original lineages. Each original village had a group of descendant villages, each one surrounded by irrigated fields and private ownership.

The mobile villages had been self-contained and endogamous. The settled villages were much less so. The joint family retained its religious importance, based on the worship of a common ancestor, even after its component households had been scattered. Family members would be called together on ceremonial occasions, and thus the old village isolation broke down. Intermarriages became common. In this way, the transformation from independent villages to a tribal organization took place.

The process brought further changes in the patterns of native warfare. The old village had to be defended; but not at so great a cost nor with the necessity for permanent upkeep. When the village became permanent the defenses had to be of a powerful kind, involving big investments and permanent upkeep.

Slaves, who were of no economic significance in the old system, now acquired economic importance. This gave rise to new techniques of ransom. Thus the tribal organization grew in solidity, and with the change the old tribal democracy disappeared. The next step was a king at the head who exercised control over the settled elements but not over the mobile ones. The kingdom came to an end before any adequate machinery of government could be established. This king built himself an individual tomb, thus breaking an ancient custom.

The changes were therefore, a king at the head, settled subjects, rudimentary social classes based on economic differences, and lineages of nothing but ceremonial importance. Most of these changes had already taken place among the Betsileo. The cooperative system made individual wealth impossible. Nor was the change devoid of serious stresses on the individual; a new class of interests, new life goals, and new conflicts came into being.

One of the Tanala clans, the Zafimaniry, was one of the first to take up the new wet rice cultivation. They continued it for a time, but finally abandoned it, and returned to the dry rice method. They offered as the reason for returning to the old method the fact that they had been attacked by an enemy, which scattered the men of the various households. The tribe tabooed the raising of wet rice, and still continues to refuse to take up wet rice despite depletion of the jungle.

Although we are not in possession of all the facts, and a great many unknown factors may have operated, we are justified in looking into the culture of the Betsileo for a contrast with the ultimate changes coincident with wet rice culture. The traditions of the Betsileo have it that there was a time when all people were equal and all land was held in common. Moreover, the cultural similarity to the Tanala leaves no doubt that in the main we are dealing with two cultures springing from a cognate source. Or to be more accurate, the changes we find in Betsileo culture were engrafted on a culture similar in all respects to the one we found in Tanala.

Whatever adventitious changes took place, basically we can regard Betsileo as the Tanala culture, after all the changes consequent upon wet rice had become consolidated, organized, and institutionalized. We are therefore observing an important experiment in the dynamics of social change.

In Betsileo society the gens is still the foundation of social life, descent being traced through the male line from a single ancestor. But the organization of the village as in Tanala culture is gone; it apparently disappeared according to the steps outlined above.

The local clan groups were administered by heads appointed by the king, one head for each gens. Members of several gentes live in the same village. Instead of free access to gens lands, as in Tanala culture, we have here a rigid system of ground rent levied on the land in the form of a proportion of rice produce.

Instead of the previous democracy as among the Tanala there is a rigid caste system with a king at the head, nobles, commoners, and slaves. The powers of the king are absolute over the life and property of everyone. The commoners are the bulk of the population, the nobles, to all intents, feudal lords whose chief control is over land by royal assignment; the slaves are war captives or their descendants.

The powers of the king far exceeded those of a lineage head in Tanala society and in some ways were greater than those of the ancestral ghosts. He could take the life, property, or wife of anyone; he could elevate and degrade the status of anyone at will, and no redress was possible. In accordance with these powers, a great many secondary mores, which accentuate the enhanced prestige of the king, are present. There are taboos about his person and concerning his children; there are special clothes forbidden to anyone else; special words must be used to designate the condition or anatomy of the king. A king was not sick, he was "cold." He did not have eyes, he had "clearness." The souls of dead kings were called Zanahary-so-and-so. Succession was decided from among the king's sons, but not necessarily the oldest. Notwithstanding his great powers and prestige, he might work like a commoner in the rice fields. Though his powers were absolute and he could not be dethroned, he could be counseled to mend his ways.

Though the king owned all the land, he allotted it for use on a basis which was a charter of ownership, revokable at his will. The king dispensed this land in quantities proportional to the importance of, and the potential return from, the individual concerned. He would give the biggest allotments in return for the greatest support. The large landowner, a noble, could now rent any portion of this land to tenant farmers, who would pay rent in the form of a proportion of produce. Land thus owned could be sold or bequeathed as long as it did not become subject to another king. In short, here was a feudal system of a kind.

The staple crop was rice by the wet method; but other crops were cultivated as well—manioc, maize, millet, beans, and sweet potatoes. The chief adjunct to wet rice cultivation was the possibility of transporting water by irrigation, a factor which added to the permanency of the whole organization and took something of the premium away from the swamps and valleys. Irrigation methods made it possible to use the terraced hillsides for agriculture. But control of irrigation, and even perhaps its installation, made a strong central power essential.

The significance of cattle was the same as in Tanala culture; they had little economic but high prestige value. Cows were used chiefly for sacrifice and hence an instrument of power with the gods. The chief source of meat food was chickens, as with the Tanala.

Parallel to the powers of the king were the powers of the father in the individual household; in Betsileo he exercised an unchecked absolutism. All property belonged to the father during the latter's lifetime except his wives' clothes and the gifts he might make to his wives or children. The profits from exploitation of the land went to him. The inheritance laws resembled those of the Tanala except that land could now be inherited.

In the life cycle of the individual we begin to note important changes. The approaching birth of a child is not announced, for fear of sorcery. The afterbirth is buried and various superstitions are connected with it. As in Tanala culture, some days are propitious for birth, others are not. A child born on a certain day (the equivalent of Sunday) must be thrown on the village rubbish heap for a while, or washed in a jug of dirty dishwater. This is supposed to avert evil destiny. The belief is that a child born on one of these unlucky days will destroy its family. Children born in the month of *Alakaosy* are killed either by drowning, or by having cattle walk over them. Should they survive these exposures, they are kept, with the due precaution of changing their destiny through an *ombiasy*. Adoption is frequent; so also is the changing of names.

The basic disciplines are like those of the Tanala. But here in Betsileo society strong emphasis falls on the training in various shades of deference to elders and rank. Manners elevate the status of one individual as against another: the father is served separately, etc.

Incest taboos are the same as those of the Tanala, and observance is with the same general laxity. Premarital chastity is expected of women and punishment is sterility—as with the Tanala. The endogamy of marriage is now within caste lines, though elevation in status of a slave can take place. There is considerably more homosexuality than in Tanala.

The levirate is practiced in Tanala culture but not in Betsileo. A man who married his brother's widow would be strongly suspected of having killed his brother with sorcery or poison. Polygamy is the rule, as in Tanala.

The disciplinarian in Betsileo society is the father. He has the sole right to punish his children, a right which is, however, rarely exercised. Children may desert their parents in Betsileo, something which is almost inconceivable in Tanala. In one family eight children deserted their parents, whereupon the father changed his name to mean, "I have wiped away excrement for nothing."

The religion of Betsileo is much like that of Tanala, but significant changes can be noted. The rigid belief in fate is changed somewhat to mean that god arranges everything in advance. Sorcery (mpamosavy) is now the cause of illness, but the sorcerer is only an executive of god. We find new concepts in Betsileo culture which are unknown in Tanala. For example, god is angry if anyone oppresses the poor. There is a strong belief now in retaliation for aggression against anyone. A man is rich because his Zanahary is good.

The immediate supernatural executives are ghosts and spirits of various kinds. There are for example the vazimba, who once lived in the land of the Betsileo and were driven out. Their souls did not go to heaven but remained in the tombs and are, therefore, hostile. Mpamosavy bury bait in the tombs of the vazimba to kill the person from whom the bait was taken. They also believe in several other varieties of evil spirits in the form of birds or animals. The Betsileo make a clear distinction between life and soul. Life ceases with death, the soul continues. The soul may leave the body by breaking a taboo, through excessive chagrin or fright. The souls of the dead observe the same caste distinctions as obtained in life. The souls of the disowned are evil, and can seduce good souls to do mischief to their own families. A good funeral for a relative insures his good will after death. The soul of a king is transformed into a snake.

Possession by spirits is much more common than in Tanala. In the latter we noted occasional tromba (possession by a ghost), and very rarely mpamosavy. In Betsileo one is possessed by evil spirits. The incidence is very common and the manifestations much more severe. These spirit illnesses are due to either human or nonhuman spirits. In one type of possession (aretondolo) the victim sees these spirits which are invisible to everyone else. They persecute the victim in a large number of ways. They pursue him and he flees across the country; he may be dragged along and made to perform all varieties of stunts. But the remarkable thing is that the victim never shows marks of injury. These seizures come suddenly, and after the first attack, the victim is liable to others. His seizure ends in a spell of unconsciousness from which he awakes normal. Another form of possession is called salomanga, which is possession by a once human spirit.

The chief method of worship is by means of sacrifice and thanks. The Betsileo make sacrifices for favors desired or received; they sacrifice for plenty and for scarcity. There is, however, a novelty in the form of taking a vow, which in essence is a promise to make a sacrifice, usually a cow or fowl, pending the outcome of certain events in the individual's favor. The rituals are filled with all kinds of repetitious ceremonials; the same thing must be done a certain number of times to be effectual.

The ombiasy has the same functions as in Tanala. He cures the sick, performs sikidy, designates good and bad days for undertakings, and makes charms. The ombiasies are as in Tanala, nkazo and ndolo, the latter being chiefly women.

There are in addition to the legitimate ombiasies the malevolent sorcerers, mpamosavy. These are very scarce in Tanala, but very numerous—or at least suspected to be so—in Betsileo. The practice is secret, and hereditary. The mpamosavy is an agent of Zanahary and is possessed by the god. These sorcerers do evil deeds at night, and run out of their homes naked except for a turban. Everyone is suspected of being mpamosavy. They work chiefly by planting charms in places where they can do harm. The techniques by which the mpamosavy work are similar to those in Tanala. One such charm is a small wooden coffin containing medicines and a small dead animal. When this is destroyed the charm is broken. Nail parings, hair cuttings, leftover food, clothing, earth from a footprint, can be used to injure its owner; urine, feces, and spittle are not so used. In Tanala we noted that these could not be used for malevolent magic as "bait." As a result in Betsileo all nail parings, hair cuttings, etc., are kept in one common heap. The charms used by *mpamosavy*, powerful in themselves, are strengthened and reinforced by evil ghosts. Anyone apprehended in the practice of *mpamosavy*, is ostracized or driven into exile.

There is perhaps one additional concept in Betsileo culture not found in Tanala; the breaking of a taboo can be atoned for by an act of purification.

Much more general apprehension exists in Betsileo than Tanala, as shown by the increase in belief in omens, dreams, and superstitions. The difference is quantitative. Some of the superstitions are rather telling. When a person dies at the moment of a good harvest, he has been killed by his wealth. The superstitions all indicate some fear of retaliatory misfortune. The type of reasoning is largely by analogy. Thus, if anyone strikes a snake but does not kill it, the offender will suffer as the snake suffers; if it is sick he will be sick, if it dies, he will die.

There is also considerable increase in crime, stealing in particular, but also murder. For this latter crime there is indemnity and retaliation by vendetta. The Tanala do not engage in boxing; the Betsileo do. Suicide is very uncommon; but I have heard of a case of suicide in which the man vowed to use his soul to persecute the man who drove him to it. Blood brotherhood exists as in Tanala.

One additional custom should be noted, as of contrast to Tanala. There the village tomb contains all the dead. In Betsileo, burial was in individual family tombs, the women being laid on one side, the men on the other. The king's body was mummified, with special rituals insuring the liberation from the body of a small embryo which later turns into a snake. Tombs became one of the favorite ways of displaying wealth and ostentation. Technological development of weaving and pottery in Betsileo was very much more highly developed than in Tanala. However, the Betsileo made contact with several neighboring peoples where these arts were highly developed, whereas the Tanala did not.

In conclusion we can say that Tanala and Betsileo cultures were identical in the main. The differences are traceable to the change in productive methods from dry to wet rice cultivation. This is proved by several circumstances: The traditions in Betsileo indicate an old culture very like Tanala; the institutions of both indicate a common source, and many of them are still identical; the changes in Tanala were gradual, and were well on the way to becoming identical with Betsileo when the French took over; and finally some of the Tanala tribes took over the wet rice method and abandoned it because of the serious incompatibilities it created in the social structure. The spread of wet rice cultivation cannot be attributed solely to diffusion; wet rice culture was endemic in Tanala and coincident with dry rice. Its spread was favored largely by the exhaustion of the dry method. Hence in examining the changes secondary to this main innovation, we need not depend exclusively on diffusion for an explanation.

Gossip and Scandal

Max Gluckman

From *Current Anthropology,* Vol. 4, No. 3, 1963, pp. 307–315. Copyright 1963, Wenner-Gren Foundation for Anthropological Research. By permission of the author, the publisher, and the copyright holder.

It has taken the development of anthropological interest in the growth and break-up of small groups to put gossip and scandal into their proper perspective, as among the most important societal and cultural phenomena we are called upon to analyse. Perceptive anthropologists dealt with these phenomena from the early days of field observation. Paul Radin, in his *Primitive Man as a Philosopher,* described the way in which

> *primitive people are indeed among the most persistent and inveterate of gossips. Contestants for the same honours, possessors of the sacred rites of the tribe, the authorized narrators of legends, all leave you in little doubt as to the character and proficiency of their colleagues. "Ignoramus," "braggart," and not infrequently "liar" are liberally bandied about. . . .*

Before I examine a study which demonstrated this fully, I glance in general terms at our problems. Their importance is indicated by the fact that every single day, and for a large part of each day, most of us are engaged in gossiping. I imagine that if we were to keep a record of how we use our waking-time, gossiping would come only after "work"—for some of us—in the score. Nevertheless, popular comments about gossip tend to treat it as something chance and haphazard and often as something to be disapproved of. It is against the canons of the Church. Yet is possible to show that among relatively small groups, gossip, in all its very many varieties, is a culturally determined process, which has its own customary rules, trespass beyond which is heavily sanctioned. I propose to illustrate the social affiliations of this process and to suggest that gossip, and even scandal, have important positive virtues. Clearly they maintain the unity, morals and values of social groups. Beyond this, they enable these groups to control the competing cliques and aspiring individuals of which all groups are composed. And finally, they make possible the selection of leaders without embarrassment. . . .

The more exclusive the group, the greater will be the amount of gossip in it. There are three forms of social group which test this hypothesis. The one is the professional group, like lawyers or anthropologists, whose gossip is built into technical discussion so tightly that the outsider cannot always detect the slight personal knockdown which is concealed in a technical recital, or the technical sneer which is contained in a personal gibe. This is, therefore, the most irritating kind of group to crash into, because one has no clue to the undercurrents, no apparatus for taking soundings. And this is why old practitioners of a subject can so easily put a comparative newcomer into his place, can make him feel a neophyte. They have only to hint in a technical argument at some personal fact about the person who advanced the theory discussed, to make the eager young student feel how callow he is. Again, the more highly organized the profession, the more effective is the role of gossip here.

I have glanced already at the second type of highly exclusive group—that feels it has high social status from which it wishes to exclude parvenus. But we must notice that these groups tend to become hereditary; and once they are, it means that each group comprises not only the present members of the group, but also the past dead members. And here lies great scope for gossip as a social weapon. To be able to gossip properly, a member has to know not only about the present membership, but also about their forebears. For members can hit at one another through their ancestors, and if you cannot use this attack because you are ignorant, then you are in a weak position. Gossip here is a two-edged weapon; for it also means that you have no ancestors in the group to be attacked through—in short that you have no ancestors. And each time that someone in your presence refers to a scandal about another's ancestor, or even his own ancestor, he is gently rubbing in the fact that you have no ancestors and do not belong properly to the group, and are a parvenu.

The third type of exclusive group is that which has exclusiveness thrust upon it—either by being a minority, by isolation of locality, or by other distinguishing criterion which the members cannot overcome. I shall illustrate the function of gossip and scandal in this type of group in detail, since here (as far as I know) these important phenomena were most fully subjected to an illuminating anthropological investigation. . . .

The Makah Indians were a small group of Red Indians resident in the Puget Sound area at the tip of Cape Flattery, opposite Vancouver Island. It was estimated that in 1780 they numbered some 2,000 people. A century later, smallpox and other vicissitudes had reduced them in number to under 700 and in 1942, when Dr. Colson studied them, there were 400-odd on the tribal roll. The Makah belonged to the Northwest Coast group of American Indians, famous in anthropological literature for their performance of the *potlatch*. A *potlatch* was a ceremonial feast to which one group or individual invited social rivals in order to demonstrate family prerogatives. The host aggressively asserted his and his family's ownership of particular property in resources, titles, songs and ceremonial privileges while feasting and made presents to the visitors. The visitors then had to give a return feast on a bigger scale or lose face.

Before the Makah came under American protection and care by treaty they lived in five villages, divided into longhouses in which dwelt extended families. The people were divided into chiefs, commoners, and slaves.

The American Indian Service set out a century ago to turn the Makah into American citizens—agriculturalists in an environment suitable only for fishing, hunting and collecting; Sunday School addicts, aware of the value of money and averse to destroying their own property, living in houses by small families, wearing clothes, eating off tables and the like. Children were taken by compulsion from their parents and sent to boarding school to cut them off from their parents and Indian tradition. All things Indian were prohibited by the local agent of the Indian Service. This process of indoctrination was kept up until 1932, when the policy of the Indian Service changed, and it began to encourage the development of Indian cultural individuality within the general American pattern.

Colson tried, in her study, to assess how far this process of Americanization had succeeded. She found that the Makah in practice had made a satisfactory adjustment to the modern American world. From the beginning, they had paid their way economically, unlike the Plains Indians, who had been put on Government rations after the destruction of the buffalo. The Makah were protected in a part of their ancient territory by their treaty with the United States Government; and from their Reservation they had been able to earn a living first at sealing, and then at fishing for halibut, and also by working for the lumber company exploiting the forests on the Reservation. . . .

Colson saw that the Makah were able to adapt themselves to the new conditions and that this was possible because they were able to earn a good living from the sea and from work on their Reservation as well as outside it. Yet they still cling together as a group, partly because they have economic interests in being Indians. As wards of the United States Government, they cannot be taxed by State or local authorities, either directly or through purchase sales tax, entertainment tax, petrol tax, etc. They are not subject, while on the Reservation, to certain processes of law, such as garnishee orders on their wages or attachment of goods acquired by hire purchase and taken on the Reservation. They are entitled to free dental and medical treatment, and their children to free lunches at school as Whites are not. There are many advantages in being an Indian and also in being a Makah. This entitles a man to free rights in the Makah Reservation and ultimately to a share in the proceeds when the Reservation or parts of it are sold as provided in the Treaty. Therefore the Makah collectively and theoretically strive to keep their numbers low in total, in order that shares shall be greater, though in practice individuals will try to insure that the descendants of their own relatives are on the tribal roll, whatever their parentage, while they try to keep the descendants of others off.

I have summarized a beautifully presented argument and analysis to give a background to Colson's perception of the virtues of gossip and scandal among the Makah. Here we have a very small group (400 people) set against the mighty mass of the American population. They are hostile in many ways to the Whites with whom they associate. They feel that the Whites have robbed them of a culture and a way of life that was theirs, that the Whites have despoiled them and their Indian brothers of land, and so forth. One would expect that they would array themselves in unity in order to maintain their independence and their identity as Makah. Far from it. They are torn by internal dissension and struggles for status and they constantly use the tongue of scandal to keep one another in proper place.

Colson, knowing that the Makah had previously been divided into chiefs, commoners, and slaves, sought to establish the nature of this ranking in the past. She found great certainty about the rules as expressed by various people. But, unfortunately, some rules contradicted others, and the application of each was always uncertain. Someone would tell her that chieftainship was determined absolutely by birth, both on father's and mother's sides; and add, of course, that he was thus descended. Others would corroborate these rules, but would point out that the first informant was descended from a Nootka slave woman, and therefore was low class. Then others would say that birth was of some account, but it was more important that a man, to be high-class, should achieve something himself, by being a doctor or whale-hunter, or the like, and of course his father was a great whale-hunter or doctor or the like. Yet others would then run down these pretensions. Again, under the *potlatch* system, a man had had to give feasts to show his greatness; so today a man ought to be generous if he is to be esteemed. But now that anyone can earn money, if a man gives feasts his rivals can say that he is a *nouveau riche* trying to cover his low-class and that the real high-class people do not need to do this since their status is well known. Others will then accuse them of meanness, inappropriate to high-class, until they become prodigal, when they are *nouveau riche*. Finally, you can always down another by alleging that his family is addicted to sorcery (poisoning). And to use sorcery means that one is of low class—for the man or woman who is secure in social position does not need to use sorcery to secure his ends. Everyone is likely to accuse others of being sorcerers and to be accused in turn. . . .

> So it went from person to person until I found that everyone in the village accused others of being low-class and not entitled to speak for the Makah or to hold up their heads in front of the really good people.
>
> The result is that in Neah Bay today a class system theoretically exists, but it is impossible for the observer to place any single person in his proper class because there are no generally accepted standards as to what constitutes a valid claim to class status. Nor is there any generally accepted placing of individuals in various classes recognized by all Makah themselves. Yet, they are conscious of class and it enters into their thinking with references to other Makah to an extent that is incomprehensible to a newcomer. Each individual claims high-class status for himself and his immediate ancestors; each usually derides the claims of other Makah unless they happen to be close relatives—and even a close relative is not safe since his claims to status can always be derided on the ground that through some line not shared with you he descends from low-class people, or it may be claimed that he has not achieved enough to justify his equal position with your own. . . .

In this analysis Colson clearly establishes the important point that specific and restricted gossip within a group marks it off from other groups, both like and unlike. The gossip and scandal which are so biting in Makah life unite them into a group outside of general American society. And, as she points out, since this gossip and scandal involve the criticism and assessment of people against the traditional values of Makah society, they maintain the tribe as Indians against Whites, and as Makah against other Indians. These Makah values and traditions largely persist in the gossip and in no other way. To be a

Makah, you must be able to join in the gossip, and to be fully a Makah you must be able to scandalize skillfully. This entails that you know the individual family histories of your fellows; for the knowledgeable can hit at you through your ancestry, and you must be able to retort in kind. You have also got to have some knowledge of the old ways of the Makah tribe. . . .

Hence, I suggest, Makah gossip does not show merely that general interest in the doings, and the virtues and vices, of others, which characterizes any group. The gossip passes beyond this stage and becomes vicious scandal, aimed at demonstrating that the other parties are not worthy to be Makah. The different groups and individuals in the tribe fight an unceasing battle to demonstrate their own true Makahship, as against the failure of others to attain Makahship. But this involves them in a continual process of remaining Makah, which (as Colson says) gives high importance to the scandalizing itself, as a mechanism for maintaining the Makah as a group encysted in the American nation, whose other members are excluded from this war of scandal. And the practice of this scandal is developed to a high art, culturally defined. Scandalizing is one of the principal means by which the group's separateness is expressed, even though it is also the principal manner in which internal struggles are fought. This combination of functions of scandal makes the hostility itself a mode through which the tribe remains united. . . .

Gossip and even scandal unite a group within a larger society, or against another group, in several ways. Firstly, all groups try to thrust their roots into the past; scandal by creating a past history for the members in relation to one another, into which newcomers have to be inducted if they are to be full members, achieves this; secondly, no groups are completely undifferentiated. All of them consist in the first place, of individuals, and, secondly, most consist of smaller groupings of individuals, cliques. These individuals and cliques may be competitively aligned against each other. They struggle for status and prestige. These struggles have to be kept within bounds, while the general values of the group are asserted, if the group is to survive. The values of the group are clearly asserted in gossip and scandal, since a man or woman is always run down for failing to live up to these values. But the struggles to fulfil those values by individuals and cliques are also restrained because the methods of achieving them are defined by gossip and scandal: and these themselves punish any excess. For they control disputation by allowing each individual or clique to fight fellow members of the larger group with an acceptable, socially instituted customary weapon, which blows back on excessively explosive users. For the battle of scandal has its own rules, and woe to him who breaks these rules. By the act of carrying his scandalizing too far, he himself oversteps the values of the group and his scandal will turn against him, will prove that he or his small clique is unworthy of the larger group. And the scandal will in fact redound to the credit of the person attacked, since he will have been unfairly assailed. Colson tells the story of two Makah women who were on bad terms. On one occasion one woman in the streets hurled strings of insults at the other, who kept walking along, singing, "The bear went over the mountain." "Both women knew that one was behaving like a 'low-class' person, the other like a 'high-class' person, and the advantage lay with the one who ignored the insults." Thus the gross scandalmonger overreaches himself and is hoist with his own slander. (Similarly, gamesmanship is the art of winning games without actually cheating.) In this way, the internal struggles within the group are fought with concealed malice, by subtle innuendo, and by pointed ambiguities. Yet all of these have their own moral norms, which must not be overstepped. The main moral norm is that you must scandalize about an opponent behind his back, if your allegations are at all open; to his face, you must be delicate and never give him ground to state that you have insulted him. For insults of this kind, if open, make impossible the pretence of group amity. Similarly, misplaced behind-the-back gossip may force the group either to expel the person slandered or to turn on the

gossiper. More than this, the process of scandal enables a group to evaluate people for their work, their qualities of leadership, and their moral character, without ever confronting them to their faces with failures in any sphere. Thus animosities between individuals and cliques are built into the larger social order through the cultural techniques of gossip and scandal. . . .

The important things about gossip and scandal are that generally these are enjoyed by people about others with whom they are in a close social relationship. Hence when we try to understand why it is that people in all places and at all times have been so interested in gossip and scandal about each other, we have also to look at those whom they exclude from joining in the gossiping or scandalizing. That is, the right to gossip about certain people is a privilege which is only extended to a person when he or she is accepted as a member of a group or set. It is a hallmark of membership. Hence rights to gossip serve to mark off a particular group from other groups. There is no easier way of putting a stranger in his place than by beginning to gossip: this shows him conclusively that he does not belong. On the other hand, if a man does not join in the gossip and scandal, he shows that he does not accept that he is a party to the relationship; hence we see that gossiping is a duty of membership of the group. That is why it is good manners to gossip and scandalize about your dearest friends with those who belong, even though it be their dearest friends—but it is bad manners—which is a moral judgment and hence a sanction—to tell unpleasant stories about your friends to strangers. For when you gossip about your friends to other mutual friends you are demonstrating that you all belong to one set which has the duty to be interested in one another's vices as well as virtues. When you gossip about your friends to strangers you are either showing the strangers that they do not belong, or you are admitting them to a privilege and to membership of a group without consulting the other people involved. So that if you want to run down a friend to a stranger you should first ask that friend's permission. You do not need his permission to run him down to mutual friends—provided that they are in the same set of relationships with yourself. I think it would be bad manners to run two people down to one another, even though they are mutually acquainted, if you are not associated with them in the same way. . . . For scandal is only virtuous if its aim be to demonstrate some kind of social unity. Scandal when directed by members of a group against another group is unifying in another, and an obvious, way—it asserts the superiority of the scandalizing group.

I am sure that if you reflect on your own experience you will realise how sound Colson's analysis is. Its significance emerges most clearly if we consider the way in which a new member of a group is inducted into the group. He may learn the rules of technique which keep the group in being, and he may be on excellent terms with the other members of the group, but he does not belong to the group until it is impossible for him to be rude to one of its members unintentionally. That is, he must know so much about each of the members' histories and likings and dislikes, that he will never say something which is hurtful to anyone unless he wants to hurt him (or her). Correspondingly, the badge of membership is that a person can quite allusively, and apparently naively, cut another member to the quick by a seemingly innocent statement. And of course, it is important that the person offended knows that the allusion is intended but not be able to pin it down, and that the injurer should know that the offended knows, and that the offended should know that the injurer knows that the offended knows—and so on *ad infinitum.*

Therefore a most important part of gaining membership of any group is to learn its scandals: what you can say with apparent innocence and what you may say by indirect rude allusion. Anthropology is a very tightly knit profession: it is one of the few professions which still has an initiation ceremony. You must have studied some exotic community. We maintain our tight bonds of friendship by a vast store of scandal and gossip as well as by legends. A most im-

portant part of my duty in training research workers is to teach them the scandals. I believe I am not alone among senior anthropologists in finding it more interesting to teach students about anthropologists than about anthropology. It is worth noting here that the Greek Lexicon defines "anthropologist" not as "anthropos plus logos," a "student of man," but only as "a scandalmonger and in the *Nicomachean Ethics,* Aristotle—who anticipated us all—says of the great-souled man: "He is no scandalmonger (*anthropologos*): he will not talk either about himself or another person." . . .

I note finally that I have discussed gossip only within small groups. Gossip about royalty, by the lower classes about the upper, and the upper by the lower, has to be related to other areas of social relations. I think we can say that men and women do wish to talk about personal matters, for reasons on which I am not clear, and in the great conurbations the discussion of, for example, stars of film and sport, produces a basis on which people transitorily associated can find something personal to talk about. Frankenberg reports that when he was studying the Welsh village, the first time he went to buy a loaf of bread he was back in five minutes. His landlady said scornfully: "Back already? It takes me an hour to buy a loaf of bread." When Frankenberg had been in the village for some time, as soon as he went into a shop, the tea-kettle was put on the fire: after all, as *anthropologos,* he was the scandalmonger par excellence. And I myself have found through my interest in soccer and cricket, that I have steadily expanded my commercial transactions with shopkeepers into warm friendships, even into a kind of blood brotherhood, in which our ritual alliance moves jerkily from elation to despair with the fate of our city's teams, and our county eleven at cricket. To buy a packet of tobacco may take me twenty minutes. But this field of gossip and scandal still awaits the study of the kind deployed by Colson upon the Makah. Meanwhile, for small groups alone, my conclusion is that we might formulate a law to say, the more exclusive a social group is, the more will its members indulge in gossip and scandal about one another. And the more persistently will they repeat the same gossip again and again and again without getting bored. . . .

Outsiders frequently complain that anthropologists are able to find that anything social has a useful function and they may therefore conclude that anthropologists approve of everything. Thus it has been argued that the criminal classes are as important as the police for the maintenance of law in a society; they provide people who commit crimes but who can easily be caught by the police and publicly tried. Their trials demonstrate to the society at large, and particularly to its growing youngsters, not only that crime is wrong—which is true, but also that crime does not pay—which is not true. Amateur criminals, less easily caught, are not so useful. But this does not mean we approve of crime. We argue only that the commission of a crime, provided that the criminal is caught, tried, and punished, serves useful ends in maintaining the law, and therefore society. My argument about gossip and scandal is similar; if I suggest that gossip and scandal are socially virtuous and valuable, this does not mean that I always approve of them. Indeed, in practice I find that when I am gossiping about my friends as well as my enemies I am deeply conscious of performing a social duty; but that when I hear they gossip viciously about me, I am rightfully filled with righteous indignation.

selection 48

Steel Axes for Stone Age Australians

Lauriston Sharp

From *Human Problems in Technological Change,* Edward H. Spicer (ed.), Russell Sage Foundation, 1952, pp. 69–90. Copyright 1952, Russell Sage Foundation. By permission of the author, and the publisher and copyright holder.

The Problem

Like other Australian aboriginals, the Yir Yoront group at the mouth of the Coleman River on the west coast of tropical Cape York Peninsula originally had no knowledge of metals. Technologically their culture was of the old stone age or paleolithic type; they supported themselves by hunting and fishing, obtaining vegetable foods and needed materials from the bush by simple gathering techniques. Their only domesticated animal was the dog, and they had no domesticated plants of any kind. Unlike some other aboriginal groups, however, the Yir Yoront did have polished stone axes hafted in short handles, and these implements were most important in their economy.

Toward the end of the nineteenth century metal tools and other European artifacts began to filter into the Yir Yoront territory. The flow increased with the gradual expansion of the white frontier outward from southern and eastern Queensland. Of all the items of western technology thus made available, none was more acceptable, none more highly valued by aboriginals of all conditions than the hatchet or short-handled steel axe. . . .

What changes in the life of the Yir Yoront still living under aboriginal conditions in the Australian bush could be expected as a result of their increasing possession and use of the steel axe? . . .

In 1915 an Anglican mission station was established near the mouth of the Mitchell River in the territory of a tribe neighboring the Yir Yoront on the south and about three days' march from the heart of the Yir Yoront country. Some of the Yir Yoront refused to have anything to do with the mission or to go near it, others visited it on occasion, while a few eventually settled more or less permanently in one of the three "villages" at the mission.

Thus the majority of the Yir Yoront continued to live their old self-supporting life in the bush, protected until 1942 by the government reserve and the intervening mission from the cruder realities of the encroaching new order which had come up from the south. To the east was poor country, uninhabited. To the north were other bush tribes extending on along the coast to the distant Archer River Presbyterian mission with which the Yir Yoront had no contact. Westward was the expanse of the shallow Gulf of Carpentaria, on which the natives saw only a mission lugger making its infrequent dry-season trips to the Mitchell River. In this protected environment for over a generation the Yir Yoront were able to recuperate from former shocks received at the hands of civilized society. During the 1930's their raiding and fighting, their trading and stealing of women, their evisceration and two- or three-year care of their dead, their totemic ceremonies continued apparently uninhibited by western influence. In 1931 they killed a European who wandered into their territory from the east, but the investigating police never approached the group whose members were responsible for the act. In 1934 the anthropologist observed a case of extra-tribal revenge cannibalism. The visitor among the bush Yir Yoront at this time found himself in the presence of times past, in an essentially paleolithic society which had been changed,

to the casual eye, chiefly by the addition of oddments of European implements and goods put to a variety of uses.

As a direct result of the work of the Mitchell River mission, all Yir Yoront received a great many more western artifacts of all kinds than they ever had obatined before. As part of their plan for raising native living standards, the missionaries made it possible for aboriginals at the mission to earn some western goods, many of which were then given or traded out to natives still living under bush conditions; or they handed out gratis both to mission and to bush aboriginals certain useful articles which were in demand. They prevented guns, liquor, and damaging narcotics, as well as decimating diseases, from reaching the tribes of this area, while encouraging the introduction of goods they considered "improving." As has been noted, no item of western technology that was available, with the possible exception of trade tobacco, was in greater demand among all groups of aboriginals than the short-handed steel axe. A good supply of this type of axe was therefore always kept in stock at the mission for sale; and at Christmas parties or other mission festivals steel axes were given away to mission or visiting aboriginals indiscriminately and in considerable numbers. In addition, some steel axes, as well as other European goods, were still traded in to the Yir Yoront by natives in contact with cattle stations established south of the missions. Indeed, such axes had probably come to the Yir Yoront along established lines of aboriginal trade long before any regular contact with whites had occurred.

Relevant Factors

If we concentrate our attention on Yir Yoront behavior centering about the original stone axe, rather than on the axe—the thing—we should get some conception of the role this implement played in aboriginal culture. This conception, in turn, should permit us to foresee with considerable accuracy some of the results of the displacement of stone axes by steel axes acquired directly or indirectly from Europeans by the Yir Yoront.

The production of a stone axe required a number of simple skills. With the idea of the axe in its various details well in mind, the adult men—and only the adult men—could set about producing it, a task not considered appropriate for women or children. First of all, a man had to know the location and properties of several natural resources found in his immediate environment: pliable wood, which could be doubled or bent over the axe head and bound tightly to form a handle; bark, which could be rolled into cord for the binding; and gum, with which the stone head could be firmly fixed in the haft. These materials had to be correctly gathered, stored, prepared, cut to size, and applied or manipulated. They were plentifully supplied by nature, and could be taken by a man from anyone's property without special permission. Postponing consideration of the stone head of the axe, we see that a simple knowledge of nature and of the technological skills involved, together with the possession of fire (for heating the gum) and a few simple cutting tools, which might be nothing more than the sharp shells of plentiful bivalves, all of which were available to everyone, were sufficient to enable any normal man to make a stone axe.

The use of the stone axe as a piece of capital equipment for the production of other goods indicates its very great importance in the subsistence economy of the aboriginal. Anyone—man, woman, or child—could use the axe; indeed, it was used more by women, for theirs was the onerous, daily task of obtaining sufficient wood to keep the campfire of each family burning all day for cooking or other purposes and all night against mosquitoes and cold (in July, winter temperature might drop below forty degrees). In a normal lifetime any woman would use the axe to cut or knock down literally tons of firewood. Men and women, and sometimes children, needed the axe to make other tools, or weapons, or a variety of material equipment required by the aboriginal in his daily life. The stone axe was essential in making the wet-season domed

huts, which keep out some rain and some insects; or platforms, which provide dry storage; or shelters, which give shade when days are bright and hot. In hunting and fishing and in gathering vegetable or animal food the axe was also a necessary tool; and in this tropical culture without preservatives or other means of storage, the native spends more time obtaining food than in any other occupation except sleeping.

In only two instances was the use of the stone axe strictly limited to adult men: Wild honey, the most prized food known to the Yir Yoront, was gathered only by men who usually used the axe to get it; and only men could make the secret paraphernalia for ceremonies, an activity often requiring use of the axe. From this brief listing of some of the activities in which the axe was used, it is easy to understand why there was at least one stone axe in every camp, in every hunting or fighting party, in every group out on a "walk-about" in the bush.

While the stone axe helped relate men and women and often children to nature in technological behavior, in the transformation of natural into cultural equipment, it also was prominent in that aspect of behavior which may be called conduct, primarily directed toward persons. Yir Yoront men were dependent upon interpersonal relations for their stone axe heads, since the flat, geologically recent alluvial country over which they range, provides no stone from which axe heads can be made. The stone they used comes from known quarries four hundred miles to the south. It reached the Yir Yoront through long lines of male trading partners, some of these chains terminating with the Yir Yoront men, while others extended on farther north to other groups, having utilized Yir Yoront men as links. Almost every older adult man had one or more regular trading partners, some to the north and some to the south. His partner or partners in the south he provided with surplus spears, and particularly fighting spears tipped with the barbed spines of sting ray which snap into vicious fragments when they penetrate human flesh. For a dozen spears, some of which he may have obtained from a partner to the north he would receive from a southern partner one stone axe head. . . . Thus trading relations, which may extend the individual's personal relationships out beyond the boundaries of his own group, are associated with two of the most important items in a man's equipment, spears and axes, whether the latter are of stone or steel. Finally, most of the exchanges between partners take place during the dry season at times when the aboriginal fiestas occur, which center about initiation rites or other totemic ceremonials that attract hundreds and are the occasion for much exciting activity besides trading.

Returning to the Yir Yoront, we find that not only was it adult men alone who obtained axe heads and produced finished axes, but it was adult males who retained the axes, keeping them with other parts of their equipment in camp, or carrying them at the back slipped through a human hair belt when traveling. Thus, every woman or child who wanted to use an axe—and this might be frequently during the day—must get one from some man, use it promptly, and return it to the man in good condition. While a man might speak of "my axe," a woman or child could not; for them it was always "your axe," addressing a male, or "his axe."

This necessary and constant borrowing of axes from older men by women and children was done according to regular patterns of kinship behavior. A woman on good terms with her husband would expect to use his axe unless he were using it; a husband on good terms with his wives would let any one of them use his axe without question. If a woman was unmarried or her husband was absent, she would go first to her older brother or to her father for an axe. Only in extraordinary circumstances would she seek a stone axe from a mother's brother or certain other male kin with whom she had to be most circumspect. A girl, a boy, or a young man would look to a father or an older brother to provide an axe for her or his use, but would never approach a mother's brother, who would be at the same time a potential father-in-law, with such a request. Older men, too,

would follow similar rules if they had to borrow an axe.

It will be noted that these social relationships in which the stone axe had a place are all pair relationships and that the use of the axe helped define and maintain the character of the relationships and the roles of the two individual participants. Every active relationship among the Yir Yoront involved a definite and accepted status of superordination or subordination. A person could have no dealings with any other on exactly equal terms. Women and children were dependent on, or subordinate to, older males in every action in which the axe entered. Among the men, the younger was dependent on the older or on certain kinds of kin. The nearest approach to equality was between brothers, although the older was always superordinate to the younger. Since the exchange of goods in a trading relationship involved a mutual reciprocity, trading partners were usually a kind of brother to each other or stood in a brotherly type of relationship, although one was always classified as older than the other and would have some advantage in case of dispute. It can be seen that repeated and widespread conduct centering on the axe helped to generalize and standardize throughout the society these sex, age, and kinship roles, both in their normal benevolent and in exceptional malevolent aspects, and helped to build up expectancies regarding the conduct of others defined as having a particular status. . . .

The stone axe was an important symbol of masculinity among the Yir Yoront (just as pants or pipes are among ourselves). By a complicated set of ideas which we would label "ownership" the axe was defined as "belonging" to males. Everyone in the society (except untrained infants) accepted these ideas. Similarly spears, spear throwers, and fire-making sticks were associated with males, were owned only by them, and were symbols of masculinity. But the masculine values represented by the stone axe were constantly being impressed on all members of society by the fact that non-males had to use the axe and had to go to males for it, whereas they never borrowed other masculine artifacts. Thus, the axe stood for an important theme that ran all through Yir Yoront culture: the superiority and rightful dominance of the male, and the greater value of his concerns and of all things associated with him. We should call this androcentrism rather than patriarchy, or paternal rule. It is the recognition by all that the values of the man (*andros*) take precedence over feminine values, an idea backed by very strong sentiments among the Yir Yoront. Since the axe had to be borrowed also by the younger from the older, it also represented the prestige of age, another important theme running all through Yir Yoront behavior. . . .

Analysis

The introduction of the steel axe indiscriminately and in large numbers into the Yir Yoront technology was only one of many changes occurring at the same time. It is therefore impossible to factor out all the results of this single innovation alone. Nevertheless, a number of specific effects of the change from stone axes to steel axes may be noted; and the steel axe may be used as an epitome of the European goods and implements received by the aboriginals in increasing quantity and of their general influence on the native culture. The use of the steel axe to illustrate such influences would seem to be justified, for it was one of the first European artifacts to be adopted for regular use by the Yir Yoront; and the axe, whether of stone or steel, was clearly one of the most important items of cultural equipment they possessed.

The shift from stone to steel axes provided no major technological difficulties. While the aboriginals themselves could not manufacture steel axe heads, a steady supply from outside continued; and broken wooden axe handles could easily be replaced from bush timbers with aboriginal tools. Among the Yir Yoront the new axe never acquired all the uses it had on mission or cattle stations (carpentry work, pounding tent pegs, use as a hammer, and so on); and, indeed, it was used for little more than the stone axe had been, so

that it had no practical effect in improving the native standard of living. It did some jobs better, and could be used longer without breakage; and these factors were sufficient to make it of value to the native. But the assumption of the white man (based in part on a realization that a shift from steel to stone axe in his case would be a regression) that his axe was much more efficient, that its use would save time, and that it therefore represented technical "progress" toward goals which he had set for the native was hardly borne out in aboriginal practice. Any leisure time the Yir Yoront might gain by using steel axes or other western tools was invested, not in "improving conditions of life," and certainly not in developing aesthetic activities, but in sleep, an art they had thoroughly mastered.

Having acquired an axe head through regular trading partners of whom he knew what to expect, a man wanting a stone axe was then dependent solely upon a known and an adequate nature and upon his own skills or easily acquired techniques. A man wanting a steel axe, however, was in no such self-reliant position. While he might acquire one through trade, he now had the new alternative of dispensing with technological behavior in relation with a predictable nature and conduct in relation with a predictable trading partner and of turning instead to conduct alone in relation with a highly erratic missionary. If he attended one of the mission festivals when steel axes were handed out as gifts, he might receive one simply by chance or if he had happened somehow to impress upon the mission staff that he was one of the "better" bush aboriginals (their definition of "better' being quite different from that of his bush fellows). Or he might—but again almost by pure chance—be given some brief job in connection with the mission which would enable him to earn a steel axe. In either case, for older men a preference for the steel axe helped create a situation of self-reliance and a behavior shift from situations in technology or conduct which were well structured or defined to situations in conduct alone which were ill defined. It was particularly the older ones among the men, whose earlier experience or knowledge of the white man's harshness in any event made them suspicious, who could avoid having any relations with the mission at all, and who thus excluded themselves from acquiring steel axes directly from that source.

The steel axe was the root of psychological stress among the Yir Yoront even more significantly in other aspects of social relations. This was the result of new factors which the missionary considered all to the good: the simple numerical increase in axes per capita as a result of mission distribution; and distribution from the mission directly to younger men, women, and even children. By winning the favor of the mission staff, a woman might be given a steel axe. This was clearly intended to be hers. The situation was quite different from that involved in borrowing an axe from a male relative, with the result that a woman called such an axe "my" steel axe, a possessive form she never used for a stone axe. (Lexically, the steel axe was differentiated from the stone by an adjectival suffix signifying "metal," the element "axe" remaining identical.) Furthermore, young men or even boys might also obtain steel axes directly from the mission. A result was that older men no longer had a complete monopoly of all the axes in the bush community. Indeed, an old man might have only a stone axe, while his wives and sons had steel axes which they considered their own and which he might even desire to borrow. All this led to a revolutionary confusion of sex, age, and kinship roles, with a major gain in independence and loss of subordination on the part of those able now to acquire steel axes when they had been unable to possess stone axes before.

The trading partner relationship was also affected by the new situation. A Yir Yoront might have a trading partner in a tribe to the south whom he defined as a younger brother, and on whom as an older brother he would therefore have an edge. But if the partner were in contact with the mission or had other easier access to steel axes, his subordination to his bush colleague was obviously decreased. Indeed, under the new dispensation he might prefer to give his axe to a bush

"sweetheart" in return for favors or otherwise dispose of it outside regular trade channels, since many steel axes were so distributed between natives in new ways. Among other things, this took some of the excitement away from the fiesta-like tribal gatherings centering around initiations during the dry season. These had traditionally been the climactic annual occasions for exchanges between trading partners, when a man might seek to acquire a whole year's supply of stone axe heads. Now he might find himself prostituting his wife to almost total strangers in return for steel axes or other white men's goods. With trading partnerships weakened, there was less reason to attend the fiestas, and less fun for those who did. A decline in one of the important social activities which had symbolized these great gatherings created a lessening of interest in the other social aspects of these events.

Not only did an increase in steel axes and their distribution to women change the character of the relations between individual and an individual, the paired relationships that have been noted, but a new type of relationship, hitherto practically unknown among the Yir Yoront, was created in their axe-acquiring conduct with whites. In the aboriginal society there were almost no occasions outside the immediate family when one individual would initiate action to several other people at once. For in any average group, while a person in accordance with the kinship system might be superordinate to several people to whom he could suggest or command action, at the same time he was also subordinate to several others, in relation with whom such behavior would be tabu. There was thus no over-all chieftainship or authoritarian leadership of any kind. Such complicated operations as grass-burning, animal drives, or totemic ceremonies could be carried out smoothly because each person knew his roles both in technology and conduct.

On both mission and cattle stations, however, the whites imposed upon the aboriginals their conception of leadership roles, with one person in a controlling relationship with a subordinate group. Aboriginals called together to receive gifts, including axes, at a mission Christmas party found themselves facing one or two whites who sought to control their behavior for the occasion, who disregarded the age, sex, and kinship variables among them of which they were so conscious, and who considered them all at one subordinate level. Or the white might impose similar patterns on a working party. (But if he placed an aboriginal in charge of a mixed group of post hole diggers, for example, half of the group, those subordinate to the "boss," would work while the other half, who were superordinate to him, would sleep.) The steel axe, together, of course, with other European goods, came to symbolize for the aboriginal this new and uncomfortable form of social organization, the leader-group relationship.

The most disturbing effects of the steel axe, operating in conjunction with other elements also being introduced from the white man's subcultures, developed in the realm of traditional ideas, sentiments, and values. These were undermined at a rapidly mounting rate, without new conceptions being defined to replace them. The result was a mental and moral void which foreshadowed the col-

lapse and destruction of all Yir Yoront culture, if not, indeed, the extinction of the biological group itself.

From what has been said it should be clear how changes in overt behavior, in technology and conduct, weakened the values inherent in a reliance on nature, in androcentrism or the prestige of masculinity, in age prestige, and in the various kinship relations. A scene was set in which a wife or young son, his initiation perhaps not even yet completed, need no longer bow to the husband or father, who was left confused and insecure as he asked to borrow a steel axe from them. For the woman and boy the steel axe helped establish a new degree of freedom which was accepted readily as an escape from the unconscious stress of the old patterns, but which left them also confused and insecure. Ownership became less well defined, so that stealing and trespass were introduced into technology and conduct. Some of the excitement surrounding the great ceremonies evaporated, so that the only fiestas the people had became less festive, less interesting. Indeed, life itself became less interesting, although this did not lead the Yir Yoront to invent suicide, a concept foreign to them. . . .

The Backwash of the Frontier: The Impact of the Indian on American Culture

A. Irving Hallowell

From *Annual Report of the Board of Regents of the Smithsonian Institution,* 1958, publication 4354, U.S. Printing Office, 1959, pp. 447–472, as reprinted from Walker D. Wyman and Clifton B. Kroeber (eds.), *The Frontier in Perspective.* The University of Wisconsin Press, 1957, pp. 229–257. Copyright, 1957 by The Regents of the University of Wisconsin. By permission of the author, the publishers, and the copyright holder.

Although Frederick Jackson Turner and his disciples have made little point of the influence of the American Indian upon our civilization, it is the Indian's continuing presence throughout our whole colonial and national history that has given many aspects of our culture a special coloring. In this respect, our national experience differs from that of any western European nation, though our culture is continuous with that of Europe. . . .

Discernible Indian influences of this sort have formed what I have called "the backwash of the frontier," fertile silt carried on the currents and eddies left by the turmoil on the borderlands. Many other factors besides frontier conditions were involved in the further development of these influences—factors too complex to analyze here. And the problem is complicated by the extreme diversity of America's reactions to the Indian and his cultures; by the manner in which Indian influences have been mediated, the varying forms they have assumed at different periods of our national existence, and their depth. Most often they have been manifested at the vernacular level of American culture, one expression of our cultural provincialism, which is perhaps the reason so little systematic attention has been paid to them. *Our contacts with the Indians have affected our speech, our economic life, our clothing, our sports and recreations, certain indigenous religious cults, many of our curative practices, folk and concert music, the novel, poetry, drama, and even some of our basic psychological attitudes, and one of the social sciences, anthropology* [Italics added].

To the outside world there is a closer association of the Indian with the image of America than perhaps we are aware of. For example, Cooper's "The Last of the Mohicans" is not only read by every American schoolchild, but it has been said to be the best-known American novel in the world. So too, "Hiawatha," Longfellow's poetic image of the Indian, is widely read and translated in other countries. Ivan Bunin, the Russian poet and novelist, "is probably as well recognized for his translation of 'Hiawatha' as for any of his original works."

Americans have created a whole succession of images of the Indian, some literary and interpretative, some growing out of direct contact with particular types of white men with him and changing with historical circumstances. Although the Pope declared as far back as 1512 that the natives of America were descended from Adam and Eve, in colonial New England Cotton Mather thought "probably the *Devil* decoy'd . . . [them] . . . hither, in hopes that the gospel of the Lord Jesus Christ would never come here to destroy or disturb his absolute empire over them." As God's elected agents and under his "wonder-working Providence," the colonists must convert these "tawney serpents" or annihilate them. However, the Indian was never simply The Enemy. On the earliest frontiers, the colonists were befriended by the natives. Who has not heard of Squanto? White men from the beginning profited in many practical ways from the Indians' knowledge of their own country and through intimate contacts learned about their customs, manner of thought, and character, and were influenced by them.

During the 18th century, when in England and on the Continent a literary image of the noble savage, partly derived from ideas about the Indian, was being created, the colonists greatly deepened their firsthand knowledge of the American natives. Trading activities brought tribal groups over a wider range into contact with the colonists.The Indians were not always fought against; on occasion they were comrades-in-arms, and aboriginal methods of fighting influenced the colonists. The speeches made by Indians in treaty negotiations aroused so much interest in native oratory that a novel literary form, with no prototype in Europe, emerged. Verbatim reports of these conferences were widely circulated and read in printed form. It has even been said that information about the organization and operation of the League of the Iroquois, which Franklin picked up at various Indian councils, suggested to him the pattern for a United States of America. In any case it was Franklin whose appreciation of the attitude of Indians toward their own culture led

him to express the anthropological principle of the relativity of culture norms when, in 1784, he wrote: "Savages we call them, because their manners differ from ours, which we think the Perfection of Civility: they think the same of theirs."

As the eastern frontier receded westward and for most Americans the contemporary Indians could be viewed at a comfortable distance, it was their decline that became a romantic literary theme. As expressed in poetry, drama, and the novel, it was an early backwash of the frontier. But it was by no means always the noble savage that was depicted; a double image was created—the savage as ignoble as well as noble. During this period, the first half of the 19th century, when the Indian was such a popular figure in American literature, it is particularly significant that most of the authors who dealt with Indian themes derived their information from written sources rather than from direct observation. Cooper depended on Heckewelder's writing, and Longfellow on Schoolcraft's "Algic Researches" (1839). It has been said that "Cooper poured the prejudices of John Heckewelder into the Leatherstocking mold, and produced the Indian of nineteenth century convention." The authors who were busy writing about the Indians were far removed from the men who faced them on the new frontiers.

Two and a half centuries after Englishmen on the eastern frontier faced the Indian, American frontiersmen in the Mississippi Valley and the Far West found themselves in a parallel situation and regarded him in much the same hostile light—the Indian blocked the path of America's "manifest destiny." In 1867, the Topeka Weekly Leader spoke for the West when it characterized the Indians as "a set of miserable, dirty, lousy, blanketed, thieving, lying, sneaking, murdering, graceless, faithless, gut-eating skunks as the Lord ever permitted to infect the earth, and whose immediate and final extermination all men, except Indian agents and traders, should pray for." Cotton Mather's terser characterization of the "tawney serpents" seems almost mild and dignified beside this scathing blast.

Wrestling with his own day-to-day problems, with the Long Hairs not far off, the trans-Mississippi frontiersman was in no position to appreciate the extent to which the Indians already had affected American culture. And it would be interesting to know how many Americans on this frontier had read "Hiawatha." Certainly, few of them could have imagined that, when the West was won and the Indians were safely settled on reservations, native arts and crafts would be appreciated for their esthetic values and widely exhibited, musicians and poets would visit these remaining enclaves of Indian culture to study their music and songs at firsthand, and a museum devoted exclusively to the preservation and exhibition of Indian objects would be established in the largest city of the Nation. What would have surprised them more, perhaps, if they could have looked at a Boy Scout Handbook of the 20th century, is the statement that it "is a pity that most boys think of headdresses, war whoops, tomahawks, and scalps the instant Indians are mentioned. . . . There are so many thousands of beautiful and desirable things in their lives that it is safe to say that they can offer boys a mighty good code of sport and happiness." And among the other things that would strike the frontiersman forcibly would be the requirement that, in order to win a merit badge in Indian lore, the Boy Scout must learn the Omaha Tribal Prayer. Yes, the Omaha, one of those dastardly Siouan tribes—the gut-eating skunks!

But if the Midwestern frontiersman had been interested enough, he would have discovered that the word "skunk," which he could so glibly hurl at the Long Hairs as a derogatory epithet, was derived from an Indian language and had entered American speech in the 17th century. The borrowing of words as well as traits of Indian culture, like the use of corn, had been going on for a long time. Referred to by anthropologists as cultural diffusion, this kind of cultural borrowing is a process that has been occurring throughout the entire history of man. It has been one of the main stimuli of cultural change. When people of different cultures meet and social interaction takes place, this situation inevitably eventuates in some cultural borrowing on the part of either or both peoples.

In the past two decades, cultural anthropologists in this country have devoted increasing attention to detailed studies of the effects of Euro-American culture upon the Indians, that is, acculturation, rather than confining themselves, as was once the case, primarily to the collection of data that would make it possible to reconstruct an ethnographic picture of aboriginal life in its undisturbed form. On the other hand, although recognizing that in principle acculturation is seldom if ever a one-way process, anthropologists have paid scarcely any attention to the total effects upon American culture of our continuing contacts with Indians.

One of the things that anthropologists have discovered is that while Indians may "clothe" themselves, so to speak, with many of the accouterments of white man's culture, this is often no more than skindeep. Even when the Indian is brought into close contact with the white man for more than a generation, and despite missionary efforts and educational opportunities, there is a psychological lag to be taken into account which indicates a dimension of the acculturation process about which we know too little.

In contrast to this side of the acculturalization picture in the United States, it is interesting to recall, when white adults, and especially children, were captured in the 17th, 18th, and early 19th centuries by many different groups of Indians and lived among them in daily intimacy, the apparent ease with which these individuals adjusted themselves to Indian culture. Turner speaks of the "occasional instances of Puritans returning from captivity to visit the frontier towns, Catholic in religion, painted and garbed as Indians and speaking the Indian tongue, and the halfbreed children of captive Puritan mothers." While there were many hundreds of white captives taken, we have detailed and reliable information on only a few cases, including individuals who were abducted as children. These "white Indians" often refused to return to the mode of life into which they had been born, even when given an opportunity. In the 18th century Crève-coeur asked: "By what power does it come to pass, that children who have been adopted when young among these people, can never be prevailed on to readopt European manners?" Such individuals sometimes forgot their native speech, like Cynthia Ann Parker, captured by the Comanches in 1836 at the age of 9. When recaptured by the whites as a grown woman, all she could remember was her name. Other captives praised Indian character and morals and some of them adopted an Indian world view and religious beliefs. It was said of Mary Jemison, abducted in 1758 at the age of 15, that "she was as strong a pagan in her feelings as any Indian," that all her religious ideas conformed to those of the Senecas, and that "the doctrine taught in the Christian religion she is a stranger to." Of William Failey, abducted in 1837, his brother-in-law and biographer wrote: "In fact, his long residence among the Indians has made him an Indian." Don Ryan in "The Warriors' Path" (1937) and Conrad Richter in "The Light in the Forest" (1953) have given this theme modern novelistic treatment. The latter book was soon republished in paperback form (1954), and Walt Disney has made a movie of it.

Benjamin Franklin must have been highly impressed by the attitude which the Six Nations assumed toward the values of their own culture as compared with that of the whites. An anecdote, in several forms, appears in his writings which presumably was derived from the considered response these Indians made when, during the Lancaster conference in 1744, it was suggested that if they so desired some of their boys might be sent to Williamsburg for a white education. The Iroquois countered with the proposition that "if the English Gentlemen would send a Dozen or two of their children to Onondago, the great council would take care of their Education, bring them up in really what was the best Manner and make men of them."

These Indians not only felt secure in their own values; they felt free to appraise those of the white man. And the captives who became "white Indians" discovered that the actual manner of life of the natives was something other than the literary images of the noble savage or the fiendish red man. The Indian cultures contained values which the white child could assimilate, live by, and in adulthood refuse to relinquish. Old White Boy and all his sons became Seneca chiefs. Even aside from captives, there were white men on the frontier who became semiacculturated to Indian ways. Sam Houston, in his early days, lived with the Cherokees. It has not been sufficiently stressed that Leatherstocking, the most famous internationally of all characters in American fiction, falls into this category. Although a white man by "natur," he had Indian "gifts." He is said to have "acquired some knowledge of most of the Indian dialects." During his early life, he lived among the Delawares and long before they called him Deerslayer, he had successively borne three other Indian nicknames. On occasion, he identified himself with the Delawares and their aboriginal values. When contemplating torture by the Hurons, he says he will strive "not to disgrace the people among whom I got my training." And the Huron chiefs, uncertain about his return from the brief furlough granted him, entertained "the hope of disgracing the Delawares by casting into their teeth the delinquency of one held in their villages." While they would have preferred to torture his Indian comrade Chingachgook, they thought the "pale face scion of the hated stock was no bad substitute for their purposes." Quite aside from his characterization as the honest, resourceful, intrepid frontiersman and scout, the uniqueness of Leatherstocking as the first white man in fiction represented as acculturated in his youth to Indian languages, customs, and values, should not be overlooked.

From a contemporary vantage point, I believe that our relations with the Indians involve one distinct peculiarity which might have been difficult to predict at an earlier period of our history. Despite our achievement of political dominance, considerable race mixture, and the effects of acculturation on the native peoples, neither the Indian nor his culture has completely vanished from our midst. The question arises, have the Indian cultures of the postfrontier period completely ceased to influence us? The answer is no. One effect of the reservation system has been the conservation of those aspects of the native cultures that had survived all the vicissitudes of previous contacts with the white race. A new potential source of influence on our 20th-century culture was created. Before we can turn to the nature of this influence, however, it is necessary to obtain the wider historic perspective that a more systematic consideration of the older lines of influence will provide us.

In the first place, it could have been predicted that, as a result of the colonization of the New World, loan words would appear in various Indo-European languages that could be traced to aboriginal American languages. Besides the nouns borrowed to designate objects unknown in England, there are many expressions in American English that reflect Indian influence—*burying the hatchet, Indian summer, Indian giver, happy hunting ground,* and *war paint,* used by the American woman. *Buck* as a slang expression for *dollar* harks back to the Indian fur trade when prices had reference to beavers or buckskins. Place names of Indian origin are, of course, legion—the names of 26 states, 18 of our largest cities, thousands of small towns, most of the long rivers and large lakes, and a few of the highest mountains are of Indian derivation.

Having come to a country new to them, it was inevitable that the colonists, whose traditional culture had not prepared them to live as they had to live here, should be influenced by those aspects of Indian culture that had immediate practical advantages in daily life. In any case, the determinative importance of the fact that this was not in any sense a virgin land must not be forgotten. The countless generations of Indians had left their imprints upon the landscape. Without the plow, the soil had been cultivated, and the raising of native crops was as typical over wide areas as was hunting and fishing. It is still debatable how far the actual virgin terrain had been radically modified by burning, girdling, and tilling. There were narrow forest trails, trodden by moccasined feet, that were already old, and the whites made use of them in their own system of overland communication, developing some of them into highways eventually connecting great centers of American civilization. Then there were the earth-works of an older Indian population in the old Northwest Territory which influenced the patterning of some early settlements. The "pilgrims" who founded Marietta, Ohio, found it convenient to moor their flatboats "at the foot of a raised terrace the Mound Builders had once used as an avenue between their temple and the river." Circleville takes its name from the fact that in the laying out of the original town, concentric circles of aboriginal earthworks were closely followed by the outlying streets. An octagonal courthouse, surrounded by a circular green, became the hub of the town. And it is said that "in the Wabash River bottoms, in the early spring many farmhouses stand high and dry on a wooded burial mound while all the fields are under water."

Among the early settlers, communication by water was everywhere the most important. While they were familiar with certain types of watercraft in their own culture, they and their descendants have been influenced by at least two types used by the Indians, the Chesapeake Bay log canoe and the bark canoe of the north.

From a European point of view, the Indians wearing moccasins, leggings, and breechclouts were considered to be relatively naked compared to themselves. However, considered in a very broad culture-historical perspective, their own style and that of the aborigines shared a generic trait in common: throughout the boreal regions of the Northern Hemisphere, clothing of the fitted or tailored type prevails, standing in marked contrast to the untailored style once found in the ancient Mediterranean region, Africa, and Central and South America. In all these latter regions, for example, nothing like the fitted footgear represented by the boot, shoe, or moccasin is found. While the practice never spread beyond the frontier itself, nevertheless there were white men who adopted the wearing of not only Indian moccasins, but leggings and a breechclout as well. The moccasin, of course, is the most noted item of Indian clothing that was used by white men very early. It was a fitted type of footgear, and if the colonists had been Romans, this item of clothing might not have been borrowed so quickly, or its use continued. Turner has noted that the General Court of Massachusetts once ordered 500 pairs each of snowshoes and moccasins for use in the frontier countries. Much later, footgear of this type was used by lumbermen. In the backwoods of Manitoba in the 1930's, a clergyman of my acquaintance always wore a pair of his best beaded moccasins in the pulpit on Sundays. It would be interesting to know more about the commercialization of the moccasin type of shoe which we see increasingly on the feet of Americans today.

It was, however, the discovery of the plants cultivated by the New World aborigines that from the very first produced the most profound impact on both European and American culture, revolutionizing the food economy and diet of Old World peoples and at the same time laying one of the foundations on which was to rise the distinctive structure of American agriculture. Of the several plants —maize, beans, pumpkins, squash, and others—maize in particular was important from the start, taking precedence over the grain which the settlers had brought from Europe. It became a primary factor in the acculturation of the Englishmen to an American way of life. We need think only of corn on the cob, cornbread, Indian pudding, hominy, mush, grits, succotash, and corn sirup; of breakfast cereals, cornstarch, and popcorn; or of corncob pipes and bourbon, to understand the extent of this Indian contribution to our civilization today.

Tobacco is an equally significant "gift" of the American Indians, symbolized by the once-familiar figure of the "wooden Indian" inextricably linked with the tobacco shop in the 19th century. The history and use of it in our culture present a number of features in cultural borrowing at large. Readaptation to the values of the borrowing people is well illustrated. The consumption of tobacco was completely divorced from the ceremonial context in which it appeared among the Indians and became purely secular.

Peruvian bark, now known as quinine, proved highly sensational since it was a specific for malaria. It reached Spain before the middle of the 17th century and was soon introduced into the English colonies. In Virginia, Governor Berkeley said in 1671 that whereas formerly one person in five had died of fever in his first year, now almost no one succumbed. When one considers that in this same century Governor Winthrop's famous remedy for ulcers consisted of "one ounce of crabbe's eyes and four ounces of strong wine vinegar," the general state of colonial medicine can be well appreciated, and the reason why Peruvian bark, an Indian herbal, achieved such high fame can easily be understood. Indian medicine was likewise given a boost when, in 1738, Dr. John Tennent was awarded 100 pounds by the Virginia House of Burgesses for curing pleurisy with Seneca rattlesnake root. As William Fenton well says, when Western medicine met Indian herbalism, the former "was still carrying a heavy burden of medieval practices so that the first few physicians in the colonies were but several centuries advanced from the Indian shaman who selected his herbs thinking of the effect that their appearance might contribute to the disease, and guaranteed their efficiency with incantations and feats of magic. Moreover, the average settler had brought from the Old World a knowledge of herbs that in kind was not unlike that of the Indian, but as newcomers they were unfamiliar with New World plants, and although the level of their own popular medicine did not set them above adopting Indian remedies, the Indian herbalist whose knowledge was power was not always a ready teacher." In "The Pioneers," Cooper pictures for us how "Doctor" Elnathan Todd managed to steal one of John Mohegan's remedies.

Popular confidence in Indian medicine remained strong during the early 19th century, when the population was flowing over the Appalachians. The "yarb and root" doctor, red or white, played a prominent role in many communities. In 1813 in Cincinnati there was published "The Indian Doctor's Dispensatory." Other books followed, including Selman's "The Indian Guide to Health" (1836) and Foster's "The North American Indian Doctor, or Nature's Method of Curing and Preventing Disease According to the Indians" (1838). In a lecture given at the New York Academy of Medicine in 1936, Dr. Harlow Brooks (emeritus professor of clinical medicine, New York University) said:

> The universal testimony of those qualified to judge has been that even within the memory of my generation we have incorporated into our pharmacopoeia and practice a good many practices and drugs of our Indian predecessors. . . . The leading doctor in my boyhood memory, in the district in which my parents settled, was an old Sioux medicineman, whose services were considered by the territorial government so valuable that when his tribe was removed to a reservation he was asked to remain with his white patients, among whom were my own parents. I am sure that much of the medicine I received as an infant and child was derived directly from the lore of this fine, learned, and much respected old man. In those days it was on the service of these men that our pioneers relied for medical help; otherwise, little or none at all was available to the early settler.

What is particularly interesting is not merely the incorporation in our pharmacopoeia of some aboriginal drugs, but the positive attitude toward Indian medicine and charms that has persisted into the 20th century. For instance, old Seneca families still sell wild flowers and sassafras on certain street corners in Buffalo, and the Pamunkey Indians of Virginia until a decade ago went to Washington every spring to sell sassafras and other herbs. In "Triple Western" (fall, 1954) there is a short item on "Medicine Man's Wisdom."

The potencies attributed to Indian herbal remedies have had still other manifestations in our culture, an important one being the medicine show. While not all these shows made use of the Indian, most of them did. It has been said that "as a symbol" the native "was as important to the med-show platform

as the wooden Indian was to the tobacco shop." It exploited the image that had already been created of him as a "healer." When Chief Chauncey Kills-in-the-Bush Yellow Robe died, eulogies appeared in the theatrical press. Rolling Thunder, the owner of the Kiowa Indian Medicine and Vaudeville Company, commented on these as follows:

> It is fine to see this intelligent recognition of the life work of an Indian. Too many people have always thought of the American Indian as next to a beast. There are some who are now learning the truth: that the Indian's drugstore was always the field and the forest, where the herbs he uses in his medicines are gathered as God placed them for him to use, and God gave the Indian the knowledge to gather and compound them. That is why the Indian as a healer has been a success.

The authors of "Show Biz" say that "when the Kickapoo Indian Medicine Company went on the block in 1911, after 30 years roaming the American plains and hamlets, it still brought $250,000. At one time, there were 150 medicine shows on the road, all of them featuring one or more Kickapoo Indians." It may be pointed out in passing that at the same time that the image of the Indian as a healer was being exploited in the medicine show, the old image of him as a bloodthirsty enemy was being dramatized by the Wild West show that William F. Cody took on the road in 1883 and which in various incarnations and imitations continued until 1931, when the 101 Ranch closed down.

The red man also became involved in another characteristic area of American cultural development in the years before the Civil War—religion. In Spiritualism, the United Society of Believers (Shakers), and the Church of Latter-day Saints (Mormons), the American Indians had special significance for the founders or adherents. According to Shaker tradition, "it was a native of the forest who first recognized the saintliness of Mother Ann. One poor Indian saw a bright light around her, and prophesied that the Great Spirit had sent her to do much good. In another story it is related that when Ann was returning from her eastern mission, she was met at the Albany ferry by a number of Indians, who joyfully cried: 'The good woman is come! The good woman is come!'" What other religious sect in the world has turned to an aboriginal people for validation of the saintliness of the founder? Besides this, some of the Shaker "gift songs" received in trance came from Indian spirits. Once the spirits of a whole tribe of Indians, who had died before Columbus discovered America and had been wandering homeless ever since, turned up at a Shaker meetinghouse, where they were made welcome. As described by an eyewitness, more than a dozen of the Shakers present became possessed by these Indian guests. A pow-wow ensued. There were yells, whoops, and strange antics. The Indian spirits asked for succotash, which they ate, and after some instruction were sent off under guidance "to the Shakers' heavenly world."

Although "speaking in tongues" had a long history in Europe as well as in America, one of the striking facts in the early developmental phases of American Spiritualism is the frequency of references to mediums speaking Indian languages and to those who had an Indian "control" or "guide." The names of more than a dozen mediums, men and women and their Indian controls, appear in the "Encyclopaedia of Psychic Science." Such historic figures as Red Jacket, Black Hawk, and Tecumseh are on the list, as well as spirits with such names as White Feather, Bright Eyes, and Moonstone. What is particularly significant is that these Indian spirits were thought to be beneficent in their influence, especially because of their healing powers, although they often manifested themselves at seances in a somewhat rambunctious manner. As time went on and spirit photography was introduced, some of these spirits appeared in native costume in the photographs.

It would seem that no other American religious sect, with the possible exception of the Shakers, felt such a genuine affinity with the aborigines. While there was no question of borrowing Indian beliefs as such, neverthe-

less the Spiritualists saw analogies to their own views and practices. One of these was the "shaking tent" rite of the Algonkians of the eastern woodlands (which has been described elsewhere). Into a framework of poles covered with birchbark or canvas a conjurer goes; the tent sways and voices are heard which, however, are usually believed to be nonhuman. An early historian of American Spiritualism, writing in 1870, after referring to some of these rites, says:

Such are some of the phases in which communication exhibits itself amongst a people whom we call "savage" and whom, in comparison to our more advanced civilization, we may justly call so; and yet, does our knowledge of the occult and invisible forces in nature furnish us with any clue to the mystery of these astounding manifestations or the power by which the unlettered "savage" can avail himself of a knowledge which all our control over the elements fails to compete with? In a word, the red Indian can do what we can neither explain nor imitate.

This interest of the Spiritualists in the Indian and his ways has continued down to the present. At Lily Dale, N.Y., the summer mecca of Spiritualists, which commemorated its 50th anniversary in 1929, it has been customary to celebrate Indian Day with parades and dances given by natives from nearby reservations.

To turn now to the Church of Jesus Christ of Latter-day Saints, the attitude of the adherents of this indigenous American sect toward the Indians is in sharp contrast with that of the Spiritualists. According to "The Book of Mormon," the red men are essentially the degenerate posterity of a rebellious segment of a small group of Jews who, migrating to the New World before the beginning of the Christian era, brought with them an advanced culture. Consequently, it is said that "The Book of Mormon" supplements the Bible, since it is a history of God's dealings with remnants of Israel and the Saviour's ministrations among them in the Western Hemisphere. For in America, the great Nephrite prophecy has been fulfilled—the second coming of Christ. After the Resurrection He appeared to a multitude of nearly 3,000 people in Mexico, before a greater assembly the next day, and after this "he did show himself unto them oft." The occurrence of the legendary figure of a so-called "white god" with certain associated attributes among the Incas, Mayas, Aztecs, and Toltecs, the Mormons interpret as supporting evidence for the historic appearance of Christ in America.

In the Mormon view the aborigines of the United States were the descendants of the Lamanites, the "bad" people of the Mormon epic. Unlike the Spiritualists, the Mormons had nothing they could look to them for; still, a strange affinity connected them with the Indians. In Mormon hymnals there are songs about the red man. In the days before the rise of archeology or anthropology in the contemporary sense, "The Book of Mormon" was representative of the speculations that had been going on in Europe for several centuries about the peopling of the New World. These earlier theories had to be reconciled first of all with the account given in the Bible of man's creation and dispersal. What is peculiar in the Mormon case, however, is the fact that a particular theory of the peopling of the New World was incorporated as a dogma of a religious sect. This could hardly have occurred anywhere but in early 19th-century America. The early Mormons easily reconciled their theory with the Bible, but since the sect has survived into a period of American culture when an enormous increase in our knowledge of New World prehistory from archeological investigations has taken place, a further reconciliation of the inspired history found in "The Book of Mormon" with this new knowledge is now being sought.

Outside the Mormon church, the consensus is that in its nondoctrinal aspects "The Book of Mormon" is derived from a romance written but not published by Solomon Spaulding, a clergyman who left the church and was in business in Ohio by 1812. There he dug into some mounds and became interested in the origin of the extinct people who had erected them. The theory that they were of Jewish origin was not original with him,

since it was maintained by many prominent men in this country. If Spaulding's manuscript had been printed in its original form as fiction, he would have anticipated those writers in America who were soon to exploit the Indian in the historical novel. Even when "The Book of Mormon" was published in 1830, it fell precisely in the period when the Indian was assuming great prominence in American literature. Three of Cooper's "Leatherstocking Tales" had met with acclaim by this date, and at least 39 novels published between 1824 and 1834 included Indian episodes.

There was a parallel development in the drama. Barker's "Indian Princess" (Pocahontas), staged in 1808, had a long line of successors. There were at least 30 so-called Indian plays staged between 1820 and 1840 and 20 or more between the latter date and the Civil War. Some of these were dramatizations of the novels of Cooper, Bird, and Simms. The peak in the popularity of these Indian dramas also falls within the period (1830–70) that has been called "the golden days of the American actor." Perhaps the most outstanding example is "Metamora, or The Last of the Wampanoags," which was in the repertoire of Edwin Forrest for almost 40 years. It was played in Philadelphia every year—except two—for a quarter of a century. Forrest had specifically advertised in 1828 for a play in which "the hero, or principal character, shall be an aboriginal of this country." William Cullen Bryant was the chairman of the committee which selected "Metamora" from the 14 plays submitted. It proved to be one of the most popular plays of the 19th-century American theater. "Metamora" was played even after Forrest's death, and a radio version was broadcast in 1939. During its theatrical lifetime, more Americans are said to have seen "Metamora" than "Abie's Irish Rose" or "Tobacco Road" in the 20th century.

In Poetry, the Indian had appeared as a subject ever since the time of Freneau, but there was nothing that could compare with the initial impact and continuing popularity of "Hiawatha." It became *the* poem of the American Indian. Before publication in 1855, there was an advance sale of 4,000 copies; in 5 months the sale had risen to 50,000 copies. It has been said that what was unique about Longfellow's poem was the fact that "'Hiawatha' was the first poem of its kind in America based on Indian legend rather than on Indian history." While true enough, it is clarifying to note that until 1839, when Schoolcraft published his "Algic Researches," there were no reliable collections of Indian myths or tales on which a poet could draw. It was, therefore, a historical accident that Longfellow came to exploit Ojibwa material; he had no other choice. Paradoxically, Schoolcraft himself published a poem dealing with the Creek Indian wars 12 years before "Hiawatha" appeared. He did not know the Creeks at first hand, while he knew the Ojibwas intimately, his wife being of that tribe. Evidently it never occurred to him to use his Ojibwa myths as the basis of a narrative poem. Thus Schoolcraft epitomizes the force of the traditional literary approach to the use of Indian themes.

Longfellow bore the same sort of relation to Schoolcraft as Cooper did to Heckewelder. Generally speaking, there was no inclination on the part of eastern novelists, dramatists, or poets who selected Indian themes to become acquainted with living Indians of the contemporary frontiers as a background for their productions. Indeed, a volume of short stories, "Tales of the Northwest," about Indians in the Upper Mississippi region, written by one who knew them intimately, was ignored after its publication in 1839. William Joseph Snelling, the author, had insisted that "a man must live, emphatically, live with Indians; share with them their lodges, their food, and their blankets, for years, before he can comprehend their ideas, or enter their feelings." American writers were not yet ready for this early call to realism. But for American readers, a novel entitled "Altowan; or Incidents of Life and Adventure in the Rocky Mountains," by Sir William Drummond Stewart, an eccentric Scot, who during the 1830's had spent 6 years in the West, was published in New York in 1846. Although the novel was undistinguished in writing and had some romantic

trappings, in this case the author *had* seen a great deal of Indian life. What makes the book unique is that one of the leading characters, as pointed out by De Voto, is an Indian transvestite—a berdache—and this individual is depicted in highly realistic terms. The author pictures his behavior and dress in detail, and no doubt is left about what he was. "I know of no English or American novel of that time or for many years later that is half so frank about homosexuality," writes De Voto.

In painting and popular music there was a parallel romantic tradition. Gleanings from historical documents or tradition were tinctured by an extremely free use of imagination. It is obvious, for instance, that the artist who provided the frontispiece for Mrs. Morton's "Ouabi, or The Virtue of Nature" (1790) knew as little about Indians at first hand as did the author of this poem in the noble savage tradition. And Benjamin West's painting of one of Penn's treaties with the Indians, dating from about 1771, offers a direct parallel to the literary artist who drew on historical documents for his source material.

Part of Mrs. Morton's poem was set to music by Hans Gram the year after its publication. This composition, the first orchestral score published in the United States, was entitled "The Death Song of an Indian Chief," although there is no evidence that the composer knew anything about aboriginal music. In 1799, a musical arrangement of "Alk'-amoonok, the Death Song of the Cherokee Indians," reputedly based on a genuine Indian melody, was published and soon became very popular. It had been sung in "Tammany" (1794), the first American opera. An eccentric musician, Anton Philip Heinrich, who died in 1861, was the composer of the "Pocahontas Waltz" for piano and is said to have been the first to use Indian themes in larger orchestral works. The heroine of the big song hit of 1844, "The Blue Juniata," was an Indian girl, "Bright Alforata."

Actually, it is at this vernacular level that the backwash of the frontier is most clearly discernible in American music of the 19th century. This was due to the role of the Indian played in the subject matter of folk songs.

In one group of songs, the Indian appears "merely as an incidental personality" and the attitudes toward him are vague. In a second group, however, negative attitudes are sharply defined since many songs in this class are long narrative ballads which depict actual frontier conflicts. Folksongs about historic events, "including songs about dramatic episodes in the relationships of Indians and White, have been sung regularly since the earliest days of colonization and have faithfully reflected changing relationships between the two culture groups at least down to the present century when modern techniques for the commercialization of popular songs may have beclouded the issue." A third category of songs reflects a positive attitude toward the Indian varying "from vague references to good Indians or Indians with heroic qualities, to songs and ballads exclusively about romanticized Indians, who are admired for their stamina and other heroic qualities." An anonymous, undated example of America's folk painting, depicting the rescue of John Smith, belongs to this earlier period. The same motif was subsequently as popular in prints as it was in fiction, drama, poetry, and music.

However, in the midst of all this romanticizing of the Indian, a trend toward greater realism developed, particularly in painting. Here and there in colonial times there had been some realistic paintings of the Indians; for example, the masterly portraits of Lenape chiefs painted in 1735 by Gustavus Hesselius (1682–1755). But about 1821, many of the western chiefs who came to Washington on business with the Government sat for their portraits. A collection of these became the nucleus of the famous "Indian Gallery." The magnificent reproduction of 120 of these portraits in a folio edition of 3 volumes (McKenny and Hall, "History of the Indian Tribes of North America, 1836–44") gave the eastern public an opportunity to see what contemporary Indians looked like. On the other hand, artists themselves began to go west (Seymour, Rindisbacher, Lewis, Catlin, Miller, Eastman, Stanley, Kane, Bodmer, Kurz), so that greatly enriched images of the natives,

the kind of life they led, and the grandeur of the country they inhabited soon became more widely known to those living far removed from the contemporary frontier. It was the author of "Altowan" who induced Alfred Jacob Miller—now one of the most famous of these artists, whose true accomplishments have only become known to the public in recent years—to accompany him west in 1837. Catlin is particularly important, however, not only because he was a pioneer, but because he was a showman. He toured eastern cities in the late 1830's exhibiting his "Indian Gallery," which has been called the first Wild West show. It included Indian "curios," featuring pipes, and in exhibition halls he erected a real Crow tepee. Catlin appeared in person and, taking selected pictures as a point of departure, lectured to his audiences about Indian life. He would dress lay figures in Indian clothing and frequently had some Indians on hand to pantomime native activities. Although Catlin was not an anthropologist, his Indian Gallery did mediate to Americans a more realistic type of knowledge about the Plains tribes than had been available. After touring American cities, he took his show to England and the Continent. In 1954, an exhibition of Catlin's work, sponsored by the United States Information Agency, was again on tour in Europe, while in this country Bodmer's watercolors were being exhibited.

Even though Catlin "had been there," he had detractors, like Audubon, who challenged the accuracy of his paintings. The same thing had happened to Cooper and Longfellow. The romantic tradition in America was strong, and the application of a purely realistic standard of judgment was, in effect, an attack upon the tradition. Cooper may have idealized the Indian in some respects and erred in many details, but he idealized the pioneer and backwoodsman too. The Indian was enveloped in the romantic tradition and what is interesting is how long he has remained a part of it.

When the dime novel sprang into popularity in the 1860's, the Indians of the Cooper tradition became an integral part of this literature. In one way or another, Indians play a role in at least 45 percent of the 321 stories in the original dime-novel series. "Maleska, the Indian Wife of the White Hunter" (1860), the first one published by Beadle and Adams, actually was a reprinting of a story that had been serialized in 1839. "The death of the dime novel, if it ever really occurred, was accompanied by the birth of the nickelodeon, the motion picture, and the radio, which simply transferred the old stories of cowboys, desperadoes, and Indians to more dynamic forms." In fact, as soon as the silent cinema began to flicker, the Indian of the old romantic tradition was in. There was a screen version of "Hiawatha" as early as 1909, the "Deerslayer" was shown in 1911, the "Last of the Mohicans" in 1920. And, until very recently, what Stanley Vestal called the "Hollywooden Indian" has persisted in that typically American movie genre—the western.

On the other hand, there was an increasing awareness that authentic knowledge of the aboriginal cultures was relevant and desirable in the arts. Perhaps this attitude developed along with the emergence of a more realistic tradition in American writing. However this may be, I think that the publication of Edna Dean Proctor's "Song of the Ancient People" in 1893 represents a transitional case. While it is in the high romantic tradition, there is an appended commentary to this poem by F. H. Cushing (1857–1900), a pioneer anthropologist who went to the Southwest in 1879 and lived among the Zuñi for 5 years. He says he can bear witness to the poet's "strict fidelity of statement, and attempt to show, as one of the Ancient People themselves would be glad to show, how well she has divined their spirit." The volume was illustrated with realistic aquatints made by Julian Scott in the Hopi country. No other Indian poem had ever been offered to the public with such an aura of authenticity about it—it was bound in buckskin with a design taken from Southwestern pottery on the cover.

The inauguration of genuine Indian themes in American concert music is ordinarily attributed to Edward MacDowell, whose "Indian Suite" was first performed in 1896.

But where did he find such themes? He was not a frontier boy. He entered the Paris Conservatory at the age of 14 and did not take up residence here until he was 27. The fact is that MacDowell exemplifies a repetition of the same kind of relationship to the source of his thematic material as was noted in the case of Cooper and Longfellow. He got them from Theodore Baker, the first trained musician to go into the field and study Indian music at first hand. Baker, a German, visited the Seneca Reservation and the Carlisle Indian School in the summer of 1880, offering the results of his analysis to Leipzig University as a doctoral dissertation. But he was not a composer, nor was Alice C. Fletcher, whose monograph on Omaha songs (1893) initiated the study of Indian music in American anthropology. However, two of the songs she collected, "Shupida" and the "Omaha Tribal Prayer," undoubtedly have been among the most widely circulated examples of authentic Indian music in American culture. Together with three other Indian songs, they appear in "Indian Lore," a pamphlet in the Merit Badge Series of the Boy Scouts of America. In the past 6 years, approximately 47,000 copies of this booklet have been printed. Scouts who aspire to the merit badge in Indian lore must be able to "sing three Indian songs including the Omaha Tribal Prayer and tell something of their meaning." Since 1911, there have been more than 18,700 American boys who have won this distinction.

Following the lead of MacDowell, other posers began to make increasing use of Indian themes, though only a few made direct contact with the reservation Indians. Among them were Burton, Cadman, Farwell, Jacobi, Lieurance, Arthur Nevin, Skilton, and Troyer, who found native music interesting to them, because as Skilton has said, "many devices of the ultra modern composers of the present day have long been employed by Indians— unusual intervals, arbitrary scales, changing tune, conflicting rhythm, polychoral effects, hypnotic monotony." Indian songs were harmonized and arranged for performance by white musicians; Indian themes were handled freely in the composition of original works, much in the same way that Longfellow handled Ojibwa myths.

In the field of operatic composition, despite the popularity of other compositions of Herbert and Cadman, neither the former's "Natoma" (1911) nor the latter's "Shanewis" (1918) became established in operatic repertoire. Some compositions based on Indian themes have received high acclaim in the repertoire of orchestral music, others as popular songs. Skilton's "Indian Dances," along with MacDowell's "Indian Suite," were among the 27 compositions of 12 American composers which had the greatest number of performances in the United States during the 7 years following World War 1. Jacobi's "String Quartet on Indian Themes" was selected to represent American music at the International Festival of Contemporary Music at Zurich in 1926. Elliott Carter's "Pocahontas," presented in New York in 1939 (and later developed into a suite for orchestra) received the Juilliard Publication Award the following year. Cadman, who went to the Omaha Reservation in 1909 with Francis LaFlesche, an Indian anthropologist, wrote one of his most famous songs that year, "From the Land of the Sky Blue Water." It vied with "The Rosary" in popularity. He likewise wrote two operas on Indian themes. "By the Waters of Minnetonka" (1921), composed by Thurlow Lieurance, who had visited the western reservations as early as 1905, has had a phenomenal success. At midcentury it appears in the Victor Album "Twelve Beloved American Songs" along with "The Rosary" and " A Perfect Day." Nor should commercialized popular songs of a lower order—some Indian in name only—be forgotten. Among those composed early in this century were "Navajo" (1903), "Tammany" (1905), "Red Wing" (1907), and "Hiawatha's Melody of Love" (1920), to say nothing of "The Indian Love Call" (1924), and "Ramona," a hit of 1927.

In the early years of this century, some American poets, like the musicians, sought out the Indians, and those of the Southwest became a focal point of interest. These were the same people that Edna Proctor had written about. They had been the subject, too, of

a novel, "The Delight Makers" (1890), by A. F. Bandelier, said by Alfred L. Kroeber to be "a more comprehensive and coherent view of native Pueblo life than any scientific volume on the southwest."

A few American painters (Sharp, Phillips, Blumenschein) had also discovered the Southwest before the opening of the 20th century. Blumenschein's graphic commentary on the acculturation process, which shows two Indians mounted on merry-go-round horses, had appeared in Harper's Weekly in 1899.

Among the poets who became interested, Mary Austin soon took the lead. She became the key figure in the use of Indian material for literary purposes, and her extremely positive attitude toward the cultures of the Indians influenced many others to seek inspiration in their art. She characterized her "Amerindian Songs" as being "Reexpressed from the Originals." Some of these first appeared in "Poetry" (1917), along with comparable interpretations by Frank S. Gordon, Alice Corbin Henderson, and Constance Lindsay Skinner. Mary Austin wrote plays and stories, too. She seems to have moved from a romantic primitivism to a more and more realistic handling of Indian themes, as exemplified by her play "The Arrow Maker," produced on Broadway in 1911, and her "One-Smoke Stories (1934), one of her last books. Nor should the fact be overlooked that four anthologies containing translations of American Indian songs and poetry have appeared in this century (George W. Cronyn, "The Path of the Rainbow," 1918 and 1934; Nellie Barnes, "American Indian Love Lyrics and Other Verse," 1925; Margot Astrov, "The Winged Serpent," 1946; and A. Grove Day, "The Sky Clears," 1951).

In the 20th century, the Indian has also reappeared in American plays, particularly in the work of the regional dramatists. While the setting is frequently the historic past, the problems the native faces in the acculturation process are sometimes dramatized. Both "Strongheart" (1905) and "Cherokee Night" (1936) are examples of this theme. In prose fiction, we also find that anthropologists, inspired by Bandelier and the stories collected in Elsie Clews Parsons' "American Indian Life" (1922), entered the field. "Laughing Boy," a Literary Guild book of 1929, by Oliver La Farge, and "Hawk Over Whirlpools" by Ruth Underhill (1940) are outstanding illustrations. In "America in Fiction," the authors call attention to the fact that "now that he is on reservations, not a military foe, and generally not an economic competitor, the Indian is a subject of great interest, so much so that more fiction has been written about him in recent years than about any other ethnic group except the Negro. In many works of fiction, he has been given central prominence, his cultural complex has been detailed, and much attention has been paid to his problems of adjusting himself to the dominating civilization that surrounds him." Their bibliography lists 37 novels or collections of stories published between 1902 and 1947. "Where once we had melodrama about the Indian with his bloody tomahawk," they say, "now we have clear-cut realism." Whatever the art form may be, what is striking is the more intimate acquaintance with contemporary Indians that informs the work of the painter, musician, poet, dramatist, or novelist who has drawn upon aboriginal cultural forms or used the problems of the Indian for his thematic material.

Finally, it seems to me that among these more recent influences, the impact of the Indian on modern anthropology should not be omitted. The social sciences as they have developed in the United States during the past half-century have attained an unusual prominence in American culture. Among these, anthropology in its modern form was just getting under way about the time the frontier closed. It was in the 1890's that Franz Boas began to teach at Columbia University and to train students in fieldwork. Boas was a specialist in studies of the American Indian and a majority of his early students followed in his footsteps. Indeed, practically all the chief authorities on North American Indian ethnology, archeology, and linguistics have been American. A historical accident? Of course. But that is the point. It is only recently among the younger generation that more

attention is being devoted to peoples in the South Seas, Africa, and Asia. But it was the study of the Indians, and the problems that emerged from the investigation of the Indian as a subject, that gave American anthropology a distinctive coloring as compared with British, French, and German anthropology. Recently an American psychologist has remarked that "if the word 'anthropology' were presented to a sample of psychologists in a word-association test I would venture 'culture' would probably be the most popular response, with 'Indians' a runner-up." The presumption, no doubt, is that these hypothetical responses would be those of American psychologists.

The more detailed and reliable accounts of native Indian cultures that have emerged from the fieldwork of American anthropologists have made possible a more objective appraisal of the values inherent in the aboriginal modes of life. To those who look at the record, the Indian no longer appears as either a noble or ignoble savage. He has moved into a clearer focus as a human being. Like our own, his traditional cultural background and historical situation have determined the nature of his experience and made him what he is.

Viewing the panorama of our colonial and national history as a whole, I have referred to many diverse aspects of our culture—speech, economic life, food habits, clothing, transportation, medicine, religion, the arts, and even a social science—which have been influenced by our relations with the Indians at different times and in differing ways. Some of these influences have been mediated directly, others indirectly. Contacts with the Indian on the frontier have by no means been the source of all of them.

In summing up, we may ask: how deeply have such influences penetrated our culture? To what extent are our relations with the Indians one key to our differentiation as Americans, not only culturally but psychologically? Constance Rourke once wrote, "The Backswoodsman conquered the Indian, but the Indian also conquered him. He ravaged the land and was ravaged in turn."

Phillips D. Carleton, concluding his comments on the captivity literature, writes: "It emphasizes the fact that it was the line of fluid frontiers receding into the West that changed the colonists into a new people; they conquered the Indian but he was the hammer that beat out a new race on the anvil of the continent." Carl Jung, who has probably analyzed more persons of various nationalities than anyone else, thought he could discern an Indian component in the character structure of his American patients, and D. H. Lawrence asked whether a dead Indian is nought. "Not that the Red Indian will ever possess the broadlands of America," he said and then added, "But his ghost will."

In America we faced the Indian on receding frontiers for a long period; but outside the frontier there was the shadow of the Indian. This shadow is still upon us. We still mouth words and idioms that reflect intimate contacts with the aborigines of our land. We still make use of plants originally cultivated by them. We wear derivative forms of the footgear they wore. We have collected objects made by them in our homes and in our museums. Our artists have found inspiration in their artistic modes of expression. We constantly see the Indian sweep past our eyes on the movie screen. He persists in our historical novels and westerns. In 1954, "The Leatherstocking Saga" reappeared, compressed into one handsome volume. We Americans have seen the Indian come and go on the commonest national coins we have fingered. The first Bible to be printed in colonial America was in the Indian language, John Eliot's translation of the Old and New Testament into an Algonkian tongue. Over the generations thousands of American men have belonged to the more-than-a-century-old Improved Order of Red Men. American anthropologists have labored most industriously to provide more and more authentic information about aboriginal modes of life and the influence of American culture on the Indian. The Indian has never been rejected from the American consciousness. Perhaps his shadow upon us is even disappearing—he has become a part of us: in the "Dictionary of American Biography" will be found side by side with other famous Americans, Pontiac and Tecumseh, Blackhawk and Osceola. In 1931 a brief popular biography of Osceola—only a few pages in length—was printed at Palm Beach; it was entitled "Osceola the Seminole. Florida's Most Distinguished Historical Character!" And it is said that more statues have been erected of Sacajawea than of any other American woman.

Now that the frontier has passed, our children discover the Indian in the comic books, as well as in the library. They are familiar with Cooper's tales in "Classics Illustrated." Indeed, there appears to have been a marked increase in number, variety, and quality of children's books about Indians published in the last two or more decades. There are biographies of Indians famous in our history as well as historical romances. The stories of famous white captives have been retold; there are excellent books on Indian crafts and simplified but accurate accounts of tribal life, besides well-written stories which center around Indian children as major characters. Nevertheless, the average American is by no means aware of all the ramifications of Indian influence upon our culture. Perhaps the Red Indian ghost D. H. Lawrence saw here and what Jung discerned in the character of his patients provide clues to an aspect of the American ethos that invites deeper scrutiny in the future.

Where Are We Going If Anywhere? A Look at Post-Civilization

Kenneth E. Boulding

From *Human Organization,* Vol. 21, No. 2, 1962, pp. 162–167. © 1962, The Society for Applied Anthropology. By permission of the author, and the publisher and copyright holder.

We are living in what I call the second great change in the state of man. The first great change is the change from pre-civilized to civilized societies. The first 500,000 years or so of man's existence on earth were relatively uneventful. Compared with his present condition he puttered along in an astonishingly stationary state. To judge by his artifacts, at least, generation succeeded generation with the sons exactly like their fathers, and the daughters exactly like their mothers. There may have been changes in language and culture which are not reflected in the artifacts, but if there were these changes are lost to us. The evidence of the artifacts, however, is conclusive. Whatever changes there were, they were almost unbelievably slow. About 10,000 years ago, we begin to perceive an acceleration in the rate of change. This becomes very noticeable 5,000 years ago with the development of the first civilization. The details of this first great change are probably beyond our recovery. However, we do know that it depended on two phenomena: the first was the development of agriculture, and the second was the development of exploitation. These two great inventions seem to have developed about the same time, perhaps independently—although we do not know this—in the Nile valley, in the lower valley of the Euphrates, and in the valley of the Indus. Agriculture, that is the domestication of crops and livestock and the planting of crops in fields, gave man a secure surplus of food from the food producer. In a hunting and fishing economy it seems to take the food producer all his time to produce enough food for himself and his family. The moment we have agriculture with its superior productivity of this form of employment of human resources means that the food producer can produce more food than he and his family can eat. But this in itself is not enough to produce civilization. In some societies in these happy conditions, the food producer has simply relaxed and indulged himself with leisure. As soon, however, as we get politics, that is exploitation, we begin to get cities and civilization. Civilization, it is clear from the origin of the word, is what happens in cities, and the city is dependent in its early stages at any rate on there being a food surplus from the food producer and on there being some organization which can take it away from him. With this food surplus, the political organization feeds kings, priests, armies, architects, and builders and the city comes into being. Political science in its earliest form is the knowledge of how to take the food surplus away from the food producer without giving him very much in return.

Now I argue that we are in the middle, perhaps not even in the middle, of the second great change in the state of man, which is as drastic and as dramatic, and certainly as large if not larger, as the change from pre-civilized to civilized society. This I call the change from civilization to post-civilization. It is a strange irony that just at the moment when civilization has almost completed the conquest of pre-civilized societies, post-civilization has been treading heavily upon its heels. The student of civilization may soon find himself in the unfortunate position of the anthropologist who studies pre-civilized societies. Both are like the student of ice on a hot day—the subject matter melts away almost before he can study it.

These great changes can be thought of as a change of gear in the evolutionary process, resulting in progressive accelerations of the rate of evolutionary change. Even before the appearance of man on the earth, we can detect earlier evolutionary gear-shiftings. The formation of life obviously represented one such transition, the movement from the water to the land represented another, the development of the vertebrates another, and so on. Man himself represents a very large acceleration of the evolutionary process. Whether he evolved from pre-existing forms or whether he landed from a space ship and was not able to get back to where he came from, is immaterial. Once he had arrived on earth, the process of evolution could go on within the confines of the human nervous system at a greatly accelerated rate. The human mind is an enormous mutation-selection process. Instead of the mutation-selection process being confined, as it were, to the flesh, it can take place

within the image and hence, very rapid changes are possible. Man seems to have been pretty slow to exploit this potentiality, but one suspects that even with primitive man, the rate of change in the biosphere was much larger than it had been before, because of the appearance of what de Chardin calls the nöosphere, or sphere of knowledge.

Civilization represents a further acceleration of the rate of change, mainly because one of the main products of civilization is history. With the food surplus from agriculture it becomes possible to feed specialized scribes. With the development of writing, man did not have to depend on the uncertain memories of the aged for its records, and a great process of accumulation of social knowledge began. The past can now communicate, at least in one direction, with the present, and this enormously increases the range and possibility of enlargements of the contents of the human mind.

Out of civilization, however, comes science, which is a superior way of organizing the evolution of knowledge. We trace the first beginnings of science, of course, almost as far back as the beginning of civilization itself. Beginning about 1650, however, we begin to see the organization of science into a community of knowledge, and this leads again to an enormous acceleration of the rate of change. The world of 1650 is more remote to us than the world of ancient Egypt or Samaria would have been to the man of 1650. Already in the United States and Western Europe, in a smaller degree in Russia and in some other parts of the world, we see the beginnings of post-civilized society—a state of man as different from civilization as civilization is from savagery. What we really mean, therefore, by the anemic term "economic development" is the second great transition in the state of man. It is the movement from civilized to post-civilized society. It is nothing short of a major revolution in the human condition, and it does not represent a mere continuance and development of the old patterns of civilization.

As a dramatic illustration of the magnitude of the change, we can contemplate Indonesia. This is a country which has about the same extent, population, and per capita income as the Roman Empire at its height. For all I know it is producing a literature and an art at least comparable to that of the Augustan age. It is, therefore, a very good example of a country of high civilization. Because of this fact, it is one of the poorest countries in the world. It is very unhappy about its present state and visualizes itself as a poor country and it is desperately anxious to break out of its present condition. Jakarta is a city about the size of ancient Rome, although perhaps a little less splendid. All this points up the fact that the Roman Empire was a desperately poor and underdeveloped society, with a civilization that existed always on a shoe-string. The Roman cities seemed to have been always within about three weeks of starvation, and even at its height it is doubtful whether the Roman empire ever had less than 75–80 percent of its population in agriculture.

Civilization, that is, is a state of society in which techniques are so poor that it takes about 80 percent of the population to feed the 100 percent. But we do have about 20 percent of the people who can be spared from food producing to build Parthenons, and cathedrals, to write literature and poetry, and to fight wars. By contrast, in the United States today we are rapidly getting to the point where we can produce all our food with only 10 percent of the population and still have large agricultural surpluses. But for the blessings of agricultural policy, we might soon be able to produce all our food with 5 percent of the population. It may even be that agriculture is on its way out altogether and within another generation or so we can produce our food in a totally different way. Perhaps both fields and cows are merely relics of civilization, the vestiges of a vanishing age. This means, however, that even in our society, which is at a very early stage of post-civilization, we can now spare about 90 percent of the people to produce bath-tubs, automobiles, and H-bombs, and all the other luxuries and conveniences of life. Western Europe and Japan are coming along behind the United States very fast. The Russians,

likewise, are advancing towards post-civilization, although by a very different road. At the moment their ideology is a handicap to them in some places—especially in agriculture, where they still have 45 percent of the people. Even this, however, is a lot better than ancient Rome. And, if the Russians ever discovered that super-peasants are a good deal more efficient than collective farms, they may cut away some of the ideology that hangs around their neck and move even more rapidly toward post-civilized society.

I am not at all sure what post-civilization will look like and, indeed, I suspect there will be several varieties of it. But it will certainly be radically different from the civilized society which it is displacing. It will certainly be a worldwide society. Until very recently each civilized society was a little island in a sea of barbarism which constantly threatened to overwhelm it. Civilization is haunted by the spectre of decline and fall, although it is noteworthy that in spite of the rise and fall of particular civilizations, civilization itself expanded steadily in geographical coverage from its very beginnings. We must face the fact, however, that post-civilized society will be worldwide, if only because of its ease of communication and transportation. I flew last year from Idlewild to Brussels, and on glimpsing the new Brussels Airport out of the corner of my eye, I thought for a moment we had come back and landed at Idlewild again. I had for a moment a horrifying vision of a world in which we went faster and faster to places which were more and more like the places we left behind, until in the end of the process we flew at infinite speed to a place that was identical with what we left behind, and we might as well have stayed home. For the first time in history there is now a world style, at least in airports, which is a symbol of the coming post-civilization. We see this in art, in architecture, in music, in literature, and in all fields of life. What in Europe looks like Americanization, in America looks like Japanification. It is simply the creeping onset of post-civilized style.

The great problem of our age, however, is the disintegration of the institutions of civilization under the impact of advancing post-civilization. The characteristic institutions of civilization are, as we have seen, first agriculture, then the city, then war, in the sense of clash of organized armed forces, and finally, inequality, the sharp contrast between the rich and the poor, between the city and the country, between the urbane and the rustic. In classical civilization both birth and death rates average about forty per thousand, the expectation of life at birth is about twenty-five years. The state is based very fundamentally on violence and exploitation, and the culture tends to be spiritually monolithic, with a single church or spiritual power perpetuating its doctrines because of its monopoly of the educational processes. . . .

In post-civilization all these institutions suffer radical change. Agriculture, as we have seen, diminishes until it is a small proportion of the society, the city, likewise, in the classical sense, disintegrates. Los Angeles is perhaps the first example of the post-civilization, post-urban agglomeration—under no stretch of the imagination could it be called a city. War, likewise, is an institution in process of disintegration. National defense as a social system has quite fundamentally broken down on a world scale. The ICBM and the nuclear warhead has made the nation-state as militarily obsolete as the city-state, for in no country now can the armed forces preserve an area of internal peace by pushing violence to the outskirts. Poverty and inequality, likewise, are tending to disappear, at least on their classical scale. Post-civilized society is an affluent society and it produces large quantities of goods, even though it may fall rather short on services. It is a society furthermore in which the technology almost prohibits great inequalities in consumption. In civilized societies the king or the emperor could live in a Versailles and the peasant in a hovel. In post-civilized society, the proletariat disappears, everybody becomes at least middle-class, and when the product mix of the economy consists of automobiles, mass-produced clothing, domestic appliances, and the prefabricated homes, it is almost impossible for the rich to consume on a scale which is more,

let us say, than ten times that of the poor. There is no sense in having more than ten automobiles!

Another profound change in the passage from civilization to post-civilization is the change in the expectation of life. In civilized society, as we have seen, birth and death rates tend to be about forty per thousand and the expectation of life at birth is twenty-five years. In post-civilized society the expectation of life at birth rises at least to seventy and perhaps beyond. At the moment we do not have the knowledge or techniques for prolonging the expectation of life much beyond seventy. We do not know, however, what lies in the future. It may be that we are on the edge of a biological revolution, just as dramatic and far-reaching as the discovery of atomic energy and that we may crack the problem of aging and prolong human life much beyond its present span. Whether or not, however, we go forward to Methuselah, the mere increase of the average age of death to seventy is a startling and far-reaching change. It means, for instance, that in an equilibrium population, the birth and death rate cannot be more than about fourteen-per-thousand. This unquestionably implies some form of conscious control of births and of the number of children per family. It means also a radical change in the age distribution of the population, with a much larger proportion of the population in later years.

There are, unquestionably, going to be many varieties of post-civilization and some are going to be more unpleasant than others. It is perfectly possible to paint an anti-utopia in which a post-civilized society appears as universally vulgar, or even universally dull. On the whole, however, I welcome post-civilization and I have really very little affection for civilization. In most pre-civilized societies the fact that the life of man is for the most part nasty, brutish, and short, does not prevent the poets and philosophers from sentimentalizing about the noble savage. Similarly we may expect the same kind of sentimentalizing about the noble Romans and civilized survivals like Winston Churchill. On the whole, though, I will not shed any tears over the grave of civilization any more than I will over pre-civilized society. Post-civilization is a realization of man's potential. On the whole its credit balance is large. It at least gives us a chance of a modest utopia, in which slavery, poverty, exploitation, gross inequality, war, and disease—these prime costs of civilization—will fall to the vanishing point. Neither the disappearance of the classical city nor the disappearance of the peasant fill me with much sorrow. Even in post-civilized society, of course, we can have cities of a kind, if we want to. We may even find culture cities in which vehicular traffic is prohibited and in which the rich indulge in the costly luxury of walking. In the meantime the masses will live scattered about the surface of the earth, commuting occasionally to quasi-automatic factories and offices, or will snuggle down with three dimensional T.V. at the end of the day.

Modest as these visions of utopia may be, there is no guarantee that we will reach them. The second great transition may be under way, but there is no guarantee that it will be accomplished. What we have at the moment is a chance to make this transition—a chance which is probably unique in the history of this planet. If we fail, the chance will probably not be repeated in this part of the universe. Whatever experiments may be going on elsewhere, the present moment indeed is unique in the whole four billion years of the history of the planet. In my more pessimistic moments, I think the chance is a slim one, and it may be that man will be written off as an unsuccessful experiment. We must, therefore, look at the traps which lie along the path of the transition, which might prevent us from making it altogether.

The most urgent trap is, of course, the trap of war. War, as I have suggested is an institution peculiarly characteristic of civilization. Pre-civilized societies have sporadic feuding and raiding, but they do not generally have permanently organized armed forces, and they do not generally develop conquest and empire; or if they do, they soon pass into a civilized form. An armed force is essentially a mobile city designed to throw things at another mobile or stationary city with presumably evil intent. As far as I know, not more than two or three civilizations have existed without war. The Mayans and the people of Mohenjodaro, seem to have lived for fairly long periods without war, but this was an accident of their monopolistic situation and they unquestionably occupied themselves with other kinds of foolishness. If pre-civilized society, however, cannot afford war, post-civilized society can afford far too much of it, and hence will be forced to get rid of the institution because it is simply inappropriate to the technological age. The breakdown in the world social system of national defense really dates from about 1949, when the United States lost its monopoly of nuclear weapons. A system of national defense is only feasible if each nation is stronger than its enemies at home, so that it can preserve a relatively large area of peace within its critical boundaries. Such a system is only possible, however, if the range of the deadly missile is short and if the armed forces of each nation lose power rapidly as they move away from home. The technological developments of the twentieth century have destroyed these foundations of national defense, and have replaced it with another social system altogether which is "deterrence." . . .

Even if we avoid the war trap, we may still fall into the population trap. Population control is an unsolved problem even for the developed areas of the world, which have moved the furthest toward post-civilization. We have not developed any social institutions which can adequately deal with the establishment of an equilibrium of population. An equilibrium of population in a stable post-civilized society may represent a fairly radical interference with ancient human institutions and freedoms. In a stable post-civilized society, as I have suggested, the birth and death rates must be of the order of fourteen per thousand, and the average number of children per family cannot much exceed two. There are many social institutions which might accomplish this end. So far, however, the only really sure-fire method of controlling population is starvation and misery. Insofar as this is true, the Malthusian spectre still broods over us.

In many parts of the world—indeed, for

most of the human race for the moment—the impact on certain post-civilized techniques of civilized society has produced a crisis of growth, which may easily be fatal. In the tropics especially with DDT and a few simple public health measures it is easy to reduce the death rate to nine or ten per thousand, at the same time that the birth rate stays up at forty per thousand. This means an annual increase of population of three percent per annum, almost all of it concentrated in the lower age groups. We see this phenomenon dramatically in places like the West Indies, Ceylon, and Formosa; but thanks to the activity of the world health organization, it is taking place rapidly all over the tropical world. It is not the ultimate Malthusian equilibrium which is the problem here, but the strain which is put on the society by the very rapid growth of population, a rate of growth without precedent in history. Perhaps the most important key to the transition to post-civilization is heavy investment in human resources—that is in education. The conquest of disease and infant mortality, however, before the corresponding adjustment to the birth rate, produces enormous cohorts of children in societies which do not have the resources to educate them—especially as those in the middle-age groups, who after all must do all the work of a society, come from the much smaller cohorts of the pre-DDT era. There is an uncomfortable analogy here to 2-4-D, the hormone which kills plants by making them grow too rapidly. At the moment the human race is heading for monumental disasters in many parts of the world. The population disaster is perhaps retrievable in the sense that it may be confined to certain parts of the world and may simply delay the spread of post-civilization in these areas, without seriously threatening the transition in the already developed areas.

Even in the developed countries, however, population control presents a very serious problem. The United States, for instance, at the moment is increasing in population even more rapidly than India. The time when we thought that the mere increase in income would automatically solve the population problem has gone by. In the United States,

and certain other societies, in the early stages of post-civilization, the child has become an object of conspicuous domestic consumption. The consumption patterns of the American spending unit seem to follow a certain *gestalt* in which household capital accumulates in a certain order such as the first car, the first child, the washer and dryer, the second child, the deep freeze, the third child, the second car, the fourth child, and so on. The richer we get, the more children we can afford to have at least on current income and the more children we do have. We now seem to be able to afford an average of something like four children per family, and as in a post-civilized society, these four children all survive, the population doubles every generation. A hundred years of this and even the United States is going to find itself uncomfortably crowded. It can be argued, indeed, that from the point of view of the amenities of life we are already well beyond the optimum population. One sees this clearly in California, which was a much more agreeable place thirty years ago than it is today. When the United States gets to have a billion people, which we could easily have in less than a hundred years, its standards of life may be substantially reduced.

My only positive contribution to this problem is the suggestion that everyone should come into the world with a license to have just one child. A market can then be organized in these licenses and people who wish to be childless can sell their licenses to the philoprogenitive for a price determined by supply and demand. Nobody, I may add, has taken the suggestion very seriously up till now.

The third trap on the road to post-civilization is the technological trap. Our present technology is fundamentally suicidal. It is based on the extraction of concentrated deposits of fossil fuels and ores, which in the nature of things are exhaustible. Even at present rates of consumption they will be exhausted in a time span which is not very long, even measured against human history and which is infinitesimally small on the geological time scale. If the rest of the world advances to American standards of consumption, these resources will disappear almost overnight. Economic development, it appears is the process of bringing closer the evil day when everything will be gone—all the oil, all the coal, all the ores—and we will have to go back to primitive agriculture and scratching in the woods.

There are indications, however, that suicidal technology is not absolutely necessary and that a permanent high-level technology is possible. Beginning in the early part of the twentieth century it is possible to detect an anti-entropic movement in technology. This begins perhaps with the Haber process for the fixation of nitrogen from the air. A development of similar significance is the Dow process for the extraction of magnesium from the sea. Both these processes are anti-entropic. They take the diffuse and concentrate it, instead of taking the concentrated and diffusing it, as do most processes of mining and economic production. Sir William Crookes in the last years of the nineteenth century predicted that we would all be starving by the middle of the twentieth century because of the exhaustion of Chilean nitrates. This prediction was fortunately falsified by the Haber process. These anti-entropic processes foreshadow a technology in which we shall draw all the materials we need from the virtually inexhaustible reservoirs of the sea and the air and draw our energy from controlled fusion—either artificially produced on the earth or from the sun.

It may even be that the major consequence of space research will be the development of a more self-subsistent high technology on earth. From a strictly economic point of view I suspect space is not even for the birds. It seems to be remarkably empty of economic goods. The technology necessary to send man into space, however, may be much the same technology that will enable him to manage his own larger space ship, the good planet earth, with a true high-level husbandry. One can perhaps even visualize the almost completely self-sufficient household of the future living in a kind of grounded spaceship in which the water circulates endlessly through the kidneys and the algae, the protein and carbohydrates likewise. The power comes from solar batteries on the roof and the food from the algae tanks and man, thereby, greatly reduces the scale of the circulation in the midst of which he has to live. In this happy day everyone will live under his own vine and his own fig tree and presumably none shall make them afraid. This may be a long way off, or it may be closer than we think. It is clear, however, that a fundamental technological transition is still to be accomplished. . . .

Beyond these three traps one sees a distant fourth trap—the trap of inanition. Man is a profoundly problem-solving animal. He reacts best to situations of challenge and difficulty. If he succeeds in solving the problems which now so thoroughly possess him, will he not in the very moment of his success die of sheer boredom? Our answers to this question must depend on our view of man's capabilities; but even here there is evidence, I think, in his religious life that he might survive even heaven. This is a problem, however, that I am prepared to let future generations take care of when they come to it. The business of our generation is more immediate. . . .

What we have to do now, however, is to develop almost a new form of learning. We have to learn from rapidly changing systems. Ordinarily we learn from stable systems. It is because the world repeats itself that we catch on to the law of repetition. Learning from changing systems is perhaps another step in the acceleration of evolution that we have to take. I have been haunted by a remark which Norman Meier, the psychologist, made in a seminar a few months ago, when he said that a cat who jumps on a hot stove never jumps on a cold one. I believe the remark may originally be attributed to Mark Twain. This seems precisely to describe the state we may be in today. We have jumped on a lot of hot stoves and now perhaps the cold stove is the only place on which to jump. In the rapidly changing system it is desperately easy to learn things which are no longer true. Perhaps the greatest task of applied social science, therefore, at the moment is to study the conditions under which we learn from rapidly changing systems. If we can answer this question, then there may still be hope for the human race.

Part 9

Ecology

The Cultural Ecology of India's Sacred Cattle

Marvin Harris

In this paper I attempt to indicate certain puzzling inconsistencies in prevailing interpretations of the ecological role of bovine cattle in India. My argument is based upon intensive reading—I have never seen a sacred cow, nor been to India. As a non-specialist, no doubt I have committed blunders an Indianist would have avoided. I hope these errors will not deprive me of that expert advice and informed criticism which alone can justify so rude an invasion of unfamiliar territory.

I have written this paper because I believe the irrational, non-economic, and exotic aspects of the Indian cattle complex are greatly overemphasized at the expense of rational, economic, and mundane interpretations.

My intent is not to substitute one dogma for another, but to urge that explanation of taboos, customs, and rituals associated with management of Indian cattle be sought in "positive-functioned" and probably "adaptive" processes of the ecological system of which they are a part, rather than in the influence of Hindu theology.

Mismanagement of India's agricultural resources as a result of the Hindu doctrine of *ahimsa,* especially as it applies to beef cattle, is frequently noted by Indianists and others concerned with the relation between values and behavior. Although different antirational, dysfunctional, and inutile aspects of the cattle complex are stressed by different authors, many agree that *ahimsa* is a prime example of how men will diminish their material welfare to obtain spiritual satisfaction in obedience to nonrational or frankly irrational beliefs. . . .

In spite of the sometimes final and unqualified fashion in which "surplus," "useless," "uneconomic," and "superfluous" are applied to part or all of India's cattle, contrary conclusions seem admissible when the cattle complex is viewed as part of an *eco-system* rather than as a sector of a national price market. Ecologically, it is doubtful that any component of the cattle complex is "useless," i.e., the number, type, and condition of Indian bovines do not per se impair the ability of the human population to survive and reproduce. Much more likely the relationship between bovines and humans is symbiotic

From *Current Anthropology,* Vol. 7, No. 1, 1966, pp. 51–59. Copyright 1966, Wenner-Gren Foundation for Anthropological Research. By permission of the author, the publisher, and the copyright holder.

The editor regrets that we cannot reprint here the several pages of interesting *Comment.* nor the author's *Reply,* that were published in the same issue of *Current Anthropology* with this article. The commentators were Nirmal K. Bose, Morton Klass, Joan P. Mencher, Kalervo Oberg, Marvin K. Opler, Wayne Suttles, and Andrew P. Vayda.

instead of competitive. It probably represents the outcome of intensive Darwinian pressures acting upon human and bovine population, cultigens, wild flora and fauna, and social structure and ideology. Moreover presumably the degree of observance of taboos against bovine slaughter and beef-eating reflect the power of these ecological pressures rather than *ahimsa;* in other words, *ahimsa* itself derives power and sustenance from the material rewards it confers upon both men and animals. To support these hypotheses, the major aspects of the Indian cattle complex will be reviewed under the following headings: (1) Milk Production, (2) Traction, (3) Dung, (4) Beef and Hides, (5) Pasture, (6) Useful and Useless Animals, (7) Slaughter, (8) Anti-Slaughter Legislation, (9) Old-Age Homes, and (10) Natural Selection.

Milk Production

In India the average yield of whole milk per Zebu cow is 413 pounds, compared with the 5,000-pound average in Europe and the U.S. In Madhya Pradesh yield is as low as 65 pounds, while in no state does it rise higher than the barely respectable 1,445 pounds of the Punjab. According to the 9th Quinquennial Livestock Census among the 47,200,000 cows over 3 years old, 27,200,000 were dry and/or not calved.

These figures, however should not be used to prove that the cows are useless or uneconomic, since milk production is a minor aspect of the sacred cow's contribution to the *eco-system.* Indeed, most Indianists agree that it is the buffalo, not the Zebu, whose economic worth must be judged primarily by milk production. . . .

In this new context, the fact that U.S. cows produce 20 times more milk than Indian cows loses much of its significance. Instead, it is more relevant to note that, despite the marginal status of milking in the symbiotic syndrome, 46.7% of India's dairy products come from cow's milk. How far this production is balanced by expenditures detrimental to human welfare will be discussed later.

Traction

The principal positive ecological effect of India's bovine cattle is in their contribution to production of grain crops, from which about 80% of the human calorie ration comes. Some form of animal traction is required to initiate the agricultural cycle, dependent upon plowing in both rainfall and irrigation areas. Additional traction for hauling, transport, and irrigation is provided by animals, but by far their most critical kinetic contribution is plowing.

Although many authorities believe there is an overall surplus of cattle in India, others point to a serious shortage of draught animals. According to Kothavala, "Even with . . . overstocking, the draught power available for land operations at the busiest season of the year is inadequate. . . . " For West Bengal, the National Council of Applied Economic Research reports:

> However, despite the large number of draught animals, agriculture in the State suffers from a shortage of draught power. There are large numbers of small landholders entirely dependent on hired animal labour. . . .

The . . . number of cattle in India is insufficient to permit a large portion, perhaps as many as $1/3$, of India's farmers to begin the agricultural cycle under conditions appropriate to their techno-environmental system.

Much has been made of India's having 115 head of cattle per square mile, compared with 28 per square mile for the U.S. and 3 per square mile for Canada. But what actually may be most characteristic of the size of India's herd is the low ratio of cattle to people. Thus India has 44 cattle per 100 persons while in the U.S. the ratio is 58 per 100 and in Canada, 90. Yet, in India cattle are employed as a basic instrument of agricultural production.

Sharing of draught animals on a cooperative basis might reduce the need for additional animals. Chaudhri and Giri point out that the "big farmer manages to cultivate with a pair of bullock a much larger area than the small cultivators." But, the failure to develop cooperative forms of plowing can scarcely be traced to *ahimsa*. If anything, emphasis upon independent, family-sized farm units follows intensification of individual land tenure patterns and other property innovations deliberately encouraged by the British. Under existing property arrangements, there is a perfectly good economic explanation of why bullocks are not shared among adjacent households. Plowing cannot take place at any time of the year, but must be accomplished within a few daylight hours in conformity with seasonal conditions. These are set largely by summer monsoons, responsible for about 90% of the total rainfall. Writing about Orissa, Bailey notes:

> As a temporary measure, an ox might be borrowed from a relative, or a yoke of cattle and a ploughman might be hired . . . but during the planting season, when the need is the greatest, most people are too busy to hire out or lend cattle.

According to Desai:

> . . . over vast areas, sowing and harvesting operations, by the very nature of things, begin simultaneously with the outbreak of the first showers and the maturing of crops respectively, and especially the former has got to be put through quickly during the first phase of the monsoon. Under these circumstances, reliance by a farmer on another for bullocks is highly risky and he has got, therefore, to maintain his own pair.

Dube is equally specific:

> The cultivators who depend on hired cattle or who practice cooperative lending and borrowing of cattle cannot take the best advantage of the first rains, and this enforced wait results in untimely sowing and poor crops.

Wiser and Wiser describe the plight of the bullock-short farmer as follows, "When he needs the help of bullocks most, his neighbors are all using theirs." And Shastri points out, "Uncertainty of Indian farming due to

dependence on rains is the main factor creating obstacles in the way of improvements in bullock labor."

It would seem, therefore, that this aspect of the cattle complex is not an expression of spirit and ritual, but of rain and energy.

Dung

In India cattle dung is the main source of domestic cooking fuel. Since grain crops cannot be digested unless boiled or baked, cooking is indispensable. Considerable disagreement exists about the total amount of cattle excrement and its uses, but even the lowest estimates are impressive. An early estimate by Lupton gave the BTU equivalent of dung consumed in domestic cooking as 35,-000,000 tons of coal or 68,000,000 tons of wood. Most detailed appraisal is by National Council of Applied Economic Research, which rejects H. J. Bhabha's estimate of 131,-000,000 tons of coal and the Ministry of Food and Agriculture's 112,000,000 tons. The figure preferred by the NCAER is 35,000,000 tons anthracite or 40,000,000 tons bituminous, but with a possible range of between 35–45,000,000 of anthracite dung-coal equivalent. This calculation depends upon indications that only 36% of the total wet dung is utilized as fuel, a lower estimate than any reviewed by Saha. These vary from 40% (Imperial Council on Agricultural Research) to 50% (Ministry of Food and Agriculture) to 66.6% (Department of Education, Health and Lands). The NCAER estimate of a dung-coal equivalent of 35,000,000 tons is therefore quite conservative; it is nonetheless an impressive amount of BTU's to be plugged into an energy system.

Kapp, who discusses at length the importance of substituting tractors for bullocks, does not give adequate attention to finding cooking fuel after the bullocks are replaced. The NCAER conclusion that dung is cheaper than coke seems an understatement. Although it is claimed that wood resources are potentially adequate to replace dung the measures advocated do not involve *ahimsa* but are again an indictment of a land tenure system not inspired by Hindu tradition. Finally, it should be noted that many observers stress the slow burning qualities of dung and its special appropriateness for preparation of *ghi* and deployment of woman-power in the household.

As manure, dung enters the energy system in another vital fashion. According to Mujumdar, 300,000,000 tons are used as fuel, 340,-000,000 tons as manure, and 160,000,000 tons "wasted on hillsides and roads." Spate believes that 40% of dung production is spread on fields, 40% burned, and 20% "lost." Possibly estimates of the amount of dung lost are grossly inflated in view of the importance of "roads and hillsides" in the grazing pattern (see Pasture). (Similarly artificial and culture- or even class-bound judgments refer to utilization of India's night soil. It is usually assumed that Chinese and Indian treatment of this resource are radically different, and that vast quantities of nitrogen go unused in agriculture because of Hindu-inspired definitions of modesty and cleanliness. However, most human excrement from Indian villages is deposited in surrounding fields; the absence of latrines helps explain why such fields raise 2 and 3 successive crops each year. More than usual caution, therefore, is needed before concluding that a significant amount of cattle dung is wasted. Given the conscious premium set on dung for fuel and fertilizer, thoughtful control maintained over grazing patterns (see Pasture), and occurrence of specialized sweeper and gleaner castes, much more detailed evidence of wastage is needed than is now available. Since cattle graze on "hillsides and roads," dung dropped there would scarcely be totally lost to the *eco-system*, even with allowance for loss of nitrogen by exposure to air and sunlight. Also, if any animal dung is wasted on roads and hillsides it is not because of *ahimsa* but of inadequate pasturage suitable for collecting and processing animal droppings. The sedentary, intensive rainfall agriculture of most of the subcontinent is heavily dependent upon manuring. So vital is this that Spate says substitutes for manure consumed

as fuel "must be supplied, and lavishly, even at a financial loss to government." If this is the case, then old, decrepit, and dry animals might have a use after all, especially when, as we shall see, the dung they manufacture employs raw materials lost to the culture-energy system unless processed by cattle, and especially when many apparently moribund animals revive at the next monsoon and provide their owners with a male calf.

Beef and Hides

Positive contributions of India's sacred cattle do not cease with milk-grazing, bullock-producing, traction, and dung-dropping. There remains the direct protein contribution of 25,000,000 cattle and buffalo which die each year. This feature of the *eco-system* is reminiscent of the East African cattle area where, despite the normal taboo on slaughter, natural deaths and ceremonial occasions are probably frequent enough to maintain beef consumption near the ecological limit with dairying as the primary function. Although most Hindus probably do not consume beef, the *eco-system* under consideration is not confined to Hindus. The human population includes some 55,000,000 "scheduled" exterior or untouchable groups, many of whom will consume beef if given the opportunity, plus several million more Moslems and Christians. Much of the flesh on the 25,000,000 dead cattle and buffalo probably gets consumed by human beings whether or not the cattle die naturally. Indeed, could it be that without the orthodox Hindu beef-eating taboo, many marginal and depressed castes would be deprived of an occasional, but nutritionally critical, source of animal protein?

It remains to note that the slaughter taboo does not prevent depressed castes from utilizing skin, horns and hoofs of dead beasts. In 1956 16,000,000 cattle hides were produced. The quality of India's huge leather industry— the world's largest—leaves much to be desired, but the problem is primarily outmoded tanning techniques and lack of capital, not *ahimsa*.

Pasture

The principal positive-functioned or useful contributions of India's sacred cattle to human survival and well-being have been described. Final evaluation of their utility must involve assessment of energy costs in terms of resources and human labor input which might be more efficiently expended in other activities.

Direct and indirect evidence suggests that in India men and bovine cattle do not compete for existence. According to Mohan:

> . . . the bulk of the food on which the animals subsist . . . is not the food that is required for human consumption, i.e., fibrous fodders produced as incidental to crop production, and a large part of the crop residues or by-products of seeds and waste grazing.

On the contrary, "the bulk of foods (straws and crop residues) that are ploughed into the soil in other countries are converted into milk."

> The majority of the Indian cattle obtain their requirements from whatever grazing is available from straw and stalk and other residues from human food-stuffs, and are starved seasonally in the dry months when grasses wither.
> . . . .
> In Bengal the banks and slopes of the embankments of public roads are the only grazing grounds and the cattle subsist mainly on paddy straw, paddy husks and . . . coarse grass.

According to Dube ". . . the cattle roam about the shrubs and rocks and eat whatever fodder is available there." This is confirmed by Moomaw: "Cows subsist on the pasture and any coarse fodder they can find. Grain is fed for only a day or two following parturition." The character of the environmental niche reserved for cattle nourishment is described by Gourou, based on data furnished by Dupuis for Madras:

> Il faut voir clairement que le faible rendement du bétail indien n'est pas un gaspillage: ce bétail n'entre pas en concurrence avec la consommation de produits agricoles . . . ils ne leur sacrifient pas des surfaces agricoles, ou ayant un potential agricole.

NCAER confirms this pattern for Tripura: "There is a general practice of feeding livestock on agricultural by-products such as straw, grain wastes and husks"; for West Bengal: "The state has practically no pasture or grazing fields, and the farmers are not in the habit of growing green fodders . . . livestock feeds are mostly agricultural by-products"; and for Andhra Pradesh: "Cattle are stall-fed, but the bulk of the feed consists of paddy straw. . . ."

The only exceptions to the rural pattern of feeding cattle on waste products and grazing them on marginal or unproductive lands involve working bullocks and nursing cows:

> The working bullocks, on whose efficiency cultivation entirely depends, are usually fed with chopped bananas at the time of fodder scarcity. But the milch cows have to live in a semi-starved condition, getting what nutrition they can from grazing on the fields after their rice harvest.
> At present cattle are fed largely according to the season. During the rainy period they feed upon the grass which springs up on the uncultivated hillsides. . . . But in the dry season there is hardly any grass, and cattle wander on the cropless lands in an often halfstarved condition. True there is some fodder at these times in the shape of rice-straw and dried copra, but it is not generally sufficient, and is furthermore given mainly to the animals actually working at the time.

There is much evidence that Hindu farmers calculate carefully which animals deserve more food and attention. In Madras, Randhawa, et al. report: "The cultivators pay more attention to the male stock used for ploughing and for draft. There is a general neglect of the cow and the female calf even from birth. . . ."

Similar discrimination is described by Mamoria:

> Many plough bullocks are sold off in winter or their

rations are ruthlessly decreased whenever they are not worked in full, while milch cattle are kept on after lactation on poor and inadequate grazing. . . . The cultivator feeds his bullocks better than his cow because it pays him. He feeds his bullocks better during the busy season, when they work, than during the slack season, when they remain idle. Further, he feeds his more valuable bullocks better than those less valuable. . . . Although the draught animals and buffaloes are properly fed, the cow gets next to nothing of stall feeding. She is expected to pick up her living on the bare fields after harvest and on the village wasteland. . . .

The previously cited NCAER report on Andhra Pradesh notes that "Bullocks and milking cows during the working season get more concentrates. . . . " Wiser and Wiser sum up the situation in a fashion supporting Srinivas' observation that the Indian peasant is "nothing if he is not practical":

Farmers have become skillful in reckoning the minimum of food necessary for maintaining animal service. Cows are fed just enough to assure their calving and giving a little milk. They are grazed during the day on lands which yield very little vegetation, and are given a very sparse meal at night.

Many devout Hindus believe the bovine cattle of India are exploited without mercy by greedy Hindu owners. *Ahimsa* obviously has little to do with economizing which produces the famous *phooka* and *doom dev* techniques for dealing with dry cows. Not to Protestants but to Hindus did Gandhi address lamentations concerning the cow:

How we bleed her to take the last drop of milk from her, how we starve her to emaciation, how we ill-treat the calves, how we deprive them of their portion of milk, how cruelly we treat the oxen, how we castrate them, how we beat them, how we overload them . . . I do not know that the condition of the cattle in any other part of the world is as bad as in unhappy India.

Useful and Useless Animals

How then, if careful rationing is characteristic of livestock management, do peasants toler-

ate the widely reported herds of useless animals? Perhaps "useless" means 1 thing to the peasant and quite another to the price-market-oriented agronomist. It is impossible at a distance to judge which point of view is ecologically more valid, but the peasants could be right more than the agronomists are willing to admit.

Since non-working and non-lactating animals are thermal and chemical factories which depend on waste lands and products for raw materials, judgment that a particular animal is useless cannot be supported without careful examination of its owner's household budget. Estimates from the cattle census which equate useless with dry or non-working animals are not convincing. But even if a given animal in a particular household is of less-than-marginal utility, there is an additional factor whose evaluation would involve long-range bovine biographies. The utility of a particular animal to its owner cannot be established simply by its performance during season or an animal cycle. Perhaps the whole system of Indian bovine management is alien to costing procedures of the West. There may be a kind of low-risk sweepstakes which drags on for 10 or 12 years before the losers and winners are separated.

As previously observed, the principal function of bovine cows is not their milk-producing but their bullock-producing abilities. Also established is the fact that many farmers are short of bullocks. Cows have the function primarily to produce male offspring, but when? In Europe and America, cows become pregnant under well-controlled, hence predictable, circumstances and a farmer with many animals, can count on male offspring in half the births. In India, cows become pregnant under quite different circumstances. Since cows suffer from malnutrition through restriction to marginal pasture, they conceive and deliver in unpredictable fashion. The chronic starvation of the inter-monsoon period makes the cow, in the words of Mamoria, "an irregular breeder." Moreover, with few animals, the farmer may suffer many disappointments before a male is born. To the agriculture specialist with knowledge of what healthy dairy stock look like, the hot weather herds of walking skeletons "roaming over the bare fields and dried up wastes" must indeed seem without economic potential. Many of them, in fact, will not make it through to the next monsoon. However, among the survivors are an unknown number still physically capable of having progeny. Evidently neither the farmer nor the specialist knows which will conceive, nor when. To judge from Bombay city, even when relatively good care is bestowed on a dry cow, no one knows the outcome: "If an attempt is made to salvage them, they have to be kept and fed for a long time. Even then, it is not known whether they will conceive or not."

In rural areas, to judge a given animal useless may be to ignore the recuperative power of these breeds under conditions of erratic rainfall and unpredictable grazing opportunities. The difference of viewpoint between the farmer and the expert is apparent in Moomaw's incomplete attempt to describe the life history of an informant's cattle. The farmer in question had 3 oxen, 2 female buffaloes, 4 head of young cattle and 3 "worthless" cows. In Moomaw's opinion, "The three cows . . . are a liability to him, providing no income, yet consuming feed which might be placed to better use." Yet we learn, "The larger one had a calf about once in three years"; moreover 2 of the 3 oxen were "raised" by the farmer himself. (Does this mean that they were the progeny of the farmer's cows?) The farmer tells Moomaw, "The young stock get some fodder, but for the most part they pasture with the village herd. The cows give nothing and I cannot afford to feed them." Whereupon Moomaw's *non sequitur:* "We spoke no more of his cows, for like many a farmer he just keeps them, without inquiring whether it is profitable or not."

The difficulties in identifying animals that are definitely uneconomic for a given farmer are reflected in the varying estimates of the total of such animals. The Expert Committee on the Prevention of Slaughter of Cattle estimated 20,000,000 uneconomic cattle in India. Roy settles for 5,500,000, or about 3.5%. Mamoria, who gives the still lower estimate of 2,900,000, or 2.1%, claims most of these are

males. A similarly low percentage—2.5%—is suggested for West Bengal. None of these estimates appears based on bovine life histories in relation to household budgets; none appears to involve estimates of economic significance of dung contributions of older animals.

Before a peasant is judged a victim of Oriental mysticism, might it not be well to indicate the devastating material consequences which befall a poor farmer unable to replace a bullock lost through disease, old age, or accident? Bailey makes it clear that in the economic life of the marginal peasantry, "Much the most devastating single event is the loss of an ox (or a plough buffalo)." If the farmer is unable to replace the animal with one from his own herd, he must borrow money at usurious rates. Defaults on such loans are the principal causes of transfer of land titles from peasants to landlords. Could this explain why the peasant is not overly perturbed that some of his animals might turn out to be only dung-providers? After all, the real threat to his existence does not arise from animals but from people ready to swoop down on him as soon as one of his beasts falters. Chapekar's claim that the peasant's "stock serve as a great security for him to fall back on whenever he is in need" would seem to be appropriate only in reference to the unusually well-established minority. In a land where life expectancy at birth has only recently risen to 30 years, it is not altogether appropriate to speak of security. The poorest farmers own insufficient stock. Farm management studies show that holdings below 2/3 of average area account for 2/5 of all farms, but maintain only 1/4 of the total cattle on farms. "This is so, chiefly because of their limited resources to maintain cattle." . . .

Natural Selection

Expert appraisers of India's cattle usually show little enthusiasm for the typical undersized breeds. Much has been made of the fact that 1 large animal is a more efficient dung, milk, and traction machine than 2 small ones. "Weight for weight, a small animal consumes a much larger quantity of food than a bigger animal." "More dung is produced when a given quantity of food is consumed by one animal than when it is shared by two animals." Thus it would seem that India's smaller breeds should be replaced by larger, more powerful, and better milking breeds. But once again, there is another way of looking at the evidence. It might very well be that if all of India's scrub cattle were suddenly replaced by an equivalent number of large, high-quality European or American dairy and traction animals, famines of noteworthy magnitude would immediately ensue. Is it not possible that India's cattle are undersized precisely because other breeds never could survive the atrocious conditions they experience most of the year? I find it difficult to believe that breeds better adapted to the present Indian *eco-system* exist elsewhere. . . .

Not only are scrub animals well adapted to the regular seasonal crises of water and forage and general year-round neglect, but long-range selective pressures may be even more significant. The high frequency of drought-induced famines in India places a premium upon drought-resistance plus a more subtle factor: A herd of smaller animals, dangerously thinned by famine or pestilence, reproduces faster than an equivalent group of larger animals, despite the fact that the larger animal consumes less per pound than 2 smaller animals. This is because there are 2 cows in the smaller herd per equivalent large cow. Mohan is one of the few authorities to have grasped this principle, including it in defense of the small breeds:

> *Calculations of the comparative food conversion efficiency of various species of Indian domestic livestock by the writer has revealed, that much greater attention should be paid to small livestock than at present, not only because of their better*

conversion efficiency for protein but also because of the possibilities of bringing about a rapid increase in their numbers.

Conclusion

The probability that India's cattle complex is a positive-functioned part of a naturally selected *eco-system* is at least as good as that it is a negative-functioned expression of an irrational ideology. This should not be interpreted to mean that no "improvements" can be made in the system, nor that different systems may not eventually evolve. The issue is not whether oxen are more efficient than tractors. I suggest simply that many features of the cattle complex have been erroneously reported or interpreted. That Indian cattle are weak and inefficient is not denied, but there is doubt that this situation arises from and is mainly perpetuated by Hindu ideology. Given the techno-environmental base, Indian property relationships, and political organization, one need not involve the doctrine of *ahimsa* to understand fundamental features of the cattle complex. Although the cattle population of India has risen by 38,000,000 head since 1940, during the same period, the human population has risen by 120,000,000. Despite the anti-slaughter legislation, the ratio of cattle to humans actually declined from 44:100 in 1941 to 40:100 in 1961. In the absence of major changes in environment, technology or property relations, it seems unlikely that the cattle population will cease to accompany the rise in the human population. If *ahimsa* is negative-functioned, then we must be prepared to admit the possibility that all factors contributing to the rapid growth of the Indian human and cattle populations, including the germ theory of disease, are also negative-functioned.

Archeological Systems Theory and Early Mesoamerica

Kent V. Flannery

From *Anthropological Archeology in the Americas,* 1968, Anthropological Society of Washington. By permission of the author, publisher and copyright holder.

Introduction

As work on the early periods of Mesoamerican prehistory progresses, and we learn more about the food-collectors and early food-producers of that region, our mental image of these ancient peoples has been greatly modified. We no longer think of the preceramic plant-collectors as a ragged and scruffy band of nomads; instead, they appear as a practiced and ingenious team of lay botanists who know how to wring the most out of a superficially bleak environment. Nor do we still picture the Formative peoples as a happy group of little brown farmers dancing around their cornfields and thatched huts; we see them, rather, as a very complex series of competitive ethnic groups with internal social ranking and great preoccupation with status, iconography, water control, and the accumulation of luxury goods. Hopefully, as careful studies bring these people into sharper focus, they will begin to make more sense in terms of comparable Indian groups surviving in the ethnographic present.

Among other things, the new data from Mesoamerica strain some of the theoretical models we used in the past to view culture and culture change. One of these was the model of a culture adapted to a particular environmental zone: "oak woodland," "mesquite-grassland", "semitropical thorn scrub", "tropical forest", and so on. New data suggest, first, that primitive peoples rarely adapt to whole "environmental zones." Next, as argued in this article, it appears that sometimes a group's basic "adaptation" may not even be to the "micro-environments" within a zone, but rather to a small series of plant and animal genera whose ranges cross-cut several environments.

Another model badly strained by our new data is that of culture change during the transition from food-collecting to sedentary agriculture. Past workers often attributed this to the "discovery" that planted seeds would sprout, or to the results of a long series of "experiments" with plant cultivation. Neither of these explanations is wholly satisfying. We know of no human group on earth so primitive that they are ignorant of the connection between plants and the seeds from which they grow, and this is particularly true of groups dependent (as were the highland Mesoamerican food-collectors) on intensive utilization of seasonal plant resources. Furthermore, I find it hard to believe that "experiments with cultivation" were carried on only with those plants that eventually became cultivars, since during the food-collecting era those plants do not even seem to have been the principal foods used. In fact, they seem to have been less important than many wild plants which never became domesticated. Obviously, something besides "discoveries" and "experiments" is involved.

I believe that this period of transition from food-collecting to sedentary agriculture, which began by 5000 B.C. and ended prior to 1500 B.C., can best be characterized as one of gradual change in a series of procurement systems, regulated by two mechanisms called seasonality and scheduling. I would argue that none of the changes which took place during this period arose *de novo,* but were the result of expansion or contraction of previously-existing systems. I would argue further that the use of an ecosystem model enables us to see aspects of this prehistoric culture change which are not superficially apparent. . . . Man and the Southern Highlands of Mexico will be viewed as a single complex system, composed of many subsystems which mutually influenced each other over a period of over seven millennia, between 8000 B.C. and 200 B.C. This systems approach will include the use of both the "first" and "second" cybernetics as a model for explaining pre-historic culture change.

The first cybernetics involves the study of regulatory mechanisms and "negative feedback" processes which promote equilibrium, and counteract deviation from stable situations over long periods of time. The second cybernetics is the study of "positive feedback" processes which amplify deviations, causing systems to expand and eventually reach stability at higher levels. Because I am as distressed as anyone by the esoteric terminology of systems theory, I have tried to sub-stitute basic English synonyms wherever possible.

Procurement Systems in the Preceramic (Hunting and Gathering) Era

Let us begin by considering the subsistence pattern of the food-collectors and "incipient cultivators" who occupied the Southern Highlands of Mexico between 8000 and 2000 B.C.

The sources of our data are plant and animal remains preserved in dry caves in the Valley of Oaxaca and the Valley of Tehuacan. Relevant sites are Guilá Naquitz Cave, Cueva Blanca, and the Martínez Rock Shelter (near Mitla, in the Valley of Oaxaca), and Mac-Neish's now-famous Coxcatlán, Purrón, Abejas, El Riego, and San Marcos Caves, whose food remains have been partially reported. Tens of thousands of plants and animal bones were recovered from these caves, which vary between 900 and 1900 meters in elevation and occur in environments as diverse as cool-temperate oak woodland, cactus desert, and semi-tropical thorn forest. Because most of the material has not been published in detail as yet, my conclusions must be considered tentative.

Preliminary studies of the food debris from these caves indicate that certain plant and animal genera were always more important than others, regardless of local environment. These plants and animals were the focal points of a series of procurement systems, each of which may be considered one component of the total ecosystem of the food collecting era. They were heavily utilized—"exploited" is the term usually employed—but such utilization was not a one-way system. Man was not simply extracting energy from his environment, but participating in it; and his use of each genus was part of a system which allowed the latter to survive, even flourish, in spite of heavy utilization. Many of these patterns have survived to the present day, among Indian groups like the Paiute and Shoshone or the Tarahumara of northern Mexico, thus allowing us to postulate some of the mechanisms built into the system, which allowed the wild genera to survive.

Each procurement system required a technology involving both implements (projectiles, fiber shredders, collecting tongs, etc.) and facilities (baskets, net carrying bags, storage pits, roasting pits, etc.). In many cases, these implements and facilities were so similar to those used in the ethnographic present by Utoaztecan speakers of western North America that relatively little difficulty is encountered in reconstructing the outlines of the ancient procurement system.

I. Plants

Literally hundreds of plant species were used by the food-collectors of the Southern Mexican Highlands. There were annual grasses like wild maize *(Zea)* and fox-tail *(Setaria),* fruits like the avocado *(Persea)* and black zapote *(Diospyros),* wild onions *(Allium),* acorns and pinyon nuts, several varieties of pigweed *(Amaranthus),* and many other plants, varying considerably from region to region because of rainfall and altitude differences. However, three categories of plants seem to have been especially important wherever we have data, regardless of altitude. They are:

(1) The maguey (*Agave* spp.), a member of the Amaryllis family, which is available year-round; (2) a series of succulent cacti, including organ cactus (*Lemaireocereus* spp.) and prickly pear (*Opuntia* spp.), whose fruits are seasonal, but whose young leaves are available year-round; and (3) a number of related genera of tree legumes, known locally as mesquites (*Prosopis* spp.) and guajes (*Lucaena, Mimosa,* and *Acacia),* which bear edible pods in the rainy season only.

System 1: Maguey procurement. Maguey, the "century plant," is most famous today as the genus from which pulque is fermented and tequila and mezcal are distilled. In prehistoric times, when distillation was unknown, the maguey appears to have been used more as a source of food. Perhaps no single plant element is more common in the

dry caves of southern Mexico than the masticated cud or "quid" of maguey. It is not always realized, however, that these quids presuppose a kind of technological breakthrough: at some point, far back in preceramic times, the Indians learned how to make the maguey edible.

The maguey, a tough and phylogenetically primitive monocotyledon which thrives on marginal land even on the slopes of high, cold, arid valleys, is unbearably bitter when raw. It cannot be eaten until it has been roasted between 24 and 72 hours, depending on the youth and tenderness of the plant involved.

The method of maguey roasting described by Pennington [for the Tarahumara] is not unlike that of the present-day Zapotec of the Valley of Oaxaca. A circular pit, 3 to 4 feet in diameter and of equal depth, is lined with stones and fueled with some slow-burning wood, like oak. When the stones are red-hot, the pit is lined with maguey leaves which have been trimmed off the "heart" of the plant. The maguey hearts are placed in the pit, covered with grass and maguey leaves and finally a layer of earth, which seals the roasting pit and holds in the heat. After one to five days, depending on the age and quantity of maguey, the baking is terminated and the hearts are edible: all, that is, except the indigestible fiber, which is expectorated in the form of a "quid" after the nourishment is gone. Evidence of the roasting process can be detected in maguey fragments surviving in desiccated human feces from Coxcatlán Cave.

The Zapotecs of the Valley of Oaxaca, like most Indians of southern Mexico, recognize that the best time to cut and roast the maguey is after it has sent up its inflorescence, or *quiote.* The plant begins to die after this event, which occurs sometime around the sixth or eighth year of growth, and a natural fermentation takes place in the moribund plant which softens it and increases its sugar content. The sending up of this inflorescence is a slow process, which can culminate at any time of the year. The large numbers of *quiote* fragments in our Oaxaca cave sites indicate that the Indians of the preceramic food-collecting era already knew that this was the best point in the plant's life-cycle for roasting.

The discovery that maguey (if properly processed) can be rendered edible was of major importance, for in some regions there is little else available in the way of plant food during the heart of the dry season. And the discovery that maguey was best for roasting *after* sending up its inflorescence and starting its natural fermentation meant that the plants harvested were mostly those that were dying already, and had long since sent out their pollen. Thus the maguey continued to thrive on the hillsides of the southern highlands in spite of the substantial harvests of the preceramic food-collectors: all they did was to weed out the dying plants.

System 2: Cactus fruit procurement. Organ cacti of at least four species were eaten at Tehuacán and Oaxaca, and their fruits—which appear late in the dry season—are still very common in Mexican markets. Most are sold under the generic terms *pitahaya* and *tuna,* but the best known "tuna" is really the fruit of the prickly pear (*Opuntia* spp.), the ubiquitous cactus of Mexican plains and rocky slopes. Most cactus fruit appears some time toward the end of the dry season, depending on altitude, but the tender young leaves may be peeled and cooked during any season of the year.

The collecting of cactus fruit had to take place before the summer rains turned the fruit to mush, and had to be carried on in competition with fruit bats, birds, and small rodents, who also find the fruit appetizing. The fruits are spiny, and some of the Tehuacán caves contained wooden sticks which may have been "tongs" for use in picking them off the stem. The spines can be singed off and the fruits transported by net bag or basket, but they cannot be stored for long. By sun-drying, the fruit can be saved for several weeks, but eventually it begins to rot. It is worth noting, however, that harvest of most of these wild fruits must be done quickly and intensively because of competition from wild animals, rather than spoilage.

The harvesting and eating of cactus fruits, no matter how intensive it may be, does not appear to diminish the available stands of cactus nor reduce subsequent generations of tuna and pitahaya—for the seeds from which the plant is propagated almost inevitably survive the human digestive tract and escape in the feces, to sprout that very year. It is even possible that such harvests are beneficial for the prickly pear and columnar cacti, in affording them maximum seed dispersal. This is only one example of the self-perpetuating nature of some of the procurement systems operating in preceramic Mexico.

System 3: Tree legume procurement. Mesquite is a woody legume which prefers the deep alluvial soil of valley floors and river flood plains in the highlands. During the June to August rainy season it bears hundreds of pods which, while still green and tender, can be chewed, or boiled into a kind of syrup (called "miel" in the Oaxaca and Tehuacán Valleys).

Such use of mesquite extended from at least the Southern Mexican Highlands (where we found it in caves near Mitla) north to the Great American Southwest, where it was evident at Gypsum Cave and related sites. *Guajes,* whose edible pods mature in roughly the same season, characterize hill slopes and canyons, and were abundant in both the Mitla and Tehuacán caves. . . .

The pod-bearing pattern of mesquite and guaje demands a seasonal, localized, and fairly intensive period of collecting. The pods can be hand-picked, and probably were transported in the many types of baskets and net carrying bags recovered in the Oaxaca and Tehuacán caves. Both pods and seeds can be dried and stored for long periods, but they must be picked at the appropriate time or they will be eaten by animals, like deer, rabbit, and ring-tailed cat.

II. Mammals

Mammals were an important year-round resource in ancient Mesoamerica, where winters are so mild that many animals never hibernate, as they do at more northern latitudes. Deer, peccary, rabbits, raccoons, opossums, skunks, ground squirrels, and large pocket gophers were common in the prehistoric refuse. However, wherever we have adequate samples of archeological animal bones from the Southern Highlands of Mexico, it appears that the following generalization is valid: white-tailed deer and cottontail rabbits were far and away the most important game mammals in all periods, and most hunting technology in the preceramic (and Formative) eras was designed to recover these two genera. Our discussion of wild animal exploitation will therefore center on these animals.

System 4: White-tailed deer procurement. The white-tailed deer, a major food resource in ancient times, continues to be Mesoamerica's most important single game species. Part of its success is due to the wide range of plant foods it finds acceptable, and its persistence even in the immediate vicinity of human settlement and under extreme hunting pressure. White-tailed deer occur in every habitat in Mesoamerica, but their highest populations are in the pine-oak woodlands of the Sierra Madre. The tropical rain forests, such as those of the lowland Maya area, are the least suitable habitats for this deer. Within Mesoamerica proper, highest prehistoric populations would have been in areas like the mountain woodlands of the Valley of Mexico, Puebla, Toluca, Oaxaca, and Guerrero.

These deer have relatively small home ranges, and although they often spend part of the daylight hours hiding in thickets, they can be hunted in the morning and evening when they come out to forage. Deer have known trails along which they travel within their home ranges, and where ambush hunters can wait for them. In other words, they are susceptible to daylight hunts, on foot, by men armed with nothing more sophisticated than an atlatl or even a fire-hardened spear, such as used by the Chiapanecs of the Grijalva Depression. On top of this, they can stand an annual harvest of 30 to 40 per cent of the deer population without diminishing in numbers. Archeological data suggest that the hunters

of the Tehuacán and Oaxaca Valleys did not practice any kind of conservation, but killed males, females, fawns and even pregnant does (as indicated by skeletal remains of late-term foetuses). This does not seem to have depleted local deer populations in any way. In fact, by thinning the herds during times of optimum plant resource availability, it may even have prevented the starvation of deer during the heart of the dry season.

System 5: Cottontail procurement. . . . Cottontails are available year round (though most abundant in the rainy season) and can best be taken by means of traps or snares. Throwing sticks are also effective, and the Indians of northern Mexico use a figure-four rock trap or "deadfall." In the Tehaucán caves there were fragments of whittled sticks and fiber loops or slip knots which may be trap fragments; similar fragments showed up in one of our Oaxaca caves in 1966. The best feature of cottontail trapping is that the only investment of labor is in the manufacture and setting of the trap; it works for you while you go about other tasks. And cottontails are such prolific breeders that no amount of trapping is likely to wipe them out.

Regulatory Mechanisms

The ecosystem in which the hunters and collectors of ancient Mexico participated included many regulatory mechanisms, which kept the system successful, yet counteracted deviation from the established pattern. I will discuss only two of these—"seasonality" and "scheduling." "Seasonality" was imposed on man by the nature of the wild resources themselves; "scheduling" was a cultural activity which resolved conflict between procurement systems.

I. Seasonality
The most important divisions of the Mesoamerican year are a winter season (October to May), which is dry, and a summer season (June to September), when most of the annual rain falls. Many edible plants and animals

of the area are available only during one season, or part of a season. For example, in the semiarid highlands of Mexico some plants like the *pochote* or kapok tree *(Ceiba parvifolia),* as well as many species of columnar cacti, bear fruit in the late winter just before the rains begin, so that their seeds will sprout that same year. Other trees, like the oak *(Quercus* spp.) and the *chupandilla (Cyrtocarpa* sp.) bear fruit after the summer season, so their seeds will lie dormant through the winter and sprout during the following year. These differences, which are of adaptive value to the plant (allowing each species to flower and seed itself during the time of year when it is most advantageous), somewhat predetermined the collecting schedule of the pre-agricultural bands in Mesoamerica: often these Indians had to be able to predict to within a week or two when the maturation of the plant would take place, and then they would have to harvest furiously before the plants were eaten by birds, rodents, or other small mammals.

MacNeish has shown some of the ways in which human groups reacted to seasonality. During the rainy season, in areas where many wild plant resources were available, they often came together in large groups which MacNeish calls "macrobands," probably consisting of a series of related families. During the heart of the dry season, when few edible plants are available, the group fragmented into "microbands," which may have been individual family units. These small units scattered out widely over the landscape, utilizing resources too meager to support a macroband.

The seasonally-restricted nature of resources made it impossible for groups to remain large all year, and effectively counteracted any trends toward population increase which might have been fostered by the intensive harvest of the rainy-season macrobands. Thus populations never grew to the point where they could effectively over-reach their wild food resources. MacNeish postulates that as late as 3000 B.C. the population of the Tehuacán Valley was no higher than 120–240 persons, in an area of 1400 square miles.

II. Scheduling

So many possibilities for exploitive activity were open to these ancient Mesoamericans that it would have been impossible to engage in all of them, even seasonally. It happens that there are times of the year when a number of resources are available simultaneously, producing a situation in which there is some conflict for the time and labor of the group. Division of labor along the lines of sex, with men hunting and women collecting, is one common solution to these conflicts, but not all conflicts are so easily resolved.

The solution for more complex situations may be called "scheduling," and it involves a decision as to the relative merits of two or more courses of action. Such "scheduling decisions" are made constantly by all human groups on all levels of complexity, often without any awareness that a decision is being made.

It is not necessarily true that the lower the level of social complexity, the fewer the conflict decisions, for hunting and gathering groups of arid America had many scheduling problems to resolve. Food gathering bands of the Great Basin, for example, often depended on "scouting reports" from relatives who had passed through certain areas several weeks in advance. If they noticed an unusually high concentration of antelope or rabbit in a particular valley, or if they saw that a particular stand of wild fruit would come ripe within the next two weeks, they would advise other scattered bands of foragers about this resource. Often, while they descended on the area to harvest that particular species, new reports would come in from other areas concerning still another resource. This was not the kind of "hit and miss" pattern of exploitation one might think, for the Great Basin Indians had a rough idea that acorns and pinyon nuts would be available in the autumn, wild legumes and grasses in the rainy season, and so on. The outlines of a schedule, albeit with conflicts, were present; the "scouting reports" helped resolve conflicts and gave precision to the dates of each kind of resource exploitation, depending on individual variations in growing season from year to year.

These individual variations, which are a common feature of arid environments, combined with the scheduling pattern to make it unlikely that specialization in any one resource would develop. This prevented over-utilization of key plants or animals, and maintained a more even balance between varied resources. Because scheduling is an opportunistic mechanism, it promoted survival in spite of annual variation, but at the same time it supported the *status quo:* unspecialized utilization of a whole range of plants and animals whose availability is erratic over the long run. In this sense, scheduling acted to counteract deviations which might have resulted in either (1) starvation, or (2) a more effective adaptation.

Evidence for Scheduling in the Food-Collecting and "Incipient Cultivation" Eras (8000–2000 B.C.)

Thanks to the plants and animal bones preserved in the dry caves of Oaxaca and Tehuacán, we can often tell which season a given occupation floor was laid down in. Because of the work of botanists like Earle Smith, Lawrence Kaplan, and James Schoenwetter, we know the season during which each plant is available, and hence when its harvest must have taken place. Even the use of animal resources can often be dated seasonally; for example, in the Tehuacán Valley, we studied the seasonality of deer hunting by the condition of the antlers, which indicates the time of year when the animal was killed.

Assuming that each occupation floor in a given cave represents the debris of a single encampment, usually dating to a single season (an assumption that seems to be borne out by the quantity and nature of the refuse), the combinations of plant and animal remains observed in a given level tell us something about prehistoric scheduling decisions. Analyses of our Oaxaca caves and MacNeish's Tehuacán Caves, by roughly the same group of specialists, suggest the following tentative generalizations:

1. *Dry season camps* (October-March), de-pending on their elevation above sea level, may have great caches of fall and winter plants—for example, acorns in the Mitla area, or Ceiba pods in the Coxcatlán area—but in general they lack the variety seen in rainy season levels. And perhaps most significantly, they have a high percentage of those plants which, although not particularly tasty, are available year-round: maguey, prickly pear leaf, *Ceiba* root, and so on. These are the so-called "starvation" plants, which can be eaten in the heart of the dry season when little else is available. These same levels also tend to have high percentages of deer bone. Some, in fact, have little refuse beyond maguey quids and white-tailed deer.

2. *Rainy season camps* (May-September), as might be expected, show great quantities of the plants available at that time of the year: mesquite, guajes, amaranth, wild avocado, zapotes, and so on. They also tend to be rich in small fauna like cottontail, opossum, skunk, raccoon, gopher, and black iguana. Although deer are often present in these camps, they frequently represent only a small percentage of the minimum individual animals in the debris. Nor are the "starvation" plants particularly plentiful in these rainy-season levels.

3. What these generalizations suggest, for the most part, is that scheduling gave preference to the seasonality of the *plant* species collected; and when conflict situations arose, it was the *animal* exploitation that was curtailed. I would reconstruct the pattern as follows:

A. In the late dry season and early rainy season, there is a period of peak abundance of wild plant foods. These localized resources were intensively harvested, and eaten or cached as they came to maturity; this appears to have been a "macroband" activity. Because "all hands" participated in these harvests, little deer hunting was done; instead the Indians set traps in the vicinity of the plant-collecting camp, an activity which does not conflict with intensive plant harvests the way deerhunting would.

B. In the late fall and winter, most plants have ceased to bear fruit, but deer hunting is at its best. Since this is the mating season, male deer (who normally forage by themselves) fall in with the does and fawns, making the average herd larger; and since this is also the season when the deciduous vegetation of the highlands sheds its leaves, the deer can be more easily followed by hunters. As the dry season wears on, however, the deer grow warier and range farther and farther back into the mountains. This is the leanest time of the year in terms of plant resources, and it was evidently in this season that man turned most heavily to plants available year round, like the root of the Ceiba (which can be baked like sweet manioc) or the heart of the maguey plant (which can be roasted). These appear to have been "microband" activities.

C. By chewing roots and maguey hearts, the preceramic forager managed to last until the late spring growing season, at which point he could wallow in cactus fruit again. Essentially, his "schedule" was keyed to the seasonal availability of certain wild plants, which climaxed at those times of the year which were best suited for small-game-trapping. He scheduled his most intensive deer hunting for the seasons when big plant harvests were not a conflicting factor.

D. Climatic fluctuations, delays in the rainy season, or periodic increases in the deer herds at given localities probably kept the picture more complex than we have painted it, but this cannot be detected in the archeological record. The constant evolution of new bags, nets, baskets, projectile points, scrapers, carrying loops, and other artifacts from the caves of the Southern Highlands suggests slow but continual innovation. To what extent these innovations increased the productivity of the system is not clear.

Because the major adaptation was to a series of wild genera which crosscut several environmental boundaries, the geographic extent of the ecosystem described above was very great. This adaptation is clearly reflected in the technological sphere. Implements and facilities of striking similiarity can be found in regions which differ significantly in altitude and rainfall, so long as the five basic categories of plants and animals are present. . . .

Coxcatlán Cave, type site for the phase, occurs at 975 meters in an arid tropical forest characterized by dense stands of columnar cacti; kapok trees (Ceiba parvifolia); chupandilla (Cyrtocarpa sp.); cozahuico (Sideroxylon sp.); and abundant Leguminosae, Burseraceae, and Anacardiaceae. Cueva Blanca occurs at 1900 meters in a temperate woodland zone with scattered oaks; Dodonaea; ocotillo (Fouquieria); wild zapote (Diospyros); and other trees which (judging by archeological remains) may originally have included hackberry (Celtis) and pinyon pine.

In spite of environmental differences, implements at the two sites are nearly identical; even the seasonal deer hunting pattern and the size of the encamped group are the same. In the past, such identity would have inspired the traditional explanation: "a similar adaptation to a similar arid environment." But as seen above, the two environments are not that similar. The important point is that the basic adaptation was not to a zone or even a biotope within a zone, but to five critical categories—white-tail deer, cottontail, maguey, tree legumes, prickly pear and organ cactus. These genera range through many zones, as did the Indians who hunted them, ate them, propagated their seeds, and weeded out their dying members. This is not to say that biotopes were unimportant; they played a role, but they were also crosscut by a very important system.

Seasonality and scheduling, as examined here, were part of a "deviation-counteracting" feedback system. They prevented intensification of any one procurement system to the point where the wild genus was threatened; at the same time, they maintained a sufficiently high level of procurement efficiency so there was little pressure for change. Under the ecosystem operating in the

Southern Mexican Highlands during the later part of the food-collecting era, there was little likelihood that man would exhaust his own food resources or that his population would grow beyond what the wild vegetation and fauna would support. Maintaining such near-equilibrium conditions is the purpose of deviation-counteracting processes.

Positive Feedback and Culture change

Under conditions of fully-achieved and permanently-maintained equilibrium, prehistoric cultures might never have changed. That they did change was due at least in part to the existence of positive feedback or "deviation-amplifying" processes. These Maruyama describes as "all processes of mutual causal relationships that amplify an insignificant or accidental initial kick, build up deviation and diverge from the initial condition."

Such "insignificant or accidental initial kicks" were a series of genetic changes which took place in one or two species of Mesoamerican plants which were of use to man. The exploitation of these plants had been a relatively minor procurement system compared with that of maguey, cactus fruits, deer, or tree legumes, but positive feedback following these initial genetic changes caused one minor system to grow all out of proportion to the others, and eventually to change the whole ecosystem of the Southern Mexican Highlands. Let us now examine that system.

System 6: Wild grass procurement. One common activity of the foodcollecting era in the Southern Highlands was the harvesting of annual grasses. Perhaps the most useful in pre-agricultural times was fox-tail grass *(Setaria)*, followed by minor grasses like wild maize *(Zea mays)*, which may have been adapted to moist barrancas within the arid highland zone.

We know very little about the nature of the early "experiments" with plant cultivation, but they probably began simply as an effort to increase the area over which useful plants would grow. For example, Smith has suggested that the preceramic food-collectors may

have attempted to increase the density of prickly pear and organ cactus stands by planting cuttings of these plants. For the most part, judging by the archeological record, these efforts led to little increase in food supply and no change in emphasis on one genus or another, until—sometime between 5000 and 2000 B.C.—a series of genetic changes took place in a few key genera. It was these genetic changes, acting as a "kick," which allowed a deviation-amplifying system to begin.

As implied by Maruyama, many of these initial deviations may have been accidental and relatively minor. For example, beans (1) became more permeable in water, making it easier to render them edible; and (2) developed limp pods which do not shatter when ripe, thus enabling the Indians to harvest them more successfuly. Equally helpful were the changes in maize, whose genetic plasticity has fascinated botanists for years. While *Setaria* and the other grasses remained unchanged, maize underwent a series of alterations which made it increasingly more profitable to harvest (and plant over wider areas) than any other plant. Its cob increased in size; and, carried around the highlands by Indians intent on increasing its range, it met and crossed with its nearest relative, *Zea tripsacum,* to produce a hybrid named *teocentli.* From here on its back-crosses and subsequent evolution, loss of glumes, increase in cob number and kernel row number, have been well documented by MacNeish, Mangelsdorf, and Galinat.

Another important process, though somewhat less publicized, was the interaction between corn and beans recently emphasized by Kaplan. Maize alone, although a reasonably good starch source, does not in itself constitute a major protein because it lacks an important amino acid—lysine—which must therefore be made up from another source. Beans happen to be rich in lysine. Thus the mere combining of maize and beans in the diet of the southern highlands, apart from any favorable genetic changes in either plant, was a significant nutritional breakthrough.

Starting with what may have been (initially) accidental deviations in the system, a positive feedback network was established which eventually made maize cultivation the most profitable single subsistence activity in Meso-america. The more widespread maize cultivation, the more opportunities for favorable crosses and back-crosses; the more favorable genetic changes, the greater the yield; the greater the yield, the higher the population, and hence the more intensive cultivation. There can be little doubt that pressures for more intensive cultivation were instrumental in perfecting early water-control systems, like well-irrigation and canal-irrigation. This positive feedback system, therefore, was still increasing at the time of the Spanish Conquest.

What this meant initially was that System 6, Wild Grass Procurement, grew steadily at the expense of, and in competition with, all other procurement systems in the arid highlands. Moreover, the system increased in complexity by necessitating a *planting* period (in the spring) as well as the usual *harvesting* season (early fall). It therefore competed with both the spring-ripening wild plants (prickly pear, organ cactus) and the fall-ripening crops (acorns, fruits, some guajes). It competed with rainy-season hunting of deer and peccary. And it was a nicely self-perpetuating system, for the evolution of cultivated maize indicates that no matter how much the Indians harvested, they saved the best seed for next year's planting; and they saved it under storage conditions which furthered the survival of every seed. Moreover, they greatly increased the area in which maize would grow by removing competing plants.

As mentioned earlier, (1) procurement of "starvation" plants like *Ceiba* and maguey seems to have been undertaken by small, scattered "microbands," while (2) harvests of seasonally-limited plants, abundant only for a short time —like cactus fruits, mesquite and guajes, and so on—seem to have been undertaken by large "macrobands," formed by the coalescence of several related microbands. Because of this functional association

between band size and resource, human demography was changed by the positive feedback of early maize-bean cultivation: an amplification of the rainy-season planting and harvesting also meant an amplification of the time of macroband coalescence. . . .

Actually, it may not be strictly accurate to say that sedentary village life was "allowed" or "made possible" by agricultural production; in fact, increased permanence of the macroband may have been *required* by the amplified planting and harvesting pattern. . . .

Conclusions

The use of a cybernetics model to explain prehistoric cultural change, while terminologically cumbersome, has certain advantages. For one thing, it does not attribute cultural evolution to "discoveries," "inventions," "experiments," or "genius," but instead enables us to treat prehistoric cultures as systems. It stimulates inquiry into the mechanisms that counteract change or amplify it, which ultimately tells us something about the nature of adaptation. Most importantly, it allows us to view change not as something arising *de novo,* but in terms of quite minor deviations in one small part of a previously existing system, which, once set in motion, can expand greatly because of positive feedback.

The implications of this approach for the prehistorian are clear: it is vain to hope for the discovery of the first domestic corn cob, the first pottery vessel, the first hieroglyphic, or the first site where some other major breakthrough occurred. Such deviations from the pre-existing pattern almost certainly took place in such a minor and accidental way that their traces are not recoverable. More worthwhile would be an investigation of the mutual causal processes that amplify these tiny deviations into major changes in prehistoric culture.

A crucial period in the story of the pre-Columbian cultures of the New World is the transition from a hunting-and-collecting way of life to effective village farming. We are now fairly certain that Mesoamerica is the area in which this took place, and that the time span involved is from approximately 6500 to 1000 B.C., a period during which a kind of "incipient cultivation" based on a few domesticated plants, mainly maize, gradually supplemented and eventually replaced wild foods. Beginning probably about 1500 B.C., and definitely by 1000 B.C., villages with all of the signs of the settled arts, such as pottery and loomweaving, appear throughout Mesoamerica, and the foundations of pre-Columbian civilization may be said to have been established.

Much has been written about food-producing "revolutions" in both hemispheres. There is now good evidence both in the Near East and in Mesoamerica that food production was part of a relatively slow *evolution*, but there still remain several problems related to the process of settling down. For the New World, there are three questions which we would like to answer.

1. What factors favored the early development of food production in Mesoamerica as compared with other regions of this hemisphere?

2. What was the mode of life of the earlier hunting-and-collecting peoples in Mesoamerica, and in exactly what ways was it changed by the addition of cultivated plants?

3. When, where, and how did food production make it possible for the first truly sedentary villages to be established in Mesoamerica?

The first of these questions cannot be answered until botanists determine the habits and preferred habitats of the wild ancestors of maize, beans, and the various cucurbits which were domesticated. To answer the other questions, we must reconstruct the human ecological situations which prevailed. Some remarkably sophisticated, multidis-

Microenvironments and Mesoamerican Prehistory

Michael D. Coe and Kent V. Flannery

From *Science, Vol. 143, No. 3607, 1964, pp. 650–654.* Copyright 1964, American Association for the Advancement of Science. By permission of the authors, the publisher, and copyright holder.

ciplinary projects have been and still are being carried out elsewhere in the world, aimed at reconstructing prehistoric human ecology. However, for the most part they have been concerned with the adaptations of past human communities to large-scale changes in the environment over very long periods—that is, to alterations in the *macroenvironment*, generally caused by climatic fluctuations. Such alterations include the shift from tundra to boreal conditions in northern Europe. Nevertheless, there has been a growing suspicion among prehistorians that macroenvironmental changes are insufficient as an explanation of the possible causes of food production and its effects, regardless of what has been written to the contrary.

Ethnography and Microenvironments

We have been impressed, in reading anthropologists' accounts of simple societies, with the fact that human communities, while in some senses limited by the macroenvironment—for instance, by deserts or by tropical forests—usually exploit several or even a whole series of well-defined *microenvironments* in their quest for food. These microenvironments might be defined as smaller subdivisions of large ecological zones; examples are the immediate surroundings of the ancient archeological site itself, the bank of a nearby stream, or a distant patch of forest.

An interesting case is provided by the Shoshonean bands which, until the mid-19th century, occupied territories within the Great Basin of the American West. These extremely primitive peoples had a mode of life quite similar to that of the peoples of Mesoamerica of the 5th millennium B.C., who were the first to domesticate maize. The broadly limiting effects of the Great Basin (which, generally speaking, is a desert) and the lack of knowledge of irrigation precluded any effective form of agriculture, even though some bands actually sowed wild grasses and one group tried an ineffective watering of wild crops. Consequently, the Great Basin aborigines remained on a hunting and plant-collecting

level, with extremely low population densities and a very simple social organization. However, Steward's study shows that each band was not inhabiting a mere desert but moved on a strictly followed seasonal round among a vertically and horizontally differentiated set of microenvironments, from the lowest salt flats up to piñon forest, which were "niches" in a human-ecological sense.

The Great Basin environment supplied the potential for cultural development or lack of it, but the men who lived there selected this or that microenvironment. Steward clearly shows that *how* and *what* they adapted influenced many other aspects of their culture, from their technology to their settlement pattern, which was necessarily one of restricted wandering from one seasonally occupied camp to another.

Seasonal wandering would appear to be about the only possible response of a people without animal or plant husbandry to the problem of getting enough food throughout the year. Even the relatively rich salmon-fishing cultures of the Northwest Coast (British Columbia and southern Alaska) were without permanently occupied villages. Contrariwise, it has seemed to us that only a drastic reduction of the number of niches to be exploited, and a concentration of these in space, would have permitted the establishment of full-time village life. The ethnographic data suggest that an analysis of microenvironments or niches would throw much light on the processes by which the Mesoamerican peoples settled down.

Methodology

If the environment in which an ancient people lived was radically different from any known today, and especially if it included animal and plant species which are now extinct and whose behavior is consequently unknown, then any reconstruction of the subsistence activities of the people is going to be difficult. All one could hope for would be a more-or-less sound reconstruction of general ecological conditions, while a breakdown of the environment into smaller ecological niches would be impossible. However, much if not most archeological research concerns periods so recent in comparison with the million or so years of human prehistory that in most instances local conditions have not changed greatly in the interval between the periods investigated and the present.

If we assume that there is a continuity between the ancient and the modern macroenvironment in the area of interest, there are three steps which we must take in tracing the role of microenvironments.

1. Analysis of the present-day microecology (from the human point of view) of the archeological zone. Archeological research is often carried out in remote and little known parts of the earth, which have not been studied from the point of view of natural history. Hence, the active participation of botanists, zoologists, and other natural scientists is highly recommended.

The modern ethnology of the region should never be neglected, for all kinds of highly relevant data on the use of surrounding niches by local people often lie immediately at hand. We have found in Mesoamerica that the workmen on the "dig" are a mine of such information. There may be little need to thumb through weighty reports on the Australian aborigines or South African Bushmen when the analogous custom can be found right under one's nose. The end result of the analysis should be a map of the microenvironments defined (here aerial photographs are of great use), with detailed data on the seasonal possibilities each offers human communities on certain technological levels of development.

2. Quantitative analysis of food remains in the archeological sites, and of the technical equipment (arrow or spear points, grinding stones for seeds, baskets and other containers, and so on) related to food-getting. It is a rare site report that treats of bones and plant remains in any but the most perfunctory way. It might seem a simple thing to ship animal bones from a site to a specialist for identification, but most archeologists know that many zoologists consider identification of recent faunal remains a waste of time. Because of this, and because many museum collections do not include postcranial skeletons that could be used for identification, the archeologist must arrange to secure his own comparative collection. If this collection is assembled by a zoologist on the project, a by-product of the investigation would be a faunal study of microenvironments. Similarly, identification of floral and other specimens from the site would lead to other specialized studies.

3. Correlation of the archeological with the microenvironmental study in an overall analysis of the ancient human ecology.

The Tehuacán Valley

An archeological project undertaken by R. S. MacNeish, with such a strategy in mind, has been located since 1961 in the dry Tehuacán Valley of southern Puebla, Mexico. The valley is fringed with bone-dry caves in which the food remains of early peoples have been preserved to a remarkable degree in stratified deposits. For a number of reasons, including the results of his past archeological work in Mesoamerica, McNeish believed that he would find here the origins of maize agriculture in the New World, and he has been proved right. It now seems certain that the wild ancestor of maize was domesticated in the Tehuacán area some time around the beginning of the 5th millennium B.C.

While the Tehuacán environment is in general a desert, the natural scientists of the project have defined within it four microenvironments (Fig. 1).

1 *Alluvial valley floor,* a level plain sparsely covered with mesquite, grasses, and cacti, offering fairly good possibilities, especially along the Río Salado, for primitive maize agriculture dependent on rainfall.

2. *Travertine slopes,* on the west side of the valley. This would have been a niche useful

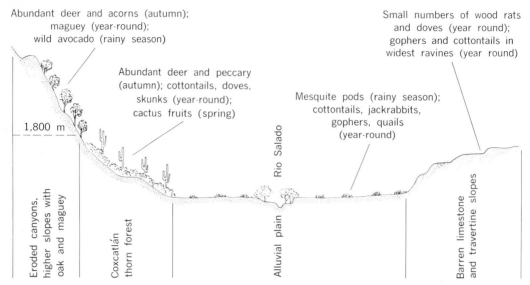

Abundant deer and acorns (autumn);
maguey (year-round);
wild avocado (rainy season)

Abundant deer and peccary
(autumn); cottontails, doves,
skunks (year-round);
cactus fruits (spring)

Small numbers of wood rats
and doves (year round);
gophers and cottontails in
widest ravines (year round)

Mesquite pods (rainy season);
cottontails, jackrabbits,
gophers, quails
(year-round)

1,800 m

Rio Salado

Eroded canyons,
higher slopes with
oak and maguey

Coxcatlán
thorn forest

Alluvial plain

Barren limestone
and travertine slopes

Fig. 1   An idealized east-west transsection of the central part of the Tehuacán Valley, Puebla, Mexico, showing microenvironments and the seasons in which the food resources are exploited. East is to the left. The length of the area represented is about 20 kilometers.

for growing maize and tomatoes and for trapping cottontail rabbits.

3. *Coxcatlán thorn forest,* with abundant seasonal crops of wild fruits, such as various species of *Opuntia,* pitahaya, and so on. There is also a seasonal abundance of whitetail deer, cottontail rabbits, and skunks, and there are some peccaries.

4. *Eroded canyons,* unsuitable for exploitation except for limited hunting of deer and as routes up to maguey fields for those peoples who chewed the leaves of that plant.

The correlation of this study with the analysis, by specialists, of the plant and animal remains (these include bones, maize cobs, chewed quids, and even feces) found in cave deposits has shown that the way of life of the New World's first farmers was not very different from that of the Great Basin aborigines in the 19th century. Even the earliest inhabitants of the valley, prior to 6500 B.C., were more collectors of seasonally gathered wild plant foods than they were "big game hunters," and they traveled in microbands in an annual, wet-season-dry-season cycle. While slightly more sedentary macrobands appeared with the adoption of simple maize cultivation after

5000 B.C., these people nevertheless still followed the old pattern of moving from microenvironment to microenvironment, separating into microbands during the dry season.

The invention and gradual improvement of agriculture seem to have made few profound alterations in the settlement pattern of the valley for many millennia. Significantly, by the Formative period (from about 1500 B.C. to A.D. 200), when agriculture based on a hybridized maize was far more important than it had been in earlier periods as a source of food energy, the pattern was still one of parttime nomadism. In this part of the dry Mexican highlands, until the Classic period (about A.D. 200 to 900), when irrigation appears to have been introduced into Tehuacán, food production had still to be supplemented with extensive plant collecting and hunting.

Most of the peoples of the Formative period apparently lived in large villages on the alluvial valley floor during the wet season, from May through October of each year, for planting had to be done in May and June, and harvesting, in September and October. In the dry season, from November through February, when the trees and bushes had lost their leaves and the deer were easy to see and track, some of the population must have moved to hunting camps, principally in the Coxcatlán thorn forest. By February, hunting had become less rewarding as the now-wary deer moved as far as possible from human habitation; however, in April and May the thorn forest was still ripe for exploitation, as many kinds of wild fruit matured. In May it was again time to return to the villages on the valley floor for spring planting.

Now, in some other regions of Mesoamerica there were already, during the Formative period, fully sedentary village cultures in existence. It is clear that while the Tehuacán valley was the locus of the first domestication of maize, the origins of full-blown village life lie elsewhere. Because of the constraining effects of the macroenvironment, the Tehuacán people were exploiting, until relatively late in Mesoamerican prehistory, as widely spaced and as large a number of microenvironments as the Great Basin aborigines were exploiting in the 19th century.

Coastal Guatemala

Near the modern fishing port of Ocós, only a few kilometers from the Mexican border on the alluvial plain of the Pacific coast of Guatemala, we have found evidence for some of the oldest permanently occupied villages in Mesoamerica. We have also made an extensive study of the ecology and ethnology of the Ocós area.

From this study we have defined no less than eight distinct microenvironments (Fig. 2) within an area of only about 90 square kilometers. These are as follows:

1. *Beach sand and low scrub.* A narrow, infertile strip from which the present-day villagers collect occasional mollusks, a beach crab called *chichimeco* and one known as *nazareño,* and the sea turtle and its eggs.

2. *The marine estuary-and-lagoon system,*

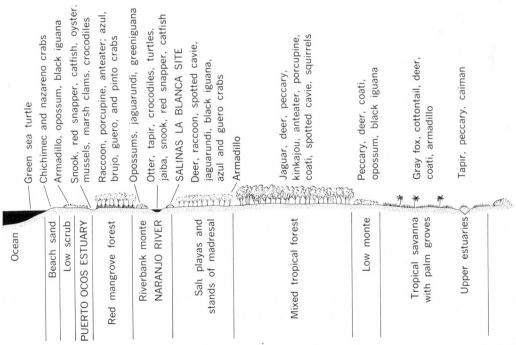

Fig. 2   Northeast-southwest transsection of the Ocós area of coastal Guatemala, showing microenvironments in relation to the site of Salinas La Blanca. Northeast is to the right. The length of area represented is about 15 kilometers.

in places extending considerably inland and utimately connecting with streams or rivers coming down from the Sierra Madre. The estuaries, with their mangrove-lined bands, make up the microenvironment richest in wild foods in the entire area. The brackish waters abound in catfish (*Arius* sp. and *Galeichthys* sp.), red snapper *(Lutjanus colorado),* several species of snook (*Centropomus* sp.), and many other kinds of fish. Within living memory, crocodiles *(Crocodylus astutus)* were common, but they have by now been hunted almost to extinction. The muddy banks of the estuaries are the habitat of many kinds of mollusks, including marsh clams *(Polymesoda radiata),* mussels *(Mytella falcata),* and oysters *(Ostrea columbiensis),* and they also support an extensive population of fiddler and mud crabs.

3. *Mangrove forest,* consisting mainly of stilt-rooted red mangrove, which slowly gives way to white mangrove as one moves away from the estuary. We noted high populations of collared anteater *(Tamandua tetradactyla)* and arboreal porcupine *(Coendu mexicanus).* A large number of crabs (we did not determine the species) inhabit this microenvironment; these include, especially, one known locally as the *azul* (blue) crab, on which a large population of raccoons feeds.

4. *Riverine,* comprising the channels and banks of the sluggish Suchiate and Naranjo rivers, which connect with the lagoon-estuary system not far from their mouths. Freshwater turtles, catfish, snook, red snapper, and mojarra (*Cichlasoma* sp.) are found in these waters; the most common animal along the banks is the green iguana *(Iguana iguana).*

5. *Salt playas,* the dried remnants of ancient lagoon-and-estuary systems which are still subject to inundation during the wet season, with localized stands of a tree known as *madresal* ("mother of salt"). Here there is an abundance of game, including whitetail deer and the black iguana *(Ctenosaura similis),* as well as a rich supply of salt.

6. *Mixed tropical forest,* found a few kilometers inland, in slightly higher and better

drained situations than the salt *playas.* This forest includes mostly tropical evergreens like the ceiba, as well as various zapote and fan palms, on the fruit of which a great variety of mammals thrive—the kinkajou, the spotted cavy, the coatimundi, the raccoon, and even the gray fox. The soils here are highly suitable for maize agriculture.

7. *Tropical savannah,* occupying poorly drained patches along the upper stream and estuary systems of the area. This is the major habitat in the area for cottontail rabbits and gray foxes. Other common mammals are the coatimundi and armadillo.

8. *Cleared fields and second growth,* habitats which have been created by agriculturists, and which are generally confined to areas that were formerly mixed tropical forest.

Among the earliest Formative cultures known thus far for the Ocós area is the Cuadros phase, dated by radiocarbon analysis at about 1000 to 850 B.C. and well represented in the site of Salinas La Blanca, which we excavated in 1962. The site is on the banks of the Naranjo River among a variety of microenvironments; it consists of two flattish mounds built up from deeply stratified refuse layers representing house foundations of a succession of hamlets or small villages.

From our analysis of this refuse we have a good idea of the way in which the Cuadros people lived. Much of the refuse consists of potsherds from large, neckless jars, but very few of the clay figurines that abound in other Formative cultures of Mesoamerica were found. We discovered many plant remains; luckily these had been preserved or "fossilized" through replacement of the tissues by carbonates. From these we know that the people grew and ate a nonhybridized maize considerably more advanced than the maize which was then being grown in Tehuacán. The many impressions of leaves in clay floors in the site will, we hope, eventually make it possible to reconstruct the flora that immediately surrounded the village.

The identification of animal remains (Fig. 3), together with our ecological study and

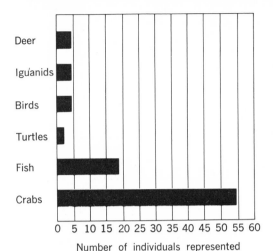

Fig. 3 Animal remains, exclusive of mollusks found in Cuadros phase levels at Salinas La Blanca.

with the knowledge that the people had a well-developed maize agriculture, gives a great deal of information on the subsistence activities of these early coastal villages. First of all, we believe they had no interest whatever in hunting, a conclusion reinforced by our failure to find a single projectile point in the site. The few deer bones that have been recovered are all from immature individuals that could have been encountered by chance and clubbed to death. Most of the other remains are of animals that could have been collected in the environs of the village, specifically in the lagoon-estuary system and the flanking mangrove forest, where the people fished, dug for marsh clams, and, above all, caught crabs (primarily the *azul* crab, which is trapped at night). Entirely missing are many edible species found in other microenvironments, such as raccoon, cottontail rabbit, peccary, spotted cavy, and nine-banded armadillo.

There is no evidence at all that occupation of Salinas La Blanca was seasonal. An effective food production carried out on the rich, deep soils of the mixed tropical forest zone, together with the food resources of the lagoon-estuary system, made a permanently settled life possible. Looked at another way,

developed maize agriculture had so reduced the number and spacing of the niches which had to be exploited that villages could be occupied the year round.

Conditions similar to those of the Ocós area are found all along the Pacific Coast of Guatemala and along the Gulf Coast of southern Veracruz and Tabasco in Mexico, and we suggest that the real transition to village life took place there and not in the dry Mexican highlands, where maize was domesticated initially.

Conclusion

The interpretation of archeological remains through a fine-scale analysis of small ecological zones throws new light on the move toward sedentary life in Mesoamerican prehistory. In our terms, the basic difference between peoples who subsist on wild foods and those who dwell in permanent villages is that the former must exploit a wide variety of small ecological niches in a seasonal pattern—niches which are usually scattered over a wide range of territory—while the latter may, because of an effective food production, concentrate on one or on only a few microenvironments which lie relatively close at hand.

Fine-scale ecological analysis indicates that there never was any such thing as an "agricultural revolution" in Mesoamerica, suddenly and almost miraculously resulting in village life. The gradual addition of domesticates such as maize, beans, and squash to the diet of wild plant and animal foods hardly changed the way of life of the Tehuacán people for many thousands of years, owing to a general paucity of the environment, and seasonal nomadism persisted until the introduction of irrigation. It probably was not until maize was taken to the alluvial, lowland littoral of Mesoamerica, perhaps around 1500 B.C., that permanently occupied villages became possible, through reduction of the number of microenvironments to which men had to adapt themselves.

Early Civilizations, Subsistence, and Environment

Robert M. Adams

From *City Invincible: A Symposium on Urbanization and Cultural Development in the Ancient Near East,* Carl H. Kraeling and Robert M. Adams (eds.), The University of Chicago Press, 1960, pp. 269–295. © 1960, University of Chicago Press. By permission of the author, the publisher and copyright holder.

. . . My task is to describe briefly some of the major ecological relationships which sustained the growth of civilizations in a number of "nuclear" areas. In addition to Mesopotamia and Egypt, the choice of pre-Spanish Mesoamerica and Peru seems most appropriate. It is supported not only by the volume and historical-archeological depth of relevant data that are available from the latter two areas but also by the likelihood that extreme geographic separation reduced their dependence on Old World precursors to a minimum. In spite of this separation there is a striking similarity, in scope and form, of nuclear American sociopolitical attainments to those of the Fertile Crescent area at a much earlier time.

J. H. Steward has argued convincingly that even the demonstrated fact of diffusion between two cultural traditions is insufficient to "explain" their likenesses. "One may fairly ask," he maintains, "whether each time a society accepts diffused culture, it is not an independent recurrence of cause and effect." From this point of view, it is possible to regard all four areas as historically distinct examples regardless of the ultimate "origins" of particular traits. This is especially true for our purposes, since cultural-environmental relationships within an area are pre-eminently a matter of independent adjustment to local conditions and resources.

Moreover, the substantive evidence in these cases for the presence of diffusion from some outside source as a determinative factor is either lacking or at best equivocal. Each of the four areas stood out over its surroundings as a highly creative rather than a passively receptive center. While the complete absence of trans-Pacific stimuli for New World high cultural development cannot be assured, the conclusion of most Americanists today is that the latter "stands clearly apart and essentially independent from the comparable culture core of the Old World." There is certainly no suggestion of any New World—Old World contact as important as the relatively brief but catalytic influence of Mesopotamia on Egypt at about 3000 B.C., yet in the latter case Frankfort took pains to point out the selective, qualified, and generally transient character of the borrowing. With respect to interrelations between Peru and Mesoamerica, it is sufficient to state that not a single object or record of influence or contact between these areas has been accepted as authentic from the long time span between the Formative (or Early Village) period and the coming of the Spaniards, although the over-all tempo of development in each is remarkably similar. In short, it is both reasonable on a priori theoretical grounds and justified by present evidence to use Mesopotamia, Egypt, Mesoamerica, and Peru as essentially independent examples for a discussion of their internal ecological relationships.

Within the limits of this discussion it is neither possible nor necessary to explore fully the similarities in cultural development among these four areas. All clearly became civilizations, in the sense in which that term is defined here as a functionally interrelated set of social institutions: class stratification, marked by highly different degrees of ownership of control of the main productive resources; political and religious hierarchies complementing each other in the administration of territorially organized states; a complex division of labor, with full-time craftsmen, servants, soldiers, and officials alongside the great mass of primary peasant producers. Each was a complex, deeply rooted cultural tradition displaying most or all of V. G. Childe's more inclusive civilizational criteria as well: monumental public works, the imposition of tribute or taxation, "urban" settlements, naturalistic art, the beginnings of exact and predictive sciences, a system of writing suitable at least for rudimentary records and accounts. The attainment of civilization, from a diachronic point of view, was expressed in each of the four areas by a series of parallel trends or processes: urbanization, militarization, stratification, bureaucratization, and the like. Of course, these processes were truncated in the New World by the Spanish Conquest—as a plausible approximation, after a level of development had been reached which was functionally equivalent to Old Kingdom Egypt or southern Mesopotamia under the Dynasty of Agade. However, this does not affect our comparisons here, which will be limited to earlier periods in the Near East for which New World equivalents are available.

It thus seems possible to group the four civilizations as representatives of a single type of class of social system. (Other members of the class would include the unknown Indus Valley polity of Harappa and Mohenjo Daro, Shang China, and perhaps certain West African city-states.) To be sure, this stress on structural and functional similarities needs supplementing by the traditional humanistic emphasis on the unique and relatively timeless qualities of each civilization for a properly balanced view. One example of the latter emphasis is the invocation of particular environmental features of different civilizations to account in part for their differing views of the natural world as reconstructed from works of ancient literature or art, for the distinctive structuring of their formal cosmologies, and perhaps even for dominant psychological attitudes. A typological approach necessarily neglects, although certainly cannot deny, the unique total patterning of every culture irrespective of what proportion of its constituent elements may have close parallels elsewhere. Probably this patterning is expressed most systematically, concisely, and impersonally in stylistic or configurational terms. But in any case these widely ramifying, largely ideational, aspects of the interrelations between man and the natural world are beyond the scope of this paper. Here we are concerned only with the generalized social order common to a group of autochthonous civilizations and with its relations to the environment.

Climate, Physiography, Resources, and Population

Beyond the limitation of each of the nuclear areas to subtropical latitudes, the combined gross catalogue of environmental features is characterized mainly by its diversity. If Egyptian and Sumero-Babylonian civilizations are restricted to great arid or semi-arid river valleys, no such uniform description holds for the zones occupied by either Mesoamerican or Peruvian civilization. Both of the latter range from sea level to high mountain slopes, with tropical, temperate, or even cold-temperate climates corresponding to their altitudes. If coastal Peru and much of highland Mesoamerica are sufficiently dry to be closely comparable with the Old World centers, this is progressively less true in the Peruvian sierra with increasing altitude and distance from the Pacific coast and not true at all in the Gulf Coastal lowlands of Middle America.

Both of the New World areas lack great inclusive river systems comparable to Egypt and the Nile or Mesopotamia and the Tigris-Euphrates. Instead, short, steeply descending watercourses that drain relatively small watersheds are common, and many of the largest of these are reduced in their pre-Hispanic importance by geographic factors. The main valley of the Rio Balsas and the intermontane basins of the Bajío on the Rio Lerma in Mexico, for example, were lightly occupied before the Spanish introduction of draft animals and the iron-tipped plow made it possible for agriculturalists to deal with heavy soils and sod. The Amazon headwaters in the eastern sierra and Montaña of Peru may be found to provide a more significant exception when they have been explored more adequately but at least the lowland rain forest of the Amazon basin proper acted as a major ecological barrier to the expansion of Peruvian civilization. Since the potentialities of the Old World rivers for disastrous floods, for large-scale irrigation, and as arteries of commerce are often thought to have promoted political unification and the growth of trade in the ancient Orient, it is worth noting that the same cultural phenomena appeared independently in regions where these potentialities were absent or at least far less important.

With respect to natural resources, it is sufficient to recall the absence of even stone in the alluvial soil of southern Mesopotamia, as well as the extremely poor quality for

building of the soft and quick-growing woods that alone were available locally. In contrast, parts at least of the New World nuclear regions were well favored, although with great altitudinal variation local self-sufficiency was often replaced by patterns of regional specialization and exchange. As with climate and terrain, then, we cannot identify a fixed constellation of raw materials which acted as a necessary precondition (much less as a ''cause''!) for the emergence of civilization in every area.

While relatively continuous settlement in linear patterns coinciding with the positions of the watercourses was possible in southern Mesopotamia and Egypt, enclaves of dense occupation separated by stretches of relatively inhospitable terrain were more characteristic of Mesoamerica and Peru. The best known and largest of the Mesoamerican enclaves is the interior drainage basin called the Valley of Mexico, which has provided the bulk of population and subsistence resources successively for the great religious center of Teotihuacan, the Toltec realm with Tula as its capital, the widespread conquests and incipient empire formation of the Aztecs, and present-day Mexico City. Yet in spite of the unparalleled importance of this region its area does not exceed 8,000 sq. km. In Peru the areas of intensive settlement and cultivation were all still smaller. Perhaps the largest of the mountain basins able to support a concentrated population is that of Huancayo, in the central highlands, with an area of only 1,200 sq. km. The arable area of the Chicama Valley, the largest in the North Coastal lowlands, is approximately the same.

In all of nuclear America, only along the Gulf Coast and on the low-lying Yucatan Peninsula were the conditions suitable for relatively uniform and continuous settlement. There, too, the rivers most nearly resemble the Nile or the Euphrates in regularity of flow and ease of control. But the lateritic soils and heavy rain-forest vegetation impose a very long recovery period after brief use for slash-and-burn agriculture, which materially reduces population density and perhaps helped to postpone for a considerable time the onset of urbanization processes which had been initiated in adjacent Mesoamerican highlands. A sharper contrast would be hard to imagine than that between Sumerians clustering in cities and Classic Mayans living in dispersed, essentially rural, hamlets while only a small elite permanently inhabited the elaborate religious centers. Yet both were civilized. In short, the distribution of population and settlements within the nuclear areas appears to have been as variable as the general environmental conditions within which they occurred, although average density in each case was surely much higher than in surrounding areas.

Variations in Agricultural Subsistence Patterns

While the essential basis for subsistence in every civilization is obviously to be found in sedentary agriculture, this rubric covers impressive technical, botanical, and zoölogical differences when it is applied to the high cultures of both the New and the Old World. Largely following C. O. Sauer, we may summarize these differences briefly.

New World agriculture, in the first place, essentially did not involve stockbreeding or the utilization of such animal products as dung fertilizer or milk. Domesticated Andean camelids such as the llama were used mainly for transport and were largely confined to the higher slopes; hence they cannot be regarded as important exceptions. Also missing in nuclear America, therefore, is the unique and powerful ambivalence of relations between herdsman and farmer, involving both symbiosis and hostility, which has shaped the social life, tinctured the history, and enriched the literature of the civilizations of the Fertile Crescent.

Second, nuclear American agriculture involves an entirely different range of cultivated plants, which nonetheless seem to have provided as balanced and adequate a diet as the cereal-date-vegetable-livestock complexes of the ancient Orient.

Third, basically different methods of cultivation were employed in the New World. In the absence of draft animals, the major implements were the digging stick and the hoe instead of the plow. Instead of a definite brief harvest season, crop-gathering was prolonged by the use of the major food crops also as green vegetables during earlier stages of their growth and by the widespread practice of interspersing different crops within a single field.

Finally, corresponding to the greater variations in climate because of altitude, New World agriculture was far more variable. There is little difference in at least the potential yields of the Assyrian uplands and the Mesopotamian alluvial plain other than that due to the inability of the date palm to flourish beyond the northern limit of the alluvium and to the greater (but not exclusive) reliance on barley rather than wheat south of that limit. By contrast, coastal Peruvian agriculture essentially revolved around a maize-beans-squash-cotton-fruits complex, while in the sierra subsistence depended on an entirely different complex composed of root crops like potatoes, oca, and quinoa. Similarly, maize, beans, and squash were the staple foods in both highland and lowland Mesoamerica, but they had been differentiated very early into altitudinally specialized varieties. Moreover, the cultivation of cotton, cacao, and many fruits was restricted to the lowlands.

Similarities in Subsistence Patterns

In spite of these profound differences, common features are not lacking. Perhaps something can be learned of the general place of subsistence in the growth of civilizations by outlining three common elements which seem to be of greatest importance.

One such significant common feature is that "farmers were persuaded or compelled to wring from the soil a surplus above their own domestic requirements and [that] this surplus was made available to support new economic classes not directly engaged in producing their own food." It must be understood that the notion of a surplus is related to fixed biological needs and the level of productive efficiency only in very general terms and that both the kinds and the quantities of available surpluses were determined to a considerable degree by the broad social contexts —"noneconomic" as well as "economic" —within which they occurred. Yet the institutional forms for the concentration and redistribution of surpluses show a high degree of uniformity among the early civilizations and serve to distinguish the latter sharply from societies in which no full-time activity other than primary food production finds sanction. Although it is impossible to quantify, it is only reasonable to assume that the proliferation of nonagricultural specialists common to all the early civilizations was correlated with a general increase in agricultural efficiency. It is, of course, quite another matter to assume that improved efficiency was independent of and prior to the whole ramifying network of concurrent social changes. Even purely technological advances, which in most instances these increased surpluses probably do not reflect, are usually linked with the social and cultural milieu, as Kroeber's study of independent and relatively simultaneous inventions was first to show.

A second common feature of some importance may be the complexity of the subsistence base on which each of the civilizations seems to have rested. We are dealing in no case with a single-crop economy or with one in which the bulk of the population normally could supply the entire range of agricultural produce for themselves. Perhaps the diversity of resources is partly to be understood as the protection against natural calamity necessary for long-term cultural growth. But also in part it must have been responsible for the development of trade, exchange, and redistributive institutions which in turn enhanced the growth of some form of centralized authority.

Mesopotamia is perhaps the best-documented example. The complementarity of dates and grain finds symbolic expression in the alabaster "Uruk vase," of late Protoliter-

ate date, where alternate palm and cereal shoots in the bottom register figuratively support the abundant ceremonial life illustrated above. Fishing was another essential subsistence pursuit; of the 1,200 or so members of the Baba temple community in Girsu in the mid-third millennium B.C., more than 100 were fishermen. The precise role of fishing in earlier times is difficult to ascertain, but quantities of fish offerings found in a late Ubaid temple at Eridu may indicate that it had already attained considerable importance by that remote period. Slightly less numerous than the Baba temple fishermen were its shepherds and herdsmen, but their numbers in that specific case do not adequately reflect the crucial position of sheep, donkeys, and oxen in the mixed economy of ancient Mesopotamia for plowing, transport, wool, and fertilizer as well as meat. Surely the prominence of the shepherd-and-byre motif in Protoliterate glyptic art reflects a high antiquity for husbandry as an essential part of the configuration of subsistence activities. In all of these cases it is interesting to note that the temple and state institutions played a vital part in the collection and redistribution of the agricultural produce.

To the far more limited degree to which there are pertinent data on diversification and specialization of subsistence in Old Kingdom Egypt, the picture is at least not inconsistent with what has been described for Mesopotamia. The idealized representations in the tombs of life on the estates of court officials record a great variety of craft activities and subsistence pursuits; since an organization of the work under foremen is sometimes illustrated, there must have been at least a partial specialization of function in the real world as well. While the great bulk of the peasant's caloric intake may always have been derived from grain, the cultivation of vegetables and fruits and fowling, fishing, and animal husbandry also play a substantial part in the tomb scenes of Old Kingdom officials. The importance of herding, in particular, may have been obscured by its limited modern role under very different conditions of land use. For obvious reasons the main center of husbandry was in the Nile Delta, and the close concern of the state for husbandry is clearly to be seen in the emphasis on livestock in lists of claimed tribute and loot, in periodic censuses of the herds, and in the appointment of numerous officials charged with responsibility of one kind or another for domestic animals.

In the New World the differentiation of subsistence pursuits seems to have been mainly on a regional basis, perhaps as a consequence of the greater environmental diversity that has previously been alluded to. But the necessity for a wide interchange of agricultural products remained the same, and the organization of this interchange similarly must have helped to expand and consolidate the position of centralized social authority. In North Coastal Peru, for example, llamas from the sierra were already being ceremonially buried in a community shrine or public building in Late Formative times. In another case, the only llama bones from a contemporary site of the same period were found in association with the burial of an individual whose relatively elaborate *Beigaben* suggest a priestly status. By the succeeding Florescent era, the relative abundance of llama bones, wool, and droppings indicates that trading contacts with the highland centers of domestication for these animals had been regularized and enlarged. Presumably cotton, maritime products, peppers, fruits, and coca were among the commodities moving in the reverse direction, as they were at the time of the Conquest. To some degree, regional specialization with regard to subsistence extended into craft production as well, as is implied by the importation of a colony of Chimu craftsmen to work for the Inca government in Cuzco. It is interesting to note that a high degree of specialization still characterizes the Quechua community.

Similar patterns of differentiation in specialized production can be identified in Mesoamerica. Cotton from the lower-lying valleys of Puebla and Morelos was already being interchanged with the Valley of Mexico in Early Formative times, and the securest archeological dating horizons of later periods are provided by distinctive pottery wares that were traded widely from their different centers of manufacture. For the Conquest period these traces of evidence can be greatly amplified with eyewitness accounts of, for example, the great and diversified market at Tlatelolco with its separate vendors for many varieties of fruit, meat, maize, vegetables, and fish and with a reputed daily attendance of 60,000 persons. From a different point of view, the heterogeneity of native resources is also underlined by the *matricula de tributos*. Although it accounts for tribute levied by the Aztecs rather than for trade, the general concentration of assignments for particular kinds of produce (other than the ubiquitous mantles) to a very few provinces surely reflects earlier patterns for the interchange of normal regional surpluses. And by Aztec times, if not earlier, the integration of interregional trading with the needs and policies of the expanding state is well known.

A third significant feature common to the agricultural pursuits of the early civilizations was the development of some degree of intensive land use. Whether or not this was accompanied by a general increase in agricultural efficiency (output/labor input), certainly it must have increased at least the total agricultural output. However, the point of current interest is not so much the effect of intensive methods of cultivation on the volume of available surplus as their effect directly on social organization. The argument, following Ralph Linton's [this volume, p. 335ff.] lucid portrayal of the introduction of wet rice cultivation in Madagascar, is that under conditions of intensive cultivation plots of land acquire different values based, for example, on cumulative improvements and the availability of water. Since water, or good bottom land, or some other similar resource was almost always relatively scarce, well-favored and improved plots came to be regarded as capital investments. While unimproved land was allotted equitably among all members of the village or extended kin group, under conditions of intensive cultivation the cohesiveness of the older social units broke down and tended to be replaced by a small number of individual families as the hereditary landholding units. The emergence of an authoritarian "king," of rudimentary social classes including nobles, commoners, and war-captive slaves, and increasing expenditures on warfare are some of the further consequences which Linton traces to the basic shift in cultivation practices. Under at least some circumstances, in other words, the social processes we have identified with the beginnings of civilization are closely interconnected , with the beginning of intensive agriculture. No necessary distinction into "cause" and "effect" is implied, be it understood, between subsistence change and institutional change. The investment of labor in land improvement and the adoption of intensive cultivation techniques were as much influenced by contemporary social forms as they influenced the latter.

Intensive agriculture, in the case of the earlier civilizations, usually is taken to be roughly synonymous with irrigation. Indeed, without some kind of irrigation agriculture is and probably always was impossible in southern Mesopotamia, Egypt, and coastal Peru. But we shall attempt to show that in most cases irrigation was part of a broader range of intensive techniques and that some of the assumed implications of irrigation as a single, gross category are misleading when applied to the four nuclear areas where the civilizations with which this paper is concerned had their beginnings. Here, then, irrigation is subsumed under the general rubric of intensive cultivation rather than equated with it.

It is important to distinguish between the functional significance of different kinds of irrigation if we are to understand better the relations between ecology and cultural growth. Small-scale irrigation, including flood-water techniques and the construction of short lengths of canal serving small landholdings, does not seem essentially different in its social effects from those observed by Linton in Madagascar. It may make available for agricultural purposes only a fraction of the potentially irrigable land surface, since it will seldom extend very far from the streams and since short canals will not be sufficient

everywhere to bring the water to fields at a high enough level. Alluvial situations, in which rivers tend to raise their beds above the level of the surrounding land, are particularly favorable for small-scale irrigation. For the same reason, they invite destruction of existing canals by silting and flooding, although this is not critical where canals do not represent a heavy investment in labor and can be quickly replaced. The construction and maintenance of this kind of irrigation, we submit, requires no elaborate social organization and does not depend on labor resources larger than those at the disposal of the individual community, kin group, or even family—or, at most, those easily available locally through patterns of reciprocity. To the extent that this kind of irrigation is important, its chief influence on social development would seem to arise from its encouragement of stratification based on differentiation of landholdings. Perhaps also it encouraged the growth of militarism associated with increasing competition for developed canal networks and the most fertile and easily irrigated lands.

Large-scale irrigation, on the other hand, imposes technical and social demands of a different order. Masses of labor must be mobilized from many scattered communities, and their activities need close co-ordination. The problem of maintenance and supervision is a continuous one and again demands a superordinate authority. Some kind of equitable distribution of the available irrigation water must be imposed on many competing communities, and disputes must be adjudicated. Since downstream users are inherently at the mercy of those higher up, large-scale irrigation networks are only durable where the entire area they serve is a politically integrated unit. As has often been observed, large-scale canal networks can only be associated with formal state superstructures in which the ultimate authority rests with an administrative elite.

The problem for us is an absolutely basic one, however sparse, refractory, and ambiguous most of the present evidence may be. To the extent that large-scale irrigation is found to have begun very early, its social requirements may be adduced as a convincing explanation for the origin of primitive states in the ancient civilizations. Processes of class stratification associated with intensive agriculture then might be a secondary and derivative phenomenon on this reconstruction; because of its monopoly over hydraulic facilities, the state bureaucracy is identified as the strongest social force. Largely following Karl Wittfogel, Julian Steward took this position with respect to Mesopotamia and Peru although not to Mesoamerica. Our view is firmly to the contrary. It is beyond the scope of a paper dealing with cultural ecology to argue that the primitive state is mainly linked instead with the emergence of a stratified society, but at least it will be suggested here that the introduction of great irrigation networks was more a "consequence" than a "cause" of the appearance of dynastic state organizations—however much the requirements of large-scale irrigation subsequently may have influenced the development of bureaucratic elites charged with administering them. The admittedly still inadequate evidence for this proposition now needs to be briefly summarized.

Our present understanding of the antiquity of irrigation in Mesopotamia is derived mainly from surface reconnaissance in Akkad and the Diyala basin and is obscured by the heavy and continuous alluviation with which the northern part of the alluvial plain has been particularly affected over the millenniums intervening since Sumerian times. At least in this region, however, there appears to have been little change in settlement pattern between the beginning of widespread agricultural occupation in the Ubaid period and the end of the third millennium B.C., or even later. There is historical documentation for the construction of occasional large canals and irrigation works as early as the Protoimperial period, but on the whole the settlements followed closely the shifting, braided channels of the major rivers.

In other words, for a long time irrigation seems to have been conducted principally on an *ad hoc* small-scale basis, which would have involved periodic cleaning and perhaps straightening of clogged natural channels, adjusting the location of fields and settlements in the closest possible conformity with the existing hydraulic regime, and for the most part constructing and maintaining only relatively small-scale field and feeder canals that were wholly artificial. Where the king explicitly claims credit for initiating dredging operations on either a canal or a natural watercourse (as in modern Iraq, the same word is used for both!), it is noteworthy that the aspect of canals as providers of irrigation water is entirely unmentioned. Moreover, whatever the rhetoric of the king's claimed responsibilities, the necessary labor forces for the maintenance work were apparently organized and directed by the individual temples. No Early Dynastic or Protoimperial record has survived of the mode of allocation of irrigation water, but at least in Ur III times this was separately handled in each temple constituency by a special official in charge of sluice gates. In short, there is nothing to suggest that the rise of dynastic authority in southern Mesopotamia was linked to the administrative requirements of a major canal system.

There are very few data yet available on the character or extent of Egyptian irrigation during the period for which it might be compared with New World equivalents, that is, up to the beginning of the Middle Kingdom. Prior to the opening of the Fayyum depression to irrigation in the Twelfth Dynasty, there is nothing less ambiguous to demonstrate state responsibility for irrigation than the statement of a Sixth-Dynasty royal architect that he had dug two canals for the king. Unfortunately, the inscription fails to make clear whether the canals were intended for irrigation or only for the movement of royal supplies like building stone, as was the case with five contemporary canals dug to bypass the First Cataract of the Nile. Still another possible explanation of the significance of the passage is that it refers to land reclamation by swamp drainage, much as a very late (and therefore doubtful) tradition credits Menes with having drained the territory around Memphis. Yet swamp drainage began long before any pharaoh appeared on the scene—if the obvious meaning is attached to the claim of a Third-Dynasty official that he "founded" twelve estates in nomes of Lower Egypt—and continued afterward without the necessity of royal initiative. In considering alternatives other than irrigation we are also confronted with a protodynastic scorpion macehead ostensibly showing the king breaking ground for a waterway of some kind. Again, an immunity charter of Pepi I protects the priesthood of the two pyramids of Snefru against any obligation for labor service on what may be a canal; here it is neither clear that the putative canal was for irrigation nor that the pharaoh was responsible for its construction. Interestingly enough, the same charter continues with an injunction against enumerating canals, lakes, wells, hides, and trees belonging to the priesthood for tax purposes and thus suggests that all of those categories were under purely local jurisdiction.

In short, considering the number of known records of royal building activity in the Old Kingdom, it seems only fair to regard their silence on the construction of irrigation works as strange if the demands of large-scale irrigation had indeed been responsible for the initial emergence of a pharaoh at the head of a unified state. On the assumption of a centrally administered irrigation system, the failure of officials with long and varied careers of public service to refer to administrative posts connected with canal maintenance or water distribution is equally puzzling. To the degree that an *argumentum ex silentio* ever carries conviction, the Egyptian case parallels that of Mesopotamia.

Although there is serious danger of overgeneralizing from it, the data on Peruvian irrigation are reasonably consistent with what has been adduced from Mesopotamia and Egypt. Drawing principally from Gordon Willey's pioneer study of settlement patterns in a typical small valley transecting the arid North Coastal strip, we cannot presently trace large-scale irrigation earlier than the Florescent era (beginning probably at about the time of Christ). The distribution of Late Formative sites suggests, however, that small-

scale experimentation with canal-building had begun in a few advantageous locales several centuries prior to this time, and some success with at least flood-water irrigation on the river flats is implied by the slow expansion inward from the valley mouth which began a millennium earlier. The Early Florescent (Gallinazo) canals, it is interesting to note, were built as integral parts of an elaborate and impressive complex of monumental construction which included fortifications and ceremonial pyramids as well; on present evidence, both of the latter types of monumental construction antedated the large canals. By mid-Florescent times at least, valley-wide systems of irrigation were in use on the North Coast (although our particular example comprises only 98 sq. km. of arable land!), and some individual canals are large by any standards: the canal of La Cumbre in the Chicama Valley, for example, is 113 km. long. A subsequent development, probably dating only from the Militaristic era (beginning after A.D. 700), was the still more extensive reshaping of natural drainage patterns through the introduction of intervalley irrigation systems in which urban zones occupied by a governing elite were set off from areas for agricultural exploitation.

Irrigation apparently developed more slowly in highland Peru than on the North Coast, although the sharpness of the contrast may be a reflection in part of the lesser amount of archeological attention that the sierra has received. Terraces for soil conservation have been reported first for the Tiahuanaco horizon, at the outset of the Militaristic era. In the characteristically steep and narrow Andean valleys rapid runoff was perhaps a more serious problem than paucity of rainfall, but in general the later terraces seem to have been associated with irrigation channels as well. The elaborate, well-cut, and extensive terrace-irrigation system for which Peru is famous all were products of the labor-service obligation imposed by the Inca state as a tax in the final century or so of its successful expansion before the coming of the Spaniards. Even the Early Inca terraces, probably postdating the onset of the Tiahuanaco horizon by four or more centuries, have been described as "small and irregular, and probably the work of individual family groups." As in North Coastal Peru, Egypt, and southern Mesopotamia, we seem to have evidence here of a very gradual evolution of irrigation practices beginning with local and small-scale terracing which emphatically did not require political organization embracing a large group of communities. Large-scale, integrated programs of canalization and terracing apparently were attempted only after the perfection of the Inca state as a political apparatus controlling the allocation of mass-labor resources. They are consequences, perhaps, of the attainment of a certain level of social development; we repeat that they cannot be invoked to explain the processes by which that level was attained.

For Mesoamerica the situation is more complex and not a little contradictory. The traditional view is that "there is little evidence that irrigation was of basic importance anywhere in Mexico, in pre-Spanish times, and that it is erroneous to speak of maize culture as having flourished most in arid or subarid regions of that country." Recently this conclusion has been controverted effectively by a number of investigators, although the full significance of their empirical findings is still open to dispute. On the whole though, the situation seems to be quite similar to that described for the other nuclear areas; in fact, it was primarily the recent findings in Mesoamerica which stimulated the reconsideration of irrigation that this paper represents.

The question of the role of irrigation in the formation of Mesoamerican civilization takes us back at least to the beginning of the Classic era (ca. A.D. 100?), if not earlier, and revolves particularly around the population and ceremonial center of Teotihuacan in the Valley of Mexico. The Pyramid of the Sun there, one of the largest pre-Hispanic structures in Mesoamerica, apparently antedates that era. It has been estimated that before its abandonment in Late Classic times (ca. A.D. 700) the site occupied 750 hectares or more of religious and civic buildings, residential "palaces," work-shops, and clusters of ordinary rooms and patios housing "at least" 50,000 inhabitants. True, the observed limits of surface debris may reflect only the aggregate area of the center over a period of several centuries and not its maximum size at any one period. Moreover, the proportion of residential units within the built-up area of the site is still not at all clear. But even if the estimate is scaled down considerably, it certainly reflects an urban civilization in being. To what extent, if at all, did it depend on irrigation agriculture? No direct evidence for canal irrigation has yet been reported. Instead we have the observations that irrigation is necessary today for cultivation of even a single yearly crop in the subregion of which Teotihuacan is a part, that according to paleoclimatic studies based on pollen analysis and fluctuating lake levels it was even more necessary during the time of emergence of Teotihuacan as a great center, and hence that the use of irrigation must be assumed. The difficulty is that a center of the enormous size of Teotihuacan must have developed on a sustaining area far larger than its immediate subregion and that a major contribution from its immediate surroundings cannot be assumed to have been indispensable for the growth of the site. Monte Alban, Xochicalco, and other examples can be found which approach Teotihuacan in size but which lie at some distance from their main agricultural hinterland. A second argument is still less conclusive. It consists of the suggestion that irrigation is implied by representation of cacao and fruit trees along the banks of streams or canals in a mural from a Teotihuacan "palace." Even if the identification of cacao is accepted as correct, the location of the scene is unknown and the crucial question of whether the waterways are natural or artificial is unanswered. There remains only a distributional argument, based on the wide extent of Mesoamerican irrigation practices at the time of the Conquest. Like all distributional arguments, it is loaded with presuppositions and provides no real clue to the antiquity of the trait in question. And so for Formative and Classic times the existence of canal irrigation still remains to be demonstrated.

For the final, or Historic, era (beginning *ca.* A.D. 900 with the founding of Tula), on the other hand, the evidence for large-scale irrigation agriculture and other hydraulic works is incontrovertible. Perhaps such works are already implied by the legendary account of the formation of Tula in the Codex Ramirez which describes the damming-up of a river in order to form an artificial lake stocked with fish and waterfowl. In any case, the Spanish conquerors were full of admiration for the scale and intricacy of the system of dikes and aqueducts that by 1519 was both supplying Tenochtitlan with potable water and controlling fluctuations in the salt- and fresh-water levels of the lakes surrounding the city. The sequence of construction of these works can be traced in some detail in historical sources, and the conclusion seems justified that they should be viewed "not so much as the result of many small-scale initiatives by small groups, but as the result of large-scale enterprise, well-planned, in which an enormous number of people took part, engaged in important and prolonged public works under centralized and authoritative leadership." Elsewhere in the Valley of Mexico, an irrigation complex in the Old Acolhua domain has been described that was roughly contemporary with the Aztec construction and also seems to have been initiated by a dynastic authority and carried out as a planned large-scale enterprise. Finally, an impressive list of places, with a wide distribution throughout Mesoamerica outside the Maya area, can be assembled for which irrigation is definitely identified or can reasonably be inferred in Spanish contact sources. In short, the position that irrigation was not important anywhere or at any period in pre-Spanish Mexico no longer seems tenable.

It needs to be stressed again, however, that distribution is a highly unreliable index to antiquity and that even the examples from the Valley of Mexico appertain only to the final century before the Conquest. Moreover, with the exception of the above-mentioned Aztec system all the known Mesoamerican irrigation networks are quite small in comparison with those of the Old World and Peru. On present evidence, then, Wolf and Palerm rightly tend to regard planned large-scale canal irrigation not as a primary cause of Mesoamerican civilization but merely as its culminating activity in the economic sphere. They recognize, to be sure, that political controls in turn probably were centralized and intensified by the introduction of major irrigation works.

But if large-scale canalization is late in Mesoamerica, there are indications that other forms of irrigation and intensive cultivation—as in Peru and Mesopotamia also—can be traced to a more remote antiquity. Canal irrigation probably never became as important a technique in the Valley of Mexico as chinampa agriculture, that is, the cultivation of artificial islands made out of plant debris and mud scooped from the lake beds. Modern chinampas are largely devoted to truck gardening, but, since the tasks of construction and maintenance do not require extensive organization and capital, they may have been used aboriginally as highly productive subsistence plots for kin groups or even families. The only example of an apparent chinampa so far subjected to archeological scrutiny contained occupational refuse dating to about the beginning of the Classic period and suggests that the technique is sufficiently old to have been a factor in the subsistence of Teotihuacan. The means were at hand early enough, in other words, for differential returns from specialized farming to have provided the material basis for the growth of a stratified society.

Since chinampas were unknown elsewhere in Mesoamerica (or depended on conditions not repeated elsewhere), their high and perennial productivity may not have been a direct factor in the development of civilization throughout the whole area. At the same time, the Valley of Mexico was in many other respects the key area of development for the greater part of Mesoamerica, for a very long time the center of its most advanced political forms, its widest and most closely intercommunicating trade network, its densest population. To a degree, then, it may have set the course of development which elsewhere was merely followed with more or less local innovation. To that degree, chinampa agriculture may far exceed in importance its highly circumscribed geographical limits. Unfortunately, having largely set aside simple diffusion studies, anthropologists are only beginning to develop more functional approaches to the analysis of interregional relations, through which the supposed primacy of the Valley of Mexico might be understood and evaluated.

Another, and broader, aspect of intensive cultivation in Mesoamerica is perhaps to be seen in the maintenance of dooryard garden plots in close symbiosis with individual houses, which augment the production of foodstuffs through the use of leavings as fertilizer and encourage stability of residence. Although not subject to archeological confirmation at present, this practice was apparently well established at the time of the Conquest and is possibly very old. Again, crudely made terraces for erosion-control purposes have been observed at many places in highland Mesoamerica and in at least one instance in the lowland rain forest of the Yucatan Peninsula. Certainly in many cases of considerable pre-Spanish antiquity, they suggest agricultural regimes of greater intensity than the milpa system as it is practiced today. Although at present impossible to document for pre-Conquest times, a more intensive application of labor in the form of hand-weeding would have prolonged cultivation and increased output, particularly in the tropical lowlands. This might make less inexplicable or even "explain" the extraordinary cultural achievements of the Classic Maya in the lowlands.

By assisting in the establishment of residential stability and in the production of surpluses, all the above-mentioned practices would have provided at least a receptive hinterland within which the new and more complex social forms could expand and consolidate. The origin of innovations such as the primitive state might then be sought in a few small strategic regions such as the Valley of Mexico where the inducements to accumulate surpluses and institutionalize class differences were probably greatest. In a wider sense, it may be granted, the florescence of the state could only take place where condi-

tions in the hinterland were also propitious, so that the pinpointing of precise points of origin is probably misleading.

Briefly to recapitulate, we have attempted to show that developments in modes of subsistence within Mesoamerica were substantially similar to those in Mesopotamia, Egypt, and Peru in that large-scale canal irrigation was a culminating, rather than an early and persistent, form of intensive cultivation. It is conceded that differences in the rate of development existed, probably in large part because of the fewer inducements and opportunities to depend on irrigation that Mesoamerica offered. But these, we suggest, are quantitative and not qualitative differences. In North Coastal Peru the culmination came in the mid-Florescent era—or even later, in the Militaristic era, if the introduction of intervalley irrigation systems is accepted as a significant later innovation. In Mesoamerica it came in late Historic or Militaristic times, as it also seems to have done in *highland* Peru. According to our Mesopotamian data, admittedly inadequate in detail and based on a possibly retarded Akkad instead of Sumer, the onset of large-scale artificial canalization did not occur until after the time of Hammurabi. Even in Sumer itself there is no justification for supposing that this process began any earlier than the late Early Dynastic or the Protoimperial period—a sound equivalent for the New World Historic or Militaristic era. In *no* area, then, at least on present evidence, was large-scale irrigation early enough to "explain" the emergence of the great theocratic centers of the Classic era or the dynastic states which closely followed them. The concern of Wolf and Palerm, and latterly of Steward, over the distinction between "Theocratic Irrigation States" (Protoliterate Mesopotamia and Florescent Peru) and "Ceremonial Trade States" (Classic Mesoamerica) thus seems groundless.

Reciprocal Effects of Human Culture on Environment

This discussion so far has assumed that the natural physiography and resources of the four nuclear areas were relatively stable. The different cultural traditions have been regarded implicitly as evolving successive patterns of ecological adjustment and land use entirely according to some internal dynamic of their own. The effect of environment, in these terms, is merely that of providing a fixed framework of potentialities and limiting conditions which somehow is then exploited selectively by the creative cultural growth within it. Such a view is obviously an oversimplification of the processes of interaction between man and the natural world, even if decisive climatic shifts no longer are regarded as likely to have occurred during the span of time that led to the emergence of any civilization.

Unfortunately the reciprocal effects of changing patterns of human activity on the land and flora cannot be traced continuously for any area. Perhaps the clearest and best-documented example is provided by recent work in central Mexico, where it has been shown that intensive hill-slope cultivation during the last centuries of Aztec dominance had gone far to destroy the capacity of the soil to sustain agriculture even before the arrival of the Spaniards. But the more remote history of occupance in even this relatively well-studied region is still insufficiently known for its environmental effects to be understood. The abandonment of the central Peten region by the lowland Classic Maya furnishes an even more dramatic case, with ecological processes such as sheet erosion, the silting-up of freshwater sources, and the gradual replacement of forest vegetation by uncultivable savanna in the course of slash-and-burn agriculture all having been suggested as contributing factors. But in spite of a generation of speculation and interest these factors still exist only as hypotheses, and in a recent general work on the Maya it is interesting to note that they are largely rejected in favor of an explanation of the collapse of at least the elaborate ceremonial life in purely historical terms.

In the alluvial valleys of the Old World civilizations, processes of erosion are less likely to have affected directly the course of cultural development. It is not impossible, however, that deforestation at the headwaters of the Tigris and Euphrates increased both the silt loads carried by those rivers and their flooding potential. In turn, this would have affected the continuity of occupation in the alluvium and the problems associated with constructing and maintaining irrigation systems. But, although deforestation undoubtedly went on, there are no empirical data at present on its rate nor on its consequences for the alluvial plain as a whole. Even the traditional assumption that the area of the plain has been continuously enlarged by the deposition of silt along the margin of the Persian Gulf has now been challenged by evidence that extensions of the land have been roughly counterbalanced by subsidence.

On the other hand, a group of different and important reciprocal effects is likely to have been initiated directly by the introduction of various techniques of intensive cultivation. Depletion of soil nutrients by inadequate crop rotation or fallowing cycle is one example. Salinization of poorly drained land as a result of continuous irrigation is another. Still a third may be the disturbance of natural patterns of drainage by the slow rise of canal beds and banks as a result of silting. To some degree all of these processes must have gone on, but their importance can only be gauged against the background of a far better understanding of ancient agriculture than we have at present for any area. To begin with, empirical studies are necessary of changes in the intensity of land use and of the exact nature of the full agricultural cycle over a long period in the past. At the time of this writing, a study along these lines has been undertaken for a small section of the Mesopotamian plain but not for any other nuclear area.

For the present, therefore, the distortions of a picture in which cultures are conceived as having evolved within a static environmental framework must remain uncorrected. If several possible types of correction have been mentioned, their effects cannot even be demonstrated satisfactorily with the evidence available from most areas, and in any case they are virtually impossible to quantify. One can only conclude that attempts to invoke changing ecological factors as "causes" of cultural development—however convenient they may appear as heuristic hypotheses—are still no more than a priori speculations.

In a broader sense, the lack of data on population density and land use underlines the purely speculative character of all those heuristic hypotheses which regard cultural change as an adaptive response to direct environmental forces. One account of the rise of militarism, for example, sees it as a consequence of the displacement of a population surplus, although there is absolutely no evidence of a concurrent reduction in the sustaining capacity of the environment or of a trend toward overpopulation in any of the nuclear areas. Another recent synthesis, going still farther, attributes not only the rise of large-scale warfare but also the cyclical character of the early empires in large part to population pressure. How population "pressure" can be defined usefully except by reference to real patterns and intensities of land utilization and settlement pressing against clearly defined ecological limits—for which, we must emphasize again, the evidence is still almost entirely lacking—is not apparent.

There is always an attraction for explanations of historical and cultural phenomena that stem from "outside" the immediate field of study. They have the advantage of providing fixed points from which analysis may proceed in a straightforward chain of cause and effect processes. But on closer inspection many such fixed points will be found to dissolve into shifting relationships which are not as separate and distinct from cultural influences as they may appear. Premature dependence upon explanations in terms of the external environment only diverts the historian or anthropologist from unraveling the complex stresses within human institutions. In all but the simplest societies, it is forces within the social order rather than direct environmental factors which have provided the major stimulus and guide to further growth.

Conclusion

In retrospect, the significant common features of land use among the early civilizations of the Old and the New World are so general that they are almost trite. If we have attempted to define the terms more closely than is usual, there is certainly nothing unusual about finding that all the great civilizational traditions rested on surpluses made available through sedentary, diversified, intensive agriculture. In addition, of course, it is implicit in this discussion that the common social institutions and processes of development identified in each of the four civilizations were bound up together with this general constellation of subsistence practices in a functionally interacting network which characterizes early civilization as a sort of cultural type.

Against this simple and limited finding of regularity, the diversity of other environmental subsistence features and the huge proliferation of cultural forms stand in sharp contrast. History is not a mathematical exercise in the application of "laws," and the meaning of human experience is not to be found by suppressing its rich variety in the search for common, implicitly deterministic, denominators. From this point of view, perhaps the lack of closer specificity in the ecological relationships that are common to the early civilizations is the single most important point to be made. Much of sociocultural development seems to proceed very largely on its own terms, including even some important aspects of ecological adjustment. Societal growth is a continuously creative process, conditioned far more by past history than by directly felt environmental forces. On the whole, then, one may reasonably conclude that for an understanding of the meaning of the early civilizations—both in their own terms and for the modern world—the natural environment serves as no more than a backdrop.

Investigating the Origins of Mesopotamian Civilization

Frank Hole

From *Science,* Vol. 153, 1966, pp. 605–611. Copyright 1966, American Association for the Advancement of Science. By permission of the author, the publisher, and copyright holder.

In southwest Asia, between 8000 and 3000 B.C., human society developed from self-sufficient bands of nomadic hunters to economically and politically integrated city dwellers who specialized in a variety of occupations. A central archeological problem is to try to discover the factors that triggered these fundamental changes in man's way of life. For want of evidence and for want of a satisfactory model of the conditions existing during the period in question, searching for origins and attempting to discover the course of events that led to civilization is difficult. Prehistorians deal with nameless cultures, trusting to reconstructions from physical remains for their picture of life in ancient times. They must work directly with geographic, technological, and demographic factors and only indirectly infer ideologies and philosophical concepts. Archeologists are thus limited in what they can hope to learn by the nature of their data and the tools they have for interpreting them. Within these limits, however, it is possible to construct some plausible theories about the origins of civilization and to test them through controlled programs of excavation and analysis. In this article I define the problem under consideration in ecological terms, review the current evidence, and suggest topics for further study.

Mesopotamian (Sumerian) civilization began a few centuries before 3000 B.C. and was characterized by temples, urban centers, writing, trade, militarism, craft specialization, markets, and art. Inferred characteristics are a class-stratified society and well-defined mechanisms for regulation of production and distribution of resources. To be sure, Sumerian civilization must have had many other important but intangible characteristics, but most of these cannot be inferred from archeological data.

The early Mesopotamian civilizations were restricted to southern Mesopotamia, the alluvial plain that stretches south from Baghdad to the Persian Gulf. Remains of immediately antecedent cultures have been excavated in the same area, and still older cultures have been excavated in the surrounding Zagros mountain valleys of Iraq and

Iran and on the steppes at the verge of plain and mountain in Khuzistan, southwest Iran.

Intensive agriculture is a precondition for civilization. The Sumerian societies for which we have some historical records were sustained by cultivation of irrigated barley and wheat, supplemented by crops of dates, and the production of sheep, goats, cattle, pigs, and fish. In 8000 B.C. people were just beginning to plant cereals, raise animals, and live in permanent villages; their societies were small, self-sufficient, egalitarian groups with little differentiation of occupation or status. These people had fewer of the artifacts and qualities of civilization than the Sumerian city dwellers had 5000 years later. In this article I use 8000 B.C. as a convenient base line and attempt to assess some 5000 years of culture history (see Table 1).

Theories of Development

Recognizing the obvious changes in society that occurred during the 5000 years, archeologists and others have proposed causal factors such as characteristics of geography to account for them. The most detailed examination of the relationship between ge-
ographic features and social forms has been made by Huntington, but other scholars working with data from Southwest Asia have had more influence on archeologists. For example, in attempting to explain the origins of agriculture, Childe proposed climatic change, specifically desiccation, as the initiating event and set off a chain of thought that is still favored by some authors. Childe argued that "incipient desiccation . . . would provide a stimulus towards the adoption of a food-producing economy. . . ." Animals and men would gather in oases that were becoming isolated in the midst of deserts. Such circumstances might promote the sort of symbiosis between man and beast implied in the word *domestication*. Although Childe's theory is attractive, there is no conclusive evidence that the climate in Southwest Asia changed enough during the period in question to have affected the beginnings of agriculture and animal husbandry.

It was once fashionable to think of culture as inevitably rising or progressing, and this trend was thought to be analogous to biological evolution. Except in a most general way, however, modern prehistorians do not think of universal stages of cultural development. Rather than focusing on evolutionary stages, many scholars have examined the role of

Table 1. *Generalized chart showing the chronology of phases and sites mentioned in the text*

DATE (B.C.)	SETTLEMENT SUBSISTENCE TYPE	CULTURAL PHASE	ETHNIC GROUP
2500		Early Dynastic III	Sumerians
		Early Dynastic II	Sumerians
		Early Dynastic I	Sumerians
2900	Walled cities	Jamdet Nasr	Sumerians
3500	Cities	Uruk	?
4000	Towns	Ubaid	?
5300	Temples	Eridu	?
5500	Irrigation	Sabz	
5800		Mohammad Jaffar	
6500	Food production	Ali Kosh	
8000	Food production and small, settled villages	Bus Mordeh	
Pre-8000	Nomadic hunters	Zarzian	

particular social and economic activities in triggering the emergence of complex forms of society. For instance, Marxists have explained the form of society (government, broadly speaking) on the basis of modes of production. Marxist evolutionists even today explain the development of social classes and political states in similar terms. They argue that, as people gained control over the production of food, the concept of private property crept in, and later the mass of people were exploited by the propertied few. "The creation of a state was necessary simply to prevent society from dissolving into anarchy due to the antagonisms that had arisen." Information on the emergence of Sumerian civilization that might support this idea, however, is lacking.

Another attempt to correlate technological systems and social advances was made by Karl Wittfogel in *Oriental Despotism*. He contended that, where people had to depend on irrigation, they inevitably led themselves into an escalating dependence on an organizational hierarchy which coordinated and directed the irrigation activities. "The effective management of these works involves an organizational web which covers either the whole, or at least the dynamic core, of the country's population. In consequence, those who control this network are uniquely prepared to wield supreme political power". Although Wittfogel's analysis seems valid in many instances, archeological investigation in both Mesopotamia and the Western Hemisphere leads to the conclusion that there was no large-scale irrigation at the time of the emergence of the first urban civilization.

An Ecological Approach

Single factors such as technology are unquestionably important, but they can be understood only within the cultural, social, and geographic context. A more comprehensive view that takes into account the interrelation of many factors is called human ecology. In a consideration of cultural development, the relevant concept in human ecology is adapta-

tion, hence the approach is to try to discover how particular factors influence the overall adaptation of a society. By means of the general approach, human ecology attempts to understand what happened in the histories of particular cultures. It does not address itself to making general statements about cultural progress or evolution.

In an ecological approach, a human society is treated as one element in a complex system of geography, climate, and living organisms peculiar to an area. To ensure survival, various aspects of a human society must be complementary and the society itself must be successfully integrated with the remainder of the cultural and physical ecosystem of which it is a part. From the ecological view, such factors as technology, religion, or climate cannot be considered apart from the total system. Nevertheless, some parts of the system may be considered more fundamental in the sense that they strongly influence the form of the other parts. Anthropologists, through their study of modern societies, and archeologists, through inference, find that such factors as geographical features, the distribution of natural resources, climate, the kinds of crops and animals raised, and the relations with neighboring peoples strongly influence the forms that a society may take. These factors comprise the major elements of the ecosystem, and societies must adapt themselves to them.

Archeological Evidence

For the period 8000 to 3000 B.C., archeological data are scattered and skimpy. This naturally limits the generality of any interpretations that can be made and restricts the degree to which we can test various theories. Ideally we would wish to work with hundreds of instances representing the range of environmental and cultural variation; instead, for the whole of Southwest Asia we can count fewer than 100 excavated and reported sites for the entire range of time with which we are dealing. Of course the number of unexcavated or unreported sites about which we know something is far greater, but we cannot but be aware of how little we know and how much there is to find out.

In all of Southwest Asia only about 15 villages that date to 8000 B.C. have been excavated, and only two of these, Zawi Chemi and the Bus Mordeh levels at Ali Kosh, give good evidence of the use of domesticated plants or animals. In short, data for the time of our base line are woefully inadequate. We have much fuller information about the villages of 5000 B.C., but, unfortunately, for periods subsequent to 5000 B.C. the *kind* of data we have changes drastically. Thus, although there is historical continuity in the series of known sites, there is discontinuity in some of the data themselves because few archeologists have worked sites spanning the whole period from 8000 to 3000 B.C. Most of the sites dating to about 3000 B.C. were excavated by "historic" archaeologists who struck levels that old only incidentally as they plumbed the depths of the cities they were digging. These scholars depended far less on artifacts than on history for their interpretations. The earliest sites were dug by prehistorians who based their inferences on results generated by an array of scientific experts. In order to understand the origins of civilizations, we thus need to bridge two quite different "archeological cultures." Archeologists and their various colleagues working in the early villages painstakingly teased out grains of charred seeds, measured metapodials and teeth of early races of sheep or cattle, and analyzed the chemical and mineral constituents of obsidian and copper; their counterparts working in the historic sites busied themselves with the floor plans of temples, the funerary pottery in the graves, the esthetics of an art style, and the translation of cuneiform impressions in clay.

Bearing in mind the reservations I have already expressed, we can begin to try to pick a coherent path through 5000 years of history. In dealing with Mesopotamia, it is usual to regard the presence of towns, temples, and cities as indicative of civilization. If we do so, we can divide our history into two parts, beginning with small food-producing villages

and following with more complex societies that include towns and cities. In the ensuing discussion I assess the available evidence and, for both forms of community, outline the characteristics and indicate how the community developed.

Food-Producing Villages

Small food-producing villages have had a long history, but here we are chiefly interested in those that existed between 8000 and 5000 B.C. None of these communities is known thoroughly, and the following descriptions are based on data from several excavated sites and from surface surveys. The fullest data come from the phases represented in Ali Kosh and Tepe Sabz, in southwest Iran, and from Jarmo, Sarab, and Guran in the Zagros mountains. Additional data derive from extensive surveys in Khuzistan and the valleys of the Zagros.

During this period villages are small and scattered, typically less than 1 hectare in size and housing perhaps 100 to 300 people. They are situated on the best agricultural land in regions where farming is possible without irrigation. From a handful of sites known to be about 10,000 years old, the number of settlements had increased by 5000 B.C., when many villages were within sight of one another and almost every village was within an easy day's walk of the next. There is no evidence of great migrations or any serious pressure of population during this time. By 4000 B.C. some villages occupy areas as large as 2 hectares.

The increase in population appears to have been a direct consequence of improved agricultural techniques. In 8000 B.C., only primitive, low-yield races of emmer wheat and two-row barley were grown; sheep and goats were both in the early stages of domestication. By 5000 B.C. a modern complex of hybrid cereals and domesticated sheep, goats, cattle, and pigs were being exploited, and irrigation was practiced in marginal agricultural areas such as Deh Luran. The effects of developed agriculture are soon apparent, for, by 4000 B.C., settlement of new areas by prehistoric pioneers can be shown clearly in such places as the Diyala region to the east of Baghdad. The age of the earliest settlements in southern Mesopotamia proper is unknown, but it would be surprising if groups of hunters and fishers had not lived along the rivers or swamps prior to the introduction of agriculture. The oldest settlement, Eridu, has been dated to about 5300 B.C., but there are no contemporary sites. In fact, there are few villages known in southern Mesopotamia that antedate 4000 B.C.

Towns and Cities

The millennium between 4000 and 3000 B.C. saw the rapid growth of towns and cities. Villages were also abundant, but some evidence suggests that they were less numerous than in earlier periods. . . . The trends I describe here pertain almost exclusively to southern Mesopotamia; in the north and in the valleys of the Zagros, the pattern remained one of small villages and—emerging later than their counterparts in the south—townships.

From southern Mesopotamia, archeological data for the period before 3000 B.C. are skimpy. Deep soundings at the bases of such sites as Eridu, Ur, Uqair, Tello, Uruk, and Susa and test excavations at Ubaid, Ras al-Amiya, and Hajji Mohammad are about all we have. Only at Ras al-Amiya is there direct evidence of agriculture, although at Eridu a layer of fish bones on the altar of temple VII suggests the importance of the sea and of fishing. Archeological evidence from several of the remaining sites consists either of temple architecture or pottery, the latter serving more to indicate the age of a site than the social or cultural patterns of its inhabitants. Some temple plans are known, but published data on domestic architecture are few, and the sizes of the communities can be inferred only roughly.

There are extensive enough excavations at sites like Uruk, Khafajah, Kish, Ur, and Nippur to indicate the scale of urbanism and many of its more spectacular architectural and artistic features for the period after 3000 B.C. The largest Early Dynastic site was evidently Uruk, where 445 hectares are enclosed by the city wall; contemporary Khafajah and Ur comprise 40 and 60 hectares, respectively. By contrast, the Ubaid portion of Uqair had about 7 hectares.

Historical Reconstructions

Pictographic writing began by about 3400 B.C., but it is difficult to interpret, and in any case early writing tells little about society; it is confined to bookkeeping. Nevertheless, by depending on myths, epics, and tales written some 1000 years later, scholars have attempted historical reconstructions of the emerging urban societies.

The oldest texts that characterize the Sumerian community are no earlier than 2500 B.C. and were written at a time when the "Temple-city" had already become the characteristic feature of the Mesopotamian landscape. In the view of many authors, the city was an estate belonging to gods of nature and maintained on their behalf by completely dependent and relatively impotent mortals. Controversy centers around the degree to which the temple controlled the economy. The extreme view is that it controlled everything while the more popular moderate view is that it controlled only part of the economy. In the Early Dynastic period, it seems clear, some, if not all, people were responsible to a temple which in turn directed most of the production and redistribution of goods and services. For practical purposes there was no distinction between the economic and the religious roles of the temples, but their administrators may not have had much political influence. Some temples listed large staffs of attendants, craftsmen, laborers, and food producers, but the precise relationship of these people to the temple is by no means clear. Moreover, such staffs would have been associated with the largest temples and not with the host of lesser temples and shrines that seem to have been present in the larger cities. Political control was vested variously in the *en* (lord), *lugal* (great man, or king), or *ensi* (governor-priest), depending on the historical period, the city referred to, and the translator of the text. In early times religious and secular titles seem not to have been held by the same person. Jacobsen describes, for pre-Early Dynastic times, a "primitive democracy" with the leader appointed by and responsible to an assembly of citizens. . . .

Environment and Subsistence

By combining the geographic, economic, and historical data, we can construct some plausible theories about the course of development and the situations that triggered it. The remarkable thing, from an ecological view, is the change in relations between men and products, and then between men and their fellows during the 5000 years. If we return for a moment to the pre-agricultural ways of life, we find small bands of hunters exploiting the seasonally available resources of a large territory by wandering from one place to another. Each community was self-sufficient, and each man had approximately the same access to the resources as his fellows. The earliest villagers seem to have maintained this pattern, although, as agriculture and stock breeding became more developed and important economically, the villagers tended more and more to stay put. People settled down where they could raise large amounts of grain, store it for the future, and exchange it for products they did not produce. In return for dependability of food supply, people gave up some of their dietary variety and most of their mobility. From a pattern of exploiting a broad spectrum of the environment, there developed a pattern of exploiting a relatively narrow spectrum.

As long as people stayed where they could find sufficiently varied resources through hunting and gathering, they could be self-sufficient. When people settled in villages away from the mountains, out of the zone of rainfall agriculture, they were no longer independent in the sense that they personally had access to the varied resources they desired or needed. Psychologically and sociologically this marked a turning point in man's relations with his environment and his fellows. Southern Mesopotamia is a land with few resources, yet in many ways this was an advantage for the development of a society. In a land without timber, stone, or metals, trade was necessary, but the role of trade in the emergence of civilization should not be overemphasized. Date palms and bundles of reeds served adequately instead of timber for most construction, and baked clay tools took the place of their stone or metal counterparts in other areas. On the other hand, travel by boat is ancient, and extensive land and sea trade is attested in early documents. It was easy to move goods in Mesopotamia.

In order to live as well as the farmers in Deh Luran did, the Sumerians had to cooperate through trade, barter, or other means with their fellow settlers. We should remember that the barren vista of modern Mesopotamia on a dusty day does not reveal the full range of geographic variation or agricultural potential of the area. Swamps and rivers provided fish and fowl and, together with canals, water for irrigation and navigation. With sufficient water, dates and other fruits and vegetables could be grown. The unequal distribution of subsistence resources encouraged the beginnings of occupational specialization among the various kinds of food producers, and this trend was further emphasized after craftsmen started to follow their trades on a full-time basis.

Economics and Management

Because of the geographic distribution of resources and the sedentary and occupationally specialized population, a social organization that could control production and redistribution was needed. Clearly, any reconstruction of the mechanics of redistribution in emerging Mesopotamian civilization is subject to the severe limitations of the evidence. If we recognize this, however, we may then seek in contemporary societies analogs that may help us imagine appropriate redistributional structures. In modern economies, money markets act as the agency of redistribution, but in virtually all "primitive" societies where surpluses or tradeable goods are produced, a center of redistribution of another kind grows. The "center" can be a person (for example, the chief); an institution, like a temple and the religious context it symbolizes; or a place, like a city with some form of free markets. Jacobsen suggests that in Sumeria temples served as warehouses, where food was stored until times of famine. . . .

In Mesopotamia, most of the surplus labor or food went directly or indirectly into building and maintaining temples. One would also have expected the chief to use a good bit of the surplus to support himself and his family, to pay the wages of craftsmen, and to buy the raw materials that were turned into artifacts, such as jewelry and clothing, that served to distinguish his rank. Others in the lord's biological or official family would also have profited from his control of the resources and ultimately have become recognized as a social class entitled to special prerogatives. This social stratification would have been associated with a similarly burgeoning system of occupational differentiation.

In an emerging system where both technology and governmental forms are relatively simple but susceptible of improvement, there is a maximum opportunity for feedback. That is, if a certain level of production will support a certain degree of social stratification, efficient management by the social elite may result in more productivity. It is interesting to speculate on how much the construction of enormous irrigation systems during later Mesopotamian history may have depended on the rising aspirations of the ruling elite.

Although the need for management of production might in itself have been sufficient cause for a developing social stratification, other factors were probably contributory. Turning now to law and politics, I should point out that, with the establishment of irrigation and the concentration of population in urban centers, man's basic attitudes toward the land must have changed. The construction of irrigation systems, even if primitive, makes the land more valuable to the builders, and this, if it did nothing else, would lead to some notions of property rights and inheritance that had not been necessary when abundant land was available for the taking. An irrigation system also implies that some men may have more direct control over the supply of water than others. This could have led to an increase in the power of individuals who controlled the supply of water, and it certainly must have led to disputes over the allocation of water. It seems inevitable that a working system of adjudicating claims over land would then have been necessary, and the task may have fallen to the chiefs (lords).

The presence of "neighbors" also has ecological implications; it is worth recalling that property invites thievery. Adams argues that the "growth of the Mesopotamian city was closely related to the rising tempo of warfare," and Service points out that the integration of societies under war leaders is common, and clearly an adaptation to social-environmental conditions. Several Early Dynastic II cities had defensive walls, attesting to conflict between cities and perhaps between settled farmers and nomadic herders, but the historical evidence for warfare begins only about 2500 B.C.

If we consider both the agricultural system and the wealth, we see conditions that enhanced opportunities for leadership and, ultimately, for direction and control. With these situations, the emerging systems of rank and status are understandable without our resorting to notions of "genius," "challenge and response," or immigration by more advanced peoples.

Religion

The role of religion in integrating emerging Mesopotamian society is frequently mentioned. By 3000 B.C. texts and temples themselves attest to the central place of religion in

Sumerian life; theoretically, at least, cities were simply estates of the gods, worked on their behalf by mortals. How closely theory corresponds to fact is a question that cannot be answered. Although we cannot date their beginnings precisely, we know that temple centers were well established by 5000 B.C., and that towns and temples frequently go together. Whether towns developed where people congregated because of religious activities or whether temples grew in the market centers where the people were cannot be decided without more data. . . .

In regard to this limited view of the role of religion, it is well to recall that major settlements had several temples. At Khafajah, for example, perhaps as early as 4000 B.C. there were three temples, and a fourth was added later. Our image of the Sumerian temple is nevertheless likely to be that of the large temple oval at Khafajah or Ubaid rather than that of the smaller temples that were contemporary and perhaps just as characteristic. The temple oval appears to have housed a society within a city, but many temples had no auxiliary buildings. More impressive even than the temple ovals were the great ziggurats erected on artificial mounds—at Uruk 13 meters high and visible for many kilometers. Again this was only one of several temples at the same site. In Ubaid, Eridu, and Uqair, for example, where temples were originally associated with residential settlements, the towns were later abandoned and only the temples with cemeteries were maintained.

Summary

It seems unlikely that Mesopotamian society took a single path as it approached the rigidly organized, hierarchal civilization of Early Dynastic times. Rather, we imagine that there was considerable experimentation and variety in the organization of society as people adapted to their physical environment and to the presence of other expanding communities.

Some towns and cities probably arose as the demographic solution to the problem of procuring and distributing resources. It would have made sense to have central "clearing houses." Similarly, it would have made sense to have the craftsmen who turned the raw materials into finished products live close to their supply (probably the temple stores). Temple centers are natural focal points of settlements. Cities and towns, however, are not the only demographic solutions to the problem of farming and maintaining irrigation canals. Both of these tasks could have been carried out by people living in more dispersed settlements. City life in Mesopotamia probably also presented other benefits. For example, as warfare came to be a recurrent threat, the psychological and physical security of a city must have been a comfort for many. Finally, to judge from some historical evidence, Mesopotamian cities were places of diversity and opportunity, no doubt desiderata for many people as long as they could also gain a suitable livelihood. . . .

A Theory of the Origin of the State

Robert L. Carneiro

From *Science,* Vol. 169, 1970, pp. 733–738. Copyright 1970, American Association for the Advancement of Science. By permission of the author, the publisher, and copyright holder.

For the first 2 million years of his existence, man lived in bands or villages which, as far as we can tell, were completely autonomous. Not until perhaps 5000 B.C. did villages begin to aggregate into larger political units. But, once this process of aggregation began, it continued at a progressively faster pace and led, around 4000 B.C., to the formation of the first state in history. (When I speak of a state I mean an autonomous political unit, encompassing many communities within its territory and having a centralized government with the power to collect taxes, draft men for work or war, and decree and enforce laws.)

Although it was by all odds the most far-reaching political development in human history, the origin of the state is still very imperfectly understood. Indeed, not one of the current theories of the rise of the state is entirely satisfactory. At one point or another, all of them fail. There is one theory, though, which I believe does provide a convincing explanation of how states began. It is a theory which I proposed once before and which I present here more fully. Before doing so, however, it seems desirable to discuss, if only briefly, a few of the traditional theories.

Explicit theories of the origin of the state are relatively modern. Classical writers like Aristotle, unfamiliar with other forms of political organization, tended to think of the state as "natural," and therefore as not requiring an explanation. However, the age of exploration, by making Europeans aware that many peoples throughout the world lived, not in states, but in independent villages or tribes, made the state seem less natural, and thus more in need of explanation.

Of the many modern theories of state origins that have been proposed, we can consider only a few. Those with a racial basis, for example, are now so thoroughly discredited that they need not be dealt with here. We can also reject the belief that the state is an expression of the "genius" of a people, or that it arose through a "historical accident." Such notions make the state appear to be something metaphysical or adventitious, and thus place it beyond scientific understanding.

In my opinion, the origin of the state was neither mysterious nor fortuitous. It was not the product of "genius" or the result of chance, but the outcome of a regular and determinate cultural process. Moreover, it was not a unique event but a recurring phenomenon: states arose independently in different places and at different times. Where the appropriate conditions existed, the state emerged.

Voluntaristic Theories

Serious theories of state origins are of two general types: *voluntaristic* and *coercive*. Voluntaristic theories hold that, at some point in their history, certain peoples spontaneously, rationally, and voluntarily gave up their individual sovereignties and united with other communities to form a larger political unit deserving to be called a state. Of such theories the best known is the old Social Contract theory, which was associated especially with the name of Rousseau. We now know that no such compact was ever subscribed to by human groups, and the Social Contract theory is today nothing more than a historical curiosity.

The most widely accepted of modern voluntaristic theories is the one I call the "automatic" theory. According to this theory, the invention of agriculture automatically brought into being a surplus of food, enabling some individuals to divorce themselves from food production and to become potters, weavers, smiths, masons, and so on, thus creating an extensive division of labor. Out of this occupational specialization there developed a political integration which united a number of previously independent communities into a state. This argument was set forth most frequently by the late British archeologist V. Gordon Childe.

The principal difficulty with this theory is that agriculture does *not* automatically create a food surplus. We know this because many agricultural peoples of the world produce no such surplus. Virtually all Amazonian Indians, for example, were agricultural, but in aboriginal times they did not produce a food surplus. That it was *technically feasible* for them to produce such a surplus is shown by the fact that, under the stimulus of European settlers' desire for food, a number of tribes did raise manioc in amounts well above their own needs, for the purpose of trading. Thus the technical means for generating a food surplus were there; it was the social mechanisms needed to actualize it that were lacking.

Another current voluntaristic theory of state origins is Karl Wittfogel's "hydraulic hypothesis." As I understand him, Wittfogel sees the state arising in the following way. In certain arid and semiarid areas of the world, where village farmers had to struggle to support themselves by means of small-scale irrigation, a time arrived when they saw that it would be to the advantage of all concerned to set aside their individual autonomies and merge their villages into a single large political unit capable of carrying out irrigation on a broad scale. The body of officials they created to devise and administer such extensive irrigation works brought the state into being.

This theory has recently run into difficulties. Archeological evidence now makes it appear that in at least three of the areas that Wittfogel cites as exemplifying his "hydraulic hypothesis"—Mesopotamia, China, and Mexico—full-fledged states developed well before large-scale irrigation. Thus, irrigation did not play the causal role in the rise of the state that Wittfogel appears to attribute to it.

This and all other voluntaristic theories of the rise of the state founder on the same rock: the demonstrated inability of autonomous political units ro relinquish their sovereignty in the absence of overriding external constraints. We see this inability manifested again and again by political units ranging from tiny villages to great empires. Indeed, one can scan the pages of history without finding a single genuine exception to this rule. Thus, in order to account for the origin of the state we must set aside voluntaristic theories and look elsewhere.

Coercive Theories

A close examination of history indicates that only a coercive theory can account for the rise of the state. Force, and not enlightened self-interest, is the mechanism by which political evolution has led, step by step, from autonomous villages to the state.

The view that war lies at the root of the state is by no means new. Twenty-five hundred years ago Heraclitus wrote that "war is the father of all things." The first careful study of the role of warfare in the rise of the state, however, was made less than a hundred years ago, by Herbert Spencer in his *Principles of Sociology*. Perhaps better known than Spencer's writings on war and the state are the conquest theories of continental writers such as Ludwig Gumplowicz, Gustav Ratzenhofer, and Franz Oppenheimer.

Oppenheimer, for example, argued that the state emerged when the productive capacity of settled agriculturists was combined with the energy of pastoral nomads through the conquest of the former by the latter. This theory, however, has two serious defects. First, it fails to account for the rise of states in aboriginal America, where pastoral nomadism was unknown. Second, it is now well established that pastoral nomadism did not arise in the Old World until after the earliest states had emerged.

Regardless of deficiencies in particular coercive theories, however, there is little question that, in one way or another, war played a decisive role in the rise of the state. Historical or archeological evidence of war is found in the early stages of state formation in Mesopotamia, Egypt, India, China, Japan, Greece, Rome, northern Europe, central Africa, Polynesia, Middle America, Peru, and Colombia, to name only the most prominent examples.

Thus, with the Germanic kingdoms of northern Europe especially in mind, Edward Jenks observed that, "historically speaking, there is not the slightest difficulty in proving that all political communities of the modern type [that is, states] owe their existence to successful warfare." And in reading Jan Van-

sina's *Kingdoms of the Savanna,* a book with no theoretical ax to grind, one finds that state after state in central Africa arose in the same manner.

But is it really true that there is no exception to this rule? Might there not be, somewhere in the world, an example of a state which arose without the agency of war?

Until a few years ago, anthropologists generally believed that the Classic Maya provided such an instance. The archeological evidence then available gave no hint of warfare among the early Maya and led scholars to regard them as a peace-loving theocratic state which had arisen entirely without war. However, this view is no longer tenable. Recent archeological discoveries have placed the Classic Maya in a very different light. First came the discovery of the Bonampak murals, showing the early Maya at war and reveling in the torture of war captives. Then, excavations around Tikal revealed large earthworks partly surrounding that Classic Maya city, pointing clearly to a military rivalry with the neighboring city of Uaxactún. Summarizing present thinking on the subject, Michael D. Coe has observed that "the ancient Maya were just as warlike as the . . . bloodthirsty states of the Post-Classic."

Yet, though warfare is surely a prime mover in the origin of the state, it cannot be the only factor. After all, wars have been fought in many parts of the world where the state never emerged. Thus, while warfare may be a necessary condition for the rise of the state, it is not a sufficient one. Or, to put it another way, while we can identify war as the *mechanism* of state formation, we need also to specify the *conditions* under which it gave rise to the state.

Environmental Circumscription

How are we to determine these conditions? One promising approach is to look for those factors common to areas of the world in which states arose indigenously—areas such as the Nile, Tigris-Euphrates, and Indus valleys in the Old World and the Valley of Mexico and the mountain and coastal valleys of Peru in the New. These areas differ from one another in many ways —in altitude, temperature, rainfall, soil type, drainage pattern, and many other features. They do, however, have one thing in common: *they are all areas of circumscribed agricultural land.* Each of them is set off by mountains, seas, or deserts, and these environmental features sharply delimit the area that simple farming peoples could occupy and cultivate. In this respect these areas are very different from, say, the Amazon basin or the eastern woodlands of North America, where extensive and unbroken forests provided almost unlimited agricultural land.

But what is the significance of circumscribed agricultural land for the origin of the state? Its significance can best be understood by comparing political development in two regions of the world having contrasting ecologies —one a region with circumscribed agricultural land and the other a region where there was extensive and unlimited land. The two areas I have chosen to use in making this comparison are the coastal valleys of Peru and the Amazon basin.

Our examination begins at the stage where agricultural communities were already present but where each was still completely autonomous. Looking first at the Amazon basin, we see that agricultural villages there were numerous, but widely dispersed. Even in areas with relatively dense clustering, like the Upper Xingú basin, villages were at least 10 or 15 miles apart. Thus, the typical Amazonian community, even though it practiced a simple form of shifting cultivation which required extensive amounts of land, still had around it all the forest land needed for its gardens. For Amazonia as a whole, then, population density was low and subsistence pressure on the land was slight.

Warfare was certainly frequent in Amazonia, but it was waged for reasons of revenge, the taking of women, the gaining of personal prestige, and motives of a similar sort. There being no shortage of land, there was, by and large, no warfare over land.

The consequences of the type of warfare that did occur in Amazonia were as follows. A defeated group was not, as a rule, driven from its land. Nor did the victor make any real effort to subject the vanquished, or to exact tribute from him. This would have been difficult to accomplish in any case, since there was no effective way to prevent the losers from fleeing to a distant part of the forest. Indeed, defeated villages often chose to do just this, not so much to avoid subjugation as to avoid further attack. With settlement so sparse in Amazonia, a new area of forest could be found and occupied with relative ease, and without trespassing on the territory of another village. Moreover, since virtually any area of forest is suitable for cultivation, subsistence agriculture could be carried on in the new habitat just about as well as in the old.

It was apparently by this process of fight and flight that horticultural tribes gradually spread out until they came to cover, thinly but extensively, almost the entire Amazon basin. Thus, under the conditions of unlimited agricultural land and low population density that prevailed in Amazonia, the effect of warfare was to disperse villages over a wide area, and to keep them autonomous. With only a very few exceptions, noted below, there was no tendency in Amazonia for villages to be held in place and to combine into larger political units.

In marked contrast to the situation in Amazonia were the events that transpired in the narrow valleys of the Peruvian coast. The reconstruction of these events that I present is admittedly inferential, but I think it is consistent with the archeological evidence.

Here too our account begins at the stage of small, dispersed, and autonomous farming communities. However, instead of being scattered over a vast expanse of rain forest as they were in Amazonia, villages here were confined to some 78 short and narrow valleys. Each of these valleys, moreover, was backed by the mountains, fronted by the sea, and flanked on either side by desert as dry as any in the world. Nowhere else, perhaps, can one find agricultural valleys more sharply circumscribed than these.

As with neolithic communities generally, villages of the Peruvian coastal valleys tended to grow in size. Since autonomous villages are likely to fission as they grow, as long as land is available for the settlement of splinter communities, these villages undoubtedly split from time to time. Thus, villages tended to increase in number faster than they grew in size. This increase in the number of villages occupying a valley probably continued, without giving rise to significant changes in subsistence practices, until all the readily arable land in the valley was being farmed.

At this point two changes in agricultural techniques began to occur: the tilling of land already under cultivation was intensified, and new, previously unusable land was brought under cultivation by means of terracing and irrigation.

Yet the rate at which new arable land was created failed to keep pace with the increasing demand for it. Even before the land shortage became so acute that irrigation began to be practiced systematically, villages were undoubtedly already fighting one another over land. Prior to this time, when agricultural villages were still few in number and well supplied with land, the warfare waged in the coastal valleys of Peru had probably been of much the same type as that described above for Amazonia. With increasing pressure of human population on the land, however, the major incentive for war changed from a desire for revenge to a need to acquire land. And, as the causes of war became predominantly economic, the frequency, intensity, and importance of war increased.

Once this stage was reached, a Peruvian village that lost a war faced consequences very different from those faced by a defeated village in Amazonia. There, as we have seen, the vanquished could flee to a new locale, subsisting there about as well as they had subsisted before, and retaining their independence. In Peru, however, this alternative was no longer open to the inhabitants of defeated villages. The mountains, the desert, and the sea—to say nothing of neighboring villages—blocked escape in every direction. A village defeated in war thus faced only grim prospects. If it was allowed to remain on its own land, instead of being exterminated or expelled, this concession came only at a price. And the price was political subordination to the victor. This subordination generally entailed at least the payment of a tribute or tax in kind, which the defeated village could provide only by producing more food than it had produced before. But subordination sometimes involved a further loss of autonomy on the part of the defeated village—namely, incorporation into the political unit dominated by the victor.

Through the recurrence of warfare of this type, we see arising in coastal Peru integrated territorial units transcending the village in size and in degree of organization. Political evolution was attaining the level of the chiefdom.

As land shortages continued and became even more acute, so did warfare. Now, however, the competing units were no longer small villages but, often, large chiefdoms. From this point on, through the conquest of chiefdom by chiefdom, the size of political units increased at a progressively faster rate. Naturally, as autonomous political units increased in size, they decreased in number, with the result that an entire valley was eventually unified under the banner of its strongest chiefdom. The political unit thus formed was undoubtedly sufficiently centralized and complex to warrant being called a state.

The political evolution I have described for one valley of Peru was also taking place in other valleys, in the highlands as well as on the coast. Once valley-wide kingdoms emerged, the next step was the formation of multivalley kingdoms through the conquest of weaker valleys by stronger ones. The culmination of this process was the conquest of all of Peru by its most powerful state, and the formation of a single great empire. Although this step may have occurred once or twice before in Andean history, it was achieved most notably, and for the last time, by the Incas.

Political Evolution

While the aggregation of villages into chiefdoms, and of chiefdoms into kingdoms, was occurring by external acquisition, the structure of these increasingly larger political units was being elaborated by internal evolution. These inner changes were, of course, closely related to outer events. The expansion of successful states brought within their borders conquered peoples and territory which had to be administered. And it was the individuals who had distinguished themselves in war who were generally appointed to political office and assigned the task of carrying out this administration. Besides maintaining law and order and collecting taxes, the functions of this burgeoning class of administrators included mobilizing labor for building irrigation works, roads, fortresses, palaces, and temples. Thus, their functions helped to weld an assorted collection of petty states into a single integrated and centralized political unit.

These same individuals, who owed their improved social position to their exploits in war, became, along with the ruler and his kinsmen, the nucleus of an upper class. A lower class in turn emerged from the prisoners taken in war and employed as servants and slaves by their captors. In this manner did war contribute to the rise of social classes.

I noted earlier that peoples attempt to acquire their neighbors' land before they have made the fullest possible use of their own. This implies that every autonomous village has an untapped margin of food productivity, and that this margin is squeezed out only when the village is subjugated and compelled to pay taxes in kind. The surplus food extracted from conquered villages through taxation, which in the aggregate attained very significant proportions, went largely to support the ruler, his warriors and retainers, officials, priests, and other members of the rising upper class, who thus became completely divorced from food production.

Finally, those made landless by war but not enslaved tended to gravitate to settlements which, because of their specialized administrative, commercial, or religious functions, were growing into towns and cities. Here they were able to make a living as workers and artisans, exchanging their labor or their wares for part of the economic surplus exacted from village farmers by the ruling class and spent by members of that class to raise their standard of living.

The process of political evolution which I have outlined for the coastal valleys of Peru was, in its essential features, by no means unique to this region. Areas of circumscribed agricultural land elsewhere in the world, such as the Valley of Mexico, Mesopotamia, the Nile Valley, and the Indus Valley, saw the process occur in much the same way and for essentially the same reasons. In these areas, too, autonomous neolithic villages were succeeded by chiefdoms, chiefdoms by kingdoms, and kingdoms by empires. The last stage of this development was, of course, the most impressive. The scale and magnificence attained by the early empires overshadowed everything that had gone before. But, in a sense, empires were merely the logical culmination of the process. The really fundamental step, the one that had triggered the entire train of events that led to empires, was the change from village autonomy to supravillage integration. This step was a change in kind; everything that followed was, in a way, only a change in degree.

In addition to being pivotal, the step to supracommunity aggregation was difficult, for it took 2 million years to achieve, But, once it was achieved, once village autonomy was transcended, only two or three millennia were required for the rise of great empires and the flourishing of complex civilizations.

Resource Concentration

Theories are first formulated on the basis of a limited number of facts. Eventually, though, a theory must confront all of the facts. And often new facts are stubborn and do not conform to the theory, or do not conform very well. What distinguishes a successful theory from an unsuccessful one is that it can be modified or elaborated to accommodate the entire range of facts. Let us see how well the "circumscription theory" holds up when it is brought face-to-face with certain facts that appear to be exceptions.

For the first test let us return to Amazonia. Early voyagers down the Amazon left written testimony of a culture along that river higher than the culture I have described for Amazonia generally. In the 1500's, the native population living on the banks of the Amazon was relatively dense, villages were fairly large and close together, and some degree of social stratification existed. Moreover, here and there a paramount chief held sway over many communities.

The question immediately arises: With unbroken stretches of arable land extending back from the Amazon for hundreds of miles, why were there chiefdoms here?

To answer this question we must look closely at the environmental conditions afforded by the Amazon. Along the margins of the river itself, and on islands within it there is a type of land called *várzea*. The river floods this land every year, covering it with a layer of fertile silt. Because of this annual replenishment, *várzea* is agricultural land of first quality which can be cultivated year after year without ever having to lie fallow. Thus, among native farmers it was highly prized and greatly coveted. The waters of the Amazon were also extraordinarily bountiful, providing fish, manatees, turtles and turtle eggs, caimans, and other riverine foods in inexhaustible amounts. By virtue of this concentration of resources, the Amazon, as a habitat, was distinctly superior to its hinterlands.

Concentration of resources along the Amazon amounted almost to a kind of circumscription. While there was no sharp cleavage between productive and unproductive land, as there was in Peru, there was at least a steep ecological gradient. So much more rewarding was the Amazon River than adjacent areas, and so desirable did it become as a habitat, that peoples were drawn to it from surrounding regions. Eventually crowd-

ing occurred along many portions of the river, leading to warfare over sections of river front. And the losers in war, in order to retain access to the river, often had no choice but to submit to the victors. By this subordination of villages to a paramount chief there arose along the Amazon chiefdoms representing a higher step in political evolution than had occurred elsewhere in the basin.

The notion of resource concentration also helps to explain the surprising degree of political development apparently attained by peoples of the Peruvian coast while they were still depending primarily on fishing for subsistence, and only secondarily on agriculture. Of this seeming anomaly Lanning has written: "To the best of my knowledge, this is the only case in which so many of the characteristics of civilization have been found without a basically agricultural economic foundation."

Armed with the concept of resource concentration, however, we can show that this development was not so anomalous after all. The explanation, it seems to me, runs as follows. Along the coast of Peru wild food sources occurred in considerable number and variety. However, they were restricted to a very narrow margin of land. Accordingly, while the *abundance* of food in this zone led to a sharp rise in population, the *restrictedness* of this food soon resulted in the almost complete occupation of exploitable areas. And when pressure on the available resources reached a critical level, competition over land ensued. The result of this competition was to set in motion the sequence of events of political evolution that I have described.

Thus, it seems that we can safely add resource concentration to environmental circumscription as a factor leading to warfare over land, and thus to political integration beyond the village level.

Social Circumscription

But there is still another factor to be considered in accounting for the rise of the state.

In dealing with the theory of environmental

circumscription while discussing the Yanomamö Indians of Venezuela, Napoleon A.
Chagnon has introduced the concept of "social circumscription." By this he means that a
high density of population in an area can
produce effects on peoples living near the
center of the area that are similar to effects
produced by environmental circumscription.
This notion seems to me to be an important
addition to our theory. Let us see how, according to Chagnon, social circumscription
has operated among the Yanomamö.

The Yanomamö, who number some 10,
000, live in an extensive region of noncircum-
scribed rain forest, away from any large river.
One might expect that Yanomamö villages
would thus be more or less evenly spaced.
However, Chagnon notes that, at the center of
Yanomamö territory, villages are closer together than they are at the periphery. Because of this, they tend to impinge on one
another more, with the result that warfare is
more frequent and intense in the center than
in peripheral areas. Moreover, it is more difficult for villages in the nuclear area to escape
attack by moving away, since, unlike villages
on the periphery, their ability to move is
somewhat restricted.

The net result is that villages in the central
area of Yanomamö territory are larger than
villages in the other areas, since large village
size is an advantage for both attack and
defense. A further effect of more intense
warfare in the nuclear area is that village headmen are stronger in that area. Yanomamö
headmen are also the war leaders, and their
influence increases in proportion to their village's participation in war. In addition, offensive and defensive alliances between villages
are more common in the center of Yanomamö territory than in outlying areas.
Thus, while still at the autonomous village
level of political organization, those Yanomamö subject to social circumscription
have clearly moved a step or two in the
direction of higher political development.

Although the Yanomamö manifest social
circumscription only to a modest degree, this
amount of it has been enough to make a
difference in their level of political organization. What the effects of social circumscription would be in areas where it was more fully
expressed should, therefore, be clear. First
would come a reduction in the size of the
territory of each village. Then, as population
pressure became more severe, warfare over
land would ensue. But because adjacent land
for miles around was already the property of
other villages, a defeated village would have
nowhere to flee. From this point on, the
consequences of warfare for that village, and
for political evolution in general, would be
essentially as I have described them for the
situation of environmental circumscription.

To return to Amazonia, it is clear that, if
social circumscription is operative among the
Yanomamö today, it was certainly operative
among the tribes of the Amazon River 400
years ago. And its effect would undoubtedly
have been to give a further spur to political
evolution in that region.

We see then that, even in the absence of
sharp environmental circumscription, the
factors of resource concentration and social
circumscription may, by intensifying war and
redirecting it toward the taking of land, give a
strong impetus to political development.

With these auxiliary hypotheses incorporated into it, the circumscription theory is
now better able to confront the entire range
of test cases that can be brought before it.
For example, it can now account for the rise
of the state in the Hwang Valley of northern
China, and even in the Petén region of the
Maya lowlands, areas not characterized by
strictly circumscribed agricultural land. In the
case of the Hwang Valley, there is no question
that resource concentration and social circumscription were present and active forces.
In the lowland Maya area, resource concentration seems not to have been a major factor,
but social circumscription may well have
been.

Some archeologists may object that population density in the Petén during Formative
times was too low to give rise to social circumscription. But, in assessing what constitutes a population dense enough to produce
this effect, we must consider not so much the
total land area occupied as the amount of

land needed to support the existing population. And the size of this supporting area depends not only on the size of the population but also on the mode of subsistence. The shifting cultivation presumably practiced by the ancient Maya required considerably more land, per capita, than did the permanent field cultivation of say, the Valley of Mexico or the coast of Peru. Consequently, insofar as its effects are concerned, a relatively low population density in the Petén may have been equivalent to a much higher one in Mexico or Peru.

We have already learned from the Yanomamö example that social circumscription may begin to operate while population is still relatively sparse. And we can be sure that the Petén was far more densely peopled in Formative times than Yanomamö territory is today. Thus, population density among the lowland Maya, while giving a superficial appearance of sparseness, may actually have been high enough to provoke fighting over land, and thus provide the initial impetus for the formation of a state.

Conclusion

In summary, then, the circumscription theory in its elaborated form goes far toward accounting for the origin of the state. It explains why states arose where they did, and why they failed to arise elsewhere. It shows the state to be a predictable response to certain specific cultural, demographic, and ecological conditions. Thus, it helps to elucidate what was undoubtedly the most important single step ever taken in the political evolution of mankind.

Post-Pleistocene Adaptations

Lewis R. Binford

From *New Perspectives in Archeology,* Sally R. Binford and Lewis R. Binford (eds.), Aldine Publishing Company, 1968, pp. 313–336. Copyright © 1968, Sally R. and Lewis R. Binford. By permission of the author, editors and copyright holders, and publisher.

This paper will examine some of the major assumptions underlying the current systematics of the archeological remains of the post-Pleistocene period. . . .

The work of the past 100 years has resulted in the accumulation of sufficient data to justify some generalizations made by workers in the field of European Mesolithic studies. Some of the generalizations made in distinguishing the Paleolithic from the Mesolithic are:

1. *There was a major shift in the centers of population growth in Western Europe.* . . .

2. *There was a major change in the form of stone tools.* . . .

3. *There is greater geographic variety in cultural remains suggesting more specific responses to local environmental conditions.* . . .

4. *There was a marked increase in the exploitation of aquatic resources and wild fowl.* . . .

5. *There was a "trend" toward small game hunting.* . . .

6. *The Mesolithic represents cultural degeneration when compared with the Upper Paleolithic.* . . .

These generalizations which summarize archeological observations have been conceived by most European scholars in the following manner:

1. There are major changes in cultural remains which serve to differentiate the cultural systems of the terminal Pleistocene from those of the immediately post-Pleistocene period.

2. This immediately post-Pleistocene period is further characterized by major changes in pollen profiles, fossil beach lines, and the geomorphology of major drainage systems.

3. The demonstrable correlation between the dramatic cultural and environmental

changes at this time is evidence for the systematic articulation of cultural and environmental systems.

Therefore:

(a) Archeological differences observed between the terminal Paleolithic and the Mesolithic can be explained by reference to environmental changes.

(b) Differences not explained by reference to environmental changes are the result of new social contacts; such social contacts were a result of movement of populations in response to local climatic deterioration. . . .

This argument is a relatively straightforward mechanistic approach and is completely compatible with a materialistic, systemic approach to the understanding of cultural change. The extent to which this approach might be questioned and the particulars of its application tested depends upon the degree to which: (1) equally radical changes in culture can be demonstrated in the absence of analogous environmental changes, and/or (2) major environmental changes can be demonstrated to vary independently of analogous changes in cultural systems.

Such test situations can be found either at a contemporary time period outside the area directly affected by the retreat of glacial ice or in the same regions under similar environmental conditions at a different time period. Researchers concerned with the initial appearance of food production, as well as those workers operating in a variety of non-Western European regions, are the ones to whom we now turn for an evaluation of the explanatory approach commonly used on Western European materials.

The shift from food-procurement to food-production has been examined by many scholars. . . . Childe's consideration of the problem was the most influential, since he presented a series of propositions specific enough to be tested through the collection of paleoenvironmental and paleoanthropological data:

Food production—the deliberate cultivation of food plants, especially cereals, and the taming, breeding and selection of animals . . . was an economic revolution. . . the greatest in human history after the mastery of fire . . . . The conditions of incipient desiccation . . . would provide the stimulus towards the adoption of a food-producing economy. Enforced concentration by the banks of streams and shrinking springs would entail an intensive search for means of nourishment. Animals and men would be herded together in oases that were becoming increasingly isolated by desert tracts. Such enforced juxtaposition might promote that sort of symbiosis between man and beast implied by the word domestication.

If it was Childe who first provided a set of testable propositions as to the conditions under which food-production was achieved, it was Braidwood who actively sought the field data to test Childe's propositions. . . . In discussing the oasis theory Braidwood states:

So far this theory is pretty much all guess-work, and there are certainly some questions it leaves unanswered. I will tell you quite frankly that there are times when I feel it is plain balderdash.

Braidwood also questioned the relevance of the postulated environmental changes to the origins of food-production:

There had also been three earlier periods of great glaciers, and long periods of warm weather in between. . . . Thus the forced neighborliness of men, plants and animals in river valleys and oases must also have happened earlier. Why didn't domestication happen earlier too, then?. . .

Braidwood's work in the "hilly flanks" zone of the Fertile Crescent was carried out over a number of years and involved the collaboration of a number of scientists from the fields of zoology, paleontology, geology, palynology, paleobotany, etc. Their investigations had been directed toward the identification of the physical effects of domestication on plants and animals and the documentation of the enviromental events of the period between 10,000 B.C. and the appearance of "settled village life." The climatological-environmental results have allowed Braidwood to generalize:

> It seems most unlikely that there was any really significant difference between then and now in the general land forms and rainfall patterns . . . [and] In southwestern Asia . . . our colleagues in the natural sciences see no evidence for radical change in climate or fauna between the levels of the Zarzian and those of the Jarmo or Hassunah phases.

Discussing specifically the relationship between environmental change and the beginnings of food-production, Braidwood states:

> We do not believe that the answers will lie within the realm of environmental determinism and in any direct or strict sense . . . we and our natural-science colleagues reviewed the evidence for possible pertinent fluctuations of climate and of plant and animal distributions. . . and convinced ourselves that there is no such evidence available. . .no evidence exists for such changes in the natural environment. . .as might be of sufficient impact to have predetermined the shift to food production.

Thus Braidwood argues that: (1) environmental conditions analogous to those at the close of the Pleistocene had occurred previously without having brought about food-production, and (2) there is no evidence to support major climatic changes in the Near East of sufficient magnitude to have "predetermined the shift to food production." These observations are not only directed against the oasis theory but also against the argument that food-production constituted an alternative adaptation to changed environmental conditions at the close of the Pleistocene. Braidwood also argues against the causative role of environmental change in his consideration of the applicability of the term Mesolithic to non-European areas. . . .

Braidwood presents a strong case that there was major cultural change in areas where environmental change was minor or absent, as well as in areas such as Western Europe where environmental change was marked. This, together with the fact that earlier interglacial warm periods were not accompanied by drastic cultural changes of analogous form, is sufficient to invalidate the argument that the magnitude of environmental and cultural change can be expected to vary directly in a simple stimulus-response pattern. These data also raise questions about the positive correlations claimed for the form of environmental and cultural changes.

Braidwood, however, is not completely consistent in his application of these findings. He argues *against* the causative role of environmental change in the Near East, yet *for* such an explanation for the cultural changes observed in Western Europe. We do not propose here that there is no relationship between environmental and cultural change in Western Europe but rather argue against the direct and simple causative role of environmental change in view of Braidwood's own findings. What we must seek is a set of explanatory variables which will be valid on a world-wide scale at the terminal- and post-Pleistocene periods.

If Braidwood rejects environmental change as the principal explanation in the Near East, what does he propose instead?. . . Braidwood offers his "nuclear zone" theory:

> In my opinion there is no need to complicate the story with extraneous "causes." The food producing revolution seems to have occurred as the culmination of the ever increasing cultural differentiation and specialization of human communities. Around 8,000 B.C. the inhabitants of the hills around the fertile crescent had come to know their habitat so well that they were beginning to domesticate the plants and animals they had been collecting and hunting. . . . From these "nuclear" zones cultural diffusion spread the new way of life to the rest of the world.

A nuclear zone is defined as follows:

> A region with a natural environment which included a variety of wild plants and animals, both possible and ready for domestication. . . .

In his statements Braidwood proposes that cultivation is the expected, natural outcome of a long, directional evolutionary trend, limited only by the presence in the environment of domesticable plants and animals. This is clearly an orthogenetic argument. The vital element responsible for the directional series of events appears to be inherent in human nature; it is expressed by Braidwood in such phrases as "increased experimentation" and "increased receptiveness." These behavioral traits made it possible for man to "settle into" his environment, and they serve as the basis for Braidwood's taxonomy of subsistence-settlement types in which three long-run trends can be seen: (1) increased localization of activity within the territory of a group, (2) more specific exploitation of the habitat, and (3) increased group size. . . . It is when we have these trends, based on inherent human nature, operating in the context of a "nuclear zone" that things begin to happen:

Now my hunch goes that when this experimentation and settling down took place within a potential nuclear area . . . where a whole constellation of plants and animals possible of domestication were available . . . the change was easily made. . . .

The explanation for absence of food production during earlier interglacial periods is that: "culture was not ready to achieve it."

It is argued here that vitalism, whether expressed in terms of inherent forces orienting the direction of organic evolution or in its more anthropocentric form of emergent human properties which direct cultural evolution, is unacceptable as an explanation. Trends which are observed in cultural evolution require explanation; they are certainly not explained by postulating emergent human traits which are said to account for the trends.

In summary, post-Pleistocene research began with the question of whether or not Western Europe was populated between the close of the Pleistocene and the first appearance of the later Neolithic settlements. When this question was answered affirmatively, emphasis shifted to the question of continuity—were the "intermediate" populations indigenous or were they intruders? In seeking to solve this problem scholars were involved in the methodological question of what archeological data could be cited as proof or disproof of continuity. As local sequences became better documented, this question was dropped, and there was an increasing tendency to view variability as a direct response to local environments which had radically changed with the retreat of the ice. This stimulus-response reasoning was generalized not only for the European foraging adaptation but was also used to explain the origins of food-production (the propinquity or oasis theory). Field investigation in the relevant parts of the Near East showed that dramatic environmental change did not characterize the crucial periods of time. The oasis theory has fallen into disfavor, and Braidwood's nuclear zone theory has tended to replace it. We have sought to demonstrate in our analysis that this theory is based on a kind of vitalism and a postulation of causal factors which are incapable of being tested. We also propose that current explanations for the form and distribution of post-Pleistocene cultures in Europe are implicitly, and often explicitly, based on simple and direct environmental determinism which the data from non-European parts of the world tend to refute. What follows is an examination of post-Pleistocene data within a different theoretical framework and the formulation of explanatory hypotheses which, it is hoped, are both more generally applicable and also testable.

If our aim is the explanation of cultural differences and similarities in different places and at different times, we must first isolate the phenomena we designate "cultural." Culture is all those means whose forms are not under direct genetic control which serve to adjust individuals and groups within their ecological communities. If we seek understanding of the origins of agriculture or of "the spread of the village-farming community," we must analyze these cultural means as adaptive adjustments in the variety of ecosystems within which human groups were participants.

Adaptation is always a local problem, and selective pressures favoring new cultural forms result from non-equilibrium conditions in the local ecosystem. Our task, then, becomes the isolation of the variables initiating directional change in the internal structuring of ecological systems. Of particular importance is understanding the conditions which favor the rearrangement of energy-matter components and their linked dependencies in a manner which alters the effective environment of the unit under study.

The term "effective environment" designates those parts of the total environment which are in regular or cyclical articulation with the unit under study. Changes in the effective environment will produce changes not only in the boundaries of the ecological community but also in the internal organization of the community. Both of these changes in turn set up conditions favoring adaptive adjustments among the components of the community. In dealing with sociocultural systems and in trying to understand the conditions under which such systems undergo adaptive change, we are necessarily concerned with the effective environment of a given system. . . .

If we hope to understand culture change in general, and the changes of the post-Pleistocene period in particular, we must seek the conditions which have brought new factors into play in the effective environments of the cultural systems at the close of the Pleistocene.

Before undertaking our analysis, one further distinction needs to be made—the distinction between functional and structural differences in ecological niches. *Functional differences* are those which result from differences in the form of the elements of a system and which do not necessarily imply differences in the kind of articulation which exists between a cultural system and the ecological community of which it is a part. *Structural differences* refer to communities made up of non-analogous components which are integrated in different ways. In citing functional variability between niches, we are referring to differences in the form of the gross environment in which ecological communities occur; in such cases there would be no necessary structural differences in the organization of the ecological communities of the system, but only in the form of their environments. A case in point might be two cultural systems, both of which are solely dependent upon terrestrial resources within their home ranges and neither of which possesses the technological means for food storage or circulation beyond the locus of procurement. If one such system were located in a tropical rain forest and the other in a temperate deciduous forest, we would observe numerous formal differences between the cultural elements in the two systems, yet both can be said to occupy similar ecological niches within their habitats. Despite obvious differences in raw materials, the form of implements, differences in phasing of activities, and even in social organization, all such differences are explicable directly by reference to differences in gross environment. Therefore, we would term these differences functional, not structural.

Structural differences in ecological niches, on the other hand, refer to differences in the modes of integration between cultural and other components within ecological communities. Such differences imply a different set of relationships between the cultural unit and the variables in the gross environment with which the cultural unit is articulated. Cultural systems which occupy different ecological niches would therefore have different effective environments. An example of two cultural systems in the same gross environment but occupying different ecological niches would be the commonly occurring case where horticulturalists and hunters and gatherers live side by side. Each cultural group is in articulation with quite different elements of the gross environment and is integrated with the environment differently. Such cultural systems would be subject to qualitatively different types of selective pressure.

We would argue that understanding the selective pressures favoring the adoption of adaptive means as radical and as new as animal husbandry and cultivation in the post-Pleistocene requires the application of the ecological principles outlined above. A first step would be to determine whether food-production constitutes a functional variant of analogous ecological niches in different environments, or whether it is a structurally new adaptive means in an ecological niche not previously occupied by cultural systems.

Braidwood's nuclear zone theory is an argument for the former interpretation; the differences between the post-Pleistocene cultures in the hilly flanks and elsewhere are explicable by reference to formally unique elements in the plant and animal populations of the piedmont regions of the Near East. Childe's position is a statement of the latter interpretation, and he cites changes in the physical environment as the cause for bringing about new structural relationships between plants, animals, and men. Our argument also favors the second interpretation but with demographic, rather than gross environmental, variables responsible for the generation of pressures favoring new ecological niches.

> At certain times and places in the course of culture history, the threat of a diminished food supply, coming from an increase of population through immigration, or from a decline in local flora due to climatic or physiographic change, was met by various measures of cultural control over plant life, which collectively, we call agriculture.

White's citation of population increase through immigration as a relevant variable in explaining the appearance of agriculture is a radical departure from traditional interpretations.

In the traditional approach, changes and variation in the available food supply have been cited as the major factors which regulate population equilibrium systems. . . .

The inference about population dynamics to be made from these statements is that populations will grow until the food requirements of the group begin to exceed the standing crop in the local habitat. No population could ever achieve a stable adaptation, since its members would always be under

strong selective pressure to develop new means of getting food. This assumption of the available food supply as the critical variable in population dynamics has prevented consideration of population variables themselves as possible sources of disequilibrium.

Recent studies in demography have argued strongly against the direct control of population density by the availability of food. . . . Most demographers agree that functional relationships between the normal birth rate and other requirements (for example, the mobility of the female) favor the *cultural* regulation of fertility through such practices as infanticide, abortion, lactation taboos, etc. These practices have the effect of homeostatically keeping population size below the point at which diminishing returns from the local habitat would come into play.

The arguments of demographers are supported by a number of recent ethnographic studies which document the abundance of food available to even marginal hunters. Some cases of importance are J. D. Clark on the Barotse, Lee on the !Kung Bushmen, Woodburn on the Hadza, and Huntingford on the Dorobo. . . .

These data suggest that while hunting-gathering populations may vary in density between different habitats in direct proportion to the relative size of the standing food crop, nevertheless within any given habitat the population is homeostatically regulated *below* the level of depletion of the local food supply.

There are two corollaries of the assumption that population size is regulated almost exclusively by food supply which we also need to examine. The first corollary is: *Man would be continually seeking means for increasing his food supply.* In other words, there would be ubiquitous and constant selective pressure favoring the development of technological innovations, such as agriculture, which serve to make larger amounts of food available to a group. There is a large body of ethnographic data which suggests that this is not the case.

Carneiro in his study of the Kuikuru, who are horticulturalists, demonstrated that these people were capable of producing several times the amount of food they did. A small increment in the amount of time devoted to planting and harvesting would have brought about substantial increases in the available food, yet the Kuikuru chose not to do this. Enough food was produced to meet local demands, and it was at that point that production stopped. Equilibrium had been reached, and neither population nor production increased. . . .

If we recognize that an equilibrium system can be established so that populations are homeostatically regulated below the carrying capacity of the local food supply, it follows that there is no necessary adaptive pressure continually favoring means of increasing the food supply. The question to be asked then is not why agricultural and food-storage techniques were not developed everywhere, but why they were developed at all. Under what set of conditions does increasing the supply of available food have adaptive advantage?

The second corollary to be examined concerns leisure time: *It is only when man is freed from preoccupation with the food quest that he has time to elaborate culture. . . .*

There are abundant data which suggest not only that hunter-gatherers have adequate supplies of food but also that they enjoy quantities of leisure time, much more in fact than do modern industrial or farm workers, or even professors of archeology. Lee, Bose, McCarthy and McArthur, and Woodburn have shown that hunters on a simple level of technology spend a very small percentage of their time obtaining food. On these grounds we can reasonably question the proposition that cultural elaboration is caused by leisure time which is available for the first time to agriculturalists.

In rejecting the assumption that hunter-gatherer populations are primarily regulated by the available supply of food, we put the problem of the development of new types of subsistence in a different light. As long as one could assume that man was continually trying to increase his food supply, understanding the "origins of agriculture" simply involved pinpointing those geographic areas where the potential resources were and postulating that man would inevitably take advantage of

them. With the recognition that equilibrium systems regulate population density below the carrying capacity of an environment, we are forced to look for those conditions which might bring about disequilibrium and bring about selective advantage for increased productivity. According to the arguments developed here, there could be only two such sets of conditions:

1. A change in the physical environment of a population which brings about a reduction in the biotic mass of the region would decrease the amounts of available food. The previous balance between population and standing crop is upset, and more efficient extractive means would be favored. This is essentially the basis for Childe's propinquity theory.

2. Change in the demographic structure of a region which brings about the impingement of one group on the territory of another would also upset an established equilibrium system, and might serve to increase the population density of a region beyond the carrying capacity of the natural environment. Under these conditions manipulation of the natural environment in order to increase its productivity would be highly advantageous.

The remainder of this paper is devoted to the exploration of this second set of conditions. The first step of our analysis is to build models of different types of population systems under different conditions. One such type of system is termed a *closed population system* in which a steady state is maintained by internal mechanisms limiting numbers of offspring at the generational replacement level. Techniques such as abortion, contraception, abstinence, and infanticide serve to lower the birth rate and increase the mortality rate so that a given population would be homeostatically regulated at a given size or density.

The second type of system, the *open population system,* is one in which size and/or density is maintained by either the budding off of new groups or by the emigration of individuals. This would be an *open system of the donor type.* If the size or density of the system is altered through the introduction of immigrants from other population groups, we have an *open system of the recipient type.*

Given these two types of population systems—closed and open, the latter including two sub-types, recipient and donor—we can begin to analyze differences in the ways in which the two system types can be articulated in a given region.

Closed Systems

We can identify the population of a region as a whole as a closed system, yet find that within the region there would be some variability in optimum group size as a response to geographical differences in the regional distribution of resources. Further, each local group within the region may operate periodically as an open system, since we would expect some variability in the degree to which local groups have achieved equilibrium. There would therefore be some redistribution of population between groups which would promote a more uniform and steady density equilibrium system over the region as a whole.

We would expect selection favoring cultural means of regulating population to occur in situations where the density equilibrium system for the region as a whole was in fact a closed system, and where there were significant imbalances in the losses and recruits for the local subsegments of the regional population. There would be differential selective advantage for cultural regulation of population growth between two closed population systems in different environmental settings if there were discrepancies between the actual birth and death rates on the one hand and the optimal rates for maintaining population size on the other.

Open Systems, Donor Type

We would expect to find this type of population system in areas which are not filled to the point at which density dependent factors are brought into play. The peopling of a new land

mass, such as the New World or Australia, would be an example of such a situation in which there would be positive advantage for this type of system.

The rate of expansion of open donor systems into uninhabited territory has been discussed in the literature, and models for this type of expansion have been built. Birdsell has made two observations which are particularly relevant here. First, the budding off of new groups occurs *before* optimum local population size has been reached. This observation demonstrates the role of emigration in bringing about and maintaining equilibrium and also shows that the unit on which selection for emigration operates is a subunit of the local population, since conditions favoring segmentation appear before the regional population is under pressure from density dependent factors.

Second, the adaptation of any given sociocultural system will determine in part the locus of selection within the social system and the particular selective advantages for different fertility rates. . . .

We have seen that two frequent means of maintaining homeostasis are emigration and cultural regulation of births and deaths. The relative importance to any group of one of these means *vs.* the other will be conditioned by such factors as mobility requirements of the group. Another conditioning factor would be the type of articulation between segments of the population which can directly affect the ease with which budding-off can occur. A third factor would be the degree to which the region as a whole is occupied which would affect the expectations of success in the establishment of daughter communities.

Open Systems, Recipient Type

This type of system could occur under only two sets of conditions; the first would be where there is the expansion of a donor system into an uninhabited region. The frontier of the region would contain a number of population units which could, for a short time, serve as recipient systems. Their change from recipient to donor systems would depend upon the extent to which optimal densities were achieved locally and the frontier continued to advance.

The second set of conditions promoting systems of the recipient type is more relevant to the consideration of early agricultural developments. This is the situation in which two or more different kinds of sociocultural systems occupy adjacent environmental zones. If the adaptation of one sociocultural unit is translatable into the adjacent environmental zone, it may expand into that zone at the expense of resident systems. Cases of this type have been cited by Kaplan as examples of the Law of Cultural Dominance, and a specific instance referred to by Sahlins are the Tiv and the Nuer. We would expect expansion of the dominant system until the zone to which the system was adapted was occupied; at this juncture there would be selection for increased efficiency of production and/or for increased regulation of the birth rate.

A different kind of situation would obtain in the case of sociocultural systems occupying adjacent zones if the adaptation of the more rapidly growing group is not translatable into the adjacent zone. Population growth within the area occupied by the parent group might well be so great that daughter communities would frequently be forced to reside in an environment which is incompatible with their particular cultural adaptation. There could be a number of effects under these circumstances.

From the standpoint of the populations already in the recipient zone, the intrusion of immigrant groups would disturb the existing density equilibrium system and might raise the population density to the level at which we would expect diminishing food resources. This situation would serve to increase markedly for the recipient groups the pressures favoring means for increasing productivity. The intrusive group, on the other hand, would be forced to make adaptive adjustments to their new environment. There would be strong selective pressures favoring the development of more efficient subsistence techniques by both groups.

It should be pointed out, however, that such advantage does not insure that these developments will inevitably occur. In many cases these problems are met by changes which might be called regressive in that the changes in adaptation which occur may be in the direction of less complex cultural forms. Examples of this sort of change can be seen among the hunter-gatherers of the non-riverine tropical forest zones in South America. . . . Lathrap has offered the possibility that perhaps all of the less sedentary South American groups are "the degraded descendants of peoples who at one time maintained an advanced form of Tropical Forest Culture."

While in these examples the adaptations along population frontiers were in the direction of less complexity, it is in the context of such situations of stress in environments with plant and animal forms amenable to manipulation that we would expect to find conditions favoring the development of plant and animal domestication. Such situations would be characterized by disequilibrium between population and resources which, in turn, would offer selective advantage to increases in the efficacy of subsistence technology. Rather than seeking the locus for the origins of agriculture in the heart of a "natural habitat zone," we would argue that we must look to those places where a population frontier or adaptive tension zone intersects a "natural habitat zone." This means that archeological investigations might well concentrate on those areas within the natural habitat zone where there is an archeologically demonstrated major shift in population density. The presence of such a shift might well indicate a population frontier where rapid evolutionary changes were taking place.

Another archeological clue to be exploited is the degree to which settlements are characterized by sedentism. The frontier zones would be expected between regions which differed widely in the degree of sedentism practiced by resident groups. In those areas with highly sedentary population, problems of transport of young and belongings would be reduced. Reduced mobility of social units in general and in the daily routines of females in particular would in turn reduce the selective advantages accruing to cultural means of controlling population growth. Therefore, under conditions of increased sedentism we would expect population growth. A consequence of such growth would be the increased relative importance of emigration as a mechanism for maintaining the local group within optimal size and density limits.

Therefore where there is a marked contrast in degree of sedentism between two sociocultural units within a relatively restricted geographical region, there would be a tension zone where emigrant colonies from the more sedentary group would periodically disrupt the density equilibrium balances of the less sedentary group. Under these conditions there would be strong selective pressure favoring the development of more effective means of food production for both groups within this zone of tension. There would also be increasing pressures against immigration, given the failure to develop more effective extractive technologies.

It is proposed here that it was in the selective context outlined above that initial practices of cultivation occurred. Such selective situations would have been the consequence of the increased dependence on aquatic resources during the terminal and immediately post-Pleistocene period. Not all portions of rivers and shorelines favor the harvesting of fish, molluscs, and migratory fowl; it is with the systematic dependence on just these resources that we find archeological remains indicating a higher degree of sedentism in both the Archaic of the New World and the terminal Paleolithic and Mesolithic of the Old World. This hypothesis is lent strong support by the fact that it is also in the terminal Paleolithic-Mesolithic and Archaic that we find, associated with increased sedentism, evidence for marked population growth and for the development of food-storage techniques, the latter being functionally linked to the highly seasonal nature of migratory fowl and anadromous fish exploited as food crops.

Since the systematic exploitation of these food sources (and of markedly seasonally available terrestrial forms as well—for example, reindeer) characterized adaptations of this time range in a wide variety of environments, we would expect that tension zones,

with their concomitant selective pressures favoring increased subsistence efficiency, would be widely distributed also. This expectation is in accord with the empirical generalizations that: (1) There were a number of independent loci of the development of cultivation techniques—the Near East, Asia, and the New World—and all the developments of these techniques occur within the time range in question; and (2) These loci were distributed across widely different environmental types—root crops in the tropics and cereals in semi-aridlands, for example.

The widespread nature of conditions favoring increased subsistence efficiency also accounts for the rapid transmission and integration of contributing innovations from one cultural system to another. Many authors have cited the rapid "diffusion" of cultural elements as characterizing the immediately post-Pleistocene period.

Finally, in the traditional view the "Neolithic Revolution" is characterized by the appearance of a number of traits which are thought to be linked to the shift to food production. The manufacture of ceramics and textiles, relatively permanent houses, and craft specialization are only a few of those frequently cited. These traits constitute part of the definition of the "village farming way of life," and the assumption is that they originated in the "nuclear area" from which they spread as a complex, the spread being achieved by diffusion, stimulus diffusion, and/or migration. As more data have been accumulated, it becomes increasingly clear that these traits are not mutually dependent; indeed, it seems to be quite clear that ceramics, for example, were first used in the Old World in coastal Japan, with a cluster of radiocarbon dates averaging ca. 7000 B.C. This is about the same time that effective grain agriculture was initially practiced in the Near East, and the occupations in question have yielded no ceramics. Given our model, such traits insofar as they are functionally linked to sedentism and/or food production would be expected to appear in a variety of regions as the result of numerous independent but parallel inventions.

Further utility for the model presented

here can be shown by the degree to which it provides explanatory answers for a series of questions posed by Braidwood and Willey— questions which cannot be satisfactorily answered within the traditional framework.

Why did incipient food production not come earlier? Our only answer at the moment is that culture was not yet ready to achieve it. . . .

We believe that a more complete answer is possible. The shift to the exploitation of highly seasonal resources such as anadromous fish and migratory fowl did not occur until the close of the Pleistocene. This shift, probably linked to worldwide changes in sea level, with attendant increase in sedentism, established for the first time conditions leading to marked heterogeneity in rates of population growth and structure of the ecological niche of immediately adjacent sociocultural systems. This new set of conditions brought about, in turn, conditions favoring improved subsistence technology. It was not that culture was unready, but rather that the selective conditions favoring such changes had not previously existed.

What were the . . . cultural conditions favoring incipient cultivation or domestication? Certainly there is nothing in the archeological record to indicate that those few instances of cultural buildup and elaboration, as manifested by the varying art styles of the upper paleolithic from western Europe into Siberia . . . provided a favorable ground for incipient food production. On the contrary, those instances of incipient cultivation or domestication of greatest potential are found in contexts of a much less spectacular character. . . .

According to our model, we would *expect* to find the selective situation favoring "incipient cultivation" in "contexts of a much less spectacular character"—in those tension zones where less sedentary populations are being moved in on by daughter groups from more sedentary populations. These are the areas where the development of greater productive means is most advantageous. . . .

If we look at the semi-arid areas where the

crops referred to (wheat and barley in the Old World; maize in the New World) were developed, it turns out that they are adjacent to areas which already supported settled (that is, sedentary) villages whose populations depended in large part upon aquatic resources. The Natufian of the Near East and the coastal settlements of Mexico and Peru are cases in point.

The explanation of the distribution noted above of the hearths of domestication of most economically significant crops within semi-arid regions lies in the nature of the seeds produced by the plants in such regions. Seeds of xerophytic plants normally have low moisture requirements and can therefore remain viable without being subject to rots which attack many other kinds of seeds. Their economic value also lies in the fact that semi-arid regions are areas with low diversity indices, which means that there will typically be many individuals of a given species within a very limited space.

We would like to note in passing that the post hoc evaluation of some "beginnings of cultivation" as "most important" (because of the ultimate economic significance of the crops produced) and the limitation of question-asking to these instances has served to prevent the recognition of the general conditions under which cultivation may have been initiated. . . .

While wheat and barley might have constituted "new influences" in Europe, it has been suggested above that cultivation arose as a response to similar pressures many times and in many places. Given the existence of the selective situation favoring food production and the response to this adaptive situation occurring in a number of places, including Europe, the adoption of easily storable high-yield crops such as wheat and barley becomes readily understandable. However, it is important not to confound the adoption of specific crops with the "spread of the village-farming way of life."

If the model presented here has value above and beyond that of a logical exercise, it must be tested by the formulation of hypotheses and the collection of data. While the outlining of a program of research is beyond the scope of and irrelevant to the aims of this paper, a few predictions follow which, if borne out by field research, would empirically validate some of our assertions.

1. Evidence for the initial domestication of plants and animals in the Near East will come from areas adjacent to those occupied by relatively sedentary forager-fishers. One such area is that adjacent to the Natufian settlements in the Jordan Valley. These settlements have yielded evidence of heavy dependence upon fish and migratory fowl and the architecture suggests a sedentary way of life. The areas just beyond these villages would have received "excess" population and would therefore have been areas of disequilibrium in which adaptive change would have been favored. Intermontane valleys and foothills which supported migratory hunters far removed from the kind of villages described above will not yield information on the earliest transition to dependence on food production, regardless of the density of wild ancestors of domesticates.

2. Evidence for independent experimentation leading to the development of agriculture as well as animal domestication will be found in European Russia and south-central Europe. We would expect the relevant areas to be adjacent to those where there was effective exploitation of anadromous fish and migratory fowl. Such areas appear to be the rivers flowing into the Black Sea.

3. As further research is carried out in Europe, Asia, and the New World, there will be evidence for numerous independent innovations paralleling forms appearing in other areas. Post-Pleistocene adaptations are viewed as the result of the operation of local selective pressures, and the development of food production is one instance of such adaptations. Parallel innovations can be expected where structurally similar ecological niches were occupied, regardless of differences in the general form of the environment.

In conclusion, it is hoped that the theoretical perspective offered here will serve to generate a new series of questions, the answers to which may increase our understanding of the major cultural changes which occurred at the close of the Pleistocene.

part 10

Economic Anthropology

Primitive Money

George Dalton

In a subject where there is no agreed procedure for knocking out errors, doctrines have a long life.

Joan Robinson

From *American Anthropologist*, Vol. 67, No. 1, 1965, pp. 44–62. By permission of the author and the publisher.

Primitive money is a complicated subject for several reasons. There is not in common use a set of analytical categories designed to reveal distinguishing characteristics of markedly different systems: economies without markets and machines still tend to be viewed through the theoretical spectacles designed for Western economy. Second, francs, sterling, and dollars are only the most recent of a long series of foreign monies introduced into primitive economies. Earlier, Arabs, Portuguese, Dutch, English, and others introduced cowrie, manillas, beads, etc., with varying permeation and varying disruption of indigenous monetary systems. Only rarely do anthropologists succeed in disentangling the foreign from the indigenous in a way which reveals the nature of the old money and the consequences of the new.

Moreover, if one asks what is "primitive" about a particular money, one may come away with two answers: the money-*stuff*—woodpecker scalps, sea shells, goats, dog teeth—is primitive (i.e., different from our own); and the *uses* to which the money-stuff is sometimes put—mortuary payments, bloodwealth, bridewealth—are primitive (i.e., different from our own).

Primitive money performs some of the functions of our own money, but rarely all; the conditions under which supplies are forthcoming are usually different; primitive money is used in some ways ours is not; our money is impersonal and commercial, while primitive money frequently has pedigree and personality, sacred uses, or moral and emotional connotations. Our governmental authorities control the quantity of money, but rarely is this so in primitive economies.

Failure to understand the reasons for such differences leads to disputes about bridewealth versus brideprice, to arguments about whether cows, pig tusks, and potlatch coppers are "really" money, to the assumption that modern coinage merely "replaces" indigenous forms of money, and to disagreement of authorities over minimal definitions of money. In these disputes the characteristics of American or European money are too often used as a model.

Some of the most respected comparisons between primitive and Western money fail to go deeply enough into comparative economic and social structure. Even Malinowski and Firth do not explain that it is nationally-integrated market organization which accounts for those Western monetary traits they use as a model of "real" money: "The tokens of wealth [*vaygua:* ceremonial axe blades, necklaces of red shell discs, and arm bracelets of shells] have often been called 'money.' It is at first sight evident that 'money' in our sense cannot exist among the Trobrianders. . . . Any article which can be classed as 'money' or 'currency' must fulfill certain essential conditions; it must function as a medium of exchange and as a common measure of value, it must be the instrument of condensing wealth, the means by which value can be accumulated. Money also, as a rule, serves as the standard of deferred payments. . . . We cannot think of *vaygua* in terms of 'money'."

Firth registers his agreement: "But according to precise terminology, such objects [strings of shell discs] can hardly be correctly described as currency or money. In any economic system, however primitive, an article can only be regarded as true money when it acts as a definite and common medium of exchange, as a convenient stepping stone in obtaining one type of goods for another. Moreover in so doing it serves as a measure of values. . . . Again it is a standard of value. . . . "

Malinowski and Firth use the bundle of attributes money has in Western market economy to comprise a model of *true* money. They then judge whether or not money-like stuff in primitive economies is really money by how closely the uses of the primitive stuff resemble our own—a strange procedure for anthropologists who would never use the bundle of attributes of the Western family, religion, or political organization in such a way. Quoting from Lienhardt—". . . most anthropologists have ceased to take their bear-

ings in the study of religion from any religion practiced in their own society." And Gluckman and Cunnison write, concerning political organizations: "One important discovery made in . . . [*African Political Systems*] was that the institutions through which a society organized politically need not necessarily look like the kinds of political institutions with which we have long been familiar in the Western world, and in the great nations of Asia."

Dollars have that set of uses called medium of exchange, means of payment, standard of value, etc., precisely because our economy is commercially organized. Where economies are organized differently, non-commercial uses of monetary objects become important, and "money" takes on different characteristics. The question is not—as it is conventionally put—are shells, woodpecker scalps, cattle, goats, dog teeth, or *kula* valuables "really" "money?" It is, rather, how are the similarities and the differences between such items and dollars related to similarities and differences in socio-economic structure?

We shall show below the connections between Western money and economy, then go on to make some points about primitive money and economy, and finally will examine the case of Rossel Island money in detail.

Capitalism: Market Integration Determines All Money Uses

In the economies for which the English monetary vocabulary was created, there is one dominant transactional mode, market exchange, to which *all* money uses relate. By contrast, in many primitive economies before Western incursion, market exchange transactions are either absent (as with Nuer) or peripheral (as in the Trobriands), but non-commercial uses of money do exist. Seeing non-commercial uses of money through the blinders of commercial money causes difficulty in understanding primitive monies. We must first be made aware of the blinders.

U.S. dollars may be called general purpose money. They are a single monetary instrument to perform all the money uses. Moreover, the same dollars enter modes of transaction to be called redistribution and reciprocity, as enter into market exchange. These features of U.S. money are consequences of economy-wide market integration and require explanation in an anthropological context.

That U.S. economy is integrated by market exchange is explained by the wide range of natural resources, labor, goods, and services transacted by purchase and sale at market-determined prices, and by the extent to which people in our national economy depend for livelihood on wage, profit, interest, and rental income got from market sale. Natural resources and capital goods (land, labor, machines and buildings of all varieties), consumption goods (food, automobiles), personal and impersonal services (dentistry, electricity), are all purchasable "on the market." Goods and services which are ceremonial and religious, or which serve as prestige indicators, are purchasable in the same way and with the same money as subsistence goods. In a market-integrated economy very different items and services are directly comparable, because all are available at prices stated in the same money. The subject of price determination of products and resources under varying conditions of supply and demand (price and distribution theory) is an important field of economics because market exchange is our dominant transactional mode.

Commercial uses of money in a market-integrated national economy

Except for economic historians, most economists and all economic theory were (until recently) concerned exclusively with European and American types of economy. Economists do not find it necessary to distinguish among the transactional modes of market exchange, reciprocity, and redistribution, because market exchange is so overwhelmingly important. For the same reason economists do not find it necessary to describe at length the different uses of money in our own economy: with only a few exceptions they all express market exchange transactions.

To make this point clear I will attach to each of the money uses an adjective describing the transactional mode, thereby pointing up how they all serve commercial transactions: medium of (commercial) exchange; means of (commercial) payment; unit of (commercial) account; standard for deferred (commercial) payment.

The medium of (commercial) exchange function of money in our economy is its dominant function, and all other commercial uses of money are dependently linked—derived from—the use of dollars as media of (commercial) exchange. For example, dollars are also used as a means of (commercial) payment of debt *arising from* market transactions. It is purchase and sale of resources, goods, and services which *create* the money functions of means of (commercial) payment and standard for deferred (commercial) payment. All the commercial uses of money are consequences of market integration, simply reflecting the highly organized credit and accounting arrangements that facilitate market purchases. This is why economists in writing about our economy need not attach the qualifier "commercial" to the money uses. Indeed, we in our market-integrated national economy sometimes regard the terms "money" and "medium of exchange" as interchangeable. But for primitive communities where market transactions are absent or infrequent, it would be distorting to identify money with medium of (commercial) exchange, as Einzig warns us: "Since, however, money has also other functions and since in many instances [of money used in primitive economies] those functions are more important than that of the medium of exchange, it seems to be unjustified to use the term as a mere synonym for 'medium of exchange'."

Non-commercial uses of money

Dollars are also used as a means of non-commercial payment: traffic fines paid to local government and taxes to all levels of government. A structural characteristic of Western economy is that redistributive transactions—obligatory payments to political authority which uses the receipts to provide community services—are made with the same money used as medium of (commercial) exchange in private transactions. The consequences are important and far-reaching.

In all societies having specialized political authority, there must be some institutionalized arrangement for the governing authorities to acquire goods and services for their own maintenance and to provide social services (defense, justice) to the community. In this sense, we may regard the redistributive function (acquiring and disbursing such goods and services) as an "economic" component of political organization. Exactly how the arrangements vary for political authority to acquire and disburse goods and services is one way of differentiating between the organization of Soviet, American, and (say) Bantu economies.

In U.S. economy the government makes use of the market in the process of redistribution: medium of (commercial) exchange money earned as private income is used by households and firms as means of (redistributive) payment of politically incurred obligation (taxes). The government then buys on the market the services and products it requires—civil servants, guns, roads—to provide community services.

In our system, the same can be said for another mode of transaction, reciprocity, or gift-giving between kin and friends. The same money serves the different transactional modes: in purchasing a gift, the money paid is used as medium of (commercial) exchange; giving the gift is part of a reciprocal transaction (a material or service transfer induced by social obligation between the gift partners). If cash is given as a gift, it is means of (reciprocal) payment of the social obligation discharged by the gift-giving.

Here is yet another reason why economists in dealing with our own economy need not distinguish among transactional modes: redistribution and reciprocity make use of market exchange and make use of the same money used in market exchange. In Western economy, therefore, tax and gift transactions appear as simple variations from the private market norm—special types of expenditure or

outlay—which present no theoretical difficulties.

American reliance upon market sale for livelihood and upon the price mechanism for allocating resources to production lines does the following: it makes the medium of (commercial) exchange use of money its dominant attribute, it makes other money uses serve market transactions, and it confers that peculiar *bundle* of traits on our general purpose money which mark off dollars from nonmonetary objects. It is our market integration which makes it necessary to institutionalize all uses of money in the same money instrument. As with Malinowski and Firth, we thereby come to think of "money-ness" as this *set* of uses conferred on the single monetary object. And because ours is a market economy, we come to think of medium of (commercial) exchange as the single most important attribute of "money-ness."

Limited-purpose monies

In primitive economies—i.e., small-scale economies not integrated by market exchange—different uses of money may be institutionalized separately in different monetary objects to carry out reciprocal and redistributive transactions. These money objects used in non-commercial ways are usually distinct from any that enter market place transactions. And the items which perform non-commercial money uses need not be full-time money, so to speak; they have uses and characteristics apart from their ability to serve as a special kind of money.

In U.S. economy, objects such as jewelry, stocks, and bonds are not thought of as money because (like cattle among the Bantu) these come into existence for reasons other than their "money-ness." Each is capable of one or two money uses, but not the full range which distinguishes dollars, and particularly not the medium of (commercial) exchange use of dollars. It is worth examining these because, we shall argue, primitive monies used in reciprocal and redistributive transactions are the counterparts of these limited or special purpose monies, and not of dollars as media of (commercial) exchange; they resemble dollars only in non-commercial uses (paying taxes and fines, and gift-giving).

Dollars serve as a store of (commercial and non-commercial) value because dollars can be held idle for future use. But this is true also for jewelry, stocks and bonds, and other marketable assets. However, in U.S. economy jewelry is not a medium of (commercial) exchange because one cannot spend it directly, and it is not a means of (commercial or non-commercial) payment because it is not acceptable in payment of debt or taxes.

As a measuring device (rather than as tangible objects) dollars are used as unit of account and standard for deferred payment of debts. Now consider the accounting and payment procedures used by a baby-sitting cooperative in which a number of households club together to draw on each other for hours of baby-sitting time. Family A uses four hours of sitting time supplied by family B. Family A thereby incurs a debt of four hours it owes the co-op; family B acquires a credit of four hours that it may draw upon in future from some member of the co-op. Here, baby-sitting labor time is a unit of (reciprocal) payments—a limited purpose money in the sense that it performs two of the subsidiary uses of dollars. Other examples (trading stamps, blood banks) could be given. The point is that even where dollars perform all the money uses for all modes of transaction, there are situations in which a limited range of money uses are performed by objects not thought of as money. These limited purpose monies become important in small-scale communities without market integration and, therefore, without a general purpose money.

Control over the quantity of money;
absence of status requisites
In national market economies, governments deliberately control the quantity of general purpose money because dollars (francs, sterling) carry out market sales which the populace depends on for livelihood. Roughly speaking, if the authorities allow too much money to come into use as medium of (market) purchase, the result is inflation. If the authorities allow too little money to come into

use, the result is deflation and unemployment (a contraction in the rate of market purchasing below the full employment capacity rate of production). The need to deliberately vary the quantity of money is a direct result of economy-wide market integration.

It has often been noted that in primitive societies there is seldom any conscious control by political authority over money objects. Such is not merely a difference between primitive *monetary* systems and our own, but one that reflects differences between their *economic* systems and ours. In economies not integrated by market exchange, non-commercial monetary transactions are only occasional events (e.g., bloodwealth, bridewealth), and non-commercial money is not usually connected with production and daily livelihood. That the non-commercial money-stuff may be fixed in quantity for all time (Yap stones), or increase in quantity only through natural growth (cows, pig tusks) does not affect production and daily livelihood (as would be the case with us if dollars were fixed in quantity).

What is also true of our market economy based on contract rather than status, is that having the money price is a sufficient condition for buying most goods. Not only is Western money anonymous, so to speak, but money users are also anonymous: the market sells to whoever has the purchase price and only rarely imposes status prerequisites on the use of money as medium of (commercial) exchange. In contrast, there usually are status prerequisites in non-commercial uses of primitive money. For example, in the use of cattle as means of (reciprocal) payment of bridewealth, status requisites such as lineage, age, rank of the persons, must be complied with. The money users are not anonymous, and a special kind of limited purpose money is necessary to the transaction.

Primitive Money and
Socio-economic Organization

Einzig points out that: "The overwhelming importance of unilateral non-commercial payments in primitive life as compared with payments arising from [commercial] trade is altogether overlooked by practically all definitions [of primitive money]. It is assumed that money must be essentially commercial in character and that any object which serves the purposes of non-commercial payments may safely be disregarded even if its use is of first-rate importance in the economic, political, and social life of primitive communities."

When anthropologists employ Western monetary terms to describe uses of money-stuff in non-commercial transactions, a crucial misunderstanding may result: when cattle or seashells perform some money uses in ways unrelated to market purchase and sale, they are not media of (commercial) exchange, or means of (commercial) payment.

The uncritical use of our general purpose money as the model of true money obscures the point that special purpose monies used for non-commercial transactions express salient features of underlying socio-economic structure. When we consider money in communities not integrated by market exchange—the Nuer, the Trobriands, the Tiv—it becomes essential to distinguish among the several transactional modes and among the several money uses: *primitive money-stuff does not have that bundle of related uses which in our economy is conferred on dollars by market integration and by the use of dollars in both commercial and non-commercial transactions.* The differences between cattle-money or shell-money and dollars are traceable to the differences in the transactional modes which call forth money uses. When Malinowski says that *kula* valuables are different from Western currency, he is really pointing out that reciprocal gift-giving is different from market purchase and sale. Indeed, anthropologists use Western monetary terms ambiguously whenever they fail to distinguish between the market and the non-commercial modes of transaction. Reining, for example, states: "There seems to have been little exchange among households although iron tools and spears made from locally smelted ore had a limited application as a medium of exchange, being used primarily for marriage payments."

If Western monetary terms are to be used by anthropologists in the meanings they convey for our own economy, the unqualified phrase "medium of exchange" must mean medium of market (or commercial) exchange. Since brides are not acquired through impersonal market transactions by random buyers and sellers, the iron tools are not used as media of (market) exchange, but as media of (reciprocal) exchange: as part of a non-commercial transaction in which a man acquires a bundle of rights in a woman and her children in return for iron tools and other indemnification payments to her kin.

It seems useful to regard the bridewealth items as special purpose "money" because the iron tools and spears—or in other societies, cows or goats—are the *required* items, and because they carry out money uses which do have counterparts in our own society. Whether one calls them special purpose monies or highly ranked treasure items necessary to the transaction for which one may not substitute other items only matters when the subject of money uses in primitive compared to Western economies is raised. Then we can show that cows and armbands of shells do perform some of the uses of dollars but in non-commercial situations. The goal is always to state the role of bridewealth or kula items, or other limited purpose money, from the viewpoint of the analyst concerned with comparative economy, but without distorting the folk-meaning of the items and the transactions they enter.

Money uses in primitive and peasant economies
Because money and money uses in market-dominated economies differ sharply from money in other economies it is useful to classify economies in accordance with the importance of market exchange transactions.

Type 1: Marketless In marketless communities, land and labor are not transacted by purchase and sale but are allocated as expressions of kinship right or tribal affiliation. There are no formal market-place sites where indigenously produced items are bought and sold. These are "subsistence" economies in the sense that livelihood does not depend on

Underdeveloped communities

PRIMITIVE (OR SUBSISTENCE) ECONOMIES		PEASANT ECONOMIES
Type I	Type II	Type III
Marketless	Peripheral markets only	Market-dominated
Sonjo	Trobriand Islanders	Malay fishermen
Nuer	Tiv	Jamaica
Lele	Rossel Islanders	Haiti
Arnhemlanders		Kipsigis
Bemba		Cantel ⎫
Kwakiutl (1840)		Panajachel ⎬ Guatemala
		Kwakiutl (1890)

production for sale. The transactional modes to allocate resources and labor as well as produced items and services are reciprocity and redistribution. In marketless economies, then, transactions of labor, resources, material goods, and services are of non-commercial sorts—obligatory gifts to kin and friends, obligatory payments to chiefs and priests, bridewealth, bloodwealth, fees for entering secret societies, corvée labor, mortuary payments, etc.—which immediately marks off as different from our own any money-stuff used. Items such as cattle, goats, spears, Yap stones, and pig tusks, take on roles as special purpose money in non-commercial transactions: they become means of (reciprocal or redistributive) payment, as is the case with bloodwealth and mortuary payments; or media of (reciprocal) exchange, as is the case with bridewealth.

Type II: Peripheral markets only Everything said above about marketless economies holds true for those with only peripheral markets, with one exception: market-place sites exist in which a narrow range of produce is bought and sold, either with some money-stuff used as medium of (commercial) exchange, or via barter in the economist's sense (moneyless market exchange). We call these market exchanges "peripheral" because land and labor are not bought and sold and because most people do not get the bulk of their income from market sales. In such small-scale subsistence economies market-place

prices do not function—as they do in our national economy—as an integrative mechanism to allocate resources to production lines: labor and land use do not respond to changes in the prices of products transacted in peripheral market places. Malinowski's *gimwali* are peripheral market transactions of an occasional sort without the formal trappings found in African market places.

Type III: Market-dominated (peasant) economies Small-scale market-dominated communities share with our own nationally integrated market economy the following features: (i) a large proportion of land and labor as well as goods and services are transacted by market purchase and sale; (ii) most people depend upon market sale of labor or products for livelihood; (iii) market prices integrate production. Labor and land move into and out of different production lines in response to profit (and other income) alternatives, as indicated by market prices. In such economies, the medium of (commercial) exchange function of money is the most important; the other commercial uses of money facilitate market transactions, and the same money is used for non-commercial transactions.

Peasant economies differ from primitive (subsistence) economies in that peasant producers depend upon production for sale. However, both peasant and primitive communities differ from large-scale, developed, nationally integrated Western economies on two counts: modern machine technology is largely absent, and traditional social organization and cultural practices are largely retained.

Rossel Island Money

Rossel Island money is famous in anthropological literature because it has for so long been a puzzler. Although it was reported at an early date, and by an economist who was in the field for only two months, re-analysis in the light of points made earlier in this paper allows a different interpretation of Rossel Island money and economy.

Armstrong's theoretical presentation

Armstrong asserts that Rossel Island money is a rough equivalent of our own: that it is a medium of exchange used to purchase a wide range of goods and services, and that it is a standard of value for stating prices. He uses Western monetary and economic terms throughout to describe the Rossel system—medium of exchange, standard of value, buy, sell, price.

Armstrong's numbering system for classes of ndap shell money (1928:62)	Number of individual ndap shells in each class
22	7
21	10
20	10
19	10
18	20
17	7
16	7
15	10
14	30
13	30–40
Total in classes 13–22 ≅ 146	

The Rossel Islanders use two types of shell money, *ndap* and *nko*. Ndap money consists of individual shells (Armstrong calls them coins), each of which belongs to one of 22 named classes or denominations, which Armstrong ranks from 1-22, a higher numbered class indicating a higher valued shell.

Armstrong could not determine the number of ndap shells in each class below 13, but he guesses there are fewer than 1,000 in all, which would mean 800 or so in classes 1-12.

Armstrong's theoretical concern is with the value relationships among the ranked shells. He tells us that (as in Western economy) all goods and services on Rossel bear a money price stated as a piece (coin) of a specific class (1-22) of ndap, so that a big house costs a No. 20 ndap shell, and a pig a No. 18. But the shells are not quite like dollar bills numbered 1-22 with a No. 20 (say), bearing twice the value of a No. 10, or an item priced at No. 20 purchaseable with two shells of No. 10 variety. In Armstrong's view it is merely an aberration due to custom, and, perhaps to unsystematic thinking that the Rossel Islanders insist that something priced at No. 20 must be paid for with a No. 20 shell, rather than with lower denomination pieces adding up to 20. He sees this as an inefficiency in their system as compared to ours—in which all bills and coins are directly convertible into each other. He therefore shows that the Rossel system requires elaborate borrowing to allow a person who does not happen to own a piece of No. 20 money to acquire an item "priced" at 20, and argues that it is the borrowing system that reveals the value relationships among the ranked coins. This is a cumbersome equivalent of our own system—a model T, so to speak—which does the same job as our own media of exchange, but with more work and fuss because one cannot substitute two $10 bills for something priced at $20. Armstrong writes: ". . . the necessity for continual loans is largely the result of the peculiar nature of the system. The same 'amount' of money, where the values are simply related and 'change' can always be given, could perform the same amount of real service (i.e., effect the same number of purchases) with perhaps a tenth or less of the amount of lending necessitated by the Rossel system."

If one borrows a No. 12 for a short time, he will have to repay a No. 13; but for a longer time he will have to repay a No. 14, 15, etc. Therefore, he says, the value relationships among the denominations 1-22 conform roughly to compound interest, which shows the relationship of an initial sum lent to its repayment equivalent, depending upon the rate of interest and the time the initial sum is outstanding. Theoretically, a No. 1 shell is related to any other number, 2-22, by the length of time a No. 1 loan is outstanding before repayment must be made in any higher number.

Armstrong's analytical interpretation may be summarized: ndap shell money functions like dollars in that it is a medium of exchange, standard of value, standard for deferred payments, etc. Debts are calculated and goods and services priced in shells of stated denomination. The peculiar (different from our own) feature of the system is that the shell denominations are not freely convertible into one another, which makes necessary frequent borrowing at interest to acquire the exact denomination shell needed for a given purchase.

Contradictory evidence

There are two faults in Armstrong's analysis from which stem the subsidiary difficulties in his interpretation of the Rossel monetary system.

1. He assumes all ndap shells function as media of (commercial) exchange. He does not distinguish among modes of transaction (reciprocity, redistribution, market exchange), but regards all transactions as commercial purchases; brides cost a No. 18 shell, just as baskets cost a No. 4 shell. He writes: ". . . any commodity or service may be more or less directly priced in terms of them [ndap shells]." Armstrong never doubts that Rossel Island money is essentially like our own media of (commercial) exchange. One could sum up his ethnocentric theorizing in a syllogism: ndap shells are "money"; money is a commercial instrument; therefore Rossel Island is a market economy.

2. This market preconception leads him to do what the Rossel Islanders do *not* do: to number the ndap classes 1-22. By so doing he can assume that convertibility via borrowing

and repayment is practiced throughout the *entire* range, so that one could start by lending a No. 1 shell, and by continual loans at interest, wind up eventually with a No. 22 shell. For example, "Any [ndap shell] value can thus be regarded as any lower value plus compound interest for the number of time units equal to the number of values by which the two are separated, so that No. 22, for example, is No. 1 plus compound interest for 21 units of time."

By ranking them 1-22 Armstrong implies that the differences between ndap shell classes are cardinal differences: that a No. 22 is 22 times more *valuable* than a No. 1, in the sense that a $20 bill is 20 times more valuable than a $1 bill. There are no such cardinal differences among ndap shells. To number them 1-22 is to give a false impression of similarity between ndap shell classes and Western money denominations and a false impression about the commensurability or the "purchasing power" relationship between lower and higher numbered ndap shells.

The characteristics of monetary transactions on Rossel that lead us to doubt Armstrong's interpretation may be set out with the following provison kept in mind: Rossel Island economy is not integrated by market exchange; ndap shells (except for the lowest few classes) are not media of (commercial) exchange; and convertibility throughout the entire range could not be practiced.

There are (on the basis of Armstrong's own data) at least three groups of ndap shells, the shells in each group being necessary for a different range of transactions, and convertibility via borrowing and repayment being possible *within* the lowest two groups, but not *within* the highest group, and not between groups.

The shells Armstrong classes 1-8 or 9 are the only ones capable of increase in quantity. The individual shells in each of these classes do not bear separate names, and some of them, at least, enter low echelon transactions, casual market exchange between individuals. In one of the rare descriptions of how shells below class No. 18 are actually used, Armstrong tells us that one may buy a basket, a lime stick, or a lime pot with a No. 4 shell. However, the question, "what goods and services will *each* shell class 1, 2, 3, . . . 22 'buy,' or what transactions does each enter?" is not answered except for ndap shells Nos. 4, 18, 20, and 21. What is clear, however, is that shell classes 18-22 are used for a very special range of important transactions which mark them off sharply from lower echelon shells, and that shells below No. 18 are not convertible into shells 18-22 by borrowing and repayment. One cannot start with a No. 1 or 17, and by lending, work it up to a No. 18-22.

Armstrong writes: "Nos. 18-22 seem to be in a somewhat different position from the lower values and one would imagine that they are not related to each other and the lower values in the precise manner set out in generalized form above [i.e., according to the compound interest formula linking the entire series, 1-22]." Convertibility via borrowing and repaying a higher class shell most certainly breaks down between Nos. 17 and 18. I suspect but cannot so readily document from the data that it does so, between Nos. 10 and 11 as well. If such is the case, convertibility is possible among Nos. 1-10, and among Nos. 11-17, but not between the two sets, and not among Nos. 18-22. It is very clear that the entire series is not linked because the uses to which shells 18-22 are put are of an entirely different order from the uses of lower shells. "As a matter of fact, a peculiarity enters as soon as we reach No. 18, which is not, as a rule [when borrowed] repaid by a coin of higher value."

Nos. 18-22 (of which there are fewer than 60 shells in all), are obviously treasure items like especially venerated kula bracelets and potlatch coppers, items with individual names and histories, which must be used to validate important social events and transactions in the same sense that bridewealth items validate a marriage. The folk-view toward these shells helps to explain their role as limited purpose money in reciprocal and redistributive transactions. "Nos. 18-22 are

peculiar in one other respect. They have a certain sacred character. No. 18, as it passes from person to person, is handled with great apparent reverence, and a crouching attitude is maintained. Nos. 19 to 22 are proportionately more sacred, are almost always kept enclosed, and are not supposed to see the light of day, and particularly the sun . . . I am inclined to think that there may be a real gap [in sacredness and prestige] . . . between Nos. 17 and 18 . . . [No. 22 shells] are said to be inherited in the male line and to be owned by the most powerful chiefs on the island."

To have regarded Nos. 18-22 as especially valuable media of (commercial) exchange—high denomination bills—with which to buy especially high-priced merchandise, is the most telling error Armstrong makes. Nos. 18-22 cannot be acquired by any amount of lower class shells, and there is no way of gauging how many times more valuable a No. 18 is compared to a No. 6 because they enter entirely different transactions.

Without exception, Nos. 18-22 enter noncommercial transactions exclusively: they are used as means of (reciprocal or redistributive) payment or exchange in transactions induced by social obligation. Payments of a No. 18 are a necessary part of ordinary bridewealth, as well as necessary payment for shared wives, and for sponsoring a pig or dog feast, or a feast initiating the use of a special kind of canoe. No. 20 is a necessary indemnity payment to the relatives of a man ritually murdered and eaten, a transaction which is part of mortuary rites for the death of a chief. Moreover, there is a connection between shells 18-22 and lineage affiliation which Armstrong notes but makes nothing of. ". . . Nos. 18 to 22 are regarded as property peculiar to chiefs, though continually lent by the latter to their subjects."

The implication throughout is that there exists (as with us) an impersonal money market in which anyone may borrow from anyone else at the going interest rate. This is doubtful. Unfortunately, Armstrong is silent on the question, "who may borrow from whom, and with what penalties for failure to repay?"

As with special purpose money for non-commercial transactions elsewhere, there are status requisites involved in the acquisition and use of the high echelon shells on Rossel. Just as marriage is not a market purchase of a wife by anyone who acquires a No. 18 ndap, but rather a reciprocal transaction between two lineage groups (the ndap payment being one of the several necessary conditions within the social situation), so too with pig feasts on Rossel. Only persons of correct status may sponsor the feast and pay the ndap shell. In this case Armstrong notes that social requisites determine who may use upper ndap shells, but he does not see this as a symptomatic difference between Rossel and Western money, i.e., between non-commercial means of (redistributive) payment, and our Western media of impersonal (commercial) exchange. What Armstrong says of pig feasts is equally true of marriage, and all the other *social events* which require payment of high echelon ndap shells:

> There are . . . complex social factors determining who shall have a pig to sell, [sic] and who shall be in a position to buy, [sic] and the buying and selling is not a simple economic occurrence, but a much more significant and complex social occurrence. We must suppose a complexity of social facts, which I am not in a position to define, that determine most of the general relations of a particular pig feast. . . . A particular individual provides a particular ndap. . . . A certain readjustment of social relations thus results from the holding of the feast . . . though we abandon the view that the monetary operations at a feast of this nature are to be regarded merely as a collective buying from a collective seller, it still remains that this is a useful way of describing these operations.

It is about as useful to describe a pig feast on Rossel as buying a pig with a No. 18 ndap as it is to describe marriage in America as buying a wife with a wedding ring. To describe the pig feast as a market purchase one must ignore the social requirements of the transaction and the folk-view of the event, both of which differentiate this redistributive transaction from market exchange. Armstrong is forced to use market terms, purchase and sale, to describe pig feasts and bridewealth, because he regards ndap shells as media of (commercial) exchange in a market system.

One bizarre feature of the Rossel system, that a transaction requires a single shell of a specifically named class, and neither a shell from a higher class nor several from lower classes would do, may be examined in the light of what has been said above. "A man may have to borrow, even though he has money of a higher value in his possession than he requires at the moment. He may have Nos. 11 and 13, but not a No. 12 which he requires at the moment. He cannot get change as a rule, for No. 13 is not a simple product of any lower value."

The higher values have nothing to do with commercial purchase and sale. One could not use five petty shells, like a No. 4 (which buys a pot), to perform a transaction such as bloodwealth (which requires that special treasure Armstrong numbers 20), for much the same reasons that in the Trobriands, one cannot "buy" a renowned kula valuable with the pots bought from the hawkers in a gimwali.

One final point. In comparing primitive money with our own, it is important that the writer describe the frequency of different kinds of monetary transactions. Only so can one gauge what role, if any, the money item(s) play in the production system. Armstrong concerns himself with social and ritual events—marriage, death, redistributive feasts, fines—and says almost nothing about production, subsistence goods, natural resource and labor transactions, and all the other ordinary concerns of money and pricing in our own economy. That he nevertheless asserts that Rossel money is much like our own, should make one wary. Einzig is properly suspicious: "It is a pity that there is not enough evidence to show to what extent, if at all, *ndap* and *nko* are used as a medium of exchange in everyday transactions, apart from the purchase [sic] of pigs."

If all the ndap shell transactions which Armstrong describes were abolished, subsistence livelihood of Rossel Islanders would remain unimpaired. It is a pity he did not hit upon that distinction which is useful to analogize economies not integrated by market exchange. DuBois writes concerning this: ". . . I should like to make a distinction between subsistence and prestige economy. By subsistence economy is meant the exploitation of the . . . natural resources available to any industrious individual. By prestige economy on the other hand, is meant a series of social prerogatives and status values. They include a large range of phenomena from wives to formulae for supernatural compulsion."

The upper values of ndap shells (and probably the middle values as well—Armstrong is silent here)—enter prestige spheres in noncommercial uses. From the Westener's viewpoint these transactions are outside the production system and subsistence livelihood. Despite Armstrong's assertion to the contrary, there is no evidence that one could opt out of the social and ritual games (through which upper ndap shells are paid and received) by converting upper shells into land, labor, or products, except perhaps as occasional events in emergency situations.

Rossel Island money: a case of red herrings
"The study of economics in simple communities should properly speaking be a job for economists. But so far few economists have tackled it, and most of the investigation has perforce been done by anthropologists."

All social scientists are either Sherlock or Mycroft Holmes. Anthropologists are Sherlock: they go to the scene, observe minutely, gather their threads of evidence from what they observe, and—like Sherlock—sometimes reach Paddington before reaching conclusions. Economic theorists are Mycroft: they do not go to the scene to observe minutely. They have no equivalent to field work because economists are not concerned with social organization or human behavior, but rather with the behavior of prices, income determinants, capital-output ratios, and other impersonal matters relating to the performance of nationally-integrated, industralized, market economies (for which fieldwork is unnecessary). Institutional matters, personal

roles, and the social implications of economic organization have long since been consigned to the limbo of sociology. Neither the problems of interest nor the methods of analysis are the same in economics and economic anthropology.

Armstrong is an economist who played at anthropology. His mistake was to bring Mycroft's tools to Sherlock's subject (and without realizing that he was doing so). The result—to mix my metaphors—was to create a sort of Piltdown Economic Man, Melanesians with monetary denominations which fit the formula for compound interest. Armstrong's pioneer work is not a hoax, but a red herring; and the lesson to be learned is not analytical—what primitive money is all about—but methodological: how not to do anthropology.

Conclusions

The distinctions spelled out in this paper may be used to answer questions of interest to economic anthropology, comparative economy, and economic development.

1. Anthropologists do not hesitate to contrive special terms for special actions and institutions when to use terms from their own society would be misleading. They do not talk about *the* family, but about nuclear, extended, and matrilineal families. The same should be done with economic matters.

Those aspects of primitive economy which are unrelated to market exchange can only be understood by employing socio-economic terms: ceremonial-prestige and subsistence goods; reciprocity and redistribution; spheres and conversions; limited purpose money. Such terms contain a social dimension and so allow us to relate economic matters to social organization, and to express the folk-view toward the items, services, persons, and situations involved. The economist dealing with monetary transactions in Western economy need not concern himself with personal roles and social situations because of the peculiarly impersonal nature of market exchange. The anthropologist dealing with marketless transactions cannot ignore personal roles and social situations and still make sense of what transpires.

Kula armbands, potlatch coppers, cows, pig tusks, Yap stones, etc., are variously described as money of renown, treasure items, wealth, valuables, and heirlooms. Malinowski says kula valuables are regarded like crown jewels or sports trophies in Western societies. Writers on East Africa say that cows are regarded like revered pets. Such treasures can take on special roles as non-commercial money: their acquisition and disposition are carefully structured and regarded as extremely important events; they change hands in specified ways, in transactions which have strong moral implications. Often they are used to create social relationships (marriage; entrance into secret societies), prevent a break in social relationships (bloodwealth, mortuary payments), or to keep or elevate one's special position (pot-latch). Their "money-ness" consists in their being required means of (reciprocal or redistributive) payment.

2. Subsidiary characteristics of Western money-stuff, such as portability and divisibility, are actually requirements for media of (commercial) exchange. In peasant and national economies integrated by market exchange, purchases of goods and services are a daily occurrence, and so money must be portable; market purchases are carried out at widely varying price, so the medium of (commercial) exchange must be finely divisible.

Yap stones, cows, kula armbands, and Rossel Island shells are not divisible, and some are not conveniently portable. But neither are they media of (commercial) exchange; they are not used for daily purchases of varying amount. Their use as non-commercial money makes their lack of divisibility and portability unimportant. Here we see one way primitive money-*stuff* is related to primitive money *usage*. As means of (reciprocal or redistributive) payment used infrequently to discharge social obligations, it does not matter that the money-stuff lacks those characteristics required of a medium of (commercial) exchange.

3. Economics textbooks err in citing primitive monies *indiscriminately* as equivalents of Western media of (commercial) exchange, for the same reason that Armstrong errs in treating Rossel Island monies as a single type and as a crude equivlent of our own. By giving the impression that *all* primitive monies perform the same primary function as dollars, they quite wrongly imply that all primitive economies may be regarded as crude market systems.

Economists are correct in saying that some unusual money-stuffs have functioned as media of (commercial) exchange. They have in mind situations such Colonial America where "primitive money-stuffs" (commodity money such as tobacco and cotton) functioned just as dollars do today, or Prisoner of War camps where cigarettes (primitive money-stuff) became used as media of (market) exchange.

But to conclude that because some primitive money-*stuffs* do perform the primary function of dollars, *all* primitive monies may be regarded as crude media of (commercial) exchange, is an important error. As we have seen in the case of Rossel Island, this market preconception impedes our understanding of marketless economies and those with peripheral markets only. It implies that market exchange is the only transactional mode ever to exist, and so—as economists do in our own economy—one may ignore the social situations in which monetary transactions occur and the folk-view toward the persons, events, and items involved. It is precisely this sort of ethnocentrism that regards all "exchanges" as commercial transactions, and equates all money payments with market purchases, with the result that brides and murder are said to have a price, just as pots and yams in the market place have a price.

4. A situation of special interest is one where cowrie (in times past), or sterling or francs (in recent times), acquired initially in external market exchange, became used in-

ternally for commercial and non-commercial transactions. Such cases of monetary incursion deserve examination for reasons which are of interest to students of community economic development as well as economic anthropology.

Cowrie inflation, wampum inflation, and bridewealth inflation are related cases. Cowrie and wampum became used as media of (commercial) exchange through external trade with Europeans in situations where the quantity of money-stuff was uncontrolled and increased rapidly in supply. Similarly, where bridewealth comes to be paid in sterling or francs, the sum increases when earnings of Western money through market sale of labor or produce increase faster than the number of marriageable females. What might be called "potlatch copper inflation" is a similar case: when the Kwakiutl became increasingly enmeshed in Canadian market economy, they used their market earnings to increase the stakes in the potlatch. The limited number of coppers (like the limited number of brides, elsewhere) fetched a larger bundle of market-purchased goods. All such cases may be described as "upward conversions": newly expanded market earnings are used to acquire treasure items and brides which indigenously were not transacted through market exchange.

Western money does much more than merely displace primitive monies where the latter were not media of (commercial) exchange indigenously. It allows non-commercial payments and obligations of traditional sorts (such as bridewealth) to be discharged with general purpose money earned in market transactions—instead of with traditional items of special-purpose money. In economies which formerly were marketless or had peripheral markets only, a structural link—Western cash—now exists between spheres of exchange which formerly were separate. Western money therefore has inevitable repercussions on traditional social organization and cultural practices. In brief, market earnings can now be used for reciprocal and redistributive payments (just as in Western economy goods purchased on the market

enter gift-giving, and money earnings are used to pay taxes and tithes).

5. One source of ambiguity in the literature is the quest for a single, all-purpose definition of money that would include our own kind (and presumably Soviet money), as well as the welter of types in use in primitive and peasant economies widely differing in organization. Einzig writes: "It must be the ultimate goal of the study of primitive money to try to find the common denominator—in so far as it exists—in terms of which both the well-established rules of modern money and the apparently conflicting conclusions on primitive money can be explained."

To concentrate attention on what all monies have in common is to discard those clues—how monies differ—which are surface expressions of different social and economic organization. Money is not an isolated case. Much the same can be said for external trade and market places, which (like money) also are made use of in economies differing markedly in organization (say, the U. S., the Soviet, and the Tiv economies). Money traits differ where socio-economic organization differs. To concentrate attention on money traits independently of underlying organization leads writers to use the traits of Western money as a model of the real thing (while ignoring the structure of Western economy which accounts for the money traits). Then any primitive money which does not have all the traits of the Western model money is simply ruled out by definition—it is not money. This does not get us very far towards understanding primitive and peasant economies.

Two distinctions which allow us to contrast primitive and Western money are the distinctions between commercial and non-commercial uses of money, and between marketless economies, those with peripheral markets only, and market-integrated economies. In sum, money has no definable essence apart from the uses money objects serve, and these depend upon the transactional modes that characterize each economy: as tangible item as well as abstract measure, "money is what money does."

The Organization of Economic Life

Manning Nash

From *Horizons in Anthropology,* Sol Tax (ed.). Aldine Publishing Company, 1964, pp. 171–180. Copyright © 1964, Aldine Publishing Company. By permission of the author, and the publisher and copyright holder.

The Economic Life of man shows a great variety over time and space. In the New Hebrides islands, the main economic concern is the accumulation of pigs. Men raise pigs, exchange pigs, lend out pigs at interest, and finally in a large ceremonial feast destroy the pig holdings of a life time. Among the Bushmen of the Kalahari desert there is no private property in productive goods, and whatever the hunting band manages to kill is shared out among the members of the group. In the Melanesian islands every gardener brings some of the yams from his plot to the chief's house. There the pile of yams grows and grows, and eventually rots, to the greater glory of the tribe. The Indians of Guatemala and Mexico live in communities each with its own economic specialty. One group produces pottery, another blankets, another lumber and wood, and the next exports its surplus maize. These communities are tied together in a complex system of markets and exchange.

How are these economic activities to be interpreted and explained? What body of ideas can make sense of the gift-giving of the Plains Indians, the personalized markets of Haiti, the elaborate ceremonial of exchange in the Solomon islands? Less than half a century ago the differences among economic systems were explained by the hypothesis of social evolution. Different economic systems were assigned to levels or states of the evolution of human society and culture. It was assumed that there had been an evolution from simple hunting bands, with communal property rules, to villages with settled agriculture and clan or family property, and that was followed by a stage of political units with advanced technology and private or state property. This view of economic evolution has not fared well in the face of modern field research. Two chief things have made this mode of explanation lose its force. First, the rising tide of field investigation of economic systems revealed a whole host of economic arrangements which this crude classification by stages could not contain. And second, the idea of stages of evolution shed very little light on the actual processes of economic change. A new model of the variables to explain economic systems and their changes over time is now being fashioned. This model rests on about four decades of accumulated information, and on methods and theories developed in the act of gathering and interpreting that data.

Method in studying economic systems is basically the same as in the rest of social and cultural anthropology. Method is a device to study social regularities, and to give meaning to those regularities. In the study of nonmonetary, or partially monetized economies, getting the basic facts is often a test of the observer's ingenuity. Many new ways of getting measurable or nearly measured data have been invented, and recent research is marked by an emphasis on quantities or relative magnitudes of economic activities.

The distinguishing features of peasant and primitive economic systems fall along four axes. The first is *technological complexity and the division of labor.* These are relatively simple societies, technologically. A simple technology means that the number of different tasks involved in any productive act are few. Usually it is the skill of a single or a few producers which carries production from beginning to end. Many primitive and peasant technologies are ingenious, marvelously fitted to a particular environment, requiring high levels of skill and performance, but still very simple. The Bemba of Rhodesia [see Selection 26, p. 190] wrest a living from poor soil with uncertain water supply by an intricate method of cultivation. With good rains and luck they harvest their crop of finger millet. The system is one of balance in a precarious ecological niche, but the task structure is simple, and the tools involved require only human energy to operate. The specialized operations involved are not the kind which make an interrelated web of occupations. Men do most of the work among the Bemba, and one man is virtually as good as another in his agricultural skills. The division of labor follows the natural axes of sex and age. An occupational list in a peasant or primitive society is not a long one. Persons tend to learn their productive skills in the ordinary business of growing up, and within age and sex categories there is high interchangeability among productive workers. Work and tasks are apportioned to the appropriate persons, without much regard to differences in skill or productivity. The technology also sets the limits of the size of the combined working parties. Except at peak periods—planting or harvesting in agricultural communities, an organized hunt at the height of the animal running season—large working parties are not found. Effort and work are closely tied to a pattern fitted to the annual and ceremonial cycle, not to the continuous demands of a highly organized economy with a wide social division of labor.

The second feature of peasant and primitive economy is the *structure and membership of productive units.* The unit of production, the social organization carrying out the making of goods, is dependent on, and derived from, other forms of social life. Peasant and primitive societies do not have organizations whose only tasks are those of production, and there are no durable social units based solely on productive activities. The bonds of kinship which structure families, clans, and kindreds are often the bonds which organize economic activities. Territorial bonds may serve to create local producing organizations. And the political structure, especially in societies with hereditary nobilities, is often used as a mechanism for forming productive units. This dependence of economic units on prior kinds of social relations has a typical series of consequences. Productive units tend to be multipurposed. Their economic activities are only one aspect of the thing they do. The economic aspect of a family, a local group, or a compound composed of patrons and clients, is just one area where the maintenance needs of the group are being met. Therefore, in these societies there tend to be many productive units, similarly structured, all doing the same sort of work. These productive units are limited in sorts of personnel they are able to recruit, the capital they are able to command, and the ways in which they may distribute their product. There does not exist a labor market, nor a capital market, nor a system of distribution to factors of production. A striking example of productive units based on relations derived from the organization of social groups only partially oriented to economic activity is the Indian pottery-making community in south-eastern Mexico. This community is composed of 278 households. Each household is engaged in the production of pottery for sale, with virtually the same technology. Every household looks like every other in its productive organization. Or again, from Mexico, among the people of Tepoztlan many make their living by the sale of services at a wage. Yet people must be sought out for employment, and hiring a fellow member of the community is a delicate social job. The transaction cannot appear as a strictly economic one.

The third distinguishing feature of peasant and primitive economies is *the systems and media of exchange.* In an economy with a simple technology, productive units which are multipurposed and derived from other forms of social organization, and with a division of labor based chiefly on sex and age, a close calculation of the costs of doing one thing or another is often impossible, or merely irrelevant. The advantages of a change in the use of time, resources, and personnel are arrived at through the logic of social structure, through a calculus of relative values, not in terms of the increase of a single magnitude such as productivity. This inability to estimate closely the costs and benefits of economic activity is aggravated by the absence of money as *the* medium of exchange. Most of the world now has some familiarity with the use of money. In fact, some societies developed full, all purpose money prior to contact with the industrial and commercial West. And many societies have standards of exchange like the Polynesian shell currencies, or the tusked pigs of Melanesia, the salt currency of the horn of Africa, or the cocoa beans of the Aztecs. But this is quasi-money, or special purpose money; it is merely the standard with the widest sphere of exchange. Special purpose money is confined to a particular circuit of exchange, and the circuits of exchange in

the economy are only partially tied together. Among the Siane of New Guinea there are different kinds of exchange of goods, and each kind of goods is limited to its particular circuit. Some goods can be exchanged only for subsistence items, others only for luxury items, and others only for items which confer status and prestige. The Tiv of Nigeria have a similar multicentered exchange system with media appropriate to each sphere of exchange. Food is exchanged for food, and can be exchanged for brass rods; brass rods exchange for the highest valued goods, women and slaves. And a reverse or downward movement of exchange items was severely resisted and considered illogical and unfortunate among the Tiv.

The media of exchange and the circuits of exchange are set into various kinds of systems of exchange. The most common systems of exchange are markets, redistributive system, reciprocal exchange, and mobilization exchange. The market system is widespread among peasants, and in Meso-America tends to be free, open, and self-regulating. In Haiti the market is competitive, free, and open, but special bonds of personal attachment grow up between some buyers and some sellers which cut down some of the risk and uncertainty involved in small peasant trading. Rotating market centers, with a central market and several subsidiary markets, are a fairly common feature in Burma among the Shans, in several parts of Africa, north and south of the Sahara, and in many places in the Near and Far East. These market systems usually operate without the presence of firms, and lack investment in expensive facilities of exchange, including the spread of information. The single complex of markets, firms, capital investments, entrepreneurs, deliberate technical investment, and property rules to facilitate accumulation and exchange is apparently a historical precipitate peculiar to the West. In the ethnographic record it does not appear as a necessary bundle or sequence of events.

Reciprocity of exchanges is exemplified by the practices of gift-giving or kula exchange of the Solomon Islands and tends to lack much bargaining between, to rest on fixed sets of trading partners, and to occur between equivalent units of the social structure. Thus clans exchange with clans; barrios or wards with wards; households with households; tribes with tribes; or communities with communities. The reciprocal exchange is for near equivalences in goods and services. The rates of exchange tend to be fixed. Redistributive trade takes place in societies with some systems of social stratification, but not organized for market exchange. An African paramount chief may collect tribute in the form of goods and redistribute it down the social hierarchy through his clients and kinsmen. Or administered trade at fixed prices, with a political center exchanging with its peripheries is another common example. Redistributive exchange keeps a political and status system operating without great gaps in wealth between the different classes of status groups. A system of mobilization for exchange collects goods and services into the hands of an elite for the broad political aims of the society. The irrigation empires of the early civilizations apparently had these sorts of exchange systems, and some of the new nations of Asia and Africa have systems like this in conjunction with some aspects of market, redistribution, and reciprocal exchange.

The fourth dimension of variation in economic systems is in *the control of wealth and capital.* Generally, investment takes the form of using resources and services to buttress or expand existing sets of social relations. The chief capital goods in peasant and primitive societies are land and men. Tools, machines, terraces, livestock, and other improvements in productive resources are controlled in a manner derived from the conventions of control and allocation of land and human beings. Land tenure is an expression of the social structure of a peasant and primitive society, and the allocation of land results from the operation of the system of kinship, inheritance, and marriage, rather than through contracts or transactions between economic units. Even in those societies where corporate kin groups like clans do not exist as

landholding bodies, special devices like the establishment of titles, or kindred-based landholding corporations may be invented as on Truk. Manpower, like land, is also organized to flow in terms of given social forms, not to abstract best uses.

For peasants and primitives to maintain their societies, capital, or property rules, or economic chance may not be permitted to work in ways disruptive of the values and norms of the society. A fairly common device for insuring that accumulated resources are used for social ends is the leveling mechanism. The leveling mechanism is a means of forcing the expenditure of accumulated resources or capital in ways that are not necessarily economic or productive. Leveling mechanisms may take the form of forced loans to relatives or coresidents; a large feast following economic success; a rivalry of expenditure like the potlatch of the Northwest Coast Indians in which large amounts of valuable goods were destroyed; or the ritual levies consequent on office holding in civil and religious hierarchies as in Meso-America; or the give-aways of horses and goods of the Plains Indian. At any rate most peasant and primitive societies have a way of scrambling wealth to inhibit reinvestment in technical advance, and this prevents crystallization of class lines on an economic base.

This schematic presentation of the major features of peasant and primitive economies serves to place them in a comparative series of economic organizations and to extend the range of social contexts for economic analysis. But charting the range and diversity of economic systems is only a part of the task of anthropology. How economic systems relate to the total social system is a question of major theoretical importance. Economic action is only a part of the system of social action. It is tied to the whole social system in three ways: First by normative integration, second by functional interdependence, and third by causal interaction. The ends sought in the economic sphere must be consonant, or complementary, with goals in other spheres. Economic activity derives its meaning from the general values of the society, and people engage in economic activity for rewards often extrinsic to the economy itself. From this point of view, there are no economic motives, but only motives appropriate to the economic sphere. In peasant and primitive societies the norms and values used to define a resource, a commodity, control over goods and services, the distributive process, and standards of economic behavior, are the norms governing most social interaction. The economy is not so different from the rest of society so that one set of values holds there, and other values hold in other contexts. The economic system does not exhibit an ethic counterposed to the regnant value system.

The functional interdependence of economy and society stems from the fact that the same persons are actors in the economic, the kinship, the political, and the religious spheres. The role of father must fit in some way with the role of farmer, and these must fit with the role of believer in the ancestor cult, and these must fit with authority position in the lineage, to take an example from the Tallensi. The interdependence of parts of society means that there are limits to the sorts of economies and societies that may coexist in one time and space continuum. These limits only now are being charted. But it is plain that a system of reciprocal exchange rests on social units that are nearly equivalent in status, power, and size. The marriage and descent system of the Nayar (whose husbands were warriors who lived away from wives and where descent was matrilineal) is an instance of the functional compatibility of an occupational and status system with a marriage and descent system.

The causal interaction of economy and society turns on the pivot of the provision of facilities. For given forms of social structure a given variety and volume of goods and services are required, and if there are shifts in facilities available, there will be shifts in the rest of society. Conversely, shifts in the social structure will change the volume and variety of goods and services a society produces. The empirical way of finding these causal interactions is to study peasant and primitive societies undergoing change. The facts of

change are the only sure guides to generalizing on the sequences, forms, and processes of economic and social interaction. Much of the change in the economic life of peasants and primitives comes from the expansion and spread of the Western forms of economic activity.

The expansion of the economic frontier can be seen in places like Orissa, the hilly tribal region of India. Here economic opportunity in the wake of the spread of the money economy has allowed some castes to move quickly up the status ladder and forced some traditional high status castes downward. The economic frontier in the form of money and new opportunities tends to change the role of corporate kin groups and place more emphasis on smaller familial units, to introduce a re-evaluation of the goods of a society, and to put pressures on traditional authority systems.

The chief way that peasants and primitives get involved in the world economy is through entering a wage-labor force, or by producing something that can sell in international trade. The effects of entering a wage-labor force often start conflicts between generations, raise problems about the control of income, and sometimes depopulate the society so that its social structure collapses. A rural proletariat may replace a tribal society. Income from entrepreneurial activity by peasants poses larger problems for the social system. It may result in greater wealth differences, in modifications in the use of capital, in loosening the integration of the society, and in changing the authority patterns. The boom involved in peasant agriculture often involves a change in religious and ethical concepts, and an increase in the importance of economic activity relative to other forms of social activity.

The introduction of factories to peasant primitive societies provides, in theory, the widest possibilities for transformation. The change induced by a factory may be akin to that from the increased use of money from wage labor, or the expansion of the economic frontier, but it tends to tie the community more closely to a national and international economic network, to provide a new context for political change, to give a base for new voluntary groupings, and to exert great pressures on extended familial networks, and above all to demand a sort of flexibility and mobility of persons and institutions usually not found in traditional societies.

What the studies of economic change have taught is that modifications in economic activity set up a series of pressures and tensions in the society and culture and that there are limited possibilities for their resolution. There is no generally agreed upon sequence of change, and hardly more consensus on final forms, but the evidence seems to indicate that economic systems are among the most dynamic parts of a society, and that economic activity, in the sense of the provision of facilities for the organization of the rest of society, is one of the most pervasive and determinative aspects of social life. It sets the limits within which social structures and cultural patterns may fall.

The field of economic anthropology has mainly, thus far, worked on the description and interpretation of small-scale societies, but by principle and method it is not limited to them. It is moving into problems of economic and social change, and illuminating the relations of economy and society, and the causal interaction of economic variables and other parts of society and culture. Its greatest challenge and potential is the fashioning of a theory encompassing both economic and non-economic variables in a single explanatory system. It may then provide a framework for a truly comparative study of the form, function, and dynamics of economic systems.

The Impact of Money on an African Subsistence Economy

Paul Bohannan

From *The Journal of Economic History*, Vol. 19, No. 4, 1959, pp. 491–503. Copyright 1959, The Economic History Association. By permission of the author, and the publisher and copyright holder.

It has often be claimed that money was to be found in much of the African continent before the impact of the European world and the extension of trade made coinage general. When we examine these claims, however, they tend to evaporate or to emerge as tricks of definition. It is an astounding fact that economists have, for decades, been assigning three or four qualities to money when they discuss it with reference to our own society or to those of the medieval and modern world, yet the moment they have gone to ancient history or to the societies and economies studied by anthropologists they have sought the "real" nature of money by allowing only one of these defining characteristics to dominate their definitions.

All economists learned as students that money serves at least three purposes. It is a means of exchange, it is a mode of payment, it is a standard of value. Depending on the vintage and persuasion of the author of the book one consults, one may find another money use—storage of wealth. In newer books, money is defined as merely the means of unitizing purchasing power, yet behind that definition still lie the standard, the payment, and the exchange uses of money.

It is interesting that on the fairly rare occasions that economists discuss primitive money at all—or at least when they discuss it with any empirical referrent—they have discarded one or more of the money uses in framing their definitions. Paul Einzig, to take one example for many, first makes a plea for "elastic definitions," and goes on to point out that different economists have utilized different criteria in their definitions; he then falls into the trap he has been exposing: he excoriates Menger for utilizing only the "medium of exchange" criterion and then himself omits it, utilizing only the standard and payment criteria, thus taking sides in an argument in which there was no real issue.

The answer to these difficulties should be apparent. If we take no more than the three major money uses—payment, standard and means of exchange—we will find that in many primitive societies as well as in some of the ancient empires, one object may serve one money use while quite another object serves another money use. In order to deal with this situation, and to avoid the trap of choosing one of these uses to define "real" money, Karl Polanyi and his associates have labeled as "general purpose money" any item which serves all three of these primary money uses, while an item which serves only one or two is "special purpose money." With this distinction in mind, we can see that special purpose money was very common in pre-contact Africa, but that general purpose money was rare.

This paper is a brief analysis of the impact of general purpose money and increase in trade in an African economy which had known only local trade and had used only special purpose money.

The Tiv are a people, still largely pagan, who live in the Benue Valley in central Nigeria, among whom I had the good fortune to live and work for well over two years. They are prosperous subsistence farmers and have a highly developed indigenous market in which they exchanged their produce and handicrafts, and through which they carried on local trade. The most distinctive feature about the economy of Tiv—and it is a feature they share with many, perhaps most, of the premonetary peoples—is what can be called a multi-centric economy. Briefly, a multi-centric economy is an economy in which a society's exchangeable goods fall into two or more mutually exclusive spheres, each marked by different institutionalization and different moral values. In some multi-centric economies these spheres remain distinct, though in most there are more or less institutionalized means of converting wealth from one into wealth in another.

Indigenously there were three spheres in the multi-centric economy of the Tiv. The first of these spheres is that associated with subsistence, which the Tiv call yiagh. The commodities in it include all locally produced foodstuffs: the staple yams and cereals, plus all the condiments, vegetable side-dishes and seasonings, as well as small livestock—chickens, goats and sheep. It also includes household utensils (mortars, grindstones, calabashes, baskets and pots), some tools

(particularly those used in agriculture), and raw materials for producing any items in the category.

Within this sphere, goods are distributed either by gift giving or through marketing. Traditionally, there was no money of any sort in this sphere—all goods changed hands by barter. There was a highly developed market organization at which people exchanged their produce for their requirements, and in which today traders buy produce in cheap markets and transport it to sell in dearer markets. The morality of this sphere of the economy is the morality of the free and uncontrolled market.

The second sphere of the Tiv economy is one which is in no way associated with markets. The category of goods within this sphere is slaves, cattle, ritual "offices" purchased from the Jukun, that type of large white cloth known as tugudu, medicines and magic, and metal rods. One is still entitled to use the present tense in this case, for ideally the category still exists in spite of the fact that metal rods are today very rare, that slavery has been abolished, that European "offices" have replaced Jukun offices and cannot be bought, and that much European medicine has been accepted. Tiv still quote prices of slaves in cows and brass rods, and of cattle in brass rods and tugudu cloth. The price of magical rites, as it has been described in the literature, was in terms of tugudu cloth or brass rods (though payment might be made in other items); payment for Jukun titles was in cows and slaves, tugudu cloths and metal rods.

None of these goods ever entered the market as it was institutionalized in Tivland, even though it might be possible for an economist to find the principle of supply and demand at work in the exchanges which characterized it. The actual shifts of goods took place at ceremonies, at more or less ritualized wealth displays, and on occasions when "doctors" performed rites and prescribed medicines. Tiv refer to the items and the activities within this sphere by the word shagba, which can be roughly translated as prestige.

Within the prestige sphere there was one item which took on all of the money uses and hence can be called a general-purpose currency, though it must be remembered that it was of only a *very limited range.* Brass rods were used as means of exchange *within the sphere;* they also served as a standard of value within it (though not the only one), and as a means of payment. However, this sphere of the economy was tightly sealed off from the subsistence goods and its market. After European contact, brass rods occasionally entered the market, but they did so only as means of payment, not as medium of exchange or as standard of valuation. Because of the complex institutionalization and morality, no one ever sold a slave for food; no one, save in the depths of extremity, ever paid brass rods for domestic goods.

The supreme and unique sphere of exchangeable values for the Tiv contains a single item: rights in human beings other than slaves, particularly rights in women. Even twenty-five years after official abolition of exchange marriage, it is the category of exchange in which Tiv are emotionally most entangled. All exchanges within this category are exchanges of rights in human beings, usually dependent women and children. Its values are expressed in terms of kinship and marriage.

Tiv marriage is an extremely complex subject. Again, economists might find supply and demand principles at work, but Tiv adamantly separate marriage and market. Before the coming of the Europeans all "real" marriages were exchange marriages. In its simplest form, an exchange marriage involves two men exchanging sisters. Actually, this simple form seldom or never occurred. In order for every man to have a ward *(ingol)* to exchange for a wife, small localized agnatic lineages formed ward-sharing groups ("those who eat one Ingol"—*mbaye ingol i mom*). There was an initial "exchange"—or at least, distribution—of wards among the men of this group, so that each man became the guardian *(tien)* of one or more wards. The guardian, then, saw to the marriage of his ward, exchanging her with outsiders for another woman (her

"partner" or *ikyar*) who becomes the bride of the guardian or one of his close agnatic kinsmen, or—in some situations—becomes a ward in the ward-sharing group and is exchanged for yet another woman who becomes a wife.

Tiv are, however, extremely practical and sensible people, and they know that successful marriages cannot be made if women are not consulted and if they are not happy. Elopements occurred, and sometimes a woman in exchange was not forthcoming. Therefore, a debt existed from the ward-sharing group of the husband to that of the guardian.

These debts sometimes lagged two or even three generations behind actual exchanges. The simplest way of paying them off was for the eldest daughter of the marriage to return to the ward-sharing group of her mother, as ward, thus cancelling the debt.

Because of its many impracticalities, the system had to be buttressed in several ways in order to work: one way was a provision for "earnest" during the time of the lag, another was to recognize other types of marriage as binding to limited extents. These two elements are somewhat confused with one another, because of the fact that right up until the abolition of exchange marriage in 1927, the inclination was always to treat all non-exchange marriages as if they were "lags" in the completion of exchange marriages.

When lags in exchange occurred, they were usually filled with "earnests" of brass rods or, occasionally, it would seem, of cattle. The brass rods or cattle in such situations were *never* exchange equivalents *(she)* for the woman. The only "price" of one woman is another woman.

Although Tiv decline to grant it antiquity, another type of marriage occurred at the time Europeans first met them—it was called "accumulating a woman/wife" *(kem kwase)*. It is difficult to tell today just exactly what it consisted in, because the terminology of this union has been adapted to describe the bridewealth marriage that was declared by an administrative fiat of 1927 to be the only legal form.

Kem marriage consisted in acquisition of sexual, domestic and economic rights in a woman—but not the rights to filiate her children to the social group of the husband. Put in another way, in exchange marriage, both rights *in genetricem* (rights to filiate a woman's children) and rights *in uxorem* (sexual, domestic and economic rights in a woman) automatically were acquired by husbands and their lineages. In *kem* marriage, only rights *in uxorem* were acquired. In order to affiliate the *kem* wife's children, additional payments had to be made to the woman's guardians. These payments were for the children, not for the rights *in genetricem* in their mother, which could be acquired only by exchange of equivalent rights in another woman. *Kem* payments were paid in brass rods. However, rights in women had no equivalent of "price" in brass rods or in any other item—save, of course, identical rights in another woman. *Kem* marriage was similar to but showed important differences from bridewealth marriage as it is known in South and East Africa. There rights in women and rights in cattle form a single economic sphere, and could be exchanged directly for one another. Among Tiv, however, conveyance of rights in women necessarily involved direct exchange of another woman. The Tiv custom that approached bridewealth was not an exchange of equivalents, but payment in a medium that was specifically not equivalent.

Thus, within the sphere of exchange marriage there was no item that fulfilled any of the uses of money; when second-best types of marriage were made, payment was in an item which was specifically not used as a standard of value.

That Tiv do conceptualize exchange articles as belonging to different categories, and that they rank the categories on a moral basis, and that most but not all exchanges are limited to one sphere, gives rise to the fact that two different kinds of exchanges may be recognized: exchange of items contained within a single category, and exchanges of items belonging to different categories. For Tiv, these two different types of exchange are marked by separate and distinct moral attitudes.

To maintain this distinction between the two types of exchanges which Tiv mark by different behavior and different values, I shall use separate words. I shall call those exchanges of items within a single category "conveyances" and those exchanges of items from one category to another "conversions." Roughly, conveyances are morally neutral; conversions have a strong moral quality in their rationalization.

Exchanges within a category—particularly that of subsistence, the only one intact today—excite no moral judgments. Exchanges between categories, however, do excite a moral reaction: the man who exchanges lower category goods for higher category goods does not brag about his market luck but about his "strong heart" and his success in life. The man who exchanges high category goods for lower rationalizes his action in terms of high-valued motivation (most often the needs of his kinsmen).

The two institutions most intimately connected with conveyance are markets and marriage. Conveyance in the prestige sphere seems (to the latter-day investigator, at least) to have been less highly institutionalized. It centered on slave dealing, on curing and on the acquisition of status.

Conversion is a much more complex matter. Conversion depends on the fact that some items of every sphere could, on certain occasions, be used in exchanges in which the return was *not* considered equivalent *(ishe)*. Obviously, given the moral ranking of the spheres, such a situation leaves one party to the exchange in a good position, and the other in a bad one. Tiv says that it is "good" to trade food for brass rods, but that it is "bad" to trade brass rods for food, that it is good to trade your cows or brass rods for a wife, but very bad to trade your marriage ward for cows or brass rods.

Seen from the individual's point of view, it is profitable and possible to invest one's wealth if one converts it into a morally superior category: to convert subsistence wealth into prestige wealth and both into women is the aim of the economic endeavor of individual Tiv. To put it into economists' terms: conversion is the ultimate type of maximization.

We have already examined the marriage system by which a man could convert his brass rods to a wife: he could get a *kem* wife and *kem* her children as they were born. Her daughters, then, could be used as wards in his exchange marriages. It is the desire of every Tiv to "acquire a woman" *(ngoho kwase)* either as wife or ward in some way other than sharing in the ward-sharing group. A wife whom one acquires in any other way is not the concern of one's marriage-ward sharing group because the woman or other property exchanged for her did not belong to the marriage-ward group. The daughters of such a wife are not divided among the members of a man's marriage-ward group, but only among his sons. Such a wife is not only indicative of a man's ability and success financially and personally, but rights in her are the only form of property which is not ethically subject to the demands of his kinsmen.

Conversion from the prestige sphere to the kinship sphere was, thus, fairly common; it consisted in all the forms of marriage save exchange marriage, usually in terms of brass rods.

Conversion from the subsistence sphere to the prestige sphere was also usually in terms of metal rods. They, on occasion, entered the market place as payment. If the owner of the brass rods required an unusually large amount of staples to give a feast, making too heavy a drain on his wives' food supplies, he might buy it with brass rods.

However, brass rods could not possibly have been a general currency. They were not divisible. One could not receive "change" from a brass rod. Moreover, a single rod was worth much more than the usual market purchases for any given day of most Tiv subsistence traders. Although it might be possible to buy chickens with brass rods, one would have to have bought a very large quantity of yams to equal one rod, and to buy an item like pepper with rods would be laughable.

Brass rods, thus, overlapped from the prestige to the subsistence sphere on some occasions, but only on special occasions and for large purchases.

Not only is conversion possible, but it is encouraged—it is, in fact, the behavior which proves a man's worth. Tiv are scornful of a man who is merely rich in subsistence goods (or, today, in money). If, having adequate subsistence, he does not seek prestige in accordance with the old counters, or if he does not strive for more wives, and hence more children, the fault must be personal inadequacy. They also note that they all try to keep a man from making conversions; jealous kinsmen of a rich man will bewitch him and his people by fetishes, in order to make him expend his wealth on sacrifices to repair the fetishes, thus maintaining economic equality. However, once a conversion has been made, demands of kinsmen are not effective—at least, they take a new form.

Therefore, the man who successfully converts his wealth into higher categories is successful—he has a "ṣtrong heart." He is both feared and respected.

In this entire process, metal rods hold a pivotal position, and it is not surprising that early administrators considered them money. Originally imported from Europe, they were used as "currency" in some part of southern Nigeria in the slave trade. They are dowels about a quarter of an inch in diameter and some three feet long; they can be made into jewelry, and were used as a source of metal for castings.

Whatever their use elsewhere, brass rods in Tivland had some but not all of the attributes of money. Within the prestige sphere, they were used as a standard of equivalence, and they were a medium of exchange; they were also a mode for storage of wealth, and were used as payment. In short, brass rods were a general purpose currency *within the prestige sphere*. However, outside of the prestige sphere—markets and marriage were the most active institutions of exchange outside it—brass rods fulfilled only one of these functions of money payment. We have examined in detail the reasons why equivalency could not exist between brass rods and rights in women, between brass rods and food.

We have, thus, in Tivland, a multi-centric

economy of three spheres, and we have a sort of money which was a general purpose money within the limited range of the prestige sphere, and a special purpose money in the special transactions in which the other spheres overlapped it.

The next question is: what happened to this multi-centric economy and to the morality accompanying it when it felt the impact of the expanding European economy in the 19th and early 20th centuries, and when an all-purpose money of very much greater range was introduced?

The Western impact is not, of course, limited to economic institutions. Administrative organizations, missions and others have been as effective instruments of change as any other.

One of the most startling innovations of the British administration was a general peace. Before the arrival of the British, one did not venture far beyond the area of one's kinsmen or special friends. To do so was to court death or enslavement.

With government police systems and safety, road building was also begun. Moving about the country has been made both safe and comparatively easy. Peace and the new road network led to both increased trade and a greater number of markets.

Not only has the internal marketing system been perturbed by the introduction of alien institutions, but the economic institutions of the Tiv have in fact been put into touch with world economy. Northern Nigeria, like much of the rest of the colonial world, was originally taken over by trading companies with governing powers. The close linkage of government and trade was evident when taxation was introduced into Tivland. Tax was originally paid in produce, which was transported and sold through the Hausa traders, who were government contractors. A few years later, coinage was introduced; taxes were demanded in that medium. It became necessary for Tiv to go into trade or to make their own contract with foreign traders in order to get cash. The trading companies, which had had "canteens" on the Benue for some decades, were quick to cooperate with the government in introducing a "cash crop" which could be bought by the traders in return for cash to pay taxes, and incidentally to buy imported goods. The crop which proved best adapted for this purpose in Tivland was beniseed *(Sesamum indicum),* a crop Tiv already grew in small quantities. Acreage need only be increased and facilities for sale established.

There is still another way in which Tiv economy is linked, through the trading companies, to the economy of the outside world. Not only do the companies buy their cash crops, they also "stake" African traders with imported goods. There is, on the part both of the companies and the government, a desire to build up "native entrepreneurial classes." Imported cloth, enamelware and iron-mongery are generally sold through network of dependent African traders. Thus, African traders are linked to the companies, and hence into international trade.

Probably. no single factor has been so important, however, as the introduction of all-purpose money. Neither introduction of cash crops and taxes nor extended trading has affected the basic congruence between Tiv ideas and their institutionalization to the same extent as has money. With the introduction of money the indigenous ideas of maximization—that is, conversion of all forms of wealth into women and children—no longer leads to the result it once did.

General purpose money provides a common denominator among all the spheres, thus making the commodities within each expressible in terms of a single standard and hence immediately exchangeable. This new money is misunderstood by Tiv. They use it as a standard of value in the subsistence category, even when—as is often the case—the exchange is direct barter. They use it as a means of payment of bridewealth under the new system, but still refuse to admit that a woman has a "price" or can be valued in the same terms as food. At the same time, it has become something formerly lacking in all save the prestige sphere of Tiv economy—a means of exchange. Tiv have tried to categorize money with the other new imported goods and place them all in a fourth economic sphere, to be ranked morally below subsistence. They have, of course, not been successful in so doing.

What in fact happened was that general purpose money was introduced to Tivland, where formerly only special purpose money had been known.

It is in the nature of a general purpose money that it standardizes the exchangeability value of every item to a common scale. It is precisely this function which brass rods, a "limited-purpose money" in the old system, did not perform. As we have seen, brass rods were used as a standard in some situations of conveyance in the intermediate or "prestige" category. They were also used as a means of payment (but specifically not as a standard) in some instances of conversion.

In this situation, the early Administrative officers interpreted brass rods as "money," by which they meant a general purpose money. It became a fairly easy process, in their view, to establish by fiat an exchange rate between brass rods and a new coinage, "withdraw" the rods, and hence "replace" one currency with another. The actual effect, as we have seen, was to introduce a general purpose currency in place of a limited purpose money. Today all conversions and most conveyances are made in terms of coinage. Yet Tiv constantly express their distrust of money. This fact, and another—that a single means of exchange has entered all the economic spheres—has broken down the major distinctions among the spheres. Money has created in Tivland a unicentric economy. Not only is the money a general purpose money, but it applies to the full range of exchangeable goods.

Thus, when semi-professional traders, using money, began trading in the foodstuffs marketed by women and formerly solely the province of women, the range of the market was very greatly increased and hence the price in Tiv markets is determined by supply and demand far distant from the local producer and consumer. Tiv react to this situation by saying that foreign traders "spoil" their markets. The overlap of marketing and

men's long-distance trade in staples also results in truckload after truckload of foodstuffs exported from major Tiv markets every day they meet. Tiv say that food is less plentiful today than it was in the past, though more land is being farmed. Tiv elders deplore this situation and know what is happening, but they do not know just where to fix the blame. In attempts to do something about it, they sometimes announce that no women are to sell any food at all. But when their wives disobey them, men do not really feel that they were wrong to have done so. Tiv sometimes discriminate against non-Tiv traders in attempts to stop export of food. In their condemnation of the situation which is depriving them of their food faster than they are able to increase production, Tiv elders always curse money itself. It is money which, as the instrument for selling one's life subsistence, is responsible for the worsened situation—money and the Europeans who brought it.

Of even greater concern to Tiv is the influence money has had on marriage institutions. Today every woman's guardian, in accepting money as bridewealth, feels that he is converting down. Although attempts are made to spend money which is received in bridewealth to acquire brides for one's self and one's sons, it is in the nature of money, Tiv insist, that it is most difficult to accomplish. The good man still spends his bridewealth receipts for brides—but good men are not so numerous as would be desirable. Tiv deplore the fact that they are required to "sell" *(te)* their daughters and "buy" *(yam)* wives. There is no dignity in it since the possibility of making a bridewealth marriage into an exchange marriage has been removed.

With money, thus, the institutionalization of Tiv economy has become unicentric, even though Tiv still see it with multi-centric values. The single sphere takes many of its characteristics from the market, so that the new situation can be considered a spread of the market. But throughout these changes in institutionalization, the basic Tiv value of maximization—converting one's wealth into the highest category, women and children—has remained. And in this discrepancy between values and institutions, Tiv have come upon what is to them a paradox, for all that Westerners understand it and are familiar with it. Today it is easy to sell subsistence goods for money to buy prestige articles and women, thereby aggrandizing oneself at a rapid rate. The food so sold is exported, decreasing the amount of subsistence goods available for consumption. On the other hand, the number of women is limited. The result is that bridewealth gets higher: rights in women have entered the market, and since the supply is fixed, the price of women has become inflated.

The frame of reference given me by the organizer of this symposium asked for comments on the effects of increased monetization on trade, on the distribution of wealth and indebtedness. To sum up the situation in these terms, trade has vastly increased with the introduction of general purpose money but also with the other factors brought by a colonial form of government. At the same time, the market has expanded its range of applicability in the society. The Tiv are, indigenously, a people who valued egalitarian distribution of wealth to the extent that they believed they bewitched one another to whittle down the wealth of one man to the size of that of another. With money, the degree and extent of differentiation by wealth has greatly increased and will probably continue to increase. Finally, money has brought a new form of indebtedness—one which we know, only to well. In the indigenous system, debt took either the form of owing marriage wards and was hence congruent with the kinship system, or else took the form of decreased prestige. There was no debt in the sphere of subsistence because there was no credit there save among kinsmen and neighbors whose activities were aspects of family status, not acts of money-lenders. The introduction of general purpose money and the concomitant spread of the market has divorced debt from kinship and status and has created the notion of debt in the subsistence sphere divorced from the activities of kinsmen and neighbors.

In short, because of the spread of the market and the introduction of general purpose money, Tiv economy has become a part of the world economy. It has brought about profound changes in the institutionalization of Tiv society. Money is one of the shatteringly simplifying ideas of all time, and like any other new and compelling idea, it creates its own revolution. The monetary revolution, at least in this part of Africa, is the turn away from the multi-centric economy. Its course may be painful, but there is very little doubt about its outcome.

part 11

Applied Anthropology

The Uses of Anthropology

Sol Tax

From *Horizons in Anthropology*, Sol Tax (ed.). Aldine Publishing Company, 1964, pp. 248–257. Copyright © 1964, Aldine Publishing Company. By permission of the author, and the publisher and copyright holder.

In this series of essays, nineteen of our younger anthropologists have described some of the directions of their thought and their research. In so doing they have given us some views of man and his works, past and present. They have also given us a view of the sciences of mankind which together we call anthropology. It will be recalled that in 1859 the leading anthropologist of France, Paul Broca, called for just such a "general anthropology" to unite the several disciplines studying man. This has become now a reality, perhaps more in America than in any other land. Each of the nineteen anthropologists has described particular phenomena of biology and of culture; of archeology, linguistics, or ethnography; of politics, society, economics, religion, or the arts. All of us are specialists, but despite the diversity of our interests, we are nevertheless closely united in the science of man.

General anthropology today not only unites scholars of all of the disciplines which converge to study mankind; it also is the most world-wide of sciences, uniting scholars of mankind wherever they are. For over a century, anthropologists more than any other group of scientists have vigorously maintained personal communication, through congresses and correspondence and travel. . . . It is not surprising that we are the first to find a way to overcome the formidable political and financial barriers that isolate the pieces of a world otherwise so shrunken in size. Through the journal *Current Anthropology* we have developed a "communications coöperative" through which almost all of the anthropologists of the world ("wherever the post office reaches") are in constant contact, aware of who the others are and what they are doing.

The science of man thus marches on with new vigor. More and more scholars are trained; the methods of study improve every year; the exchange of ideas and knowledge increases rapidly; and the results of our labors accumulate at an ever increasing rate. These results—some of the newest of which have been recounted in these essays—and the interesting discoveries just beyond the horizon, are sufficient justification for anthropology. The discovery of man and culture is one of the noblest endeavors of the human spirit. But we also live in a world beset with problems; thus it is a fair question whether anthropology also has something to offer to help to solve them.

Like other scientists, we anthropologists believe that our greatest service to mankind is in pursuit of knowledge. This is why society trains us. If we stop being scientists and scholars, what are we? So for the most part we pursue scientific problems, not practical or political or social problems. . . .

The question remains, then, as to how anthropology finds its uses.

One answer to this question might be suggested by the phrase "applied anthropology." Engineering and medicine are professions which can be said to apply the knowledge gained by the physical and the biological sciences. After this pattern, some have awaited the development of a profession that would apply the findings of anthropology. Indeed, since 1941 we have had in the United States a Society for Applied Anthropology which has attempted to build such a profession. Although this society has encouraged the use of anthropological knowledge by government and private organizations, a profession of applied anthropologists has not come into being, either in the United States or elsewhere. Anthropological knowledge is used by administrators and managers with the wit to use it. If they wish professional assistance, they must turn to anthropologists. Anthropologists indeed become involved in management and administration, just as in social work, education, and public health. These anthropologists are sometimes distinguished from those who work for museums, research institutions, and universities; but in contrast to analogous medical sciences, they do not form a class of practitioners. Instead, all anthropologists conceive of themselves both as pursuing academic research and as putting their knowledge to social use. If an outsider seeks anthropological counsel, he must search out a genuine anthropologist; the anthropologist who gives him counsel will not dissociate himself from either the name of his discipline or his academic pursuits.

Anthropologists study man. Each anthropologist pursues a particular special study—this is what we mean by research—but all are actively interested in the whole study. We are highly specialized as social anthropologists, or human paleontologists, or linguists, for example, but we are equally general anthropologists. As we learn and we teach our specialties, we also learn from other specialists and we teach in a context which we share with them.

Here then we come to the second answer to the question. It is as teachers of the lessons of the whole of anthropology that we put our science to use; and we teach not only in the classroom, important as that is to most of us, but wherever we work and live. Anthropology has become for us a way of life, a set of values to pass on to whomever we touch: our parents and our children; our colleagues at work or play; our fellow citizens wherever they are. . . . The first attraction of anthropology is the very breadth of our subject matter—the study of mankind as a whole—which brings and holds us together, and gives us the special character which we then pass on. Man as an animal, as a population, as a species; man's behavior and his culture, and the behavior of his culture; the origin, characteristics, and distribution of the varieties of man, his language, social forms, ideas; man's genetics, prehistory and history, and the laws of history, which explain all of these in all time over the whole earth; comparative anatomy, personality, religion and ethics, law, sociology, and science; national characteristics, acculturation, socialization—all of these and whatever else may become relevant are parts of the grand problem which anthropologists have chosen to study.

The original anthropologists were anatomists, philologists, geographers, and antiquarians who met together in Paris, in London, in Moscow, or in New York to listen each to the others. It was their interest in the all-inclusive problem that drew them together and that made all-inclusiveness a virtue to be felt and extolled. The anatomists might come to read papers on craniometry to philologists and to students of customs, and to listen in turn to papers on chipped-stone industries, on grammar or on folklore. Those first anthropologists surely contributed not only breadth, but a great tolerance for variety in subject matter and in techniques of study. They established these as values for which anthropology ever since has tended to select.

It is not surprising that anthropology should characteristically form a society of scholars open to new techniques, tools, ideas, and men. The tools brought in range from the "law of uniformity" from geology to a Freudian model, on a Carbon-fourteen dating from chemistry. We have freely adopted, reinterpreted, and made our own whatever has appeared useful to our varied problems. People of other fields are drawn in because they are wanted and needed. But if men are not so drawn in, their ideas still are. Sometimes whole new fields of study are added, like culture and personality, but of course all that are added are new answers to the heterogeneous problems already there. Anthropology always has been as broad in conception as it is possible to be; in wandering correspondingly widely for its data and tools, it absorbs into the tradition of the discipline those new men with special ideas who accept the breadth of anthropology.

The breadth, eclecticism, and openness of boundaries of our subject matter are associated not only with an unusual tolerance for a variety of subjects and tools, but also for surprising ambiguity. It is not possible to be (as we say) "wholistic," to take into account all at once all aspects of a problem if we also require a clear structure. Given a choice between fully understanding one piece of a whole, but not in context, or only half understanding a larger whole, we generally prefer the second. This choice is related to our predilection for dealing with the real world. Unlike economists and others who deal with abstractions comfortably, we reflect our origins in natural history by feeling more comfortable the closer we are to nature, and to substantive rather than to theoretical or methodological problems.

The original interest of anthropologists in "other people" is also related to our concern with the reality of man through all time and space. Knowing mankind is to know all varieties of mankind; knowing people means seeing them as people. This is one source of our "liberal" view of other peoples and cultures. When it is recalled that the original Ethnological Society of Paris was formed by members of the Aborigines Protection Association, it is not surprising that anthropologists have generally taken the side of the oppressed. But it is not only tradition, and the circumstance of our founding, that lends us our character. Our tradition takes us out to study different peoples and cultures; though we see them in the broadest context, it is living people whom we come to know. It is because we live with them and come to know them that we learn from them. We keep our liberal tradition because we are the pupils of other peoples. Even if the "other peoples" are only archeological remains (or even not "peoples" at all, but baboons or gorillas!) our point of reference is still other living peoples and cultures, whose accomplishments give us humility and perspective and make us, too, "other" people.

It is precisely our tradition of general anthropology that makes it possible not only to use specialized knowledge, but also to recognize the relevance of new specialties. The question is not whether any piece of specialized knowledge is directly useful, but how the insights of general anthropology can be put to the service of society. Hence that second answer to the question posed: we serve by passing on to others the point of view and the understandings that we have ourselves gained. We have learned and we teach that the peoples of our species are equally human, thus equally able to achieve what is great and what is base. We have learned and we teach that the different peoples have from the very beginning of time developed particular ways and particular values; it is part of being commonly human to differ not simply as individuals, but systematically as communities of individuals. We teach our concept of culture and our tolerance of cultures. We have learned and we teach that a people values its identity, and resists changes which threaten it; that nobody but a people itself can judge what is important in its values, and what is threatening. Thus we teach the wisdom of discovering rather than assuming what other people want and fear, an undertaking the more difficult and the more important as the cultural difference is greater. These lessons we can teach in the classroom, on the lecture platform, in books, and hope that they will become part of a liberal education to be internalized by the many.

What else? When we are asked, we can go farther specifically to influence programs which deal with other peoples. Now it becomes important to distinguish among the kinds of people in a nation or in a community. We have learned that at an operating level we deal not with a culture at all but with many cultures; not even with the many cultures but rather with groups of people who are influenced not only by their cultures but by their position and by their interests as they perceive them. The programs in which we become involved concern what are now called "new nations." A new nation characteristically has an elite culturally perhaps less separated than we are from its tribes and its villagers, but with interests often opposed to theirs. Anthropologists generally see the problem from the village point of view, the administrators of programs, from that of the governing elite with whom they deal. The problem is now not one simply of teaching what we have learned; to be helpful means to become political, and at this point most scientists properly leave the task to others.

Suppose, however, that we stay with the problem: even now—at a time when there are differences of interest and perspectives to which education is not an effective answer—how can knowledge derived from the study of man be deliberately put to the service of man?

"The service of man" is a large phrase. If it could be limited to, say, the service of one's own country, the problem would be more manageable. The country—any nation—is governed by people—in specific Departments, Bureaus, Committees, and as administrators; the scientist simply places his knowledge at the service of one of these, and

his problems are resolved. He becomes a technician, an instrument. Indeed the capitals of nations are crowded with social scientists who do just this. This is not to say that they are weak, immoral, dishonorable. Often they will have personal points of view to press: recently I met a young economist working with the Alliance for Progress, in Washington, who described how the younger men in the agency were fighting to change a philosophy inherited from an older agency. They obviously were passionately working from the inside and probably effecting policy more than if they operated on the outside as independent critics. . . . The anthropologist who puts his knowledge to the service of his country need not therefore lose his integrity or his freedom of action, although he may well lose his patience. The difference between serving one's conscience and one's boss; one's boss and one's country; one's country and mankind—the difference in each case is neither clear nor absolute. It is easy to rationalize one's own behavior—whatever it may be—or to blame the next anthropologist.

It is characteristic of the anthropologist that if he does continue his work of education into what is close to the political realm, he acts as an independent agent, taking upon himself the ultimate responsibility for satisfying his conscience in terms of the obligations he feels toward his colleagues and toward his fellow men. It may be because anthropologists cannot comfortably have clients or work for others that a class of applied anthropologists does not develop. The scientist has, as Broca said, but one master, the truth as he learns it, and to teach it requires also the freedom of the academic profession.

Let us accept the independence of the anthropologist. Supposing him to be a research scientist serving only the one master and responsible only to his conscience and to his colleagues, let us give him this problem: What are the circumstances in which a community of people achieves its own goals, or is on the contrary frustrated? Assuming that there is basic agreement on what is wanted, communities of people still fall short of their goals. This happens whether the community one has in mind is a modern city unable to keep itself clean and orderly; or a nation unable to control the growth of a strangling bureaucracy; or even the faculty of a University unable to protect its academic freedom. The problem is one for the tools as well of political science, economics, and sociology; but it is the sort of general problem which anthropologists characteristically tackle, borrowing what tools we need. We would think of beginning the anthropological research in a small community of a culture different from our own, since this is our special method of objectifying the problem; but we would hope to end up with some general understanding of the processes involved. Should we succeed in learning how any community of people can better achieve its own goals, we would have put anthropology to important use.

The method of research that is suited to this problem, however, appears to violate the canon that the anthropologist should not become involved in public affairs. In the three or four cases where the problem has been successfully pursued, the anthropologists found that they had to interfere quite deliberately in social processes. To study such a problem requires helping the people of the community to discover their goals; but since there are competing goals and wants and forces in the society, this cannot be a simple educational process. (If it were so simple, there would be no problem to begin with.) So the anthropologist takes a special position in the community and becomes an actor as well as an observer. He helps people to try various ways of discovering their goals and the ways of achieving them which suit their own cultural norms and their own self-perceived interests. One well-known example of this sort of research is Allen Holmberg's work at Vicos in Peru, where the researchers from Cornell University had to lease a plantation and become the *patrón* of the serf-like Indian community in order to bring the community into a position where it could act freely for itself. The community responded remarkably; and Holmberg's experiment proved an important point not only for anthropology but also for

the people of Vicos and Peru, for all others in similar circumstances, and for the policymaking powers in the world. Similarly the University of Chicago's experiment in helping a small community of North American Indians to resolve its problems has led to understandings not only about American Indian problems in general, but about those of other population enclaves like the Maori of New Zealand or tribal peoples in India or Africa. The general lesson that they will adjust to the modern world when their identity and their own cultural values are not threatened is important because such threats may not really be necessary. The understandings gained by this method of research by the anthropologists of Cornell and Chicago could probably not have come in any other way. The results are proving themselves in an understanding of the problems of new nations, of North American cities, even of the organization of universities. Indeed, the unique community of anthropologists of the world that I mentioned as being now in existence was helped into being directly by what was learned from American Indians. The same understanding may some day help the peoples of the world to achieve the common goal of peace.

This new method of research . . . is often called "action anthropology." It does not fit the distinction frequently made between pure and applied research. It requires the intellectual and the political independence that one associates with a pure researcher; it depends upon university and foundation connections and support rather than those of a client or government. But it also requires that the anthropologist leave his ivory tower and that without losing his objectivity he enter into some world of affairs which becomes for the time being his laboratory. But since we are ethical men, and our laboratory is a community of people who are not to be sacrificed for our purposes or for science or even for some larger humanity, the anthropologist who undertakes such research is selected from those who are willing and able to take on unusual burdens and risks. Like a physician with his patients, he accepts the problems of a whole community as his own prob-

lems. Since he can never be wholly successful, he must be prepared for disappointments
and frustrations, without even the satisfaction
of blaming others besides himself. It is no
wonder that this method of research has not
become common, or indeed fully accepted as

legitimate. The stakes are high and the game
dangerous; but action anthropology is nevertheless quite in the tradition and spirit of
general anthropology, and promises to provide the best demonstration of its meaning
and its use.

selection 62

Anthropology as an Applied Science

H. G. Barnett

From *Human Organization,*
Vol. 17, No. 1, 1958, pp. 9–11.
Copyright 1958, The Society
for Applied Anthropology. By
permission of the author, and
the publisher and copyright
holder.

I

. . . A concern over the future of applied anthropology led, in 1951, to an experiment in
the use of anthropology in the administration
of the Micronesians who are under the jurisdiction of the United States. At that time
seven anthropologists held civil service positions with the governing agency, the Trust
Territory of the Pacific Islands, one anthropologist being associated with each of the six
regional divisions of the area and one with
the Headquarters Staff of the Commissioner
for the Territory. All had been employed on a
so-called job description. As it happened, this
was a very permissive professional charter
laying out broad areas of activity with respect
to research, advice, and program evaluation.
It was positively phrased and was so inclusive
in its implications that no generally understood boundary existed between the duties of
the anthropologists and other personnel concerned with the same problems. A more ob-
jectionable feature of the situation, as it was
viewed in the latter part of 1951, was the
engagement of the anthropologist in the policy-making process at both the Headquarters
and the District levels. This often produced
differences of opinion, based upon what was
considered to be good or bad for the Micronesians, with the views of the anthropologist—avowedly a specialist on human behavior—at stake.

In order to eliminate this source of confusion, as well as to lay out an area for scientific

contribution, it was decided to restrict the anthropologist's participation in decision making to the submission of data for which he could show evidence, and to relieve him of any duty requiring the implementation of a decision. He was thus to be treated as a technical specialist and not as an administrative officer. He was to accept directives and refer policy-making to his executive associates, confining his efforts to social, economic, and other analyses which would enable those officers to arrive at their decision or take into account the consequences of their past actions for future determinations.

This generalized statement of the anthropologist's role in the Trust Territory administration was ultimately particularized and a rationale given for its premises and safeguards in a memorandum issued by the Commissioner in 1952. The key assertions in this document were as follows:

1. Since anthropologists are concerned with collecting information about, and maintaining an intimate knowledge of, the indigenous cultures of the area, they should be in a position to contribute to effective administration in three principal ways:

a. Advising on the implementation of departmental, i.e., educational, economic, judicial, etc. projects and on the solution of problems arising from such implementation. . . .
b. Evaluating the success of particular departmental programs in the light of their objectives. . . .
c. Independently formulating and implementing researches of theoretical interest to the anthropological profession and/or of practical importance to the administration. . . .

2. The anthropologist has the obligation to collect, in a reliable and systematic way, information that is useful to the administrator. This obligation cannot be met adequately if he assumes or is called upon to assume, the role of an agent of control or enforcement. Apart from the question of job training, there is the important fact that the anthropologist

must maintain, insofar as possible in the eyes of the people, a neutral position with respect to administrative policy and action. Anything which tends to identify him as a government official invested with the power to impress his ideas detracts by so much from his usefulness as a source of unbiased information, because it jeopardizes confidential relationships with his informants and frequently involves him in factional struggles. . . .

3. In line with the observations contained in the last section, it is desirable that the anthropologist be accorded the freedom and the facilities to interview informants under the most favorable conditions. It is to be expected that at times information will be given him in confidence. Allowance should be made for this in local housing and office arrangements wherever possible. . . .

4. . . . It is evident that the anthropologist's familiarity with, and his acceptance by, the people [Micronesians] of his district give him knowledge that is otherwise unobtainable by outsiders. . . . From both an ethical and a practical standpoint, he is obligated to preserve confidences. . . .

II

While the announced purpose of this work plan was to promote more effective cooperation between administrators and anthropologists, its significance was more far-reaching than that. Behind it lay the conviction that anthropology is or can be an applied science. Under it lay the premise that science can demonstrate means but not ends. Supporting it was the understanding that the anthropologist must confine himself to statements of fact and probabilty, leaving to the administrator the responsibility for making policy decisions based on those facts and probabilities.

It is appreciated that these determinants of the role of anthropology in Trust Territory administration are not widely accepted as guides to action by anthropologists or other social scientists. They derive by analogy from

484

Applied Anthropology

the characteristics of the applied physical sciences. Since on that count their validity may be debatable, and since they raise questions of truth or necessity, it may be well to elaborate on them.

As to the possibility of a scientific application of anthropological knowledge, it must be admitted at once that the findings and the constructs of academic anthropology are rather sterile for this purpose. For one thing, as Gouldner has emphasized, theoretical science of any kind can rarely be translated directly into practice. At the least it must be adapted; and in many instances it must be modified to accommodate empirically derived concepts. Beyond that, applied science must develop its own insights and methods. This is especially true of applied social science, for its primary concern is with change, whereas theoretical sociology and anthropology deal with structures which are inherently static even though one is supposed to flow into or become another. Serious attention to the results of empirical studies of cultural change cannot fail to reveal that much has been learned or can be learned about dynamic regularities in human behavior. It is not too much to say that we are often in a position to predict and control such changes, granted the ordinary limitations imposed upon any applied science; namely, the demands for rigor in analysis, attention to specificity, stipulation of conditions, and conclusions stated as probabilities.

III

There is yet another reason for the valid objection that traditional anthropology offers little insight into practical problems, and it is intimately related to the first. In spite of its acknowledgments of, and gestures toward, psychology and psychiatry it does not incorporate their insights into its contributions to the study of man. It satisfies itself with abstract forms and hypostatized forces rather than with human beings and their motivations. Presumably an unapplied anthropology

can operate with this separation of man from his works; but the student of change, observing human beings reacting to the stresses of novelty, cannot long remain insensitive to its artificiality and its unproductivity. It is difficult to escape the conclusion that human behavior is a socio-psychological phenomenon to the understanding of which psychology and psychiatry have quite as much to offer as does anthropology. A conjunction of these disciplines, and others, to form a social instead of a departmental science, holds considerable promise for the future. That the effort can be significant and useful is evident from the formulations attempted by such workers as Leighton and Mead.

The anthropologist seeking to apply his knowledge must further beware of the illusion that science means certainty. Modern science does not state its propositions as absolutes. All generalizations and the predictions based upon them are conditional and probability statements. It is true that the most assured social scientist is an amateur in forecasting and control as compared with the laboratory physicist or the engineer. He has much more in common with the meteorologist, who must take daily and hourly readings and even then refuse to forecast the weather for point X at time Y except within wide limits and when subject to stipulated conditions.

The course of human affairs runs no more smoothly than does the weather, but social scientists know more about its turbulences and their causes than most people are willing to grant. There seems to be no reason for assuming that a human being is more difficult to understand or control than is an atom. In all science, including that of things social, it is the prediction of causes, not effects, that is risky. Under natural conditions—that is, conditions which are not externally manipulated—the conjunction of events that is necessary and sufficient to produce another event has itself such a complex of antecedents that it is rarely possible to do more than to say that it is likely to occur. For this reason, in anthropology as in physics, a regularity, hence a prediction, is properly phrased in the conditional tense: if A happens, then B is likely to follow.

Anthropological forecasting in the Trust Territory was not pretentious and it was not spectacular. It was undertaken with hesitation and with full realization of its fallibility, but in the conviction that any rational guide to procedure is better than one based on preconception, ignorance, or dedication. It was replete with qualifications: a particular sequence *could* occur or *might* occur; it is more likely or less likely, possible, or expectable. The reasoning which produced such projections rested on analogy with what is known to have occurred elsewhere or at another time among the same people under comparable conditions. Sometimes the result was nothing more than an objectively organized compilation of common sense; but even this can be valuable in an emotionally charged atmosphere.

Scientific activity, like any other, is governed by a set of values. In himself, the scientist prizes open-mindedness, caution, and detachment. In his work he strives for rigor, evidence, thoroughness, and proof. Whether he is right is less important than whether his methodology is appropriate to its purposes; that is, whether it answers the questions asked in ways which can be verified by others. Adherence to this set of values is the result of a choice—opposed, for example, to reliance upon answers by doctrine or intuition—and it is a preference which cannot be supported by employment of scientific methods. It is true that values can be studied scientifically; so can science itself. In any case, though, the method operates under the dictates of its supraordinate value system representing ends which may be accepted or rejected—by appeal to other values—but cannot be shown to be true or false.

IV

Just as science cannot turn upon itself and validate its goals, neither can it justify other goals or procedures except by granting the values which dictate them. It can grade, rate, and evaluate alternatives and preferences, granting the ends they seek as givens; but it cannot evaluate those ends except by reference to other ends accepted as givens. In short, science can deal with means and not ends, but neither ends nor means are absolutes. What is an end in one value framework, may become a means or an instrument in another. There are scientific means to save human lives, but no scientific justification for them—unless we can demonstrate that they are means to some other granted end, such as happiness, which may in its turn be demonstrated to be a means to social solidarity or some other unquestioned value, and so on indefinitely. The suitability of means to relative ends can therefore be demonstrated. So can the wisdom of a choice between alternative means; but again, only under the command of a scientifically extrinsic criterion operating as a value. There are costly as well as inexpensive means to save life, healthful as well as unhealthful avenues to happiness.

The crux of the matter is that science can ascertain properties; it cannot discover or adjudicate their virtues. It can rate them in terms of stated criteria, not in terms of their desirability. Its findings cannot be translated into good and evil. That requires the imposition of a scale of moral values about the validity of which there can be debate but no proof. In Kant's terms, science deals with hypothetical not categorical imperatives.

The allocation of policy making to the Trust Territory administrator arose from the desire not only, or even primarily, to establish effective collaboration with the anthropologist, but even more to ensure a division of function based on competence and acknowledged responsibility. The administrator, by the terms of his employment, was expected to make decisions concerning Micronesian welfare and to assume responsibility for their consequences. Since there could be no scientific determination of the ends to be sought in this decision-making process, it followed that the anthropologist, acting as a scientist, was not professionally qualified, nor was he charged with the responsibility, to define the purposes of government. It may be argued that the administrator was not qualified either, but this is a matter of opinion and cannot be demonstrated except, again on certain value assumptions. In any case, the argument does not qualify the anthropologist, for it does not follow that those who know a people best know what is best for them.

This division of function did not preclude expressions of opinion or value judgments by the Trust Territory anthropologist. Indeed, he was often urged to state his opinions, and probably offered them more often than he was asked. It did place on him the obligation to make clear when he was expressing a personal taste, a preference, or a prejudice with acknowledgment of the values from which it stemmed. Contrary to the contention sometimes voiced by social scientists, this obligation did not require a schizophrenic personality any more than do the demands on a man to act both as a father and a physicist, or a biologist and a Democrat. It does ask that men claim no more distinction for their preferences than they are entitled to as social philosophers. And it is a safeguard against the prevalent view that anthropologists are just another brand of intellectual with an axe to grind.

V

This brings us to the heart of the matter as far as the utilization of anthropology is concerned. Quite apart from the question of whether we should aspire to the ideal of an objective treatment of our data, there is the fact that the anthropologist is not widely regarded as an authority on human affairs and his reputation in this respect does not show evidence of increasing. Even more important, however, can be the damaging effects of a reaction against a discipline of knowledge which offers opinions under the panoply of science. Today, when opportunities for nonacademic employment are multiplying, this prospect might well be a matter for serious reflection.

This leads to a more serious question which will not have escaped the reader; namely, do we want a rigorous science of human behavior? And if so, are we prepared to deal with its consequences? We share this dilemma with the physicists, but are more deeply involved; for we propose to understand and, by so much, to provide a basis for the human direction of human affairs. The decision weighs heavily because science, any science, and its applications are neutral instruments; and they can operate for the good or ill of mankind, depending on the value system of the man who puts them into play.

Intervention and Applied Science in Anthropology

Lisa R. Peattie

From *Human Organization,*
Vol. 17, No. 1, 1958, pp. 4–8.
Copyright 1958, The Society
for Applied Anthropology. By
permission of the author, and
the publisher and copyright
holder.

I

. . . "Applied anthropology" and "action anthropology" as the terms are now used seem to be new. If intervention and taking-up causes are as old as organized anthropology, the whole notion of scientific intervention seems on the whole to be a more modern phenomenon in the profession. The members of the Ethnological Society in working for the abolitionist cause, seem to have been expressing an interest which they naturally felt *as anthropologists* in the native peoples, but they do not seem to have felt that their work for the cause was in itself an application of general scientific principle to solve particular practical problems either. "Applied anthropology" in this sense is thought of as the general moral and practical enlightenment which anthropology can provide men in considering the problems of their day. . . .

Applied anthropology as it appears today may be looked upon as having two roots. One is the element of concern and of special knowledge arising out of the peculiar position of the anthropologist. He is a member of the western peoples who have been rapidly making themselves rulers of the world, and whose way of life is still sweeping over the other peoples. He nevertheless knows the native peoples in the path of that civilization as informants and friends, and, to a degree unique among westeners, he sees the natives as having moral systems, esthetic sensibilities, and ways of life complete and proper in their own terms. His own society will accept this special concern because his special knowledge is useful to that society, trying to cope with the job of dealing with all sorts of people of different ways of life. The anthropologist is thus the man in the middle, and he tends to take on himself the job of speaking for the native to the west, and at the same time interpreting and filtering the forces of the west down to the native. This root— represented in those early ethnological societies—is the older of the two.

On the other hand, applied anthropology may be seen as part of a general movement of social science away from the humanistic studies, and toward the model of the physical and biological sciences. So anthropology strives for a higher degree of predictive precision, and sees as a goal the possibility of scientific management of social situations. It becomes possible to think of anthropology as doing more than giving men a certain enlightened perspective on themselves and their problems in the way that Brinton and Boas thought. Now we imagine the applied anthropologist as curing the ills of society through science, as the doctor of medicine uses science to cure the ills of the body.

If modern applied anthropology and action anthropology are looked upon as springing from these two roots, one sees that there is at times a tendency of one or another root to appear the dominant one, and even at times for there to be marked lines of cleavage, of incompatibility, between these two aspects of anthropology in action. The first root arises out of the special interest of the anthropologist in native and minority peoples. The second affirms the possibility and urges the value of disinterested consideration of social phenomena—as a biologist might view protozoa on his microscope slide. Action anthropology is in part an attempt to treat interest disinterestedly. Applied anthropology tries to move back and forth between value-interest and disinterested consideration of relevant fact. Anthropology in action is suspended between these two poles and swings between them.

II

There are many different kinds of applied or action anthropologists, and . . . even more kinds of applied or action anthropology.

In the first place, the action and scientific components of the hyphenated creature are variously divided. At one extreme, there is the kind of applied anthropology represented by a considerable part of research in Africa, in which the anthropologist is supported by government funds in order to do what is essentially pure research relevant to administration. The anthropologist's job is here to describe the cultural reality with which the administrator must deal; he tells the adminis-

trator what the golden stool means to the Ashanti, or describes the native legal system of the Tswana. In other instances, the anthropologist has a closer relationship to the taking of action and the exercise of power; he may be commissioned to find the facts with regard to some particular problem with which administrators are to take action—ritual murders in Basutoland, or the functioning of medical services in Latin America. Still more closely allied to action are those anthropologists who become regular, specialized members of the administrative group, with a mandate like that of the Staff Anthropologist in the Trust Territory to "recommend practical measures to achieve given program objectives." From this role it is not far to the single individual who combines under one hat the roles of scientific observer and actor, whether anthropologist turned administrator, administrator with anthropological training, or "action anthropologist" with a diffuse personalized power ("influence") not derived from a role in a formal managerial system.

Applied anthropologists have also variously conceived the balance between science and action in their work. Applied anthropology has been thought of as scientific experiment, with the interests of the subjects enhanced as well as protected: as social service using the conceptual apparatus of anthropology; and (as in the Fox program) a blend in which "helping" and learning-from are equal goals, inextricably blended. But even the most "scientific" of the applied anthropologists seem to worry a good deal about the ethics of their operations.

There have been a number of instances in which anthropologists have worked among people of their own general culture, in ways which are more or less "applied" science. The field of "anthropology in industry," the community studies made for the Bureau of Agricultural Economics, and some more recent studies in the mental health field are examples. But it is still true that the largest part of the situations in which applied anthropology comes into being are those in which western government impinges upon peoples of other culture, whether in European colonies in Africa, technical assistance programs in the underdeveloped countries, or on Indian reservations in the United States. The typical applied anthropologist works in a cross-cultural situation, and tends to find his patent to practice in the traditional concern of his profession with non-western and especially the primitive peoples.

The typical applied anthropologist works with such peoples in a situation of great disparity of power, and, most typically, he is supported by and responsible to management (or is, as in Vicos, himself management). Although I know of anthropologists who have informally put themselves at the service of the "underdog," I do not know of any clear case of the underdogs hiring themselves an anthropologist.

The typical situation of the applied anthropologist is thus to find himself working for or at least with those who have power over other people with different values from themselves, and with regard to whose values the anthropologist is somewhat more sensitive than the other members of the administering group. It is not remarkable, then, that applied anthropology is sensitive on the subject of values and is attentive to the ethical problems surrounding the ends towards which power may legitimately be exercised and the degree to which the anthropologist may legitimately associate himself with the exercise of power. This concern in turn adds force to the anthropologist's worries lest the applied branch of his profession fail to measure up as science. The attempt to remain value-neutral in the interests of science may appear a dodging of the responsibilities inherent in his relation to power; the attempt to use his skill and his relation to power to "do good" may appear unscientific special pleading; the attempt to avoid power while using his special skills to clarify and to mediate between conflicting values may seem to involve him in . . . difficulties of hopeless complexity.

III

The roles which applied anthropologists have taken have been shaped in part by the necessities of particular situations, and in part by the feelings of the anthropologists concerned toward these problems. So, too, criticism of these various roles must recognize that there are various sets of postulates, usable and used by anthropologists, relevant to such judgment.

The first axis along which the species and varieties of applied and action anthropologists range themselves may be identified by the question: What sort of science should anthropology be?

There is, at one extreme, a group of anthropologists who hope for, from their profession, a kind of prediction and control and of precise, compendent generalization similar to that in the natural sciences. There are, at the other end of the scale, those for whom their profession's center of gravity lies somewhere closer to the humanities, and who conceive of their science as offering mainly illuminating insights and useful organizing concepts for experience and action. Men in the former category are likely to conceive of applied anthropology, on the action side, as a process of applying scientific generalization to particular practical instance and, on the scientific side, as a process of experimental testing of generalizations. They strive for a precise stating of goals and predictions and for a paring-down of a factorial complexity in such a way as to make their science-action program fit the picture of the laboratory experiment. Those in the second category tend to operate in the way which Sol Tax speaks of as "clinical"; they "work in a way that does not assume or require much firmness or precision in (their) predictive findings"; they are characterized by "empiricism," "trial and error correction," ad hoc "inventiveness," and sensitivity to a "multiplicity of cues." Workers in the first category try to so arrange their intervention that its nature, time, and place are clearly marked, and then withdraw—actually or conceptually—to watch the results, as the laboratory technician, having planted a bit of tissue in his mouse, waits to see its growth. Men in the second or "clinical" mode of working tend to remain in continuing involvement with the social situation which is their subject-matter, and which they are both altering and observing at the same time. They find in this way of working a greater stimulus to the illuminating observation and the useful new concept which is for them the chief fruit of scientific endeavor; an accompanying loss of precision which would distress the scientific applied anthropologist does not so much distress them, partly because they hoped for less from that precision at the outset.

Anthropologists differ also in their conceptions as to the prevailing and proper relationships between science and values. Within anthropology, the extreme positivist viewpoint which would debar value from the field of proper *subjects* of study is not importantly represented; values, indeed, have for many social anthropologists occupied the center of their field of subject-matter. Anthropologists have differed, and continue to differ, however, as to the *bearing of values on science* and of *science on values*.

With regard to the first of these issues, the way in which values should properly affect scientific anthropology, three general sorts of position may be distinguished. There is first the "conservative" view that anthropology is and must be an intellectual discipline in its own right, needing no justification in practical utility, and indeed in danger of digressing from its own proper aims or of ceasing to be science at all if it is too responsive to the demands of men of affairs for help in solving practical problems. Thus Evans-Pritchard writes:

> It may be that it is laudable for an anthropologist to investigate practical problems. Possibly it is, but if he does so he must realize that he is no longer acting within the anthropological field but in the non-scientific field of administration. Of one thing I feel quite certain: that no one can devote himself wholeheartedly to both interests; and I doubt whether anyone can investigate fundamental and practical problems at the same time.

Men holding this view are unlikely to hold any great enthusiasm for applied anthropology; in any case, they do not comfortably become applied anthropologists.

A second view is frequently held today by those who are glad to own themselves applied anthropologists. In this view, it is proper and indeed laudable for the anthropologist to let values and practical concerns set his problem and define his subject matter, but he must then, in the interest of proper scientific objectivity, keep his values strictly out of his work. Men conceiving of their work in this way may or may not hold it proper for the anthropologist also to express his own value-based preferences for what should happen. But in any event, it is considered that the more the anthropologist can keep his observations and descriptions separate from his valuings, the better the quality of his scientific production will be.

There is a third view—that in Nadel's words "value judgments are inseparable from an investigation" and may indeed contribute to it. So Redfield finds that without the personal value-laden reactions which the ethnologist brings to the cultural reality he is observing he would not observe so well nor be able to describe that reality so precisely; "valuing is part of the ethnologist's work." This view of the science of anthropology is by no means the same as an insistence that anthropology should be of practical utility, that its problems should be set in terms of values. For both men cited, this value-infused observation is a way of carrying out scientific enterprises of no direct practical utility. But from this position, the value-involvement of the applied or action anthropologist in his scientific problem may appear less a disadvantage than it does to the would-be "pure scientist." It may even seem an advantage to be maximized and used, rather than a kind of "friction" to be reduced.

We come then to the question: What is the relevance of science for values? What can knowledge of the Is tell us of the Ought? A good many anthropologists—including applied anthropologists—have taken Max Weber's position with regard to this question; their answer is that knowledge of fact can never tell us anything as to what should be; science can never contribute to making a choice between *values*. In this view, the applied anthropologist can in his professional role only point out the factual consequences of alternative modes of action, or recommend the best technical means for bringing about an end previously value-determined. If he presumes to urge one course of action as against another, he has moved outside the realm of science.

Within anthropology there have been, however, many who have considered it possible to draw value-deductions from science. There is, first, a point of view connected with functionalism, and related to the notion of biological adaptability, in which that is good which can be shown to contribute to the survival of men—and by extension, of cultures. There has been also the attempt to identify "universal" values and to find a sanction for these in the demonstration of their universality. At the opposite pole, there is that anthropologically based value theory which finds the sanction for value-systems to lie not in universality but in particularity; the doctrine of cultural relativism. Although in the first instance asserting the relativity of values and thus negative in reference, this has clearly been expanded into positive injunctions to protect other cultures from destruction and to conform to one's own culture. There have also been in anthropology those who have found the good, not in comparing cultures laterally, but in tracing the evolution of cultural life vertically along the axis represented by time: evolutionists, old and new. So even Boas in 1908 seems to have seen a more than descriptive significance in the observation that mankind was evolving away from narrow nationalisms. So Kroeber sees trends in human history which make it possible to speak of "higher" cultures.

But these various tendencies to derive at least some Ought from the descriptions of the Is which anthropologists make have, by and large, not been so much an occasion for intervention, or for taking action, as a third position, standing somewhere outside the question as to whether or not science can tell us anything of values. This is the position which finds the anthropologist obligated to speak or to act just because of his special knowledge. Anthropologists need not, in feel-ing such obligation, believe that they can prove their values by their science; they know that they do hold some values, and when these are endangered in a field which touches their subject-matter and in which they feel involvement—Nazi racism, government policy towards the American Indian, racial segregation in education—they feel somehow a *duty* to act. Nor do they feel in most cases that, in thus stepping outside the realm of descriptions of what is, they cease to be anthropologists; it is because they are anthropologists, with certain special knowledge and special interests, that they feel obliged to act as they do.

This is intervention in the tradition of the early ethnological societies—or it is disciplined and combined with a scientific discovery goal into action anthropology, or cast still more into the traditional mold of science as an "experiment" in cultural change.

IV

In such action, it must be noted, anthropologists do in fact draw value deductions from their science—even when they claim the impossibility of doing so on a logical basis. Is not the emphasis placed on cultural self-determination an example of an implicit extension of methodology into ethical imperative? In studying the various ways of life other than his own the anthropologist learned to suspect judgment, to regard, for that time, those practices and beliefs as having their own internal logic and their own validity. The study of culture demanded cultural relativism. So also the stress, in many statements on applied anthropology, on restoration of equilibrium and the prevention of friction and violence in social relations, while representing a value general in the society from which the anthropologists are drawn, seems to be given special force by the functionalist approach in anthropological theory, and the general tendency of many descriptions to center around the concepts of equilibrium and integration.

It may even be argued that the recent

tendency of anthropologists to put greater stress on values surrounding the well-being and self-fulfillment of individuals, as contrasted with the stability and integration of cultural wholes, is in itself partially a result of the experience of anthropologists with applied anthropology and the underdeveloped peoples. Anthropologists have been drawn into the great current of change connected with the attempts of such peoples to get the things which the West has, and they have become identified with it, and come to see the needs of the peoples who are their subject matter in a new way because of it.

Applied anthropology thus contains within itself two distinct strains of value-emphasis: one concerned with "the relativity of values," the "right of cultural self-determination," the values of "integration"; the other speaking of universal individual needs, satisfied better by some cultures than others. "Every cultural shoe pinches somewhere." Typically, a single anthropologist uses both these sets of values, implicitly carrying in his own mind a working separation of areas into one category or the other. Technology is usually seen as an area in which one has a right to work for change, as also medical care; they are thought of as means, farther from a central core of value, and as closely related to the universal biological needs of man. So new plows yes, new religion no. Sorcery is seen as violating some universal right to mental health, a particular kinship structure as representing the right of cultural self-determination. Such a gradient may be argued as one representing greater to less disturbance to the person, or it may appear simply as a given.

V

In summary, then, the following seem to be some of the main problems for discussion—in most cases, continuing, not-capable-of-resolution discussion—with regard to applied or action anthropology.

Applied anthropology will always continue to raise the great unsolvable questions of ethics. What is the good life for man? To what extent is it proper for present generations to undergo discomfort in the interest of the (presumed) advantage of future generations? To what extent has one man or group of men a right to exert power over others, even in their own interest? To what extent may men ever be said to have free choice, and in what circumstances?

These fundamental philosophical questions raise also others which are, in theory at least, capable of some empirical investigation. It would seem worthwhile, for example, to investigate the forms of power and influence in applied anthropology. To what extent, for instance, may the members of the Fox field project be said to be exerting power over the Fox through their questioning, clarifying, and occasionally persuading functions? How may the rationality of human choices be increased? And how may mechanisms be developed for expressing these choices?

It seems clear that applied or action anthropology is bound to be qualitatively different, as science, from traditional anthropology. At least it is evident that it is adding to anthropology a greater interest in process, in small group dynamics, in what has been called "mood," in the relations between social groups, and in phenomena, such as leadership and factionalism. In the literature of the Fox project we find described, for instance, a field of interpersonal relations in which relations of power and items of "mood" are quite as important as those societal bonds and cultural uniformities more traditionally at the center of the anthropologist's field of investigation.

The methodology of such investigations is still in need of refinement. Most especially we need in applied anthropology attention to the methodology of validation. Much of the literature of applied anthropology is a fairly impressionistic description of "what happened when." We need better. Anthropology will have to develop ways of better recording of process and better measurement of change—in attitudes and in interpersonal relationships. Most especially I am struck by the lack, so far as I know, of any really thorough and convincing account of how a group of applied anthropologists are seen by their "clients"—and this although one of the advantages of applied anthropology should be that it takes the effects of the investigator into account in description. To put a group of "pure" scientists to studying the interaction of the applied scientists with their clients may be a humiliating solution, but it is at least a logically possible one.

selection 64

The Research and Development Approach to the Study of Change

Allan R. Holmberg

From *Human Organization,* Vol. 17, No. 1, 1958, pp. 12–16. Copyright 1958, The Society for Applied Anthropology. By permission of the author, and the publisher, and copyright holder.

I

... In 1952, quite by design, although unexpectedly and suddenly, I found myself in the delicate position of having assumed the role of *patrón* (in the name of Cornell University) of a Peruvian *hacienda,* called Vicos, for a period of five years, for the purpose of conducting a research and development program on the modernization process.

As you can readily imagine, such action on my part clearly shook (or perhaps I should say shocked) the Board of Trustees—to say nothing of the 2,000 residents of the *hacienda* and no few of my anthropological colleagues—to the extent, I might add, that had events subsequently taken other turns than they eventually did, I would probably not be writing this and would be much more in disgrace as an anthropologist and human being than I presently am. Moreover, had I known then what I now know, I am not so sure that I would be willing to repeat the experience, even though it has been one of the most rewarding ones of my whole professional career. My doubts lie not so much with the fruitfulness or legitimacy of the research and development, as contrasted with the strictly research, approach to the study of the social process but more with the wear and tear that it might cause to the inadequately financed or inadequately staffed anthropologist or other behavioral scientist who is brash enough to attempt to apply it, especially in a foreign area. On this point I shall have more to say later. For the moment, suffice it to say that having recently retired—again quite by design—from playing the dual role of God and anthropologist (the status of Vicos has recently changed from a dependent to an independent community) and having again assumed the role of a plain anthropologist, I find the change in status a highly comforting one. Nevertheless, on the basis of the past five years of experience at Vicos, I remain convinced that the interventionist or action approach to the dynamics of culture, applied with proper restraint, may in the long run provide considerable payoff in terms both of more rational policy and better science. My concern here, therefore, will be with some of the reasons why I believe this to be the case. What, then, are some of the implications—the advantages and disadvantages, the gains and losses—of the application of the research *and* development approach to the study of change, both from a value and scientific point of view?

II

On the question of values—in the ethical sense—I really have little to say, more than to state my stand. No one—professional or layman—can scientifically justify intervention into the lives of other people, whether they be of his own kind or of a different breed. However, by its very nature, the social process is an influencing process among individuals and social groups, one upon which the very existence of society depends. It is no less a necessary condition for the study of social life. Even the most "pure" anthropologist imaginable, conducting his research with "complete" detachment and objectivity, cannot avoid influencing his subjects of study or in turn of being influenced by them. In some instances, I believe, this has led to very salutary effects, both on anthropologists and their informants. Certainly the science of anthropology has been greatly enriched by those informants who were influenced by anthropologists to become anthropologists, even though it may be more questionable, perhaps, that native cultures have been correspondingly enriched by those anthropolo-

gists who were influenced by their informants to go native. While this may seem beside the point, I simply want to emphasize the fact that influence and consequently the values which motivate that influence are always part of the process of human interaction and while they can be studied by science, their validation must rest on other grounds.

This does not mean that any anthropologist—pure or applied—can manipulate his subjects without restraint. Some code of ethics must govern his behavior, as the Society for Applied Anthropology long ago recognized. In the case of Vicos, however, where power was held by us, this became an especially delicate issue because having assumed the role of *patrones* we expected and were expected to intervene in the lives of the people. It was at this point that the question of values entered and it was at this point that it was very necessary to take a value stand. What then was this stand?

I long ago made the decision for myself, which is shared by a great many people and communities of the world, that the best kind of a community in which to live is one that is, to quote Aldous Huxley, "just, peaceable, morally and intellectually progressive" and made up of "responsible men and women." To my way of thinking, and I am by no means unique in this view, the best way of approaching this Utopian state of affairs is to pursue as a goal the realization of basic human dignity to which every individual is entitled. And by basic human dignity I mean a very simple thing: a wide rather than a narrow sharing of what I regard as positive human values, some expression of which, as Professor Harold Lasswell has so clearly shown, is found in every society and towards a wider sharing of which, if I interpret Professor Robert Redfield correctly, the broader course of civilization itself has been moving for a considerable period of time.

For lack of better terms of my own to express the meaning I wish to convey, let me again refer to Lasswell who speaks of the following categories of value: power, wealth, enlightenment, respect, well being, skill, affection and rectitude. The wide sharing of such values among members of the Vicos community was essentially the overall basic value position and policy goal to which we subscribed. In other words, everyone, if he so desired, should at least have the right and the opportunity, if not the responsibility, to participate in the decision-making process in the community, to enjoy a fair share of its wealth, to pursue a desire for knowledge, to be esteemed by his fellowmen, to develop talents to the best of his ability, to be relatively free from physical and mental disease, to enjoy the affection of others, and to command respect for his private life. While no such value stand, of course, can ever be validated by science we and a surprising number of Vicosinos, as I have said elsewhere, and, as revealed by a baseline study, believed them "to be good and desirable ends."

Movement towards such goals, of course, rests on a couple of fundamental assumptions (or better, expectations) in which I happen to have a very strong faith: 1) that human traits are such that progress can be made towards the realization of human dignity, and 2) that the natural order (physical nature) is such that with greater knowledge and skill, human beings can turn it progressively to the service of social goals.

In stating this overall value position, I have not meant to suggest that movement towards these goals can occur only through a single set of institutional practices. Like most anthropologists I subscribe to the doctrine of the relativity of culture and I firmly believe that people have the right of self-determination, as long as they respect that right in others. From the very beginning at Vicos we recognized this principle. In short, we used our power to share power to a point where we no longer hold power, which is just as matters should be.

Before leaving these value and policy matters let me simply cite a few of the developmental changes that have come about as a result of the application of the research *and* development approach to change at Vicos:

1. *Organization*
1952. Vicos had an *hacienda*-type organization. Outside renters not only had free use of *hacienda peones* for labor and per-

sonal services, but also of their animals and tools. Power was concentrated in the hands of *patrón.*

1957. Hacienda system and free services have been abolished; new system of community organization now in march is based on shared interests and local control.

2. *Land ownership*
1952. No title to land, although Vicosinos had tried on numerous occasions to purchase the land on which they had been living as *peones* for 400 years.

1957. Based on reports of development by the Cornell-Peru Project, the Institute of Indigenous Affairs asked the Peruvian Government to expropriate Vicos in favor of its indigenous population. This expropriation has now taken place.

3. *Local Authority*
1952. Under the *hacienda*-type organization there were no responsible secular authorities within the community.

1957. The Vicosinos have organized a board of their own delegates elected from each of 6 zones of the *hacienda.* They have the legal responsibility for the direction of community affairs.

4. *Income*
1952. The indigenous community of Vicos had no source of income of its own.

1957. Former *hacienda* lands are now farmed for the public good, providing a steady income for the payment of lands and the development of public service.

5. *Education*
1952. In the aspect of education Vicos had a very small school, with one teacher, 10–15 students.

1957. Vicos now possesses the most modern school in the whole region, recently made a *nucleo escolar,* with a capacity of 400 students. There are now 9 teachers and about 200 students, many of whom have had five years of continuity in school.

6. *Production*
1952. Low economic production—each *hectare* of potato land produced a value of only $100.

1957. Each *hectare* of potato land is now producing a value of $400–$600.

7. *Health facilities*

1952. There were no modern health facilities.

1957. A modern health center has been built by the Vicosinos and a neighboring community; a clinic is held twice a week and a public health program is underway.

Most of the cost of these developments have been borne by members of the community themselves.

As a final development outcome I should perhaps mention that the Cornell-Peru Project has had considerable impact outside of the area of Vicos. When originally undertaken there was not a single project of its kind in Peru. At the present time, the Institute of Indigenous Affairs is directing five programs of a similar nature in other areas of the country. And attached to all are Peruvian anthropologists, many of them trained in part at Vicos.

But more important have been the effects on the outside produced by the Vicosinos themselves. Word of their freedom has got around. Let me cite but one example. Recently an *hacienda* community, in conditions similar to those obtaining at Vicos in 1952, sent a commission to Vicos for advice. Their *hacienda,* a public one as Vicos had been, was about to be rented at public auction for a period of ten years and they were desirous of freeing themselves from service to a *patrón.* One of the ways in which this can be done is for the residents of an *hacienda* to rent it directly from the government themselves. But in the case of this community sufficient funds were not immediately available.

The Vicosinos sent a return commission to *Huascarán,* a fictitious name for the community under discussion. On the recommendation of this commission the community of Vicos, which had funds in the bank, lent the community of Huascarán sufficient money to rent their *hacienda* directly from the government, thus freeing them from service to a *patrón.* More than that when the commis-

sion from Vicos first went to Huascarán they noticed that the Huascarinos planted their fields by somewhat antiquated methods and suggested more modern methods of agriculture which were originally introduced into Vicos by the Cornell-Peru Project. These are the kind of developmental effects that give the applied anthropologist an occasion for joy.

III

Now what of the scientific implications of the research and development approach to the study of change? Here again I take a positive view, particularly in a situation like Vicos, where it was possible to work in a complete cultural context, where it was possible to specify social goals for almost all aspects of culture, and where it was possible for the anthropologist to maintain some control over the interventions and variables involved. In such an environment, hypotheses can be tested by comparing actual goal achievement with predicted goal achievement.

Actually in the natural sciences, research and development are inseparable. It is even common to join them in one formal project as is the case in many technologically advanced industries, in government, and in private institutions. But whether formally joined or not, scientific discovery is sooner or later inevitably put to the test of success or failure through the application of research results in engineering and technology. In other words, a great strength of, if not a necessary condition for, natural science is feedback through development.

Anthropology, like other behavioral sciences, profits little from such corrective feedback. In part this is because it is not systematically employed in social decision-making, as let us say, physics is employed in missile or building construction. But even if it is employed the results are either not fed back to the anthropologist or they are fed back too slowly to facilitate rapid scientific advance. Moreover, research and development work in behavioral science are seldom joined, even though they were to some extent in Vicos, for the systematic exploitation of their reciprocal benefits, as they are in the research and development laboratories of the natural sciences. To get the feedback necessary for rapid advance in a behavioral science like anthropology, policy is needed, even if policy does not need science.

The connection between research and development in anthropology and other behavioral sciences is probably even closer than it is in the natural sciences. In science, as everyone knows, every generalization is both an insight and a prediction, even though its explicit statement is usually cast in one form or another. Now when a generalization on behavior is communicated to people who are also its subjects, it may alter the knowledge and preferences of these people and also their behavior. Thus a scientific generalization on behavior, by altering behavior, appears to falsify or obsolesce itself. This is called "pliancy factor" by my philosophical colleague at Cornell, Max Black.

In general this complication has been viewed as a cross that the behavioral scientist must bear. Actually, a generalization about behavior is not falsified when predictions based upon it are made obsolete when the subject to whom it is made known prefers to modify himself rather than to conform to an earlier prediction. It is simply that the possibility of modification of behavior must be taken into account and turned to scientific advantage. In the continuous interplay between scientific generalization and goal-seeking behavior, the insight-feedback of a scientific generalization can be employed both for goal revision and as empirical data for research. This is one of the great advantages of the research and development approach. Perhaps an example will illustrate what I mean.

One of the developmental goals of the Vicos program was to bring decision-making bodies of the community up to a level of competence at which we, the *patrones,* could be dispensed with but without the community's falling victim to its most predatory members as has sometimes been the case. Thus,

arrangements had to be made for group survival and stability and, through controlling the complexity of the problems dealt with and by other devices, the groups gradually brought to their highest level of competence. This required that hypotheses be formulated and acted upon—hypotheses concerning the requirements of viability and competence of groups. Once acted upon the hypotheses were tested by their results. Hence each successive developmental step was a step in the isolation of another variable for research.

Concretely, both development and research interests merge in following the consequences of such successive steps as the following, at least some of which were taken for one group of potential decision-makers at Vicos: 1) the group was asked for advice in the settlement of land disputes; 2) it was invested with prestige by calling public attention to its role; 3) the group was given the opportunity to settle land disputes; 4) the group was provided, through skilled observers, the feedback of an understandable analysis of its performance; 5) the *patrón* was withdrawn from the group meeting, reserving only the right to veto under certain conditions; 6) the jurisdiction of the group was enlarged with gradually decreasing veto.

While this detail is much abbreviated, it suggests how research on the developmental steps provides an opportunity for the dogged pursuit of whatever variables one wishes to isolate. Every insight into variables can be put to a test; and, where predictions are disappointed, a reformulation of the hypothesis can be followed by a further test until predictions are no longer disappointed. By no means will all the unknowns of human behavior become unveiled, but development requires correct insights, hypotheses, and analytic models. It compels their never-ending revision until they pass the test of application.

The essence of the connection between research and development in this illustration is that each developmental intervention—say, introducing legal principles by which land disputes might be resolved—is both a necessary step towards reaching community goals and in the research sense a method of varying the group situation to isolate another variable in group dynamics—in this instance isolating the effect of introducing formal principles against which individual cases are to be judged. It is precisely because of feedback to the researcher from the development application that research needs development just as much as development needs research.

Whatever the particular example, the story is much the same. The researcher is compelled to follow through, to keep on trying for the refinement of an hypothesis or model that will stand the test of application. If, for example, he wants to know what is necessary to break down prejudice between Indians and Mestizos, his research is not terminated when he has tested one popular hypothesis and found it invalid, because his developmental objectives require that he try a whole series of interventions until prejudice begins to decline.

In the case of Vicos, attempts were made in collaboration with several colleagues to lay out about 130 specific possible lines of research and development, each matched to a specific developmental goal such as the diversification of agriculture, the development of community leadership, the reduction of social distance between Indians and Mestizos, the increase of educational opportunities for both children and adults, etc. Wherever possible an attempt was made to make fairly precise statements about the goals in question. To lay out the various possibilities in order subsequently to develop a strategy of research and development, each line of possible intervention was represented in a semi-diagrammatic way by a column on a very large bulletin or map board taking up the walls of a room. The diagram shown represents how 3" x 5" cards were used to lay out visually the research and development sequences, subject to constant revision as research and development continues.

At the top of the column is posted for some end-point date the particular goal in question to be reached. At the bottom of the column are posted the counterpart institutional and

An ideological goal or end point

A corresponding institutional goal or end point

Program plans for probes, pretests, interventions, and appraisals

Present ideological situation with respect to above goals summarized

Present institutional situation with respect to above goals summarized

Record of past interventions

Base line ideological situation

Base line institutional situation

ideological situations found at the base line period before interventions. Above them are summarized any interventions so far made, and above them the present institutional and ideological situation with respect to this one line of development. The remainder of the column is given over to a proposed schedule of probes, pretests, interventions, and appraisals.

By utilizing such a method, interventions are not likely to be hit or miss and their developmental and research gains can be fully appreciated. Scheduling them requires careful appraisal of the facts describing the existing situation and trends, probes of readiness of the community to take the proposed step, pretests of interventions on a small scale, then the intervention itself and subsequent appraisal, which in turn becomes the first step in a still further intervention. Hence in diagrammatic terms, the upper part of the column, including the goals themselves, is constantly undergoing revision on the basis of the growing lower part of the column representing past experience.

To illustrate the distinctiveness of research, where the whole life of the community is available for study, as it was to a considerable extent in Vicos, it may be helpful to visualize a great many columns such as have just been described, set side by side. The interrelationships among these columns can hardly go unnoticed, and it becomes both possible and necessary to consider these interrelationships in devising a research and development strategy.

One more thing should be said about this contextual mapping in a research and development approach to change. It makes possible, for *development,* an economy of intervention. For example, one way in which to reduce social inequality between Mestizos and Indians is to schedule public functions in Vicos attractive enough to draw neighboring Mestizos in and then conduct these functions in such a way as to break down the traditional acceptance of segregation. One can conceive of an experiment along this line that might test the hypothesis that prejudice between Indians and Mestizos will be reduced by contact under conditions of social equality.

Now with reference to quite a different goal of reducing communal binges, movies are an effective competitor with alcohol because the Vicosinos prefer to be sober when watching a movie. Movies are also an obvious method for adult education, including literacy. Finally, the importation and showing of films may become the nucleus of a small-scale experiment of Indian entrepreneurship. Hence a variety of lines of desirable research and development converge on a movie program for Vicos. Actually such an experiment is now underway at Vicos and a skillful plan for introducing movies into the community may turn out to be a strategically sound intervention because many birds may be killed with one small stone.

I have now said enough to indicate what I believe some of the value and scientific implications of the research and development approach to the study of change to be. Most of what I have said is positive and I have not suggested that this approach be applied to the exclusion of others. My greatest doubts about it, on the basis of my experience at Vicos, stem from the unlikelihood of mobilizing sufficient funds and personnel to do a research and development job well. It is a man's job that a boy cannot be sent to do. I hope that the powers supporting research will soon take cognizance of this fact.

Some Relations of School and Family in American Culture

Robert F. Spencer

From *Symposium: A School is to Learn*. . . . Proceedings of the Minnesota Academy of Science, Vol. 29, 1961. pp. 129–239. Copyright by the Minnesota Academy of Science. By permission of the author, the publisher, and the copyright holder.

Virtually any statement made about the contemporary American system of education can be subjected to infinite documentation. What the school should accomplish, what its curricula ought to be, how far it should or has become a kind of surrogate for the family, church or other institution, emerge as vital questions for the professional educators, questions, clearly, for which there is no single answer. Judgments become normative, ameliorative, critical, and certainly, nearly always fraught with overtones of emotionalism. This leaves the non-specialist who attempts to gain an over-view of the nature and image of the educator and his field in the dilemma of adequately finding his way. Still, the school is a social institution. As such, it can be subjected to analysis in quite the same behavioral terms as any other human group activity. Rather, therefore, than to move into the areas of the ideal—what a school and the system associated with it ought to be—it may be possible to consider the educational institutions in terms of their structure and function, thereby analyzing the interrelations between school system and other institutional facets of contemporary society.

This paper is written from the point of view of the behavioral sciences, specifically, from the vantage point of the anthropologist whose concern lies in the comparison of the various aspects of human behavior at all times and places. For indeed, if a society seeks to learn about itself, it gains perspective only through an observation of alternative solutions to human problems which have been reached by human groups possessing different historical backgrounds and whose view of man, his nature and destiny, is couched in fundamental assumptions and premises different from those of *Homo americanus.*

Further, the anthropologist is accustomed to see a society and its associated culture in holistic terms, arguing that all aspects of behavior in a historically conditioned and determined context are intimately interrelated that they interact with each other and are so systematically fashioned as to support one another. In other words, any facet of behavior in a society has a function, the end of which is to maintain and perpetuate the whole. From comparative studies of other peoples, whether civilized or so-called primitives, the anthropologist affirms the essential dynamically functional nature of any institution in society. This can never exist in a vacuum but becomes an integral element in a complex system. By this reasoning, it is rank error to divorce the educational institution of this or any other human society from the total social matrix.

But to speak of a total American society and culture poses an almost insurmountable problem for some investigators. Ours is, it is true, a vastly proliferated system what with its many interest groups, its varied ethnic backgrounds, its abundant organizations, or its geographical and ecological diversity. Yet a failure to admit the organic integrity of American culture and society is to ignore the forest. Indeed, there is enough of a uniformity in contemporary American society to suggest that size does not necessarily make for complexity and that the concept of complexity is stressed far too much. In this paper, I submit that there is an American culture, that the school system is a vital part of the total society, and that, in intereacting with other social institutions, e.g., the family, the school functions to affirm and preserve not only ideological and ideational norms, but more pointedly, aspects of behavior which promote the maintenance of the totality of American society as we know it.

The anthropologist is aware at once that the analytic points he makes are not necessarily reflective of popular consensus or wish. A question which nearly always confronts him at once relates to the applications of what he and his fellow behavioral scientists have to say. This is, in fact, a recognizable pattern in American culture, one which demands constantly applications of any line of scientific inquiry. A point which must be left open here is that respecting science itself. Even if science is a vital part of contemporary culture, something which seems to offer a panacea to modern man, scientific values are not necessarily social values. Indeed, one may ask if science, taken as an entity essentially supercultural, can ever be normative. Theoretically,

of course, it should not be. A description of the physiological function of the pancreas is not the same as a course of treatment prescribed for diabetes. In this paper, I seek to do no more than call attention, on the basis of what is empirically known about American society and culture, to some of the existing interrelationships between school system, family, and society. I should wish respectfully to leave to the investigator whose interest is application the solutions to the specific problems which arise out of culture pattern and human behavior.

It is possible to make a series of statements, a summary of propositions which reflect an empirically derived scientific commitment to the problem at hand. These are, in effect, to "call the shots" as one sees them; they are not to define solutions. They are:

1. There is a total system definable as American culture and society.

2. This system, tightly bound in some areas, extremely loosely in others, depends on essentially ephemeral human relationships.

3. The ephemeral quality of the human relationship is an outgrowth of the primary cultural definition of the worth of the individual.

4. On the significant formative level, i.e., that of socialization, making the individual one with his culture and society, family and school function together to produce a desired result.

It may thus be affirmed that the family and the system of contemporary American education meet in the area of a dynamic social cross-fertilization. If the ensuing processes are examined functionally, a picture reflecting the vitality of institutional relations can be proffered.

American Culture and Society

To say that contemporary America constitutes not one, but a series of diffuse subcultures is to do violence to the anthropological concept of culture. To identify, as some sociologists do, a depressed urban area where crime is rampant as a criminal subculture fails to take into account the fact that even deviant behavior is structured and patterned according to the norms of the so-called majority. Sub-culture as concept is not only unfortunate but is dangerous in presenting a distortion of existing uniformity. One need not move into the psychoanalytic formulations of national character as has been done for America by Margaret Mead or Geoffrey Gorer to recognize that there is an essential structural sameness to American life. Into this, individuals and groups, whether in the form of the Sons of Erin, the Sons of Hermann, or the Japanese-American Citizens' League, are inextricably drawn. An ethnic minority is a separate cultural segment only if it refuses to be assimilated into the prevailing modes of the majority, such as may be the case of the traditional Chinatown. Here, however one is not dealing with a Chinese subculture but rather with a segment of Chinese culture encysted within the larger body. When the minority of whatever kind comes to act within the majority group and framework it has forfeited its distinctness. Thus in the fieldwork experience of the writer, it is noted that the Buddhist temple of Japan, when transplanted to America, possesses the organization of the Christian churches. It has a minister, an order of service, a Sunday School, a board of deacons or elders, a hymnology, and so on. There is every indication that the aspirations of American life, indeed, the problem of survival itself, are met by conformity. If one considers merely that the individual is confronted with a value system, a legal system, a uniform pattern of aims, aspirations, and goals, there is an organic integrity and wholeness to American culture.

The concept of culture as employed by anthropologists has been subject to some rather unfortunate misunderstandings on the part of other social scientists, whether objective or applied. For culture is not necessarily behavior, however much the terms society and culture are confused. In the concept of culture one may understand the definitions which lie behind action and behavior. In other words, men act because they hold certain truths to be self-evident. It is the ostensibly self-evident truth with which one is concerned in the culture concept; it is the definition of the situation, the evaluation of the relations between man and man, between man and the supernatural, between man and his universe. The line between culture and values is admittedly difficult to draw. But culture and values are not the same things; given the definition of the situation, men proceed to build systems of values on the basis of truths which they consider to be fundamental and intrinsic. Values, as a result, can only be viewed as relative, never as absolutes. But it is in culture that there lies a basis of prediction, not of the course of specific events, but rather of what the individual will do in a given circumstance. If I remark to my small boy—"but boys don't cry," I have not only indicated that such behavior falls short of the expected, i.e., the predictable, but I have also gone far to enculturate. I have not only informed the child of the behavior expected of him but I have succeeded in some measure in internalizing in the child the beginnings of self-image in the male role in this culture.

It is often said that society precedes culture. Men, in other words, must live together before they can establish the ground rules necessary to further living together. It is here that the comparative knowledge brought out by the anthropological approach is of assistance. One may consider, for example, the case of the Apache Indians for whom the anthropologist Morris Opler notes: "Childhood is not an end in itself, but a period of preparation for adulthood." This statement is significant only when American and Apache norms are compared. Clearly, in American culture of today, childhood is viewed, however implicitly, as an end in itself. One has merely to consider the vast array of items designed to preoccupy children—the school itself, the toy industry, television programs, Santa Claus, the Easter Rabbit, and Disneyland with its complex associations. It is evident also that the transition from childhood to adulthood, given this cultural definition among ourselves, can be traumatic and result in the storm and stress of adolescence. As Margaret Mead has shown, the Samoans, with a different cultural definition of childhood, never experience the griefs of transition.

Or one might go further down the line and consider other cultural premises as they affect man in modern society in the United States. American action, for example, clearly rests on the premise that the world and the nature of man are inherently good and improvable. This means, of course, that contemporary society accepts the view that man can triumph over nature and that man can and does rise to new heights of progress. This premise rests, one may be sure, in the history of Western civilization and in the Judeo-Christian ideology of the triumph of good over evil. But whatever the origins of the concept, behavior among ourselves is couched in terms of these fundamental assumptions, so much so, in fact, that individuals are not only not capable of verbalizing them, but tend to start in alarm when the question of their validity is raised. American culture welcomes change, technological change especially, forgetting that this may have marked repercussions for the total social structure, the way in which the individual relates to his fellows, and to the place occupied by him. On the sociological level, this is the time-honored example of the cultural lag: the disparity between material achievement and the solution to the problem of living socially with it.

It is scarcely necessary to call attention to the corollaries of the fundamental assumptions of American culture. With the sociologist, for example, one can point to the changing composition of rural populations, to the fact that they no longer exist as such but are, by virtue of increased communications and mobility, drawn into the urban orbit. Or one may show how urbanism in the traditional sense is gone, being replaced by the burdens of an industrialized society with its decentralization of industry and its growing pattern of suburban living. Again, one can point to the whole problem of mobility as an important factor in the fragmentation of human relationships, as for example, in the increasing nucleation of the family, the breakdown of deeper, more permanent, and supportive relationships, with both kinsmen and friends.

Here is obviously not the place to consider at length the area of individuation and the essential isolation of the person as features characteristic of American society. One may consider Weber's view, as well as that of Tawney, of the individualized capitalistic Protestant ethic, go with Max Lerner into his analysis of the distinctive attributes of American culture, or hold with Riesman and Whyte in respect to mass society and its nature. Regardless of prophecies of doom, one can be objective. There does seem to be a loss, as a result of individualized separateness, of some of the features which characterized the frontier or which anthropologists find diagnostic of peasant or folk societies. Such a loss is seemingly a concomitant of our cultural surroundings and is perhaps a reflection of industrialization and its effects on social living. The Soviet Union, for all its vaunted collectivism, obviously faces the same kind of problem. Nor does totalitarian control do other than shift men's loyalties away from the organic society to the artificially conceived state. While American society has not done this, and happily never will, it still pays a price for increasing industrialization, a price measured in the gradual departure from the deep roots of tradition. If there is regarded as desirable in human activity a sense of support, a deeply founded series of expressions relating to dependence between man and man rather than independence (points which are of course debatable), American society has tended to lose in depth in favor of momentary fulfillment. Such statements, it is true, could not be made were it not for the data collected from other cultures which make comparison possible. Nor is this to say that American society and culture are found wanting. It is merely to note that there are alternative solutions to the problems of human living. If American society can be viewed with greater objectivity, some of the issues which confront the social worker and the educator might more readily be resolved.

The American Family

It is axiomatic that no society can operate effectively without the family. This is the primary institution, the instrument of procreation, the agent of socialization. One need examine only a fraction of the extensive literature on the family, that produced by the professional sociologist, to gain the impression that in American life today the family and its associated kinship system have taken on a special coloring. The sense of personal independence and autonomy relates closely to family aspirations with the result that the extended kinship unit of the past is in eclipse. Perhaps, as family size increases, and we are told that this is a trend, the individualism which is fostered by the present system will to some degree fade. But in these present decades the notion that the young married couple should forage for itself, set up its independent household, raise its children independently of the grandparental generation or the extended family, find its social outlets in a peer group of like age, retain the most casual relations with the extended kindred of both, and so on through a host of isolating features like these remains uppermost. It is significant that the cultural premises of American life create a situation in which the unmarried person creates a problem; his status both socially and psychologically remains in doubt. This may, in fact, be an important factor in reducing the age of marriage in American society. It is curious that a society which stresses so heavily a moral tone should find it easier to accommodate the divorced person than the bachelor. But it is also significant that the primary function of the family, that of socializing the young, is not materially altered. Conceptually, at least, in legalistic terms, in terms of societal expectations, the family assumes a responsibility at this level. What has changed is the depth and extent of the view of the family as a socializing agent. At what point, it may be asked,

does family responsibility for a child come to be shared with the total society itself?

The above suggests then that there are some quite specific functions of the family in American society. This is a tightly structured society in its quite limited prescription of the ways in which a child may be handled and the extent of freedom accorded the parent. One has only to consider the overview of American culture and society which comes from the pen of Dr. Benjamin Spock and his imitators or from the accurate predictive analysis of Gesell and Ilg. Conversely, however, the parent has certain alternative ways of acceptable action open to him. Both parents may be employed and the very young child farmed out to the sitter or the nursery school. There is marked mobility in American culture with the result that the nucleated family may move at random to any part of the geographical limits of the society. These are elements which suggest a looseness of organization and which point to an important aspect of modern American life—the family must operate within quite precisely defined vertical limits, even if these are not wholly deeply rooted, but it is free to expand horizontally. On the level of child rearing, and bearing generally help from an extended kinship group, this means that the society must utilize institutions other than the family to enhance the socialization process. It is here that there is a functional and structural reason for the school and the educational institutions generally. A school is not to learn. It is in large measure to substitute for the socializing and social institutions which in the European ethnic backgrounds out of which most Americans come were of another kind.

One should anticipate some disagreement with these remarks on the part both of the social worker and the educator. In answer, attention may be called to a discussion based on social system, on the issue of how the American family exists as an entity different from the family of the Japanese, the Arabs, or various of the modern Europeans. Because of the nature of the social system of which the American family forms a part, it can be asserted that there is actually little latitude in behavior or choice for individuals. This is not to say that freedom of choice is wholly precluded. But such freedom is meaningful only with defined limits. The polygynous family, for example, cannot exist. Or one may learn from the sociologist that there may be differences in expectations on the parts of persons coming from different backgrounds. And there is a profuse and consistent body of information on matters of this kind. Not only is the nature of the American child rearing process known in some detail, but the expectations and goals of varying elements in the society are also understood. Thus the differences as between social classes, that defined on the basis of economic status as well as educational attainment, are further reflected in attitudes toward child rearing, toward goals in education, and in respect to the achievement and expectation of success. These are important and meaningful on certain levels. In the end, however, they become minutiae when viewed against individualized, competitive, and isolating elements characteristic of the total social fabric.

How does the family in American society act as a socializing agent? Students of personality as related to socio-cultural systems have repeatedly demonstrated how the socializing elements resident in social systems reach the individual, are channeled integrated, intensified, internalized, so as to produce a personality oriented in a specific direction. Ego strength, development of the super-ego, the severity or laxness of pressure in one or another direction have their bearing on the development of the adult personality and its relations to the values systems which become characteristic of any cultural milieu. Thus as one anthropologist has pointed out, there are those cultures which stress sanctions of shame as against those which concern themselves more deeply with an internalized sense of guilt. Or similarly, the whole problem of integrated anxiety or of any other aspect of covert development is involved here. Since it is generally regarded as axiomatic that the child is father to the man, socialization, enculturation, the fixing of values and personality patterns occur at the earliest age levels.

Clearly, in American society, the moral role attributed to the family in inculcating the value systems of American life suggests that the family is by no means becoming blurred in its functional outlines. That it has changed in composition is unquestionable. The days are clearly gone when the socializing agency might lie in alternate generations, such as between grandparent and grandchild. The parent himself in the nucleated family system of today is obliged to assume a good many socializing roles, more indeed than would have been the case among pioneer and rural families of tradition, and certainly more than is true of other Western areas, such as in Europe. The child learns at home, from his peer groups, through mass media, and through the recognized moral institution of the church, the latter especially becoming a surrogate for the family and implementing and complementing the school system. Not only does the family in American society fix the primary personality patterns, those which reflect the unconscious orientations leading to the formation of a modal personality type, but regardless of social class and background, the child learns certain kinds of information. His orientations toward the world, his views about acceptable and unacceptable behavior, his basic moral code, i.e., the total "good" and "bad" pattern, folkways and folklore are imparted through the socializing agencies relating to the very young, to the infant and child whose world the culture itself must define. But more than this, learning involves initially language, it relates to the formation of the major motor responses, and it does not omit such aspects as food preferences, manner of sleeping, postures, gestures, and a host of related psycho-biological features. Thus when the child finally comes to school, he has already been patterned, his likes and dislikes are defined, his moral sense is on the way to realization, and it is to all these that the educational institutions give additional enforcement. The child, in short, approaches the school system as a functioning member of society.

What has been said here of the enculturative process is of course true of all societies.

Differences lie not only in the varying kinds of information imparted and the kind of personality system developed, but also in the depth or intensity of the processes of internalization and learning. It has been so often remarked of contemporary society and culture that its variations preclude any generalizations. From what has been noted above this criticism is scarcely applicable. When social class, for example, is viewed as an independent variable influencing the enculturative process among ourselves, as a good many studies have attempted to show, there is a corresponding lack of attention to differences or variations in the consequent personality type. The demands of the culture, in spite of conceptual pluralism, create an American personality mode, one operative within the framework of individualized competitiveness but at the same time one which must accommodate itself to the demands of mass society. This paradox creates a modern problem. It is a problem which becomes vital in regard to the interrelations of school and society or family in American life and it reflects the great difficulty of defining the functions of school and family and their respective allocation. If the age of school attendance is reduced, and clearly this seems to be happening, then some of the traditional functions of the family are being arrogated by impersonal social institutions.

The Educational Institutions— Manifest and Latent Functions

Traditionally, "a school is to learn . . . ." This means, of course, that in the history of Western culture, especially as it has unfolded since the Protestant Reformation, the emphasis on individual responsibility and achievement has grown over the centuries, reaching a kind of apogee in the scientism of the nineteenth century. Since then, learning for learning's sake has tended to be refocused. A Ph.D., that degree reflective of German pedantry and ostensibly pointless investigation, tends now to require that the holder occupy a position of service in society, at

least, that his researches find some ultimate or, more likely, some immediate application. These views stand in sharp contrast to the old-fashioned view that the person be learned and cultured and that this is the primary of education.

In terms of the concepts which underlie education in modern society the mere idea that only academic skills are to be acquired is clouded by the multi-pronged aims of the school. Philosophies of education do, it is true, differ from community to community, but the pendulum seems to swing gradually away from an orthodox Deweyism. Despite marked variation in approach, at least as they are seen and defended by vocal protagonists, the problems of the educator, as indeed of the social worker, appear to arise in the contrast between training for individual attainment and achievement for the ends of society. "Helping people to help themselves," the cliche of the social worker, a view implicit in professional education, poses a paradox in pitting social desiderata against individual realization. The resolution at present seems to lie at varying points on a complex continuum. But the issue, as seen by the social analyst, is not which method is better but rather how the educational institutions function to stabilize the total social fabric.

The school, in addition to the problem of imparting knowledge and skills, is confronted with wholly new issues. One can readily sympathize with the educator whose task is to fashion a frame of reference in which to resolve them. What the school does, therefore, is not a cause of the disharmonies in the social body; it is apparent that education must come to grips with a change in the total configuration and patterning of American social behavior and values. On the manifest level, with the increasing nucleation of the family over the past five decades, the school has the task of molding sound character and enhancing the formation of a wholesome personality. Inevitably, it is faced with the problem of creating a sound social adjustment for those entrusted to its care, a fact which is probably borne out in the "conformist" tendencies of the modern teen-ager.

Similarly, in effecting preparation for life, the school becomes the guardian of the culture, being left with the necessity for instilling the sense of democratic citizenship and of spiritual and moral values. Add to this the concerns with vocational skills and their inculcation, the problem of helping the individual "discover himself," and the task is endless. It is small wonder that points of view differ and that the spirit of individualism should conflict with the ends of the social aggregate.

But of course these are areas in which the educator as professional has been vitally concerned. He is aware of the problems but finds difficulty in drawing the lines of definition. Whether he does so in terms of the so-called "child-centered school" or whether he moves into a more conservative area, he is still operating in terms of the overt, in the area of the socio-cultural commonality of understanding which assigns manifest functions to the school system. In other words, while there may be disagreement in detail and implementation, the concept that the "school is to learn" continues to underlie any concept of education.

From a strictly objective viewpoint, however, one which attempts to utilize the methods of science without associated value judgments, any institution has latent functions. There are aspects of institutional organization of which those involved, whether in a participant or directive capacity, are not necessarily wholly aware. To take a cross example, while all of us, as citizens, welcome the changing social status of the Negro in America and applaud the legal edicts which have made this so, we may also, as scientists, recognize that racial tensions, particularly in the Deep South, reflect a stability of social institutions, that the scapegoat psychology directed toward the Negro may have a function in channeling the aggressive and hostile drives of some individuals and groups. To modify these by legislation is not wholly to resolve the problem. In other words, racial tensions as they have existed among ourselves, however much we as individuals may dislike them, have to be seen objectively as serving some kind of purpose and function.

Hearts may, it is true, bleed for the Negro; this does not alleviate the hatred, the hostility, or indeed the anxiety arising because of the appearance of certain kinds of disreputable conservatism.

Thus, if the school has taken over all the manifest functions noted above, what is left? What does the educational institution do covertly in maintaining the social whole and how does it interfunction with other segments of the society? Because institutions interact, it may be affirmed that the changing functions of the family cause the school to assume a greater share of the burden of socialization than was formerly the case. Are the schools creating a longer and longer day for the child because the parent wishes to be free of the obligations of parenthood? Or conversely, is there talk of reducing vacation time because the school believes that its sphere of influence is being intruded upon? This is not a "chicken and egg" proposition but rather one which is reflective of an interaction between school and family. The effects, in any case, are clear; the child is removed more and more from his family group. The number of people who formerly would be thrown into closest contact with children becomes increasingly reduced. This takes place not only through the general length of the school day but also through the group aims of the educational system and its ancillary elements.

If one considers that the child in America of today has a long school day, one realizes that his activities are highly diffuse and that he is put in the position of interacting with a host of people and groups. Monday through Friday, involved in the day itself, a period of hours, it may be noted, far longer than is the case in the school system of the various countries of Europe, the child becomes further involved in a mass of extra-curricular activities. In American life today, urbanized as it is, Saturday calls for still further activity ranging from the involvements of the various voluntary associations, participation in spectator or consumer activities and sports, the cinema, the television medium, while Sunday is frequently given to yet another aspect of education in church and Sunday School, and otherwise follows the pattern of Saturday. The total result, one which even the most dedicated of educators in the American system must recognize, is the shift toward greater impersonality. Time is simply lacking to pause, to assess personal achievement, or to formulate depth in human relationships. There is, as the folklorists have shown, a great change in levels of participation—the spontaneous games which some of us knew as children are on the way out, being replaced by play engineered by institutional authority—and the end is worth spelling out. It is loss of creativity and a lessening dependence on the rich traditions of the culture.

The constant push to be occupied, the "busyness" of which American culture makes so much, unquestionably has its effects on the formation of the value system of the child. The idealized adult tends less to be a family member and more to involve an impersonal associate of the society at large—a teacher, a minister, a scoutmaster. This means that images become inconsistent, undependable, and that the cultural traditions take on a diffuse quality. Where formerly an authoritarian grandparental figure might emerge, one predictable in terms of his strengths or weaknesses, but wholly predictable also in terms of enforcing cultural norms, the child of today can readily transfer his allegiance and find his ideal in a host of vaguely defined figures. The end result is that the skill of the child in interacting with other individuals is in itself changed. He is not necessarily less efficient nor yet less able but he lives in a society which accords worth to horizontal human relationships and tends to veer away from those reflecting emotional depth. By the same token, he is trained and socialized to accept essentially ephemeral human relationships. This is no more than affirmation of the

fact that the cultural traditions are not deeply set. It is here that a real problem lies. It is expressed pointedly in a recent evaluation of the views of James B. Conant.

There is strong evidence that our ideal of classless middle-class society has been translated to mean that children must be molded into so-called democratic "look-alikes," if not "think-alikes." Our experience in two world wars has done much to encourage the idea of national society in uniform and in lock-step. There is a possibility that in a society influenced so greatly by the media of mass communication the individual, as an individual, can be lost. We may be in a new crisis in which it is necessary to defend the right of the individual as a scholar, as an artist, as a person, to discover himself and to express himself.

The educational institutions are confronted with the dilemma of substituting in some measure, indeed, extensively, for the family, of reaching the individual at a younger and younger age. The school has been concerned with the "needs" of the individual in his development but finds difficulty in defining these needs as against those of the society itself. The end result is makeshift. Our culture is confronted with the dilemma of abhorring the collective and yet at the same time of realizing the Judeo-Christian ethic of the responsibility of man for man. Progressive education did not resolve the issue nor does a return to the rigid disciplining of pure subject matter curricula seem to hold much promise. What is indeed more practical is a recognition on the part of the educational system of its specific function in the whole society, an awareness that ours is a cultural tradition worth imparting and worth preserving both in its historic past and in its changing present.

Healing Ways

Lyle Saunders

From *Cultural Difference and Medical Care.* Russell Sage Foundation, 1954, pp. 141–173. Copyright 1954, Russell Sage Foundation. By permission of the author, and the publisher and copyright holder.

With regard to illness and its treatment, as in other aspects of their culture, the Spanish-speaking people of the Southwest have many traits in common with the Anglos. Like most other people, they have minor ailments that they tend to disregard. Like all people, they occasionally have aches and pains, chills and fever, and other insistent symptoms that force them to seek relief. And, as in the case of most other people, what they do, how they do it, and when, are determined by the "knowledge" thay have of the meaning and cause of their symptoms, and of what can or should be done about them. Such knowledge as a product of association with other people may be as restricted or expansive, as consistent or contradictory, as the range of their associations permits it to be. . . .

Illness and disease, it must be remembered, are social as well as biological phenomena. On the biological level they consist of adaptations of the organism to environmental influences; on the social level they include meanings, roles, relationships, attitudes, and techniques that enable members of a cultural group to identify various types of illness and disease, to behave appropriately, and to call upon a body of knowledge for coping with the condition as defined as an illness. *What is recognized as disease or illness is a matter of cultural prescription* [italics added], and a given biological condition may or may not be considered an "illness," depending on the particular cultural group in which it occurs. Infestation by intestinal worms is generally regarded as a type of disease by people in the United States. Among other people, for example the inhabitants of the island of Yap, worms are thought to be a necessary component of the digestive process. *Mal ojo, susto,* and *empacho* are examples of diseases that are common in Latin America but unknown in the United States—with the exception of the Spanish-speaking Southwest—although the symptoms which give rise to diagnoses of any or all of these are fairly common in this country. What should be done about a given condition defined culturally as "illness" and the proper relationships of a sick person to other people are also culturally prescribed. An individual thus has cultural guides that enable him to know when he or others may be regarded as sick, something about the cause and nature of the sickness, what may be done to alleviate or remedy the condition, and the behavior expected of him and of others in the situation. . . .

In adopting new ideas about illness and new materials and techniques for treating it, the Spanish-speaking people have not necessarily abandoned any of their old ideas or healing methods. Some individuals may have dropped certain practices used by their parents or grandparents in treating certain disease conditions, or may have failed to learn them, but in the Spanish-speaking population viewed as a whole most of the old ways persist in some form. Drugstores in the "Mexican" sections of Anglo cities in the Southwest do a thriving business in herbs and other folk remedies. *Parteras, curanderas, médicas, albolarias,* and even *brujas* still find a demand for their services in both rural and urban areas. Alternative types of medical service and methods of treatment are seldom mutually exclusive, so that the adoption of the new does not necessitate giving up the old. The new is merely added to the old body of knowledge or belief, and either or both are drawn upon, depending on the circumstances. The Spanish-speaking person who puts himself in the hands of an Anglo institution and practitioner for a surgical operation expects to receive the utmost benefit from Anglo knowledge and skill. If, subsequently, he wears a piece of *oshá* over the incision, this does not necessarily indicate any lack of faith in Anglo methods but rather his reliance on a wider range of "knowledge" than that possessed by the Anglos who are treating him. Penicillin and the other antibiotics admittedly reduce or prevent infection, but so, in his opinion, does *oshá,* and it does no harm to be doubly certain of results by using both.

Folk Medicine

Three of the four sources from which the Spanish-speaking people derive their ideas

about sickness and its treatment provide them with types of knowledge, belief, and practice that may be classified as folk medicine. Folk medicine differs from "scientific" medicine in a number of ways. In any culture, it is generally the common possession of the group. In a folk culture, there is relatively little division of knowledge with respect to medicine, so that what one adult knows about illness and its treatment is usually known by all other adults. Although knowledge of the origins of folk medical practices and beliefs may have largely been lost, the practices and beliefs themselves are often so rooted in tradition that they seem a part of the natural order of things and are as much taken for granted as is the daily rising and setting of the sun. Folk medical lore is transmitted from person to person and generation to generation by informal methods and through what sociologists like to call unstructured situations. One learns it, much as he learns other elements of his culture, as an incidental part of his everyday associations. Folk medicine is usually well integrated with other elements of a folk culture and is reinforced by them. The expected attitude toward a given element of folk medicine is one of uncritical acceptance. Failure does not invalidate a practice or shake the belief on which it is based. A remedy is tried, and if it works no surprise is evinced, since that is what was expected. If it does not work, the failure is rationalized and something else tried. In most illnesses the patient ultimately either recovers or dies. If he gets well, the remedial technique is credited with effecting the cure. If he dies, the reason is not that the remedy was inappropriate, but that the patient was beyond help. Folk medicine, like scientific medicine, undoubtedly derives much of its prestige and authority from the fact that the majority of sick persons get well regardless of what is done.

If practitioners of scientific medicine think of folk medicine at all, they are likely to regard it as mere superstition or as a somewhat curious and outdated survival, having about the same relationship to medical science that astrology has to astronomy. But folk medicine, even in cultures with a well-developed tradition of scientific medicine, is a flourishing institution, and many folk practices have survived because they undoubtedly do get results. Although they are in general uncritically accepted by those using them, folk medical practices are subjected over a period of time to a rough empirical evaluation. Those that seem successful frequently come to be more and more used and thus firmly entrench themselves in the minds and behaviors of the group using them. Those that consistently fail to do what is expected of them tend to be used less and less frequently and, in time, may be dropped altogether. There thus operates a selective process that tends to weed out the ineffective practices and to strengthen those that prove to be effective.

Between scientific medicine and folk medicine there is a constant two-way interchange. Remedies that have been developed by scientific medicine become a part of the pharmacopoeia of folk medicine (for example, aspirin to relieve headaches or other minor aches and pains) and others with a long history of use are "discovered," analyzed, tested, and ultimately become a part of scientific medicine (for example, curare, quinine, cocaine). It is not the materials or procedures that determine whether a given technique represents folk or scientific medicine, but rather the way in which they are used and the body of knowledge or belief that lies behind the use. Scientific medicine is rooted in a precise knowledge of cause and effect relationships and a critical attitude toward both practices and results. Folk medicine is neither precise nor critical. It is rooted in belief, not knowledge, and it requires only occasional success to maintain its vigor.

The folk medicine of a given people, however, is usually not a random collection of beliefs and practices; rather, *it constitutes a fairly well-organized and fairly consistent theory of medicine* [italics added]. The body of "knowledge" on which it is based often includes ideas about the nature of man and his relationships with the natural, supernatural, and human environments. Folk medicine flourishes because it is a functional and integrated part of the whole culture, and because it enables members of cultural groups to meet their health needs, as they define

them, in ways that are at least minimally acceptable.

The Spanish-speaking people of the Southwest, as has been indicated, draw their medical beliefs and practices from many sources. One of these, and one that particularly influences the medical beliefs and practices of the two groups we have called Mexicans and Mexican-Americans, is the folk medicine of Mexico. . . .

One widely dispersed body of knowledge and practice is that related to concepts of heat and cold as qualities both of disease conditions and of materials used in therapy. These concepts provide a means of determining what remedy may be used for a particular illness and what the consequences are likely to be if the wrong treatment is used. Illnesses are classified as hot and cold, without respect to the presence or absence of fever, and the correct therapy is to attain a balance by treating "hot" diseases with "cold" remedies and "cold" diseases with "hot" remedies. Foods, beverages, animals, and people possess the characteristics of "heat" or "cold" in varying degree, and it is thought wise always to maintain a proper regard for the principles of balance. "Hot" foods, for example, should never be combined, but rather should be taken in conjunction with something "cold," with care being used to see that extremes of heat and cold are not taken together. A person with a "cold" disease is endangered by being given "cold" remedies or foods, since these are likely to aggravate his condition. There is no general agreement on exactly what is "hot" or "cold"; therefore, the classification of a given material or condition may vary from place to place.

Another fairly common body of belief and practice in Mexico relates to the concept of the clean stomach and includes the idea that the maintenance of health requires a periodic purging of the stomach and intestinal tract. At least one disease, *empacho,* is thought to be directly due to failure to achieve a clean stomach, and the rather large number of purgatives used are evidence of the extent to which the concept is accepted.

Blood is considered important in the balance of health and disease and many folk remedies serve the function of purifying the blood or otherwise improving its quality. Loss of blood for any reason, even in the small amounts necessary for laboratory tests, is thought to have a weakening effect, particularly on males, whose sexual vigor is thereby believed to be impaired.

Illness is conceived primarily in terms of not feeling well. Conditions that are not accompanied by subjective feelings or discomfort are generally *not classified as illness* [italics added]; hence, there is no obligation to do anything about them. Health is looked upon as a matter of chance and it is felt that there is very little that a person can do to keep it. Minor discomforts usually are not sufficient motivations to seek treatment, and frequently persons are seriously ill before they begin to seek or accept help. There is a tendency to conceal illness, partly deriving from the idea that to be sick is a manifestation of weakness.

Air is considered potentially dangerous, particularly if cold or if it is blowing over one. Night air is more dangerous than day air, and persons already ill are thought to be particularly susceptible to the harm that air can bring. Consequently, sickrooms are not ventilated, and special care is taken to see that all windows and doors are closed at night.

Pregnancy requires adherence to many dietary restrictions and a reduction in the amount of water drunk, lest the head of the foetus grow too large for an easy delivery. Frequent bathing and regular exercise in the prenatal period are thought to facilitate the delivery process, which frequently takes place with the woman in a squatting or kneeling position. After the delivery the mother remains in bed for an extended period of time, and then she takes or is given a steam bath. During the first three days following delivery the diet is restricted to a small amount of "cold" foods. Thereafter, "hot" foods again may be eaten.

With respect to etiological factors, three types of causation are recognized: empirical, magical, and psychological. Empirical or "natural" diseases are those in which a known external factor operates directly on the organism to produce the illness. Any disorders resulting from exposure to bad air, invasion by microorganisms, contact with an infected person, eating improper foods, failure to keep a clean stomach, and similar hazards are considered "natural" diseases. A long list of illnesses, including pneumonia, rheumatism, diarrhea, colds, smallpox, worms, tuberculosis, and venereal disease, is placed in this category. Magical diseases are those in which the causative factors lie outside the realm of empirical knowledge and cannot be thus verified. Such a disease is *mal ojo,* or evil eye, which is produced in young children, often without intention, by persons who have a "strong glance." Some kinds of *susto,* a type of illness resulting from fright, are of magical etiology in that they are felt to be caused by the possession of an individual by an evil spirit. And there are, of course, many kinds of bewitchment in which a person with evil intent and magical power can cause illness symptoms in another. Psychological diseases are those in which a strong emotional experience causes the appearance of the disease symptoms. Examples are *susto* when it occurs in young children who have suffered a severe fright, or epilepsy, which is believed to result from strong emotional feelings.

For most illnesses there are appropriate remedies. The number and range of remedial measures are so great that only some of the major categories can be indicated here. Herbs are widely used in a variety of ways and for a large number of conditions. Tea made by boiling leaves or stems in water is a common remedy. Herbs are also taken with foods, are used in aromatic preparations whose fumes may be inhaled, are applied to external surfaces in the form of powder, and are worn in bags or cachets over parts of the body, much as the Anglos not so many years ago wore asafetida to ward off colds. Massage or some other form of manipulation of body parts is considered efficacious for some illnesses, and poultices and plasters of various kinds are used to produce both mechanical and magical effects. Salves and ointments are not uncommon; foods are both prescribed and withheld for remedial purposes; and various types of bathing are practiced. Prayer and the reciting of religious formulas are common forms of dealing with sickness, and where the illness is thought to be magical in nature, spells, charms, incantations, and other ritualistic practices may be utilized. In recent times, practices and materials have been borrowed from scientific medicine, and injections or "shots" have become a common form of treatment.

Mild disorders are treated by the afflicted person or by some member of his family. More serious cases, or those that do not yield to home treatment, may require calling in someone with more specialized knowledge. Who is called and when, depends on the type and seriousness of the disease, the degree of discomfort, the availability of specialized help, and the probable cost of obtaining assistance. If the disease is a "natural" one that is fairly serious or uncomfortable, a physician may be called in to assist rather early in its course, provided a doctor is available and the problem of payment is not insuperable. Physicians, it is felt, understand "natural" diseases and are able to do something about them. But if the disease is thought to be of magical or psychological origin, assistance is more likely to be sought from a *curandera,* a *bruja,* or some other type of folk specialist, since they are assumed to be more familiar with and, hence, better able to treat such diseases. A complaint of *susto* or *mal ojo* will be listened to understandingly by a folk specialist, and the patient will be assured that his ailment is being treated. But to make such a complaint to a practitioner of scientific medicine would be to expose oneself to the possibility of skeptical disbelief, condemnation, or even ridicule, a circumstance that most patients and their families prefer to avoid. . . .

Probably one of the most widely used, and certainly one of the most efficacious, remedies of the Spanish-American villages was *oshá,* a plant of the parsley family, to which reference has already been made, whose properties were probably learned from the Indians. The healing qualities of *oshá* are largely concentrated in the root, which may be used in many ways to treat a wide variety of illnesses. Chewed raw or ground into a powder and made into a tea, it prevents flatulency and soothes the stomach. Drunk in hot water with sugar and whiskey, it will break up a cold and help to cure such respiratory illnesses as influenza, pneumonia, and pulmonary tuberculosis. Taken internally it will also reduce fevers. Applied directly to a wound in powdered form, or worn over a wound, *oshá* promotes healing. An ointment for the relief and cure of cuts and sores can be made from mutton fat, candle wax, and turpentine into which is mixed some powdered *oshá* root, *manzanilla* (camomile), and *contrayerba* (caltrop). Mixed with olive oil, *oshá* can be used as a liniment in the treatment of rheumatic pains, and it is also useful, in the form of a paste, to draw out the poison from snakebites. In addition, this highly versatile plant is used as the basis of an enema, as a remedy for colic in children, and as a means of protection against snakes, which are believed to be repelled by its pungent odor. *Oshá* has recently entered into Anglo folk medicine as an ingredient in a cough remedy prepared and sold by a Denver druggist. It is also useful as a seasoning for soups and stews.

The familiar onion of Anglo home remedies is also put to many uses by the Spanish-Americans. Roasted and applied hot, *cebollas* are thought to be effective in treating chilblains. Teething babies are allowed to chew the leaves and stems to relieve the pain of swollen gums. A cough syrup made of the juice of fried or roasted onions sweetened with honey or sugar is thought to be an excellent treatment for colds, particularly in the case of babies. *Inmortal* (spider milkweed) likewise has many uses. Powdered and mixed with water, it can be drunk to reduce headache or chest pains or to bring down a fever. Made into a paste and used as a poultice, it will relieve pains of various kinds. It is also useful in childbirth. Rubbed on the abdomen or taken with cold water it will reduce labor pains, and drunk with hot water after delivery it helps to expel the placenta. Asthma, shortness of breath, and similar afflictions may be helped by drinking a tea made of *inmortal.*

Not even a representative sample of the many plants used in the folk medicine of Spanish-Americans can be given here. But some indication of the extent of the list and of the familiarity to Anglos of many items on it may be obtained from a brief mention of the popular Anglo names of a few of the plants used: cattails, garlic, cottonwood, basil, apricot, camphor, alfalfa, lavender, aster, licorice, sunflower, anise, sagebrush, cocklebur, pumpkin, thistle, elderberry, lupine, algae, oleander, milkweed, corn, mustard, goldenrod, tansy, and mint. And not only plants but animals, animal products, and nonorganic substances find their place in the list of remedies, as can be seen in a mention of rattlesnake oil, cowhide, lime, rennet, milk, red ants, bones, alum, earth, and rock of various kinds, each of which, along with many other substances, is used in the treatment of some type of illness. . . .

Folk Medicine and Scientific Medicine

Anglo practice and village practice with regard to childbirth differ in several important respects. Anglo physicians, who are in a position to advise practicing midwives, recommend that the patient be delivered in bed to lessen the possibility of postpartum hemorrhage. They adivse that the mother should remove her clothing, that the *partera* should scrub her hands and arms with strong soap before approaching the mother, that the scissors used for severing the cord be washed in soapy water, that the mother be given a sponge bath soon after delivery. There has been a strong tendency, however, for many of the *parteras* to look upon Anglo medical ways as different from but not appreciably better than their traditional medicine and to continue to use their own more familiar methods. Or, if the Anglo methods are adopted, their efficacy may be reduced by the failure of the *partera* to grasp the reasons behind their use. The scissors, after being washed with soap, may be dried with an unsterile cloth or placed on a table that has not been cleaned. Water that has been boiled may be poured when cool into an unsterile container. The acceptance of Anglo ways may represent merely

the adoption of new elements into an old pattern in which the new procedures are not understood in terms of the Anglo reasons for their use, but instead are fitted into the already existing pattern of understanding with respect to causation and healing of illness and disease. Just as Anglo medical personnel tend to see many of the Spanish-American folk practices as either worthless or dangerous, so Spanish-Americans are inclined to be skeptical about the efficacy, necessity, and safety of some of the Anglo healing practices, and may be at times reluctant to accept them. Surgical procedures, in particular, are frequently regarded as harmful, dangerous, and unnecessary, and many villagers can tell of someone who was done irreparable damage by an operation or who, being advised by an Anglo physician that an operation was absolutely necessary, was thereafter cured by some folk procedure.

The transition from Spanish-American folkways to the acceptance and use of Anglo scientific medicine is complicated by the fact that folk medical knowledge is widely disseminated, so that anyone giving medical care is subject to the critical attention of relatives and friends of the patient, who are always ready to step in and insist on changes in treatment or to add to what is being done if they feel that proper care is not being given. Thus, the *partera* who has learned some new techniques from a physician or from the training program of the State Department of Public Health may find herself constrained by the pressure of family opinion to forego her new knowledge and to continue with old ways. Knowing as well as she what herbs may be used to hasten delivery or check postpartum bleeding, the family have provided them, and they are likely to interpret the failure of the *partera* to use them as resulting from ignorance or indifference to the welfare of the patient. They *know* these traditional remedies assure comfort and safety for the patient, and they are likely to feel that no treatment process can be good which withholds them.

Among many Spanish-American villagers, Anglo medicine is regarded as something to be used chiefly as a last resort when all other known procedures have failed. Consequently, for a long time, the Anglo record of successful treatment was less good than it need have been because too frequently Anglo practitioners were not consulted until the case was practically hopeless. Most of the successes in treatment were thus credited to folk practices; many of the failures were charged to Anglo medicine. As a result, another barrier to the acceptance of Anglo medicine was raised through the development of the belief, which could be supported by reference to known cases, that Anglo medical institutions were places where people went to die.

The continued use of their own medical practices by Spanish-Americans sometimes leads the Anglo, who knows his ways are better, to characterize Spanish-Americans as ignorant or superstitious, to accuse them of being indifferent to the well-being of their families and friends, and to become impatient and annoyed at their failure to see the obvious benefits of Anglo procedures. What such Anglos fail to appreciate is that Spanish-Americans also *know* that their ways are superior and that their use, far from constituting neglect of or indifference to the needs of sick relatives and friends, actually constitutes the provision of first-rate medical care. The Anglo may argue that by the pragmatic test of results his *is* the best medicine and that the Spanish-American ought to have enough sense to see it. But the evidence of the superiority of Anglo medicine is not always available to the Spanish-American in a form that has meaning to him and, in any case, what is or is not "good sense" is relative to culture. In utilizing his own knowledge and that of his friends, relatives, and neighbors, and when that fails, in calling in a *médica* or *curandera* or even a *bruja,* the Spanish-American villager is acting in a way that is eminently sensible in the light of his convictions about the nature of disease and the proper ways to deal with it. To behave otherwise, to disregard what he knows and subject himself or a member of his family to a course of treatment that may bear no particular relationship to his understanding of disease, simply because some Anglos say that it is what

he should do, would constitute a very strange kind of behavior indeed.

Sickness, particularly if it be serious, is likely to be viewed as a crisis, and in situations of crisis people in all cultures tend to resort to those patterns of thinking and acting that have been most deeply ingrained in them as a result of their cultural experiences. To meet a crisis with the resources of one's culture, whatever they may be, is to behave in a manner that is both sensible and sound; it is, in fact, to behave in the only way that most human beings can under such circumstances. The Spanish-American, in utilizing the medical ways of his culture is neither ignorant nor indifferent. If he knew no way of dealing with illness, he might be called ignorant. But he does know something to do, frequently many things. If he did nothing, he might be called indifferent. But he does something, and continues to do something while his resources remain undepleted or until he achieves results. The sequence in which he does things is determined by the differential value he places on the various procedures as they apply to the particular situation. If the seeking of Anglo medical care is, for a given illness, well down on the list, it is because this is the way he sees the particular procedure in relation to the others that are available to him. That an Anglo, in a similar situation, might have a different set of resources and a different order of importance for them, cannot be expected to have any considerable influence on his behavior. . . .

Reasons for Anglo Medicine Not Being More Extensively Used

A number of explanations can be found for the failure of Spanish-speaking people in close contact with Anglo culture to adopt completely its medical ways. One such factor is certainly the extent to which Anglo medical services and facilities are available. Although the Spanish-speaking are rapidly becoming urbanized, many of them still live in rural areas where medical personnel and facilities are not readily available. Large numbers of

Spanish-speaking people live in sparsely settled areas where one has to drive many miles to see a physician or enter a hospital. A map of health facilities in New Mexico, prepared in 1946 for the New Mexico Health Council, showed four counties to be completely without medical facilities and a large part of the state to lie outside a 30-mile radius from any type of health facility. In parts of Colorado, Arizona, and Texas, similar conditions exist. The present widespread distribution of automobiles and recent improvements in rural roads have done much to make Anglo medicine more readily available to rural Spanish-speaking people and have undoubtedly contributed to its somewhat greater use. But there still remain many areas where, either because of sparseness of population or a high concentration of Spanish-speaking people among the residents of the areas, it would be quite difficult to get to an Anglo doctor or hospital even if one were highly motivated to do so.

Another factor related to availability is that of cost. Anglo medical care is expensive and the Spanish-speaking, as a group, are poor. In many instances they cannot afford, or do not feel that they can afford, the services of a physician or a sojourn in a hospital. Anglo medicine involves bills for home or office calls, some likelihood of being given an expensive prescription, and the possibility of surgery, or hospitalization for some other reason, which may be very costly. A *médica* usually does not charge much and under certain circumstances can be paid with products instead of cash, a definite advantage to those living in rural areas. Her medicines are not likely to cost much, and there is little likelihood that she will recommend hospitalization or an operation. Diagnosis and treatment by oneself and one's family cost little or nothing, and for many minor illnesses can be quite satisfactory. These differences in costs certainly constitute an influence in the readiness or reluctance with which an individual or family makes the decision to seek any given type of medical care.

Lack of knowledge of Anglo medical ways is probably another factor in the extent to which Spanish-speaking people do or do not use Anglo practitioners and facilities. The simple matter of getting in touch with a doctor and putting oneself under his care can seem complicated to a person who is not at ease in either the English language or Anglo medical culture. How does one find a doctor? How can one be sure that the chosen doctor will be either competent or *simpatico*? How is a doctor approached? How can one know in advance how much the treatment will cost or what will be the expected manner of payment? What illnesses may properly be taken to a physician? These and other questions, the answers to which most of us take for granted, can be puzzling to persons not wholly familiar with Anglo culture, and can be effective barriers to the initiation of a doctor-patient relationship, particularly when the potential patient may not be highly motivated in the direction of wanting Anglo medicine.

Closely related to a lack of knowledge of Anglo medical ways as a deterrent to seeking Anglo medical care is the factor of fear. That which is strange or unknown is often feared, and there is much in Anglo medicine that is strange and fear inducing even to Anglo laymen. The instruments used, the pain that sometimes accompanies their use, and the unfamiliar surroundings of the office, clinic, or hospital in which they are used, all can arouse fear. So can the unfamiliar elements in the medical routine—the examination procedure, the invasion of one's physical and mental privacy, the uncertainty of the diagnostic procedure, the incomprehensible language that may be used. For a Spanish-speaking person, for example, a physical examination can be a very unpleasant experience, particularly if it involves the participation of persons of the opposite sex. The fear of being examined by a man is sometimes enough to keep Spanish-speaking women away from Anglo medical practitioners and to make traumatic for others the contact they have with Anglo medicine. Foster reports the failure of a considerable proportion of women coming to a prenatal clinic in Mexico City to return for a follow-up visit after their initial experience, which included an unexpected physical examination. It is not without significance for the medical relations of Spanish-speaking and Anglos in the Southwest that most of the healing personnel in the culture of the Spanish-speaking are women, whereas proportionately more of those in the Anglo culture are men. Spanish-speaking men, too, are likely to have some reluctance to subjecting themselves to examination by Anglo physicians and to being placed in potentially embarrassing situations with Anglo nurses.

Another possible factor that may operate is resistance to being separated from one's family and being isolated for an indefinite time in an Anglo institution, where all relationships are likely to be impersonal. Good medical care, from the Anglo point of view, requires hospitalization for many conditions. Good medical care, as defined in the culture of the Spanish-Americans, requires that the patient be treated for almost any condition at home by relatives and friends, who are constantly in attendance and who provide emotional support as well as the technical skills required in treatment. In time of sickness one expects his family to surround and support him, and to supervise closely and critically, if not actually carry on, the treatment process. Members of the family, in turn, feel obligated to remain close to the patient, to take charge of his treatment, and to reassure him as to his place in and importance to the family group. The Anglo practice of hospitalization, with the treatment being taken over by professional strangers and the family relegated to the meager role permitted by the visiting regulations, runs counter to the expectation patterns of the Spanish-speaking and, thus, may be a factor in the reluctance of some members of the group to seek or accept Anglo medical care.

There are some illnesses for which Anglo medical care is not sought because, as has already been noted, the type of sickness is not ordinarily known to Anglo practitioners. A patient suffering from *mal ojo, susto,* and similar conditions seeks relief, if at all, from someone who is familiar with these diseases and who, therefore, may be expected to know something about the proper method of treatment. This difference between the two cultures in the conceptualization of disease serves to restrict the range of conditions for which Anglo medical assistance might be sought to those recognized by both cultural groups and gives to the folk practitioner almost exclusive influence in dealing with those conditions that are recognized only by the Spanish-speaking group.

A final factor that may be mentioned as possibly contributing to the hesitancy of Spanish-speaking people to use Anglo medicine is that such attempts as are made often do not provide the satisfactions that the Spanish-speaking expect. With the *curandera* and *médica* the whole process of diagnosis and treatment moves along in an atmosphere of informal cooperation and collaboration between patient, family, and the healer. Alternative procedures are discussed and courses of treatment agreed upon, with the opinions of patient and family frequently being given much weight in the final decisions. The folk practitioner works less as an independent specialist than as a consultant and technician who implements the therapeutic plans of the patient or his family, all of whom remain very much in the picture throughout the treatment period. All know what is going on and why. All are free to offer suggestions and criticisms. The diagnosis and treatment of illness thus involve active participation by the patient and members of his family in a situation in which the relationships are mainly personal and informal. Diagnosis is usually easy and swift, and treatment follows immediately.

By contrast, Anglo medicine is likely to be somewhat impersonal and formal. It is expected that the patient will be turned over to the physician, who will then direct the diagnostic and treatment procedures, largely without the benefit of advice or suggestion from either the patient or his family. Information may be sought from both, but usually only for the purpose of getting at the present complaints or learning the patient's medical history. Diagnosis may be slow and may involve techniques that are not understood by the patient or his family. Treatment may be delayed pending the establishment of a definite diagnosis and, when instituted, may involve hospitalization of the patient. The patient and his family are expected to be relatively passive participants in a situation in which most of the new relationships established are impersonal, businesslike, and, frequently, very unsatisfactory. In treatment by either folk practitioner or physician the possible range of outcomes is about the same. The patient may get better, may remain as he is, may get worse, may die. There being no conclusive evidence of the relatively greater frequency of desirable results when using Anglo medicine than when relying on folk healers, the amount of satisfaction that patient and family get in the medical relationship becomes an important factor in determining which of the two types of medicine they will select.

The most important differences between Spanish-American folk medicine and Anglo scientific medicine that influence the choice of one or the other are these: Anglo scientific medicine involves largely impersonal relations, procedures unfamiliar to laymen, a passive role for family members, hospital care, considerable control of the situation by professional healers, and high costs; by contrast the folk medicine of Spanish-American villagers is largely a matter of personal relations, familiar procedures, active family participation, home care, a large degree of control of the situation by the patient or his family, and relatively low costs. Given these differences, it is easy to understand why a considerable motivation would be necessary for a Spanish-American to have any strong preference for Anglo medicine over that which is not only more familiar and possibly psychologically more rewarding—or at least less punishing—but also less expensive.

Despite the many factors that operate to hinder the seeking and acceptance of Anglo medical care by Spanish-speaking people of the Southwest, however, Anglo medicine is rapidly coming to play an increasingly larger part in the total complex of attitudes and activities of the Spanish-speaking people with respect to illness and health. In cities where Anglo medical facilities and personnel are accessible, the use made of them by the Spanish-speaking probably is not greatly different in either amount or kind from that of Anglos of comparable social class status. In some rural areas, activities of private practitioners, medical groups, health cooperatives, local and state health departments. and, particularly, public health nurses have brought a considerable amount of Anglo medicine within the reach of Spanish-speaking people and have done much to develop the attitudes necessary to the acceptance and use of Anglo medical ways. If we think of the Spanish-speaking population as distributed along a continuum ranging from complete reliance on their own folk medicine at one pole to the complete acceptance of Anglo scientific medicine at the other, the greatest numbers would be concentrated near the center, with the highest proportion probably being found on the Anglo half of the continuum. . . .

Index